Newman and His Family

John Henry Newman by Maria Giberne circa 1840.

Newman and His Family

By
Edward Short

B L O O M S B U R Y
LONDON · NEW DELHI · NEW YORK · SYDNEY

Bloomsbury T&T Clark

An imprint of Bloomsbury Publishing Plc

50 Bedford Square	1385 Broadway
London	New York
WC1B 3DP	NY 10018
UK	USA

www.bloomsbury.com

First published 2013

British Library Cataloguing-in-Publication Data
A catalogue record for this books is available from the British Library.

ISBN: HB: 978-0-567-63385-9
PB: 978-0-567-10434-2
ePDF: 978-0-567-01471-9
epub: 978-0-567-35994-0

Library of Congress Cataloging-in-Publication Data
Short, Edward
Newman and his Family/Edward Short p.cm
Includes bibliographic references and index.
ISBN 978-0-567-63385-9 (hardcover) – ISBN 978-0-567-10434-2 (pbk.)
2012045678

Typeset by Deanta Global Publishing Services, Chennai, India
Printed and bound in Great Britain

For my darling Karina

Contents

". . . England is the country of family life."
—Queen Victoria to her daughter Victoria, Empress of Germany *(1859)*

"One happy point, as far as truth is concerned, is that it restores to Protestants
and Anglicans the liberty of speaking their minds on the Church of Rome, without
being 'snubbed' at. After due defences of transubstantiation, purgatory, etc. etc.
we shall have one for persecution. The Church of Rome has long wanted
a Champion on all these points and for truth's sake she could never have so
safe a one as J.H.N . . . But it is hard for people to write with patience and
propriety on such frightful stuff . . ."
—Harriett Mozley to Jemima Mozley *(1849)*

"'It's a devil of a thing, gentlemen,' said Mr. Swiveller,
'when relations fall out and disagree.'"
—Charles Dickens, The Old Curiosity Shop *(1841)*

"Someone has said ingeniously of you and me, that we are the two roots of the
same quadratic equation; and it is to me curious and amusing to find how much I am
sure to agree with you in spite of an utterly different conclusion. I mean I often agree
far more with you in numerous details of thought or sentiment, *than with hosts of*
others, whose conclusion is the same as mine. We met Dean Francis Close last summer
at Freshwater. . . . *He was very friendly and asked a great deal about you; and was not*
a little diverted when I said I thought my differences from you almost always turned on
matters of fact, *when in appearance we agreed as to sentiment and even in principle.*
We seem to look out on different worlds. Of course we fall in with
totally different circles."
—Francis William Newman to John Henry Newman *(1863)*

"The common defence of the family is that, amid the stress and fickleness of life,
it is peaceful, pleasant and at one. But there is another defence of the family,
which is possible and to me evident: this defence is that
the family is not peaceful and not pleasant and not at one."
—G. K. Chesterton from Heretics *(1905)*

Preface

*"It was with deep sorrow I read what you told me about your family matters,"
Newman wrote Viscount Feilding in November 1850. "Time, however, please
God, will set all to rights, or at least indefinitely soften the acuteness of feeling
which such steps as you tell me of express . . . For such a change you must pray
unceasingly."*

To what family matters was Newman referring? Father Stephen Dessain, the great
Newman scholar noted dryly how "The Earl of Denbigh, Lord Feilding's father, who
had been writing him voluminous letters on religion, had just decided that it was his
duty to disinherit his heir."[1] After attending Eton and Cambridge, Rudolph William
Basil Feilding (1823–92) converted with his wife, Louisa Pennant (1828–53), heiress
of the Downing estate near Holywell in Flintshire in August, 1850 and it was to punish
his son for betraying the family's Protestant heritage that the 7th Earl of Denbigh
drew up a will disinheriting him. Lord Feilding's conversion had been prompted by
seeing crumbs of the Anglican communion service being swept up by the sacristan at
Whitford, a village near Pantasaph in North Wales. Lady Feilding began to doubt the
legitimacy of the National Church after reading Newman's *Difficulties felt by Anglicans
in submitting to the Catholic Church* (1850), which he had written, in part, to explain
his own conversion to his family. Madeleine Beard, in her lively account of the vital
role that England's convert aristocrats played in the restoration of the English Church
in the latter part of the nineteenth century, recalled how Lord Feilding "bought books
from a Catholic bookshop in Edinburgh to further his quest for the Truth. He enquired
in the bookshop where a Catholic priest might be found . . . The bookseller suggested
a Bishop Gillis at St. Margaret's Convent. Lord Feilding set out for the convent walking
all the way and praying for God's guidance. He explained to the Bishop all that was
on his mind. After two hours, his difficulties vanished. He saw 'the Church, his own
life, everything, transfigured by his new vision.'"[2] When the Viscount was attacked
for his secession from the Church of England by Joseph Askew, a former fellow of
Queen's College, Oxford, Newman counselled against any indignant riposte.[3] "As to Mr
Askew's Letter, it is at once angry and pompous, and it would be very easy to demolish
his whole structure—but I do not think it is worth while. There is no call on you to
answer every one who chooses to make free with you . . ."[4] Then, again, when the No

---

[1]   LD, 14:129 JHN to Viscount Feilding (15 November 1850).
[2]   Madeleine Beard, *Faith and Fortune* (Herefordshire, 1997), p. 66.
[3]   See "A Letter to Viscount Feilding, on the Grounds of his Secession to the Church of Rome" by
      Joseph Askew (London, 1850).
[4]   LD, 14:129 JHN to Viscount Feilding (15 November 1850).

Popery response to the restoration of the English hierarchy was at its hysterical height, Newman wrote Lord Feilding with unflappable good sense: "As to this hubbub, I was anxious just at first, when indeed you were here—but I do not see what can come of it, except indeed inconvenience to individuals, and black looks from friends and strangers. We must take it coolly, and leave the British Lion to find he cannot touch us. If he put some of us in prison, we should but gain by it—and I suspect his keepers are too sharp-sighted for that . . ."[5] Later, Lord Feilding would go on to become treasurer of the Peter Pence Association, found the Capuchin Franciscan friary in Pantasaph, and co-found the Catholic magazine, *The Universe.* The advice that Newman gave to Lord Feilding when he wrote of his father's intention to disinherit him was the advice that he would give to all those who wrote to him of family distress: they must pray unceasingly. And since this was advice that he was obliged to take himself, when the sorrows of family arrived at his own doorstep, he could offer it to others with hard-earned humility. As it happened, in the case of Viscount Feilding, the advice bore welcome fruit. On 20 May 1859, when a son and heir was born to the Feildings, Lord Denbigh thought better of his petulant decision, tore up the will disinheriting his son, and ordered the bells to be rung at Newnham for his Catholic grandson.[6]

In choosing to write of Newman and his family, I have taken up a theme that explains a good deal about my subject and his work. Whether I have done the depth and richness of my theme the justice it deserves I shall have to leave to the judgement of my gentle readers. Certainly, in researching, writing, and rewriting the book, I was encouraged by the example of Newman himself, who never let difficulties prevent his essaying worthwhile projects. In pursuing my theme, I was surprised by how far-flung family history can be, taking in at once social, political, philosophical, artistic, and religious history. In this regard, especially in the case of Newman's nephew, John Rickards Mozley, I found myself writing not only about members of Newman's family but an entire intellectual epoch. At the same time, although the scope of *Newman and his Family* is far-ranging, I had no grand thesis in mind when I set about writing it. My only object was to share with my readers how Newman's relations with his family informed his understanding not only of himself and his contemporaries but of his faith in God. In my last book, *Newman and his Contemporaries*, I showed how friendship informed Newman's insights into faith and life. In this book, which can be read as a companion to that other book, I attempt to show how family, which is an infinitely more complicated thing, deepened and transformed those insights. And I try to show this by mining his correspondence, as well as his other writings, including his sermons.

Many of Newman's contemporaries left behind marvellously vivid accounts of how fascinating they found his sermons. William Lockhart's account is one of the best.

> Newman's sermons had the most wonderful effect on us young men. It was to many of us as if God had spoken to us for the first time. I could never have believed beforehand, that it was possible that a few words, read very quietly from

---

[5] LD, 14:130 JHN to Viscount Feilding (15 November 1850).
[6] For an excellent account of the Feilding family, see Madeleine Beard, *Faith and Fortune* (Hereford-shire, 1997), pp. 63–75.

a manuscript, without any rhetorical effort, could have so penetrated our souls. I do not see how this could have been, unless he who spoke was himself a *seer*, who saw God, and the things of God, and spoke that which he had seen, in the keen, bright, intuition of faith. We felt God speaking to us; turning our souls, as it were, "inside out," cutting clean through the traditions of human society, which are able so completely to corrupt and distort the spiritual insight of the soul.[7]

What I have tried to do in the pages that follow is to show how Newman often used his sermons to address family issues *sub specie aeternitatis*.[8] Although I draw on a number of his *Parochial and Plain Sermons* written when he was an Anglican, I also draw on his Catholic sermons, which Walter Bagehot (1826–77), a shrewd judge of literary merit, found "very keen and acute like all his writings" and yet "much more decisive and conclusive . . ."[9] Apropos the author of *Lombard Street* (1873), the bookman Augustine Birrell observed how "Mr. Bagehot must have had the *Parochial Sermons* by heart. Two of the most famous, entitled 'The Invisible World' and 'The Greatness and Littleness of Human Life' [both of which I discuss at length in the pages that follow] seem to have become incorporate with Mr. Bagehot's innermost nature. They are not obviously congruous with his pursuits. What have bankers to do with the invisible world?"[10] In my chapter on Newman and his father, I endeavour to answer that question.

When I began reading about Newman and his family in preparation for this book, I had no idea that I would be met with so much kind assistance from so many generous people. It is a pleasure to express my gratitude to them. First of all, I should like to thank Francis J. McGrath, FMS, the editor of Newman's uncollected Anglican sermons as well as the final volumes of his *Letters and Diaries*. I met with Brother McGrath at the Birmingham Oratory when I first began this project in 2004 and he could not have shown me more generous, critical, encouraging support. Another generous source of critical help was Father Dermot Fenlon of Newman's Oratory, who looked over many of my chapters in typescript and made a number of characteristically incisive recommendations. Father Ian Ker kindly read my chapters on Charles and Frank Newman and gave me the benefit of his usefully excoriating criticism. I am profoundly grateful to Dr Tracey Rowland, Dean and Permanent Fellow of the John Paul II Institute for Marriage and Family (Melbourne) and author of *Ratzinger's Faith* for her critical assistance. Richard Greene, Professor of English at the University of Toronto and biographer of Edith Sitwell and Graham Greene, was full of generous support, as was Douglas Lane Patey, Professor of English at Smith College and author of that superb critical biography of Evelyn Waugh for Blackwell. Then, again, Father Carleton Jones, OP gave me great help by making me see the self-knowledge that animates Newman's care for souls. Paul Shrimpton of Magdalen School, Oxford, read my chapter on Charles Newman and made many helpful suggestions. Prof Mary Ann Glendon of Harvard Law School was another source of generous encouragement.

---

[7] William Lockhart, *Cardinal Newman: Reminiscences of Fifty Years Since* (London, 1891), p. 24.
[8] There is a paucity of good commentary on the sermons, though Ian Ker and Eric Griffiths have written perceptively about them. See Ker's introduction to his anthology of select sermons and Griffith's essay in *Newman After a Hundred Years*. ed. Ker and Hill (Oxford, 1990).
[9] *Collected Works of Walter Bagehot*. ed. Norman St. John-Stevas (London, 1986), XV, p. 249.
[10] Ibid., p. 200.

Frank Bowles of the Manuscript Reading Room at Cambridge University Library provided me with invaluable assistance in my research on Jemima's second son, John Rickards Mozley, with whom Newman entered into a lively correspondence in 1875. Ruth Long, from the Cambridge Library's photographic department, gave me efficient help with the splendid photograph of Mozley that I include among my plates. Father Gregory Winterton, late of Newman's Oratory, kindly granted me permission to use photographs of Newman's family in the Oratory's archive of photographs, which I have reproduced from Meriol Trevor's volumes. Madeleine Beard, the author of *Faith and Fortune*, gave me her good counsel and good company. The crack historian and biographer Andrew Roberts, whose life of Lord Salisbury is such an indispensable guide to the political and diplomatic history of the later part of Victoria's reign, which Newman followed so closely, was exceedingly generous in his interest in my work. Conrad Black shared with me his great regard and deep knowledge of Newman. My good friend Robert Crotty, the Director of the Guild of Catholic Lawyers, gave me the benefit of his critical sympathy over several festive lunches in New York. My dear friends Jack and Nuala Scarisbrick introduced me to Cambridge and gave me the benefit of their prayers, good wishes, and Lucullan hospitality. Yet another friend, Father Anthony Schueller, Pastor of St. Jean Baptiste in New York also gave me vital help. A newer friend from faraway Kansas City, Sister Silvia Enriquez of the Servants of Mary, gave me her prayers when I needed them most. Another new friend, Jo Anne Sylva, the author of the indispensable *How Italy and Her People Shaped Cardinal Newman*, shared with me her insights into my many-sided subject. Angela Thirlwell, who has written so brilliantly about the Pre-Raphaelites, pulled herself away from Paris to read my MS for a very generous puff. Dwight Lindley, III, Professor of English at Hillside College, who is hard at work on what promises to be a very good book on George Eliot, also read the book for a puff and gave me much reassuring counsel when I was wracked with doubts. William and Michelle Law were also full of inspiring encouragement. Distinguished Professor Emerita, Nancy Siraisi of Hunter College, the author of several books on the history of medieval and Renaissance medicine, with whom I studied European history in my insouciant youth, was also very generous with her support, which I particularly prize, knowing her fondness for Victorian fiction. Timothy Leddy, Kaitlin Walter, and Caroline Van Horn gave me the support of their bright young brains. I should also like to thank Prof. Humfrey Butters of Warwick University, whose wit and learning and *caritas* would have greatly endeared him to the hero of my book. From Bloomsbury, I am grateful to my former editor in London, Thomas Kraft, whose initial support for this book was crucial. Anna Turton, Commissioning Religion Editor at Bloomsbury, sustained that support by kindly giving me an opportunity to pitch this book to her colleagues in Bedford Square. I am also grateful to Kara Zavada in Bloomsbury's New York office and to Katie Broomfield and Caitlin Flynn in the London office. No acknowledgments would be complete unless I expressed my immense thanks to Ken Bruce in London and Subitha Nair in India for their 'above and beyond' help with the production of the book. Then, again, I owe a very special debt to Distinguished Professor Emerita Naomi Miller of Hunter College whose learning and encouragement were a constant boon to me when I first began reading Newman's magnificent letters, at her suggestion, over 25 years ago.

What she will make of what I have made of that fascinating epistolarium I do not know, though I hope she approves. Another early influence on this book was that of my father, John Francis Short, who introduced me to Newman when I was a bookish boy on the Jersey shore. He had read the *Apologia* and the *Idea of a University* in the old Everyman editions when he was an undergraduate at Georgetown. Thirty years later, he put both books into my hands, assuring me that, for good sense and good style, they were incomparable. In all of the years that I have been reading the author whom the *Cork Examiner* called "the just man made perfect," my admiration for him and his work has only deepened. My father was right: Newman is incomparable.

Finally, I should like to thank my wife Karina, whose love and forbearance and discriminating sympathy have made the road to this finish line not only possible but joyous. And I should like to welcome a new addition to our family, Sophia Thérèse Mariana, whose grave wondering eyes bear out Newman's great insight that children are "a pledge of immortality" because, as he wrote, "in the infant soul" there is "a discernment of the unseen world in the things that are seen, a realization of what is Sovereign and Adorable, and an incredulity and ignorance about what is transient and changeable . . ."[11]

Edward Short
Astoria-Woodside-Astoria
2004–2012

---

[11] *PS*, ii, 6, p. 64.

Abbreviations and References

References to Newman's works are usually to the uniform edition of 1868–81 (36 volumes), published by Longmans Green until the stock was destroyed during the World War II. Editions of posthumous works (e.g. *Autobiographical Writings*) are noted in the references. Readers without access to the physical uniform edition can find an electronic version at *newmanreader.org*. References to the *Apologia pro Vita Sua*, *The Idea of a University*, *A Grammar of Assent*, and *Fifteen Sermons Preached before the University of Oxford* are to the Oxford critical editions. Since my study draws on only a select number of Newman's works, this is not a complete list of his published or unpublished writings.

Apo.	*Apologia pro Vita Sua.* ed. Martin J. Svaglic (Oxford, 1967)
Ari.	*The Arians of the Fourth Century*
AW	*John Henry Newman: Autobiographical Writings.* ed. Henry Tristram (London and New York, 1956)
Bygones	G. J. Holyoake. *Bygones Worth Remembering* (London, 1905)
Call.	*Callista: A Tale of the Third Century*
Contr	Frank W. Newman. *Contributions Chiefly to the Early History of the Late Cardinal Newman (1891)*
DA.	*Discussions and Arguments on Various Subjects*
Dev.	*An Essay on Development of Christian Doctrine*
Diff. i, ii.	*Certain Difficulties felt by Anglicans in Catholic Teaching*, 2 vols.
Ess, i, ii	*Essays Critical and Historical*, 2 vols.
Family	*Newman Family Letters.* ed. Dorothea Mozley (London, 1962)
GA	*An Essay in Aid of a Grammar of Assent.* ed. I. T. Ker (Oxford, 1985)
HS, i, ii, iii	*Historical Sketches*, 3 vols
Idea	*The Idea of a University.* ed. I. T. Ker (Oxford, 1976)
Jfc.	*Lectures on the Doctrine of Justification*
LD	*The Letters and Diaries of John Henry Newman.* ed. Charles Stephen Dessain et al. vols i–vi (Oxford, 1978–84), xi–xxii (London, 1961–72), xxiii–xxxii (Oxford, 1973–2008)
LG	*Loss and Gain: The Story of a Convert*
MD	*Meditations and Devotions* (London, 1893)
Mix.	*Discourses Addressed to Mixed Congregations*
Moz., i, ii	*Letters and Correspondence of John Henry Newman during his Life in the English Church.* ed. Anne Mozley, 2 vols. (London, 1891)
NO	*Newman the Oratorian: His Unpublished Oratory Papers.* ed. *Placid, Murray, OSB* (Dublin, 1969)
OS	*Sermons preached on Various Occasions*

Phases   F. W. Newman. *Phases of Faith.* ed. U. C. Knoepflmacher (Leicestershire, 1970),

PS, i-viii   *Parochial and Plain Sermons*

Prepos.   *Present Position of Catholics in England*

Rem, i., ii Thomas Mozley. *Reminiscences of Oriel College & the Oxford Movement* (London, 1882)

SD   *Sermons bearing on Subjects of the Day*

Sieveking   I. G. Sieveking. *Memoir and Letters of Francis W. Newman* (London, 1907)

SN   *Sermon Notes of John Henry Newman: 1849–1878.* ed. Fathers of the Birmingham Oratory (London, 1913)

US   *Fifteen Sermons Preached before the University of Oxford.* ed. Earnest and Tracey (Oxford, 2006)

VM, i, ii   *The Via Media*, 2 vols

VV   *Verses on Various Occasions*

Chronology of John Henry Newman and his Family

1801 Born in London: 21 February
1808 Enters Ealing School
1806 Converted to dogmatic Christianity by classical master, the Rev Walter Mayers
1817 Enters Trinity College, Oxford
1818 Wins college scholarship
1820 Obtains poor BA
1822 Elected fellow of Oriel College, Oxford
1824 Ordained deacon and curate of St Clement's, Oxford
      Death of John Newman (1767–1824)
1825 Appointed Vice-Principal of Alban Hall and Ordained Priest
1826 Appointed tutor of Oriel
1828 Appointed Vicar of St Mary's. *Arians of the Fourth Century*. Sails for Mediter-
      ranean with Archdeacon and Hurrell Froude
      Death of Mary Newman (1808–28)
1833 May: Succumbs to life-threatening fever in Sicily
      July: Returns to England
      July: Keble delivers Assize Sermon "On National Apostasy", which inaugurates
      Oxford Movement
1834 Publishes first volume of *Parochial and Plain Sermons*
1836 Death of Jemima (née Fourdrinier) Newman (1771–1836)
1837 *Lectures on the Prophetical Office of the Church*
1838 *Lectures on the Doctrine of Justification*
1841 *The Tamworth Reading Room*. Tract 90
1842 Moves to Littlemore
1843 *Oxford University Sermons*
      September: Resigns the living of St Mary's
      Sermons on Subjects of the Day
1845 Resigns Oriel Fellowship: 3 October
      Received into Roman Catholic Church: 9 October
      Essay on the Development of Christian Doctrine
1846 23 February: leaves Oxford for Marvvale, near Birmingham
1847 30 May: ordained priest in Rome. *Loss and Gain*
1848 1 February: founds the Oratory of St Philip Neri at Birmingham
1849 *Discourses Addressed to Mixed Congregations*

1850   *Lectures on Certain Difficulties felt by Anglicans in submitting to the Catholic Church*
        Restoration of Catholic hierarchy in England: period known as "papal aggression"
1851   *Lectures on Present Position of Catholics in England*
        Appointed Rector of Catholic University of Ireland (resigns 1858)
1852   *Discourses on the Scope of University Education*
        Death of Harriett (née Newman) Mozley (1803–52)
1856   *Callista: A Sketch of the Third Century*
1857   *Sermons Preached on Various Occasions*
1859   *Lectures and Essays on University Subjects*
        "On Consulting the Faithful in Matters in Doctrine" published in *Rambler*
1864   *Apologia pro vita sua*
1865   *The Dream of Gerontius*
1866   *A Letter to the Rev E.B. Pusey*
1868   *Verses on Various Occasions*
1870   *An Essay in Aid of a Grammar of Assent*
        Papal infallibility defined by First Vatican Council
1873   *The Idea of a University*
1875   *A Letter to the Duke of Norfolk*
1877   *Via Media*
        Elected honorary fellow of Trinity College, Oxford
1879   Created cardinal by Leo XIII
        Death of Jemima (née Newman) Mozley (1808–79)
1884   Death of Charles Robert Newman (1802–84)
1890   Death of John Henry Cardinal Newman: 11 August
1897   Death of Francis William Newman (1805–97)
1931   Death of John Rickards Mozley (1840–1931)
1991   John Henry Cardinal Newman Declared Venerable
2010   Blessed John Henry Cardinal Newman beatified by Pope Benedict XVI: 19 September

Introduction

On Sunday, the 15th of August, 1773, before their tour of the Hebrides, Johnson and Boswell were in Edinburgh dining with Dr William Robertson, the antiquary and historian of Greece, when the topic of Edmund Burke came up. "What I most envy Burke for," Johnson observed, "is his being constantly the same. He is never humdrum; never unwilling to begin to talk, nor in haste to leave off . . . Burke, sir, is such a man, that if you met him for the first time in a street where you were stopped by a drove of oxen, and you and he stepped aside to take shelter but for five minutes, he'd talk to you in such manner, that, when you parted, you would say, this is an extraordinary man."[1] John Henry Newman, in contrast, for all of his many talents, lacked this sort of conspicuous distinction. One can see this in his photographs, even in his portraits, where he clearly refuses to play the great man. William Lockhart (1820–92), the first of his friends to convert, captured something of this aspect of the man when he recalled seeing Newman walking in the street. "I have a vivid remembrance of my first seeing John Henry Newman when I was quite a youth at Oxford. He was pointed out to me in the High-street. I should not have noticed him if his name had not been mentioned by my companion. I looked, and then, I saw him passing along in his characteristic way, walking fast, without any dignity of gait and earnest, like one who had a purpose; yet so humble and self-forgetting in every portion of his external appearance, that you would not have thought him, at first sight, a man remarkable for anything. It was only when you came to know him that you recognized or began to recognize what he was."[2] One of the great paradoxes of Newman's life is that it was his cultivation of the unremarkable, his disavowal of pomp and prestige, his delight in the ordinary that made him so very remarkable indeed. In this respect, he reminds one of Saint Francis de Sales, who knew how "humility resembles that tree of Tylos, which at night folds up and conceals its beautiful flowers . . . So humility enfolds and conceals all our virtues and human perfections, producing them only at the call of charity, which is not an earthly but a heavenly virtue, not a moral but a divine perfection, and the very sun of all the other virtues, over which she should always preside . . ."[3] The remarkable thing about Newman that I highlight in this book is the deep love he had

---

[1] *Johnson's Journey to the Western Islands of Scotland and Boswell's Journal of a Tour to the Hebrides with Samuel Johnson, LL.D.* ed. R. W. Chapman (Oxford, 1933), pp. 179–80.

[2] William Lockhart. *Cardinal Newman: Reminiscences of Fifty Years Since* (London, 1891), p. 1.

[3] St Francis De Sales. *An Introduction to the Devout Life* (Philadelphia, 1942), p. 127. It is fitting that this insight should come from Saint Francis de Sales because in Newman's own chapel at the Birmingham Oratory the patron saint of authors has pride of place over the altar, to the right and left of which are portraits of Newman's many friends.

for his family, despite their many difficulties and differences, which can be understood best as his own response to the "call of charity." This is an aspect of his character that has not been given the attention it deserves. It is true that Meriol Trevor provided a good deal of information about the different family members in her indispensable two-volume biography, as did the lively storyteller Sean O'Faolain in his rather more impressionistic study, *Newman's Way* (1952). Dorothea Mozley did a good job of bringing together a sampling of the family correspondence in *Newman Family Letters* (1962), on which I have drawn extensively. But I believe that mine is the first book to consider the ways in which Newman's family helped him to respond to the "call of charity." Readers can see this most vividly in the chapters that follow here on Charles, Frank, Harriett, and Jemima, where that call could not have been more demanding. Then, again, I don't know that anyone else has endeavoured to show, as I have, how Newman's family enabled him to understand the faith of the English generally, in all its redoubtable dissidence. It was, after all, Newman's brothers and sisters who first acquainted him with the barriers that stood in the way of his sharing his dogmatic faith with a Protestant society that regarded the Roman Church as tyrannical, corrupt, backward, and traitorous. In the chapters that follow, I show how Newman's family gave him a useful foretaste of what he could expect from the world beyond the family circle, especially after he grew disenchanted with Anglicanism in the late 1830s and moved closer and closer to Rome.

In one of his early uncollected sermons, written in 1824, the year of his ordination into the Anglican ministry, Newman spoke of how his very priesthood compounded these barriers, especially with loved ones. Referring to the "dispensers of the word of life," he spoke of how "Their office is as arduous and tremendous as it is honourable. To have to answer for the souls of men is an awful consideration.

> They are of the same fallen nature as their brethren; yet they must learn to be better than they, and not only purify themselves but others also. They have to wrestle not only with sin, but with the author of sin—and are in an especial way of objects of attack from the evil one, for he knows that in slaying them, he slays the leaders of the host. But the most difficult and painful circumstances is one which relates to their flock itself. They have to convert and admonish those, who (without God's grace) oppose the very efforts that are made for their good. Thus in one sense they are at war with the very individuals they love. They have to wrestle with the pride and selfishness of the heart. They have to probe before they can cure. They are seemingly unkind. Thus they must be content with the affection of some, and meekly bear the opposition of many. They must not wonder if they are misunderstood and misrepresented.[4]

Considering the generosity and devotion with which Newman assumed his pastoral duties, it is not surprising that he should have warmed to Fra Cristoforo in Manzoni's best-selling novel, *I Promessi Sposi* ("The Betrothed"), which provided Newman with one of his first glimpses into the Roman clergy, an otherwise exotic species

---

[4] Sermon 1, No. 42, "On Attending the Ordinances of Grace," preached 12 December 1824 *in John Henry Newman: Sermons 1824–1843* (Oxford, 2011), IV, p. 9.

in nineteenth-century England.[5] "I have lately been reading a novel you spoke of, I Promessi Sposi," he wrote his sister Jemima in 1837, and am quite delighted with it . . . It is most inspiring—it quite transported me in parts."[6] Two years later, he wrote his friend Frederic Rogers of how "The Capuchin in the 'Promessi Sposi' has stuck in my heart like a dart. I have never got over him. Only I think it would be, in sober seriousness, far too great an honour for such as me to have such a post, being little worthy or fit for it."[7] Later, after his conversion, in 1846, Newman would write Jemima of missing Manzoni in Milan. "I will not leave Milan, which I intend to do tomorrow, without sending you a line. We have *not* seen Manzoni—and I believe he is even more sorry for it than we are. Not that we are not sorry, but it is so great a thing to be in the city of St Ambrose. I never was in a city which has so enchanted me. To stand before the tombs of such great saints as St Ambrose and St Carlo—and to see the places where St Ambrose repelled the Arians, where St Monica kept watch through the night with the 'pia plebs' as St Augustine calls them, and where St Augustine himself was baptized. Our oldest Churches in England are nothing in antiquity to those here, and then the ashes of the Saints have been scattered to the four winds. It is so great a thing to be where the 'primordia,' the cradle, as it were, of Christianity is still existing."[8] In my chapter on Jemima, I show how such communications strained a relationship that was strained enough after he abandoned the English faith of the Tractarians for the foreign faith of St Ambrose and St Augustine. Still, it was nicely ironic that Jemima, who would never entirely reconcile herself to her brother's conversion, should have introduced him to a priest in Fra Cristoforo that so splendidly personified his pastoral ideal.[9]

Had Newman been still alive when his brother Frank published his vituperative memoir, *Contributions Chiefly to the Early History of the Late Cardinal Newman* (1891), he might have been hurt but not surprised by it. In this respect, for Newman, his family became something of a microcosm of the larger English world beyond the family, a little England, in which he encountered many of the same prejudices that animated the larger world. If his sisters embodied many of the assumptions of those loyal to the National Church, his brothers embodied many of the assumptions of those disloyal to that Church, with the exception of those, of course, whose disloyalty led them to the Church of Rome. No two men were more disinclined to consider following Newman's lead than his two brothers.

In the chapters that follow, I look at Newman's relationships with his parents and with his siblings to show how each of them helped shape his understanding of his contemporaries but also of himself. In my chapter on Newman's relationship with his father, I show how John Newman was similar to many fathers of families, intent on

---

[5]   Alessandro Manzoni (1785–1873) was a Milanese poet and novelist for whom Verdi wrote his *Requiem*. After falling under Voltaire's sway and drifting away from the Church in his youth, Manzoni became a staunch Catholic. For James Hope-Scott, Manzoni's Ultramontanism was the result of his former unbelief, "And what more natural than for a stray sheep to be attracted by the voice of the shepherd?" See Note 3, LD, 30: 267 JHN to Robert Ornsby (22 October 1883).

[6]   LD, 6: 150 JHN to Mrs John Mozley (6 October 1837).

[7]   LD, 7: 151 JHN to Federic Rogers (15 September 1839).

[8]   LD, 11: 264 JHN to Mrs John Mozley (22 October 1846).

[9]   See Jo Anne Cammarata Sylva's *How Italy and her People Shaped Cardinal Newman: Italian Influences on an English Mind* (New Jersey, 2010) for an excellent account of Newman's interest in Manzoni.

providing for his wife and children but perfunctory when it came to his Christian faith. Still, his father gave him, among many other things, insights into the religion of the nineteenth-century English, as well as into the world that set itself in opposition to the Church, which always reminded his son of how anathema religion was to the natural man. He was also the person to whom he first confided his failure in the BA examination at Trinity and his triumph when he won his Oriel fellowship in 1822. Nothing could have summed up his joy on that occasion better than this: "I am just made Fellow of Oriel. Thank God. Love to all," to which his mother responded with characteristic thankfulness and solicitude.

> I am quite at a loss to express my surprise, pleasure and gratitude at your success. What a great blessing you should be spared the labours and anxiety of another year's probation. For that I feel most thankful, as my great dread has been lest your health should be injured by such close application. Your Father was quite affected at the intelligence. He desires his love, and concurs with me in all I have said.[10]

Then, again, in my chapter on Newman's eldest sister, Harriett, I show how her anti-Romanism mirrored his own, until he began to see that Rome was not accurately reflected in the defamatory caricatures of English Protestantism. On 6 October 1845, three days before he would convert, Newman published his famous "Retractation of Anti-Catholic Statements," averring:

> It is now above eleven years since the writer of the following pages, in one of the early numbers of the Tracts for the Times, expressed himself thus:—"Considering the high gifts, and the strong claims of the Church of Rome and its dependencies on our admiration, reverence, love, and gratitude, how could we withstand it, as we do; how could we refrain from being melted into tenderness, and rushing into communion with it, but for the words of Truth itself, which bid us prefer it to the whole world? 'He that loveth father or mother more than Me, is not worthy of Me.' How could we learn to be severe, and execute judgment, but for the warning of Moses against even a divinely-gifted teacher who should preach new gods, and the anathema of St. Paul even against Angels and Apostles who should bring in a new doctrine?" He little thought, when he so wrote, that the time would ever come, when he should feel the obstacle, which he spoke of as lying in the way of communion with the Church of Rome, to be destitute of solid foundation.[11]

In his splendidly unwhiggish *A History of the Protestant Reformation in England and Ireland* (1827), William Cobbett recalled how, "From our very infancy, on the knees of our mothers, we have been taught to believe, that to be a Catholic was to be a false, cruel, and bloody wretch; and 'popery and slavery' have been wrung in our ears, till, whether we looked on the Catholics in their private or their public capacity, we have inevitably come to the conclusion, that they were every thing that was vicious and

---

[10] LD, 1: 129.
[11] *VM*, ii, p. 427.

vile."[12] In my chapter on Harriett, I show how Newman spent most of his Anglican career coming to terms with this traditional bugbear. Once he recognized that the objections to Rome were indeed "destitute of solid foundation," Newman would go on to write many responses to the sort of anti-Romanism that he encountered in Harriett, both in his letters and in his published works, but one of his most eloquent responses can be found in a piece he wrote on Pius IX for whose "independence in policy and vigour in action" he had such deep admiration.[13] Speaking of the rabid opposition that greeted the reconstitution of the hierarchy in England in 1850, the period known as "Papal Aggression," Newman wrote:

> It may strike one at first with surprise, that, in the middle of the nineteenth century, in an age of professed light and liberality, so determined a spirit of persecution should have arisen, as we experience it, in these countries, against the professors of the ancient faith. Catholics have been startled, irritated, and depressed, at this unexpected occurrence; they have been frightened, and have wished to retrace their steps; but after all, far from suggesting matter for alarm or despondency, it is nothing more or less than a confession on the part of our adversaries, how strong we are, and how great our promise. It is the expression of their profound misgiving that the Religion which existed long before theirs, is destined to live after it. This is no mere deduction from their acts; it is their own avowal. They have seen that Protestantism was all but extinct abroad; they have confessed that its last refuge and fortress was in England; they have proclaimed aloud, that, if England was supine at this moment, Protestantism was gone.

In my chapter on Harriett, I show how she and her husband Tom Mozley did indeed see how "Protestantism was all but extinct abroad" when they visited Normandy in 1843. And in my chapter on Frank Newman I show how his opposition to Rome betrayed immense misgivings about the subjectivism that he cobbled together for his own faith. In fact, Frank's opposition to Rome was so virulent that it even led him to imagine that his brother converted *without* believing in the authority of the Magisterium, something which Newman might certainly have had him in mind when he wrote these clarion sentences during the period known as "Papal Aggression":

> Twenty years ago England could afford, as much in contempt as in generosity, to grant to Catholics political emancipation. Forty or fifty years ago it was a common belief in her religious circles that the great Emperor, with whom she was at war,

[12] William Cobbett. *A History of the Protestant Reformation in England and Ireland* (London, 1846), II, p. 4.
[13] *HS*, iii, p. 148. Readers should contrast what Newman has to say here with what the historian Eamon Duffy says in *The New York Review of Books* (23 December 2010), where he claims that Newman "was scathingly critical of the authoritarian papacy of Pope Pius IX . . . and . . . opposed the definition of papal infallibility in 1870 as an unnecessary and inappropriate burden on consciences." In fact, Newman was not critical of Pius IX or his papacy; he was critical of how the English Ultramontanes misrepresented Pius and his papacy. Moreover, Newman did not oppose the definition of infallibility; he regarded it as inopportune. When it was finally decreed, at the First Vatican Council, he welcomed it, not least because he saw it as a necessary rebuff to the extravagances of the English Ultramontanes.

was raised up to annihilate the Popedom. But from the very grave of Pius the Sixth, and from the prison of Pius the Seventh, from the very moment that they had an opportunity of showing to the world their familiarity with that ecclesiastical virtue of which I have said so much, the Catholic movement began. In proportion to the weakness of the Holy See at home, became its influence and its success in the world. The Apostles were told to be prudent as serpents, and simple as doves. It has been the simplicity of the Sovereign Pontiffs which has been their prudence. It is their fidelity to their commission, and their detachment from all secular objects, which has given them the possession of the earth.[14]

By rejecting the anti-Romanism of Harriett and Frank and embracing the faith that was so objectionable not only to his sisters and brothers but to his parents, Newman showed how fully he grasped the import of Christ's warning, which is at the very heart of the theme of this book: "He that loveth father or mother more than Me, is not worthy of Me." By the same token, I show how Newman's mother and father (often unwittingly) helped him to live out his faith, especially when adversity and heartbreak came knocking at the family's door.

Indeed, it was adversity and heartbreak that enabled Newman to understand the true character of the Christian faith. In his sermon, "The Weapons of Saints" (1837), he drove home to his audience just how revolutionary Christianity was. Before one could understand sanctity, Newman contended, one had to understand the source of sanctity, and here he explicated those ringing words from St Matthew: "Many that are first shall be last, and the last shall be first."

These words are fulfilled under the Gospel in many ways. Our Saviour in one place applies them to the rejection of the Jews and the calling of the Gentiles; but in the context, in which they stand as I have cited them, they seem to have a further meaning, and to embody a great principle, which we all indeed acknowledge, but are deficient in mastering. Under the dispensation of the Spirit all things were to become new and to be reversed. Strength, numbers, wealth, philosophy, eloquence, craft, experience of life, knowledge of human nature, these are the means by which worldly men have ever gained the world. But in that kingdom which Christ has set up, all is contrariwise. "The weapons of our warfare are not carnal, but mighty through God to the pulling down of strongholds." What was before in honour, has been dishonoured; what before was in dishonour, has come to honour; what before was successful, fails; what before failed, succeeds. What before was great, has become little; what before was little, has become great. Weakness has conquered strength, for the hidden strength of God "is made perfect in weakness." Death has conquered life, for in that death is a more glorious resurrection. Spirit has conquered flesh; for that spirit is an inspiration from above. A new kingdom has been established, not merely different from all kingdoms before it, but contrary to them; a paradox in the eyes of man,—the visible rule of the invisible Saviour.[15]

---

[14] *Rise and Progress of Universities*, in *H.S.*, iii, pp. 145–6.
[15] *PS*, VI, pp. 22, 313–14.

Having reaffirmed the Christian faith in these luminous terms, Newman could begin to encourage his auditors to see the personal appeal of sanctity. "Now let us apply this great truth to ourselves," he exhorted his listeners, "for be it ever recollected, *we* are the sons of God, *we* are the soldiers of Christ. The kingdom is within us, and among us, and around us. We are apt to speak of it as a matter of history; we speak of it as at a distance; but really we are a part of it, or ought to be; and, as we wish to be a living portion of it, which is our only hope of salvation, we must learn what its characters are in order to imitate them."[16] Newman wrote this sermon in 1837 but it could describe his entire apostolate. And his family was instrumental in helping him not only to understand but to live it.

Then, again, in his *Meditations and Devotions*, Newman shows how family figures in the self-sacrifice necessary to receive what he calls "The Forty Days' Teaching."

> O my Saviour, I adore Thee for Thy infinite wisdom, which sees what we do not see, and orderest all things in its own most perfect way. When Thou didst say to the Apostles that Thou wast going away, they cried out, as if Thou hadst, if it may be so said, broken faith with them. They seemed to say to Thee, "O Jesu, did we not leave all things for Thee? Did we not give up home and family, father and wife, friends and neighbours, our habits, our accustomed way of living, that we might join Thee? Did we not divorce ourselves from the world, or rather die to it, that we might be eternally united and live to Thee? And now Thou sayest that Thou art leaving us. Is this reasonable? is this just? is this faithfulness to Thy promise? Did we bargain for this? O Lord Jesus, we adore Thee, but we are confounded, and we know not what to say!"
>
> Yet let God be true, and every man a liar. Let the Divine Word triumph in our minds over every argument and persuasion of sensible appearances. Let faith rule us and not sight. Thou art justified, O Lord, when Thou art arraigned, and dost gain the cause when Thou art judged. For Thou didst know that the true way of possessing Thee was to lose Thee. Thou didst know that what man stands most of all in need of, and in the first place, is not an outward guide, though that he needs too, but an inward, intimate, invisible aid. Thou didst intend to heal him thoroughly, not slightly; not merely to reform the surface, but to remove and destroy the heart and root of all his ills. Thou then didst purpose to visit his soul, and Thou didst depart in body, that Thou mightest come again to him in spirit. Thou didst not stay with Thy Apostles therefore, as in the days of Thy flesh, but Thou didst come to them and abide with them for ever, with a much more immediate and true communion in the power of the Paraclete.[17]

Another reason why Newman's family was so important to his development is that they introduced him to the extent to which the very idea of dogmatic religion revolted the English. "It is not at all easy (humanly speaking) to wind up an Englishman to a dogmatic level," Newman remarked in his *Apologia* with amusing understatement. A good example of the uncomprehending contempt with which most of his contemporaries

16 Ibid., pp. 317–18.
17 *MD*, pp. 384–5.

regarded dogmatic religion and the prayer that sustains it can be found in Ruskin's autobiography, *Praeterita* (1889), in which the great art critic described encountering a monk who gave him a tour of his alpine monastery.

> Having followed him for a time about the passages of the scattered building, in which there was nothing to show, —not a picture, not a statue, not a bit of old glass, or wellwrought vestment or jewellery, nor any architectural feature in the least ingenious or lovely, we came to a pause at last in what I suppose was a type of a modern Carthusian's cell, wherein, leaning on the window sill, I said something in the style of *Modern Painters*, about the effect of the scene outside upon religious minds. Whereupon, with a curl of his lip, "We do not come here," said the monk, "to look at the mountains." Under which rebuke I bent my head silently, thinking however all the same, "What then, by all that's stupid, do you come here for at all?"[18]

For his own part, from the time that he was a boy, Newman set great store by dogma. "From the age of fifteen," he wrote in his autobiography, "dogma has been the fundamental principle of my religion. I know no other religion; I cannot enter into the idea of any other sort of religion; religion as a mere sentiment, is to me a dream and a mockery. As well can there be filial love without the fact of a father, as devotion without the fact of a Supreme Being. What I held in 1816, I held in 1833, and I hold in 1862."[19] Even Gladstone recognized the importance of the dogmatic principle, when, musing in 1851 on what he suspected would be the imminent demise of the pope's temporal power, he told Manning:

> The temporal power of the Pope, that great, wonderful, and ancient creation, is *gone*; the problem has been worked out, the ground is mined, the train is laid, a foreign force, in its nature transitory, alone stays the hand of those who would complete the process by applying the match . . . When that event comes it will bring about a great shifting of parts . . . God grant it may be for good. I desire it because I see plainly that justice requires it, and God is the God of justice. Not out of malice to the Popedom: for I cannot at this moment dare to answer with a confident affirmative the question, a very solemn one: "Ten, twenty, fifty years hence, will there be any other body in Western Christendom witnessing for fixed dogmatic truth?" With all my soul, I wish it well . . .[20]

Newman's grasp of the indispensability of the dogmatic principle was confirmed by his reading of the Fathers, whose hearts and minds were dedicated to defining dogma as a means of ascertaining the deposit of the faith. Indeed, the profound patristic cast of Newman's thinking was noticeable even to those who did not share his religious views. Sir James Knowles (1831–1908), who edited the *Contemporary Review* and the *Nineteenth Century*, designed the Grosvenor Hotel in Victoria, as well as St Stephen's,

[18] John Ruskin. *Praeterita* (Oxford World Classics, 2012), p. 305.
[19] *Apo.*, p. 54.
[20] Gladstone to Manning (26 January 1851) in *Correspondence on Church and Religion of W. E. Gladstone.* ed. D. C. Lathbury (London, 1910), I, p. 359.

St Philip's and St Saviour's in Clapham, and served as impresario of the Metaphysical Society from 1869 to 1881, was entirely latitudinarian in his own religious beliefs, and yet even he could see that Newman stood "in our century," as he said, "as if one of the early Fathers had strayed into it." In fact, with St Athanasius in mind, Knowles thought Newman "ought to have lived in Alexandria." He particularly recalled Newman telling him that *"It will be a very very long time before the English people listens to dogma again."*[21]

Throughout his long life, Newman's English contemporaries would richly bear out this prediction. Augustine Birrell (1850–1933), the essayist and Liberal statesman, who was unfortunate enough to be caught unawares by the Easter Rebellion in Dublin in 1916 when he was chief secretary there, spoke for many nineteenth-century Englishmen when he recalled in 1884 how, "It was common talk at one time to express astonishment at the extending influence of the Church of Rome, and to wonder how people who went about unaccompanied by keepers could submit their reason to the Papacy, with her open rupture with science and her evil historical reputation. From astonishment to contempt is but a step. We first open wide our eyes and then our mouths."[22] Even Richard Holt Hutton shared this distrust of dogma, writing in his brief biography of Newman, "Dogma is essential in order to display and safeguard the revelation; but dogma is not itself the revelation. And it is conceivable that in drawing out and safeguarding the revelation, the Church may not unfrequently have laid even too much stress on right conceptions, and too little on right attitudes of will and emotion."[23] But for Newman the person who exhibited the English contempt for dogma most distressingly was his brother Frank, who summed up his own view of the matter by exclaiming "Oh Dogma! Dogma! how dost thou trample under foot love, truth, conscience, justice! Was ever a Moloch worse than thou?"[24]

At the same time, it is important to stress that Newman, for all of his insistence on the primacy of dogma, never sought to palliate the occasional enormities of the Roman Church in her strictly human aspects, which, he recognized, only reinforced the English aversion to Roman Catholicism. Writing to his good friend Lady Georgiana Fullerton, the convert peeress, whose novel *Ellen Middleton* (1844) created such a sensation by reacquainting the English with the power of the confessional, Newman observed of the Massacre of St Bartholomew's Day, which resulted in the murder of some 10,000 Huguenots in Paris and other French cities on the night of 23 August 1572: "It seems to me that we are not drawn to uphold the policy of Catherine de Medici, a woman whom no one thinks well of, merely because the Pope of the day [Gregory XIII], ill-informed perhaps and profoundly moved by the fierce and unprincipled conduct of the Huguenots, showed joy at the news of the massacre. Nor does the

[21] Knowles quoted in Priscilla Metcalf. *James Knowles: Victorian Editor and Architect* (Oxford, 1980), p. 357. W. G. Ward paid Knowles a handsome compliment when he said of the charming, clubbable, talented man who managed to bring together so many different men of differing faiths: "In conversation he had the very happy art of finding the subject on which different members of the company could and would talk freely, and of himself putting in the right word, and, as it were, winding up the clock." See Ward quoted in Metcalf, p. 358.

[22] "Via Media," in Augustine Birrell. *Obiter Dicta* (London, 1884), p. 184.

[23] R. H. Hutton. *Cardinal Newman* (London, 1890), p. 24.

[24] *Phases*, p. 37.

event reconcile us to it—for, I suppose, it is by such acts, deeply impressing the English mind, that Catholics in England suffer to this day. It has *not* turned out to the greater glory of God."[25]

Admitting one's mistakes meant a good deal to Newman, even though it was the admission of his own erroneous views of religion that led so many of his family and friends to turn against him. Still, this readiness to criticize himself was part and parcel of his intellectual honesty and it can be seen in nearly every aspect of the man and his work. Dean Church, the author of what remains the greatest history of the Oxford Movement, made a number of observations in his obituary of his close friend in the *Guardian* (an Anglican paper in the nineteenth century) which nicely corroborates this point. "It is common to speak of the naturalness and ease of Cardinal Newman's style in writing," Church observed. "It is, of course, the first thing that attracts notice when we open one of his book," though he also recognized that "there are people who think it bald and thin and dry. They look out for longer words, and grander phrases, and more involved constructions, and neater epigrams. They expect a great theme to be treated with more pomp and majesty, and they are disappointed. But the majority of English readers seem to be agreed in recognising the beauty and transparent flow of language, which matches the best French writing in rendering with sureness and without effort the thought of the writer." It is amusing that Church should have singled out the French in this regard because it was the Frenchman Buffon (1707–88), who famously said that *Ces choses sont hors de l'homme, le style est l'homme,* an apothegm with which Newman would not have entirely agreed. For him, subject matter was *not* external to the man. Certainly, in all the subjects he essayed—whether education, philosophy, theology or literature—he took a profoundly personal interest. Still, for Church, "what is more interesting than even the formation of such a style—a work, we may be sure, not accomplished without much labour—is the man behind the style."

> For the man and the style are one in this perfect naturalness and ease. Any one who has watched at all carefully the Cardinal's career, whether in old days or later, must have been struck with this feature of his character, his naturalness, the freshness and freedom with which he addressed a friend or expressed an opinion, the absence of all mannerism and formality; and where he had to keep his dignity, both his loyal obedience to the authority which enjoined it and the half-amused, half-bored impatience that he should be the person round whom all these grand doings centred. It made the greatest difference in his friendships whether his friends met him on equal terms, or whether they brought with them too great conventional deference or solemnity of manner. He was by no means disposed to allow liberties to be taken or to put up with impertinence; for all that bordered on the unreal, for all that was pompous, conceited, affected he had little patience; but almost beyond all these was his disgust at being made the object of foolish admiration. He protested with whimsical fierceness against being made a hero or a sage; he was what he was, he said, and nothing more, and he was inclined

---

[25] LD, 32:262 JHN to Lady Georgiana Fullerton (21 October 1864).

to be rude when people tried to force him into an eminence which he refused. With his profound sense of the incomplete and the ridiculous in this world, and with a humour in which the grotesque and the pathetic sides of life were together recognised every moment, he never hesitated to admit his own mistakes.[26]

These are the qualities that make the *Apologia Pro Vita Sua* (1864), Newman's great spiritual autobiography such a special book. Far from being an exercise in self-vindication, as some have claimed, it is full of self-deprecatory honesty. It is also as much an account of his disenchantment with the Church of England, as his conversion to Rome, which necessarily required him to "admit his own mistakes."

Few eminent Victorians can be understood without reference to their families. We need to know about Thackeray's relationship with his intensely Evangelical mother in order to understand not only his fascination with the vanity of the world but his longing for some antidote to that vanity.[27] We need to know about the coddling that Ruskin received from his parents to understand how it both sustained and stultified him.[28] We need to know about Dickens' attachment to his wayward father to understand his immense sympathy with the outcast, as well as his will to succeed where his father had failed. We need to know about the Brontë family in order to know how it helped to produce the extraordinary talents that gave us *Wuthering Heights* and *Jane Eyre*. Similarly, no one can understand Newman's warm affectionate playful gregarious generous nature unless he knows something of the love he received from and gave back to his family, even though his evolving religious convictions would, in many cases, alienate that love.

Considering the number of friends that Newman not only made but retained during his long life—the number is staggeringly large: there are hundreds and hundreds of people with whom he was friendly—one sometimes wonders if he did not possess some friend-inducing talisman. In *Travels in West Africa* (1897), Mary Kingsley (1862–1900), the niece of Newman's most famous critic, Charles Kingsley (1819–75), relates how she encountered a "friendship-compelling charm" when she was visiting tribesmen along the Ivory Coast. As she described it, this popular charm ". . . is obtained on the death of a person you know really cared for you—like your father or mother, for example—by cutting off the head and suspending it over a heap of chalk, as the white earth that you find in river beds is called here, then letting it drip as long as it will and using this saturated chalk to mix in among the food of any one you wish should think kindly of you . . ."[29] It is unlikely that Newman ever went to quite these lengths to make himself agreeable to the many people who thought kindly of him—he rarely dined outside college when he was at Oxford or outside the refectory when he was at the Birmingham Oratory—but it is still astonishing how many friends he had. And it is extraordinary

---

[26] LD, 32:602.

[27] John Aplin. *The Inheritance of Genius 1798–1875* and *Memory and Legacy 1876–1919* (London, 2011) and *Thackeray Family Letters* (London, 2011).

[28] Something of the adulation Ruskin received at home can be gleaned from his father's exclaiming, "Oh! how dull and dreary is the best society I fall into compared with the circle of my own Fire Side with my Love sitting opposite irradiating all around her, and my most extraordinary boy." Ruskin quoted in Judith Flanders. *The Victorian House* (London, 2003), p. xxiv.

[29] Mary Kingsley. *Travels in West Africa* (Folio Society, 2007), p. 159.

how many entire families he befriended. One thinks of the Arnolds, the Badeleys, the Bowdens, the Bowles, the Froudes, the Hope-Scotts, the Howards, the Mozleys, the Puseys, the Ryders, the Simeons, and, of course, the Wilberforces. If there is such a thing as versatility in friendship, no one ever possessed it to the degree that Newman possessed it. He was a master, a *virtuoso* of friendship.

Indeed, when one thinks of all of the distinctly different personalities in these families—for example, in the Froude family, not only the scrupulously devout Hurrell and the blithely irreverent Anthony but the earnestly sceptical William and the High Church paterfamilias, Archdeacon Froude, with his positively Wildean addiction to paradox—one can begin to see that for any one individual to befriend all of them showed a very catholic appreciation for the good points in others.

Considering the legendary barbs that Newman directed at the quintessentially liberal Dr Arnold, it is extraordinary that he should have been befriended by both his sons: Matthew, the dutiful inspector of schools, poet and critic and Thomas, the modestly heroic convert and schoolmaster who, in following Newman *twice* into the arms of the papists, overcame not only his love of the quiet life but his formidable wife, Julia *née* Sorrell, who blamed Newman for the straitened finances her husband's conversions caused the family. (Her daughter, Mary, later Mrs Humphry Ward recalled seeing Newman walking along the streets of Edgbaston and "shrinking from him in dumb, childish resentment as from some one whom I understood to be the author of our family misfortunes.")[30] Tom Arnold recorded a vivid account of his last meeting with Newman following Newman's last note to him, which demonstrated that Newman's ability to appeal to widely varied families was part and parcel of his appeal to English Protestants as a whole, an appeal which he continues to exert. On 16 July 1879, Newman had written:

> My Dear Arnold,
>
> Don't suppose I was neglectful of your kind letter of April 18 because I have left it so long unanswered. But, when it was written, I was between Paris and Turin, and I have been so busy, so ill, and so oppressed with arrears of work since, that I left many friendly letters unanswered, and yours in the number.
>
> It is a strange phenomenon which we heard at the Vatican, that the Pope had been deluged with letters from England by Protestants, stating their satisfaction at his having promoted me.
>
> Ever yours affectly., John H. Card. Newman.[31]

Nine years later, Arnold found himself in Birmingham and, as he said, "called at the Oratory," where the "Cardinal's quarters were now on the ground floor. He received me with the greatest kindness, and we had a long conversation, chiefly on the Irish University question. I noticed then, and not for the first time, how much more distinguished his features had become, for regularity, dignity, and even beauty, since

---

[30] John Sutherland. *Mrs. Humphry Ward: Eminent Victorian, Preeminent Edwardian* (Oxford, 1990), p. 22.

[31] LD, 29:155–6 JHN to Thomas Arnold (16 July 1879).

he had become a very old man. There was not the least sign in his talk of the infirmities of age. When I rose to go, I spoke of the pleasure it had given me to find him in such comparatively good health and strength. He replied with a smile, 'But you know, Arnold, I am so *very* old.'" Then, after his death, Arnold recalled how "In 1890 I was at the funeral service celebrated for him in the old Oratory church at Brompton. Bishop Clifford preached; a large number of Protestants were present."[32]

"Soapy" Sam Wilberforce, the eventual Bishop of Oxford, whose Broad Church elasticity came to epitomize English Protestantism after Arnold's death, might have looked askance at Newman for what he considered his excessive intellectual rigor (Cardinal Manning, for different reasons, would do the same), but his brothers, Henry and Robert felt enormous respect and indeed love for Newman, even emulating his conversion, at considerable personal sacrifice. A few days before Newman's birthday in 1835, Henry wrote him, "I cannot help sending you a line today . . . to say how very often I think of you and with what earnest desires for your happiness and usefulness. I must send you these same wishes today, because I want them to reach you on the 21st." Although he had married the year earlier, he never lost his deep affection for Newman, always maintaining the candor that had characterized their friendship when Henry was Newman's pupil at Oriel. "I think the natural fault of my mind is that of thinking less than I ought of my absent friends," Henry admitted in his birthday greetings to his dear friend, "but I can truly say that you are an exception, for there has been, I think, hardly a day (indeed I think I might say not a day) since I saw you, in which I have not thought with grateful affection of your kindness to me, and the benefits which I hope I have received from it."[33]

In 1873, when Newman received word from Henry's wife that her husband was dying, he wrote one of his characteristically moving letters of sympathy. The sorrows that he had suffered in his own family gave him the ability to enter into those of other families.

The Oratory April 21. 1873

My dear Mrs Wilberforce,

 Your letter has just come – Thank you much for writing.

 I have known Henry so long that I feel as if I were sinking and departing myself; for I am much older than he.

 What must you feel! but God supports husbands and wives in such extreme trials, and He will not fail you.

 I mean to say Mass daily for dear Henry till other news come to me – and then I shall say Mass for you and your children.

 God is good in all He does

Yours most affectly John H Newman[34]

Louis Bouyer (1913–2004), the French Oratorian, who wrote a good book on Newman in 1952, for which Monsignor H. Francis Davis, the Oratorian and first Postulator

---

[32] Thomas Arnold. *Passages in a Wandering Life* (London, 1900), p. 205.
[33] LD, 5:29 Henry Wilberforce to JHN (19 February 1835).
[34] LD, 26: 295 JHN to Mrs Wilberforce (21 April 1873).

of Newman's cause, wrote a discriminating foreword, once aptly observed: "In our perplexities, in our hopes, in our unshakeable trust in the Church, no voice beyond the grave speaks to us as powerfully as Newman does; because there is no one who speaks more directly to the heart, as there is no one who speaks more directly from the heart."[35] His letters to the Wilberforce family exemplify this. When, days later, Newman received word that Henry had died, Newman wrote his son, Wilfrid how, "There never was a man more humble than your dear father – never one who so intimately realised what it was to die – and how little we know, and how much we have to know about it. Now he knows all: he knows all that we do not know. He has the reward of all his prayers; there is an end of all his fears. He has served God with a single aim all through his life, and he now understands how good it has been to have done so. I have known him most intimately for forty-seven years and he has always been the same. Of course I shall say Masses for his soul; but I wish and pray that each of us, when our time comes, may as little need them as I think he does. None of us are fit to enter God's Holy Presence, but he has been preparing himself for it all through his life."[36] Here, Newman showed how he reciprocated Henry's love and admiration. And yet in this and in so many other condolences that he wrote for the loved ones of departed friends, Newman always bore witness to the truth that the loss of his sister Mary had impressed upon him:

> The earth that we see does not satisfy us; it is but a beginning; it is but a promise of something beyond it; even when it is gayest, with all its blossoms on, and shows most touchingly what lies hid in it, yet it is not enough. We know much more lies hid in it than we see. A world of Saints and Angels, a glorious world the palace of God, the mountain of the Lord of Hosts, the heavenly Jerusalem, the throne of God and Christ, all those wonders, everlasting, all-precious, mysterious, and incomprehensible, lie hid in what we see. What we see is the outward shell of an eternal kingdom; and on that kingdom we fix the eyes of our faith.[37]

Another remarkable thing about Newman's friendships is how many of his friends became friends of his family. On the very day in July of 1833 that Newman returned from his Mediterranean tour with the Froudes, where he succumbed to a near fatal fever in Sicily, Henry wrote him from Bath, "I heard this morning, I need not say with how much thankfulness, that you have passed through London towards Oxford. Nor need I tell you now, how much I felt on hearing indirectly that you had been so dangerously ill in the heart of a nearly barbarous country; nor even the anxiety one could not but feel at your long absence. May God, who has thus preserved you through so much, keep you now for his own great and good purposes, and make you a blessing to our country, to His Church and the world. It would indeed give me the greatest delight to hear how you are and some particulars of your late deliverance. I have thought much of Mrs Newman of your sisters, and of the sufferings which they must have undergone. Pray be so good as to assure [them] of my most sincere sympathy in their fears and their

---

[35] Louis Bouyer. *Newman: His Life and Spirituality* (London, 1958), p. 423.
[36] LD, 26: 296 JHN to Wilfrid Wilberforce (23 April 1873).
[37] *PS*, iv, p. 210. For a strenuous denial of these rudimentary truths, see Keith Thomas. *The Ends of Life: Roads to Fulfillment in Early Modern England* (London, 2009).

joy."[38] In 1880, Frederic Rogers, Lord Blachford (1811–89), Newman's old pupil from Oriel, who became such a staunch Tractarian, but with whom he had so painful a falling out when he converted, before they were finally reconciled in 1865, wrote to Newman from Menton to reminiscence about the time he spent with Mrs Newman and her daughters at Iffley in 1831: "I often think of those old Iffley days in which she [Jemima] added so much to the pleasure of all about her, and certainly – I am going to say not least – to mine. What a long time back it is – and how pleasant to remember. Before Germany or Italy or a Reformed Parliament – and when so many other things were so little what they are, and Froude used to say 'When will anything happen to disturb this stagnancy.'"[39] Isaac Williams (1802–65), the poet and Fellow of Trinity who wrote the controversial Tract 80, "On Reserve in communicating Religious Knowledge," and to whom Newman dedicated his *Church of the Fathers* (1840), was another Tractarian friend who became very fond of Newman's family, especially his mothers and sisters. For Williams, Newman, who "had so much poetry, love of scenery and associations of place and country, and domestic and filial affection. . . . never seemed . . . so saintlike and high in his character as when he was with his mother and sisters. The softness and repose of his character then came out, and so corrected that restless intellect to which he has been a prey."[40] Newman did delight in the company of his mothers and sisters, though they inspired more than "softness and repose" in him. As the chapters that follow show, Newman never hesitated to speak his mind to his mothers and sisters, especially when this involved their religious differences, and this sometimes introduced a decided contrariety, which would no doubt have disconcerted Isaac Williams, who did not understand Newman's true character or his evolving faith.

Family and friends meant so much to Newman because he recognized that they put us on the path to love of God, a theme which he nicely set out in one of his best sermons, "Love of Relations and Friends" (1831), in which he wrote:

> St. John the Apostle and Evangelist is chiefly and most familiarly known to us as "the disciple whom Jesus loved." He was one of the three or four who always attended our Blessed Lord, and had the privilege of the most intimate intercourse with Him; and, more favoured than Peter, James, and Andrew, he was His bosom friend, as we commonly express ourselves. At the solemn supper before Christ suffered, he took his place next Him, and leaned on His breast. As the other three communicated between the multitude and Christ, so St. John communicated between Christ and them. At that Last Supper, Peter dared not ask Jesus a question himself, but bade John put it to Him,—who it was that should betray Him. Thus St. John was the private and intimate friend of Christ. Again, it was to St. John that our Lord committed His Mother, when He was dying on the cross; it was to St. John that He revealed in vision after His departure the fortunes of His Church.[41]

For Newman, the import of this special affection on Christ's part is deeply revealing. We might assume that "as being All-holy," God "would have loved all men more or less,

---

[38] LD, 4:6 Henry Wilberforce to JHN (13 July 1833).
[39] Lord Blachford quoted in LD, 29: 216.
[40] *Autobiography of Isaac Williams* (London, 1892), p. 17.
[41] *PS*, ii, pp. 51–2.

in proportion to their holiness." Yet this is not the case. Instead, "we find our Saviour had a private friend; and this shows us, first, how entirely He was a man, as much as any of us, in His wants and feelings; and next, that there is nothing contrary to the spirit of the Gospel, nothing inconsistent with the fulness of Christian love, in having our affections directed in an especial way towards certain objects, towards those whom the circumstances of our past life, or some peculiarities of character, have endeared to us." Jonathan Swift, wishing to mock the false philanthropy of his own century, would famously say that he hated mankind but had a soft spot for Tom, Dick, and Harry. Newman, in his century, would be surrounded by legions of insufferable do-gooders who claimed to love mankind but had no time whatever for Tom, Dick, or Harry. Of the hollowness of such grandiose benignity he was in no doubt.

> There have been men before now, who have supposed Christian love was so diffusive as not to admit of concentration upon individuals; so that we ought to love all men equally. And many there are, who, without bringing forward any theory, yet consider practically that the love of many is something superior to the love of one or two; and neglect the charities of private life, while busy in the schemes of an expansive benevolence, or of effecting a general union and conciliation among Christians. Now I shall here maintain, in opposition to such notions of Christian love, and with our Saviour's pattern before me, that the best preparation for loving the world at large, and loving it duly and wisely, is to cultivate an intimate friendship and affection towards those who are immediately about us.[42]

From the love of those closest to us, we can begin to appreciate the love that we owe to others beyond our circle of family and friends. And the fact that this is usually a very gradual process was, for Newman, providential, because he recognized how "the great difficulty in our religious duties is their extent. This frightens and perplexes men,— naturally; those especially, who have neglected religion for a while, and on whom its obligations disclose themselves all at once. This, for example, is the great misery of leaving repentance till a man is in weakness or sickness; he does not know how to set about it. Now God's merciful Providence has in the natural course of things narrowed for us at first this large field of duty; He has given us a clue. We are to begin with loving our friends about us, and gradually to enlarge the circle of our affections, till it reaches all Christians, and then all men." Yet Newman cautions his readers against imagining that the more extensive love he describes can be easily attained. On the contrary, "it is obviously impossible to love all men in any strict and true sense. What is meant by loving all men, is, to feel well-disposed to all men, to be ready to assist them, and to act towards those who come in our way, as if we loved them. We cannot love those

---

[42] Cf. Aquinas, "Some spiritual writers have been persuaded that we should love all our neighbors equally, even our enemies. They were speaking of inward affection, not of outward effect, for where the giving of benefits is concerned the order of love puts the persons who are close to us before those who are distant. Their position, however, is quite unreasonable, for the affection of charity, following the predilection of grace, is no less unequally distributed than is natural love . . . The intensity of charity is measured with reference to the subject, the lover, and here the governing principle is this, the nearer the dearer . . ." *Summa Theologica*, 2a-2ae, xxvi, 6 and 7.

about whom we know nothing; except indeed we view them in Christ, as the objects of His Atonement, that is, rather in faith than in love." And here, Newman's wonderfully practical intelligence recognized that love cannot be simply a sentiment or emotion, however well-intended. It must be exercised, like any virtue, in real life with real people, for "love is a habit, and cannot be attained without actual *practice*, which on so large a scale is impossible." It follows from this that it is absurd "when writers (as is the manner of some who slight the Gospel) talk magnificently about loving the whole human race with a comprehensive affection, of being the friends of all mankind, and the like. Such vaunting professions, what do they come to? that such men have certain benevolent *feelings* towards the world,—feelings and nothing more;—nothing more than unstable feelings, the mere offspring of an indulged imagination, which exist only when their minds are wrought upon, and are sure to fail them in the hour of need. This is not to love men, it is but to talk about love.—The real love of man *must* depend on practice, and therefore, must begin by exercising itself on our friends around us, otherwise it will have no existence."[43]

Readers should keep these distinctions in mind when they dip into my chapters on Frank and Charles because Newman had them in mind when he wrote this vital sermon, especially their profoundly misguided notions of 'social justice,' which bear an uncomfortably close resemblance to those of our own canting age. He also had in mind his own family's difficulties, which were considerable. "By trying to love our relations and friends, by submitting to their wishes, though contrary to our own, by bearing with their infirmities, by overcoming their occasional waywardness by kindness, by dwelling on their excellences, and trying to copy them, thus it is that we form in our hearts that root of charity, which, though small at first, may, like the mustard seed, at last even overshadow the earth. The vain talkers about philanthropy . . . usually show the emptiness of their profession, by being morose and cruel in the private relations of life, which they seem to account as subjects beneath their notice."[44]

No one who delves into the history of the Enlightenment can doubt the accuracy of Newman's point, for it is a history full of bossy visionaries whose love of reason left them indifferent or even hostile to those closest them. Jean-Jacques Rousseau (1712–78), the would-be benefactor of children, abandoned his own illegitimate children to foundling hospitals, while Augustus Comte (1798–1857), the founder of his own highly idiosyncratic humanitarian faith, could never stick his devoutly Catholic family, despite his mother's cosseting. Indeed, he later blamed them for refusing to fund his various literary projects.[45] The wonderful ninth edition of the *Encyclopedia Britannica* sums up Comte's character nicely. Notwithstanding the subscription taken up for him by friends and well-wishers, which eventually gave him a competence of £200 per year, he still managed to annoy many of his benefactors, including John Stuart Mill, with his "high pontifical airs," though Mill and others remained loyal to the haughty savant. "We are sorry not to be able to record any

---

[43] *PS*, ii, pp. 54–5.
[44] Ibid., p. 55.
[45] For a more sympathetic reading of Rousseau, see Mary Ann Glendon. *The Forum and the Tower: How Scholars and Politicians Have Imagined the World from Plato to Eleanor Roosevelt* (Oxford, 2011), pp. 113–30.

similar trait of magnanimity on Comte's part," the *Britannica* entry remarks. "His character, admirable as it is for firmness, for intensity, for inexorable will, for iron devotion to what he thought the service of mankind, yet offers few of those softening qualities that make us love good men and pity bad ones. He is of the type of Brutus or of Cato—a model of austere fixity of purpose, but ungracious, domineering, and not quite free from petty bitterness."[46]

The appeal that St John had for Newman was of an altogether contrary order. "Far different indeed . . . utterly the reverse of this fictitious benevolence was his elevated and enlightened sympathy for all men. We know he is celebrated for his declarations about Christian love. 'Beloved, let us love one another, for love is of God. If we love one another, God dwelleth in us, and His love is perfected in us. God is love, and he that dwelleth in love dwelleth in God, and God in him.' Now did he begin with some vast effort at loving on a large scale? Nay, he had the unspeakable privilege of being the *friend of Christ*. Thus he was taught to love others; first his affection was concentrated, then it was expanded. Next he had the solemn and comfortable charge of tending our Lord's Mother, the Blessed Virgin, after His departure. Do we not here discern the secret sources of his especial love of the brethren? Could he, who first was favoured with his Saviour's affection, then trusted with a son's office towards His Mother, could he be other than a memorial and pattern (as far as man can be), of love, deep, contemplative, fervent, unruffled, unbounded?"[47] Certainly, this was precisely the sort of "especial love" that Newman sought to show his different family members.

As in *Newman and his Contemporaries*, my last book, which can be read as something of a companion volume to *Newman and his Family*, I have drawn extensively on Newman's vast correspondence, as well as the correspondence of his siblings. It is not possible to overstate the importance or indeed the richness of this epistolary record. Like most of their English contemporaries, Newman and his family delighted in the penny post, a system devised by Henry Cole (1808–82) and Sir Rowland Hill (1795–1879) and introduced into Britain in January of 1840. Cole, who mounted the Great Exhibition and served as the first director of the South Kensington Museum, was a great friend and admirer of Newman, singling him out for praise as the writer of "the finest specimens of our modern English language."[48] Hill and Cole revolutionized the way the English communicated with each other. As one historian of the English postal service noted:

> The reform brought about a profound social change by making communication so easy. Harriet Martineau was glad that now the poor can at last write to one another, "as if they were all M.P.'s." Richard Cobden found it a "terrible engine for upsetting monopoly and corruption," and believed the success of the Anti-Corn Law League in 1846 was assisted in no small degree by cheap postage. Disraeli in his novel *Endymion* looked back to the forties as to another world: "It is difficult for us who live in an age of railroads, telegraphs, penny posts,

---

[46] *The Encyclopedia Britannica*, Ninth Edition (New York, 1890), VI, p. 230.
[47] *PS*, ii, pp. 55–6.
[48] *LD*, 28: 326, Note 1.

and penny newspapers, to realize how limited in thought and feeling, as well as incident, was the life of an English family of retired habits and limited means only years ago"[49]

The Pre-Raphaelite painter and designer, Edward Burne-Jones (1833–98) took full advantage of the new frequency of the mails, corresponding with one of his mistresses, on average, five times a day. Indeed, he wrote her over 700 letters in just two years. In one of his more whimsical missives, he even confessed to how, as he said, "I wish I could post myself . . . I'm flat enough and stamped on enough I'm sure for post—and a penny is my full value," though he recognized that it might be awkward for her to see him handed in on a tray with her other letters.[50] Nonetheless, not all Victorians saw the point of more frequent and more accelerated mail delivery. The great laureate signed off one of his letters, "Believe me, tho penny-post maddened, yours ever, A. Tennyson." For the keenly private poet, whose letterbox was besieged by supplicants, the penny post became an absolute curse. To one old friend, after sending him £10, he wrote: "You should . . . pity us for our worse than Egyptian plague of letters, books, MSS etc not from England alone but from the colonies, U.S., even France, Germany—nay Liberia and the negroes: and the demands for churches, chapels, hospitals, schools— horseleeches all crying Give, give . . . When we are both dead of pennypost softening of the brain you will have to sprinkle a repentant tear over our ashes and believe in us as old."[51] Newman was similarly besieged and yet one of the signs of his sanctity was the generosity and indeed good-hearted care with which he answered his myriad correspondents, many of whom he did not know.

Tennyson's complaints notwithstanding, most Victorians were grateful for the ability to share their thoughts through the post so easily and so cheaply.[52] The Newman family was no different. One of the discoveries that I made in delving into the family letters is how marvellously expressive they are. Newman, of course, is one of the great English letter writers—his letters are so full of point and variety and charm and insight—but his siblings were also capable of epistolary élan.[53] Charles and Harriett were particularly good correspondents, as my chapters on them show.

Frank, on the other hand, was in a class all his own. Writing to a correspondent in March of 1850, he observed: "I am not easy (far from it) until we get out of this Chinese scrape. I have for years maintained that the more we fight against China the more we shall teach them the art of war; and unless we tear the empire in pieces by aiding insurrections, they must beat us at last, and become masters in the Indian seas. We

---

[49] Howard Robinson. *Britain's Post Office: A History of Development from The Beginnings to the Present Day* (Oxford, 1953), p. 153.

[50] Burne-Jones to Helen Mary Gaskell in Fiona McCarthy. *The Last Pre-Raphaelite: Edward Burne-Jones and the Victorian Imagination* (Harvard University Press, 2012), p. 412.

[51] *Collected Letters of Alfred Lord Tennyson.* ed. Lange and Shannon (Cambridge, 1981), I, p. xxix.

[52] Tennyson to W. C. Bennett (22 October 1864).

[53] Lytton Strachey's reputation never recovered from the flippancy of *Eminent Victorians* (1916) but his essays are still full of good things. In *Characters and Commentaries* (London, 1933), for example, he has a brilliant piece on English letter writers where he observes how: "The most lasting utterances of a man are his studied writings; the least are his conversations. His letters hover midway between these two extremes; and the fate which is reserved for them is capable of infinite gradations, from instant annihilation up to immortality." It is safe to say that none of Newman's letters merit the former.

cannot contend against three hundred and eighty millions of ingenious, industrious, homogeneous men under a single monarch with compact country, splendid rivers and harbours, unsurpassed soil and climate . . . But I seem to be *insanus inter sobrios*, for nobody accepts this thought from me."[54] When not considering foreign affairs, Frank took up local matters with the same opinionated zest. "I am becoming quite zealous for my daily swim," he wrote to his good friend James Martineau, the Unitarian sage, when he was living in Ventnor, "even when (as to-day) the south-west gives us rather too much sea, to the chagrin of the bathing men. Perhaps you have seen various letters in *The Times*, etc., on the indecency of promiscuous bathing . . . I cannot understand why they all direct their attack to the wrong point, and insist on driving people into solitudes and separations very inconvenient, instead of demanding that, as on the Continent, both sexes be clad in the water. Last year I saw an article that expressed disgust at ladies bathing within reach of *telescopes!*"[55] These extracts show the ludicrous side of Frank's viewiness; there was also a darker side, as my chapter on him reveals.

Considering how preeminently gregarious and practical Newman's genius was, it is not surprising that he should have excelled at letter writing. Of all profound thinkers, Newman is the least ponderous. In whatever he writes, he is always a man speaking to other men, and, as such, he eschews what Wordsworth called the "gaudiness and inane phraseology" that mar the prose of so many writers of English.[56] He was also careful to avoid the turgidity and pedantry that often spoils the work of the learned. When Pusey published his first book, a scholarly treatise on the state of theology in Germany, Newman wrote his sister Harriett, "It is sadly deformed with Germanisms; he is wantonly obscure . . . he invents words." Of course, Newman appreciated the warning Pusey's book was written to give about a German theology going off the rails but he also recognized that it would be "sadly misunderstood . . . from his difficulty in expressing himself."[57] Newman, in his own writing, was never unmindful of this difficulty. In a letter to Jemima, he speaks of it in a way that shows that his very awareness of it helped him to overcome it.

> It is so great a gain to throw off Oxford for a few hours . . . The country, too, is beautiful; the fresh leaves, the scents, the varied landscape. Yet I never felt so intensely the transitory nature of this world as when most delighted with these country scenes . . . I wish it were possible for words to put down those indefinite, vague, and withal subtle feelings which quite pierce the soul and make it sick.[58]

This wish to share with others his response to the great miracle of life is everywhere in Newman's wonderful correspondence. In this, he reminds one of something T. S. Eliot

---

[54] *Sieveking*, pp. 144–5. The English went to war with China in 1839–42 and 1856–60 principally to secure the interests of free trade. As Prof Hoppen notes, it was Sir John Bowring who said that "Jesus Christ is Free Trade and Free Trade is Jesus Christ." Where little wars became necessary to affirm this faith, then little wars were mounted in China and elsewhere. See K. Theodore Hoppen. *The Mid-Victorian Generation 1846–1886* (Oxford, 1998), p. 156.

[55] *Sieveking*, pp. 89–90.

[56] Wordsworth and Coleridge. *Lyrical Ballads with some Other Poems* (London, 1798), p. ii.

[57] LD, 2:74 JHN to Harriett Newman (4 June 1828).

[58] LD, 2:69 JHN to Jemima Newman (10 May 1828).

once wrote in an unpreserved lecture that he gave to Yale in 1933: "The desire to write a letter, to put down what you don't want anybody else to see but the person you are writing to, but which you do not want to be destroyed, but perhaps hope may be preserved for complete strangers to read, is ineradicable. We want to confess ourselves in writing to a few friends, and we do not always want to feel that no one but those friends will ever read what we have written."[59] At the same time, Newman encouraged others to regard their correspondence to him in this deeply personal way. To Jemima, for example, he wrote how "it is not so much for the *matter* of letters that I like to read them as for their being written by those I love."[60]

It was Newman's ability to put himself so wholeheartedly into whatever he wrote that many found so inspiring. When Edward Elgar finished his great oratorio *Gerontius* (1900), for example, which he based on Newman's long poem of the same name, he considered it "far better than anything I have ever done" and quoted a line from Ruskin's *Sesame and Lilies* to express how much it meant to him, "This is the best of me; for the rest, I ate, and drank, and slept, loved and hated, like another: my life was a vapour and is not; but *this* I saw and knew; this, if anything of mine, is worth your memory."[61] In giving of himself so thoroughly in this greatest of his compositions, Elgar was being distinctly Newmanian. In many of the chapters that follow, I show how Newman's sisters also delighted in the wholeheartedness with which their brilliant brother gave of himself in all that he did, especially when he was still at Oxford. Far from suffering from self-absorption, as some have contended, Newman realized that one has to have a self to give in order to prosper the work of love, and not only a self but a personality, and this naturally demands interiority. On this often misunderstood score, Newman was always one with Jacques Maritain (1882–1973), who observed how, "Personality means interiority to oneself."

> But precisely because it is the spirit which—in a manner unknown to the plant and animal—makes man cross the threshold of independence, properly speaking, and of interiority to oneself, consequently the subjectivity of the person has nothing in common with the unity without doors and windows of the Leibnitzian monad; it demands the communication of intelligence and love. Because of the very fact I am a person and that I express myself to myself, I seek to communicate with *that which is other* and with *others*, in the order of knowledge and love. It is essential to personality to ask for a dialogue, and for a dialogue wherein I really give myself, and wherein I am really received. Is such a dialogue actually possible? That is why personality seems to be linked in man to the experience of suffering even more deeply than to that of creative conflict. The entire person is relative to the absolute, in which alone it can find its fulfillment. Its spiritual fatherland is the whole order of goods having an absolute value, and which serve as an introduction to the absolute Whole, which transcends the world. Finally, the human person not only bears to God the common resemblance born by other creatures; it resembles Him

---

[59] Valerie Eliot brilliantly chose this as the epigraph of her first volume of Eliot's letters. See *The Letters of T. S. Eliot Volume I: 1898-1922.* ed. Valerie Eliot and Hugh Haughton (New Haven, 2011), p. v.
[60] LD, 1:297 JHN to Jemima Newman (5 September 1826).
[61] Michael Kennedy. *Portrait of Elgar* (Oxford, 1968), p. 138 and 113.

in a proper and peculiar fashion. It is the image of God. For God is spirit, and the person proceeds from Him, having as its principle of life a spiritual soul, a spirit capable of knowing and loving, and of being elevated by grace to participate in the very life of God, so as to finally love Him and know Him even as He knows and loves Himself.[62]

One does not need to be entirely conversant with *Leibnitzian monads* to take Maritain's point. In the chapters that follow, I show how it was indeed suffering that acquainted Newman with his own interiority, though this never made for the sort of introspective shilly-shally that plagued Arthur Hugh Clough and his Cambridge admirer Henry Sidgwick. Newman's interest in that utterly fascinating creature, John Henry Newman calls to mind Rembrandt's fascination with Rembrandt: which was as much about the glory and mysteriousness of life as it was about the self's discovery of that which transcends the self. The art critic Kenneth Clark is good on this in his portrait of Rembrandt, where he speaks of the same immersed detachment in Rembrandt's contemplation of self that Newsman also exhibited. "Vitality, an insatiable appetite for life," Clark pointed out, "that surely is the chief characteristic of all the greatest novels and of all the autobiographies we still care to read; and when we compare Rembrandt with some other portrait-painters—with his most famous contemporaries, Velasquez and Van Dyck—his total immersion in human life seems to give his portraits, particularly his self-portraits, a new dimension. But with this whole-hearted engagement went an equally great detachment, the two sides of his character mingling as imperceptibly as the two sides of a spinning disc. This is what makes his self-portraits unique. His appetite urged him to gobble up his own image, but his detachment freed him from all the evasions, excuses and self-pity which are the normal human reaction to that clamorous, irrepressible thing—the self."[63]

Another reason why I mine Newman's correspondence is that it highlights the deep concern that he had for the rise of unbelief in nineteenth-century England, a concern which is expressed again and again in his letters to his family. Wilfrid Ward touched on this concern in his two-volume biography, which is still worth reading. "There is one further feature in the correspondence," he wrote, "which calls for special notice."

Newman's lifelong preoccupation with the prospect of an unprecedented movement towards unbelief in religion led him from an early date to give close attention to the question,—How can the reasonableness of religious belief be brought home to all the men of goodwill? The Oxford University Sermons (on "The Theory of Religious Belief"), which began as early as 1826, have this for their main object. The "Grammar of Assent" pursued it further. His own friendship with Blanco White, with Mark Pattison, with William Froude, the brother of Hurrell, brought closely home to him the fact that there were honest inquirers to whom the mode in which

[62] Jacques Maritain. *Scholasticism and Politics* (Liberty Fund, 2011), p. 64.
[63] Kenneth Clark. *An Introduction to Rembrandt* (London, 1978), pp. 37–8. Apropos the veracity of Newman's self-awareness, one of Anthony Froude's biographers spoke for generations of Newman detractors when he observed how: "we need not impugn Newman's honesty. The fault lay in himself: he was honestly self-deluded." Waldo Hilary Dunn. *James Anthony Froude: A Biography 1857–1894* (Oxford, 1963), II, p. 600.

Christianity was presented to them had made its acceptance impossible. In early years he felt the deficiency to lie largely in the fact that the apologetic current in the Anglican Church did not take adequate account of the actual state of inquiring minds or of their special difficulties. And he regarded the result not only as a matter deeply serious in its bearing on the happiness and welfare of men who were dear to him, but as of overwhelming concern for the faith of the rising generation. He gradually came to see in the Catholic Church the one hope for withstanding a movement towards unbelief which threatened to be little less than a devastating flood. There are traces of this thought even before he joined her communion. The special power of Catholicism in this direction, as he came gradually to believe, was twofold. First, the Church was, as he expressed it, "the concrete representative of things invisible." She upheld dogmatic truth with all the authority of immemorial tradition. Her insistence on the whole of revelation, and jealous refusal to mutilate it, was a part of this aspect of her strength. And she was, moreover, a living power specially adapted to resist the excesses of Rationalism—the errors to which the human reason is liable if left to itself.[64]

This is true as far as it goes but what Ward omits to point out is how Newman first encountered the effects of these "excesses of Rationalism" in his brothers Charles and Frank, both of whom exchanged their Christian faith for the doctrinaire doubts of scepticism. In my chapters on Charles and Frank, I show how this exchange may have tried Newman's fraternal patience but never entirely exhausted it, even though his brothers were not always prepared to reciprocate his love.

In the chapters that follow, another theme that figures prominently is that of home and how it affected Newman's relationships not only with his parents and siblings but with his contemporaries. In a letter to his friend Mary Holmes, the convert governess, for example, Newman showed how much the very notion of home meant to him by urging his friend not to lose the home that the Old Catholic Blount family offered her as a part of her position at Mapledurham.

The Oratory Birmingham August 3/64

My dear Miss Holmes

I write you a line to congratulate you on your having got to Mapledurham. Now don't leave it, please. Don't be angry, if I say that you like strangers at first, but you tire of them, when they become acquaintances. No one, but yourself, can know the penances which you undergo in any family, be it ever so near perfection— much more in families which are not perfect—but you can't tell how it distresses me when I see one like yourself, who deserve so much better things, tossing on the waves—and this distress both makes me pleased, as now, that you have come into port again, and desirous that in port you should continue.

I was saying Mass for you the other day, and am always

Yours affectionately John H Newman of the Oratory[65]

---

[64] Wilfrid Ward. *The Life of John Henry Cardinal Newman* (London, 1912), I, pp. 22–3.
[65] LD, 21:182 JHN to Miss Holmes (3 August 1864).

Most of the Victorians were very keen on their homes and this fondness reinforced their religious allegiances, especially those Anglican allegiances that Newman's sisters Jemima and Harriett were so unwilling to repudiate. In choosing to embrace Roman Catholicism, Newman left the cozy, well-appointed, familiar home of Englishry for what his family and friends and most of his contemporaries regarded as at once foreign and disreputable—indeed, the very antithesis of home. In contemplating leaving his Anglican friends, Newman himself wrote his good friend Keble, "No one could have a more unfavorable view than I have of the present state of the Roman Catholics—so much so that any who joined them would be like the Cistercians at Fountains, living under trees till their house was built . . ."[66] Anne Thackeray Ritchie, the great novelist's daughter, epitomized the view of many of her contemporaries when she wrote of Newman, "Did you see that kind but feeble letter of Newmans about my Fathers death—Hoping he had had some presentiment Vanitas Vanitatum &c. It's a beastly religion where you want a lot of little ceremonies to propitiate & my dear daddy doing his work & putting by for his family seems to me ever such a much better life than the celibate saint."[67] The letter that had inspired Ritchie's outburst was a typically heartfelt letter from Newman to Mary Holmes, in which he spoke of "the piercing sorrow that I feel at Thackeray's death." For Newman, "now the drama of his life is closed," the novelist himself was "the greatest instance of the text, of which he was so full, Vanitas vanitatum, omnia vanitas. . . . one should be very glad to know that he had presentiments of what was to come. What a world this is – how wretched they are, who take it for their portion. Poor Thackeray . . ."[68]

At the same time, it is interesting to read Newman telling his fellow Oratorians in one of his Oratory papers, apropos the character of the Oratorian as opposed to the Jesuit: "The Jesuits do not know the word 'home;' they are emphatically strangers and pilgrims upon earth; whereas the very word 'nido'"—the Latin word for *nest*—"is adapted to produce a soothing influence and to rouse a fraternal feeling in the heart of the Oratorian."[69] In choosing to become an Oratorian, Newman showed how much the "soothing influence" of home meant to him, although it also measured the sacrifices he made when he left his Anglican for his new Catholic home. In a passage from his charming Oxford novel, *Loss and Gain* (1847), Newman gives very moving expression to the appeal of this Anglican home, saying of his hero, Charles Redding:

> Charles was an affectionate son, and the Long Vacation passed very happily at home. He was up early, and read steadily till luncheon, and then he was at the service of his father, mother, and sisters for the rest of the day. He loved the calm,

---

[66] LD, 10:476 JHN to John Keble (29 December 1844).
[67] *Correspondence and Journals of the Thackeray Family* (London, 2011), IV, p. 257.
[68] LD, 20:566 JHN to Mary Holmes (27 December 1863).
[69] Newman's "Oratory Papers, No. 6" in *Newman the Oratorian: His Unpublished Oratory Papers*. ed. Placid Murray (London, 1980), p. 215. If Newman thought that the Oratorians were soothingly domestic, Balzac found the French Oratorians (no relation to those founded by St. Philip) otherwise. In fact, it was the French Oratorians who turned Balzac into an insatiable reader by denying him food when he was studying with them as a schoolboy in the Vendôme. Later, as an adult, he would compensate for this juvenile asceticism by gorging himself whenever he finished one of his novels. See Anka Muhlstein. *Balzac's Omelette* (New York, 2012), p. 9.

quiet country; he loved the monotonous flow of time, when each day is like the other; and, after the excitement of Oxford, the secluded parsonage was like a haven beyond the tossing of the waves. The whirl of opinions and perplexities which had encircled him at Oxford now were like the distant sound of the ocean—they reminded him of his present security. The undulating meadows, the green lanes, the open heath, the common with its wide-spreading dusky elms, the high timber which fringed the level path from village to village, ever and anon broken and thrown into groups, or losing itself in copses—even the gate, and the stile, and the turnpike road had the charm, not of novelty, but of long familiar use; they had the poetry of many recollections. Nor was the dilapidated, deformed church, with its outside staircases, its unsightly galleries, its wide intruded windows, its uncouth pews, its low nunting table, its forlorn vestry, and its damp earthy smell, without its pleasant associations to the inner man; for there it was that for many a year, Sunday after Sunday, he had heard his dear father read and preach; there were the old monuments, with Latin inscriptions and strange devices, the black boards with white letters, the Resurgams and grinning skulls, the fire-buckets, the faded militia-colours, and, almost as much a fixture, the old clerk, with a Welsh wig over his ears, shouting the responses out of place—which had arrested his imagination, and awed him when a child. And then there was his home itself; its well-known rooms, its pleasant routine, its order, and its comfort—an old and true friend, the dearer to him because he had made new ones. "Where I shall be in time to come I know not," he said to himself; "I am but a boy; many things which I have not a dream of, which my imagination cannot compass, may come on me before I die—if I live; but here at least, and now, I am happy, and I will enjoy my happiness."[70]

Mark Girouard, the lively architectural historian, shows how religion influenced not only the moral life but the country houses of Victorian country gentlemen. "A portrait of Lord Armstrong, the millionaire arms dealer," Girouard writes, "shows him reading the newspaper in his dining room inglenook at Cragside, over the fireplace of which is inscribed 'East or West, Home is Best.' An essential part of the new image cultivated by both new and old families was their domesticity; they were anxious to show that their houses, however grand, were also homes and sheltered a happy family life." And as Girouard stresses, "This life often contained a strong element of religion. Accounts of going to church, visiting the poor, or reading religious books filled the diaries of upper-class girls, as well as, and sometimes instead of, descriptions of parties and clothes.

In Jane Austen's *Mansfield Park*, when Fanny visits the family chapel at Sotherton, she finds to her regret that daily prayers are no longer said there. But family prayers came back in force under the Victorians; family chapels began to be built again in considerable numbers, and in houses where there was no chapel the whole household assembled for prayers every morning in the hall or dining

[70] *LG*, p. 93.

room. On Sundays the household walked through the garden or across the park to the church—often newly built or restored at the pious expense of the owner of the house. The family walked too, so that grooms and coachmen could be free to observe their Sunday duties.[71]

On the impact that this domestic piety had on country houses, Girouard remarks: "Houses of the gothic style had the extra advantage that, as a result of Pugin, Ruskin and others, gothic was increasingly associated both with Christianity and truthfulness . . . Especially pious families could give their gothic houses an extra flavour of religion by an admixture of tracery and stained glass—or by building a chapel and tower grand enough to dominate the whole building, as was the case at Eaton Hall in Cheshire . . . Others contented themselves with having pious inscriptions carved or painted in appropriate places: 'Except the Lord buildeth the house they labour in vain that build it' was a special favourite."[72]

G. K. Chesterton roundly rejected the notion that family prayers had somehow made the domestic life of the Victorians religious, claiming that the "sanctity of the home" to which the Victorian merchant was fond of referring was little more than a phrase and a misleading one at that. For Chesterton, this suppositious merchant "never really meant sanctity, he only meant security . . . When he went to China (which he did occasionally in search of money) he saw a Pagan civilization very like the old Greek and Roman civilization. There also the house was a temple. There the religion of the family flowered . . ." Yet Chesterton's merchant regarded such traditional "domestic festivity" as "ridiculous," "barbarous," and "alien." It might have been true that "he had something at home called Family prayers" but the "mere memory of them" had "murdered religion for two generations." For Chesterton, this was the "real Victorian hypocrisy": Victoria's contemporaries posed as the great defenders of hearth and home, when, in fact, they were the "great anti-traditionalists" and "destroyed a thousand traditions."[73]

If there was hypocrisy, there was also a yearning for integrity in the group most responsible for this new domestic ideal, however elusive that integrity might prove. "Evangelicals," Judith Flanders notes in her insightful book, *The Victorian House*, "hoped to find a Christian path in all their actions, including the details of daily life; a true Christian must ensure that the family operated in a milieu that could promote good relations between family members and between the family members and their servants, and between the family and the outside world. The home was a microcosm of the ideal society, with love and charity replacing the commerce and capitalism of the outside world. This dichotomy allowed men to pursue business in a suitably capitalist—perhaps even ruthless—fashion, because they knew they could refresh the inner man by returning at the end of the day to an atmosphere of harmony, from which competition was banished. This idea was so useful that it was internalized by many who shared no religious beliefs with the Evangelicals, and it rapidly became a

---

[71] Mark Girouard. *Life in the English Country House* (New Haven and London, 1978), pp. 270–1.
[72] Ibid., p. 273.
[73] G. K. Chesterton, "The True Victorian Hypocrisy" from *Sidelights* (1932) in *Collected Works* (San Francisco, 1990), XXI, pp. 512–13.

secular norm."[74] Thackeray's daughter Annie nicely exemplified this, embracing the Evangelical idealization of home without any of the underpinnings of Evangelical religiosity, which, in any case, she had found so off-putting in her grandmother. Yet it was in the very reactionary zeal of Evangelicalism that G. M. Young saw the seeds of its undoing.

> Evangelicalism had imposed on society, even on classes, which were indifferent to its religious basis and unaffected by its economic appeal, its code of Sabbath observance, responsibility and philanthropy; of discipline in the home, regularity in affairs; it had created a most effective technique of agitation, of private persuasion and social persecution. On one of its sides, Victorian history is the story of the English mind employing the energy imparted by Evangelical conviction to rid itself of the restraints which Evangelicalism had laid on the senses and the intellect; on amusement, enjoyment, art; on curiosity, on criticism, on science. The Evangelical discipline, secularized as respectability, was the strongest binding force in a nation which without it might have broken up, as it had already broken loose.[75]

Here, Young was echoing Queen Victoria, who confessed to her daughter Vicky, "You know I am not at all an admirer or approver of our very dull Sundays, for I think the absence of innocent amusement for the poor people a misfortune and an encouragement of vice . . ."[76]

The tensions that the Evangelicals introduced into English society were noted not only by Chesterton, Young and Queen Victoria but by Thackeray, who nicely measured the strains the new religiosity placed on his countrymen. In a passage from his early burlesque, *The History of Samuel Titmarsh* (1841), the novelist observed how "Every morning on week-days, punctually at eight, Mr. Brough went through the same ceremony, and had his family to prayers, but though this man was a hypocrite, as I found afterwards, I'm not going to laugh at the family prayers, or say he was a hypocrite *because* he had them.

> There are many bad and good men who don't go through the ceremony at all; but I am sure the good men would be the better for it, and am not called upon to settle the question with respect to the bad ones; and therefore I have passed over a great deal of the religious part of Mr. Brough's behaviour: suffice it, that religion was always on his lips; that he went to church thrice every Sunday, when he had not a party; and if he did not talk religion with us when we were alone, had a great deal to say upon the subject upon occasions, as I found one day when we had a Quaker and Dissenter party to dine, and when his talk was as grave as that of any minister present. Tidd was not there that day,—for nothing could make him forsake his Byron riband or refrain from wearing his collars turned down; so he sent Tidd

---

[74] Judith Flanders. *The Victorian House* (London, 2003), pp. xxi–ii.
[75] G. M. Young. *Portrait of an Age* (Oxford, 1934), pp. 4–5.
[76] Queen Victoria to Princess Victoria (27 April 1859) in *Letters to Vicky: The Correspondence between Queen Victoria and her Daughter Victoria, Empress of Germany, 1858–1901.* ed. Andrew Roberts (Folio, 2011), p. 52.

with the buggy to Astley's. "And hark ye, Titmarsh my boy," said he, "leave your diamond-pin upstairs: our friends to-day don't like such gewgaws; and though for my part I am no enemy to harmless ornaments, yet I would not shock the feeling of those who have sterner opinions. You will see that my wife and Miss Brough consult my wishes in this respect." And so they did,—for they both came down to dinner in black gowns and tippets; whereas Miss B. had commonly her dress half off her shoulders.[77]

What makes the Evangelical ideal of domesticity interesting for our purposes is that it first flourished in the suburb of Edgbaston, where Newman established his Birmingham Oratory in 1848. "Our house is rising at Edgbaston," he wrote his dear friend Mrs Bowden in 1851, "we have been able to build all through the winter. It is quite frightful, the space of ground it covers."[78] It must certainly have amused Newman, with his fine sense of the comedy of class, that this spacious suburb, which had been planned by Lord Calthorpe to offer "genteel homes for the middle classes," was known as the "Belgravia of Birmingham." As Judith Flanders points out, "Its homes were for the families who owned and ran the industries on which the town thrived—but who did not want to live near them. The leases for houses in Edgbaston were clear: no retail premises were permitted, nor was professional work to be undertaken in these houses. Edgbaston was the first residential area that assumed that people wanted to live and work in different locations. Over the century this same transformation occurred across the country. In London the City became a place of work, the West End a place of residence; gradually, as the West End acquired a work character too, the suburbs became the residential areas of choice."[79]

Newman, on whom so little of the passing scene was lost, for all his delight in devout retirement, was well aware of this new hankering for tranquillity on the part of the trade-bedraggled middle classes. In a wonderful sermon entitled "The Church a Home for the Lonely" (1837), he wrote of how "the outward world is found not to be enough for man, and he looks for some refuge near him, more intimate, more secret, more pure, more calm and stable.

> This is a main reason and a praiseworthy one, why a great number of the better sort of persons look forward to marriage as the great object of life. They call it being settled, and so it is. The mind finds nothing to satisfy it in the employments and amusements of life, in its excitements, struggles, anxieties, efforts, aims, and victories. Supposing a man to make money, to get on in life, to rise in society, to gain power, whether in a higher or lower sphere, this does not suffice; he wants a home, he wants a centre on which to place his thoughts and affections, a secret dwelling-place which may soothe him after the troubles of the world, and which may be his hidden stay and support wherever he goes, and dwell in his heart, though it be not named upon his tongue.

---

[77] *The History of Samuel Titmarsh* in *The Works of William Makepeace Thackeray* (London, 1898), XII, p. 59.
[78] LD, 14:232 JHN to Mrs Bowden (10 March 1851).
[79] Flanders, p. xxiii.

So far, one imagines, Lord Calthorpe would have agreed; but then Newman made an observation about this desire for domestic refuge that few of his contemporaries would have ventured. "The world may seduce, may terrify, may mislead, may enslave, but it cannot really inspire confidence and love," he wrote. "There is no rest for us, except in quietness, confidence, and affection; and hence all men, without taking religion into account, seek to make themselves a home, as the only need of their nature, or are unhappy if they be without one. Thus they witness against the world, even though they be children of the world; witness against it equally with the holiest and most self-denying, who have by faith overcome it." And it followed from this that "Here . . . Christ finds us, weary of that world in which we are obliged to live and act, whether as willing or unwilling slaves to it. He finds us needing and seeking a home, and making one, as we best may, by means of the creature, since it is all we can do. The world, in which our duties lie, is as waste as the wilderness, as restless and turbulent as the ocean, as inconstant as the wind and weather. It has no substance in it, but is like a shade or phantom; when you pursue it, when you try to grasp it, it escapes from you, or it is malicious, and does you a mischief. We need something which the world cannot give: this is what we need, and this it is which the Gospel has supplied." Here, Newman gave expression to his own worldly disappointments but also to that hunger for reality, beyond the evanescence of mortal life, which the loss of so many of his friends and family only accentuated. And it is this hunger which made him not only receptive to the truths of religion but ready to cooperate with the many graces that came his way. "I say, that our Lord Jesus Christ, after dying for our sins on the Cross, and ascending on high, left not the world as He found it, but left a blessing behind Him. He left in the world what before was not in it,—a secret home, for faith and love to enjoy, wherever found, in spite of the world around us. Do you ask what it is? the chapter from which the text is taken describes it. It speaks of 'the foundation of the Apostles and Prophets, Jesus Christ Himself being the chief corner-stone;' of 'the Building fitly framed' and 'growing unto an Holy Temple in the Lord;' of 'a Habitation of God through the Spirit.' This is the Church of God, which is our true home of God's providing, His own heavenly court, where He dwells with Saints and Angels, into which He introduces us by a new birth, and in which we forget the outward world and its many troubles."[80]

Of course, after he became disenchanted with the National Church, Newman would be rather more specific about the identity of this "Church of God," though even as an Anglican he had already begun to recommend a haven to his restless contemporaries that was very much different from that which the Evangelicals were setting up in places like Edgbaston. For Newman, the Evangelicals could hardly claim to have distinguished themselves from their Latitudinarian neighbours. After all, they were "in cordial and intimate sympathy with the sovereign Lord and Master of the Prayer-Book, its composer and interpreter, the Nation itself . . ." They were "on the best terms with Queen and statesmen, and practical men, and country gentlemen, and respectable tradesmen, fathers and mothers, school-masters, churchwardens, vestries, public societies, newspapers, and their readers in the lower classes."[81] Indeed, more than the

---

[80] *PS*, iv, p. 12.
[81] *Diff.*, pp. 15–16.

Anglicans themselves, the Evangelicals had "the spirit of the age with them. . ."[82] And the false notions of home that they extolled were inseparable from the false notions of nationalism that propped up the tottering national religion. Newman's brothers and sisters would have varying attitudes towards the Established Church—Harriett and Jemima would remain loyal to it, while Charles and Frank would repudiate it—but they would all reject their eldest brother's Catholicism on the grounds that it was foreign, not only the reverse of but a threat to home. In the pages that follow I endeavor to show how in leaving the home of his family and the home of his nation, Newman discovered his true home, even if leaving beloved family and beloved places was "like going on the open sea."[83]

Once Newman converted to Rome, many Anglicans took him to task for betraying the life that he had breathed into the Anglican Communion—his sister Jemima most plaintively. Yet his own treatment of the Anglicanism that he had left behind was hardly treacherous. After all, he was only telling his old Anglican friends what they already knew but dared not admit. "Doubtless the National religion is alive," Newman conceded.

> It is a great power in the midst of us, it wields an enormous influence; it represses a hundred foes; it conducts a hundred undertakings; it attracts men to it, uses them, rewards them; it has thousands of beautiful homes up and down the country where quiet men may do its work and benefit its people; it collects vast sums in the shape of voluntary offerings, and with them it builds churches, prints and distributes innumerable Bibles, books, and tracts, and sustains' missionaries in all parts of the earth. In all parts of the earth it opposes the Catholic Church, denounces her as anti-christian, bribes the world against her, obstructs her influence, apes her authority, and confuses her evidence. In all parts of the world it is the religion of gentlemen, of scholars, of men of substance, and men of no personal faith at all. If this be life, if it be life to impart a tone to the Court and Houses of Parliament, to Ministers of State, to law and literature, to universities and schools, and to society, if it be life to be a principle of order in the population, and an organ of benevolence and alms giving towards the poor, if it be life to make men decent, respectable, and sensible, to embellish and reform the family circle, to deprive vice of its grossness and to shed a glow over avarice and ambition; if, indeed, it is the life of religion to be the first jewel in the Queen's crown, and the highest step of her throne, then doubtless the National Church is replete, it overflows with life; but the question has still to be answered: life of what kind?[84]

Once Newman left his Anglican for his Roman Catholic home, he would spend a good deal of his Catholic life trying to explain to his Protestant contemporaries what had impelled him to pack his bags. Love of family was an essential part of that explanation and in the chapters that follow I shall endeavour to give this special, difficult, sanctifying love the closer look it deserves.

---

[82] Of course, there were Anglican Evangelicals and Evangelical Anglicans but here I contrast the unalloyed.
[83] LD, 12:95 JHN to Ambrose St John (20 January 1846).
[84] *Ess*, i, pp. 381–2.

1

Father and Son

Beginnings

When he was composing the *Apologia*, John Henry Newman relates how the words
"'*Secretum meum mihi*,' [kept] ringing in my ears,"—"My secret is my own." This is
perhaps the most revelatory of all the things he has to say in that revelatory book.
What little we know about his relationship with his father shows that he was adamant
about protecting its privacy. Although forthcoming enough when documenting other
aspects of his life—his letters and diaries span over 30 volumes—he left behind a
record about his relationship with his father that is scrappy. Whenever he writes of
his father or of his dealings with his father, he writes with marked astringency. But
his reticence did not arise from any want of love or respect. On the contrary, no one
had a deeper influence on Newman in his formative years than his genial, astute,
broadminded father. If Newman chose to be reticent about this relationship, it was
because the relationship was precious to him. Moreover, Newman's reticence was in
keeping with the approved practice of Victorian autobiography. Herbert Spencer, the
founder of evolutionary philosophy, to whom we owe the calamitous notion that,
ethically speaking, we can do as we please, so long as we do not appear to be harming
others, was not someone with whom Newman could share much common ground,
but he agreed with him that it would "be out of taste to address the public as though it
consisted of personal friends."[1] Anthony Trollope, an altogether more congenial figure,
many of whose novels Newman read with keen pleasure, affirmed the same principle:
"That I or any man should tell of everything of himself I hold to be impossible. Who
could endure to own the doing of a mean thing?"[2] Tennyson was similarly taciturn in
this regard, telling Leigh Hunt, "It goes somewhat against the grain to give any account
of myself or mine to the public . . . I am the son of Rev. George Clayton Tennyson, LLD.
I was born at Somersby, a small village in Lincolnshire, I was chiefly educated by my
father, who was a man of considerable acquirements and when about 18 years of age I
was entered at Trinity College, Cambridge. Will these dry dates serve . . .?"[3] Montague
Rhodes James, the Cambridge don and Provost of Eton who beguiled his bachelorhood
by writing incomparable ghost stories, was convinced, as he said, that "Reticence may

---

[1]   Herbert Spencer. *An Autobiography* (London, 1904), p. 7.
[2]   Anthony Trollope. *An Autobiography* (Oxford, 1950), p. 1.
[3]   See Tennyson to Leigh Hunt (13 July 1837) in *Alfred Tennyson: The Major Works* (Penguin, 2009),
      p. 494.

be an elderly doctrine to preach, yet from the artistic point of view I am sure it is a sound one. Reticence conduces to effect, blatancy ruins it . . ."[4] Considering what an indelible impression Horatio Nelson made on Newman in his childhood—his first memory was of candles being lit to celebrate Nelson's victory at Trafalgar—it is fitting that the great naval hero should have also followed this great tradition of reticence, ending his 19-page autobiography with a conclusion that was as amusing as it was terse:

> Thus may be exemplified by my life, that perseverance in any profession will most probably meet its reward. Without having any inheritance, or having been fortunate in prize-money, I have received all the honours of my profession, been created a peer of Great Britain, etc. And I may say to the Reader,
>
>   'GO THOU AND DO LIKEWISE'[5]

In the portrait Newman drew of his father in his various autobiographical writings and his letters, we can see how he used a comparable reticence to capture a relationship that lay the groundwork for all that culminated in what Lord Rosebery nicely described as Newman's "strange, brilliant, incomparable end."[6]

In this chapter, I shall show the extent of John Newman's influence on his son by revisiting the record of their relationship as it appears in Newman's correspondence and his autobiographical writings, taking into account how John Newman's banking career might have figured in his influence, and contrasting Newman's relationship to his father with the relationships that some of his contemporaries had with their fathers.

John Henry Newman was born in the City of London at 80 Old Bond Street (around the corner from the "Sign of the Globe" public house) on 21 February 1801. His birthplace, long ago demolished, is now commemorated with a plaque on the visitor's entrance to the London Stock Exchange. His father, John Newman (1767–1824), was a banker, the son of a grocer with roots in Cambridgeshire. His mother, Jemima (1772–1836) was the daughter of Henry Fourdrinier, a wealthy paper maker, whose family were originally French Huguenot refugees who had come to England after the revocation of the Edict of Nantes (1685).[7] John and Jemima married in 1799, when he was 32 and she was 27, and had 6 children, John, Charles, Harriet, Francis, Jemima, and Mary. The family grew up at 17 Southampton Street (later Southampton Place), Bloomsbury, where, Newman recalled how "one of my first memories even

---

[4] Montague Rhodes James. *Collected Ghost Stories* (Oxford, 2011), p. 414.
[5] See Nelson's autobiography (1799) appended to Robert Southey. *Life of Nelson* (Collins, n.d.), p. 19.
[6] Rosebery quoted in Robert Rhodes James. *Rosebery* (London, 1963), p. 217.
[7] "The revocation of the edict of Nantes," wrote Saint-Simon in his diary, "without the least pretext or any necessity, depopulated a quarter of the kingdom, ruined its commerce and weakened it in all its parts." Alfred Cobban added that "It has been estimated that in spite of efforts to close the frontiers to those flying from persecution, hundreds of thousands of Huguenots, including many of the industrial, commercial, and maritime classes, escaped abroad, while those who remained in France, in the wild country between Gard and Lozère, broke out in the terrible and prolonged revolt of the Camisards. In the cause of religion, Sorel writes, Louis XIV had lost more than he could have gained by the most victorious war, or than could have been demanded by his enemies as the price of the most disastrous peace." See Alfred Cobban. *A History of Modern France: Volume 1: 1715–1799* (London, 1963), p. 15.

before . . . 1803 [was] my admiring the borders of the paper in the drawing rooms," as well as Ham Court in Surrey and Fulham. Newman's recall of the family's London home was so vivid, even more than 30 years after leaving it, that he wrote how "every part of it is as clearly before my mind, as if I lived in it ever since."[8] He also recalled reciting "The Cat and the Creambowl" there when he was all but 4 years of age. Southampton Place still contains handsome Georgian houses of the 1740s designed for the 4th Duke of Bedford by Henry Flitcroft, who also designed St Giles-in-the-Fields.

The Newman family was mildly Calvinistic, not, as is sometimes claimed, Evangelical. Unlike many of his other contemporaries, Newman's early faith was founded on more than the Bible. "I was brought up from a child to take great delight in reading the Bible," he wrote in the *Apologia*, "but I had no formed religious convictions till I was fifteen. Of course I had a perfect knowledge of my Catechism." In the autumn of 1816, when he was 15, he "fell under the influences of a definite Creed, and received into my intellect impressions of dogma, which, through God's mercy, have never been effaced or obscured."[9] The Rev Walter Mayers, who had studied at Pembroke College, Oxford and was Newman's classical master at Ealing School, engaged him in long conversations about the Christian faith and put into his hands, among other books, Thomas Scott's account of his conversion from Unitarianism to Calvinist Christianity, *The Force of Truth*, (1779), in which he extolled not only the paramount importance of truth but conscience as its inerrable guide. No other book made as deep an impression on Newman's formative development. Speaking of his book in his preface, Scott wrote of how it contained "little more than the history of my heart, that forge of iniquity; and my conscience, that friendly, but too often neglected monitor. By men in general, this latter is hated, because, as far as informed, it boldly tells the truth; and their grand endeavour seems to be, to lay it asleep, or to render it as insensible, as if seared with an hot iron. Through the deceitfulness of the human heart, the allurements of the world, and the artifices of Satan, this, at length, is commonly accomplished; and in the mean time, they deafen themselves to its remonstrances, by living in a continual noise and bustle." Pages and pages of Newman's Anglican and Catholic sermons hammer home those vital truths.

But it is the personal conviction with which Scott expresses them that must have first struck Newman. "The conflict in my soul between these two is here related," Scott writes, "and some account given of the artifices, which Satan, in confederacy with my heart, made use of, to keep my conscience quiet, and silence its remonstrances; and also of the means, which the Lord employed to defeat this conspiracy, to give conscience its due ascendancy, and to incline my before unwilling heart to become obedient to its friendly admonitions; with the effect thereof upon my religious views and conduct." Here are the same humility, the same gratitude for God's grace, the same appreciation for the redemptive force of conscience that one finds in Newman's *Apologia* and his devotional payers. "As to the effect of this publication, respecting my character and worldly interest, myself, and all that is dear to me, I would leave in his hands, who causeth all to work together for good to them, that love Him, whom he hath called according to his purpose. And he hath so evinced his care over me, and goodness to

[8] LD, 16:391 JHN to Henry Bittleston (27 February 1855).
[9] *Apo.*, pp. 15–17.

me, in all the concerns of my past life, that it were shameful, if I did not most willingly cast all my care upon him for the future. But, reader, the effect of it respecting thee, I have much at heart; and have had, still have, and shall, I trust, continue to have it much in my prayers." Scott's deep solicitude for the spiritual well-being of his reader was something else that Newman would emulate in his own work, especially his vast correspondence.

> If thou art a believing servant of God, I hope thou wilt see cause to bless God in me, and wilt be established and comforted thereby, according to the fervent desire of my soul, for all that love the Lord Jesus Christ in sincerity. If thou art one, whose experience answers in many things, to what is related in the former part of this narrative, as face answers to face in the water, may the Lord, the Spirit, who convinceth of sin, alarm thy drowsy conscience, and bring thee under a serious concern for thy precious soul, and its eternal interests; may he incline thine heart diligently to use the means here spoken of, as far as conscience evidences it to be thy duty; and may he bless the means for enlightening thy mind with the knowledge of the truth, as it is in Jesus; and for guiding thy wandering feet into the ways of peace. This, be assured, is my hearty prayer for thee; and with this prayer I commend this work unto the Lord, that, if it be his blessed will, he may employ it, as an instrument for advancing his glory, and the salvation of souls. THOMAS SCOTT. Weston Underwood, Feb. 26, 1779.[10]

More than a mere preface, this was a testament of faith and it had an electrifying influence on Newman's understanding of the life of faith.

In the "former part of this narrative," Scott might have been speaking directly to Newman's own concerns about his own falling away from God, about which he is so forthcoming not only in the *Apologia* but his diaries and prayers. "Until the sixteenth year of my age," Scott wrote, "I do not remember, that I ever was under any serious conviction of my being a sinner, in danger of wrath, or in need of mercy: nor did I ever, during this part of my life, that I recollect, offer one hearty prayer to God in secret. Being alienated from God through the ignorance that was in me, I lived without him in the world; and as utterly neglected to pay him any voluntary service, as if I had been an Atheist in principle. But about my sixteenth year I began to see, that I was a sinner, a leper in every part, 'there being no health in me;' out of many external indications of inward depravity, conscience discovered, and reproached me with one; and I was, for the first time, disquieted with apprehensions of the wrath of an offended God. My attendance at the Lord's table, being expected about the same time, (though I was very ignorant of the meaning and end of that sacred ordinance,) this circumstance, united with the accusations of my conscience, brought an awe upon my spirits, and interrupted my before undisturbed course of sin."[11] If we compare this to Newman's prayers, we can see how closely Scott's experiences paralleled those of Newman. "I know perfectly well, and thankfully confess to Thee, O my God," Newman wrote in a journal entry in 1859. "that thy wonderful grace

---

[10] Thomas Scott. *The Force of Truth* (London, 1814), p. v.
[11] Ibid., pp. 7–8.

turned me right round when I was more like a devil than a wicked boy, at the age of fifteen, and gave me what by thy continual aids I never lost. Thou didst change my heart, and in part my whole mental complexion at that time, and I never should have had the thought of such prayers, as those I have . . . but for that great work of thine in my boyhood . . ."[12] Scott, as we can see, was crucial in helping Newman first seek out and cooperate with these "continual aids."

In summing up his debt to Scott, Newman wrote: "Besides his unworldliness, what I also admired in Scott was his resolute opposition to Antinomianism, and the minutely practical character of his writings. They show him to be a true Englishman, and I deeply felt his influence; and for years I used almost as proverbs what I considered to be the scope and issue of his doctrine, 'Holiness rather than peace', and 'Growth the only evidence of life.'"[13] Both principles would assume enormous importance in his conduct of his relationship with his family. And it is also important to stress that it might very well have been the example of his father's practicality that first disposed Newman to value Scott's practicality, even though John Newman did not take the practical steps necessary to make his Christian faith more central to his life.

Then, again, another deeply attractive aspect about Scott for Newman was "his bold unworldliness and vigorous independence of mind. He followed wherever truth led him . . ." Later, at Oxford, Newman would read Scott's famous commentaries on the Bible. In fact, Newman "so admired and delighted in his writings" that when he was an undergraduate at Trinity, as he said, "I thought of making a visit to his Parsonage [at Aston Sandford, about 16 miles from Oxford], in order to see a man whom I so deeply revered."[14] For Newman, collectively, these "deep religious impressions," received from Scott and the books he recommended, were "the beginning of a new life."[15] Indeed, in this regard, Scott had something of the same impact on Newman that Saint Ambrose, another master of Scripture, had on Saint Augustine. This is why Newman would later claim that Scott was someone, as he said, "to whom (humanly speaking) I almost owe my soul."[16]

Like Ambrose, Newman saturated his writings in Scripture, especially his sermons. In "Preparation for the Judgement" (1848), for example, he invoked the words of the Apostle John to warn not only his Victorian contemporaries but all men that the evasions of the world can be neither indefinite nor inconsequential.

> Many men like to live in a whirl, in some excitement or other which keeps their minds employed, and keeps them from thinking of themselves. How many a man . . . employs all his leisure time in learning merely the news of the day. He likes to read the periodical publications, he likes to know what is going on in the four quarters of the earth. He fills his mind with matters which either do not concern him, or concern only his temporal welfare; with what they are doing in various parts of England, what Parliament is doing, what is done in Ireland, what

---

[12] *AW*, p. 250.
[13] *Apo.*, pp. 18–19.
[14] Ibid., p. 18.
[15] *AW*, p. 29.
[16] *Apo.*, p. 18.

is done on the Continent; nay he descends to little matters of no importance, rather than entertain that thought which must come on him, if not before, at least in the evening of life and when he stands before his Judge. Others are full of projects for making money; be they high or be they low, that is their pursuit, they covet wealth and they live in the thought how they may get it. They are alive to inventions and improvements in their particular trade, and to nothing else. They rival each other. They as it were, run a race with each other, not a heavenly race, such as the Apostle's who ran for a crown incorruptible, but a low earthly race, each trying by all means in his power to distance his neighbour in what is called the favour of the public, making this their one end, and thinking nothing at all of religion. And others take up some doctrine whether of politics or of trade or of philosophy, and spend their lives upon it; they go about to recommend it in every way they can. They speak, they write, they labour for an object which will perish with this world, which cannot pass with them through the grave. The holy Apostle says "Blessed are they that die in the Lord, for their works do *follow them*." Good works follow us, bad works follow us, but everything else is worth nothing; everything else is but chaff. The whirl and dance of worldly matters is but like the whirling of chaff or dust, nothing comes of it; it lasts through the day, but it is not to be found in the evening. And yet how many immortal souls spend their lives in nothing better than making themselves giddy with this whirl of politics, of party, or religious opinion, or money getting, of which nothing can ever come.[17]

Reading this, one can see how much the appeal of Scripture fortified Newman's faith. One can also see why Anthony Froude found Newman's sermons so captivating. Although Froude eventually became Carlyle's tout after writing some marvellously barbed histories of the Tudors, he never forgot the power of the sermons Newman gave from the pulpit of St Mary's. "No one who heard his sermons in those days can ever forget them. They were seldom directly theological. We had theology enough and to spare from the select preachers before the university. Newman, taking some scripture character for a text, spoke to us about ourselves, our temptations, our experiences. His illustrations were inexhaustible. He seemed to be addressing the most secret consciousness of each of us . . . He never exaggerated; he was never unreal. A sermon from him was a poem, formed on distinct ideas, fascinating by its subtlety, welcome—how welcome!—from its sincerity, interesting from its originality, even to those who were careless of religion; and to others who wished to be religious, but had found religion dry and wearisome, it was like the springing of a fountain out of the rock."[18]

Considering how important the Bible was to Newman's development in his formative years, it is fitting that it was his father who should have given him his first Bible, in which the inscription appears "J H N – from his dear Father. 1807," to which

---

[17] *Faith and Prejudice and other Unpublished Sermons* (London, 1956), pp. 36–8.

[18] J. A. Froude. "The Oxford Counter Reformation," in *Short Studies on Great Subjects* (London, 1883), p. 236. For a detailed reading of Froude's work, which, however, fails to take into account the true character of the historian's respect for Newman, see Ciaran Brady. *James Anthony Froude* (Oxford, 2013).

Newman added "I suppose I have used no Bible so much as this." This gift should be borne in mind when one reads in Frank's memoirs of how John Newman "had learned his morality more from Shakespeare than from the Bible . . ."[19] Newman's father was indeed fond of Shakespeare—a fondness which he bequeathed to his children, especially Harriett, who was a shrewd admirer of the Shakespearian acting of Kean and Macready—but he was also steeped in the Bible.[20]

Fulham

Newman received his love of the Bible not only from his parents but from his paternal grandmother and from his father's sister, Elizabeth, known as Aunt Betsey, who had a house in Fulham, where Newman spent his first five summers. In July 1844, when still undecided as to whether to convert to Roman Catholicism, he had occasion to acknowledge his profound debt to their influence. He visited the house in Fulham one hot summer day and found that it had been converted into a chemist's shop. "I wanted to have a peep at the house, but the good chemist, civil as he was, did not take my hints—so I saw nothing, except the hall through the door. I saw too the staircase which I had forgotten. But I described to him the lie of the house, which he confirmed. I told him where the kitchen was, where I recollect you going to superintend the making of apple puffs. And the room opening on the garden where were the two card-racks with a lion (I think) on them; and the pictures of the prodigal son, and giving alms to the poor, and the unjust steward . . . There you used to breakfast—at least I recollect coming down in the morning and seeing the breakfast things looking bright and still—and I have some vague reminiscence of dry toast . . . I told the worthy man where the drawing room was—and I spoke of a sort of loft above, in which I have a dim vision of apples on the floor and a mangle. And of the garden—the summerhouse, he said was gone . . . How strange it is, I wish I could describe it, to stand in a house which was so much to me, as that house was, and it is different, and I so different! Whatever good there is in me, I owe, under grace, to the time I spent in that house, and to you and my dear Grandmother, its inhabitants. I do not forget her Bible and the prints in it . . ."[21] Then, again, in December 1844, he wrote his aunt: "This cold weather is a reason for thinking of you especially. I fear it tries you a great deal. Be sure you are continually in my thoughts. No one more so, or more tenderly so. You, my dear Aunt, and you alone, connect me in my thoughts with my first years, and you had so much to do with giving a direction to my mind. I trust that in the day of account I shall be able to answer well for the advantages I enjoyed in your and my dear Grandmother's care. May you be rewarded a thousand times over for what you did for me . . ."[22] When his Aunt received this moving letter, it might very well have reminded her of an earlier one she had received from her

---

[19] F. W. Newman. *The Soul: Its Sorrows and Its Aspirations* (London, 1905), p. 7.
[20] See Harriett's animadversions on Charles Keane's Shylock and Hamlet in *Family*, pp. 183–4.
[21] LD, 10:303 JHN to Aunt Elizabeth Newman (25 July 1844).
[22] LD, 10:452 JHN to Aunt Elizabeth Newman (9 December 1844).

nephew. "I write a few lines as I think it will show more fully, (what I do not suspect you mistrust,) my continual remembrance of you," he had written in 1826, after he received his Oriel Fellowship, "than if I merely sent my love by another . . . I have quite changed my life, and instead of being busied in the affairs of a parish, am busy with those of College . . . Wherever I am placed however I trust I shall never forget that I am not my own, but made over to a Master whose interests I must continually promote – I feel I have a great responsibility laid upon my shoulders, and hope I shall be directed and strengthened to make use of the talents put into my hands. – It will be something if I can in any measure promote the cause of God and spread the influence of the Gospel of Christ, and I am willing (I trust) to spend my life in the cause."[23]

Newman's vivid evocation of the house at Fulham proves how attentive he was to the glory of the material world—even when embodied in apple puffs and mangles. By contrast, when Walter Pater described how an old staircase, old wainscoting, "the perfumed juice of . . . fallen fruit" affected a fictional child in his sketch, "The Child in the House" (1873), he treated their aesthetic effect as an end in itself. In his character Florian, who suggests nothing so much as Walter Pater in short trousers, "desire of physical beauty mingled . . . [with] . . . the fear of death—the fear of death intensified by the desire of beauty."[24] This sense of pagan fatality was in keeping with Pater's claim in the conclusion of *The Renaissance* that "Not the fruit of experience, but experience itself, is the end."[25] Newman might have agreed with Pater that "it is false to suppose that a child's sense of beauty is dependent on any choiceness or special fineness;" in his *Apologia*, Newman related how he spent hours of his early childhood admiring the wallpaper in his parent's drawing rooms; but he never followed Pater in attempting to treat aesthetics as an end in itself. Indeed, Pater's essay proves the point that Newman makes in *The Idea of a University*, that individual fields of knowledge, like aesthetics, "have their own department, and, in going out of it, [they] attempt to do what they really cannot do . . ."[26] For Newman, exalting any particular field of knowledge beyond its proper boundary led directly to that "multitude of off-hand sayings, flippant judgments, and shallow generalizations, with which the world abounds. . . . Hence the misconceptions of character, hence the false impressions and reports of words or deeds, which are the rule, rather than the exception . . . hence the extravagances of undisciplined talent, and the narrowness of conceited ignorance; because though it is no easy matter to view things correctly, nevertheless the busy mind will ever be viewing. We cannot do without a view, and we put up with an illusion, when we cannot get a truth."[27] At the same time, in making such extravagant claims for his own limited field of study, Pater did that study no favours. As the shrewd literary critic and classicist Richard Jenkyns observes, "The importance of Pater in the context of classical studies lies in his lack

[23] LD, I: 284 JHN to Elizabeth Newman (29 April 1826).
[24] Walter Pater. "The Child in the House" from *Selected Writings of Walter Pater* (New York, 1974), p. 11.
[25] Walter Pater. *The Renaissance* (Oxford, 1986), p. 152.
[26] *Idea*, p. 58.
[27] Ibid., pp. 56–7.

of importance: this literary demigod, who wrote what Yeats was to call the sacred book for his generation, seems to have made no impression at all upon the study of classical literature within the University . . . His picture of Greek society in *Plato and Platonism* is both naïve and self-indulgent; the polished surface of his essay on Euripides' *Bacchae* conceals . . . startling crudities of judgement . . ."[28] As we shall see, one of the benefits bestowed on Newman by his father was to instil in him a certain critical balance alien to Pater.

Ham

In 1804, Newman's father bought a house in the country—Grey Court House near Ham Common, Surrey, where the family lived for 5 years. As his recollections of Fulham demonstrate, Newman had an acute sense of place; his descriptions of places and their associations animate some of his most vivid writing. In this, he reminds one of the Brontës, of what Mrs Gaskell wrote when she first visited the Haworth moors in 1853: "Oh! Those high, wild, desolate moors, up above the whole world, and the very realms of silence!"[29] No place left as enduring an impression on Newman as Ham. "If I had known it," Graham Green wrote in that marvellous autobiography of his, *A Sort of Life* (1971) "the whole future must have lain all the time along those Berkhamstead streets."[30] Newman could have said the same about Ham. When he was 81, he wrote his old friend Dean Church about one of his more memorable tormentors: "Poor Golightly! I half hoped I should have met him in Oxford two years ago [when Newman received his honorary degree from Trinity] . . . I knew his mother almost before he was born and recited to her on Ham Common 'The Butterfly's Ball and the Grasshopper's Feast'."[31] To his sister Jemima, whose recall of the family's history could be extraordinarily accurate, Newman once observed: "What an odd gift memory is, so long latent, yet so sure."[32]

Newman had once befriended Golightly—even offering him the curacy of Littlemore until his former friend's detestation of Roman Catholicism turned him against Newman and the Tractarians. Indeed, Golightly played an energetic role in orchestrating the outcry against Tract 90. Later, before his death in 1885, he received his just desserts when he began suffering from apparitions. Still, without Golightly, we might never have the charming picture of Master John reciting:

> And there was the Gnat and the Dragon-fly too,
> With all their Relations, Green, Orange, and Blue.
> And there came the Moth, with his Plumage of Down,
> And the Hornet in Jacket of Yellow and Brown;

[28] Richard Jenkyns. "Classical Studies 1872–1914," in *The History of the University of Oxford*. Volume VII: Nineteenth-Century Oxford, Part 2. ed. Brock and Curthoys (Oxford, 2000), p. 329.
[29] Gaskell quoted in *The Brontes: A Life in Letters*. ed. Juliet Barker (Folio Society, 2006), p. 192.
[30] Graham Greene. *A Sort of Life* (New York, 1971), p. 13.
[31] LD, 30:65 JHN to R. W. Church (6 March 1882).
[32] LD, 22:82 JHN to Mrs John Mozley (24 October 1865).

> Who with him the Wasp, his Companion, did bring,
> But they promis'd, that Evening, to lay by their Sting.
> And the sly little Dormouse crept out of his Hole,
> And brought to the Feast his blind Brother, the Mole.

Ham figures again and again in Newman's letters. On his 18th birthday, he wrote his mother from Oxford of how he "awoke in the morning of February 21, and without recollecting it was my birthday my mind involuntarily recurred to the day . . . I was six years old [and] spoke Cowper's 'Faithful Friend' at Ham."[33] In 1861, he wrote Mary Holmes, the governess with whom he would have a long correspondence: "I have been going about seeing once again, and taking leave for good, of the places I knew as a child. I have been looking at the windows of our house at Ham near Richmond, where I lay aged 5 looking at the candles stuck in them in celebration of the victory at Trafalgar. I have never seen the house since September 1807—I know more about it than any house I have been in since, and could pass an examination in it. It has been in all my dreams."[34]

In 1854, he was presented with one of his boyhood books and noted in his journal: "This book I had at Ham, i.e., before September 1807. I have just received it from T. Mozley, and . . . I recollect perfectly rhodomontading out of it to my nursery maid in the shrubbery there, near the pond, at the end of the diagonal of the paddock or field from the house . . ." Later, when he was 85, he would tell a correspondent of the profound love he felt for the place, "which I dreamed about when a school boy as if it was Paradise."[35]

On board the Hermes on his way to Corfu in December 1832, with his dear friend Hurrell Froude, Newman revealed how central Ham was to his imagination. Gladstone devoted much time to studying Homer—mostly in a fantastic attempt to show how the work of the pagan poet presaged Christianity.[36] Newman saw in Homer more personal parallels and in this he was closer to James Joyce than to the Liberal Prime Minister.

> I have not always had the . . . deepest attachment to old Homer . . . But when I was for hours within half a mile of Ithaca, as I was this morning, how shall I describe my feelings. They were not caused by any classical association, but by the thought that I now saw before me in real shape those places which had been the earliest vision of my childhood. Ulysses and Argus inhabited the very isle I saw. It answered the description most accurately – a barren huge rock, of limestone (apparently) a dull grey poorly covered with brushwood, broken into roundish masses with deep ravines, which were the principal points where cultivation had dared to experimentalize – tho' the sides of the hills were also turned up. Olive trees have made their appearance, the vines being cut down in the winter and invisible looking from the water. On a height in the centre and narrowest part of

---

[33] JNH to Mrs Newman (24 February 1819) LD, 1:62.
[34] JHN to Mary Holmes (5 August 1861) LD, 20:23.
[35] JHN to Thomas William Morton, S. J. (24 February 1886) LD, 31: 119.
[36] See David Bebbington. *The Mind of Gladstone* (Oxford, 2004).

the island is a height called the tower of Ulysses – We could see through the glass parts of the Cyclopean (as they are called) ruins which surmount it – their make is far anterior to the historical period – and, tradition having assigned them to Ulysses, antiquarians do not hesitate to admit the fact. Homer calls the island dear and little – and so it is – I gazed upon it by the quarter of an hour together, being quite satisfied with the sight of the rock. I thought of Ham and of all the various glimpses, which memory barely retains and which fly from me when I pursue them, of that earliest time of life when one seems almost to realize the remnant of a pre-existent state. Oh how I longed to touch the land and satisfy myself it was not a mere vision I saw before me.[37]

Ham was home for Newman in a way that no other place could be. William James once observed of his brother Henry that he was "a native of the James family, and has no other country."[38] Newman had neither the cosmopolitan upbringing that James had nor the concomitant sense of being *déraciné*. Despite entering into and adopting views foreign or unfathomable to many of his compatriots, he had a relationship with England that had nothing of the obliquity of James' relationship with America. Indeed, as Dean Church remarked: "He was, after all, an Englishman; and with all his quickness to detect and denounce what was selfish and poor in English ideas and action, and with all the strength of his deep antipathies, his chief interests were for things English—English literature, English social life, English politics, English religion. He liked to identify himself, as far as it was possible, with things English, even with things that belonged to his own first days. He republished his Oxford sermons and treatises. He prized his honorary fellowship at Trinity; he enjoyed his visit to Oxford, and the welcome which he met there. He discerned how much the English Church counted for in the fight going on in England for the faith in Christ. There was in all that he said and did a gentleness, a forbearance, a kindly friendliness, a warm recognition of the honour paid him by his countrymen, ever since the *Apologia* had broken down the prejudices which had prevented Englishmen from doing him justice."[39] Nevertheless, for all his undoubted Englishness, Newman was very much a native of the Newman family, without ever losing sight of his true country, his eternal home, beyond the region of thunder, for which Ham became a kind of earthly emblem.

John Newman

In his diverting autobiography, *First Childhood* (1934), Lord Berners painted a memorable portrait of his father, about whom he recalled.

He never attempted to take any active part in my education. Once when my mother suggested that, for some offence or other, he should beat me, he merely said that he couldn't be bothered. I suppose I ought to have been grateful to him,

---

[37] LD, 3:172 JHN to Mrs Newman (30 December 1832).
[38] Jean Strouse. *Alice James: A Biography* (New York, 1980), p. x.
[39] R. W. Church. *Occasional Papers* (London, 1897), II, p. 477.

but I remember feeling a little offended by his lack of interest. It is said that a child's idea of God is often based on the characteristics of its male parent. If this is the case, it may perhaps account for the somewhat peculiar ideas I entertained, in my childhood, with regard to the Deity. I remember, on an occasion when I was misbehaving, my nurse saying, "If you're not careful, one of these days God will jump out from behind a cloud and catch you such a whack!" The threat was an alarming one, but I was not perturbed, and retorted, "Nonsense! God doesn't care WHAT we do."[40]

Although John Newman took an active and indeed benign part in his son's education, it is fair to say that he did not give him his understanding of God. He did, however, impart several other valuable things to him: his independence, his self-confidence, his love of music, his interest in the uses of failure, his interest in that once highly intricate thing, the English gentleman, and, perhaps most importantly, his quick, elastic, eminently practical, eminently supple critical intelligence. The fact that John Newman was not particularly devout was never surprising to his son. Indeed, after converting, Newman made a shrewd observation on this score. "Heroic, by which I mean self-sacrificing, virtues are, as a general rule, less applicable to fathers of families, simply because all duties being relative, the duty of a man to his wife and children comes before a larger number of more distant duties. This it is which has led, in the Catholic Church, to the celibacy of the clergy: which is no dogma, but a mere consequence of what I may call *the division of labour* consequent on a more developed state of Christian civilization. The attire of the glorified Church is to be wrought about with a variety of ornament."[41]

At the same time, in a sermon entitled "The Duty of Self-Denial" (1830), he also observed how "even in affection towards our relations and friends, we must be watchful over ourselves, lest it seduce us from the path of duty. Many a father, from a kind wish to provide well for his family, neglects his own soul. Here, then, is a fault; not that we can love our relations too well, but that that strong and most praiseworthy affection for them may, accidentally, ensnare and corrupt our weak nature." Newman's own familial trials enabled him to see that family could sometimes actually tempt one to deny the true "call of charity," which must be rooted in love of God. Yes, Christ "has sanctioned and enjoined love and care for our relations and friends. Such love is a great duty; but should at any time His guidance lead us by a strange way, and the light of His providence pass on, and cast these objects of our earthly affection into the shade, then they must be at once in the shade to *us*,—they must, for the time, disappear from our hearts. 'He that loveth father or mother more than Me, is not worthy of Me.' So He says; and at such times, though still loving them, we shall seem to hate them; for we shall put aside the thought of them, and act as if they did not exist. And in this sense an ancient and harsh proverb is true: we must always so love our friends as feeling that one day or other we may perchance be called upon to hate them,—that is, forget them in the pursuit of higher duties."[42] Newman was always prepared to show his parents and his siblings

---

[40] Lord Berners. *First Childhood* (Oxford, 1983), p. 27.
[41] LD, 19:540. *The Rambler* (July 1859), pp. 234–6.
[42] "The Duty of Self-Denial" (1830) in *PS*, vii, pp. 7, 96–7.

genuine love in season and out of season, but there was never anything sentimental about it and he never allowed it to get in the way of his duty to God.

How John Newman regarded the Anglican faith is impossible to say with any exactitude: he left behind nothing that speaks of his religious views. However, a passage from George Eliot's *Scenes from a Clerical Life* (1858) captures a few aspects of the National Church with which Mr Newman, even as a City man, must have been familiar. And certainly the Newmans from Cambridgeshire would have recognized the accuracy of Eliot's depiction. In "Mr. Gilfil's Love-Story," she observes how:

> . . . the Vicar did not shine in the more spiritual functions of his office; indeed, the utmost I can say for him in this respect is, that he performed those functions with undeviating attention to brevity and despatch. He had a large heap of short sermons, rather yellow and worn at the edges, from which he took two every Sunday, securing perfect impartiality in the selection by taking them as they came without reference to topics; and having preached one of these sermons at Shepperton in the morning, he mounted his horse and rode hastily with the other in his pocket to Knebley, where he officiated in a wonderful little church, with a checkered pavement which had once rung to the iron tread of military monks, with coats of arms . . . Here, in an absence of mind to which he was prone, Mr Gilfil would sometimes forget to take off his spurs before putting on his surplice, and only become aware of the omission by feeling something mysteriously tugging at the skirts of that garment as he stepped into the reading-desk. But the Knebley farmers would as soon have thought of criticising the moon as their pastor. He belonged to the course of nature, like markets and tollgates and dirty bank-notes; and being a vicar, his claim on their veneration had never been counteracted by an exasperating claim on their pockets. Some of them, who did not indulge in the superfluity of a covered cart without springs, had dined half an hour earlier than usual—that is to say, at twelve o'clock—in order to have time for their long walk through miry lanes, and present themselves duly in their places at two o'clock, when Mr Oldinport and Lady Felicia, to whom Knebley Church was a sort of family temple, made their way among the bows and curtsies of their dependants to a carved and canopied pew in the chancel, diffusing as they went a delicate odour of Indian roses on the unsusceptible nostrils of the congregation.

It is also tantalizing to consider what Newman's father would have made of Eliot's amusing portrait of the fathers of families in her story. "The farmers' wives and children sate on the dark oaken benches," she writes, "but the husbands usually chose the distinctive dignity of a stall under one of the twelve apostles, where, when the alternation of prayers and responses had given place to the agreeable monotony of the sermon, Paterfamilias might be seen or heard sinking into a pleasant doze, from which they infallibly woke up at the sound of the concluding doxology. And then they made their way back again through the miry lanes, perhaps almost as much the better for this simple weekly tribute to what they knew of good and right, as many a more wakeful and critical congregation of the present day."[43] Doubtless, both Mr. Newman and

[43] George Eliot. *Scenes of a Clerical Life* (Edinburgh and London, 1868), pp. 159–62.

his son would also have recognized the point of this passage, in which Eliot remarks how "Mr. Gilfil's sermons . . . were not of a highly doctrinal . . . cast. They perhaps did not search the conscience very powerfully . . . but, on the other hand, they made no reasonable demand on the . . . intellect—amounting indeed, to little more than an expansion of the concise thesis that those who do wrong will find it the worse for them, and those who do well will find it the better for them; the nature of wrong doing being exposed in special sermons against lying, backbiting, anger, slothfulness, and the like; and well-doing being interpreted as honesty, truthfulness, charity, industry, and other common virtues, lying quite on the surface of life, and having very little to do with deep spiritual doctrine."[44]

Newman took an altogether dim view of George Eliot, which is not surprising considering the ethical agnosticism to which she, like so many of her contemporaries, succumbed. Still, in her nicely satirical way, she poked fun at many of the same aspects of the National Church that he found wanting: its dogmatic vacuity, its perfunctoriness, its confusion of religious faith with ethics. In one letter to his itinerant friend, Mary Holmes, the governess, he wrote: "Talking of Trollope, I don't think it fair of him to be charging 5/a part for his scanty new novel. [*The American Senator*, which was serialized in Temple Bar from May 1876 to July 1877.] You may say that George Eliot (for what I know) does the same—but George Eliot may do what he likes for me, who am no great admirer of his, whereas Trollope's writings are the best of their kind."[45] Eliot, for her part, was fascinated by Newman. She read his *Lectures on the Present Position of Catholics in England* (1851) "with great amusement (!)," finding them "full of clever satire and description."[46] And after reading the *Apologia*, she wrote a friend, "I envy you your opportunity of seeing and hearing Newman and should like to make an expedition to Birmingham for that sole purpose." The book had "breathed much life" into her and she was keen on meeting the man who had so brilliantly exposed what she characterized as the "arrogance," "coarse impertinence," and "unscrupulousness with real intellectual incompetence" of Charles Kingsley, whose gratuitous calumny had inspired Newman to write the book in the first place.[47] As it happened, the meeting never took place, but if it had, Eliot might very well have left behind a more extensive response to the works of a man whom she never ceased to admire, especially since, as she said, "the *Apologia* mainly affects me as the revelation of a life—how different in form from one's own, yet with how close a fellowship in its needs and burthens—I mean spiritual needs and burthens."[48] Then, again, Richard Holt Hutton, the editor of the *Spectator* and first biographer of Newman, recalled how Newman's fellow Oratorian, J. J. Dalgairns, whom he regarded as "a man of singular sweetness and openness of character, with something of a French type of playfulness in his expression," spoke movingly to him of "the noble ethical character of George Eliot's novels, and the penetrating disbelief in all but human excellence by which they are pervaded. Implicitly he intended to convey to me, I thought, that nowhere but in the Roman Church could you find any

[44] Eliot, p. 126.
[45] LD, 28:74 JHN to Mary Holmes (3 June 1876).
[46] See *The George Eliot Letters*. ed. Gordon Haight (New Haven, 1954), 1, p. 160.
[47] *The George Eliot Letters*, 2:387.
[48] *The George Eliot Letters*, 4:158–9.

real breakwater against an incredulity which could survive even the aspirations of so noble a character as hers."[49]

John Newman's appearances in the *Letters and Diaries* are fewer than those of any other family member, and yet they give one the impression of a strong, decisive, independent man. His first letter to his son has rather a business-like air.

> This is the first Letter your Papa ever wrote to his Son. I request you will read it to your Mamma and also to Charles that, when he sees how well you can read writing, he will be very desirous of minding his Book that he may also be able to do the same—but you will observe that you must learn something new every Day or you will no longer be called a clever Boy. I therefore hope that by Thursday next you will have got your Multiplication Table by Heart and have also began to learn your Pence Table. I mean to examine you as to your Multiplication Table and if I find you improve I intend after a time to buy you a nice Copy Book and teach you to write . . .[50]

John Newman clearly recognized how clever his eldest son was and had high expectations for him. Newman's father, in other words, was preparing his son to join what Hurrell Froude would later refer to as the "aristocracy of talent."[51] There was ambition in John Newman, which his son also inherited, though he would deliberately chasten this aspect of his character in ways that would baffle his father. Still, the very fact that John Newman was the son of a grocer who rose to become a private banker demonstrates extraordinary enterprise, an enterprise which he inherited from his father, who moved from Cambridgeshire to Mayfair to sell groceries to the rich and yet found time to provide his eldest son and daughter (Newman's beloved Aunt Elizabeth) with enough education and culture to prepare the one for a career in the City and the other with a position as mistress in a finishing school in Strand-on-the-Green. That grocers could ply a lucrative trade was borne out by John Sainsbury (1844–1928), whose commitment to high quality and low prices transformed his Holborn dairy into one of the most successful food chains in Victorian Britain, and this at a time when he and his wife were bringing up a family of six sons and five daughters; at his death, Sainsbury was estimated to be worth £300,000. Of course, neither Newman's grandfather nor the other 4,980 grocers operating in Victorian London were as fabulously successful as Sainsbury but by setting up shop in Mayfair John Newman could certainly afford to give his family advantages that many other tradesmen could not.

Doubtless it was this family history that impelled Newman's father to have the high expectations he had for his son and to prepare him to realize those expectations with the practical support he needed. Indeed, his practical approach to education was one that Newman would always extol. In *The Idea of a University*, he defended the practical benefits of liberal education in terms that his father would have readily recognized and approved. For Newman, university training was "the great ordinary means to a great but ordinary end" because "it aims at raising the intellectual tone of society, at cultivating

---

[49] Wilfrid Ward. *William George Ward and the Catholic Revival* (London, 1893), p. 303.
[50] LD, 1:3 John Newman to JHN (24 November 1806).
[51] *Apo.*, p. 257.

the public mind, at purifying the national taste, at supplying true principles to popular enthusiasm and fixed aims to popular aspiration, at giving enlargement and sobriety to the ideas of the age, at facilitating the exercise of political power, and refining the intercourse of private life." Moreover, university training "gives a man a clear conscious view of his own opinions and judgments, a truth in developing them, an eloquence in expressing them, and a force in urging them. It teaches him to see things as they are, to go right to the point, to disentangle a skein of thought, to detect what is sophistical, and to discard what is irrelevant." This training in critical thinking—which is so rarely instilled in our own universities—prepares the graduate "to fill any post with credit, and to master any subject with facility . . ." It also equips him with a certain collegiality. "It shows him how to accommodate himself to others, how to throw himself into their state of mind, how to bring before them his own, how to influence them, how to come to an understanding with them, how to bear with them." Consequently, the beneficiary of university training "is at home in any society, he has common ground with every class . . ." More than this, university training develops those personal reserves on which any graduate will need to draw in making his way in the world, for "He has the repose of a mind which lives in itself, while it lives in the world, and which has resources for its happiness at home when it cannot go abroad. He has a gift which serves him in public, and supports him in retirement, without which good fortune is but vulgar, and with which failure and disappointment have a charm. The art which tends to make a man all this, is in the object which it pursues as useful as the art of wealth or the art of health, though it is less susceptible of method, and less tangible, less certain, less complete in its result."[52]

Ealing

John Newman made sure that his eldest son got a good education at a school suited to his temperament. Rather than one of the more rough-and-tumble public schools, he chose Great Ealing School, a private school founded in 1698, which, in its nineteenth-century heyday, was said to rival neighbouring Harrow.[53] Newman entered the school as a boarder in May 1808 at the age of 7 and left in December 1816 at the age of 15. The school was run by the Rev George Nicholas of Wadham College, Oxford, a capable, discerning, lovable man, who "was accustomed to say," as Newman recalled, "that no boy had run through the school, from the bottom to the top, so rapidly as John Newman."[54] Later, his mother suggested that he might wish to transfer to Winchester but Newman wisely stayed put. The idea of what Winchester might have made of him is intriguing. It certainly did not make much of Anthony Trollope. "It is the nature of schoolboys to be cruel," Trollope recalled in his *Autobiography*, "I have sometimes doubted whether among each other they do usually suffer much, one from the other's cruelty but I suffered horribly! I could make no stand against it. I had no friend to whom I could pour out my sorrows. I was big, and awkward,

---

[52] *Idea*, pp. 154–5.
[53] W. S. Gilbert attended the school from 1849 to 1852 and became head boy in his last year.
[54] *AW*, p. 29.

and ugly, and I have no doubt skulked about in a most unattractive manner. Of course I was ill-dressed and dirty. But ah! How well I remember all the agonies of my young heart; how I considered whether I should always be alone; whether I could not find my way up to the top of that college tower, and from thence to put an end to everything."[55]

Ealing was a good choice on his father's part because Newman would probably not have flourished in a public school; he was too gentle, too intelligent and, in his quiet, studious way, too independent. He was also indifferent to games. Frank Newman, the youngest of the three Newman brothers, recalled of John: "I cannot remember seeing him at any play, though we had plenty of games . . . As far back as my memory reaches, in none of these was John Henry Newman to be seen. He did go to our bathing-pond, but he never *swam*."[56] (An Oxford wag, who also happens to know rather a lot about Newman, once suggested to me that this indifference on the part of the youthful Newman to the local bathing-pond proved his heterosexuality, because if he had had any homosexual leanings, he would hardly have been indifferent to the puerile nudity with which such places abounded.) Newman himself recalled that although "in no respect a precocious boy, he attempted original compositions in prose and verse from the age of eleven, and in prose showed a great sensibility and took much pains in matters of style."[57] The boy who was intent on figuring out what constituted good English style could not be expected to find much diversion in marbles and tops.

Moreover, as Harriett pointed out in her fictionalized account of the Newmans' early home life, *Family Adventures* (1852), her brothers never cared for toys. In one passage of the book, Newman and his brother Charles are taken to a toy store by their Aunt Elizabeth and told that they can purchase what they like, but as Harriett relates, "these little boys never seemed at home among toys; so very few seemed to come within the range of their understanding. It was in vain a shopman and shopwoman spread before them the choicest stores of their warehouse. All were declined—one was stupid, another babyish. Toys of all sorts Henry [Newman's name in the book] gravely declared he never could understand, and Robert [Charles's name] could abide no horse not alive except a rocking horse." However, they are fond of books and they ask the shopkeeper if there are any in the shop "besides the ABC and picture books on the counter."

> The man replied, "Yes," and in half a minute both the boys were deeply engaged over a heap of neat, but not gay looking story books.
>
> "These have the most pictures, sir," said the man, civilly bringing out a more tempting looking set.
>
> "No, thank you," replied Robert, after looking at one or two, "we do not care for pictures; we like as much printing as possible."
>
> "Very strange young gentlemen," thought the shopman . . .[58]

[55] Anthony Trollope. *Autobiography* (Oxford, 1950), p. 9.
[56] *Contr*, pp. 2–3.
[57] *AW*, p. 29.
[58] Harriett Mozley. *Family Adventures* (London, 1852), pp. 185–8.

One can see something of the wit that became so characteristic of Newman in a letter he wrote his father from Ealing when he was 11. In the letter, he transcribed a prologue from a Terence play, *The Andrian*, which he recited at a school production, including these verses:[59]

> If Patriot Ardour, unabated Zeal
> And toil incessant for the Public Weal
> If mildest manners and a mind full fraught
> With all the wisest and the best have taught
> If Eloquence, Integrity and Worth,
> If true Religion, could protect on earth
> Surely such splendid virtues had been spared
> Nor basest arm to aim at thee had dared,
> Yet all dies not, thy name on Natures tomb,
> Raised by the Country to record thy doom,
> Shall speak enough in Ages yet to Come . . .

Apropos the prologue, Newman quoted from Addison's *Cato* (1713): "In this you will perceive that 'I must dissemble, and speak a language foreign to my heart.'" Then, in a postscript, he apologized for any bafflement the letter might have caused: "It will appear odd to you when the letter is half-opened to see something about Britons, Religion, Integrity, Honor, Ages, Country, Race, young attempts, splendid virtues, one accord etc etc etc."[60] Clearly, this gentle boy, for all his shyness, had a good sense of humour and a discriminating eye for humbug.

At Ealing, he showed the flair for making friends that would never leave him. Hans Henry Hamilton, his dearest school friend, went on to a distinguished legal career. From Trinity College, Dublin, he was called to the Irish Bar in 1823, became a Q.C. in 1852, and was chairman of the Quarter Sessions for Galway from 1852 to 1858 and for Armagh from 1858 until death in 1875. Another school friend, Richard Westmacott the Younger (1799–1872), was the son of Sir Richard Westmacott (1775–1856), the sculptor responsible for the wonderful figures on the pediment of the British Museum, as well as memorials to the Younger Pitt, Charles James Fox, and Lord Nelson. His son followed closely in his footsteps by becoming a notable sculptor himself, as well as an Academician and RA professor of sculpture. His most renowned work was the pediment of the Royal Exchange. In 1820, Newman loaned Westmacott money to help him stage a farce that he had written to pay off creditors. Newman even helped with rewriting the play, securing the star comedian (a Mr Harley) and composing some songs for the production. "After my usual manner," he wrote in a memorandum of 1874, "I strove to throw myself into the swing of his mind," though he was also concerned that, "what I wrote was out of keeping with

---

[59] Newman's lifelong fondness for the work of Terence recalls another brilliant English convert, Ben Jonson (1572–1637), who was equally fond of the Roman playwright, to whose work he was introduced at Westminster School, where he studied under William Camden. See Ian Donaldson's *Life of Ben Jonson* (Oxford, 2011).

[60] LD, 1:13 JHN to John Newman (10 November 1812).

my then religious profession, and would raise a laugh against me, did it ever come to light." As Westmacott himself predicted, the collaborative farce sank "*undamned into oblivion.*"[61] In 1841, Westmacott, no longer strapped for cash, executed his magnificent bust of his friend, which of all the likenesses of Newman best captures his unassuming nobility. Two years later, Westmacott served as one of the judges for Parliament's fresco competition, which was won by John Tenniel, the *Punch* artist who would go on to illustrate *Alice in Wonderland*. In 1849, Westmacott oversaw the building of Nelson's monument in Trafalgar Square. He was also one of the commissioners for the Great Exhibition of 1851.

It is some mark of the trust Newman placed in his old school friend that he should have shared with him so candidly the deliberations that preceded his conversion. On 11 July 1845, Newman confided in Westmacott: "It is morally certain I shall join the R. C. Church, though I don't wish this *told* from me.

> My conviction has nothing to do with events of the day. It is founded on my study of early Church history. I think the Church of Rome in every respect the continuation of the early Church. I think she is the early Church *in* these times, and the early Church is she *in* these times. They differ in doctrine and discipline as child and grown man differ, not otherwise. I do not see any medium between disowning Christianity, and taking the Church of Rome . . . I have at various times been reluctant to tell it to you . . . I was afraid. I will be frank with you, and tell you why. It was because I had got a notion that you had been inclined to skepticism— and it seemed a most serious thing to tell a person so inclined that one's own conviction was that he must believe every thing or nothing . . . I think you are stronger now than to be put out by such an avowal on my part. But for myself I say fairly, that I cannot believe only as much as our Reformers out of their own heads have chosen we should believe—I must believe less or more. If Christianity is one and the same at all times, then I must believe, not what the Reformers have carved out of it, but what the Catholic Church holds.[62]

In this candid letter, one can see the insights taking shape that would inform Newman's *Essay on the Development of Christian Doctrine* (1845), which shows how the development of doctrine resembles the development of the human individual from an undeveloped child into an adult. Westmacott certainly had no trouble seeing how the brilliant adult in Newman evolved from the brilliant boy that he had found so companionable at Ealing. When Westmacott's father died in 1856, Newman wrote his old schoolfellow a letter of condolence, to which Westmacott replied: ". . . I assure you that of the numerous letters I have received none has so moved me as yours – reminding me of those days of friendship in boyhood and manhood, to which I always refer with feelings of satisfaction – Though we have been separated now for many years I have never forgotten you – nor ceased to feel a deep interest in you."[63] It was this special bond between the two friends that doubtless moved Newman to commission Westmacott

[61] LD, 1:77–9 Memorandum on Helping Richard Westmacott.
[62] LD, 10:729 JHN to Richard Westmacott (11 July 1845).
[63] LD, 18:374–5 Richard Westmacott to JHN (8 September 1856).

to design a commemorative tablet for his mother in the Chapel at Littlemore, which invokes so strongly Newman's poignant regret: "Little did I think, when she laid the first stone at the new Church, she would not live to see it finished."[64]

Ealing also introduced Newman to the Reverend Walter Mayers, who imbued him with the Evangelical faith that roused him from his boyish neglect of God. By inculcating principles of religion among his schoolboys, Mayers influenced Newman's own pastoral understanding of the tutorial office, which would create such trouble for him when he became a tutor himself at Oriel. Eulogizing his indispensable mentor, Newman said of him something that could have been said of himself: "His was a life of prayer . . . the unseen things of the spiritual world were always uppermost in his mind"—though of course, Newman's career, both as an educator and a priest, also involved him in relentless administrative work of various sorts, which he always handled with dutiful dispatch.

Oxford

When it came to whether his eldest son should go to Oxford or Cambridge, John Newman exhibited unusual indecisiveness. Perhaps what rattled him was the sheer excitement of the momentous day. Whatever the cause, it was only when the post chaise was at the door and a neighbour who took an interest in young Newman recommended Oxford that the decision was made. Exeter, the neighbour's own college, was his first choice but since it had no vacancies, Newman settled on Trinity, which Dr Nicholas later pronounced "a most gentlemanlike college."[65] Newman matriculated when he was 16. Although he won a college scholarship in 1818, he did miserably in his final examination, failing completely in mathematics and receiving a fourth (the lowest grade possible) in classics. This poor showing was all the more disappointing because Newman had prepared for and indeed set his heart on a double first. Although there are grounds for attributing this failure to overwork—his diaries and letters show that in the months leading up to the examination, from July to April, he was reading on average 16 hours a day—other factors might also have contributed to his failure, which, as I shall endeavour to show, had more to do with his father than with mental or bodily fatigue. Since his scholarship was good for 9 years, Newman returned to Oxford and in 1822 sat for and won the prestigious Oriel fellowship. In Oriel's Senior Common Room, Newman would meet the formidable dons—nicknamed the Noetics for their fondness for logic—who reasoned him out of his youthful Evangelical phase.

After settling in at Trinity in June, 1817, Newman described life in college for his father: "At dinner I was much entertained with the novelty of the thing. Fish, flesh and fowl, beautiful salmon, haunches of mutton, lamb etc and fine, very fine (to my taste) strong beer, served up on old pewter plates, and mis-shapen earthenware jugs. Tell Mama there are gooseberry, raspberry, and apricot pies. And in all this the joint did not go round, but there was such a profusion that scarcely two ate of the same joint.

---

[64] LD, 5:299 JHN to Elizabeth Newman (17 May 1836).
[65] *AW*, p. 30.

Neither do they sit according to their ranks, but as they happened to come in."[66] In these letters, Newman described things that he knew his father would recognize as worth describing: the cost of things, tutorial rigor (Newman was pleased to find that Thomas Short, destined to become one of Trinity's most famous dons, was disliked for his rigor), the sumptuousness of the college board, the college pecking order, the social life of the undergraduates. In another letter, written a few days later, he described an aspect of his new life with which he would never become reconciled:

> I am not noticed at all, except by being silently stared at. I am glad they do not wish to be acquainted with me, not because I wish to appear apart from them and illnatured, but because I really do not think I should gain the least advantage from their company. For Hollis the other day asked me to take a glass of wine with two or three others of the College, and they drank and drank all the time I was there. I was very glad that prayers hindered their staying together longer than half an hour after I came to them – for I am sure I was not entertained with either their drinking or their conversation. They drank while I was there very much, and I believe intended to drink again. They sat down with the avowed determination of each making himself drunk. I really think, if any one should ask me what qualifications were necessary for Trinity College, I should say there was only one, – Drink, drink, drink.[67]

Doubtless Newman was familiar with Thackeray's description of these bibulous gatherings: "One looks back to what was called 'a wine party' with a sort of wonder. Thirty lads round a table covered with bad sweetmeats, drinking bad wines, telling bad stories, singing bad songs over and over again. Milk punch—smoking—ghastly headache—frightful spectacle of dessert table next morning, and smell of tobacco—your guardian, the clergyman, dropping in in the midst of this—expecting to find you deep in algebra, and discovering the gyp administering soda water"[68] Some might see priggishness in Newman's objections to these parties but it was not drink *per se* but drunkenness that he found objectionable. It also needs to be remembered that the drunkenness of Regency Oxford, like Regency London, was far worse than the "dull and deep potations" that Gibbon encountered at Magdalen in the 1750s. Thomas Creevey's papers make that plain. Of course, there are many wonderful drinking stories in Creevey, but here is one that shows how very much less well behaved the 11th Duke of Norfolk was compared to Newman's friend and patron, the 15th Duke.

> It used to be the Duke of Norfolk's custom to come over every year from Arundel to pay his respects to the Prince and to stay two days at Brighton, during which he always dined at the Pavilion. In the year 1804, upon this annual visit, the Prince had drunk so much as to be made very seriously ill by it, so that in 1805 (the year that I was there) when the Duke came, Mrs. Fitzherbert, who was always the Prince's best friend, was very much afraid of his being again made

[66] LD, 1–35 JHN to John Newman (11 June 1817), p. 35.
[67] LD, 1–36 JHN to John Newman (17 June 1817).
[68] W. M. Thackeray. *The Book of Snobs* (Oxford, 1918), p. 325.

ill, and she persuaded the Prince to adopt different stratagems to avoid drinking with the Duke. I dined there on both days, and letters were brought in each day after dinner to the Prince, which he affected to consider of great importance, and so went out to answer them, while the Duke of Clarence went on drinking with the Duke of Norfolk. But on the second day this joke was carried too far, and in the evening the Duke of Norfolk showed he was affronted. The Prince took me aside and said—"Stay after everyone is gone tonight. The Jockey's got sulky, and I must give him a broiled bone to get him in good humour again." So of course I stayed, and about one o'clock the Prince of Wales and Duke of Clarence, the Duke of Norfolk and myself sat down to a supper of broiled bones, the result of which was that, having fallen asleep myself, I was awoke by the sound of the Duke of Norfolk's snoring. I found the Prince of Wales and the Duke of Clarence in a very animated discussion as to the particular shape and make of the wig worn by George II.[69]

Creevey, incidentally, shared Newman's distrust of Henry Brougham (1778–1868), the Whig lawyer who would become one of Newman's *bête noirs*. While he conceded Brougham's oratorical powers, remarking of a speech he gave in memory of Pitt that it "shook the very square and all the houses in it from the applause it met with," he was never altogether keen on the man himself. "I cannot like him," he confessed; "He has always some game or underplot out of sight . . ."[70]

Newman's objections to the heavy wine drinking that he encountered at Oxford was also an objection to a certain impiousness. Since the young men who got drunk on Gaudy Night (celebrated every year on the Monday after Trinity Sunday) were not only making nuisances of themselves but making a mockery of Holy Communion, one can see why Newman found them offensive. At the same time, Newman looked askance at the abstemious. When Frank tried to interest him in Manning's crusade against drink, Newman famously demurred: "As to what you tell me of Archbishop Manning, I have heard that some also of our Irish bishops think that too many drink-shops are licensed. As for me, I do not know whether we have too many or too few."[71] Considering Newman's impatience with drunkenness, it is interesting that William Lockhart should have recalled this perhaps not entirely apocryphal episode in his recollections of Newman at Oxford:

There was a tradition in my time at Oxford, that once on market day when the upper end of High Street, near Carfax Church, was much crowded with roughs, and the "Town" and "Gown" element were apt to come into collision, Newman was walking past All Saints' Church in the line of march of a furiously drunken butcher, who came up the street foul-mouthed and blasphemous. When they were near together, Newman stood in his path; my informant, who was a "muscular Christian," the stroke of his college boat, expecting violence, came close up to the

[69] *The Creevey Papers* (New York, 1904), pp. 50–1.
[70] See entry for 17 October 1812 in *Creevey*, p. 107.
[71] LD, 23:363 JHN to Francis W. Newman (End of October 1867).

butcher, and was just making ready to fell him, when he saw the man stop short; Newman was speaking to him. Very quietly he said, "My friend, if you thought of the meaning of your words you would not say them." The savage was tamed on the spot; he touched his hat, turned round and went back.[72]

Later, after Newman became a Fellow of Oriel in April 1822, he would make it a point not to ingratiate himself with the rich hard-drinking gentleman commoners. In one of the autobiographical fragments he left behind, he wrote of himself: "He was one out of four Tutors, and the junior of them, and, though it would be very unjust to say of him that he intentionally departed from the received ways of the College, it cannot be denied that there was something unusual and startling in his treatment of the undergraduate members . . . He began by setting himself fiercely against the Gentlemen-Commoners, young men of birth, wealth or prospects, whom he considered (of course with real exceptions) to be the scandal and the ruin of the place . . . and he behaved towards them with a haughtiness which incurred their bitter resentment."[73] This explodes the charge, sometimes brought against Newman that he was somehow prejudiced in favour of the well-born and only engaged in a kind of slumming when he settled in Birmingham.[74] One can see this in the aristocratic convert George Talbot's assumption that Newman would naturally prefer to preach to "an audience of Protestants more educated than could ever be the case in England," to which Newman responded by reminding his correspondent that "However, Birmingham people have souls; and I have neither taste nor talent for the sort of work, which you cut out for me; and I beg to decline your offer."[75] It is true that he was later friendly with many aristocratic Catholics but this was due to their shared faith, not to any snobbery on Newman's part. Indeed, he had no illusions about the spiritual deficiencies of the upper classes. To his dearest Oxford friend, John Bowden, he wrote:

> I much fear society is rotten . . . As far as I have means of seeing the Upper Classes, it certainly is so. Doubtless there are many specimens of excellence in the higher walks of life . . . but I am tempted to put it to you whether the persons you meet generally are (I do not say, consistently religious, we can never expect that in this world) but believe in Christianity in any true meaning of the word. No, they are

---

[72] William Lockhart, *A Retrospect of Fifty Years* (London, 1891), p. 2.

[73] *AW*, p. 89.

[74] One of Newman's earliest biographers has another theory: "Newman's ultimate settling at Birmingham," Wilfrid Meynell wrote, "has been assigned to a variety of solemn causes: by some to his desire to hide himself; by others to the desire of his new authorities that he should be hidden. We have even heard about the banishment to Birmingham of this apostle for whom, in truth, fine society had no fascinations, of this man of letters who preserved in his seclusion an almost uninterrupted literary mood. And, after all, as Father Bowles has told me, the determining reason was a weighty one—the weight of his books. These had been carted to Maryvale at an incredible expense—a sum making a good hole in what would have been a year's income of his old Oxford days, when that income, all told, never exceeded £500 a year. He had been moved already to Cotton Hall from Maryvale and from his books, not greatly liking the separation. They were a sort of magnet to him, and as he could get to them more easily and less expensively than they to him—to them he went." See Wilfrid Meynell. *Cardinal Newman* (London, 1907), pp. 76–7.

[75] LD, 21:167 JHN to George Talbot (25 July 1864).

liberals, and in saying this, I conceive I am saying almost as bad of them as can be said of any man. What will be the case if things remain as they are? Shall we not have men placed in the higher stations of the Church who are anything but real Churchmen? the Whigs have before now designed Parr for a Bishop, we shall have such as him – I would rather have the Church severed from its temporalities and scattered to the four winds than such a desecration of holy things. I dread above all things the pollution of such men as Lord Brougham affecting to lay a friendly hand upon it. This vile Ministry, I cannot speak of them with patience.[76]

Lord Malmesbury would claim in 1884 that Newman had been an ineffectual tutor, a figure of fun incapable of commanding the respect of the undergraduates in his charge. Frederic Rogers, one of Newman's most brilliant pupils, who went up to Oriel in October 1828, a few months after Malmesbury left, and later went on to join Gladstone's cabinets as head of the Colonial Office, refuted the claim by recalling a more recognizable Newman, "a tutor with whom men did not venture to take a liberty," whose "formidable and speaking silence" was "calculated to quell any ordinary impertinence." In this regard, Newman was reminiscent of St Anselm, whose magnetism, as R. W. Southern remarks, "inflamed" his pupils "with intellectual zest."[77] Something of Newman's youthful self-possession, despite all his shyness, must have come from sparring with his father, not to mention his redoubtable colleague in the Oriel Senior Common Room, Richard Whately, about whom *The Times* once remarked: "He walked over ignorance, stupidity and conceit as a man crushes the shells on the seashore."[78]

Proof of the easy sympathy between father and son is evident from Newman's readiness to share little jokes with his father. "Whenever I go out," he wrote him from Trinity in 1817, "I am stared at; and the other day there was a party of people laughing at my dress. I am the head of the table at dinner, because I am the only one; at least I sometimes nearly finish my dinner before the few remaining drop in. The other day I had a nice dinner set before me of veal cutlets and peas, so much to myself that I could hear the noise I made in chewing through the empty hall; till at length one came in, and sat opposite to me, but I had not been introduced to him, and he could not speak to me. Consequently we preserved an amicable silence, and conversed with our teeth."[79] Then, again, on 18 May 1820, he wrote to tell his father how, as he said, "I intend to be at home a week in the middle of June, the first week in August, and a week in October. In the intervening time the Green Gate and venerable roof of Trinity College, will, I hope, keep me in an uninterrupted, calm, delightful course of study."[80] Before he sat for his BA examination in 1820, he found time to assure his father: "I write this to deny in the strongest terms the anxious declaration of my Mother 'that *I* am very anxious.' I am quite the reverse. I will not deny that I have *moments* of terror, but, except those moments, I am cool and in spirits."[81]

[76] LD, 2:317 JHN to John William Bowden (13 March 1831).
[77] R. W. Southern. *St. Anselm: A Portrait in A Landscape* (New Haven, 1990), p. 119.
[78] Bryan MacMahon. *Eccentric Archbishop: Richard Whately of Redesdale* (Dublin, 2005), pp. 11–12.
[79] LD, 1:40 JHN to John Newman (27 June 1817).
[80] LD, 1:73 JHN to Mr Newman (18 May 1820).
[81] LD, 1:92 JHN to Mr Newman (18 November 1820).

The rapport between father and son can also be seen in how Newman shared with his father his literary enthusiasms. With one letter, for example, he sent his father George Crabbe's *Tales of the Hall* (1819), "a work," as he said, "of which I am excessively fond," though he was also aware that its "monotonous gloominess" would probably not win it "many admirers." Nevertheless, Newman refused to allow this to sway his own judgement. "Hardly one of his Tales has a fortunate ending; hardly one of his Tales but has the same ending; hardly one of his Tales but is disfigured by the most prosaic lines, and degraded by familiar vulgarity. However, for all this, he seems to me one of the greatest poets of the present day."[82] He also took pride in sharing with his father his accustomed erudition. "By the end of this week," he wrote him in May 1820 when he was studying for his BA degree, "I shall have finished, thoroughly I hope, Æschylus, Newton, and half of my Livy. I am now reading at the rate (I whisper a great secret) of from 13 to 14 hours a day. I make hay while the sun shines."[83] Later, after he became a fellow at Oriel, he wrote his father of how "they know very little of me and judge very superficially of me, who think I do not put a value on myself *relatively* to others. I think (since I am forced to speak boastfully) few have attained the facility of comprehension which I have arrived at, from the regularity and constancy of my reading, and the laborious and nerve-bracing and fancy-repressing study of Mathematics, which has been my principal subject."[84] By the same token, he took palpable pleasure in sharing with his father the heady reality of his new position when he said of the Senior Common Room: "All the Oriel Fellows are so kind, I hardly know how to behave. I am now a member of 'the School of Speculative Philosophy in England,' to use the words of the Edinburgh Review; and it is not the least advantage, that, I have, whenever I wish, the advice and direction of the first men in Oxford."[85] One must keep in mind this unabashed delight in distinction to appreciate the self-sacrifice that Newman would later exercise in embracing St Philip Neri's call to humility. As he wrote his good friend Ambrose St John from Dublin in 1855, "Again 'As a crowning maxim, [St Philip] laid it down as a rule, that to obtain the gift of humility perfectly, four things were necessary, *spernere mundum, spernere nullum, spernere se ipsum, spernere se sperni.*'" He scarcely ever had this sentence of St Bernard out of his mouth, "to despise the world, to despise no one, to despise self, to despise being despised."[86]

That John Newman was proud of his talented son is clear from a memorandum that Newman wrote in 1874, recalling the fondness that Thomas Short, his tutor at Trinity felt for him, which memorably pleased his father. "At Easter 1818 my Father came to Oxford and took me home with him. When we got to London, he determined to go with me to Dr Nicholas at Ealing, for he was quite overcome with Short's warmth about me. He said Short went to meet him as an old friend, and holding out his hands said, 'O, Mr Newman, what have you given us in your Son,' or words to that effect. This was before I got the Scholarship."[87]

[82] LD, 1:83 JHN to Mr Newman (28 August 1820).
[83] LD, 1:87 JHN to Mr Newman (28 September 1820).
[84] LD, 1:125 JHN to Mr Newman (16 March 1822).
[85] LD, 1:135 JHN to Mr Newman (16 April 1820).
[86] LD, 17:49 JHN to Ambrose St John (9 November 1855).
[87] LD, 1:50.

Still, John Newman was not uncritical of his son. In his autobiographical writings, Newman was candid about his father's concern that he was becoming overly zealous—religiose rather than merely devout. This concern was confirmed when Newman joined his younger brother Frank's in refusing to transcribe urgent letters for their father on a Sunday afternoon. For the two brothers, the stricture against working on the Sabbath was inviolable; for John Newman, it was impudence.

> After Church my Father began to speak to me as follows: – "I fear you are becoming etc . . . Take care. It is very proper to quote Scripture, but you poured out texts in such quantities. Have a guard. You are encouraging a nervousness and morbid sensibility, and irritability, which may be very serious. I know what it is myself, perfectly well. I know it is a disease of mind. Religion, when carried too far, induces a softness of mind. You must exert yourself and do every thing you can. Depend upon it, no one's principles can be established at twenty. Your opinions in two or three years will certainly, certainly change. I have seen many instances of the same kind. Take care, I repeat. You are on dangerous ground. The temper you are encouraging may lead to something alarming. Weak minds are carried into superstition, and strong ones into infidelity. Do not commit yourself. Do nothing ultra. Many men say and do things, when young, which they would fain retract when older, but for shame they cannot."[88]

Later, when John Newman reconciled with his sons, Newman confided in his journal: "When I think of the utter persuasion he must entertain of the justice of his views of our apparent disobedience, the seeming folly of our opinions, and the way in which he is harassed by worldly cares, I think his forgiveness of us an example of very striking candor, forbearance, and generosity."[89] One of the reasons Newman's father objected to Evangelical fervour in his son was that he recognized that it jarred with his natural reserve. Newman confirms this in an autobiographical fragment in which he describes the passing of his Evangelical phase. Instrumental in this were his Oxford mentors, Edward Hawkins, who impressed upon him the importance of tradition and Charles Lloyd, who "bullied" him into reconsidering the Evangelical notions that Walter Mayer had first inculcated in him.[90] "The critical peculiarities of evangelical religion," Newman spoke of himself in the 3rd person, "had never been congenial to him, though he had fancied he held them. Its emotional and feverish devotion and its tumultuous experiences were foreign to his nature . . ." Moreover, for Newman, another reason why evangelical religion took no hold on him was "his great attraction to what may be called the literature of Religion, whether the writings of [the] Classics, or the works of the Fathers."[91] This was an accurate self-assessment. The charge occasionally made against Newman of self-absorption is false. Newman paid close attention to his religious opinions because he rightly recognized that they were instructive. His distaste for enthusiasm on the one hand, and his reasoned faith on the other, supported by a

---

[88] *AW*, p. 179.
[89] Ibid., p. 176.
[90] William J. Baker. *Beyond Port and Prejudice. Charles Lloyd of Oxford, 1784–1829* (Maine, 1981), p. 106.
[91] *AW*, p. 82.

thorough familiarity with the Fathers, freed him from the "intense introversion" as G. M. Young called it, that hobbled so many of his contemporaries in their religious development, from Mark Pattison to William Gladstone.[92]

The row between Newman and his father on the Sabbath reveals another aspect about their relationship: it was not the usual chilly one that so many other early nineteenth-century upper middle-class sons had with their fathers. J. W. Clark, the Victorian historian of Cambridge, is droll on this score, pointing out how "In the last century a man addressed his father as 'Sir,' and, so far as we can judge from contemporary literature, regarded him with fear, and not unfrequently with dislike. In the first half of the present century the new literary tastes and new political opinions that became prevalent among young Englishmen, made the breach wider still. A college tutor, popularly supposed to stand towards his pupils in the relation of a father, came to know so little about them, that the following anecdote is not incredible. One of the tutors of a large college desired his servant to go and invite a pupil, whom he had not seen for some time, to take wine with him after hall. 'Mr. So-and-so, sir? He died three terms ago.' 'You ought to tell me when my pupils die,' replied the Don."[93] Of course, when Newman became a don himself, he would work to remove this artificial divide between tutors and undergraduates by infusing his tutoring with pastoral care, even against keen and finally insuperable opposition.

Some sense of the mutual respect that Newman and his father felt for each other can be seen from the journal entry Newman jotted down for 11 January 1822: "My Father this evening said I ought to make up my mind what I was to be . . . So I chose; and determined on the Church. Thank God, this is what I have prayed for."[94] Of course, his father had hoped that his son might pursue a legal career—Newman even enrolled in Lincoln's Inn in November 1819. (Gladstone enrolled in 1833.) But when Newman opted for the Church, his father responded with "full acquiescence."[95] This entry shows how important it was for Newman that his father should approve his decision to be ordained a priest. Indeed, as another letter shows, Newman was eager to share his pastoral life with his father, if only to disabuse him of the notion that it was somehow intrusive.

> So far from this invasion of an Englishman's castle being galling to the feelings of the poor, I am convinced by facts that it is very acceptable. In all places I have been received with civility, in most with cheerfulness and a kind of glad surprise, and in many with quite a cordiality and a warmth of feeling. One person says, 'Aye, I was sure that one time or other we should have a proper minister—another that 'she had understood from such a one that a nice young gentleman was to come to our parish'—a third 'begged I would do him the favour to call on him, whenever it was convenient to me' (this general invitation has been by no means uncommon) Another speaking of the parish she came from said, 'the old man preached very good doctrine but did not come to visit people at their houses as the new one did.'

[92] G. M. Young. *Portrait of an Age: Victorian England* (Oxford, 1953), p. 67.
[93] J. W. Clark. *Cambridge: Historical and Picturesque Notes* (London, 1902), pp. 307–8.
[94] *AW*, p. 180.
[95] Ibid.

Singularly enough, I had written down as a memorandum a day or two before I received your letter, I am more convinced than ever of the necessity of frequently visiting the poorer classes—they seem so gratified at it, and praise it. Nor do I visit the poor only—I mean to go all through the parish; and have already visited the shopkeepers and principal people . . . I have not tried to bring over any regular dissenter—indeed I have told them all, I shall make no difference between you and churchgoers—I count you all my flock, and shall be most happy to do you a service out of Church, if I cannot within it. A good dissenter is of course incomparably better than a bad Churchman—but a good Churchman I think better than a good dissenter. . . Thank you for your letter and pardon my freedom of reply.[96]

If in his letters and autobiographical writings, Newman maintained a reserve about his father, Frank Newman was more forthcoming.

My father, whatever his inferiority in culture to his son, had an earnest zeal for *justice*, and in temperament as an arbitrator would have dealt equably with contending parties . . . [He was] an admirer of Benjamin Franklin and Thomas Jefferson. I had heard him say, "I do not pretend to be a religious man;" also, "I am a man of the world;" nay once: "I wonder that clever men do not see that it is *impossible* to get back to any certainty where they are so confident,"—he meant in *religious history*. So I painfully whispered to myself: "He is not a Christian." But, as I grew up, I began to honour a breadth, serenity, and truthfulness in my father's character. He was rather fond of a coarsely-worded maxim: *Give the devil his due*. After I had outgrown the shuddering at heresy and unbelief (a tedious process with me), I saw him, in my memory, as an unpretending, firm-minded Englishman, who had learned his morality more from Shakespeare than from the Bible, and rejected base doctrine from whatever quarter. The main elements of his character were in entire contrast to those of his eldest son. The only quality which I am aware that they had in common was—*love of music*.[97]

This is from *Contributions Chiefly to the Early History of the Late Cardinal Newman* (1891), the rebarbative memoir that Frank wrote after Newman's death to prove, as he said, that "the existing generation [had] seen [his brother] through a mist:" the real Newman being neither as truthful nor as admirable as his countrymen imagined. Frank's recollection of his father consequently says more about his animus against his brother than it does about his father. Nevertheless, it does confirm the differences between Newman and his father. In contrast to his son, John Newman was sympathetic to the republican ideas of the age and not particularly devout in his Christian faith. Still, such differences did not separate father and son as much as Frank imagined. Nor is it true that the "main elements of his [father's] character" were "in entire contrast to those of his eldest son." On the contrary, considering their differences, it is remarkable how similar they were. Probity, unpretentiousness, enterprise, and a readiness to give the devil his due were as characteristic of the one as the other. And of course, they

---

[96] LD, 1:184 JHN to John Newman (9 August 1824).
[97] *Contr*, pp. 6–7.

both loved music, which, as we all know, binds together even the most disparate souls. (In 1822, Newman wrote his father how, as he said, "I was at a Music party at the President's last Friday. We played chiefly Haydn's Symphonies.")[98] Indeed, Newman might have been thinking of this delight in music that he shared with his father when he wrote to one of the parents of his Oratory School boys:

> To my mind music is an important part of education, where a boy has a turn for it. It is a great resource when they are thrown on the world–it is a social amusement–perfectly innocent–and what is so great a point employs their thoughts . . . It is often a great point for a boy to escape from himself . . . He cannot be playing difficult passages on the violin, and thinking of any thing else.[99]

If much in Frank's memoir is merely scurrilous, some of his recollections ring true. When one recalls Newman's youthful shyness—how he could not abide being stared at, for example—it is not difficult to credit Frank's claim that "His taste was fastidious. He could not bear the coarseness of the vulgar." Then, too, it is easy seeing Newman adopting certain political views. "In reading History to our family," Frank recalled, "while my father's business preoccupied him, John often commented severely, especially against the opponents of our Charles I, and against French Republicans." One can readily see Newman coming to the defence of the monarch whom Lionel Johnson described so memorably.

> Comely and calm he rides
> Hard by his own Whitehall:
> Only the night wind glides:
> No crowds, nor rebels, brawl.
>
> Gone, too, his Court: and yet,
> The stars his courtiers are:
> Stars in their stations set;
> And every wandering star . . .
>
> Vanquished in life, his death
> By beauty made amends:
> The passing of his breath
> Won his defeated ends.

Here was a king who succeeded by failing—for the young Newman a most prophetic figure. According to Frank, both Newman's father and his father's mother "charged George III, as the chief criminal for two cruel, needless wars, both ruinous, the American ignominious also." Newman wrote a prologue for a Terence play at the behest of George Nicholas, the headmaster of Ealing School that "was a panegyric on George III . . . unbroken panegyric."

Newman was no less disinclined to criticize George IV. "When the coronation of George the IV was coming into view, a widespread excitement dislocated classes and

---

[98] LD, 1:126 JHN to Mr Newman (27 March 1822).
[99] LD, 1:42 JHN to Edward Bellasis (4 September 1865).

families on the tidings that the King wished to discard his wife, the Princess, by an odious accusation." In 1820, George the IV attempted to have Parliament pass a Bill of Pains and Penalties which would divorce him from his wife Caroline on the grounds of her alleged adultery with Bartolomeo Pergami, by all accounts an arrestingly handsome young courier, whose curly black hair, dark flashing eyes and splendid physique dazzled the northern Princess. Frank vividly recalled the family fracas to which the controversy of the proposed Bill gave rise.

> In Oxford, it caused a battle between Gown and Town. It distracted my father's drawing room also by a scene which was almost a quarrel, from the vehement part taken by J.H.N. against his father. The Ministry had given notice of prosecution: the trial was begun only. My age was just fifteen, but the strangeness of the affair was hard to forget, though seventy years have passed. It would be unfair to my brother to pretend memory of his arguments; yet I may say that I remember none, and can imagine none, except that the fact of the Ministry ordering the trial ought to bias us against the Queen.[100]

Frank's recall of how general the controversy was is corroborated by other accounts. "The discussion of the Queen's business is now become an intolerable nuisance in society," the diarist Charles Greville recorded, "no other object is ever talked of. It is an incessant matter of argument and dispute what will be done and what ought to be done. All people express themselves bored with the subject. It is a great evil when a single subject of interest takes possession of society; conversation loses all its lightness and variety, and every drawing-room is converted into an arena of political disputation."[101] Frank's recollection of how his brother viewed the matter also sounds plausible. Although Coleridge and Macaulay (then an undergraduate at Cambridge) favoured the Queen's case, most of her support came from radicals, artisans, mechanics, and ruffians—not the sort who would have appealed to Newman.[102] Nor would he have found her case any less unappealing for being represented by Henry Brougham, whose trumpery summation would have confirmed Newman's low opinion of the man.

> I pray your lordships to pause. You are standing on a precipice . . . Save the country, my lords, from the horror of this catastrophe—save yourselves from this situation—rescue the country, of which you are the ornament, but in which you could flourish no longer, when severed from the people . . . Save that country, that you may continue to adorn it—save the Crown, which is in jeopardy—the aristocracy, which is shaken—the altar itself . . .

From this early quarrel with his father, we can trace the beginning of Newman's opposition to Brougham, whom, later, after he took up the cause of Catholic Emancipation, Newman branded "the very patriarch of . . . liberalism in religion."[103]

---

[100] *Contr*, pp. 7–8.
[101] Charles Greville, entry for 25 June 1820 from *Greville's England: Selections from the Diaries of Charles Greville: 1818–1860* (London, 1981), pp. 21–2.
[102] Christopher Hibbert. *George IV* (London, 1976), p. 565.
[103] LD, 2:126, Note 1.

What motivated Brougham to defend Pergami's exuberant paramour cannot be given any brief answer. Flora Fraser, Queen Caroline's elegant biographer, patiently unpeels the layers of duplicity in Brougham's association with Caroline petal by deceitful petal. The politician whom she charitably describes as "a man with no fixed principles" wove a tangled web.

> In the course of the negotiations [between the Regent and his estranged wife Princess Caroline] Brougham began by acting in the Princess's interests, and treated with the Tory Government . . . He then secretly abandoned the Princess's interests, while ostensibly continuing to act as her agent in the negotiations. He hoped thereby to obtain the silk gown of a King's Counsel—a prerequisite for the office of Lord Chancellor, to which he aspired. But he did not only aspire to be Lord Chancellor, he had hopes of the premiership. It was common knowledge that the Regent detested Lord Liverpool. Brougham would be led to a point in his Parliamentary ambitions where he wondered if he could not give the Regent what he wanted, get rid of his wife and then form a government himself. . . .[104]

Newman's attitude to Brougham is best summed up in "The Tamworth Reading Room," (1841), one of the wittiest of all his writings, where he speaks of him as "the great sophist."[105] His attitude to Brougham's client was probably not dissimilar to the one expressed in a popular verse circulated at the time:

> O, Gracious Queen, we thee implore
> To go away and sin no more
> Or, if the effort be too great
> To go away at any rate.[106]

John Newman's view of the matter appealed more to emotion than logic. As Frank transcribed it, his father's argument was this: "The Prince, who is now King, overwhelmed with debt, wanted money. The King, his father, forbade Parliamentary aid unless the Prince would marry the Princess Caroline. But the Prince loved another lady, whom he had married, illegally, yet with all holy rites. To get the money he sacrificed the lady of his love, and accepted the Princess as his wife, when he had no *heart* to give her. Of course, dislike soon followed; she was unhappy in his home, and virtually was driven into exile. Now, if it shall be proved that, scorned by her legal husband, she sought solace from some other lover, hers is a case that deserves great pity, not insult and punishment; and of all living men this King George IV is the last

---

[104] Flora Fraser. *The Unruly Queen: The Life of Queen Caroline* (London, 1996), p. 323.

[105] *DA.*, p. 260. Taking Peel to task for undertaking the Tamworth Reading Room scheme in tandem with Brougham, Newman wrote: "It is, indeed, most melancholy to see so sober and experienced a man practicing the antics of one of the wildest performers of this wild age; and taking off the tone, manner, and gestures of the versatile ex-Chancellor, with a versatility almost equal to his own. Yet let him be assured that the task of rivaling such a man is hopeless, as well as unprofitable. No one can equal the great sophist. Lord Brougham is inimitable in his own line."

[106] See *The Correspondence and Diaries of the late Right Honourable John Wilson Croker, Secretary to the Admiralty 1809–1830.* ed. Louis Jennings (New York, 1884), 1, p. 165.

that has a right to censure her." Subsequently, as Frank records, the Cabinet itself split about the matter; Canning, for example, came round to Caroline's defence. But what struck Frank was his brother's intrepidity: "How wonderful, that J.H.N. at the age of nineteen, and not likely to know the facts, all fresh in my father's mind, should stand up against him thus."[107] It was rash of Frank to assume that his brother did not know the facts of the matter. Nevertheless, what Frank did not recognize was that it was their father who fostered Newman's independence by encouraging him to speak his mind, even, as in this case, when he strongly disagreed with him. Frank recalls that his father was so incensed by his son's position that he made sure he got in the last word, "Well, John! I suppose I ought to praise you for knowing how to rise in the world. Go on! Persevere! Always stand up for men in power and in time you will get promotion." Frank's comment regarding this is characteristically barbed: "Years afterwards, I discerned that my father had mistaken fanaticism for self-seeking."[108] Frank might have had any number of eccentricities, including a horror of alcohol, red meat, tobacco, and vaccination, but when it came to the Roman Church, he was thoroughly conventional. In him, and indeed in his other siblings, Newman encountered all the usual anti-Catholic prejudices. It was hardly surprising, then, that Frank should find his brother's youthful points of view harbingers of what he always called 'fanaticism.' Nonetheless, insinuating that his brother was guilty of self-seeking showed more incomprehension than spite. Self-seeking was the last charge that could be levelled against the man who exchanged Oxford for what the Pre-Raphaelite painter Edward Burne-Jones (1833–98) called "Blackguard, button-making, blundering, beastly, brutal, bellowing, blustering, bearish, boiler-bursting, beggarly, black Birmm."[109]

John Newman and the City of London

To understand John Newman and his relationship with his son, it is necessary to know something of the City of London. In 1815, when John Newman was living with his family at Southampton Street and making a good living as partner of the Ramsbottom, Newman and Ramsbottom bank at 72 Lombard Street, the City's population was 122,000, or one tenth of the total London population. There were 8,500 firms doing business there, and most, like John Newman's bank, were relatively small, though the Bank of England, between 1792 and 1813, had increased its staff of clerks from 300 to 900.[110] By 1783, London had supplanted Antwerp as the world's financial centre. With Paris, it was the premier clearing house for financial transactions and the leading market for insurance services and securities.[111] Nathan Rothschild and Alexander Baring were the two preeminent bankers, the one dominating the bullion and securities markets and acting as the unofficial banker of the British government and the other financing

---

[107] *Contr,* pp. 8–10.
[108] Ibid., p. 9.
[109] Fiona McCarthy. *The Last Pre-Raphaelite: Edward Burne-Jones and the Victorian Imagination* (Harvard, 2012), p. 24.
[110] David Kynaston. *The City of London: Volume I: A World of Its Own 1815–1890* (London, 1994), p. 30
[111] Boyd Hilton, *A Mad, Bad and Dangerous People? England 1783–1846* (Oxford, 2006), p. 13.

Anglo-American trade and acting as the unofficial banker of the US government.[112] The two personified the expansiveness and the confidence characteristic of banking at the time, despite the inevitable ups and downs of the market. Lord Byron celebrated their incomparable sway in memorable verses from *Don Juan*.

> Who hold the balance of the world? Who reign
> O'er congress, whether royalist or liberal?
> Who rouse the shirtless patriots of Spain?
> (That make old Europe's journals 'squeak and gibber' all)
> Who keep the world, both old and new, in pain
> Or pleasure? Who make politics run glibber all?
> The shade of Bonaparte's noble daring?—
> Jew Rothschild, and his fellow-Christian, Baring.

It was this puissant City that reinforced John Newman's marked independence. In David Kynaston's brilliant history of the City, one can see how independence was woven into the very fabric of the place. "The City had its own culture, its own traditions, and altogether a pride that rendered it not entirely susceptible to aristocratic buyouts."[113] City men occasionally went into Parliament but only to profit their businesses, and throughout the eighteenth century they tended to oppose whatever government was in power.[114] The independence of the City was also a product of its cosmopolitanism. "I am infinitely delighted in mixing with these several Ministers of Commerce," Joseph Addison wrote of the eighteenth-century Royal Exchange, "as they are distinguished by their different Walks and different Languages: Sometimes I am justled among a Body of Armenians; Sometimes I am lost in a Crowd of Jews; and sometimes make one in a Group of Dutchmen. I am a Dane, Swede, or Frenchman at different times, or rather fancy my self like the old Philosopher, who upon being asked what Countryman he was, replied that he was a Citizen of the World."[115] This cosmopolitanism would come naturally to John Newman's son, who, for all of his undoubted Englishness, was always prepared to enter into points of view different from those of his compatriots. One can see this not only in his embrace of Roman Catholicism, than which, for most of the nineteenth-century English, nothing was more outlandishly foreign, but also in his views of France, America, Italy and, especially Ireland.[116] "I am amused at the great cleverness of the Irish," Newman wrote back to the Oratory when he was staying at 22 Lower Dorset Street in Dublin, while setting up the Catholic University, "which far surpasses any thing I ever saw elsewhere. The very ticket takers in the room followed my arguments, and gave an analysis of the Discourse afterwards."[117] Indeed, one of the last letters he wrote was to a man named Sir John Eardley Eardley-Wilmot (1810–92), the former M.P. for South Warwickshire, who took great interest in Irish

[112] Ibid., p. 155.
[113] Kynaston, p. 22.
[114] Ibid.
[115] *Selections from The Tatler and The Spectator of Addison and Steele* (Penguin, 1982), p. 437.
[116] *The Selected Writings of Thomas Carlyle* (Penguin, 1971), p. 354.
[117] LD, 15:88–9 JHN to Nicholas Darnell (16 May 1852).

affairs, assuring him that "Though I have not any very great influence in the matter I very gladly take part in a movement in which you are interested for the advance of the Industries of Ireland and I am sorry I have so long left your letter unanswered before sending you my name."[118] If Newman rarely spoke ill of the Irish, Carlyle, like many of the Victorian English, rarely spoke well of them. When he recalled the 'architect,' as he called him, of his dilapidated house in Chelsea, a fellow named Parsons, he could only think of "His men of all types, Irish hodmen," who, "for real mendacity of hand, for drunkenness, greediness, mutinous nomadism, and anarchic malfeasance . . . excelled all experience or conception."[119]

Dickens has fun with the English infatuation with Englishry in *Our Mutual Friend* (1864–65), where he has Mr Podsnap explain to a foreign gentleman, "We Englishmen are Very Proud of our Constitution, Sir. It Was Bestowed Upon Us By Providence. No Other Country is so Favoured as This Country . . ."

> "And if we were all Englishmen present, I would say", added Mr. Podsnap, looking round upon his compatriots, and sounding solemnly with his theme, "that there is in the Englishman a combination of qualities, a modesty, an independence, a responsibility, a repose, combined with an absence of everything calculated to call a blush into the cheek of a young person, which one would seek in vain among the Nations of the Earth."[120]

That Dickens should have made Mr Podsnap a City man, who "got up at eight, shaved close at a quarter-past, breakfasted at nine, went to the City at ten, came home at half-past five, and dined at seven" shows that he was not entirely free of a certain insularity himself, though he was right enough in recognizing that his contemporaries were, by and large, proud of their Englishness.[121]

A rather different send-up of Englishry can be found in Newman's *Lectures on the Present Position of Catholics in England*, (1851), in which the newly converted Newman got at the root of the Englishman's fanciful notions about his national identity by locating them squarely in his even more fanciful views of Christianity. If any of my readers have not read anything by Newman, they should start with this satirical masterpiece. There, Newman explains that for most English Protestants, "Christianity was very pure in the beginning, was very corrupt in the middle age, and is very pure again in England now, though still corrupt everywhere else . . ." Moreover, as Newman explains, "in the middle age, a tyrannical institution called the Church arose and swallowed up Christianity . . ." Gratefully, however, "the Church is alive still, and has not yet disgorged its prey, except, as aforesaid, in our own favoured country. . ." The reason this should be so is simple. As Newman describes it, "in the middle age, there was no Christianity anywhere at all, but all was dark and horrible, as bad as paganism, or rather much worse. No one knew anything about God, or whether there was a God or no, nor about Christ or His atonement; for the Blessed Virgin, and Saints, and the Pope, and images, were worshipped instead; and thus, so far from religion benefitting

[118] LD, 31: 298 JHN to Sir John Eardley Eardley-Wilmot (31 July 1890).
[119] *The Selected Writings of Thomas Carlyle* (Penguin, 1971), p. 354.
[120] Charles Dickens. *Our Mutual Friend* (Oxford, 1952), p. 133.
[121] Ibid., p. 128.

the generations of mankind who lived in that dreary time, it did them infinitely more harm than good."[122]

Anthony Trollope would skewer this same comical John Bullism in *Orley Farm* (1862), where the bemused narrator observes: "We cannot bring ourselves to believe it possible that a foreigner should in any respect be wiser than ourselves. If any such point out to us our follies, we at once claim those follies as the special evidence of wisdom. We are so self-satisfied with our own customs that we hold up our hands with surprise at the fatuity of men who presume to point out to us their defects."[123]

If John Bull suspected the Church of Rome of every conceivable enormity, he could look on the rather foreign City of London, as Kynaston points out, with something of the same distrust.

> Successive generations of social satirists and caricaturists made savage butts of City people, pointing up their corpulence, their mundane recreations, their general lack of elegance. The culminating example was Peter Pindar's depiction of the prominent, grossly overweight self-made merchant-cum-banker Sir William Curtis ("Sir William Porpoise"), with his "nose as red as roses in June." The other strand was even less benign and came out implicitly in 1785 when the Marquis of Landsdowne urged Francis Baring to stand for the House of Commons: "It's the highest Injustice to consider every Merchant as a Jew, as if he were incapable of looking forward to anything but a Fraudulent Contract or a Line of Stockjobbing— the consequence of which is that their talons are left to prey upon the Publick instead of serving it . . ." Anti-Semitism was a crude perspective on the City that had plenty of mileage left in it.[124]

For R. H. Mottram (1883–1971), who had begun his career as a banker with Gurney's in Norwich before becoming a popular author, Mayfair, in the early nineteenth century, "solidly based on landed values, still looked down on the City, much as the County Magnate shoo'd the railway line from his park walls." The toff in *Punch* epitomized this view when he reacted to the proposed demolition of Temple Bar: "What? . . . why, it's the only Bawwier between us and the howwid city!"[125]

Nevertheless, by the late eighteenth century, the historical tensions between landed and moneyed men began to ease. When Samuel Johnson was asked by a young nobleman in 1770 where the gallantry and military spirit of the old English nobility had gone, the great Londoner replied: "Why, my Lord, I'll tell you what is become of it; it is gone into the City to look for a fortune."[126] Once gentlemen began becoming financiers, attitudes towards the City became less unfavourable. Then, too, as Kynaston points out, the City played an indispensable role in "managing the national debt, thereby enabling the ruling landed class simultaneously to enhance national power through protracted warfare, consolidate the Hanoverian settlement and keep taxation not only low but also thoroughly regressive. The economic case was compelling for bringing

---

[122] *Prepos.*, pp. 12–13.
[123] Anthony Trollope. *Orley Farm* (Oxford World Classics, 1985), Ch. 18, p. 179.
[124] Kynaston, pp. 20–1.
[125] R. H. Mottram, "Town Life", in *Early Victorian England 1830–1865* (Oxford, 1934), I, p. 182.
[126] James Boswell. *Life of Johnson*. ed. George Birbeck Hill (Oxford, 1934), II, p. 126.

the moneyed men on board."[127] Yet, whatever common cause landed and moneyed men might occasionally recognize, they always remained wary of one another. Private bankers were a breed apart.[128]

And within this special breed, there was a tension between the old and the new bankers not unlike the tension Newman saw between authority and theological inquiry within the Church. Walter Bagehot, an incisive critic of the City and a great admirer of Newman's, described how the City benefited from this tension.

> No country of great hereditary trade, no European country, at least, was ever so little "sleepy," to use the only fit word, as England; no other was ever so prompt at once to seize new advantages. A country dependent mainly on great "merchant princes" will never be so prompt; their commerce perpetually slips more and more into a commerce of routine. A man of large wealth, however, intelligent, always thinks, more or less, "I have a great income, and I want to keep it. If things go on as they are I shall certainly keep it; but if they change I *may* not keep it." Consequently, he considers every change of circumstance a "bore" and thinks of such changes as little as he can. But a new man, who has his way to make in the world, knows that such changes are his opportunities; he is always on the look out for them, and always heeds them when he finds them. The rough and vulgar structure of English commerce is the secret of its life; for it contains "the propensity to variation," which, in the social as in the animal kingdom, is the principle of progress.[129]

If the vitality of English banking was sustained by the continual infusion of new bankers preventing "a commerce of routine," Newman shows how the vitality of the Catholic faith is sustained by theological inquiry protecting the Church against popular error on the one hand and narrow dogmatism on the other.

> Some power is needed to determine the general sense of authoritative words—to determine their direction, drift, limits, and comprehension, to hinder gross perversions. This power is virtually the *passive infallibility* of the whole body of the Catholic people. The active infallibility lies in the Pope and the Bishops—the passive in the "universitas" of the faithful. Hence the maxim "Securus judicat orbis terrarum." The body of the faithful never can misunderstand what the Church determines by the gift of its active infallibility. Here on the one hand I observe that a local sense of a doctrine, held in this or that country, is not a "sensus universitas"—and on the other hand the schola theologorum is one chief portion of that universitas—and it acts with great force both in correcting popular misapprehensions and narrow views of the teaching of active infallibilitas, and, by the intellectual investigations and disputes which are its very life, it keeps the distinction clear between theological truth and theological opinion, and is

---

[127] Kynaston, p. 21.
[128] Ibid., p. 15.
[129] *The Collected Works of Walter Bagehot*. (London, 1978), IX, pp. 54–3.

the antagonist of dogmatism. And while the differences of the School maintain the liberty of thought, the unanimity of its members is the safeguard of the infallible decisions of the Church and the champion of its faith.[130]

Ian Ker neatly encapsulates Newman's understanding of how the prophetical and the sacerdotal offices of the Church interact in what Newman called "this ever-dying, ever nascent world." "Like his idea of the university, Newman's idea of the Church is of a wholeness and unity comprising a variety of elements and parts held together in creative tension, each sustained by mutual dependence rather than threatened by the collision of interaction. The keynote in both cases is equipoise as opposed to encroachment."[131]

If Newman's father was one of the new men in Bagehot's scheme of English banking, he was not one of the "rough companions" with "rude manners" with which Bagehot compared the "old-fashioned trader, the man who trades on his own capital."[132] Newman's interest in what constitutes a true gentleman, so memorably set out in *The Idea of a University*, might very well have sprung from his father's belonging to a profession that was also interested in gentlemen. In a witty *Saturday Review* essay, Bagehot looked at the often delicate relationship between gentlemen and their bankers:

> One would think that the English nation, with its vast and undoubted wealth, might afford to be candid in this respect and to acknowledge any occasional scarcity of cash under which it may chance to labour. Yet the fact is never frankly admitted . . . "My wants," says the Count in one of Mr. Disreali's tales, "are few; a fine carriage, fine horses, a complete wardrobe, the best opera box, the first cook, and pocket money—that is all I require. I have these, and I get on pretty well." "Well," said Charles Doricourt, "you are a lucky fellow, Mirabel; I have had horses, houses, carriages, opera boxes and cooks, and I have had a great estate, but pocket money I never could get. Pocket money was the thing which it cost me most of all to buy." The reserve in the Bank of England is the pocket money of the nation.[133]

In addition to independence, the City gave Newman's father an intellectual acuity, a sharpness that would also distinguish his son. In 1808, Robert Hawker, a clergyman from Plymouth visited the Royal Exchange and left a vivid picture of the City at work: "On our arrival, my mind was wonderfully arrested with all I saw and heard. The place, though spacious, was full of persons; and earnestness was strongly pictured upon every countenance . . . One general feature marked every character, whether buyer or seller:—I mean the unwearied perseverance, uniformly distinguishing all, to accomplish the object of their distinct pursuits. Here were no vacant countenances. Nothing like the shew of indifference. Every one appeared alive, zealous, and indefatigable."[134] The

---

[130] LD, 27:337–8 JHN to Isy Froude (28 July 1875).
[131] Ian Ker. *John Henry Newman* (Oxford, 1990), p. 707.
[132] *The Collected Works of Walter Bagehot* (London, 1978), IX, p. 52.
[133] *Collected Works of Walter Bagehot* (London, 1978), IX, p. 295.
[134] Kynaston, p. 33.

picture evoked here is reminiscent of what Newman had to say of the Duomo in Milan, which he visited less than a year after he converted.

> I have said not a word about that overpowering place, the Duomo. It has moved me more than St Peter's did – but then, I studiously abstained from all services etc. when I was at Rome, and now of course I have gone when they were going on and have entered into them. And, as I have said for months past that I never knew what worship was, as an objective fact, till I entered the Catholic Church, and was partaker in its offices of devotion, so now I say the same on the view of its cathedral assemblages. I have expressed myself so badly that I doubt if you will understand me; but a Catholic Cathedral is a sort of world, every one going about his own business, but that business a religious one; groups of worshippers, and solitary ones – kneeling, standing – some at shrines, some at altars – hearing Mass and communicating – currents of worshippers intercepting and passing by each other – altar after altar lit up for worship, like stars in the firmament – or the bell giving notice of what is going on in parts you do not see – and all the while the canons in the choir going through [[their hours]] matins and lauds [[or Vespers]], and at the end of it the incense rolling up from the high altar, and all this in one of the most wonderful buildings in the world and every day – lastly, all of this without any show or effort, but what every one is used to – every one at his own work, and leaving every one else to his.[135]

For some, seeing any resemblance between a cathedral and a counting house might seem sacrilegious, but for Newman, whose faith was always nourished and renewed by the most sedulous practical application, the resemblance was natural.

When Newman wrote to describe to his father his first parish, St Clement's, Oxford, where he was appointed curate, he did so with an attention to detail that must have pleased the banker in his father.

> June 3. 1824
>
> [[To my Father]]
> The Parish of St Clements is situated beyond Magdalen Bridge, on each side of the London Road. In the return of 1801 it contained about 400 inhabitants—in 1821 about 800. Since that time Oxford has become more commercial than before, owing to the new canals etc all which have tended to increase the population. But the increase of this particular parish has been also owing to the improvements in the body of the town. Old houses, which contained perhaps several families, have been pulled down, to make way for collegiate buildings, to widen streets, to improve the views. This has made building a very profitable speculation in the outskirts of the place, and the poor families once unpacked, have not been induced to dwell so thickly as before. The parish, in which I am interested, I find consists at present of 2000 inhabitants, (at first I understood 1450) and it is still increasing. The living, I am told, is worth about £80. I do not suppose the curacy will be

---

[135] LD, 11:253 JHN to Henry Wilberforce (24 September 1846).

more than £40 or £50. The Church, as I before mentioned, holds but 300—this it is proposed to rebuild.

As I shall be wanted as soon as possible, my present intention is to run away from Oxford by a night coach on Trinity Sunday night [[This shows that as early as 1826, I was thinking of studying the Fathers.]] or Monday morning, stopping an hour or two at Strand; then proceeding to London, and returning to Oxford Wednesday or Thursday. More time neither my pupils nor the duties of the Curacy will allow; and I wish, if possible, to see you all, before I am nailed down to Oxford.

I finished the Cicero on Friday last—finished the corrections etc by Tuesday, and despatched my parcel to town by a night coach. It will appear, I expect, in the course of a month or five weeks.[136]

What is also remarkable about this letter is how it prefigures the capable man of business in Newman who would work so resourcefully to put together the Catholic University of Ireland and, later, the Oratory School, projects which required precisely the sort of administrative aplomb that he exhibited first as deacon of St Clement's.

Another trait that was prized in the City, which "consists," as one foreigner described it, "of little narrow, crooked streets, forming a labyrinth, out of which it is not easy to extricate yourself when you have once entered it," was integrity.[137] The attributes that Robert Barclay II praised in John Henton Tritton, the head of Barclays were universally emulated: "He was the most deliberate and exact man I ever knew," Barclay recalled. "He followed up the details of every part of our concern with minute particularity which kept all the clerks up to the mark, silently overlooking their work and making all his observations in a low tone of voice, so that the same quiet habit of transacting business prevailed throughout the House. Extreme caution, inflexible integrity and firmness were his characteristics as a man of business, and to these he added punctuality and self-command . . ."[138] Mottram saw a similar reliance on integrity in his overview of the early nineteenth-century City: ". . . in *Pickwick*, Sergeant Snubbin's Mr. Mallard was probably as well off as the head of a department in the Bank of England, though he did nothing but make appointments for his master. But he had of course to provide for his own old age and sickness, and those of his dependants. In this body . . . we have the central distinctive type of our period. The classes above it, royal, noble, or propertied, legislators, merchants, member of learned professions, had existed before, but for the first time they became dependent on the . . . negative virtues of a body of men who made noting with their hands, except figures in books of account, and whose great quality was not manual skill, but probity as regards other people's affairs entrusted to them."[139] Of course, Mottram was speaking of bank clerks, who were nothing as exalted as private bankers; still, probity was indispensable to both.

[136] LD, 1:176 JHN to Mr Newman (3 June 1824).
[137] Kynaston, p. 29.
[138] Ibid., p. 15.
[139] R. H. Mottram, "Town Life", in *Early Victorian England 1830–1865*. ed. G. M. Young (Oxford, 1934), I, p. 180.

Lastly, as Kynaston nicely puts it, "bottom, not brilliance . . . made a private banker."[140] *Bottom*, in this sense, is not a word one hears much nowadays but it describes many of the qualities that John Newman would instil in his son: resourcefulness, staying power, substance, stability—though, of course, the extraordinary thing about Newman was that he had both bottom *and* brilliance.

"The Privilege of Misfortune"

The years between the American War of Independence and Waterloo were boom years. After Waterloo, the boom burst. In December 1815, John Newman penned a poem in which he voiced what must have seemed an innocuous hope:

> Oh, may all wars from henceforth be confined
> To mimic pictures and the scenes behind![141]

Unfortunately, in 1816, his wish came true and England experienced one of her severest commercial crises ever, "characterized by restricted trade, restricted money and countless failures."[142] Mottram echoes this, pointing out how, "it now strikes the observer, from a longer perspective, that although the top-hat had crowned the respectability of business, and the umbrella had replaced the sword as part of the daily wear, there still lurked an omnipresent and perpetual precariousness."[143] This would be borne out in the case of John Newman when his bank closed its doors on 8 March 1816. Three years later, when the post-war depression reached its nadir, Charles Churchill summed up the market's calamitous collapse. "Thus closes a trying Year in the Commercial World, having been full of successive Shocks on Confidence—with falling Markets in every Branch of Trade—& from month to Month going from bad to worse—we have to thank God for having hitherto escaped without any Losses of Consequence . . . If in the hurry of Business and cares of the World, I forget thee, do not thou Oh God forget me."[144]

After John Newman's bank stopped payment, the family scrambled to decide what to do. Newman would remain in Ealing; and it was during that summer that he experienced the first of the three illnesses that he later recognized as pivotal in his spiritual development—"the first keen, terrible one, when I was a boy of 15," which, as he said, "made me a Christian, with experiences before and after, awful and known only to God."[145] Here, again, he chose to be mum. *Secretum meum mihi.* Nonetheless,

[140] Kynaston, p. 16
[141] Sean O'Faolain. *Newman's Way* (New York, 1952), p. 49.
[142] Kynaston, p. 44.
[143] R. H. Mottram, "Town Life", in *Early Victorian England 1830–1865.* ed. G. M. Young (Oxford, 1934), 1, p. 182.
[144] Kynaston, p. 43.
[145] *AW*, p. 268 "My second, not painful, but tedious and shattering was that which I had in 1827 when I was one of the Examining Masters, and it too broke me off from an incipient liberalism— and determined my religious course. The third was in 1833, when I was in Sicily, before the commencement of the Oxford Movement."

it is telling that one of the defining experiences of his life occurred in tandem with his father's failure.

It is also remarkable that it was to his father that he first confided his later academic failure, when he obtained the poorest possible BA degree.

Trinity College December 1st 1820

My dear Father,

The pain it gives me to be obliged to inform you and my Mother of it I cannot express. What I feel on my own account is indeed nothing at all, compared with the idea that I have disappointed you; and most willingly would I consent to a hundred times the sadness that now overshadows me if so doing would save my Mother and you from feeling vexation. I will not attempt to describe what I have gone through; but it is past away, and I feel quite lightened of a load.—The Examining Masters were as kind as it was possible to be; but my nerves quite forsook me and I failed. I have done every thing I could to attain my object, I have spared no labour and my reputation in my College is as solid as before, if not so splendid.—If a man falls in battle after a display of bravery, he is honoured as an hero; ought not the same glory to attend on him who falls on the field of literature?

Believe me, My dear Father Your dutiful Son
John Henry Newman.[146]

Newman's failure in his final examination at Trinity was so pivotal in his development because after it he would come to see failure as God-sent, a providential test of faith, as well as an opportunity for him to reaffirm his readiness to do without worldly success and to devote himself wholly to God. Whether his failure at schools was accidental or an involuntary or wilful emulating of his father's failure is impossible to say. Meriol Trevor attributed it to "nerves" and proof that "nothing was to come to him easily. So many less gifted than he, born into the upper and ruling class, who never had to worry about money, passed comfortably into whatever career they chose to enter; Newman had to slave for all he gained, and to suffer humiliating defeat for every prize."[147] At the same time, the epistolary record shows that Newman himself often hinted at parallels between his own and his father's failure.

The cares of the world did not cause Newman to forget God or His blessings. "When I look round, I see few families but what are disturbed from within," he wrote his mother in 1821. "Many are wasted by death – many distracted by disagreements – many scattered. We have not had to weep over the death of those we love. We are not disunited by internal variance – we are not parted from each other by circumstances we

---

[146] LD, 1:94 JHN to Mr Newman (1 December 1820). Apropos his academic debacle, Newman wrote in the third person of how "He had overread himself, and, being suddenly called up a day sooner than he expected, he lost his head, utterly broke down, and after vain attempts for several days had to retire, only making sure first of his B.A. degree. When the class list came out, his name did not appear at all on the Mathematical side of the Paper, and in Classics it was found in the lower division of the second class of honours, which at that time went by the contemptuous title of 'Under-the-line', there being as yet no third and fourth classes." A.W., p. 47; cf. pp. 39–40, 50–3

[147] Meriol Trevor. *Newman: The Pillar of the Cloud* (London, 1962), p. 31.

cannot control. We have kind and indulgent parents, and our tastes, dispositions, and pursuits are the same. How grateful ought we to be!"[148] This reminder of the familial blessings was particularly welcome at a time when Newman's family was bracing for rough seas ahead. The brewery at Alton that John Newman had undertaken was not doing well. The next day John Newman wrote to commend his eldest son for the exemplary pluck he was showing during a difficult time:

> I trust when this dreadful Storm is over under Providence that my Mind will be settled and calm enough to consider well which my state of agitation has hitherto disabled me from the advantages which you so feelingly and with such good practical sense describe. To me none of the least are the Blessings of having such Children so deeply endowed with the best of Principles both as to religion [and] high honor and I am proud to say of not contemptible abilities. Amongst them let this be a consolation to you that as the Eldest you have by example as well as by precept and instruction so greatly contributed to the Moral Beauty as well as to the cultivation and enlargement of their Minds. I shall go to Church tomorrow and I know I shall have your Prayers for Support from on high on this trying occasion and it is a solacing feeling that amongst the institutions of our excellent Church one of the finest is the knowledge that dear Family and relations however divided by distance are putting up their devotions to the Throne of Mercy at the same moment and in the same words and who knows but they may unseen to us mingle there and descend upon us in the results of spiritual support and the confidence of humble hope and assurance of divine assistance, however negligent we may have been of our duties to God and ungratefully insensible of our advantages – The same fixed Star is viewed by the Eye at Oxford as in London and appears to each observer to be in the same Place.[149]

On 1 November 1821, the pelting of this pitiless storm reached its long-dreaded crescendo: John Newman was declared bankrupt.

The worldly failure encountered by Newman's father would make a lifelong impact on him. In this respect, few of his contemporaries would have as great an impact on him. In his autobiographical writings, his *Apologia* and his letters, Newman gave consistent credit to such early influences as Walter Mayers, Thomas Scott, Bishop Butler, and Joseph Milner. They put him on his way to understanding the faith that he would spend his life practising. But he never mentions his father's influence in any of these grateful acknowledgements. Why? Partly because he recognized that his father's faith was tinged with the undogmatic vagueness that he saw in the faith of the various Broad Church followers of Thomas Arnold. But even more because the debt he owed his father for helping him to understand his faith was too deep, too personal, too all-embracing. Whenever he mentions Scott or Milner or Butler, he mentions books of theirs that fired his youthful mind. His father, of course, left behind no books and yet, through all Newman's voluminous writings, from The *Arians of the Fourth Century* (1833) to the *Letter to his Grace the Duke of Norfolk* (1875) there is very little in that

---

[148] LD, 1:113, JHN to Mrs Newman (26 October 1821).
[149] LD, 1:114 John Newman to JHN (27 October 1821).

huge output that is not without some trace of his father's influence. Certainly, one can see this influence in a letter he wrote to *The Christian Observer* on 22 September 1822, in which he addressed the trials faced by the Christian student, but in a way that made clear that his father's troubles had forced him to rethink his own academic ambitions. The Christian student faced a perennial dilemma: "He must labour diligently for honors which he professes not to desire: he must exert every nerve to gain an eminence which, trembling at the thought of its numerous temptations, he often sincerely fears to reach . . . The man of business may shew that his affections are not set on worldly possessions by his works of charity and love; but how can a religious student inform the world that he seeks not honour for its own sake? Failure perhaps is the only thing that can prove the state of his heart, by manifesting his cheerfulness under disappointment; and there may be moments in which he may feel disposed to pray even for failure, if failure be necessary to vindicate, either to himself or to others, the real character of his religious principles."[150] Newman's father read the letter with wholehearted contempt. "I know you write for the Christian Observer," Newman recalled his father telling him. "My opinion of the Christian Observer is this, that it is a humbug. . . . That letter was more like the composition of an old man, than of a youth just entering life with energy and aspirations."[151] Well, what John Newman did not appreciate (understandably enough) was that it was his own failure that had inspired the piece and what he took to be humbug was really more a testament of faith. His son would not labour, at Oxford or anywhere else, for "the idol of fame."[152] Failure, not success, would be the badge of his faith, and for that he had his father to thank. For his part, his father could not understand why his son should harp so on failure, especially after he had worked so hard to give him a proper launch in the world. Later, as a Catholic, Newman would reassert the connection between failure and faith. "We should not expect to see nations prosperous in proportion to their Catholicity . . . Since the coming of our Saviour on earth, humiliation, suffering, and poverty are to be looked on as His livery; and His prophecies to His Church rather foretell thorns than roses, strife than peace, and humiliation than triumph."[153]

Eminent Failures

Growing up with a father who had met with failure put Newman in distinguished company. Charles Dickens' father was a naval clerk whom one of his colleagues in the Navy Pay Office recalled as ". . . a fellow of infinite humour, chatty, lively, and agreeable." John Dickens saw himself as one of life's born optimists, "a cork which, when submerged, bobs up to the surface again none the worse for the dip." Handsome, always smartly turned out and impeccably polite, he was the prototypical Micawber. He was also genuinely beloved. "Never was a Man more unselfish," his wife recalled

---

[150] LD, 1:151 JHN to *The Christian Observer* (22 September 1822).
[151] *AW*, p. 179.
[152] LD, 1:151.
[153] LD, 19:540 from a letter to *The Rambler*, "Temporal Prosperity, Whether a Note of the Church" (July 1859), pp. 234–6.

after his death, "ever a Friend to those whom he could serve and a most affectionate kind Husband and father."[154] Yet he could also fly into rages. Once, backstage at one of his son's theatricals, he caught sight of a figure he took to be an intruder and leapt at him, only to find that the figure was his own reflection in a glass. At other times, with his grandiloquent patter and elaborate manners, he seemed a character of his own theatrical making, detached from those around him, always resisting reality. If there was something endearing about his eccentricity, his improvidence was intolerable: he was constantly in debt, constantly strapped, constantly borrowing. In February 1824, a Camden baker would not be fobbed off any longer and had him arrested for what was then a considerable debt of £40. From the "sponging house" where debtors were given the chance to clear their debts, Charles was sent to see if his uncle would lend his brother the needed blunt to set him free, but he refused: the well was empty; and so on 20 February 1824, John Dickens was imprisoned in the Marshalsea as an insolvent debtor.

For Dickens, the upshot was grim. At the age of 12, he was plucked from school and set to work in a blacking factory. As Dickens unforgettably recalled, Warren's Blacking at 30 Hungerford Stairs was located in "a crazy, tumbledown old house, abutting . . . on the river, and literally overrun with rats. Its wainscoted rooms and its rotten floors and staircase, and the old grey rats swarming down in the cellars, and the sound of their squeaking and scuffling coming up the stairs at all times, and the dirt and decay of the place . . ." left an indelible impression on him. Most children are prone to fearful imaginings but Warren's was not phantasmal: it was real. This was the nightmare of nightmares from which Dickens spent his life struggling to escape. His father would get out of the Marshalsea in a matter of months but Dickens would remain in the blacking factory for over a year. Indeed, in all that time, he had no idea when he would get out or indeed whether he would ever get out. He was only removed from the place after his father quarrelled with the proprietor. His mother actually did what she could to try to keep him there after his father extricated him which may account for why Dickens was never at his best in drawing his female characters.[155]

Once free of the blacking pots, Dickens followed his father into journalism and swiftly established himself as a popular author. The poverty he had known as a child would never return. Yet the spectre of his father's failure remained with him always. It opened the eyes of the future novelist to the manifold evils of the world. Indeed, in nearly all his books, the world is a place of dispossession, where the only things truly possessed are dreams or heartbreak. In *Little Dorrit* (1857), an ancient inmate of the Marshalsea defends the prison as a refuge from the world. "Elsewhere people are restless, worried, hurried about, anxious respecting one thing, anxious respecting another. Nothing of the kind here, sir. We have done all that—we know the worst of it; we have got to the bottom, we can't fall, and what have we found? Peace."[156] Yet such fatal resignation is conspicuously absent from most of Dickens's novels. Whether in *David Copperfield* or *Oliver Twist*, *Nicholas Nickleby* or *Great Expectations*, resiliency rules. If the failure of John Dickens acquainted his son with evil, it also acquainted him

---

[154] Peter Ackroyd. *Dickens* (London, 1990), p. 11
[155] Ackroyd, pp. 67–75.
[156] Charles Dickens. *Little Dorrit* (Oxford, 1953), p. 63.

with the joy of fighting evil. As G. K. Chesterton put it in one of his brilliant essays on Dickens, "This world can be made beautiful again by beholding it as a battlefield. When we have defined and isolated the evil thing, the colors come back into everything else. When evil things have become evil, good things, in a blazing apocalypse, become good. There are men who are dreary because they do not believe in God; there are many others who are dreary because they do not believe in the devil . . ."[157]

When John Dickens died, his son was sleepless with grief, and spent three successive nights walking the streets of London. "When a church clock strikes, on houseless ears in the dead of the night," he wrote in a piece called "Night Walks" describing his noctambulations, "it may be at first mistaken for company and hailed as such. But, as the spreading circles of vibration, which you may perceive at such a time with great clearness, go opening out, for ever and ever afterwards widening perhaps (as the philosopher suggested) in eternal space, the mistake is rectified and the sense of loneliness is profounder."[158] Well, there might be some faint rumor of despair in that. Dickens was in the dumps. But he resisted despair. (On this occasion he might even have thought of what Edward Copleston, the Provost of Oriel from 1814 to 1827 once told the lonesome young Newman: *"Nunquam minus solus, quam cum solus."*) Despite being occasionally despondent, Dickens was at heart a fighter, the antithesis of Charles Kingsley, who, for all his muscular Christianity, was always inclined to see the war half lost:

> We fall on our legs in this world,
> Blind kittens, tossed in neck and heels;
> 'Tis Dame Circumstance licks Nature's cubs into shape,
> She's the mill-head, if we are the wheels . . .

This was never Dickens' way. No Dame Circumstance accounts for the resipiscence of Scrooge or the loyalty of Pip or Nicholas Nickleby's gallant care for Smike. Or indeed the terrible scrapes into which John Dickens fell. Such scrapes were caused by individual character, not Dame Circumstance.

Now, of course, Newman's father was no John Dickens: he was not feckless and certainly never irresponsible with money. If he encountered failure, it was the result of the vagaries of the market. Newman even speculates that his banking partners might have been unduly precipitate in closing the bank. Had they kept their doors open, they might have weathered the storm. Nevertheless, while the source of each man's failure might have been different, the reaction of their sons to their reversals had certain aspects in common. Both drew closer to their fathers; both grew tougher; both viewed the world with a certain wary detachment, though, as Chesterton shows, Newman's attitude to the world never had Dickens's peculiar optimism.

Charles Dickens, who was most miserable at the receptive age when most people are happy, is afterwards happy when most men weep. Circumstances break men's

---

[157] G. K. Chesterton. "On the Alleged Optimism of Dickens", *The Collected Works of G. K. Chesterton.* Volume XV: Chesterton on Dickens (San Francisco, 1989), p. 202.
[158] Charles Dickens. From "Night Walks", in *The Uncommercial Traveller and Reprinted Pieces* (Oxford, 1958), p. 133.

bones; it has never been shown that they break men's optimism . . . . Higher optimists, of whom Dickens was one, do not approve of the universe; they do not even admire the universe; they fall in love with it. They embrace life too close to criticize or even to see it. Existence to such men has the wild beauty of a woman, and those love her with most intensity who love her with least cause.[159]

Dame Sybil Thorndike heartily agreed with Chesterton when she wrote in her introduction to *Nicholas Nickleby* (1839), "The name 'incurable optimist,' often hurled at Dickens's head is surely the title of a man of faith who knows there is a Way, and the finding of that Way is the main business of each of us. 'Incurable optimist,' yes, and a god-like sense of the ridiculous—a sense of Youth—the Youth of God."[160]

Another of Newman's contemporaries can serve as an illuminating contrast. Anthony Trollope's father failed as an heir, a lawyer, a farmer and an author. For years he dedicated himself to writing what he called his *Encyclopaedia Ecclesiastica*, a Church history, which, as Trollope's biographer, Victoria Glendinning writes, promised to "explain all ecclesiastical terms, rites and ceremonies, and all the orders and subdivisions of monks and nuns."[161] In his *Autobiography*, Trollope described the appalling odds against which the unhappy project was pursued. "During the last ten years of his life, [his father] spent nearly half of his time in bed, suffering agony from sick headaches. . . . Under crushing disadvantages, with few or no books of reference, with immediate access to no library, he worked at his most ungrateful task with unflagging industry. When he died, three numbers out of eight had been published by subscription; and are now, I fear, unknown, and buried in the midst of that huge pile of futile literature, the building up of which has broken so many hearts."[162] Here is a solicitude for ill-conceived literary ambition that all writers of books about Cardinal Newman should find consoling.

In her splendid biography, Glendinning quotes something from *Ralph the Heir*, which would undoubtedly have caught Newman's eye. "In the midst of calamities caused by the loss of fortune," the narrator remarks, "it is the knowledge of what the world will say that breaks us down; – not regret for those enjoyments which wealth can give, and which had long been anticipated."[163] This was certainly not the case with Newman—he was never discountenanced by what the world might say—but he would nevertheless have seen the accuracy of the observation in a commercial society where bankruptcy always signified deep, immitigable, personal disgrace.

Trollope's relationship with his father offers a striking contrast to the relationship that Newman enjoyed with his father. Where Newman took confidence and independence from his father, Trollope took from his only a sense of grinding oppressiveness. "From my very babyhood, before those first days at Harrow, I had

---

[159] G. K. Chesterton. From "The Boyhood of Dickens", in *Collected Works of G. K. Chesterton*, V. 15 Chesterton on Dickens (San Francisco, 1989), pp. 61–2. See also Michael Slater. *Charles Dickens* (New Haven, 2009), pp. 14–30.
[160] Dame Sybil Thorndike. Introduction. *Nicholas Nickleby* (Oxford, 1950), p. xiii.
[161] Victoria Glendinning. *Anthony Trollope* (New York, 1993), p. 34.
[162] Anthony Trollope. *Autobiography* (Oxford, 1950), pp. 13–14.
[163] Glendinning, p. 38.

had to take my place alongside of him as he shaved at six o'clock in the morning, and say my early rules from the Latin Grammar, or repeat the Greek alphabet; and was obliged at these early lessons to hold my head inclined towards him, so that in the event of guilty fault, he might be able to pull my hair without stopping his razor or dropping his shaving-brush. No father was ever more anxious for the education of his children, though I think none ever knew less how to go about the work."[164] John Newman, on the other hand, refused to resort to any authoritarianism in the upbringing of his son, an approach that Newman would emulate when he took charge of the education of the young himself. Indeed, it also informed the rule he adopted for the Birmingham Oratory, which was based not on any authoritarianism but on mutual trust, shared sanctity and love. Newman is amusing about this in one of his Oratorian papers, where he remarks:

It was St. Philip's object . . . instead of imposing laws on his disciples, to mould them, as far as might be into living laws, or, in the words of Scripture, to write the law on their hearts. This is what the great philosopher of antiquity had considered the perfection of human nature; that is what is so frequently brought before us in Scripture, especially in St. Paul's Epistles. It is what the holy Patriarchs of the Regulars, St. Benedict, St. Dominic, St. Francis, St. Ignatius, and the rest, had felt to be beyond them (and which is, humanly speaking, impossible when any extended body is concerned). . . .But here we have touched upon a distinction which separates the Oratory from all monachism, early as well as late. . . .It is impossible to mistake the character of religious and regular discipline stamped on the exterior of the Jesuits by the influence of the long spiritual exercises and the almost military usages of their tradition. His look is imposing; his speech measured. Look at him as represented in a picture. You know by his staid and upright figure, his downcast or uplifted eyes, his abstracted countenance; and his high biretta. Contrast this with the picture of one of the first Oratorians and a contemporary of St. Philip in the Borghese collections at Rome, by Andrea Sacchi. He sits in an easy chair, in a lounging posture, one hand stretched on a table, with bright sparkling eyes and a merry countenance. Here you have a type of the exterior of an Oratorian compared with a regular.[165]

John Newman's paternal rule, like the rule of the Oratorians, was chary of rule. Certainly, he gave his brilliant son freedom to come to his own conclusions about philosophical issues with which he knew they differed, which is evident from the *Apologia*. "When I was fourteen," Newman recalled, "I read Paine's Tracts against the Old Testament and found pleasure in thinking of the objections which were contained in them. Also, I read some of Hume's Essays; and perhaps that on Miracles. So at least I gave my Father to understand; but perhaps it was a brag. Also, I recollect copying out some French verses, perhaps Voltaire's, in denial of the immortality of the soul, and saying

---

[164] Ibid., p. 14.
[165] *Newman the Oratorian: His Unpublished Oratory Papers* (London, 1980), p. 215. The picture to which Newman refers is Sacchi's portrait of Monsignor Clemente.

to myself something like 'How dreadful, but how plausible!'"[166] Here it seems likely that it was his father who suggested at least some of this reading. Otherwise, Newman would hardly have regarded telling his father that he had read the books a "brag." Clearly, Newman's father encouraged him to question different points of view. And this readiness to enter into different points of view is what gives so much of Newman's analysis of the psychology of faith its credibility. It is also why indifferentism, heresy, latitudinarianism, unbelief, all the intellectual barriers to union with Almighty God and His Church at once fascinated and appalled him.

Another writer—an Edwardian rather than a Victorian, but still very much influenced by Newman—sheds a different light on Newman's response to his father's failure. James Joyce (1882–1939) never recalled his own father John Stanislaus without filial generosity. "I was very fond of him always, being a sinner myself, and even liked his faults. Hundreds of pages and scores of characters in my books came from him . . . I got from him his portraits, a waistcoat, a good tenor voice, and an extravagant licentious disposition (out of which, however, the greater part of any talent I have springs) . . ."[167] What Joyce omitted to mention was that it was also his father who impelled him to leave Ireland and to make his home on the Continent. In *The Portrait of an Artist as a Young Man* (1914), Joyce fictionalized the cause of this exile to make it seem the stuff of artistic heroism. But in reality, Joyce fled Ireland to escape his father's all-consuming fondness for John Jameson Irish whisky, which sent his mother to an early grave and plunged the Joyce family into degrading poverty. If Joyce himself inclined to look forbearingly on his father, his brother Stanislaus refused to palliate the old man's sins.

> He had a jolly time of it with his hard-drinking friends of that hard-drinking generation. But however uncritical of himself he may have been, he must have suffered in his self-esteem. He had failed in all the careers that had seemed open so promisingly before him—as a doctor, as an actor, as a singer, as a commercial secretary, and lastly as a political secretary. He belonged to that class of men regarding whom it is impossible to postulate any social system of which they could be active members. They are saboteurs of life though they have the name of *viveurs*.[168]

Although Joyce preferred to present his father as a life-enhancing Falstaffian figure, a raconteur and wit, who personified Dublin's defiant bonhomie, he realized that remaining in Dublin would entrap him in his father's saloon-bar notoriety, which his pride would have found intolerable, even though this same steely pride stemmed in large part from the high regard in which his father held him. So he left *Errorland* and dedicated himself to recreating the family in art that his father had so spectacularly ruined in life. Thus, the artist in Joyce was not "like the God of creation . . . behind or beyond or above his handiwork, invisible, refined out of existence, indifferent, paring

---

[166] *Apo.*, p. 3 and LD, 1:18, Note 1.
[167] Richard Ellmann. *James Joyce* (New York, 1982), p. 643.
[168] Stanislaus Joyce. *My Brother's Keeper* (New York, 1958), pp. 29–30.

his fingernails" but a highly interested revisionist.[169] If Joyce's father had frittered away the Joyce legacy in Irish whiskey and "slackjawed blackguardism," to use Bernard Shaw's memorable phrase, Joyce would redeem it by turning even his father's failures into the wellsprings of art.[170]

Newman, in contrast, turned his father's failure into the wellsprings of faith. He transformed it, not, as Joyce did his father's failure, by romanticizing it, but by accepting it, by taking it to heart, by making it his own, out of empathy and love. He also came to appreciate, thanks to his father, that an understanding of failure, of the infirmity inseparable from our fallen human nature, was instrumental to understanding, accepting and responding to God's love. Later, St Paul would reinforce this crucial lesson but it was Newman's father who first imparted it, which gives his influence on his son an importance that is often overlooked.

The lesson of failure that Newman first learnt from his father would reappear again and again under different guises. After the ordeal of the Achilli trial, for example, Newman wrote to a correspondent of "the long course of self-denying and persevering exertions in my favour . . . which could only have been found in that Communion whose life is supernatural charity." And he saw the graces of this Communion against the backdrop of the restoration of the English hierarchy, which, as he said, "amid a thousand duties and cares, has inaugurated its history by an act simply directed to the vindication [of] the Catholic name . . ." Just as friends and well-wishers had come to his aid, so "the poor remnant of a nation once Catholic, priesthood and laity . . . vindicated their place in the great family of God" by coming to the aid of the restored English Catholic Church. Failure, in other words, brought the faithful closer to God. As Newman attested at the end his letter, "What is good, endures; what is evil, comes to nought."

> As time goes on, the memory will simply pass away from me of whatever has been done in the course of these proceedings, in hostility to me or in insult, whether on the part of those who invoked, or those who administered the law; but the intimate sense will never fade away, will possess me more and more, of that true and tender Providence which has always watched over me for good, and of the power of that religion which is not degenerate from its ancient glory, of zeal for God, and of compassion towards the oppressed.[171]

---

[169] See James Joyce. *Portrait of an Artist as a Young Man* (New York, 1968), p. 215.
[170] GBS to Sylvia Beach (11 June 1921) in Bernard Shaw. *Collected Letters* (New York, 1985), III, p. 719 "I have read several fragments of Ulysses in its serial form," Shaw told Sylvia Beach, when she tried to get him to fork over for the immensely expensive first edition of *Ulysses*. "it is a revolting record of a disgusting phase of civilization; but it is a truthful one . . . I have walked those streets and know those shops and have heard and taken part in those conversations. I escaped from them to England at the age of twenty; and forty years later have learnt from the books of James Joyce that Dublin is still what it was and young men are still driveling in slackjawed blackguardism just as they were in 1870 . . . I must add, as the prospectus implies an invitation to purchase, that I am an elderly Irish gentleman, and that if you imagine that any Irishman, much less an elderly one, would pay 150 francs for a book, you little know my countrymen."
[171] LD, 15:319–20 JHN to Robert Whitty (2 March 1853).

This is the long view of how Newman responded to his father's failure. But how did he react to the immediate shock of the thing? He left no record of that. *Secretum meum mihi.* Whenever his deepest personal feelings were engaged, Newman tended to keep his own counsel. Still, the account that Henry Edward Manning (1808–92) left behind of how he responded to his father's bankruptcy might give us some clue as to how Newman might have felt about his own father's bankruptcy. Certainly, in the case of both young men, it must have been a terrible blow. For years, until his own business failed, William Manning (1763–1835) was a lobbyist for the West Indian merchants in the House of Commons and a Governor of the Bank of England. In his prime he commuted to the City from his home in Totteridge in a resplendent coach and four. When disaster struck, it devastated him and left an indelible mark on his son. The two future cardinals were worlds apart in many respects but they both knew intimately the insecurity that wracked England's upper-middle classes at a time when commercial crashes and the fear of crashes had become general. Indeed, as Boyd Hilton notes, "Insecurity was endemic among the upper-middle classes as business crashes and the rumour of crashes spread throughout the community. (Even holdings in the funds did not bring reassurance, given the underlying fear of revolution and radical demands for debt repudiation). So-called gentlemanly capitalism turns out to have been a roller coaster, on which it was possible for individuals to rise to huge prosperity, only for the next wave of bankruptcies to plunge them into economic doom and social obloquy."[172]

Manning's account of how his father met his own ordeal in this inescapable instability is moving.

> After the peace of 1815, the great incomes of our merchants began to fall. The West Indian commerce suffered first and most. This shook his commercial house, and from 1820 to 1830 he had great cares . . . During those days he was in London most days in the week. When he came down to Combe Bank [an estate near Sevenoaks where had had moved in 1815 from Totteridge], he was worn and weary. He was fond of fishing, and would stand for hours by the water at Combe Bank. He used to tell me that his chief delight was the perfect quiet after the strain and restlessness of London. We used to ride often together, but his time was too much broken, and his mind too full to allow of conversation on any subjects beyond the commonest . . . Just after I had taken my degree in the winter of 1830-31 the ruin came. I was with my father in 3 New Bank Buildings . . . I heard him say to one of the correspondents of the house who came for business that "the house had suspended payments." After that all went into bankruptcy, and I went with my father to Guildhall, before a Commissioner in Bankruptcy, and saw him surrender his last possession in the world, his gold watch, chain, and seals, which he laid down on the table. It was returned to him as the custom is. After that I took him away, leaning on my arm. I remember some time before his saying to me with much feeling, "I have belonged to men with whom bankruptcy was synonymous with death." It was so to him.[173]

[172] Hilton, p. 156.
[173] E. S. Purcell. *Life of Cardinal Manning* (London, 1895), I, 8 and 71 quoted in Kynaston, pp. 82–3.

His father's catastrophe gave Manning's opposition to the world a marked combativeness. "Believe me," he wrote to his brother, "Mercury, the God of Merchants, was the God of Rogues—rogues and merchants are convertible terms, and have ever been so from the establishment of the Port of Tyre to that of the Port of London . . ."[174] Such views inspired him to champion the cause of the dock workers in 1889, securing them their "tanner" from the outmanoeuvred Dock Directors and causing Lord Buxton to remark: "For a month past I have seen the Thames as stagnant as the Dead Sea. To-morrow I hope to see it once more full of life and motion and worthy of the Port of London."[175] Manning's victory even won the praise of Edward White Benson, the Archbishop of Canterbury, who conceded how: "Manning in his final little speech says he should have been guilty of dereliction of duty if he had not tried to do what his position demanded. Whatever that may be, he has done it well and with deserved honour."[176] Newman also congratulated him (through an amanuensis), even though in the moral Manning drew from the episode he might have seen a forgivable demagoguery. As Manning told Lord Buxton: "A clergyman said last week: The Dockers' Strike succeeded because the police did not do their duty; the Gas Strike has failed because the police did their duty. The freedom of contract is maintained by the truncheon. There is no justice, mercy, or compassion in the Plutocracy. There is my creed."[177] Manning's readiness to fight for the workers notwithstanding, he never took an egalitarian line when it came to his prelatical dignity. "I remember once walking with my father along Kensington High Street," G. K. Chesterton once recalled, "and seeing a crowd of people gathered by a rather dark and narrow entry on the southern side of that thoroughfare."

> I had seen crowds before: and was quite prepared for their shouting or shoving. But I was not prepared for what happened next. In a flash a sort of ripple ran along the line and all these eccentrics went down on their knees on the public pavement. I had never seen people play any such antics except in church; and I stopped and stared. Then I realised that a sort of little dark cab or carriage had drawn up opposite the entry; and out of it came a ghost clad in flames. Nothing in the shilling paint-box had ever spread such a conflagration of scarlet, such lakes of lake; or seemed so splendidly likely to incarnadine the multitudinous sea. He came on with all his glowing draperies like a great crimson cloud of sunset, lifting long frail fingers over the crowd in blessing. And I looked at his face and was startled with a contrast; for his face was dead pale like ivory and very wrinkled and old, fitted together out of naked nerve and bone and sinew; with hollow eyes in shadow; but not ugly; having in every line the ruin of great beauty. The face was so extraordinary that for a moment I even forgot such perfectly scrumptious scarlet clothes. We passed on; and then my father said, "Do you know who that was? That was Cardinal Manning."[178]

---

[174] Henry Edward Manning quoted in Shane Leslie. *Henry Edward Manning: His Life and Labours* (London, 1921), p. 34.
[175] Leslie, p. 372.
[176] Ibid., p. 373.
[177] Ibid., p. 376.
[178] G. K. Chesterton. *Autobiography* (London, 1936), pp. 49–50.

"The Rule of God's Providence"

Two weeks after his father was declared bankrupt, Newman set his sights on the Oriel fellowship. "It may be called audacious for various reasons," he wrote in his third-person memoir, "and certainly would seem to others; but in truth he had never himself accepted his failure in the schools as the measure of his intellectual merits, and, in proportion as the relief of mind ceased to be felt, consequent at first upon his freedom from scholastic work and its anxieties, a reaction too place within him; and he began to think about retrieving his losses, and to aspire to some honourable and permanent place in his loved University . . ."[179] This was one version of what prompted his standing for the prized fellowship; but there was another, less flattering version, which showed the extent to which Newman continued to find ambition a spiritual liability.

> I passed this evening with the Dean, whose Oriel cousin was there. He said the principal thing at the examination for Fellows was writing Latin. I thought I ought to stand; and indeed, since, I have nearly decided on so doing. How active still are the evil passions of vain glory, ambition &c in my soul! After my failure last November, I thought that they would be unruly again, for I felt so resigned through God's grace that it seemed as if honours of the world had no longer any charm in themselves to tempt me with. Alas! no sooner is any mention made of my standing for a fellowship, than every mound and barrier seems swept away, and the tides of passion spread and overflow and deluge me in every direction, and without thy help, O Lord, what will be the end of this? ὥσπερ ξυν ἵπποις ἡνιστροφῷ δρόμου &c.[180]

If Newman found his fondness for success unwelcome proof of his ambition, he never lost his fascination with failure. Or put another way, the allure that success held for him always reminded him of what a difficult discipline he had imposed on himself. Accepting the mortifications of failure would never come easily to him. After his failure in the schools in December 1820, he wrote Walter Mayers, vividly describing how the experience affected him:

> For some time, even when appearances were most favorable, I had a sort of foreboding what would happen. About two months before my trial, the probability of success in my own judgment declined to a first in mathematics and a second in classics; when I went up, to two seconds – after the examination to one second; the Class List came out, and my name was below the line . . . My failure was most remarkable. I will grant I was unwell, low-spirited, and very imperfect in my books; yet, when in the Schools, so great a depression came on me, that I could do nothing. I was nervous in the extreme, a thing I never before experienced, and did not expect – my memory was gone, my mind altogether confused. The Examiners behaved with great kindness to me, but nothing would do. I dragged a sickly examination from Saturday to Friday, and after all was obliged to retire

[179] *AW*, p. 49.
[180] Ibid., p. 177.

from the contest. I will not attempt to describe the peace of mind I felt when all was over. Before there was darkness and dread – I saw the cataract, to which I was hurrying without the possibility of a rescue. It was as if a surgical operation was day after day being carried on upon me, and tearing away something precious; and all the while "omnes omnia bona dicebant, et laudabant fortunas meas." They looked at me, and envied me, and laughed at my fears, and could hardly believe them real. There is a great difference between believing a thing to be good, and feeling it; now I am thankful to say, I am not only enabled to believe failure to be best for me, but God has given me to see and know it. I never could before get my mind to say heartily "Give me neither poverty nor riches." I think I can now say it from my soul. I think I see clearly that honour and fame are not desirable. God is leading me through life in the way best adapted for His glory and my own salvation. I trust I may have always the same content and indifference to the world, which is at present the prevailing principle in my heart – yet I have great fears of backsliding.[181]

His father's bankruptcy, less than 2 years later, brought these insights into unforgettable focus. Writing to his beloved Aunt Elizabeth, a week after his father was declared bankrupt, he revealed the profound kinship he felt for his father without ever mentioning him—which was characteristic of how reticent he could be about matters that affected him most. Although in many respects a deeply autobiographical writer, he had nothing of the confessional glibness of Boswell or Rousseau. Newman always reveals most by seeming to reveal least. Unless one recognizes the fellow feeling that he expresses for his father in this letter, however obliquely, one will miss its import. Vincent Blehl grossly misread the letter by regarding it as "preachy" and "perhaps the most Evangelical letter he ever wrote." It may be full of the "language of enthusiasm," even of "stock phrases," as Blehl complains, but it is emblematic of something that was essential in Newman: his determination to give his faith practical, sacrificial expression.[182] Here, the bond between father and son could not have been more indissolubly sealed, even though it was founded on something that John Newman would probably have preferred to ignore.

A person, who is in a situation which the world would call calamitous, has at least this advantage over his more prosperous neighbour, that he may talk on religious topics without offence; the glory of religion is seen in affliction, and the hearer can hardly feel and cannot express dislike to that which he sees of such sovereign efficacy to calm, to solace, and to comfort. This privilege of what is called misfortune, I shall in many cases take advantage of; in my present letter, however, I need bring forward no such excuse for the introduction of that sublime subject which ought to be ever uppermost in our thoughts and the end of all our actions. Thank God, the severe dispensation, which has visited us, has as yet no terrors for me – God grant I may continue in the same state of mind – I really quite hail it and rejoice in it; for I think it very likely to be productive of great good to all of

---

[181] LD, 1:99 JHN to Walter Mayers (January 1821).
[182] Vincent Blehl, S. J. *Pilgrim Journey: John Henry Newman 1801–1845* (London, 2001), pp. 39–40.

us. Surely it is a mark, a striking mark, of the divine care and protection; for He seems to be withdrawing from us all those "things of the earth" on which we might be tempted to "set our affections", in order that we may look upwards, and "lay up treasure in Heaven", and sit loose to all earthly objects, and seek all our joys and pleasures from holiness and the love of God. I am convinced that nothing can be a greater snare and evil to a person than unalloyed prosperity. I cannot say how I should behave were the offer of possessing them made to me, but in my present state of mind there is nothing I would rather deprecate than wealth, or fame, or great influence. Every reflection suggests more strongly and more strongly the conclusion of the Apostle – "having food and raiment let us be therewith content" – a conclusion infinitely more cheering than a dry submission or a cold acquiescence in what is deemed unavoidable; for it is attended by a conviction that God gives us that which is best for us to have. To those who are conscious that they long to love God and to be perfectly holy, every dispensation of Providence, which the dull world is accustomed to regard as unfortunate, gives rise to the most fervent gratitude; and they exult in undergoing trials and passing through the flames of calamity, for they trust and expect to come forth purified and refined, with the dross of human corruption purged away. It is thus, through God's grace, that I feel with respect to our present circumstances; they may be painful, they may be grievous; but I exult and triumph, and my heart beats high at the thought that God is cutting away all ties which might bind me to the world and preparing me for that Kingdom of which perfect holiness is the characteristic glory. – When I add to this reflection, the delightful thought that those I love most may be undergoing the same blessed discipline and preparation as myself, how can I but rejoice with joy unspeakable at the event that has taken place? This may be called enthusiasm, but it is an enthusiasm which I wish never to lose; it is a feeling which I am persuaded is alone powerful to support under suffering, and which I pray God all who smile at, may soon themselves experience. I have been scribbling on, hardly connectedly; but since I think you will like to hear from me and I have no particular news to communicate from Oxford, I have not been very sollicitous with regard to novelty of matter.[183]

Newman at 21 might have been concerned that what he had to say here lacked "novelty" but it is remarkable that at 81 he would still be giving thanks for the "privilege of misfortune." When his friend Lord Braye, an old Etonian and Christ Church man, who had converted in 1868 and went on to become Lieutenant Colonel of the Leicestershire Regiment during the South African War, complained of not accomplishing enough, Newman wrote him back: "Your case is mine. It is for years beyond numbering – in one view of the matter for these 50 years – that I have been crying out 'I have laboured in vain, I have spent my strength without cause and in vain: wherefore my judgment is with the Lord, and my work with my God.' Now at the end of my days, when the next world is close upon me, I am recognized at last at Rome. Don't suppose I am dreaming of complaint – just the contrary. The Prophet's words, which expressed my keen pain,

---

[183] JHN to Elizabeth Newman (7 November 1821) LD, pp. 115–16.

brought, because they were his words, my consolation. It is the rule of God's Providence that we should succeed by failure; and my moral is, as addressed to you, Doubt not that He will use you – be brave – have faith in His love for you – His everlasting love – and love Him from the certainty that He loves you."[184] Lord Braye followed this up by asking Newman to write him a letter of introduction; he was keen on serving the Church in some direct personal way. Newman obliged by referring him to Archbishop Siciliano Di Rende in Rome, though he was careful to warn his friend, "I am not at all sure that my name will be of service to you in some quarters."[185]

The Death of John Newman

On 27 September 1824, Newman recorded in his diary that his father was gravely ill but conscious enough to recognize him and his sister Harriett. Then he "said his last and most precious words to my Mother." The next day Frank, Jemima and Mary arrived for the family death watch. That night, Newman and his brother Charles sat up until 4 a.m. with their father, after which Charles, Frank and Newman slept in the parlour in their clothes. On 29 September at 10 o'clock in the evening, John Newman drew his last breath. When he returned to Oxford, Newman wrote his Mother a brief letter.

> Our treasure is in heaven.' We must rejoice in the future. Here we must 'rejoice with trembling.' Here we may be separated by ten thousand accidents, and death at least must eventually tear us from each other. The days will come, when one after another we shall drop away like leaves from the tree. But, being, as we trust, in Christ, we shall meet one and all in heaven to part no more.

Nearly 40 years later, in 1860, Newman wrote Mary Holmes a letter that brought his earlier musings full circle, though the same undertone of unfathomable mystery remained. "You were right in thinking that your family reminiscences would interest me," he told the itinerant governess. "I think nothing more interesting, and it is strange to think how evanescent, how apparently barren and result-less, are the ten thousand little details and complications of daily life and family history. Is there any record of them preserved any where, any more than of the fall of the leaves in Autumn? or are they themselves some reflexion, as in an earthly mirror, of some greater truths above? So I think of musical sounds and their combinations – they are momentary – but is it not some momentary opening and closing of the Veil which hangs between the worlds of spirit and sense?"[186]

When John Newman died, his son jotted down his father's last utterances in a diary entry full of the abbreviated eloquence of loss.

> I got to Town Sunday morning. He knew me, tried to put out his hand and said, "God bless you." Towards the evening of Monday he said his last words. He seemed in great peace of mind. He could, however, only articulate, "God bless you, thank

---

[184] LD, 30:141–2 JHN to Lord Braye (29 October 1882).
[185] LD, 28:181–2 JHN to Lord Braye (9 February 1883).
[186] LD, 19:415 JHN to Mary Holmes (4 November 1860).

my God, thank my God—and lastly 'my dear.'" Dr. C. came on Wednesday, and pronounced him dying; he might live 12 hours. Towards evening we joined in prayer, commending his soul to God. Of late, he had thought his end approaching. One day on the river, he told my Mother, "I shall never see another summer." On Thursday, he looked beautiful, such calmness, sweetness, composure, and majesty were in his countenance. Can a man be a materialist who sees a dead body? I had never seen one before. His last words to me, or all but his last, were to bid me read to him the 53rd chapter of Isaiah. "Who hath believed, etc."[187]

The profound words from Isaiah would always have a special place in Newman's heart. "He is despised and rejected of men; a man of sorrows, and acquainted with grief; and we hid as it were our faces from him; he was despised, and we esteemed him not. Surely he hath borne our griefs, and carried our sorrows: yet we did esteem him stricken, smitten of God, and afflicted. But he was wounded for our transgressions, he was bruised for our iniquities; the chastisement of our peace was upon him; and with his stripes we are healed." And certainly these words would have appealed deeply to the dying man whose own sorrows had reunited him with Christ.

In 1825, a year after his father's death, Newman made an entry in his private journal. "The death of my dear Father had from time to time come across my mind in a most cutting way; and I have sometimes thought with much bitterness that I might have softened his afflictions much by kind attentions which I neglected. I was cold, stiff, reserved. I know I hurt him much . . . When . . . he noticed to me his pain . . . I hardly said a word. Why could I not have said how much I owed to him, his kindness in sending me to Oxford &c &c. It is over, irrevocable. O for a moment to ask for his forgiveness . . ."[188] Newman's own ellipses here bespeak a terrible distress. Yet it is difficult to gauge how warrantable his guilt was. The guilt sons feel when fathers die is often extravagant. Was Newman culpably cold to his dying father or was he merely being overly compunctious? The record does not say. "*Secretum meum mihi.*"

In 1874, after sorting out his early papers, Newman wrote a memorandum marked "Most Private," in which he revisited the events leading up to the dénouement of his father's bankruptcy: "Some of my letters between 1817 and 1819 will be found dated from or directed to Alton in Hampshire. I wish no reference to be made, in any Memoir of me, to my or my family's residence there, which took place at that time; but here for the sake of those into whose hands my papers come on my death, and because there are those still alive who know it, I will set down how it arose. My Father's partners in the Banking House were great brewers at Windsor, and had successively, uncle and nephew, represented that place in Parliament. When then the Banking House wound up its accounts in 1816, these gentlemen were the means or occasion of my Father's undertaking an old and well established brewery in Alton from the hands of a friend of theirs. Did I imply that there was any thing in their conduct to complain of, I should be slandering them without the shadow of excuse for doing so; but any how the undertaking turned out most unfortunate for him. He found himself on an entirely

---

[187] *AW*, pp. 202–3.
[188] *AW*, p. 208. See also "The Mind of Newman on Christian Death," in *John Henry Newman: Sermons 1824–1843*. ed. Francis J. McGrath and Placid Murray (Oxford, 2010), pp. 414–23.

new field of work in advanced years and with the first symptoms of that complaint upon him of which he eventually died. Before three years were over, a flaw was found in the title to the freehold, and this was only one of a series of troubles. He returned to London, and after a few years his anxieties brought him to his end. For his sake who loved and wearied himself for us all with such unrequited affection, I wish all this forgotten."[189]

In tackling the day-to-day crises that arose at the Oratory School, Newman came to appreciate the strains that his father must have suffered when he was working to make a success of the bank: "I have heard my dear Mother say that Bankers had all the responsibility of all pursuits and trades upon them, for, whenever any one was in pecuniary difficulty, he went to his Banker. And so a schoolmaster has the anxieties of all the parents of his boys – and more so – for parents would not blame themselves, if their children fell ill at home – but they are naturally disposed to think that school-carefulness which they do not see to judge of, might be greater than it is."[190] If the cares of running a school bound Newman to his father, so too did the demands of the priesthood, which he always insisted on seeing in the most practical terms possible. When he was ordained on 13 June 1824, he wrote in his journal, "It is over. I am thine, O Lord; I seem quite dizzy, and cannot altogether believe and understand it. At first, after the hands were laid on me, my heart shuddered within me; the words, 'for ever' are so terrible . . . I feel as a man thrown suddenly into deep water." The next day, he could still not quite take it in. "'For ever', words ever to be recalled. I have the responsibility of souls on me to the day of my death . . ."[191]

Newman made another important reference to his father in a letter he wrote to his mother in September 1834, two years before her death, after he had completed his first *Tract of the Times*: "There are many little incidents, stored in my memory, which now waken into life. Especially I remember that first evening of my return to Oxford in 1818, after gaining the scholarship at Trinity, and my Father saying, 'What a happy meeting is this!' Often and often such sayings of his come to my mind and almost overpower me; for I consider he did so very much for me at a painful sacrifice to himself—and was so generous and kind; so that whatever I am enabled to do for you and my sisters I feel to be merely and entirely a debt on my part, a debt which he calls me to fulfill."[192] In this same letter, written from Alton, whither he had returned for one last look at a place so fraught with lacerating family history, Newman wrote: "As I got near the place, I many times wished I had not come, I found it so very trying. So many strong feelings, distinct from each other, were awakened. The very length of time since I was here was a serious thought, almost half my life; and I so different from what a boy, as I then was, could be;—not indeed in my having any strong stimulus of worldly hope then, which I have not now—for, strange though it may seem, never even as a boy had I any vision of success, fortune, or worldly comfort to bound my prospects of the future . . ."[193] Looked at in this light, his father's failure confirmed Newman's deepest, earliest premonitions.

---

[189] Memorandum by JHN (12 September 1874) LD, 1:27–8.
[190] LD, 21:4 JHN to Mrs John Mozley (2 January 1864).
[191] *AW*, pp. 200–1.
[192] LD, 4:331 JHN to Mrs Jemima Newman (20 September 1834).
[193] Ibid., pp. 331–2.

Yet more than that, it confirmed his faith in God and it confirmed what would be his one true calling. "There was something so mysterious . . . in seeing old sights, half recollecting them . . . It is like seeing the ghosts of friends. Perhaps it is the impression it makes on one of God's *upholding* power, which is so awful – but it seemed to me so very strange, that every thing was in its place after so long a time. As we came near, and I saw Monk's Wood, the Church, and the hollow on the other side of the town, it was as fearful as if I was standing on the grave of some one I knew, and saw him gradually recover life and rise again. Quite a lifetime seems to divide me from the time I was here. I wished myself away from the pain of it."[194]

The ghost of Newman's former self would be laid to rest. The ghost of John Newman would haunt him for the rest of his life, constantly reminding him that his "treasure was in heaven."

---

[194] Ibid., p. 332.

2

Mrs Newman and *Amor Matris*

"For myself," Newman's mother wrote in response to her son's letter about revisiting the family home at Alton, where her husband went bankrupt, after trying unsuccessfully to make a go of a brewery, "it was a period of such anxiety and fearful augury of greater trials progressively advancing, that I scarcely think I should wish to revisit the place.

> For, although at all times and places I have had much to enjoy and be grateful for, yet I think there the sorrowful would press foremost . . . . Your recollection of your dear Father's 'greeting' cheers me greatly. I have always a nervous dread lest you all can recall him only in pain and sorrow. I have ever felt it a source of deep thankfulness, that we were enabled to put you in the way of those advantages, that your gifts and merit claimed . . . and I often reflect with heartfelt delight and gratitude on the prospect of your labours being valuable to future generations. But you must not spend yourself too much . . . . In these times, with your talents and energy, you cannot say what you may be called to, and no one can be very efficient without spirits and health.[1]

At each point of the family ordeal, Mrs Newman understood that her son's "gifts and merit" were being refined in "pain and sorrow." She recognized that his "labours" would indeed be "valuable to future generations." She knew that her personal prize would also benefit others. In hindsight, this might seem inevitable enough: surely a loving mother would have seen that so talented a son would do great things and have great influence; but such insight was not inevitable. Most of Newman's contemporaries—including his brothers and sisters—were not convinced that his influence would be good. Before the publication of the *Apologia* (1864) made admiring Newman acceptable, many of Newman's contemporaries treated him as a brilliant failure. Of course, Mrs Newman died in 1836 before Newman converted and walked away from becoming what many thought he was destined to become, "one of the great future pillars of the Anglican Church."[2] But if she had lived to see her son vindicated in his controversy with Charles Kingsley, she would have seen others recognizing talents that she had acknowledged decades before, perhaps more clearly than anyone, though it is rather less likely that she would ever have come round to appreciating his Roman Catholic faith.

[1]   LD, 4:332 Mrs Jemima Newman to JHN (26 September 1834).
[2]   See "Men of the Day", No. 145, *Vanity Fair*, 20 January 1877.

For his part, Newman took from his mother's love an immense respect and sympathy for mothers in general. His correspondence shows how readily he could enter into their trials. For example, in a letter to his friend Lady Henry Kerr, who followed her husband Lord Henry Kerr (1800–82) into the faith with her six children after the Gorham Case, he gives a good example of his appreciation for the concomitant anxieties of a mother's love.[3] Writing at the height of the Indian Mutiny, which put so many of the English in India in peril, after sepoys in the Indian army objected to the grease coating cartridges for their new Enfield rifles, an amalgam of beef and pork offensive alike to Mussulmen and Hindus, Newman wrote: "My dear Lady Henry, I was very glad to hear from you and about you. Several times had I asked others what had become of William, whom last year Lord Henry and you saw on his journey towards India. It is indeed a most fearful awful time for those who have friends in those parts. When the Crimean war began I wondered how friends could endure the mocking tantalizing telegraphs, telling just enough to frighten and unsettle, and then leaving the truth for the slow despatch by mail. But this is a hundred times worse, and in so many different respects that I am quite puzzled to think, how it is that many gentle delicate fragile persons at home, mothers for instance advanced in years, are able to live. I think suspense and the anxiety connected with it one of the greatest of mental troubles. The Greek hero in the Poem was willing to die, so that he died in [a] day."[4] Newman gave voice to the same solicitude for mothers during the Franco-Prussian war. "What an awful thing this war is – the more so because it is so near us," he wrote. "One of our party here, who is in Switzerland, said it nearly made him cry at the railway stations to see the partings of mothers and boys."[5]

In another letter to his good friend Lady Simeon, whose son was set on attending Oxford at a time when Catholics were unsure whether what was called "mixed education" was a good thing, Newman likened priests to mothers when it came to guiding the young:

> *We* must take care of the young one by one, as a mother does, and as an Archbishop does not. *We* know our own, one by one (if we are priests with the pastoral charge as our ecclesiastical rulers cannot know them.) It were well indeed if some high prelates recollected more than they seem to do the words of the Apostle "Fathers provoke not your children to anger lest they become pusillanimous," depressed, disgusted, disappointed, unsettled, reckless. Youth is the time of generous and enthusiastic impulses, young men are imprudent, and get into scrapes. Perhaps

---

[3] In 1847, Bishop Phillpots of Exeter refused to install Charles Gorham to the living of Exeter after he rejected the doctrine of baptismal regeneration. When Gorham appealed the ruling, the Privy Council overruled the bishop, and Gorham was installed to the living after all, which outraged orthodox Anglicans and led to Gladstone's two closest friends, Henry Edward Manning and James Hope, seceding to Rome. Gladstone recognized that the Judgment went "to the very root of all life and all teaching in the Church of England" by not only undermining the doctrine of baptismal regeneration but also allowing the English State to overrule the Church on doctrinal matters. See *Correspondence of William Ewart Gladstone On Church and State* (London, 1910), II, p. 92.

[4] LD, 18:197 JHN to Lady Henry Kerr (8 December 1857) The Greek hero to whom Newman refers is Ajax in the *Iliad*, XV, pp. 511–13. Lady Kerr's eldest son, William Hobart Kerr (1836–1913) was in the Madras Service during the Indian Mutiny. After leaving Harrow, he attended Stonyhurst and Haileybury. He became a Catholic in 1852 and a Jesuit in 1867.

[5] LD, 25:189 JHN to Mrs John Mozley (19 August 1870).

they fall in love imprudently. To carry out an engagement on which they have set their hearts may seem to the parents a madness; most truly, yet it may be a greater madness to prohibit it. All of us must recollect instances when to suffer what is bad in itself is the lesser of great evils, as the event has shown. When there has been a successful prohibition it has resulted in a life-long ruin of the person, so dear to us, for whose welfare we have been mistakenly zealous. It does not do to beat the life out of a youth—the life of aspiration excitement and enthusiasm. Older men live by reason habit and self-control, but the young live by visions. I can fancy cases in which Oxford would be the salvation of a youth; when he would be far more likely to rise up against authority, murmur against his superiors, and (more) to become an unbeliever, if he is kept from Oxford than if he is sent there.[6]

Then, again, his letters also put mothers into a more far-reaching perspective. To one correspondent, in 1861, he wrote of the headlong loss of faith that Oxford experienced when he departed for Rome, when the Tractarians were left to contend with the liberals who, in publishing the incendiary *Essays and Reviews*, called into question every aspect of Christian orthodoxy. "I assure you," Newman wrote, "I look with the most anxious interest at the state of Oxford – the more so because I anticipated its present perplexities. And it was one of my severest trials in leaving it, that I was undoing my own work, and leaving the field open, or rather infallibly surrendering it to those who would break down and crumble to powder all religion whatever. As to the authors of 'Essays and Reviews,' some of them at least, I am sure, know not what they do." While Newman appreciated that "it is not right to keep up shams," he also saw that the writers involved with this irreverent project did not take into account "the termination, or rather the abyss, to which these speculations lead." In any case, "they ought to make sure that they have a firm hold of true and eternal principles. To unsettle the minds of a generation, when you give them no landmarks and no causeway across the morass is to undertake a great responsibility."[7] This was an abiding concern of Newman's, though in the case of his own highly unsettling conversion, he was careful to follow it up with lectures showing his erstwhile Anglo-Catholic brethren how their needs could only be met by the Church of Rome, needs which the Erastian National Church could only frustrate.[8] At the same time, the only alternatives that the writers of the *Essays and Reviews* offered to an exploded Christianity were the sterile assumptions of rationalism. And here, Newman stepped back from the immediate matter at hand to consider religious unsettlement from a much more searching standpoint. "The religion of England depends, humanly speaking, on belief in 'the Bible and the whole Bible,' etc., and on the observance of the Calvinistic Sabbath. Let the population begin to doubt in its inspiration and infallibility, where are they? Alas, whole classes do already; but I would not be the man knowingly to introduce scepticism into those portions of the community which are as yet sound. Consider the miseries of wives and mothers losing their faith in Scripture, yet I am told this sad process is commencing. . . . My own

[6] LD, 23:366 JHN to Lady Simeon (10 November 1867).
[7] LD, 19:487-8 JHN to Malcolm Maccoli (24 March 1861).
[8] See Newman's *Lectures on Certain Difficulties Felt by Anglicans in Submitting to the Catholic Church* (1850).

belief is, that, if there be a God, Catholicism is true; but this is the elementary, august, and sovereign truth, the denial of which is in progress. May He Himself give grace to those who shall be alive in that terrible day, to fight His battle well. All the forms of Protestantism, allow me to say, are but toys of children in the great battle between the Holy Catholic Roman Church and Antichrist."[9] That Newman should have put mothers at the very heart of this unsparing account of what he would call "the great *apostasia*" is emblematic of the vital role he accorded them in the increasingly urgent propagation of the faith.

In his uncollected sermons, there is a marvellous passage from a sermon that he delivered at St Clements in 1825, the year he was ordained a minister in the Anglican Church, in which he speaks of how indispensable a mother's instruction is to the development of a child's faith. A father's example, of course, is always vital but it is not as decisive as the nurturing of a mother, for "she is with her children from infancy, and is intrusted with all their wants, and their comforter in every little sorrow." For Newman, it followed from this that "the growth of religion in a nation depends more upon the piety of mothers than any other class of persons."

> It has been observed that some of the most distinguished religious characters have traced their spiritual mindedness to having had the blessing of good mothers. It is the mother who in the dawn of life may incline the mind to follow the leadings of conscience—to avoid all that a child feels shame in doing, and to follow that which the internal sense approves. It is for the mother to detect the first risings of sin in a child, and to punish them at once and firmly—knowing that it is only by correcting at first that bad habits are prevented. It for the mother to instill principles of obedience, honesty, openness, sincerity, truth, kindness, meekness, self-command, disinterestedness—How much has she to do, what need of fervent prayers for divine grace to direct her! Above all, she has to raise young thoughts to the consideration of God. As the mind opens, she must instruct in the duty of prayer—and teach how to pray—she must press upon her child its weakness and natural incapacity for goodness—enlarge upon the heinousness of all disobedience—describe the need *little* children have of divine grace to make them think and act aright—and on the necessity of possessing a new and good heart—and thus draw it on to the consideration of the mercy and power of Christ, who bid the infants be brought to Him . . .[10]

In specifying what he meant by the special role that mothers play in preparing their children for the reception of the faith, Newman revealed something of the nurturing that he had received himself from his own mother. As Meriol Trevor observes in her biography of Newman, Mrs Newman "was a sensible woman, not a managing dominant type. She and her husband were intelligent and cultivated, but in no sense intellectuals; nor were they ambitious for themselves or for their children—they were content with their position in the world. This created the best possible background for their clever, imaginative and lively children; there was no forcing, moral or intellectual, no strain of

---

[9]   LD, 19:488 JHN to Malcolm Maccoll (24 March 1861).
[10] Sermon 4, No. 122 in *John Henry Newman Sermons: 1824–1843*. ed. Francis J. McGrath (Oxford, 2011), III, pp. 38–9.

living up to high adult standards [which wreaked such havoc on poor Edward Pusey]. The memories of childhood were happy for all of them."[11]

Jemima was descended from an ancient family in the Northern provinces of France, whence religious persecution drove them into Holland. Her great grandfather, Paul Fourdrinier (1685–1758), a distinguished engraver and printseller, was born in Groningen in the Netherlands, the son of Jacques Fourdrinier and his wife, Jeanne Theroude, who were Huguenot refugees from Dieppe and Normandy. Paul studied engraving in Amsterdam under Bernard Picart, then regarded as one of the best engravers in Europe. He removed to London in 1719 and married Susanne Grolleau (1694–1746) at the French Church St Martin Orgar in the City of London in Martin Lane, off Cannon Street, most famous as being one of the churches invoked in the nursery rhyme, "Oranges and Lemons."

> You owe me five farthings
> Say the bells of St. Martin's.

Although most of the building was destroyed in the Great Fire of London in 1666, the tower and a portion of the nave were left standing. Paul and Susanne had five children, Paul (b. 1724), Judith (b. 1727), Marie (b. 1728), Henry (b. 1730), and Charles. Paul had established premises at Craggs Court, Charing Cross by 1727. His trade card was designed by William Kent in 1731 and advertised "Prints, Mapps, and Stationary Wares." Paul engraved Kent's designs for the illustrations to Homer's *Odyssey*, John Gay's *Fables* (1727), James Thomson's *Seasons* (1734), and Alexander Pope's *Essays on Man* (1734). In 1736, Paul engraved the architectural plans of Houghton, Norfolk, the seat of Sir Robert Walpole. In addition, Paul engraved plans for other leading architects of the day, including Lord Burlington, Colen Campbell, James Gibbs, Isaac Ware, and John Wood. From 1738 to 1741, Paul also produced prints documenting the building of Westminster Bridge. Designed by Charles Labelye, the bridge was then the longest stone bridge erected over a tidal river. His son, Henry Fourdrinier Senior (1730–99) was a wealthy paper maker and stationer with premises in Lombard Street. In May 1765, he married Jemima Manning (1730–71) of Bishopsgate, with whom he had three sons, Henry, Sealey, and Charles, as well as a daughter, Jemima, all of whom (save Charles) appear in the family painting in the possession of the National Gallery. There, in a painting that has an almost Watteauesque refinement and grace about it, this elegant Huguenot family stand in their garden in Putney, behind which Windsor Castle can be seen in the distance. It is some testament to the material solidity of the Fourdrinier family that the painter they should have chosen to present this family portrait was John Downman (1750–1824), a portrait painter, based in Cambridge, whose subjects included Benjamin West, Thomas Cole, who would later found the South Kensington Museum, Elizabeth (née Farren), Countess of Derby, Sarah Siddons, Isaac D'Israeli, and Georgiana, Duchess of Devonshire, who became Downman's patron.

Mrs Newman's brother, Henry Fourdrinier Junior (1766–1847), was born in Lombard Street on 11 February, and succeeded his father as a paper-maker and wholesale stationer. Together with his brother Sealy, Henry invented a paper-making

---

[11] Meriol Trevor. *Newman: The Pillar of the Cloud* (London, 1962), p. 7.

machine, the chief feature of which was its ability to produce continuous paper of any size at a rapid rate. Perfected at the brothers' paper mill at Two Waters, in Hertfordshire, situated at the union of the river Gade with Bulborne Brook, the machine revolutionized paper production not only in England but throughout Europe and beyond. However, between 1800 and 1807, the brothers expended £60,000 perfecting the machine and defending its patent, and as a result, in 1810, they became bankrupt—a calamity that must have made John Newman's bankruptcy in November of 1821 all the more distressing for Newman's mother. To make matters worse, in 1814, after Tsar Nicholas visited England, he commissioned the use of two of the Fourdriniers' machines for the Imperial paper works at Peterhoff for 10 years at £700 pounds a year, and while those charged with operating the machines were paid by the Imperial Treasury, the Fourdriniers never received their commission.

In 1839, Henry and his brother submitted a claim for patent infringement, after Parliament had failed to uphold their patent. In the debate that ensued, interesting evidence emerged. Marc Isambard Brunel, for example, called the Fourdriniers' machine "one of the most splendid inventions of the age."[12] According to other testimony, the machine had increased the national revenue to £500,000 a year and saved the country a total of £8,000,000. Considering the fact that John Henry Newman backed Sir Robert Inglis's successful challenge to Sir Robert Peel for the Oxford parliamentary seat in 1829 after Peel reneged on his opposition to Catholic Emancipation, it is worth remarking that Inglis recommended the compensation for Henry Fourdrinier that Peel counselled the House to reject, though Henry was eventually awarded £7,000 in May of 1840, for what the *Gentleman's Magazine* characterized as "some compensation for their loss by the defective state of the law of patents."[13] In their glowing obituary for the great inventor, the magazine noted how:

> In November last [1854] some influential members of the paper trade commenced a subscription to purchase annuities for Mr. Henry Fourdrinier and his two surviving daughters, both unmarried. Ere much progress was made Mr. Fourdrinier died, in his 89th year, at Mavesyn Rydware, in Staffordshire, where he had retired, in possession of his cheerful and benevolent spirit, and as contented in his humble cottage as he was formerly in his spacious house. His personal appearance is thus described by his daughter Harriet E. Fourdrinier, in a little work called "Our New Parish; its Privileges and Progress, 1851," dedicated to her beloved father as a tribute of veneration on the completion of his 86th year:—"His form is spare; his hair is white; he has passed that age of 'four score years' which the Psalmist so touchingly describes; but, at present, we rejoice to say, *his* strength is not 'labour and sorrow.' His walk is active; his eyes are bright; his health is good; his spirits buoyant, and his gait firm. He is the delight of his children and his 'children's children' the latter of whom, to the number of some twenty-four, make him their friend and companion. He will talk with the elder, or romp with the young ones; drive his daughters out in the carriage, or take long walks with the sons; run races with the boys, and dance

---

[12] Marjorie Plant. *The English Book Trade* (London, 1974), p. 329.
[13] See Hansard, 25 April 1839, vol. 47 cc512–22 and *Gentleman's Magazine*, Vol. LXIV (July 1855), pp. 102–3.

with the girls; shews hospitality to his friends; does duty as a master; is a loyal and devoted subject, and makes a capital churchwarden! Many worldly troubles still oppress him, but he bears the yoke as knowing by Whom it is laid on."[14]

In this Fourdrinier family history, we can see something of the same brilliance and drive that characterized the Newman family history, though in the Fourdrinier history there is an element of bold inventiveness that only Jemima's son would rival when he set about articulating his highly innovative educational, philosophical, and theological insights. What is striking about the combined family history is the extent to which it shows how Newman's genius grew out of the genius of his forbears, a phenomenon that must have struck both his parents after they named their firstborn after their respective fathers, though Newman's mother must also have found the pioneering independence in her son an uncanny echo of the same quality in her brother.

If Mrs Newman was especially fond of her firstborn, partly no doubt because he reminded her of her brother, Newman returned the compliment. Harriett in her fictionalized account of the early life of her brothers and sisters, *Family Adventures*, recalls how Newman, from his earliest boyhood, was deeply attached to his mother. In the novel, Harriett named her brothers by their middle names: so John was Henry, Charles was Robert, and Frank was William. And here one can see what a discerning family historian Harriett was.

> The first story I shall tell you concerns, principally, the eldest son. His name was Henry, and he went to school with his brother Robert; but it is not of school that I am about to tell. This little boy, Henry, was very observant and considerate. During one Christmas vacation when he came home, he saw his mamma netting a very fine veil; he thought it was exceedingly beautiful, and often watched his mamma's swift and dexterous mode of work, wondering how she could go on weaving her delicate web, and at the same time be talking and looking about her, as if she were sitting doing nothing. But there was one thing that disturbed Henry, and Charles that was, that his mamma's box was not good enough for her work. He could not rest after this thought had come into his head; for on one thing he was determined—he would buy his mamma a netting-box . . .[15]

Harriett then describes how her fictionalized brother contrives to make himself master of the sum necessary to buy the netting-box. He saves up all that he can from school and then takes out a loan from his beloved Aunt Elizabeth, after which the proud day arrives when he is actually in the shop and there Harriett describes a rather fastidious customer. "When they got to the shop," Harriett relates, "there was not one box that immediately struck his fancy, as he had expected. After opening and shutting, and locking and unlocking, half a hundred boxes, and debating betwixt red, yellow, and blue linings, and making choice after choice, and still again discarding the last for another and another, Henry, with a sigh, fixed upon one he thought not at all worthy his mamma and her netting. Poor Henry sat very disconsolate on a low stool, with the box in his lap, the image of disappointment and resignation . . ." and this despite the

---

[14] *Gentleman's Magazine* (July, 1855), pp. 102–3.
[15] Harriett Mozley. *Family Adventures* (London, 1852), pp. 13–14.

fact that "Henry had the whole range of a very pretty shop to amuse himself . . ." Still, "his heart was so full of netting-boxes, and in his search just before, he had come to understand their plan and fittings-up so thoroughly, that he passed by every thing that was not in the form of a box; peeping into every thing that was, to compare with the arrangement of his present *beau-ideal*."

> At length some boxes were brought in: Henry seized on the very first. "Oh, aunt!" cried he, "this is exactly right—not those shabby painted and patched things, with common gold balls," added he, disdainfully looking at those he had first seen, and putting aside the one he had so nearly fixed upon; "this is just what I had in my eye—exactly the thing!—No, thank you," continued he to the man, who wanted to show him others, "I don't want to see any more; this is, I say, exactly the thing; please put it in a bit of paper."[16]

Here, we can see that Harriett understood at once the discrimination and the decisiveness that characterized her eldest brother—attributes, to his sister's chagrin, that he would also bring to the forming of his religious opinions.

If Newman was keen on pleasing his mother, he also inherited from her his profound simplicity, which is an aspect of his character that is often overlooked. What does one mean by *simplicity*? What the OED means: *Free from duplicity or guile, honest, open, ingenuous; free from pride or ostentation, unpretentious; plain, unadorned; humble; pure; composed of a single substance.* Newman's contemporaries might have felt that no one as rarefied or as subtle as Newman could be simple. Lord Acton, whose dubious reputation for learning is only matched by his dubious judgement, was convinced that Newman was a "splendid Sophist."[17] Nevertheless, at heart, he *was* simple and he got this trait from his mother. Her radiant good sense, her concern for the well-being of her children, the attention she paid to keeping her family strong and united, despite their differences, all of these things were of a piece and composed of a single substance: love of God; and one can see all of these qualities in Newman's relations with his family, with his contemporaries at Oxford when he was an undergraduate and when he was a don, with friends and foes of the Oxford Movement, with the Oratory after he converted, and with the enormous network of friends and acquaintances with whom he corresponded throughout his long life. Indeed, one correspondent wrote one of his sister's apropos a letter of condolence that Newman had written: "It is a relief to see your brother so absolutely himself in his power of writing. This is quite an example of his nature and his gift of what is called *simplicity*—that power of saying exactly what he means, and going straight at his subject, putting a state of things directly before one, feelings as well as facts. I hope it all shows that he has the natural relief that the expression of natural feeling always brings."[18] Edward Pusey also saw this characteristic quality in his dear friend, remarking to a correspondent of his in the wake of the row over Tract 90: "You will be glad to hear that the immediate excitement about Tract 90 seems subsiding, although I fear (in the minds of many) into

---

[16] *Family Adventures*, pp. 18–20.
[17] Gertrude Himmelfarb. *Lord Acton: A Study in Conscience and Politics* (London, 1952), p. 157.
[18] *Moz.*, i, p. 8.

a lasting impression of our Jesuitism etc. On the other hand, they who have read what Newman has written since on the subject, must be won by his touching simplicity and humility . . . The pseudo-traditionary and vague ultra-Protestant interpretation of the Articles has received a blow from which it will not recover. People will abuse Tract 90, and adopt its main principles. It has been a harassing time for Newman, but all great good is purchased by suffering; and he is wonderfully calm . . . ."[19] William Lockhart also saw this trait in his dear friend, speaking of him as someone who was "intent on some thought, and earnest in pursuing some purpose, but who never gave a thought as to what impression he was making, or what people thought about him. When one came to know and study him, it was plain that his mind was so *objective* that his own subjectivity was well-nigh forgotten. Hence his simplicity, meekness, and humility; God, not self, was the centre of all his thoughts."[20] Dean Church noted the same quality. "Any one who has watched at all carefully the Cardinal's career, whether in old days or later, must have been struck with this feature of his character, his naturalness, the freshness and freedom with which he addressed a friend or expressed an opinion, the absence of all mannerism and formality; and where he had to keep his dignity, both his loyal obedience to the authority which enjoined it and the half-amused, half-bored impatience that he should be the person round whom all these grand doings centred. It made the greatest difference in his friendships whether his friends met him on equal terms, or whether they brought with them too great conventional deference or solemnity of manner. He was by no means disposed to allow liberties to be taken or to put up with impertinence; for all that bordered on the unreal, for all that was pompous, conceited, affected he had little patience; but almost beyond all these was his disgust at being made the object of foolish admiration. He protested with whimsical fierceness against being made a hero or a sage; he was what he was, he said, and nothing more, and he was inclined to be rude when people tried to force him into an eminence which he refused. With his profound sense of the incomplete and the ridiculous in this world, and with a humour in which the grotesque and the pathetic sides of life were together recognised every moment, he never hesitated to admit his own mistakes."[21] Ford Madox Ford was only 17 when Newman died but he, too, appreciated something of the simplicity that animated the great Cardinal's life when he said of his two dearest friends, Joseph Conrad and Stephen Crane, "They were very simple people really. All great authors are. If you are not simple, you are not observant. If you are not observant, you cannot write. But you must observe simply. The first characteristic of great writing is a certain humility."[22] But of all Newman's contemporaries, Lord Ripon, the Liberal statesman, Viceroy to India, and courageous convert probably captured this aspect of Newman best when he addressed the Catholic Union in 1879 after Newman received his red hat.

Dr Newman possessed the greatest intellectual gifts combined with the gentlest spirit. With powers which would have well fitted him to fill the highest positions in

---

[19] LD, 8:178 E. B. Pusey to J. R. Hope (18 April 1841).
[20] Lockhart, pp. 23–4.
[21] See *Guardian* obituary for Cardinal Newman by R. W. Church in LD, 32:602.
[22] *The Bodley Head Ford Madox Ford. Volume V: Memories and Impressions* (London, 1971), p. 201.

this country, he had rejected all the temptations of worldly ambition to follow with simplicity of heart the guidance of God. Thus affording a noble and encouraging example to many others to cast aside all earthly considerations, when they have felt stirring within them the call to go forth from their Father's House and all its tender recollections and overmastering attachments, and to ask in humble guise admittance to the fold of Holy Church.[23]

Newman himself described this "simplicity of heart" in *Callista* (1855), his novel about the conversion of a young woman in the third century, where he says of his heroine that the more she considered the effect of Christian teaching on her Christian friends, the "more surely did she discern that this teaching wrought in them a something which she had not. They had about them a simplicity, a truthfulness, a decision, an elevation, a calmness and a sanctity to which she was a stranger, which spoke to her heart and absolutely overcame her."[24] And yet in order to understand fully the accuracy of Lord Ripon's encomium, we must go to Newman's splendid sermon, "Ignorance of Evil" (1836), written in the year of his mother's death, where he explains how he understood *simplicity* with his usual concinnity.

Christ has purchased for us what we lost in Adam, our garment of innocence. He has bid us and enabled us to become as little children; He has purchased for us the grace of *simplicity*, which, though one of the highest, is very little thought about, is very little sought after. We have, indeed, a general idea what love is, and hope, and faith, and truth, and purity, though a poor idea; but we are almost blind to what is one of the first elements of Christian perfection, that simple-mindedness which springs from the heart's being *whole* with God, entire, undivided. And those who think they have an idea of it, commonly rise no higher than to mistake for it a mere weakness and softness of mind, which is but its counterfeit. To be simple is to be like the Apostles and first Christians. Our Saviour says, "Be ye harmless," or simple, "as doves." And St. Paul, "I would have you wise unto that which is good, and *simple concerning evil*." [Rom. xvi. 19.] Again, "That ye may be *blameless and harmless*, the sons of God, without rebuke, in the midst of a crooked and perverse nation." [Phil. ii. 15.] And he speaks of the "testimony of" his own "conscience, that in *simplicity* and godly sincerity, not with fleshly wisdom, but by the grace of God," he had his conversation in the world and towards his disciples. Let us pray God to give us this great and precious gift; that we may blot out from our memory all that offends Him; unlearn all that knowledge which sin has taught us; rid ourselves of selfish motives, self-conceit, and vanity, littlenesses, envying, grudgings, meannesses; turn from all cowardly, low, miserable ways; and escape from servile fears, the fear of man, vague anxieties of conscience, and superstitions. So that we may have the boldness and frankness of those who are as if they had no sin, from having been cleansed from it; the uncontaminated hearts, open countenances, and untroubled eyes of those

---

[23] LD, 29:428 Lord Ripon to the Catholic Union (20 February 1879).
[24] *Call*, p. 294.

who neither suspect, nor conceal, nor shun, nor are jealous; in a word, so that we may have confidence in Him, that we may stay on Him, and rest in the thoughts of Him . . .[25]

There is another lively testimony to Newman's respect for simplicity in a letter that he wrote to Sir James Stephen (1789–1859), the Evangelical workaholic and Under Secretary for the Colonies, as well as frequent contributor to the *Edingurgh Review*, whose influence was such that he was reputed to rule the British Empire single-handedly. When *Loss and Gain* appeared in 1848, Stephen described it in a review as "a novel of humour, drollery, and sarcasm, directed chiefly against those who, ten years since, were [Newman's] own zealous and affectionate disciples."

This might have been unobjectionable enough but Stephen went further and noted how "The scourge of his contempt is laid with inexorable severity on all who have been weak enough to be dazzled and misled by the glare of his sophistry."[26] These were honest, if somewhat blunt blows. In response, Newman delivered an impromptu apologia that shows him to have been very much his mother's son.

> It used to be a proverb often in the mouth of Dr Whately, "Fling dirt enough and some will stick." I have not found it true in my own case. Misconceptions from many quarters have been attached to my words, acts, and motives, for 20 years and more. But they have been inconsistent with each other, and unreal in themselves: and having no life, have faded away. It has been so in time past, it will be so in time to come. Do not think me arrogant when I say, that, with ten thousand failings, I have a witness within me to singleness of mind and purpose, and to a heart bared before my Maker and Judge. Time is the test of facts. What I am conscious of myself now, I think will one day be granted by others.[27]

That this "singleness of mind and purpose" would one day lead Newman to a Rome that his Huguenot mother could not help but abominate would be a lasting source of pain to Newman, but nevertheless their shared trials brought them closer not only to each other but to God. Days before Mr Newman was declared bankrupt, Newman wrote his mother, apropos this "very trial itself," that "there is nothing in any way to fear. 'All things work together for good to those who love God.' I am firmly and rootedly persuaded of this. Every event that happens to them is most certainly the very best in every light that could by any possibility have happened. God will give good—I will do as much as I can, and THEN I have nothing to apprehend. This is indeed a privilege, for it takes away all care after the future." His mother's response to this epitomized all that was most lovable about the woman.

> I have been very anxious about your Father's health. I am happy to say he is much better . . . I thank God, myself, I am very well; and I rely on that good Providence who can and will protect and guide us through all the trials we must expect to experience for a long time to come. Say in your next when we may expect to have

[25] *PS*, 8, pp. 267–8.
[26] Sir James Stephen. *Essays in Ecclesiastical Biography* (London, 1907), II, p. 126.
[27] LD, 15:398 JHN to Sir James Stephen (17 July 1853).

the comfort of your and Francis's company . . . I thank God sincerely, that all of us have always had our happiness in each other's society, and have not sought for pleasure beyond our own circle and domestic resources. I anticipate much comfort, nay even happiness from our approaching meeting . . . I shall only say, every thing you do or say is sure to be a comfort and make me still more proud of you. Indeed, my dear, I am convinced I am highly favoured to have six such good children.[28]

If Newman's mother taught him how trials came to bind us to the will of God, she also set him a good literary example. Mrs Newman was a natural writer, something that her son was not. In an autobiographical fragment, Newman recalled how much attention he had paid to writing as a boy at Ealing School. Speaking of himself in the third person, he wrote how

> . . . he was sent to a school of 200 boys, increasing to 300, at Ealing, near London, under the care of the Revd George Nicholas, LLD of Wadham College. As a child, he was of a studious turn, and of a quick apprehension; and Dr Nicholas, to whom he became greatly attached, was accustomed to say, that no boy had run through the school, from the bottom to the top, so rapidly as John Newman. Though in no respect a precocious boy, he attempted original compositions in prose and verse from the age of eleven, and in prose showed a great sensibility and took much pains in matters of style. He devoted to such literary exercises and to such books as came in his way, a good portion of his play-time; and his school-fellows have left on record that they never, or scarcely ever, saw him taking part in any game.[29]

In making himself a writer, making himself an exceedingly good writer, Newman acquired something of the limpidity that came naturally to his mother, but only with great and persistent labour. "It is one of my sayings (so continually do I feel it)," he told William George Ward (1842–82), the pugnacious Ultramontane and editor of the *Dublin Review*, for whom Newman always felt amused affection, despite their differences, "that the composition of a volume is like gestation and childbirth. I do not think that I ever thought out a question or wrote my thoughts, without great pain, pain reaching to the body as well as the mind. It has made me practically feel that labour 'in sudore vultûs ejus' is the lot of man; and that 'ignorance' is truly one of his four wounds. It has been emphatically a *penance*. And in consequence I have hardly written anything unless I was *called* to do so."[30] He even wrote his novel of the third century, *Callista* at the behest of Cardinal Wiseman, though there as in so many of his literary productions, what might have begun as a response to an occasion took on a life of its own. In the case of *Callista*, although the book abounds in powerful apologetics, one can still see the stylist in Newman unabashedly enjoying himself.

> The bank of the hill below him, and on the right and left, was a maze of fruit-trees, about which nature, if it were not the hand of man, had had no thought

---

[28] LD, 1:117 Mrs Jemima Newman to JHN (23 November 1821).
[29] *AW*, p. 29.
[30] LD, 20:169 JHN to W. G. Ward (15 March 1862).

except that they should be all together there. The wild olive, the pomegranate, the citron, the date, the mulberry, the peach, the apple, and the walnut, formed a sort of spontaneous orchard. Across the water, groves of palm-trees waved their long and graceful branches in the morning breeze. The stately and solemn ilex, marshalled into long avenues, showed the way to substantial granges or luxurious villas. The green turf or grass was spread out beneath, and here and there flocks and herds were emerging out of the twilight, and growing distinct upon the eye. Elsewhere the ground rose up into sudden eminences crowned with chestnut woods, or with plantations of cedar and acacia, or wildernesses of the cork-tree, the turpentine, the carooba, the white poplar, and the Phoenician juniper, while overhead ascended the clinging tendrils of the hop, and an underwood of myrtle clothed their stems and roots. A profusion of wild flowers carpeted the ground far and near.[31]

This is delightful writing. Yet for Newman, style was never an end in itself: his motivations for writing were far too practical merely to turn phrases. Thackeray once reread bits of his stuff and confessed, "I have just read such a stupid part of *Pendennis*, but how well written it is."[32] One would never say the same about Newman's work. In the *Idea of a University*, the esteem he shows for the mastery of language could not be higher, but he esteems it as a means, not an end.

If then the power of speech is a gift as great as any that can be named,—if the origin of language is by many philosophers even considered to be nothing short of divine,—if by means of words the secrets of the heart are brought to light, pain of soul is relieved, hidden grief is carried off, sympathy conveyed, counsel imparted, experience recorded, and wisdom perpetuated—if by great authors the many are drawn up into unity, national character is fixed, a people speaks, the past and the future, the East and the West are brought into communication with each other.—if such men are, in a word, the spokesmen and prophets of the human family,—it will not answer to make light of Literature or to neglect its study; rather we may be sure that, in proportion as we master it in whatever language, and imbibe its spirit, we shall ourselves become in our own measure the ministers of like benefits to others, be they many or few, be they in the obscurer or the more distinguished walks of life,—who are united to us by social ties, and are within the sphere of our personal influence.[33]

It was also from his mother that Newman inherited his admirable aplomb under duress. "To God I owe every thing," she told her son in one letter, referring to the strength God gave her when her husband's troubles became a constant worry. "He it was who taught me the necessity of resignation . . . the duty of silence on the only subject that [was] ever present to my thoughts . . . .The effort and the resolution to persevere have been so much above human power, that I do not fear saying there is nothing too hard to be

---

[31] *Call*, pp. 268–9.
[32] Lewis Melville. *The Thackeray Country* (London, 1905), p. 1.
[33] *Idea*, p. 245.

effected through His assistance."[34] Later, when Newman encountered his own troubles, whether the many vituperative attacks in print that followed the publication of Tract 90, the libel charge of the Achilli trial, or the whispering campaigns of his enemies in Rome after he had settled in Birmingham, he must often have recalled his mother's fortitude. Certainly, he emulated her unflappable faith.

Then, again, it was from his mother that Newman inherited the practical dispatch with which he tackled the troubles and crises that came his way. For example, when cholera broke out in 1831, Mrs Newman wrote her son:

> Should our fears of [the cholera's] approach increase, I wish you could have that cottage at Littlemore for head quarters for nurses to be on the spot without mixing with their uncontaminated families and for a depot of medicines etc. And I should think it a privilege, while health permits, for you to consider me head nurse. I have the whole in my head, should it be ordained that our vicinity is to suffer under the visitation. Pray take care of your own health. Your usefulness is before you, for I trust the comfort of many for many years.[35]

It is also worth noting that when Newman decided to build a church in Littlemore, the impoverished village where he later established a quasi-monastic retreat out of a disused stable, he insisted that his mother lay the cornerstone for the church, since she would often come from nearby Iffley (where Newman had helped her buy a house and keep a servant in livery) to minister to the poor of the neighbourhood.[36] Mother and son also shared something of the same gentle sense of humour, which is on charming display in their letters to one another. "I am looking forward with cheerful hope," Mrs. Newman wrote in one letter to her son, "to a 'crust of bread and *liberty*' to enjoy the increasing attainments and amiable society of all my dear Children and that, with a few additions of friendship, in which I flatter myself you will include yourself, is the summit of my ambition."[37] Newman could also share jokes with his mother. In one instance, he writes of his brother Frank, on the brink of his attaining his double first, in a letter full of poignancy in light of their later irreconcilable divisions:

Oriel College – May 25. 1826

My dear Mother,

I hereby send you a young person from Oxford, to whom I hope you will be kind for my sake. – his stay will be short, so I trust the favor I ask will not be too great. – You must indulge him in some things poor young gentleman – he has got some odd ideas in his head of his having been lately examined, of his having been thanked for the manner in which he acquitted himself, particularly in the mathematical school – and of a general belief in Oxford that his name will appear in both first classes – you must not thwart him in these fancies,

[34] LD, 1:187 Mrs Jemima Newman to Harriett Newman (26 August 1824).
[35] LD, 2:373 Mrs Newman to JHN (12 November 1831).
[36] Ian Ker. *John Henry Newman* (Oxford, 1990), pp. 106–7.
[37] Jemima Newman quoted in Maisie Ward. *Young Mr. Newman* (London, 1948), p. 17.

but appear to take no notice of them, and gently divert his attention to other subjects. – He is a great talker; be sure you do not let him talk, poor young fellow – he is particularly apt to talk when persons are in the room – you have better therefore keep him as much to himself as possible – He behaves particularly ill in the company of ladies, chattering at a great rate, young man, and especially when I or other discreet person is not by; perhaps then you had better keep him in the back building . . .

He can mend shoes, string pianos, cut out skreens, and go on errands – the last is his forte – employ him in errands while he is with you and the time will pass pleasantly enough. – I forgot to say that he could sharpen knives. – He is very docile, while kindly treated, and quite harmless. – Do not frighten him – and believe me

With love to all, Yours most dut: J H N[38]

A few months later, he would write her again: "My 'Fathers' are arrived all safe – huge fellows they are, but very cheap – one folio costs a shilling! and all are in this extravagantly moderate way. – Frank too has sent his books; so I am having a new bookcase. I have heard from Frank, who (as you say) is very happy – but I lament to see with you that his mind is warped in one respect." It was at this juncture that Frank first plunged into the Evangelical fervour that would eventually lead to his leaving the Anglican fold together with his Balliol fellowship. "Time (I hope) will set all things right," Newman wrote his mother, though he also saw his brother's increasingly undogmatical faith as distinctly cautionary. "Every fresh opinion indeed we hear, is a call upon us to search our own opinions more rigidly and to examine their soundness – yet I cannot think them wrong in this instance."[39] As it happened, they were not wrong. In less than eight years, Frank's Christian faith would be in tatters.

His mother's letters reveal a warm-hearted, intelligent, maternal woman. Although capable, like her son, of exhibiting toughness when circumstances required, she was too refined to let toughness coarsen her native grace. In the painting done of the Fourdrinier family when she was young and unmarried, one sees a figure whose grace is tinged with apprehensiveness. She appears detached from the other figures, preoccupied, looking away as into an unfathomable future. Still, in her grace, one can see where Newman got his grace. Aubrey de Vere, the Irish poet and critic, saw this quality in his friend right off the bat.

The emotion of seeing him for the first time was one of the greatest in my life. I shall never forget his appearance. I had been waiting some time, and then the door opened, and Newman, in cap and gown, entered very swiftly, and quietly, with a kind of balance of the figure, like a very great lady sweeping into the room. That was my first impression; the second of a high-bred young monk of the Middle Ages, whose asceticism cannot quite conceal his distinguished elegance.[40]

[38] LD, 1:290–1 JHN to Mrs Newman (25 May 1826).
[39] LD, 2:30–1 JHN to Mrs Newman (18 October 1827).
[40] S. M. Paraclita Reilly. *Aubrey de Vere: Victorian Observer* (Dublin, 1956), p. 91.

As this recollection shows, Newman's grace was the outward sign of inward sanctity, a reflection of what Castiglione called "the celestial, adorable and true beauty which lies hidden in the secret recesses of the Almighty where profane eyes may not see it."[41]

In addition to grace, Mrs Newman possessed uncanny prescience. When Newman wrote her before the brewery failed in Alton, in an attempt to ease her worries, she responded how, as she said,

> I thank God I . . . view our present afflictions in the light you do, though I might not have the power to express my feelings so clearly and properly as you have done. My sorrows are not personal, but they are divided and complicated. We are human beings, sent here to act a part full of trials, either from joys or sorrows. All are not so gifted (I speak with love to you and gratitude to God) as *you*, to resist the temptations of the one, and to endure with true Christian resignation the sufferings of the other. I anticipate in my anxiety for you all many evils that it may please God to avert, but yet I hope pardonable in the nature of a Mother's feelings,—the decay of friendships from which youthful expectations may have augured comfort and delight through life. Many such feelings as these for my dear children will suggest themselves to my imagination; but with humble but sure confidence I resign me and mine and to the Giver of all good, knowing that in due time we shall be relieved from our troubles, or enabled by His assistance to support them.[42]

The lives of her children would be fraught with trials. One of the reasons why she and her eldest son were so close was that, when the trials mounted, Newman readily assumed many of the responsibilities of head of the family. It is commonplace that great men do not always shine in their familial settings; the rogue's gallery that Paul Johnson shared with his readers in his *Intellectuals* (1988) vividly proves this; Newman, however, was an exception. His mother increasingly depended on him for support, good counsel, and money when money was scarce, and he never let her down. He shared most of his salary with his mother and his siblings, as well as earnings from his writing. He searched out and bought houses for them. He wrote them charming, brilliant letters. He introduced many of his lively friends to them. He helped them with their studies. He shared his own intellectual and spiritual life with them. It is true that he was often absorbed in his own projects, which, once the Oxford Movement launched in 1833, became demanding, but he always found time for his mother and his siblings. As Anne Mozley, the editor of his Anglican correspondence, observed: "His keen family feeling . . . was never blunted by the public claims upon him."[43]

His mother, for her part, always felt a unique kinship with her first son. On his 20th birthday, she wrote: "Accept our individual and united congratulations on this auspicious day; and our kindest wishes that each added year may bring an increase

---

[41] Castiglione. *The Courtier* (Penguin, 1967), p. 341.
[42] LD, 1:113–1 Mrs Newman to JHN (27 October 1821).
[43] *Moz., ii*, p. 342.

of happiness to you . . . It is one of my greatest delights to anticipate that, however chequered the scenes of this life, your well-regulated mind will ever support you under its disappointments, and increase its rational pleasures." In an earlier letter, she gave still more eloquent expression to her maternal solicitude for a son whom she knew had a tendency to overwork himself: "You do not say how you are—pray, take care not to overfag yourself."[44]

With so sympathetic a mother, Newman was always keen on sharing his early triumphs. Indeed, after he won the Oriel Fellowship in 1826, which Thomas Short, the legendary don of Trinity had encouraged him to pursue, he wrote his mother: "By-the-bye, I have not told you the name of the other successful candidate: Froude of Oriel. We were in grave deliberation till near two this morning. . . . Froude is one of the acutest and clearest and deepest men in the memory of man. I hope our election will be *in honorem Dei et sponsae suae ecclesiae salutem*, as Edward II has it in our Statutes." When he could not give his mother the attention he wished to give her, he did not make trumpery excuses for himself. "I have just received your letters," he wrote her hurriedly in the same month that he received his Fellowship, "and have just despatched my famous Essay by the night coach to Town. The first minute, after having rid myself of it, I dedicate to you. I have felt much that my engagements of late drove me from you, hindered my conversing with you, making me an exile, I may say, from those I so much love. But this life is no time for enjoyment, but for labour, and I have especially deferred ease and quiet for a future life in devoting myself to the immediate service of God."[45]

Mrs Newman will always hold a special place in the hearts of those who admire her son's work not least because she saw his gifts so clearly and long before he ever published anything. "I cannot let this 21st anniversary of your birthday pass, without a line of congratulation from me," she wrote her son in 1822. "As my words flow from the heart of a Mother, I know they will meet a kind reception. I thank God, it is a day of rejoicing to us all; to your Father and me, that it has given us a Son who has uniformly persevered in improving the talents given him, and in forming his character both morally and religiously to virtue. And now that we have no more the dear child, we may boast instead, a companion, counsellor and friend. To your dear brothers and sisters it has given a second father, to whom they are much indebted for the improvement and cultivation of their minds; and, proud and happy am I to say, you are worthy of each other. To yourself, my dear, it is a day of thankfulness and rejoicing, that you have been guided and protect[ed] in this good path to fulfil all these duties so satisfactorily to your nearest and dearest connections, and likewise to form other friendships, which promise to be permanently valuable, and that you are placed in the situation that seems most suited to your abilities and character. These and innumerable other blessings we have all of us to be grateful for, and I rely with humble but perfect confidence in that Almighty Power who has hitherto preserved you, that He will diffuse His blessings on your future years."[46]

---

[44] LD, 1:62 Mrs Jemima Newman to JHN (21 February 1819).
[45] LD, 1:283 JHN to Mrs Jemima Newman (29 April 1826).
[46] LD, 1:122 Mrs Jemima Newman to JHN (21 February 1822).

In response, Newman gave voice to a young man's ambivalent farewell to his boyhood at the same time that he looked ahead to his adult-life to-be, a transition that no one could find more bittersweet than his mother:

> Thank you for your very kind letter. When I turn to look at myself, I feel quite ashamed of the praise it contains, so numerous and so great are the deficiencies which even I can see . . . When I thought of the years that are gone, and the unknown expanse which lies before me, I felt much affected, and quite shed tears to think I could no longer call myself a boy. Not that I am sorry so great a part of life is gone,—would that all were over!—but I seem now more left to myself, and, when I reflect upon my own weakness, I have cause to shudder . . . What time I have left, I am glad, and am indeed obliged, to devote to my attempt at Oriel,— wishing to prepare for that which will not admit of preparation.[47]

In these anxious lines, his anxious mother read a lack of self-confidence. "To show you I do not think you *too old* for a Mother's correction and advice, I shall not hesitate to tell you I see one great fault in your character, which alarms me very much, as I observe it increases upon you seriously; and, as all virtues may degenerate into vices, it is every one's duty to have a strict guard over themselves to avoid extremes. Your fault is want of self confidence, and a dissatisfaction with yourself, that you cannot exceed the bounds of human nature. Else, why should you, who *at least* equal in talents, prudence, and acquirements most young men of your age, allow yourself to be so desponding as to think you need 'shudder at your own weakness.'"[48] Yet what his mother mistook for lack of self-confidence was really humility. As Newman wrote to Charles, "Now that the contest and labour is all over [exacted by the Oriel exam], I may be allowed to state that for the last month or two I have been so far from having a mean opinion of myself, which my Mother some how judged I had conceived, that I have actually considered myself as having a good chance of succeeding . . ." Having triumphed, Newman could look back on his ordeal fondly. "The examination throughout was most kind and considerate, and we were supplied with sandwiches, fruit, cake, jellies, and wine," not to mention "a blazing fire and plenty of time."[49]

Of course, other more substantial differences arose. Newman's mother and his sisters were not entirely keen on his Tractarian friends or the Romanizing tendency of Tractarianism. In a Memorandum dated June 1873, Newman wrote how: "There was always the chance of their not liking those whom I liked; and in matter of fact, they did not like some of my greatest friends." Harriet, in particular, disliked Hurrell Froude, thinking him a smarty boots, but then she was a smarty boots herself. "And, again," as Newman recalled, "they did not like the distinctive principles of the Oxford Movement; and, the more it developed, the wider did their difference from me in respect to it grow . . . These differences though they tried to hide them, made me very sore. They had a full right to their own views; but I did not imitate them in

---

[47] LD, 1:123 JHN to Mrs Jemima Newman (6 March 1822).
[48] LD, 1:124 Mrs Jemima Newman to JHN (11 March 1822).
[49] LD, 1:10–1 JHN to Charles Newman (13 April 1822).

bearing patiently what could not be helped."[50] This was a characteristically honest admission. Naturally, it must have been difficult for Newman to recognize that none of his work on behalf of what he regarded as the one true fold would persuade those whom he loved the most. But he understood that this was a mystery that it was fruitless to question. To his good friend, Maria Giberne, he wrote in July 1876: "It is certainly wonderful that no one of your or of my own family has been converted, considering how many prayers have been offered for them—but we must recollect St. Paul's words that it is 'not of him that willeth etc.' [Romans 9:16] and St. John's [1:13] that 'God's children are born not of blood etc.' Your prayers most surely are not thrown away, not one of them is lost or fails—but how they are answered is a question to be solved in the world to come."[51]

Nevertheless, if the Huguenot in Newman's mother could not always cotton to the Roman aspects of her son's point of view, this never blinded her to the appeal of his work, especially his sermons. Many of Newman's contemporaries would testify to the power of his sermons but his mother was one of the first. "I assure you your Sermons are a real comfort and delight to me," she wrote her son in 1826. "They are what I think Sermons ought to be to enlighten, to correct, to support, and to strengthen. It is, my dear, a great gift to see so clearly the truths of religion – still more to be able to impart the knowledge to others. You will, I am sure, duly appreciate the treasure, and make it valuable to many besides yourself."[52] One might ascribe this simply to a mother's partiality—and in the case of Mrs Newman, there was particular partiality, because, as she told her eldest child, "you were the *silent* pride of my early life, and I now look on you as the comfort and guide of my age."[53] Yet Mrs Newman understood the quality of the sermons well enough to know that their influence would impose a growing burden on her son. As she wrote in a letter of 1836, which would be her last to him, written a month before her death, when she was 64: "I know you must feel your position one of great responsibility, as many influential members of future times will most likely have their characters and religious opinions formed by you." Rereading this letter, Newman doubtless marvelled at how his mother had anticipated the awful responsibility that he did feel as he moved closer and closer to the Church of Rome. Whether his turning away from his familial faith would unsettle the Christian faith of his contemporaries became a constant worry in the crucial years between his first fundamental questioning of Anglicanism in 1839 and his conversion in 1845. This last maternal letter also carried an undertone of admonition: "Happy am I to think that you know yourself insufficient to such important duties and that you seek guidance and aid where alone it can be given perfect and sure. I cannot but lament when I hear suspicions cast upon your opinions as 'favouring Catholicism.' Not that I mind the reproach which all good and useful men must suffer in doing their duty, but I regret lest the surmise should weaken your influence and powers which might be great on momentous occasions."[54] Newman's mother might have recognized her son's "great

---

[50] LD, 5:314–15 Memorandum: "Apology for Myself" (June 1873).
[51] LD, 28:94 JHN to Miss M. R. Giberne (25 July 1876).
[52] LD, 1:277 Mrs Jemima Newman to JHN (6 March 1826).
[53] LD, 2:252 Mrs Jemima Newman to JHN (19 July 1830).
[54] LD, 5:276 Mrs Jemima Newman to JHN (12 April 1836).

gift," even before it was fully manifest, but she was also a Huguenot whose family had borne the brunt of Catholic persecution, and she would not have approved of anyone, least of all her son, "favouring Catholicism."[55]

Lord Macaulay's lively description of the oppression to which the Huguenots had been subjected in France would undoubtedly have won her warm approval. In his *History of England*, the great Whig historian related how "Louis XIV had, from an early age, regarded the Calvinists with an aversion at once religious and political. As a prince fond of arbitrary power, he detested those republican theories which were intermingled with the Genevese divinity." One by one he revoked the privileges "the schismatics enjoyed." Even before the revocation of the Edict of Nantes, "he interfered with the education of Protestant children, confiscated property bequeathed to Protestant consistories, and on frivolous pretexts shut up Protestant churches. The Protestant magistrates were deprived of the honour of nobility. The Protestant officers of the royal household were informed that His Majesty dispensed with their services. Orders were given that no Protestant should be admitted into the legal profession. The oppressed sect showed some faint signs of that spirit which in the preceding century had bidden defiance to the whole power of the House of Valois. Massacres and executions followed . . ." After the revocation of Nantes, the persecution took a more blatant turn—"a crowd of decrees against the sectaries appeared in rapid succession. Boys and girls were torn from their parents and sent to be educated in convents. All Calvinistic ministers were commanded either to abjure their religion or to quit their country within a fortnight." Indeed, "in a few months, fifty thousand families quitted France for ever." And these were "generally persons of intelligent minds, of industrious habits, and of austere morals. In the list are to be found names eminent in war, in science, in literature, and in art. Some of the exiles offered their swords to William of Orange, and distinguished themselves by the fury with which they fought against their persecutor. Others avenged themselves with weapons still more formidable, and by means of the presses of Holland, England, and Germany, inflamed, during thirty years, the pubic mind of Europe against the French government."[56] This history being what it was, it was only natural that Mrs Newman should have little sympathy for the faith of her ancestral oppressors.

Before her death in 1836, intimations that her son might not be altogether sound on Catholicism would make Mrs Newman increasingly uneasy. In a long letter that

---

[55] It is interesting that Maria Giberne (1802–85), who was such a close family friend of Newman and his siblings, was also of a Huguenot family. After becoming an Evangelical at 20, she went on to adopt Anglo-Catholic views, under Newman's direction. Although initially disconcerted by Newman's conversion, she eventually converted herself on 19 December 1845. In 1846, she made her way to Rome, where she supported herself by painting. In 1851, she helped identify and transport back to England witnesses for the Achilli trial. In 1856, she decided to become a nun and in 1863, at Autun, she joined the Visitation order, after which she corresponded frequently with Newman.

[56] Lord Macaulay. *History of England* (Folio Society, 2009), II, p. 13 Queen Victoria enjoyed Macaulay, about whom she wrote on his death: "He is a great national loss—though his writings were perhaps rather partial, but so fine and so powerful." *Letters to Vicky: The Correspondence between Queen Victoria and Her Daughter Victoria, Empress of Germany* 1858–1901 (Folio Society, 2011), p. 64.

Newman wrote his mother in March 1833 describing his time in Rome, he candidly shared with her the ambivalence he felt in the presence of the Pope and the one, holy, catholic, and apostolic Church.

I had seen the Pope before, who looks like other men, and tho' I think I know his face well, there is nothing to describe about it – yet it is a great thing to say that it is negatively good, – that it is not fat, or red, or ugly, or unpleasant – it becomes the Pope – it is grave. His robes, which are very long all round, are white satin with a broad facing of gold work – he had his triple crown on his head . . . He is attended by two immense fans of white (peacock?) feathers – and as he moves, blesses the people. The mode of blessing is solemn, and is a contrast to the usual attitudinizing of the preachers etc. here . . . he scarcely moves his hand, and appears to be praying as he goes. . . . The high altar was decked out sumptuously, incense swung to and fro; a crowd of priests were preparing for the service, salutations and genuflexions were making on every side, and a choir . . . were chanting. On the right on the episcopal throne was the Sovereign Pontiff, his mitre on his head, with a train, partly of gentlemen ushers . . . partly of ecclesiastics with shaven heads . . . A vast number of ceremonies went on, little of which I could understand . . . Besides, Mass was celebrated. – At the close the young girls were introduced in white with fancy crowns on their heads; a curious contrast, for tho' muffled up over the mouth even, and scarcely more than the eyes visible, they were very nicely dressed, and had apparently silk stockings on, which one could see. They are introduced to the Pope, kiss his foot, and receive the present. Then the Pope retires as he came. – All this I say is a curious sight, considered merely as a citizen of the world would consider it – a court day of a sovereign priest. – Nor, viewing it as a Christian, should I condemn it, were the ceremonies other than they are, and were it not at Rome. But, not to speak of doctrinal errors, there is much unedifying dumbshow – I cannot doubt it . . . nor can I endure the Pope's foot being kissed, considering how much is said in Scripture about the necessity of him that is greatest being as the least, nor do I even tolerate him being carried in on high. – Next it is in Rome – and Rome is a doomed city, it is one of the 4 monsters of Daniel's vision – and tho' a priest might have temporal power elsewhere, I begin to think that it was a sin, as such, in the Church's uniting itself with that enemy of God, who from the beginning sat on her 7 hills, with an enchantress's cup, as the representative and instrument of the Evil Principle. And yet as I looked on, and saw all Christian acts performing the Holy Sacrament offered up, and the blessing given, and recollected I was in church, I could only say in very perplexity my own words, "How shall I name thee, Light of the wide west, or heinous error-seat?" – and felt the force of the parable of the tares – who can separate the light from the darkness but the Creator Word who prophesied their union? And so I am forced to leave the matter, not at all seeing my way out of it. – How shall I name thee?[57]

---

[57] LD, 3:267–8 JHN to Mrs Jemima Newman (25 March 1833).

For the unreconstructed Huguenot in Jemima Newman, this must have set off loud alarm bells. Most English travellers in Rome would have agreed with Newman about the "unedifying dumbshow" and enjoyed the comforting reminder of "the 4 monsters of Daniel's vision." They were at once drawn to and repelled by Roman Catholicism and flocked to Easter and Christmas ceremonies to witness the abominations that they had been warned against since nursery days. In *The Mediterranean Passion: Victorians and Edwardians in the South* (1987), John Pemble describes how "They jostled and elbowed for the best places; avidly observed and busily noted; and then felt a rage and disgust which demanded an outlet in ostentatious misbehavior. They refused to uncover for the Pope, or to kneel to receive his blessing. At Mass they remained seated or standing when the Host was elevated, and Mrs. Trollope was told that on one occasion the popping of champagne corks was heard from the English tribune during the silence of the sacred moment. During the music they would scoff and snigger and make loud pejorative comments—to the great embarrassment of more sensitive compatriots. 'I had no conception English women could be such brutes, or exhibit themselves so contemptibly,' wrote John Ruskin after attending a service in the Chiesa del Gesu in December 1840."[58] Still, few English Protestants would have described the Roman service with the degree of detail that Newman described it or come away from the Mass asking themselves, "How shall I name thee, Light of the wide west, or heinous error-seat"? This was a question that Englishmen simply did not ask themselves. That Newman was asking it must have made his Mother feel as though the ground beneath her was buckling. Even as early as 1833, signs that her son was indeed favouring Catholicism were becoming undeniable. When he returned from his visit to the Mediterranean with the Froudes, for example, he wrote of the Eternal City:

> Is it nothing to be able to look on our Mother, to whom we owe the blessing of Christianity, with affection instead of hatred? with pity indeed, aye, and fear, but not with horror? Is it nothing to rescue her from the hard names, which interpreters of prophecy have put upon her, as an idolatress and an enemy of God, when she is deceived rather than a deceiver? Nothing to be able to account her priests as ordained of God, and anointed for their spiritual functions by the Holy Spirit, instead of considering her communion the bond of Satan?[59]

Had Mrs Newman lived longer, it is questionable whether she would have been surprised to hear Newman admit, as he did in 1841, that "She alone," that is to say the Roman Church, "amid all the errors and evils of her practical system, has given free scope to the feelings of awe, mystery, tenderness, reverence, devotedness, and other

---

[58] J. Pemble. *The Mediterranean Passion: Victorians and Edwardians in the South* (Oxford, 1987), p. 212.

[59] *Apo.*, p. 114. About this passage from his article "Home Thoughts Abroad" (1836), Newman wrote how: "This was my first advance in rescuing, on an intelligible, intellectual basis, the Roman Church from the designation of Antichrist; it was not the Church, but the old dethroned Pagan monster, still living in the ruined city, that was Antichrist."

feelings which may be especially called catholic."[60] His visit to Rome had had a greater impact on him than even he could register. In September 1839, he wrote his good friend Frederic Rogers:

> Your account of your priest is amusing. *Can* the R. C.s have any tender feeling towards Anglicanism? Who among us ever showed them any kindness? Are we not the pets of a State which made it a felony to celebrate Mass even, I believe, in private, a law which Ward declares remained in existence till 1780? *What* are the R. C.s to admire in us? our married Bishops or our Dissenting brethren? I cannot deny that my heart is with neither of these—where it is 'tis more difficult to say, but I saw yesterday (by chance in a letter which I had sent home from the Continent,) that I then considered I had left "half of it at Rome". What a sad case of divided allegiance—with one's duty one way, and one's love another—still let it be.[61]

It is striking that the great art historian Kenneth Clark, who entirely ignored the contribution that Catholic Spain made to European civilization in his popular television series, should nevertheless have echoed Newman, when he remarked in the series, with respect to the impact of the Counter Reformation, how "Rome and the Church of Rome regained many territories it had lost . . . and . . . became, once more, a great spiritual force. But was it a civilizing force? In England we tend to answer no. We have been conditioned by generations of liberal, Protestant historians who tell us that no society based on obedience, repression and superstition can be really civilized. But no one with an ounce of historical feeling or philosophical detachment can be blind to the great ideals, to the passionate belief in sanctity, to the expenditure of human genius in the service of God, which are made triumphantly visible to us with every step we take in Baroque Rome. Whatever it is, it isn't barbarous or provincial . . . the Catholic revival was a popular movement . . . it gave ordinary people a means of satisfying, through ritual, images, and symbols, their deepest impulses, so that their minds were at peace; and I think that one must agree to put off defining the word civilization till we have looked at the Rome of the Popes."[62]

After his Mother's death on 17 May 1836, Newman wrote his Aunt Betsey, "my dearest Mother is taken from us. If you knew how dreadfully she has suffered in mind, and how little her wanderings left her like herself you would feel, as we do, that it is really a release. Who would have thought it! Every thing is strange in this world—everything mysterious. Nothing but sure faith can bring us through."[63] Newman later testified to the exacting "duty of silence" in accordance with which his Mother met her innumerable trials. "It is odd that in these later years," he told a family friend in 1881, "I have never thought of asking Jemima [his sister] any question, since from her good memory, she would be sure to recollect every word my Mother let drop. But it was not

---

[60] *V.M.,* ii, p. 386.
[61] LD, 7:151 JHN to Frederic Rogers (15 September 1839).
[62] Kenneth Clark. *Civilization* (New York, 1969), pp. 17–18.
[63] LD, 5:299 JHN to Elizabeth Newman (17 May 1836).

my mother's way to talk of herself without pressing. She told me more about herself
when I was a schoolboy than at any other time. I think the troubles of life had so
oppressed, so crushed her, that she had no heart to look back at all at any thing."[64]
When her daughter looked back, it was with moving regret. In June 1836, after their
mother's death, she wrote Newman: "We have a pretty little garden badly laid out and
overgrown by neglect. I am very busy in bringing it into order [for] when Harriett
comes. As I work in it, I think continually of Mama's taste and contrivance, and what
she would have done, and how pretty she would have made it. I sometimes think it
would have been a great delight to me, if she could have been down here once."[65] When
Newman looked back on his relationship with his Mother, he felt not only remorseful
but aggrieved. "What has been to me distressing in my work, is, that it has been one
of the causes which kept me from being much with my mother lately. But there was
another cause. I mean of late years my Mother has much misunderstood my religious
views, and considered she differed from me; and she thought I was surrounded by
admirers and had everything my own way—and in consequence, I, who am conscious
to myself I never thought any thing more precious than her sympathy and praise, had
none of it."[66] It is doubtful whether Mrs Newman "misunderstood" her son's religious
views; it is more likely that she simply disagreed with them. Nevertheless, the death of
his Mother set in sharp relief the lonely road on which Newman had been travelling
for years and would continue to travel. To his sister Harriet, in June 1836, he wrote:
". . . speaking of dejection from solitude; I never feel so near heaven as then. Years ago,
from 1822 to 1826, I used to be very much by myself; and in anxieties of various kinds,
from money matters and other things, which were very harassing. I then had no friend
near me—no one to whom I opened my mind fully or who could sympathize with me.
I am but returning at worst to that state . . . Therefore, please God, I trust I shall get on
very well, and after all this life is very short, and it is a better thing to be pursuing what
seems God's call, than to be looking after one's own comfort. I am learning more than
hitherto to live in the presence of the dead—this is a gain which strange faces cannot
take away."[67]

    At the same time, throughout his father's and his own travails, his mother had
been his closest confidant and this made for a fellow feeling between mother and son
that is nicely expressed by Newman in a letter that he wrote in November of 1823
when he had begun to attend lectures that would help prepare him for his conversion
to Rome.

> What a significant intimation yesterday's snow has given us of a severe winter!
> Trees have been torn up by the wind in all directions—and today the Cherwell is
> so swollen with the rains etc that it nearly overflows Christ Church water walk.
> My lodgings are in the High Street, some way from Oriel—so you may fancy it
> is very inconvenient to paddle to dinner in thin shoes and silk stockings. I am
> beginning to attend some private lectures in Divinity by the Regius Professor,

[64] LD, 29:365 JHN to Louisa Elizabeth Deane (16 April 1881).
[65] LD, 5:315 Mrs Jemima Mozley to JHN (23 June 1836).
[66] LD, 5:313 JHN to Mrs John Mozley (26 June 1836).
[67] LD, 5:311–12 JHN to Harriett Newman (21 June 1836).

Dr Charles Lloyd, which he has been kind enough to volunteer to about eight of us—so you may fancy my time is much occupied. I have taken a ride or two, make it a practice of being in bed by eleven o'clock, and rise with the lark at half past five. When I rise, I sometimes think that you are lying awake and thinking—and only such reflections make me uncomfortable.[68]

Their religious differences notwithstanding, Newman had a deep bond with his mother—one forged in heartbreak and loss, as well as love and affection—and it showed him not only the vanity of human wishes but the wisdom of empathy.

---

[68] LD, 1:167 JHN to Mrs Newman (1 November 1823) The article by Charles Lloyd (1784–1820) entitled "View of the Roman Catholic Doctrines," which ran in the *British Critic* in 1825, paved the way for Newman's less prejudiced attitude towards the Roman Church.

3

Charles Newman and the Idea of Socialism

On 23 February 1825, Charles Newman sent his brother John a letter that became something of a milestone in both their lives. "I am glad to say I have come to a satisfactory conclusion with regard to religion, sooner than could be expected," Charles announced. After "a great deal of preparatory thought," he confessed that he had "come to a judgment which no doubt will surprise you; for it is entirely against Christianity . . ." He had assumed Christianity to be "synonymous with wisdom and knowledge," but found it "far otherwise." And the upshot could not have been more decided: "I think Mr Owen . . . beats St Paul hollow."[1] Here, of course, Charles was referring to Robert Owen, the Welsh utopian socialist. Subsequently, Newman encapsulated his brother's objections to the Christian faith. "You say that 'for practical motives to action Mr O. [Owen] beats St Paul hollow whose 'doctrines', tho' 'ingenious' are unsuitable 'to this present race of men.'—that knowledge is the great remedy for moral evil—that revealed religion 'brings evil most abundantly into the world', and gets praise when it merely cures some portion of that which it has caused. Again, it gets praise from the instances of great men who have believed it; tho', instead of being improved by it, these in reality have ennobled it by their own excellence;—and further, that its effects have been unfairly estimated by the standard of right and wrong which itself proposes. Lastly, that the doctrine of eternal punishment (according to a statement of it of your own) is ridiculous."[2] In adopting Owen's anti-Christian philosophy, Charles set himself apart not only from his brother but from his entire family. Indeed, Robert Owen and his socialist ideas would affect nearly every aspect of Charles' life, from his relations to his family and his associates, to his livelihood and his very sense of identity. But most of all it would cause him to abandon his Christian faith, which Charles threw over when he was 23 and never recovered. The letter would also be a milestone for Newman because it would be the first personal inkling he would have of what he called the "great *apostasia*," which he described so memorably in the speech he gave in 1879 when he was made a cardinal.

Hitherto, it has been considered that Religion alone with its supernatural sanctions, was strong enough to secure submission of the masses of our population to law

---

[1] LD, 1:212 Charles Newman to JHN (23 February 1825). William Cobbett referred to Charles' hero as "that 'humane', half mad, beastly fellow Owen . . ." See *Rural Rides* (London, 1830), p. 440.

[2] See LD, 2:266–81 (19 August 1830). Newman omitted this passage from a letter that he sent Charles because, as he said, he thought it "distracting the course of the narrative by over-minuteness . . ." Still, it distills the essence of Charles' exceptions to Christianity.

and order; now the Philosophers and Politicians are bent on satisfying the problem without the aid of Christianity. Instead of the Church's authority and teaching, they would substitute first of all a universal and thoroughly secular education, calculated to bring home to every individual that to be orderly, industrious, and sober is his personal interest. Then, for great working principles to take the place of religion, for the use of the masses thus carefully educated, it provides the broad fundamental ethical truths of justice, benevolence, veracity, and the like . . . As to Religion, it is a private luxury, which a man may have if he will; but which of course . . . he must not obtrude on others, or indulge in to their annoyance. The general character of this great *apostasia* is one and the same everywhere; but in detail, and in character it varies . . .[3]

To understand what prompted Newman's brother to come to so radical a judgement, it is necessary to know something of Charles' life and Owen's peculiar brand of socialism. In this chapter, I shall revisit both to show how in trying to address Charles' objections to Christianity, Newman willy-nilly prepared himself to meet the objections of an entire generation of rationalists convinced that Christianity was not only irrational but immoral.

Charles Newman, the older of Newman's two brothers, was at once the most eccentric and the most troubled of the six Newman siblings. Born in 1802, a year after John, he was also the most headstrong of the children. Proud, captious, and convinced of his own superiority, he was not easy to befriend. By the same token, he could be gentle and charming, and, in fact, inspired much love and affection. A photograph taken of him in profile when he was an older man—perhaps in his 60s—shows that he had the same prominent nose and prognathous jaw as his older brother. But what is striking is his bearing: he has the studied grandeur of one of the old actor managers—that, say, of Sir Johnston Forbes-Robertson or Sir George Alexander. The theatre critic Thomas Purnell (1834–89), who befriended Charles in his later years, vividly recalled meeting him for the first time in Tenby, the little Welsh village to which he would later retire: "He stood at the top of the topmost stair. I cannot imagine a more distinguished head and face. There was a touch of Mephistopheles in him. There was also a touch of Jupiter Olympius. Although dressed in ill-fitting clothes, and with a sort of blanket over his shoulders, he appeared to me to be the ideal of courtly grace. He bowed me without a word into his apartments. This was in the roof of the building, and the only light came from a window which opened with a notched iron bar. The room was as meagrely furnished as Goethe's study in Weimar. A bed, a chest of drawers, a table and two or three chairs, with a few books, constituted the whole goods and chattels."[4] That such lofty airs were still intact in his old age was a credit to his fortitude, for no man spent more time in the proverbial soup than Charles Newman. His misadventures give the family narrative an almost Dickensian undertone, though for Newman and the other members of the family, his improvidence was a source of continual worry and distress.

---

[3] This is from Newman's "Biglietto Speech" which he gave in 1879; see *Addresses to Cardinal Newman with his Replies*, pp. 66–7.

[4] Thomas Purnell quoted in J. M. Wheeler, "Biographical Sketch" in Charles Robert Newman. *Essays in Rationalism* (London, 1891), p. 14. Tenby, interestingly enough, was where the arch-rationalist Thomas Huxley spent his honeymoon. Huxley told James Knowles that Newman was "the slipperiest sophist I have ever met with." See *Life and Letters of T.H. Huxley* (London, 1913), II, p. 240.

His mother was forever saying prayers for him. Harriet, Newman's eldest sister, told her brother Frank, "Charles is a sore thorn to us: but oh! how much sorer it would be, if he were a rogue or a profligate."[5] Newman's conduct towards him was saintly. He was truly his brother's keeper, helping him with his studies when he was a boy, writing him letters of reference when he needed jobs; hearing out his complaints on those frequent occasions when his affairs were in a muddle; making him generous loans of money for which he expected no repayment. Charles himself was fond of telling Frank, 'John ought to have been a Prince; for he always spends money like a Prince.'"[6] In 1825, Newman secured his brother a good position at the Bank of England for £60 a year. Charles constantly quarrelled with his fellow clerks, even insulting one of the trustees, who happened to have been a good friend of John Newman, Senior.[7] Matters came to a head in 1832 when the Bank suspended Charles for misconduct. But before the Governor could give this most unusual clerk the official axe, Charles sent off a preemptive epistolary salvo:

Friday morning
14 September, 1832
53 Surrey Row

To the Secretary of the Bank,
Sir,

Mr. Bock of the Cash Book Office has called on me at my lodgings and informed me that you wish to see me, when I conclude that I am still a Clerk in the establishment. I suppose certain forms are to be gone through. Now I assure you I am quite afraid of forms and all the holy rules; and I have no doubt you would feel as I do, had you been in my place last Tuesday three weeks. The fact is these forms are like ready made clothes, and do not fit me, and I cannot help it, and I am prepared to tell you or any one else in the establishment, be they who they may, that I think it but fair you should dispense with forms in my case as much as possible, and I had much rather leave the Bank than have my feelings hurt. Having given you this notice as no doubt I have a right to do, I will wait upon you according to the message.

I am, Sir,

Your obedient Servant
(Sd.) C. R. Newman[8]

This gives a good sense of the odd charm of the man, which stemmed from a kind of imperturbable fecklessness. In a letter to his mother, who worried herself sick over her erratic son, he wrote: "I confess I went to sleep three lines back in this letter. I am just waked. But I have received no inspiration in consequence. And so conclude, your loving son, Charles Henry Newman."[9] No sooner was Charles discharged from the bank than Mrs Newman, in a fit of maternal folly, made over £1,000 to him that

---

[5] Francis W. Newman. *Contributions Chiefly to The Early History of the Late Cardinal Newman* (London, 1891), p. 96.
[6] Ibid., pp. 42–3.
[7] Sean O'Faolain. *Newman's Way* (London, 1952), pp. 138–40.
[8] O'Faolain, pp. 191–2.
[9] Ibid., p. 140.

she had intended to leave him at her death. Charles squandered it in 2 months.[10] Periodically, the family wondered if Charles was quite sane. The consensus was that he could not be considered insane. Yet he was so highly eccentric that the distinction must often have seemed moot. George Jacob Holyoake, the social reformer and secularist, who knew both Charles and Frank, recalled how, "Like Charles Lamb's poor sister, Mary, who used to put her strait waistcoat in her basket and go herself to the asylum, when she knew the days of her aberration were approaching, Charles Newman had premonitions of a like kind. He had the thoroughness of thought of his family."[11] Later, from Bonn, whither he had gone to study German literature at Frank's urging, Charles weighed in on the question himself. "My whole malady is founded, rather than received its nourishment from social causes. The state of society in England either makes people mad naturally, or gives them an artificial madness from their efforts to escape from their natural madness. The family of the Newmans is as mad a family as perhaps can be found in that mad country. Frank, the moment he gets out of his line, is the maddest person I am acquainted with. Next to him I rate either you or me, or Owen of Lanark . . ."[12]

Charles Newman fell under the influence of Robert Owen (1871–58) in 1823 when his socialist movement was still taking shape. Starting out with a firm of Manchester cotton-spinners, Owen set up on his own in 1800 when he was given a share of his father-in-law's mills in New Lanark on the Clyde, which he transformed into a paternalist factory, around which he built a village with a hospital and school. He also proposed gathering the poor into what he called "Villages of Cooperation," with the object of instilling in them habits of self-sufficiency and temperance. When William Cobbett reviewed the proposal, he was not impressed: "Mr. Owen's scheme has, at any rate, the recommendation of perfect novelty; for of such a thing as a *community of paupers*, I believe no human being ever before heard. Mr. Owen has provided a hospital and chapel for each of his communities; I wonder that he, who appears to have foreseen every other want, should have forgotten a *madhouse*."[13] Once his schemes had met with modest success in Britain, Owen found an additional audience for them in America. Nine hundred millenarians, feminists, and vagabonds flocked to New Harmony, Indiana to sample the promised benefits of communal life, legalized divorce, and birth control.[14] (Owen regarded traditional marriage, rather as Tolstoy regarded it, as a form of sexual despotism.) The land for New Harmony, for which Owen paid $125,000 in 1824, extended over 20,000 acres and included a village, chapels, four mills, a textile factory, a brewery, and various craft shops.[15] However, by 1827, the community had almost entirely disintegrated. Too many of the brethren bristled at the prohibitions against tobacco and alcohol and none found the dress code tolerable. Women were required to wear knee-length coats over pantaloons and men pantaloons

[10] Ibid., p. 193.

[11] *Bygones*, I, p. 13.

[12] LD, 9:330–1 Charles Newman to JHN (4 May 1843).

[13] W. Cobbett. "The Last Hundred Days of English Freedom" (August 1817) in *Political Works*, v, p. 230.

[14] Boyd Hilton. *A Mad, Bad, and Dangerous People? England 1783–1846* (Oxford, 2006), p. 490.

[15] John F. C. Harrison. *Quest for the New Moral World: Robert Owen & the Owenites in Britain and America* (New York, 1969), p. 164.

buttoned over a boy's jacket without collars, which resembled a kind of fantastic penal dress.[16] Owen tried to set up another community in Texas but the wildcat capitalists there showed him the door. When Owen returned to Britain, he opened Halls of Science in Glasgow, Huddersfield, Macclesfield, and Sheffield, which were designed to inculcate Owen's secularized millenarianism, according to which, as he said himself, "The first coming of Christ was a partial development of Truth to the few . . . The second coming of Christ will make Truth known to the many . . . The time is therefore arrived when the foretold millennium is about to commence."[17] The historian Michael Burleigh nicely describes the Halls as "a fusion of Mechanics Institute and Methodist chapel. They were supposed to afford members a foretaste of the New Moral World, in which dancing would go with free buns and lemonade."[18] Later, Owen would become an avid spiritualist, claiming at the end of his life that he had communicated with Benjamin Franklin, Thomas Jefferson, and the Duke of Kent (who had intended to show Queen Victoria the New Lanark Mills in 1820 but died before they could make the journey together).[19] As Burleigh remarks of Owen's senescent table-tapping, this was "an eccentric fate for the founder of Rational Society."[20]

The letter in which Charles announced that he found Owen more persuasive than St Paul prompted Newman to write seven long letters in response, which eventually filled eight exercise books. The letters began on a note of solicitude. It had been less than a year, in September 1824 that Charles and the other Newman children had lost their father. Before the loss of John Newman, the family had suffered many other trials and Newman recognized that these had seriously rattled his younger brother. "I have long observed and with painful feelings, the effects which trial, disappointment and continual mortifications have had upon you . . . you have a most sensitive and feeling mind, and they have wounded it excessively . . . You have had much to bear, and I am sometimes much affected to think of what you have borne. Do not be too proud to allow me to sympathize with you." The arguments Newman used to parry Charles's objections in 1825 were rooted in reason. Recounting those arguments in a letter of 1830, Newman called Charles's attention to the fact that we necessarily act by consulting probabilities, not proofs—a point to which he would return nearly 50 years later in *A Grammar of Assent* (1870). "Certainty in the business of life," he told Charles, "means a conviction sufficient for practice. You seem to think that no evidence for an alleged fact is certain, which admits of the chance of the fact being otherwise – i.e. you would hold that demonstration alone is certain proof. I differ – and again demand your reasons, and no reasons can I find . . . The world is against you – for every thing we do, is done on probabilities. Even when we trust our senses and memory, we rely on evidence, which, in your own words, 'is not certain and may be false.' No facts are known, no practical matters conducted, on demonstrative proof, which is found in pure mathematics alone and subjects of a similar nature: – there is always a chance of error. It is possible that Charles X is still in France – the fact that

[16] Ibid., p. 187.
[17] Michael Burleigh. *Earthly Powers: The Clash of Religion and Politics in Europe from the French Revolution to the Great War* (London, 2005), p. 240.
[18] Ibid., p. 241.
[19] Elizabeth Longford. *Queen Victoria* (Folio Society, 2007), p. 12.
[20] Burleigh, p. 241.

he is not there admits of a theoretical doubt – yet who practically doubts that he is not there?"[21]

But the issue of evidence was a red herring. It was Newman's contention that Charles, like many who repudiate their Christian faith, attacked Christianity because he objected to the content of Scripture, not because he had found proof that the evidence for that content was unreliable. "A dislike of the contents of Scripture is at the bottom of unbelief," Newman told his brother, "and since those contents must be rejected by fair means or foul, it is plain that in order to do this the evidences must in some sort be attacked . . ."[22] An entire history of nineteenth-century England could be formed around that one insight. Even Charles had admitted, in a letter to his brother, that unbelievers "have been driven to dishonorable shifts, and shuffling uncandid conduct."[23]

If Owen sought to establish an atheist new order based on cooperation between capital and labour, in which capital, playing a paternalist role, would reform and improve labour, Newman tried to warn his brother against the appeal of specious novelty, which could never produce the warrant of tradition. "Alas, how many have been overset by certain fancies, that they had discovered new principles. Do not suppose yourself the first who has imagined truth hid almost from the whole world till he rejected it. Fresh theories of morals and religion are no uncommon thing; every projector flatters himself that now at least he has hit the mark; yet in time the bubbles break and vanish: thus whether your theory be a bubble or not, you have no right to feel confident in its truth from its being different from any theory yet invented."[24] There were clear parallels here to the Jacobin impostures that Burke exposed in his writings on the Revolution in France. Of the French projectors who brought about such lasting mischief, Burke wrote: "They have no respect for the wisdom of others; but they pay it off by a very full measure of confidence in their own. With them it is a sufficient motive to destroy an old scheme of things, because it is an old one. As to the new, they are in no sort of fear with regard to the duration of a building run up in haste; because duration is no object to those who think little or nothing has been done before their time, and who place all their hopes in discovery."[25] Robert Owen proved himself an apt pupil of the Jacobins in boldly pronouncing that "the past ages of the world present the history of human irrationality only, and . . . we are but now advancing towards the dawn of reason, and to the period when the mind shall be born again."[26] Here, too, was a neat formulation of the atheist millenarianism that would be the brainchild of Owen's megalomania.

Newman charged Charles with crediting a rationalism that claimed to know more than it could prove, but at the same time he was careful to stress that he had no proofs of his own to offer for the doctrines of Christianity. "The most powerful arguments for Christianity do not convince, only silence; for there is at the bottom that secret antipathy

---

[21] LD, 2:280 JHN to Charles Newman (19 August 1830).
[22] LD, 1:219 JHN to Charles Newman (24 March 1825).
[23] LD, 1:224 JHN to Charles Newman (14 April 1825).
[24] LD, 1:214 JHN to Charles Newman (3 March 1825).
[25] Edmund Burke. *Reflections on the Revolution in France* (Everyman's Library, 1935), pp. 84–5.
[26] Robert Owen, "An Address to the Working Classes" (1819) from *A New View of Society* (Everyman's Library, 1927), p. 155.

for the doctrines of Christianity, which is quite out of reach of argument. I do not then assert that the Christian evidences are overpowering, but that they are unanswerable; nor do I expect so much to show Christianity true, as to prove it rational; nor prove infidelity false, so much as irrational. When I consider too the present flurried state of your mind to which I alluded in my last letter, I am still more bound to state these preliminary cautions."[27]

Throughout the correspondence, Newman exhibited remarkable patience and tact. He was also candid about the personal stake he took in the issue. "I write from a full heart. You may think me weak and narrow minded; and some about you may reckon every one of my professions necessarily bigoted and interested; but I am your affectionate brother; I am a natural adviser and friend; and if I am right (and I have as much right to bring forward that supposition as you the contrary one) I am a monitor of good, and they the 'bigoted' ministers of error."[28] But Charles was not prepared to listen to reason or even to defend his own assertions and Newman therefore had no alternative but to go on the offensive. "Prejudice may have had great effect in forming your opinion, it cannot sharpen your arguments or blunt mine. I am not allowed to *convince* you, I must now attempt to *confute* you."[29]

But before bringing his guns into position, Newman confessed, "I feel myself unable to commence the attack till I know in what quarter the foe is; and whether I am spending my blows on imaginary assailants, or advancing to the actual seat of war."[30] He therefore asked his brother to answer a number of questions pertaining to the claims of Christianity which would help him ascertain where Charles' real objections lay. Taken together, the questions constitute a sort of catechism for scoffers.

1. Are the Gospels and Acts as ancient as pretended?
2. Were they written by the Jews who had been concerned in the occurrences related?
3. Did the circumstance of the death of Jesus occur as they represented?
4. Was the cause the same?
5. Were any of his miracles believed by the Pharisees etc. to have been really wrought?
6. Is it true that the great men among the Jews constantly opposed his pretensions?
7. Did the people in general, and among them the apostles . . . expect (before his death) a temporal Messiah?
8. If so, why did not Jesus indulge them?
9. Would not his insight into the real meaning of the prophecies . . . inform him that the spiritual Messiah was to be put to death?
10. If so, what tempted him to assume that character?
11. Was his conduct enthusiasm or imposture?

And so on for a total of 35 fairly pointed questions. Against this fusillade, many might have sent up the white flag but Charles dug in. Newman saw an unhappy

---

[27] LD, 1:219 JHN to Charles Newman (24 March 1825).
[28] LD, 1:215 JHN to Charles Newman (3 March 1825).
[29] LD, 1:246 JHN to Charles Newman (26 July 1825).
[30] LD, 1:219 JHN to Charles Newman (24 March 1825).

augury in his brother's obduracy. "I sorrowfully prophesy waverings of opinion, wanderings, uncertainty, continual change. Or if you appear at all consistent, the only maxim in which you will be so (however you may attempt to disguise it from yourself by spreading it out into a system) is, that Christianity is wrong. Almost every other principle will be fluctuating and transitory." Here, is what Pope Benedict XVI called "the tyranny of relativism," which would extend its influence ever more widely throughout the nineteenth century.[31] "But even admitting you arrive at some certainty in principles, peace at least you will never have. In spite of the allsufficiency of knowledge, you will find it a cold and bleak state of things to be left carelessly and as it were unkindly by the God who made you, uncertain why you are placed here, and what is to become of you after death. Truth indeed is to be preferred to comfort; I only warn you not to expect more than you will find. Your greatest peace will be the calm of hopelessness."[32]

This was prescient. Charles's life was indeed one of continual wanderings and uncertainty. After being dismissed from the Bank of England, he quarrelled with his mother and refused to speak with his brothers and sisters. Still, Mrs Newman could not help but take pity on her refractory son, ". . . poor fellow, he seems at war with the whole world, particularly all Christians."[33] Charles' own explanation for his actions was hardly helpful. "In giving up the friendship of my relations," he maintained, "I acted honorably, because I knew I did not respond to their feelings . . . I considered myself as a log round the neck of my family . . . I am not to be pitied. I have chosen my own part and must take the consequences."[34] As it happened, the family was rarely spared the consequences of his folly, especially when he required pecuniary relief. Nevertheless, they never stopped praying for him. In 1834, Mrs Newman wrote her son John, "We must not permit the apparent hopelessness of our efforts to subdue our endeavors. We know not when it may please God to hear our prayers for him, or what trials He may ordain for him or ourselves."[35]

The trials came with what must have seemed tiresome frequency. In 1834, less than 2 months after his mother paid over to him the £1,000 that he was to receive on her death, Charles was found destitute in London at No. 7 Hope Place, Bird Street, West Square by a friend from the Bank named Ellis who informed Newman that he had learnt from neighbours that his brother had been living with a woman, who "not content with depriving him of the various sums sent him by his friends, had actually pawned his very clothes, and with the different sums she obtained in this and other ways, continued in a state of intoxication as long as the money lasted."[36] She must have drunk sumptuously on £1,000. Ellis then paid a visit to the lodgings himself and

---

[31] Homily of Joseph Cardinal Ratzinger, Dean of the College of Cardinals, Mass for the Election of the Supreme Pontiff, St Peter's Basilica, (18 April 2005) "We are building a dictatorship of relativism that does not recognize anything as definitive and whose ultimate goal consists solely of one's own ego and desires."

[32] LD, 1:215 JHN to Charles Newman (3 March 1825).

[33] *Family,* p. 35.

[34] LD, 4:132 Charles Newman to JHN (3 December 1833).

[35] LD, 4:238, See note 3.

[36] LD, 4:133 this comes from JHN's "Memorandum on Charles Newman" (1874).

found there a scene that left him "horror-struck." "In a room, the shutters of which were all but closed, containing not an atom of furniture but one chair, stretched upon a small quantity of straw lay this unfortunate young man with absolutely no other covering than his drawers and shirt . . . while his wife [the woman was not his wife] was decently attired . . . He appeared in no way disconcerted at my unlooked for visit merely apologizing for not having called on me . . . his manners, looks, words, and actions giving . . . proof of insanity . . ."[37] Later Ellis tried to get Charles admitted into St Bartholomew's Hospital but the doctors there, while agreeing that he suffered from some "aberration of intellect," were not convinced that it amounted to insanity.[38]

Perhaps because of Charles's travails, Frank Newman gave a good deal of thought to insanity when he was trying to interest Mussulmen in his religious views. While visiting Aleppo on his missionary expedition, he wrote of how, "madmen are looked on as sacred characters . . . there are no madhouses in the land . . . Certainly in England the results of turning all the mad loose would be awful. But when one sees the entire satisfaction there is here with so ugly and revolting a state of things and the inability people have to conceive the inconvenience of it . . . I am driven to speculate . . . Is insanity excessively rare here, so that outrages, if they occur, are naturally very few? Or is insanity, at its worst, mollified by the respectful treatment which it meets, as vicious horses by kindness? . . . Here is a people without lunatic asylums. Well, their lunatics are few or harmless; what a comfortable coincidence! If insanity among us is caused by strong passions in one class and intoxication in another, while the Turkish populations are nearly free from both . . . it implies a higher average morality. . . . Add to this there are no abandoned women there."[39]

Was the Newman family wrong to consider Charles sane? Probably not: Charles' apathy was more wilful than mad. One reason why he felt no remorse for squandering his inheritance was that he simply refused to take any responsibility for it. By the lights of Owenism, circumstances were to blame, not Charles Newman. On this point, Owen could not have been clearer:

> From the earliest ages it has been the practice of the world to act on the supposition that each individual man forms his own character, and that therefore he is accountable for all his sentiments and habits, and consequently merits reward for some and punishment for others . . . This is not a slight mistake, which involves only trivial consequences; it is a fundamental error of the highest possible magnitude; it enters into all our proceedings regarding man from his infancy; and it will be found to be the true and sole origin of evil. . . . This error cannot much longer exist; for every day will make it more and more evident *that the character of man is, without a single exception, always formed for him . . . by his predecessors . . . they give him . . . his ideas and habits, which are the powers that govern and direct his conduct. Man therefore never did, nor is it possible he ever can*

---

[37] LD, 4:133.
[38] Ibid.
[39] *Sieveking*, pp. 40–1.

form his own character. . . . Inquire of the most learned and wise of the present day, ask them to speak with sincerity, and they will tell you that they have long known the principles on which society has been founded to be false . . . Happily for man this reign of ignorance rapidly approaches to dissolution . . .[40]

After reading this, one sees what it was about Owenism that persuaded Charles to prefer it to St Paul's faith. He saw in Christianity the faith of his predecessors—the faith not only of his brother and his family but of long-established English opinion, to which he would always feel scornfully superior. Accordingly, in Owen's claiming how "the tide of public opinion, in all countries, has been directed by a combination of prejudice, bigotry, and fanaticism . . ." he found an immensely sympathetic point of view.[41] Owenism appealed to Charles's *amour propre*. In adopting Owen's new creed of atheist rationalism, Charles could flatter himself that he was enlightened where his countrymen were mistaken. He could also rest assured that he would escape his older brother's rumored fate. After converting, Newman pointed out how: "Some time since, an American Paper was sent me on some matter or other, and accidentally was an extract from some Liverpool Print, commenting on my conversion, praising me generally, or at least speaking most respectfully, but saying that it was perfectly well known to Mr N's friends that his mind was gone, that a mental alienation rendered his testimony to Catholicity quite worthless etc etc. It was a grave, sleek, imposing lie, which made one smile. People sucked it in greedily and smacked their lips."[42]

That Charles's apathy was not proof of insanity is also clear from his letters. There were times when he could be perfectly lucid. When his mother died in 1836, he wrote movingly to Newman: "How much seed has been sowed in my mother's kindness to me, which has not been reaped either by her or me; yet I am very glad I saw her a few months ago, and that she must have seen the dawn of more amity in me than I have expressed in a long while to her and my family." Speaking of his brothers in the same letter, he wrote: "How painful it is that Frank and you differ so much in opinion, I have no hope that you will ever agree, for there is a fundamental difference in your minds. I wish I had more amity of opinion with yourself, who have acted with such kindness to me . . . I do not mean to say that Frank is positively lowminded, but he is decidedly not high minded, and I believe he does not, nor ever will, do you justice, and perhaps you not him . . . I hope the time may come, when we may meet together in the way you expressed in a letter to me, but I hope Frank may not be excluded . . . Nothing can be more unfortunate than the differences of opinion that has happened between three brothers. You are the last person in the world I ought to have opposed so bitterly . . ."[43] It is noteworthy that in an interpolation to this letter, Newman corrected Charles on the cause of his falling out with Frank—which was prompted by Frank repudiating the Anglican Church and joining the Plymouth Brethren of John Nelson Darby, whom one churchman described as the "Goliath of Dissent,"—but he did not dispute Charles' analysis of their division *per se*.[44] Elsewhere, Newman would write to Frank, apropos

---

[40] Robert Owen. *A New View of Society and Other Writings* (Everyman's Library, 1927), pp. 44–6.
[41] Ibid., p. 46.
[42] LD, 13:72 JHN to Henry Wilberforce (28 February 1849).
[43] LD, 5:315 Charles Newman to JHN (26 June 1836).
[44] ODNB.

Charles, "I do believe him to be very uncomfortable at you and me for not being of one mind in religion. He has spoken so very strongly about it."[45] Indeed, for all of his periodical waywardness, Charles could be very trenchant, especially when speaking of the family. "I knew long ago that there were many evils in life," he wrote John in 1836, "but this one of disunion in our family I hoped to escape . . . Nor am I fond of truth (often it is very harsh) except so far as it produces good; but unity cannot be attained without it, nor can friendship stand on a firm foundation. If any thing could make one sick of life, it is these quarrels. Harriett said, when she called on me in Hackney, that we are all bewitched; we are so."[46]

Once free of Threadneedle Street, Charles set his sights on becoming a teacher. In 1834, he became an usher at a school at Herstmonceux in Sussex, from which he was discharged for biting one of the boys.[47] That same year he took another teaching position at Mr Barnes's, Grove Street, Hackney. In 1835, he moved on to the Rev J. Butt's, Bromley, Kent, where the headmaster gave him a glowing testimonial: "I have formed a very high opinion of Mr. N's moral worth. His habits are altogether studious . . . I conceive him to be a very valuable asset."[48] In 1836, he had taken yet another teaching position at Mr Wick's, Chippenham for 40 guineas a year, which Newman saw as proof that Charles was at least making some attempt "to get on in his profession."[49] Then in 1837 he was at Mr Read's, Stroud, Gloucestershire, from which he wrote Newman: "I was robbed when I was about a mile and a half out of Uxbridge in my way here. But I lost only my hat and a shirt and collar . . . I got off with my watch and money safe . . . But I am not at all discouraged from walking in future . . . it is less dangerous than the stage . . . in London I bought a Sophocles."[50] By the time Charles showed up at Oxford during the long vacation of 1837, he looked a fright and spoke of the Christian faith with pitiable incoherence. To his sister Jemima, Newman wrote: "I cannot quote you what Charles says of his present state of unbelief—he says he does not know whether he believes or not—but then adds something of such a nature as I am sure should have kept him from the Sacrament—In fact he seems to take religion as a medicine, which would be beneficial though he were an atheist."[51] After that awkward meeting, the two brothers only met once more, two years before Charles's death. Later in 1837, Charles took another teaching position; this time with the Rev M. Gibson at Upper Town, Boulogne. After these forays into teaching, Charles might have been tempted to think, for all his atheism, as John Betjeman thought after his school days were over:

> Luxuriating backwards in the bath,
> I swish the warmer water round my legs
> Towards my shoulders, and the waves of heat

[45] LD, 4:329, JHN to Frank W. Newman (7 September 1834).
[46] Martin J. Svaglic. "Charles Newman and his Brothers." *Modern Language Association* 71(3): (June 1956), 380.
[47] LD, 30:351, See note.
[48] LD, 4:134 Memorandum on Charles Newman.
[49] LD, 4:134.
[50] Ibid.
[51] LD, 6:23 JHN to Mrs John Mozley (8 February 1837).

Bring those five years of Marlborough through to me
In comfortable retrospect: 'Thank God
I'll never have to go through those again.'

In 1840, conceding that teaching might not be his métier, Charles rejoined the Owenite socialists, after which, as Newman noted in his Memorandum, he "claimed as a right that we should support him."[52] Charles's illimitable sense of entitlement found ready corroboration in the writings of Owen. A determinist convinced that individual character was shaped by circumstance and that free will and moral responsibility were illusions, Owen saw his socialist communities as engines of a new atheist world order that would help men realize their true untapped potential. For him, religious faith was so much "mischievous irrationalism."[53] The turbulent working man had been given too much religion and it had turned him into a mendacious, thieving, idle sot, intent not on enriching but confounding his employers. The paternalist in Owen wished to remake this unhappy man by weaning him off strong drink, instilling habits of "attention, celerity and order"[54] in him, and encouraging him to forge cooperative ties with his employers.

Charles's defence of Owenism might seem quixotic. After all, he could hardly be said to have had much in common with labourers. Nevertheless, however unstable he might have been in other respects, he never wavered in his zeal for socialism. It became something of a surrogate faith for him. He admitted as much in a letter to John. "You mistake if you think my primary object in connecting myself with the Socialists is any thing else than the recovery of my health. Now conventional society, or very religious society is no society to me. I would as soon live among the Caribs, as among persons who do not aim at least among themselves at justice as a means towards well being in this life for themselves and others. You may think this perverse, nevertheless I state it as a fact. I have often wished I could find some religious party of similar aim . . ." With the exception of the invidious reference to "the Caribs," most socialists would still agree with what Charles has to say here. The search for social justice, after all, does constitue the avowed religion of socialism, even if the search itself produces socal injustice on a massive scale. Still, if Charles was interested in the philosophical claims of Owenism, he also valued its practical benefits. In October of 1840, Charles told John that it was scholarly fatigue that rendered him unemployable: "I read for six days at the rate of 200 lines a day of Aeschylus. In consequence yesterday, I found myself ill . . . The idea of my competing with others is absurd. You cannot expect people affected as I am to act like the rest of the world. I hope you will leave off blaming me."[55] In fact, in 1840 alone, by Charles' own reckoning, John and Frank had supported him to the tune of £59.[56] This was another reason why the determinist theories of Robert Owen were so attractive to Charles: they excused his improvidence.

[52] LD, 4:135 Memorandum on Charles Newman.
[53] E. P. Thompson. *The Making of the English Working Class* (London, 1963), p. 859.
[54] Robert Owen. *A New View of Society* (1813) quoted in E. P. Thompson. *The Making of the English Working Class* (London, 1963), p. 859.
[55] LD, 4:135.
[56] Ibid.

Yet Charles's life could not have been a more resounding confutation of the claim that circumstances determine character. Frank called attention to this in a letter of July 1871 to his friend Anna Swanwick, the English author and feminist, who translated Goethe and Schiller, Tasso and Aeschylus and assisted in the founding of Girton College and Somerville Hall, Cambridge:

> He is a Cynic Philosopher in modern dress, having many virtues, but one ruinous vice, that of perpetual censoriousness, by which he alienates every friend as soon as made, or in the making, by which he ejected himself from all posts of usefulness . . . He has lived now more than thirty years in retirement and idleness. His moral ruin was Robert Owen's Socialism and Atheistic Philosophy . . . His sole pleasure in company seems to be in noting down material for ingenious, impertinent, and insolent fault-finding; hence no one can safely admit him. He formally renounced his mother, brothers and sisters about forty years ago, and wrote to other persons requesting them not to count him a Newman . . . because we were religious and he was an Atheist. He has had all the same dear sweet influences of home as all of us; yet how unamiable and useless has he become! still loving to snarl most at the hands that feed him. Is not this an admonition not to attribute too much to the single cause of home influences, however precious? I shall be happy to attend to your Aeschylus . . .[57]

If Newman's failures came as a result of lack of support for undertakings that were truly on a grand scale—his plan, for example, to create a Catholic University in Dublin that would appeal as much to Irish as to English Catholics or his plan to found an Oratory in Oxford—Charles' failures were the result of bad ideas. Theodore Dalrymple, who worked for years as a psychologist in the Birmingham criminal justice system, has written with cautionary zest about how bad ideas continue to cause mayhem in contemporary society beyond the academy. "The idea that one is not an agent but the helpless victim of circumstances, or of large occult sociological or economic forces," he writes of the bad idea that most stultified Charles Newman, "does not come naturally, as an inevitable concomitant of experience. On the contrary, only in extreme circumstances is helplessness directly experienced in the way the blueness of the sky is experienced. Agency, by contrast, is the common experience of us all. We know our will's free, and there's an end on't. The contrary idea, however, has been endlessly promulgated by intellectuals and academics . . ."[58] And, one might add, utopian socialists. Indeed, in his entry on Owen for the *Oxford Dictionary of National Biography*, Gregory Claeys rightly remarks how "the idea that character was formed by the environment and not the will—perhaps the core assumption of the Enlightenment—was in fact a fundamental one for modern thought," and no one in nineteenth-century England sought to advance it more pertinaciously than Owen, "though contemporaries found its endless repetition tedious."[59]

---

[57] *Sieveking*, pp. 217–18.
[58] Theodore Dalrymple. *Life at the Bottom: The Worldview that Makes the Underclass* (New York, 2001), p. x.
[59] ODNB.

Newman saw the irresponsibility and the dependency that such determinism would breed throughout society as a whole because he saw so clearly how it had bred these things in his brother Charles. He also saw how determinism would redound to the power of the paternalist state by promoting centralization. Writing to the Editor of the *British Magazine* in 1834, he foresaw with remarkable foresight the first stirrings of the British welfare state.

> Certainly, the principle itself [of centralization] is involved in the very notion of government, and no novelty; indeed it seems to be an admitted axiom in politics that, in respect to some branches of national power, as in the executive, a strict centralization is plainly requisite for the well-being of a state, and a division of them among several parties a great evil. Yet this being granted, it seems to have been a characteristic of the British constitution hitherto, whether rightly or wrongly, to view the principle with jealousy, as hostile in its tendency to the liberty of the subject, and to allow each neighbourhood to provide as much as possible for itself; and it is a growing peculiarity of the present age, whether rightly or wrongly, to purchase a respite from present actual evils by the introduction of it into various departments of the body politic to which it was before a stranger. In other words, it has hitherto been the English policy to make the nation the principal, and the government but an adjunct to it; it is now coming into fashion to merge the nation in the government. Many words are not required in proof of this remark; it will be enough to remind the reader, by way of illustration, of the story of the foreigner's surprise on finding Waterloo Bridge was built, not by the government, but by individuals; or, to take a very different instance, that our received English dictionary is the work of an individual, the French dictionary proceeding from the Institute; or that our theatres and travelling are left to private speculation; or that our magistrates are unpaid; or that our East India empire was acquired by a mercantile company. On the other hand, the late numerous Commissions, the Education Board in Ireland, the Metropolitan Police, the Poor Law Amendment Bill, are all evidence of the growing popularity of the centralizing system. This system cannot be denied the praise of introducing vigor, promptitude, and certainty into every department which it enters, while the national principle is un-business-like and cumbrous; and thus it has been the means of throwing us into the strange inconsistency of advocating a principle almost of tyranny, in the management of hitherto private matters, at the very time we were exulting in the triumph of a great Reform measure, which was to supersede the necessity of a government, and to make the House of Commons, and so the people, their own rulers. But in truth the inconsistency is but apparent; the destruction of local influences which centralization involves, and the disorganization of the parliament, as the seat and instrument of the administration, alike tending to the aggrandizement of the executive, as the main-spring of all national power, and virtually identical with the government.[60]

De Tocqueville had seen this same personal irresponsibility at play in *l'ancien regime* before the French Revolution, where "the lord had no longer felt bound by his traditional

---

[60] LD, 4:340 Letter to the Editor of the *British Magazine*, October 1834.

obligations. And no local authority, no poor relief committee or parish council had taken them over. Now that nobody was bound by law to see to the welfare of the poor in rural areas, the central government had, somewhat venturesomely, accepted responsibility for this duty. . . . In short, the central power had taken to playing the part of an indefatigable mentor and keeping the nation in quasi-paternal tutelage."[61] In the spectacle of Charles walking away from his personal responsibilities and delivering himself up to the direction of the Pelagian socialism of Owen, Newman saw a kind of miniature revolution playing out in his own family, with the same harvest of anarchy and apostasy which the Jacobins had reaped from their insurrection.

In the eighth of his Oxford Sermons, "Human Responsibility, As Independent of Circumstances," preached in January of 1832, Newman was clearly, if obliquely, addressing Charles when he reminded his auditors that "it has been always the office of Religion to protest against the sophistry of Satan, and to preserve the memory of those truths which the unbelieving heart corrupts." The truths Newman had in mind could not have been more universal, or more pertinent to his determinist brother: "both the freedom and the responsibility of man;—the sovereignty of the Creator, the supremacy of the law of conscience as His representative within us, and the irrelevancy of external circumstances in the judgment which is ultimately to be made upon our conduct and character."[62] Here was 'tough love' with a wallop. But Newman got tougher still when he set about delineating the psychology of determinism, or, as he called it, "fatalism."

> Fatalism is the refuge of a conscience-stricken mind, maddened at the sight of evils which it has brought upon itself, and cannot remove. To believe and tremble is the most miserable of dooms for an immortal spirit; and bad men, whose reason has been awakened by education, resolved not to be "tormented before their time," seek in its intoxication a present oblivion of their woe. It is wretched enough to suffer, but self-reproach is the worm which destroys the inward power of resistance. Submission alone makes pain tolerable in any case; and they who refuse the Divine yoke are driven to seek a sedative in the notion of an eternal necessity. They deny that they ever could have been other than they are. "What heaven has made me, I must be," is the sentiment which hardens them into hopeless pride and rebellion.[63]

If Charles read this sermon, he left behind no response. Instead, he seemed to go out of his way to personify precisely the "hopeless pride and rebellion" against which his eldest brother warned. In 1841, Newman wrote Jemima: "I am very much perplexed about him, or rather distressed. F[rank] and I—(as you may recollect) agreed to give him £1 a week till Michaelmas—by way of giving him time to look about him for something to do. Up to this time he has done nothing, or rather he sets his face against doing any thing—sends me rigmarole letters about philosophy . . . and more than hints that he has given up religion. He is very intimate with the Socialists, and

[61] Alexis de Tocqueville. *The Old Regime and the French Revolution* (New York, 1955), pp. 40–1.
[62] *US*, p. 101.
[63] Ibid., p. 106.

now does not shrink from the name."[64] Yet it was characteristic of Newman to end his uncompromising sermon with an encouraging summons. "We may amuse ourselves, for a time, with such excuses for sin as a perverted ingenuity furnishes; but there is One who is justified in His sayings, and clear when He judgeth. Our worldly philosophy and our well-devised pleadings will profit nothing at a day when the heaven shall depart as a scroll is rolled together, and all who are not clad in the wedding-garment of faith and love will be speechless. Surely it is high time for us to wake out of sleep, to chase from us the shadows of the night, and to realize our individuality, and the coming of our Judge. 'The night is far spent, the day is at hand,'—'let us be sober, and watch unto prayer.'"[65]

In 1842, Charles decided to go to Bonn to get a degree in German literature on the recommendation of Frank, who told John: "I have heard from a young Englishman at Bonn, that his whole year's expenses there, including lectures, books, and clothes (without traveling) were £50 . . . German Literature is every day more valued. Booksellers and others are constantly needing help in getting up works, from persons who are at once acquainted with German and with Greek and Latin . . . I confess I think this is the only sort of literary work, in which [Charles] might get a permanent maintenance . . . ."[66] It is some measure of Frank's judgement that he should have recommended such a course to his clearly unstable brother. Still, at first, Charles's studies seemed to go well. In 1843, Frank wrote Newman: "I have lately had a letter from Charles—after some anxiety at his long silence. On the whole it is very satisfactory . . . He has come to the conviction that Kant is a quack . . . He expresses some contempt for the puerility of the students. One of them not long back pulled his nose, which obliged Charles to pull his nose in turn; but there the matter dropped."[67] Later, however, matters deteriorated. In 1845, Charles wrote from Berne, "I am as much driven out of Bonn, as if I were driven out with sticks and stones. The students, the noisy part of them, are the masters here. I have incurred their displeasure . . . The Germans, the more I see of them . . . the less I admire them. It is great unmanliness to allow children, for such the students mentally are, to give the tone to society, and to rule public opinion . . . They are destitute of blackguardism, and they are not fierce and overbearing, but such unmanly nonentities I never yet met. I leave it to Frank to admire their 'moral refinement'."[68] Although it is not clear from Charles's letter what exactly provoked the students to run him out of town, his unconcealed disdain for them was doubtless a factor. In the same letter, Charles made no bones about his future prospects. While he thought he might earn his living by his pen, he wanted to make sure that Newman realized that this might not be possible and in that event, "you and Frank ought to look in the face my going to my parish."[69] Such minatory language could not have been easy to bear. Yet Newman's heart must have gone out to his brother when he heard of his continual scrapes. "As I have been in the arrest house at Coblenz for six days," Charles wrote him from Berne, "I had come from Bonn without a pass to Audernach, and was conducted from Audernach

---

[64] LD, 8:254 JHN to Mrs John Mozley (26 August 1841).
[65] *US*, p. 113.
[66] LD, 8:302 Frank Newman to JHN (19 October 1841).
[67] LD, 9:304 Frank Newman to JHN (10 April 1843).
[68] LD, 10:487 Charles Newman to JHN (9 January 1845).
[69] Ibid., p. 487.

to Coblenz (11 miles) in manacles, I know what prison fare or workhouse fare is, and what circumstances and society are, which are usually considered as degrading; and in respect to the fare, it was much better and more wholesome than I got in Bonn; and as to the society, one can find much better people there, than I have found any where in Bonn. It is necessary that my relations should familiarize themselves with this idea. It was necessary that I should have all my things sold, as a protest against being obliged to pay the landlords. Thus, I lost all my best clothes . . . the watch you gave me . . . the great coat which Frank gave me . . . . I have upwards of six Napoleons in my pocket."[70] Self-pity may not be the most heroic of traits but one would have to be very hard-hearted to blame Charles for indulging in it here.

If Newman was never less than *en prince* when it came to monetary support for his often indigent brother throughout his long, chequered life, Harriett never withheld her loyal love, even if, as here, she could not resist giving her eldest brother a gratuitous dig. "I think of late years Charles has struggled hard," she wrote Jemima in 1845, "and cannot now help what he is—so long as he is tolerable I will not blame him. I always thought it a mistake to send him on his own resources to a strange country. It seemed to me a means of making the name notorious through Europe, as it is already through England." Still, she showed practical good sense as well as love when she concluded, "For our own comfort I am sure the only way is to club together and say, 'there is so much for you and we will do more.' This legacy sunk for him would have saved £15 p.a., now it might as well have been thrown into the sea."[71]

In 1853, Charles retired to Tenby, to Alma Cottage, Marsh Road. For the rest of his life, he rarely chose to see visitors, preferring the society of his landlady, Mrs Eliza Griffiths and her daughter, Amy, who treated him with assiduous kindness. The view Newman took of his brother's long retirement showed what dismay their divisions had made: "He has given up the very thought of me, as if wiped out of the world, since I have become a Catholic."[72] When Frank wrote him in 1855, inquiring what they should do about their impossible brother, Newman answered with a question of his own, charged with exasperation: "How can I prescribe in a case, where 18 years have elapsed since I saw the patient, and 30 years since I could be said in any sense to know him?"[73]

Still, neither divisions nor estrangement stopped Newman from loving his brother. In 1862, he wrote Mrs Griffiths a letter that attests to this love.

The Oratory, Birmingham, March 12th, 1862

Madam,

I am the brother to Mr. Newman who lodges, I understand, at your father's, Mr. Phillips. I hear from my brother Professor Newman a very serious account of his health. I thank you the kind interest you have taken in his condition.

Whatever is necessary for his comfort he ought to have, and it will be a great point indeed if you could persuade him to see a doctor.

---

[70] Ibid., pp. 487–8.
[71] *Family*, pp. 15–16.
[72] LD, 4:135.
[73] LD, 16:464 JHN to Mrs John Mozley (10 May 1855).

I would come to him at once did I not think that in his present weak state it would make him angry and do harm, not good.

But what I especially write to you about is to beg you value the soul of a fellow creature, to bring before him the Sacred Name of Jesus. Perhaps he would listen to a woman when he would not listen to a man, much less to a professed minister.

Provided he would allow that sacred name to be brought before him I make no objection whoever does it, though I should myself wish the Catholic Priest to be the person. Of Protestants, I should prefer the Established Clergyman of the place. But I think it would be a very good thing if he would allow you to read to him the 53rd chapter of the Prophet Isaiah.

Excuse the freedom of this letter,

I am, Madam, Yours faithfully, John H. Newman[74]

Here, it is striking that Newman should have recommended that Mrs Griffiths arrange to have the 53rd chapter of Isaiah read to Charles because this was the same passage that their father had urged Newman to read to him when he was dying.

When Charles died in March 1884, Newman wrote Anne Mozley, "He must have had some curious natural gifts, for eccentric, violent and self-willed as he was, he attached to him the mother and daughter with whom he lodged, and, the mother having died, the daughter has refused a nurse and has nursed him day and night through his last illness. It is more than sixty years that he embraced and acted on the principles of Owen the Socialist."[75]

Owen's movement, so promising in the early 1820s, fizzled out in the mid-1840s when such bolder visionaries as Friedrich Engels and the Chartists began calling for more organized tactics to combat the capitalists. Class conflict, not class cooperation, was the new battle cry. Nevertheless, despite his signal contributions to the cause of socialism, Owen would always have a mixed reception across the political and philosophical spectrum. G. M. Young saw the Owenite utopia in terms of "bold peasants, rosy children, smoking joints, games on the green—Merrie England, in a word, engaged in a flourishing export trade in coal and cotton."[76] E. P. Thompson considered Owen "not the first of the modern Socialist theorists . . . but one of the last of the eighteenth-century rationalists. . . . However admirable . . . as a man, he was a preposterous thinker. . . . There comes through his writings not the least sense of the dialectical processes of social change, of 'revolutionizing practice.'"[77] Clearly, for Thompson, Owen lacked the requisite commitment to confiscation without which socialism could not prevail. In the Owenite earthly paradise, private property would not be put up for grabs. This is doubtless why Engels considered Owen "hopeless."[78] In the old *Dictionary of National Biography*, Leslie Stephen was also dismissive, though more on class than ideological grounds, referring to Owen as "one of those intolerable bores who are the salt of the earth."[79] In *The Idea of Poverty: England in the Early*

---

[74] LD, 32: 225–6 JHN to Mrs Griffiths (12 March 1862).
[75] LD, 30:335 JHN to Anne Mozley (23 March 1884).
[76] G. M. Young. *Portrait of an Age: Victorian England* (Oxford, 1953), p. 19.
[77] E. P. Thompson. *The Making of the English Working Class* (London, 1963), p. 865.
[78] Friedrich Engels quoted in Boyd Hilton. *A Mad, Bad, and Dangerous People? England 1783–1846* (Oxford, 2006), p. 491.
[79] Leslie Stephen quoted in Hilton, p. 491.

Industrial Age (1984), Gertrude Himmelfarb came to Owen's defence, seeing him and his movement as a preferable alternative to the more radical, violent programme of the Chartists. For her, "social harmony, communality, rationality, and morality . . . were at the heart of the Owenite enterprise."[80] For Michael Burleigh, Owen might have decided by the age of 10 that "all theologies were erroneous," but in the atheist schemes of his adulthood he would only succeed in replacing the genuine faith of Christianity with various gimcrack pseudo-faiths—faith in collectivism, faith in rationality, faith in what he called "community."

> Community does all possess
> That can to man be given;
> Community is happiness,
> Community is heaven.[81]

This faith in community was driven by contempt for the family and of the parish that honoured the independence of the family. In his study of Owenism in Britain and America, John Harrison recognized the fundamental importance of the Owenite campaign against the family. For Owen, the family was "the main bastion of private property and the guardian of all those qualities of individualism and self-interest to which he was opposed: 'separate interests and individual family arrangements with private property are essential parts of the existing irrational system. They must be abandoned with the system. And instead thereof there must be scientific associations of men, women, and children, in their usual proportions, from about four or five hundred to about two thousand, arranged to be as one family.' The fragmentation and disharmony which Owenites deplored in competitive society they attributed largely to the institution of the private family."[82] Thus, Owen regarded family, not class, as the great cause of discord in society, anticipating the view of Sir Edmund Leach (1910–89), the celebrated social anthropologist who once gave out that "Far from being the basis of the good society, the family, with its narrow privacy, and tawdry secrets, is the source of all of our discontents."[83] Marx and Engels might have deplored Owen's neglect of the class struggle but they applauded his readiness to dismantle the family. Harrison usefully itemized what Owen found objectionable about the family. "Protected from the world at large by strong walls of legal and religious custom the family seemed to him an autonomous and alien element in society. It served to isolate men from each other, and to breed loneliness and self-centeredness. Moreover it was an organ of tyranny, by which the wife was subjected to, and in fact made the property of her husband. She was condemned to a life of petty domestic drudgery and endless child-bearing . . . Community was an attempt to remedy this failure of the family."[84] Judging from the frequency with which Charles

---

[80] Gertrude Himmelfarb. *The Idea of Poverty: England in the Early Industrial Age* (London, 1984), p. 239.
[81] Burleigh, p. 240.
[82] J. F. C. Harrison. *Robert Owen and the Owenites in Britain and America* (London, 1969), pp. 59–60. The quote is from Owen's *Book of the New World* (London, 1844), p. 48.
[83] See BBC Reith Lectures for 1967, reprinted in the *Listener*.
[84] Harrison, p. 60.

quarrelled with his own family, Owen's aversion to the family might have particularly appealed to him.

The contemporary response to Owen and his movement was more divided still. In 1822, William Hazlitt walked 34 miles to New Lanark to see Owen's new social order in action, with the idea of writing an essay about it, but abandoned the project after encountering what he described as "its deadly monotony."[85] Henry Hetherington, the Chartist, gave his predecessor in the fight against Old Corruption full marks. In his last will and testament, he wrote: "These are my views and feelings in quitting an existence that has been chequered with the plagues and pleasures of a competitive, scrambling, selfish system; a system by which the moral and social aspirations of the noblest human beings are nullified by incessant toil and physical deprivations; by which, indeed, all men are trained either to be slaves, hypocrites, or criminals. Hence my ardent attachment to the principles of that great and good man—ROBERT OWEN."[86] John Keble took a rather less approving view. On 13 January 1840, he wrote: "Those dreadful Socialists have commenced an establishment within five miles of Romsey, and I hear that they have sermons every Sunday expressly to mock and blaspheme the Text which they select. Ought the magistrates to be applied to in such a case? or ought one to try and get the people to treat them as excommunicates? I think some thing of the latter kind might be done, and would have the collateral good effect of showing the people the meaning and use of excommunication."[87] Keble was referring to the Owenite community, Harmony Hall, Queenwood, Hampshire.[88]

Newman agreed with Keble. In his sermon "Faith and the World" (1838), Newman might have been addressing the antagonism that the world has always shown faith, but he clearly meant some of his critique to apply to the Owenite atheist utilitarianism that had so thoroughly muddled his brother.

> Another consideration which the world urges in its warfare against religion . . . is that religion does not bring the elementary and existing nature of man to its highest perfection, but thwarts and impairs it, and provides for a second and new nature. It is said, and truly, that religion treats the body hardly, and is severe with the soul. How different is the world, which conceives that the first object of life is to treat our inferior nature indulgently, that all methods of living are right which do this, and all wrong which do not! Hence men lay it down, that wealth is the measure of all good, and the end of life; for a state of wealth may be described as a state of ease and comfort to body and mind. They say that every act of civil government is wrong, which does not tend to what they thus consider to be man's happiness; that utility and expedience, or, in other words, whatever tends to produce wealth, is the only rule on which laws should be framed; that what tends to higher objects is not useful or expedient; that higher objects are a mere dream; that the only thing substantial is this life, and the only wisdom, to cherish and enjoy it. And they are

---

[85] William Hazlitt quoted in Stanley Jones. *Hazlitt: A Life* (London, 1989), p. 327.
[86] Henry Hetherington quoted in E. P. Thompson. *The Making of the English Working Class* (London, 1963), p. 887.
[87] See John Keble quoted in LD, 7:244, Note 2.
[88] See LD, 7:244, Note 2 and Harrison, pp. 216–19.

so obstinate in this their evil view of things, that they will not let other people take their own view and rest in it; but are bent on making all men (what they call) happy in their way. In their plans of social and domestic economy, their projects of education, their mode of treating the poor, the one object which they think sufficient for happiness is, that men should have the necessaries of life according to their condition. On the other hand, they think that religion in all its duties clashes with this life, and is therefore unnatural. Almsgiving they think the virtue of a barbarous or half-civilized or badly-managed community. Fasting and watching are puerile and contemptible, for such practices interfere with nature, which prompts us to eat and sleep. Prayer again is a mere indolence. It is better, they say, to put the shoulder to the wheel, than to spend time in wishing it to move. Again, making a stand for particular doctrines is thought unnecessary and unmeaning, as if there were any excellence or merit in believing this rather than that, or believing any thing at all.[89]

In 1840, Newman included Owen and his socialist followers in what he saw as a new "league of evil" working to undermine faith in Christianity. In this league he grouped Thomas Carlyle, Dr Arnold and his Latitudinarian followers, Henry Hart Milman, whose *History of Christianity* (1840) he reviewed at length in the *British Critic*, faulting its Socinianism, the political economists (especially Nassau William Senior, who had been one of Whately's pupils) "who *cannot* accept (it is impossible) the Scripture rules about almsgiving, renunciation of wealth, self-denial etc.," and geologists like Charles Lyell, whose *Principles of Geology* (1830–33) undermined confidence in the Biblical account of creation and set the stage for the evolutionary theories of Darwin and others.[90] In February, 1840, Newman wrote his sister Jemima:

I begin to have serious apprehensions lest any religious body is strong enough to withstand the league of evil, but the Roman Church. At the end of the first Millenary it withstood the fury of Satan—and now the end of a second is drawing on. It has *tried* strength; what it *has* endured during these last centuries! and it is stronger than ever! We on the other hand [that is to say, the Anglican Church] have never been tried and come out of trial without practical concessions. I cannot see that we can sustain the assault of the foe. We are divided among ourselves, like the Jews in the siege. So that it seems to me that we are coming on a great encounter between infidelity and Rome, and we should be smashed between them.[91]

In a later Memorandum, written in 1874, Newman wrote at length about the brother whose flaws of character were so terribly compounded by the destructive principles of Owenism.

My dear brother Charles, who has now for fifty years given us so much trouble, has had far more serious disadvantages in the way of his success in life than most men.

---

[89] *SD*, pp. 86–7.
[90] LD, 7:245 JHN to Mrs John Mozley (25 February 1840).
[91] Ibid.

He at length felt them so keenly himself that he thought it a reason for giving up the attempt to support himself and a claim in justice upon us to support, just as if he were a cripple or bedridden. Hence his attraction from the age of 21 or 22 to the teaching and views of the Socialists.

It was at this very early age that my Father gave it to us as his distinct judgment, that Charles would never make his way in the world – and so it has proved. From the time of my Father's death down to this time, and doubtless till his own death, he has been and will be mainly supported by his brothers. Of late years he has been, and is to be in future, supported wholly by Frank. From 1825 to 1841 he partly supported himself.

His abilities are more than ordinary. He had a good classical education, and from a youth knew French and German, and acquainted himself with the literature of both those languages. He translated various of the Poems of Schiller and others into English verse. He had a turn for philosophical research. As to his ethical characteristics, he has ever shown himself upright, sensitively honest, generous, openhanded, and affectionate. What has led to his aimless, profitless, forlorn life, has been in the first place his preposterous pride and want of common sense . . . next . . . to what otherwise would have excited a kind interest in those whom he fell in with, his deficient command of his own faculties, so as to remind me of the old man introduced into Romola, whose memory and mind gave way suddenly whenever he had come to the point of reaching to some decisive act.[92] This natural misfortune would lead men to pity and love him even with tenderness, did he not with a morbid selfconsciousness sternly refuse to be comforted, considering sadness to be a womanish weakness, and on the contrary break out into acts of wildness and cruelty, chiefly towards his relations, into mad acts, as a relief to himself of the irritation, the fierce indignation he has felt at his own distressing impotence of mind. No wonder that at times he has seemed to his friends to be mad actually . . . though twice in 1834 and 1845, when a medical judgment was taken on the point, it was to the effect that no restraint could legally be put on his liberty. Yet, in spite of this, he has attached strangers to him, whenever he has been with them long enough to be known. Mr Ellis, who knew him at the Bank, took great interest in his misfortunes . . . and Mrs Griffiths in whose house he has lodged at Tenby these last 16 years, is both greatly attached to him and shows a profound respect for his talents and learning. One great point in his favour is his gentleness and calmness of demeanour, which both surprises and wins those who come across him. He will argue with great fairness and moderation as well as clearness of intellect.[93]

---

[92] Here, Newman refers to the irresoluteness of Baldassarre in George Eliot's *Romola* (1863), which does remind one of Charles. "Along with the passionate desire for vengeance which possessed him had arisen the keen sense that his power of achieving the vengeance was doubtful. . . . He was not mad; for he carried within him that piteous stamp of sanity, the clear consciousness of shattered faculties: he measured his own feebleness. With the first movements of vindictive rage awoke a vague caution, like that of a wild beast that is fierce but feeble—or like that of an insect whose little fragment of earth has given way, and made it pause in a palsy of distrust." See *Romola* (London, 1910), p. 291.

[93] LD, 1:182–3 This is from JHN's "Memorandum on Charles Newman," 1874.

That last observation is important because, while Newman was prepared to acknowledge his brother's "great fairness," "moderation," and "clearness of intellect" as points in his favour, he nonetheless recognized that they were not enough to enable him to embrace the love of God without which he would never find happiness or peace. "I consider the rejection of Christianity to arise from a fault of the heart, not of the intellect," Newman told Charles when he was 23 in that long-ago series of letters; "unbelief arises, not from mere error of reasoning, but either from pride or sensuality."[94] For Newman, atheism was not an alternative to belief but a failure of faith. When his old Oriel colleague Blanco White's descent into scepticism became clear after the publication of his autobiography, Newman did not mince his words.

> B. White's Autobiography . . . is the most dismal horrible work I ever saw. He dies a Pantheist denying that there is an ultra-mundane God, apparently denying a particular Providence, doubting, to say the least, the personal immortality of the soul, meditating from Marcus Antonius, and considering that St. Paul's epistles are taken from the Stoic philosophy. As to Christianity he seems thoroughly to agree with Strauss, and rejects the gospels as historical documents. Yet his Biographer actually calls him in his last moment a *Confessor*—confessor to what? not to any opinion, any belief whatever—but to the Search after truth; ever wandering about and changing, and therefore great. Is this the end of Life? Can there be a greater paradox than this? But what a view does it give one of those Unitarians and *id genus omne* ["and all their ilk"]. They really do think it is no harm being an Atheist, so that you are sincerely so, and do not cut people's throats and pick their pockets.[95]

In trying to understand Newman's response to Charles's apostasy (and indeed to that of his younger brother Frank), it is necessary to appreciate that Newman was not convinced of the shibboleths of secular humanism. He did not hold that the only way to treat different beliefs is to treat them as equally true or, in effect, equally false. For Newman, as for Jacques Maritain, truth is the lifeblood of human fellowship. As Maritain wrote in *On The Use of Philosophy* (1961), those who would make "relativism, ignorance, and doubt a necessary condition for mutual toleration . . . shift their right feelings about the human subject—who must be respected even if he is in error— from the subject to the object; and thus they deprive man and the human intellect of the very act—adherence to the truth—in which consists both man's dignity and reason for living."[96] Truth will make for unpleasantness at times—or, as in the case of the Newman siblings, painful estrangement—but that is why we must be willing

---

[94] LD, 1:219 JHN to Charles Newman (24 April 1825) Owen Chadwick, speaking of Isaac Williams' tract on reserve (Tract 80) wrote: "The doctrine of reserve, though much abused and misunderstood at the time, lies near the heart of Tractarian thought; partly because its connexion with Keble's own stamp of character is so intimate, and partly because it is inseparable from the doctrine that a right state of heart is the safeguard of faith." See Owen Chadwick. *The Spirit of the Oxford Movement* (Cambridge, 1990), p. 35 What Chadwick does not acknowledge is that Newman had arrived at this conviction years before the Tracts were begun in 1833, which his letters to Charles demonstrate.

[95] LD, 10: 640 JHN to Henry Wilberforce (27 April 1847).

[96] Jacques Maritain. *On the Use of Philosophy* (Princeton, 1961), p. 23.

to exercise charity. "The conviction each of us has, rightly or wrongly, regarding the limitations, deficiencies, errors of others does not prevent friendship between minds," Maritain wrote:

> In such a fraternal dialogue, there must be a kind of forgiveness and remission, not with regard to ideas—ideas deserve no forgiveness if they are false—but regard to the condition of him who travels the road at our side . . . We can render judgment concerning ideas, truths, or errors; good or bad actions; character, temperament . . . But we are utterly forbidden to judge the innermost heart, that inaccessible center where the person day after day weaves his own fate and ties the bonds binding him to God. When it comes to that, there is only one thing to do and that is to trust in God. And that is precisely what love for our neighbor prompts us to do.[97]

This is why when Frank Newman succumbed to scepticism, Newman wrote: "His joining the Unitarians is now in the Papers. The Unitarians are pious Deists now— believing in our Lord as an eminent teacher, greater, but not in a higher sense, than Socrates. Humanly speaking, there he will remain, unless, when death comes, God has mercy upon him, and the Saviour whom he has disowned. For that great Mercy one must pray."[98] Later, he would encounter this same Unitarianism in his nephew John Rickards Mozley. And Newman's response to Frank would be the same response that he would make to Charles and his nephew: he would never stop praying for them.

It is remarkable here and in his response to Blanco White's embrace of scepticism that Newman should have made reference to classical authors, whose works were so central to the education of the men of the nineteenth century. Indeed, Charles would rarely be without a copy of Aeschylus or Sophocles. Of course, many in the nineteenth century would attempt to reduce Christ, whom St Cyprian called

> King of the saints,
> invisible Word of the Father most High,
> wisdom's Prince, Ground of exertion, eternal Joy;
> Jesus, Saviour of this mortal race . . .[99]

to a kind of parity with the sages of antiquity. For the student of the Fathers in Newman, as well as the classicist, this was as false to Christ as to those who lacked the Revelation of Christ.

In 1873, Newman sent a brilliant letter to William Leigh, Junior, who succeeded to Woodchester Park on his father's death and sent two of his sons to the Oratory School, which put the terrible pain Newman felt with regard to his brother's apostasy in some historical perspective.

> Our Lord had a full knowledge and love of fallen man. He came to save that which was lost. And St Paul had that love according to his measure after Him – and

---

[97] Maritain, pp. 35–6.
[98] LD, 28:112 JHN to Mrs John Mozley (10 September 1876).
[99] *Pedagogus* 3:12 in A. Hamman, O. F. M. *Early Christian Prayers*, trans. Walter Mitchell (London, 1961), p. 51.

so the great missionaries, as St Francis Xavier. We may gain from the classics, especially from the Latin, a good deal, in the way of that knowledge, both of man and of God. The poems of Horace, I grant, are most melancholy to read – but they bring before us most vividly and piteously, our state by nature, they increase in us a sense of our utter dependence and natural helplessness, they arm us against the fallacious promises of the world, especially at this day, the promises of science and literature to give us light and liberty. It is most piercingly sad to observe how the heathen writers yearn for some unknown good and higher truth and cannot find it – how Horace, in particular, tries to solace himself with the pleasures of sense, and how stern a monitor he has within him, telling him that Death is coming. Lucretius is another author teaching still more solemnly the same awful lesson. "We should be happy," he says, "were it not for that dreadful sense of Religion, which we all have, which poisons all our pleasures. I will get rid of it." But he could not . . . and he destroyed himself. Who can but pity such a race – so great and so little! Who does not recognize the abyss of misery which lies in that wound which sin has made in us! Who does not begin to see from such a spectacle, the Love of the Eternal Father, who felt it in fullness, and came to die for His dear rebellious children![100]

Two years before Charles' death, Newman made the journey to Tenby to visit his brother for what would be the last time. In a biographical sketch to a collection of rambling articles that Charles submitted to George Jacob Holyoake's *The Reasoner* between 1860 and 1861, J. M. Wheeler wrote how "It must have been a strange meeting, and one worthy the brush of a great artist. Surely in all England there were not two men of eighty whose thoughts were so divergent or two brothers whose lives were so diversified. The one a saintly cardinal, called by the Pope the Light of England, who, by his rare urbanity, had gained the respect of all, replete with all that should accompany old age—as honor, love, obedience, troops of friends: the other, fallen, too, into the sere and yellow leaf [but] . . . poor, solitary, unknown and despised, a scorn and wonderment to his nearest neighbors."[101]

When Charles died, Newman paid for his tomb in the Anglican cemetery overlooking the bay and what Arnold called "the unplumb'd salt, estranging sea," and chose for the inscription,

> Domine, misericordia tua in seculum,
> Opera manuum tuarum ne despicias.
>
> "O Lord, of Thy eternal mercy
> Despise not this work of Thy hands."

---

[100] LD, 26:389 JHN to William Leigh, Junior (24 November 1873).
[101] See J. M. Wheeler, "Biographical Sketch" in Charles Robert Newman. *Essays in Rationalism* (London, 1891), p. 16.

4

Frank Newman and the Search for Truth

"I have been reading . . . admirable sermons by Dr. Stanley and an admirable letter of his to the Bishop of London . . . There is also an admirable preface of Dean Milman's to a new edition of the History of the Jews *which I will send to you, as soon as I can get another copy. I am much occupied with all this searching after truth."*
—Queen Victoria to her daughter Vicky (26 May 1863)

Looking back on his younger brother's life in 1886, Newman wrote a mutual friend: "I sometimes could have cried on reading his old letters of 50 and 60 years ago—He was a thorough going Evangelical, or rather I should say deeply and fervently Christian, except there was just one thing which he revolted from more than he loved Our Lord, and that was the Sacramental principle. Now his religion seems to me as superficial as it was then deep."[1] It was ironic that Newman should have made Richard Holt Hutton, the editor of *The Spectator* the recipient of this confidence because Hutton's course had been the opposite of Frank's: He began a Unitarian and ended an Anglican. When Newman claimed that it was the "sacramental principle" that turned Frank against the Christian faith, he was being selective. After Frank finished questioning what he found dubious about Christianity, there was little left of the faith that he considered tenable. This being the case, Newman questioned whether his brother truly understood the differences that separated them. "Of course there was a 'vast chasm' in religion between my brother and me; but neither his memory nor his insight into my mind was such as to enable him to say what that chasm was. My own testimony is that it lay in such questions as Baptismal Regeneration, Infant Baptism, and a Divinely-appointed Church, its privileges and gifts." What stuck in Newman's own memory—he wrote this in 1883, at the end of his life—was something his brother had told him years before, "that he would rather say that the Apostles were mistaken than that Baptism conveyed Regeneration. That is a chasm indeed."[2] Yet Frank prided himself on being what he called a "searcher after truth," and even faulted Newman for not undertaking such a search himself.[3] According to Frank, his brother "seems never to have known what it is to search after truth. How else could he be ignorant that the searcher after truth seeks for evidence, and constantly sacrifices Prepossessions and his own Will in

---

[1] LD, 31:126 JHN to Richard Holt Hutton (15 March 1886).
[2] LD, 30:233 JHN to The Editor of the Fortnightly Review (14 June 1883).
[3] *Sieveking*, p. 346.

the search?"[4] Newman acknowledged that evidence might be taken into account in considering the claims of faith, but he put it into perspective. "If Revelation has always been offered to mankind in one way, it is in vain to say that it ought to have come to us in another. If children, if the poor, if the busy, can have true Faith, yet cannot weigh evidence, evidence is not the simple foundation on which Faith is built. If the great bulk of serious men believe, not because they have examined evidence, but because they are disposed in a certain way,—because they are 'ordained to eternal life,' this must be God's order of things."[5] By the same token, "A mutilated and defective evidence suffices for persuasion where the heart is alive; but dead evidence, however perfect, can but create a dead faith."[6] In Frank's claiming that the search for truth had required him to sacrifice his prepossessions, Newman saw an idle boast. If one of those prepossessions had been his Christian faith, what had Frank gained? Frank might have countered, as he put it in his spiritual autobiography, *Phases of Faith* (1850), that "If following truth must bring us to Socianianism, let us by all means become Socinians . . . Surely we do not love our doctrines more than the truth, but because they are the truth . . ."[7] Here was an essential difference between the brothers. Frank might imagine that truth and Socinianism could be one and the same; Newman held that they were categorically different. Yet this and many other differences gave rise to many false comparisons. At Frank's funeral, seven years after Newman's death, the Rev Temperley Grey observed, "Without depreciating in the least his illustrious brother, it may be said that while the one was a saint in the cloister, the other was a saint in the very thick of life's battle."[8] The suggestion that Newman had spent 52 years in Edgbaston in a cloister would have baffled his many parishioners and friends, not to mention the students and parents attached to the Oratory School. The *Morning Leader* made an equally ill-informed comparison, claiming that Newman was a "spiritual Tory," while Frank was a "spiritual radical."[9] The novelist William Makepeace Thackeray certainly knew Tories well enough to know that Newman was not one of their number, spiritually or otherwise.[10] In *Pendennis* (1849), he showed that what divided the brothers was not their station in life or their presumed political leanings but truth. "The truth, friend!" one of the novel's characters exclaims, "Where is the truth?"[11]

No proper comparison between the brothers can be made without understanding where each located that disputed article. After trying unavailingly to reason his apostate brother Charles into reconsidering the claims of Christianity, Newman chose to take a different tack with his younger brother. He pointedly ended a letter to Frank by assuring him that "I have written this not as thinking to convince you . . . but resolved not to let an opportunity pass of declaring to you my sentiments . . ."[12] In

---

[4] *Contr*, p. 57.
[5] "Love the Safeguard of Faith against Superstition" (1839) in *US*, p. 161.
[6] "Faith and Reason, Contrasted as Habits of Mind" (1839) in *US*, p. 142.
[7] *Phases*, pp. 70–1.
[8] *Sieveking*, p. 345.
[9] Ibid., p. 345.
[10] Avery Dulles countenanced this wild error when he claimed that "With respect to the political order, Newman was a staunch conservative, a Tory of Tories . . ." See Dulles *John Henry Newman* (London, 2002), p. 162.
[11] W. M. Thackeray. *The History of Pendennis* (Penguin, 1994), p. 801.
[12] LD, 2:184 JHN to FWN (1830).

another letter, he wrote: "I never had an idea in writing to make you 'embrace my views.' It is not worth while going into my meaning at length; but it is one thing not to aim at persuading, and another to put stumbling blocks in the way."[13] This was in keeping with his *University Sermons,* in which he had declared that "the influence of Truth in the world at large . . . [comes of] *the personal influence,* direct and indirect, of those who are commissioned to teach it."[14] Still, Frank confessed that his brother's personal influence often simply baffled him: "I could not guess what made his sense of Truthfulness so different from mine," he wrote, "and if forced to clash with him face to face, Reconciliation, I felt, would never in our life be possible."[15] In Frank's opposition to the doctrines of Christianity, Newman came to see the psychology of apostasy, with all its characteristic contempt for the miraculous and the traditional. Frank, for his part, thought his brother a sectarian fanatic. Such a profound misreading of his Catholic faith dismayed Newman, but it also prepared him for the "spiritual epidemic" that would unsettle the faith of so many in nineteenth-century England. As he informed Maria Giberne in a letter of 1876, "Poor Frank has been here – very gentle, sweet, and nice – but I fear he does not consider our Lord more than a good man – and has no scruple in criticising His words and deeds. It is a spiritual epidemic, which, in one shape or another, is going abroad."[16] If Newman saw in Frank a susceptibility to the same unbelief that unsettled so many of his contemporaries, Frank saw in Newman a personal influence that misled as much as it inspired. Looking back on their differences, Frank recalled how "My brother's very acute mind was evidently that of a barrister, not of a philosopher or searcher for truth. But his dash and generosity gave him wonderful power with young men. His scorn of worldliness and meanness, his contempt of the race for promotion in the Church, his claim that each shall lay down his interest on the altar of the Church (especially for beautiful church edifices), were all new to dons of Oxford at that time. But not to see that a sacerdotal system was that of Paganism and Judaism, and the very reverse of what Jesus taught, was in those days to me an inexplicable blindness in a learned and acute young clergyman."[17] In this chapter, I shall revisit Frank's life and work to show how his search for the truth differed from his brother's and how such irreconcilable differences impelled Newman to answer what St Francis de Sales called the "call of charity."

Born in 1805, Frank was a hearty, healthy, intelligent child. He was also the handsomest of the three Newman brothers, with jet black hair and bright cerulean eyes, though later in life, as a bust in University College shows, he came to resemble an American cigar Indian. Still, according to his good friend George Jacob Holyoake (1817–1906), the social reformer and founder of Secularism, Frank "had classical features, a placid, clear, and confident voice, and an impressive smile which lighted up all his face."[18] At Ealing School, where he followed his brothers, he was captain of the school and delighted in games. "Our playground was meadow land," he recalled,

---

[13] LD, 7:442 JHN to FWN (10 November 1840).
[14] "Personal Influence, The Means of Propagating The Truth" (1832) in *US*, p. 65.
[15] *Contr,* p. 61.
[16] LD, 28.127 JHN to Maria Giberne (21 October 1876).
[17] Francis Newman quoted in Moncure Daniel Conway. *Autobiography* (New York, 1905), I, p. 444.
[18] *Bygones,* 1, p. 13.

"slightly rising from a broad strip of fine gravel, where our boys, in large bands, enjoyed Long Rope—with us a glorious game . . . We had cricket and rounders, and in the winter months football; petty fives against every petty wall; hopping and hopscotch, patball and trapball, prisoner's base (or bars?), tops of several kinds, and multiform games of marbles."[19]

Newman, Frank remembered, was indifferent alike to hopscotch, tops, marbles, and cricket: "As far back as my memory reaches, in none of these was John Henry Newman to be seen. He did go to our bathing-pond, but never *swam*."[20] However, in her fictionalized account of the early home life of the Newmans, *Family Adventures* (1852), Harriett left an amusing account of Newman's respect for soldiers. There, Newman and his brother Charles are in a toyshop and Charles cries out for a kettle-drum. [In the book, Newman is named Henry and Charles, Robert.] The shopkeeper replies that he is "very sorry, but a kettledrum was of so expensive a make that it would never answer as a toy."

> "But I don't want it as a toy," said Robert; "I don't like toys; I want a real good large kettle-drum that I could play, just as the soldiers do," and he made a suitable flourish with the drumsticks he held in his hand, while he went on protesting against the stupidity of toy manufacturers, who would not make kettledrums instead of silly toys, which nobody cared for.
>
> The shopman took this hint. He thought the young gentleman had a fancy for military toys, and he produced some guns, swords, and bows and arrows of a superior description. They certainly were far above the usual appearance of these articles, so much so, that the boys, so far from turning away from them with the indifference they had hitherto shown, examined them with silent respect.

 Whereupon, Henry declares: "I will have a sword," a preference entirely in keeping with the future Cardinal's readiness to fight for the faith and his lifelong respect for soldiers.[21] Indeed, in Newman's estimation, a soldier, as he said, "comes more nearly than a King to the pattern of Christ. He not only is strong but is weak. He does and he suffers. He succeeds through a risk. Half his time is on the field of battle, and half of it on the bed of pain. And he does this for the sake of others; he defends us by it; we are indebted to him; we gain by his loss; we are at peace by his warfare."[22] Newman may not have had much in common with Ruskin—besides an immense familiarity with Scripture—but he would have entirely agreed with the art critic's view of the dignity of the solider. "The consent of mankind has always . . . given precedence to the soldier," Ruskin wrote. "And this is right. For the soldier's trade . . . is not slaying, but being slain . . . Our estimate of him is based on this ultimate fact . . . that put him in a fortress breach, with all the pleasures of the world behind him, and only death and his duty in front of him, he will keep his face to the front; and he knows that his choice may be put

---

[19] *Contr*, pp. 2–3.
[20] Ibid., p. 3.
[21] Harriett Mozley. *Family Adventures* (London, 1852), pp. 186–7.
[22] *SD*, p. 57.

to him at any moment—and has beforehand taken his part—virtually takes such part continually—does, in reality, die daily."[23]

The classics tutor at Ealing, Walter Mayer instilled in Frank an Evangelical faith similar to the one that he instilled in young Newman. "My religion then certainly exerted a great general influence over my conduct," he recalled, "for I soon underwent various persecution from my schoolfellows on account of it." He described it in his autobiographical *Phases of Faith* (1850) as "an unhesitating unconditional acceptance of whatever was found in the Bible. While I am far from saying that my whole moral conduct was subjugated by my creed, I must insist that it was no mere fancy resting in my intellect: it was really operative on my temper, tastes, pursuits and conduct."[24] After Ealing, Frank went up to Worcester College, Oxford, lodging first with his brother at Searle's Coffee House and then with his brother and Blanco White at Palmer's in Merton Lane, where he recalled White, the Spaniard of Irish ancestry who left the Catholic priesthood to become a Fellow of Oriel teasing his brother, "Ah! Newman! if you follow that clue it will draw you into Catholic error."[25]

Newman praised his brother's academic attainments. "To say that he knows more than most of those who take common degrees would be saying little. I am convinced he knows much more of Greek, as a language than most of those who take first classes . . . he certainly knows much more of Greek as a language, in fact is a much better Greek scholar than I . . . Again, he is a much better mathematician than I am; I mean, he reads more mathematically, as Aristotle would say."[26] Frank made good on this glowing report by obtaining a double first and becoming a fellow at Balliol. "He has astonished all Oxford," Newman wrote his mother.[27] On accepting his degree, "the whole assembly rose to welcome him, an honour paid previously only to Sir Robert Peel on taking his double first."[28]

In 1827, while tutoring the children of John Vesey Parnell, Lord Congleton in County Wicklow, Frank met John Nelson Darby, the founder of the Plymouth Brethren, and plunged more deeply still into the bibliolatry that he had imbibed at Ealing. On his return to Oxford, he refused to subscribe the 39 Articles necessary for the MA degree and resigned his fellowship. In 1830, he met a fellow Darbyite, with whom he undertook an evangelizing mission to Baghdad. On his return to England in 1833, he fell out with Darby and his associates after formulating his own idiosyncratic Deism. Shortly thereafter, he began attending Broadmead chapel, a Baptist meeting place. In November 1835, Hurrell Froude reported that he had heard Newman "accused (as a proof of unfeeling bigotry in you) of having refused to meet your brother on his return from Persia."[29] Newman explained: "I saw him and was with him for several days on his return. After that, on his determining 'to preach the gospel,' as it is called, I wrote to tell him that, while he did so, I could have no intercourse with him – my tie to the Church as a Clergyman destroying the claim of relationship . . ., and leaving

[23] John Ruskin. *Unto This Last* (London, 1892), pp. 25–6.
[24] *Phases*, p. 1.
[25] *Contr*, p. 14.
[26] LD, 1:155 JHN to Mrs Jemima Newman (5 November 1822).
[27] LD, 1:292 JHN to Mrs Jemima Newman (8 June 1826).
[28] DNB.
[29] LD, 5:155 R. H. Froude to JHN (November 1835).

the Scripture rule to act. I have heard from him quite lately – but not in a satisfactory way. I do fear his verging towards liberalism. That wretched Protestant principle about Scripture, when taken in by an independent and clear mind, is almost certain to lead to errors I do not like to name."[30] In 1836, Frank became classical tutor at the non-denominational Bristol College. A year earlier, he married Maria Kennaway, a member of the Plymouth Brethren. In 1863, Newman was relieved when he learnt that his brother's missionary wanderlust would not put Maria in harm's way: "Frank had a vision of going to Beyroot," he wrote his sister Jemima, "but he seems to think nothing will come of it. His wife would feel strange, I should think, in such a country: though I dare say a sea town, such as it, would contain certain unmistakable marks of the presence of Englishmen, and would supply a number of English comforts. But she likes visiting the poor, and the Mahometan poor present to my imagination a terra incognita."[31]

In 1840, Frank moved to Manchester New College, where he formed a long friendship with the Unitarian James Martineau, the college's Professor of Mental and Moral Philosophy, who, like Mrs Newman, was of Huguenot ancestry. For Frank, one clear point in Martineau's favour was that he agreed with Arius, the fourth-century heretic whose denial of the divinity of Christ provided Newman with the subject for his first book, *The Arians of the Fourth Century* (1833). Anyone who opposed points of view espoused by his brother tended to be met with Frank's approval. The principles underpinning Martineau's Unitarianism would find a ready convert in Frank. "That there can exist no obligation, moral or logical, to set aside the suggestion of the understanding in obedience to external authority; that no seeming inspiration can establish anything contrary to reason; that the last appeal, in all researches into religious truth, must be the judgments of the human mind; that against these judgments Scripture can have no authority"—these were the rallying cries of all the rationalists of the nineteenth-century.[32] Frank was also a great advocate of the idea of progress, convinced, as he was, that it would confirm the prescience of his hobby horses. In one of many letters to Charles Kingsley's widow, for example, Frank told her how, as he said, "The longer I live, the more hopeful and more interesting I find the whole world. In spite of crime, folly, and misery, the massive nations seem to improve. The good . . . become wiser and stronger, as well as in proportion more numerous . . ."[33]

It was fitting that Frank should have developed his heterodox views in Manchester because the city was a centre of free thinking. Part of this might have been due to the effects of rapid industrialization. Elizabeth Gaskell, in the opening of her novel *Mary Barton* (1848), described how these were ravaging the city's "careworn men," whom she described as "doomed to struggle . . . in strange alternations between work and want." She particularly noticed how "they were sore and irritable against the rich, the even tenor of whose seemingly happy lives appeared to increase the anguish caused by the lottery-like nature of their own." Consequently, it was difficult

[30]   LD, 5:164 JHN to R. H. Froude (17 November 1835).
[31]   LD, 20:399 JHN to Mrs John Mozley (22 January 1863).
[32]   Vera Wheatley. *The Life and Work of Harriet Martineau* (London, 1957), p. 306.
[33]   *Sieveking*, p. 385.

for Manchester's working men to show any "resignation to God's will."[34] Frank would follow these working men in taking issue with what he regarded as the injustice of Christianity. Then, again, many German émigrés had imported a distinctly German free thinking into the city, which was passionately anti-Catholic.[35] In his brilliant book *Iron Kingdom: The Rise and Downfall of Prussia 1600–1947* (2006), Christopher Clark describes how Roman Catholicism provided German liberalism with a perennial whipping boy. In the nineteenth-century German liberals "held up Catholicism as the diametrical negation of their own world view," Clark points out. "They denounced the 'absolutism' and the 'slavery' of the doctrine of papal infallibility." Moreover, "Liberal journalism depicted the Catholic faithful as a servile and manipulated mass (by implied contrast with a liberal social universe centered on male tax-paying worthies with unbound consciences.)" And from this carefully implanted bigotry, "A bestiary of anti-clerical stereotypes emerged: the satires in liberal journals thronged with wily, thin Jesuits and lecherous, fat priests—amenable subjects because the cartoonist's pen could make such artful play with the solid black of their garb . . ."[36] That such German liberalism reinforced the prejudices of Frank's childhood is clear from his *Contributions Chiefly to the Early History of the Late Cardinal Newman*, where he wrote, apropos his brother's Roman Faith: "I do not believe in the recurrence of dire barbarism. But a Power that wishes to imprison or kill, and cannot, will use mean tricks such as baptizing a Jewish child and then claiming him to be a Christian. There is nothing too little for its spite, or too large for its ambition. Protestants ought never to harbour an unkind thought against a private Catholic as such; yet never to forget that, where private judgment is forbidden, no man's conscience is in his own keeping."[37]

As this shows, Frank was steeped in No Popery. He might contend, in a letter to his brother, how "a deeper upturning of men's old notions is needed, before they will learn the feebleness of human judgment and that mutual forbearance without which every thing is sectarian . . ."[38] But Frank never repudiated his lifelong prejudices against the Church of Rome and although fond of recommending forbearance to others, never managed to practise it himself. Newman made a wry joke of this aspect of his brother when he remarked to Ambrose St John in 1846, from his first English Catholic address, Old Oscott, which he renamed Maryvale, "My brother is coming to see me at Maryvale . . . I think he has some obscure idea he can decide whether there are thumbscrews and the like . . ."[39]

---

[34] Elizabeth Gaskell. *Mary Barton* (Folio Society, 2004), p. 3.
[35] In 1874, Newman told Jemima's second son, John Rickards that "Germany, the native soil of the Reformation, was now the normal seat of intellectual irreligion." See LD, 27:266. JHN to John Rickards Mozley (4 April 1874). The poet John Sterling also connected Frank to Germany. While he was classical tutor at Bristol College, Frank commenced a friendship with Sterling, the companion of Coleridge and Carlyle, who spent years studying German philosophy in Germany and England. It was from Sterling that Frank got the idea that his older brother Charles might benefit from studying German literature in Bonn. When Sterling's wife and mother died of consumption in 1843 within hours of each other, Frank adopted the eldest of his orphan sons.
[36] C. Clark. *Iron Kingdom: The Rise and Downfall of Prussia 1600–1947* (New York, 2006), p. 570.
[37] *Contr*, p. 139.
[38] LD, 7:308 Frank W. Newman to JHN (15 April 1840).
[39] LD, 11:204 JHN to Ambrose St John (11 July 1846).

In 1846, Frank was appointed to the chair of Latin in University College, London, "that bleak, blank, hideous . . . whited sepulchre. . . ," as Max Beerbohm nicely called it, where he introduced the Italian pronunciation of the language and set his students the task of translating Longfellow's *Hiawatha* into Latin.[40] Outside the classroom, Frank took an interest in several ancient languages, including the Umbrian, Numidian, Libyan, Scythian, and Etruscan tongues. For over 40 years, he corresponded with the biblical orientalist John Nicholson. In one letter to his learned friend, Frank wrote: "I would not have you take any particular trouble . . . but if in your Turkish Dictionary you find . . . *tax*, at your entire leisure (no hurry at all) I should be glad to learn how you pronounce the word." In another, he confessed, "I am constantly reminded of you by the study which I have been rather closely pursuing here for nearly eight weeks, viz., the reading of *Robinson Crusoe* in Arabic." In addition to his wide-ranging linguistic interests, Frank espoused various political causes. In 1852, he joined the shilling subscription set up by the secularist Holyoake to aid Kossuth and Mazzini on behalf of Hungary and Italy. Nine thousand shillings were subscribed to the fund, after which Holyoake presented the celebrated patriots with a cheque for £450. Kossuth and Mazzini were only two of Frank's many republican heroes. In one letter, he referred to Mazzini—an anti-clerical Deist—as a "man of sorrows," who would prevail against his reactionary opponents because he exemplified "a nobler practice and a higher faith than our routine statesmen dream of."[41] Mazzini's own pronouncements about his faith were of a similarly vague turgidity. Professing to be more Christian than the "magnates" of the Roman Church, he claimed to belong to "a still purer and higher faith; but its time has not yet come; and until that day, the Christian manifestation remains the most sacred revelation of the ever-onward-progressing spirit of mankind working its way to an Ideal which must sooner or later be realized."[42]

In 1848, Frank became Principal of University Hall at London for dissenting students, though he resigned the position shortly thereafter. In 1850, he began lecturing at Bedford College for Women. In addition to advocating the rights of women, Frank was a keen abolitionist, vegetarian, and anti-vivisectionist. In 1862, he relinquished his chair of Latin in London University and embarked on an extensive career of freelancing. Starting in 1865, he made several contributions to a series of tracts published by the apostate former Catholic Thomas Scott (1808–78), whose commitment to "free enquiry and the free expression of opinion" led him to publish not only Frank but J. W. Colenso and the theosophist Annie Besant. In 1866, Frank moved back to Bristol. In 1876, he joined the British and Unitarian Association, of which he became vice president. In the same year, his wife Maria died. Two years later, he married Eleanor Williams, the 54-year-old daughter of a builder. Throughout his later years, he continued to call himself a Christian, though one who could never bring himself to believe in the divinity of Christ. In 1892, in a letter to a friend, he admitted that "while I cannot be a Christian if weighed in any historical balance yet my moral and spiritual sentiment is unchanged since I joyfully surrendered myself

---

[40] Max Beerbohm, "From Bloomsbury to Bayswater," in *Mainly on the Air* (London, 1947), p. 87.
[41] Denis Mack Smith. *Mazzini* (New Haven, 1994), p. 107.
[42] Ibid., pp. 17–18.

to God in 1819." Frank died on 4 October 1897 at 15 Arundel Crescent, Weston-super-Mare.[43]

Most of Frank's books are screeds against doctrinal religion or paeans to his own idiosyncratic Deism. About *Phases of Faith* (1850), probably his best-known book, Matthew Arnold was memorably dismissive: "One would think to read him that enquiries into articles, biblical inspiration, etc. etc. were as much the natural functions of a man as to eat and copulate. This sort of man is only possible in Great Britain and North Germany. Ireland even spews him out."[44] Apropos *The Soul: Its Sorrows and Aspirations: An Essay Towards the Natural History of the Soul as the True Basis of Theology* (1849), Charles Kingsley, speaking to fellow Christian socialists, J. M. F. Ludlow and F. D. Maurice, exclaimed "Oh yes! The s-s-s-soul and her stomach aches!"[45] Newman, from his rather different perspective, was equally critical of the book: "My dear brother Frank has published a dreadful work . . . denying Scripture . . . denying dogmatic truth in toto, railing at some doctrines etc. etc. I can't be surprised—he must with his independent mind, work out his own principles, and they tend to atheism. God grant he may be arrested in his course!"[46] Frank's principles can be gleaned from a brief history of Christianity that he included in the book: "After the first blaze of apostolic Christianity," he explained, "the heavenly flame instantly paled, the Churches declined, form and rule grew up, Bishops became proud, superstition increased, controversy raged, persecution began, this World became the prize for which the Churches fought, ecclesiastical dominion took deep root, darkness overspread the earth, polytheism invaded what should have been God's kingdom, and cruelty, sensuality, ambition and avarice hid beneath priests' robes."[47] In *On the Defective Morality of the New Testament* (1867), Frank remonstrated with the authors of Scripture for making what he considered poor ethical judgements. In 1874, he followed this up with *Hebrew Theism*, in which he sought to make his unconventional views more palatable by presenting them in iambic pentameter. The evangelical atheists in our own midst could not put the case for the villainy of Rome with more vituperative zest.

> Listen not to priests, who forbid the pious to marry
> Who make merit of fasting, who bid you renounce vanities,
> Who haply allure you to a cloistered, conventual life,
> Who talk against riches, and against enjoyment of ear and eye,
> As though the senses were impure, and affection blamable,
> The indulgence of taste a weakness, and comfort ignominious.
> Whatever enjoyment is lawful, enjoy ye with a good conscience:
> Whatever brings you most pleasure, seek for it, if it harm not your neighbor,

[43] Cf. Evelyn Waugh. *A Little Learning* (London, 1964), p. 28 "My first visual memory is of a camera obscura on the pier at Weston-super-Mare. On that day, I have been told, I suffered an absurd and nearly fatal accident. I was biting a hard-boiled egg when the yolk suddenly shot from its white case and lodged entire in my throat, threatening me with asphyxiation. Apoplectic of face I was thumped and shaken by the heels. It was a close run thing . . ."

[44] *The Letters of Matthew Arnold to Arthur Hugh Clough.* ed. Howard Foster Lowry (Oxford, 1932), p. 115.

[45] Charles Kingsley quoted in Robert Bernard Martin. *The Dust of Combat: A Life of Charles Kingsley* (London, 1960), pp. 128–9.

[46] LD, 13:415 JHN to Maria Giberne (7 February 1850).

[47] F. W. Newman. *The Soul, Her Sorrows and Her Aspirations* (London, 1849), p. 261.

Of one *instinct* only take heed and beware ye—for it is dangerous—
The instinct of religion, which seeks after God.
Cripple it, crush it, tear it out by its roots;
For from it have come wars and controversies and exclusions
And heartburnings endless; but *Truth* it will never reach.

In *Catholic Union: Essays towards a Church of the Future as the Organization of Philanthropy* (1854), a prophetic title considering how many Christian churches have reinvented themselves as philanthropic associations in the wake of the collapse of their theological pretensions, Frank argued that the catholicity proclaimed by the Church of Rome should not be abandoned but appropriated for an improved, creedless faith. "We are learning," he said, "that right creeds are but means of becoming *better men;* and that goodness (in the truest sense) is the end proposed . . ." And this was especially the case since "we have daily proof that persons who agree with us more minutely in theological creed are by no means always so trustworthy in various virtues as others who differ from us." For Frank, "The true union between man and man in the highest and closest human friendship turns on a reciprocal trust in one another's virtue; and thousands are become so sick at heart of the pretensions of creeds, that they often ask, whether the union of *good men, as such,* is for ever to be impossible. This question is nothing but the aspiring of the heart towards the true Church of the Future,—a union of those who look on that part of man, in which he is said to be like to God, as his best and noblest; and who dedicate themselves to the cultivation of this. Such a catholic union would have no religious creed whatever: and so far from bearing within it the sectarian principle of Protestantism, it would embrace Jews, Turks, Arabs, Hindoos, Chinese,—Christians, Theists, Pantheists and Atheists,—whenever they were sincere, and personally virtuous." Frank cited his own personal experience to defend his view. "Knowing, as I do, that many hearts and minds are brooding over the questions, 'Ought not the sense of Human Brotherhood to draw men together into a nobler and better church than has yet appeared? Is the time, or is it not, yet ripe?' I have thought it not unsuitable to offer my contribution towards the answer; which, in fact, takes one into the regions of Communism and of Politics, as departments of Morals. I believe Communism to be one mode in which human nature is crying out for a new and better union than has yet been achieved." To corroborate his view, Frank invoked the spirit of the age, asking his readers "what else are all the Philanthropic movements of this half century,—*against* Slavery, Cruel Punishments, Bad Jails, Intemperance,—and *for* Education, Health, Cleanliness, Relaxation,—what are they all but plain confessions that there is a vast class of duties and doctrines which the State cannot take in hand until public opinion has gone first, and on which the Church ought to form and gather public opinion, if she could; but she cannot, because she is theological and ecclesiastical, not purely moral. Few Christians are so bigoted as to refuse to co-operate with Jews, Turks, Infidels and Heretics to abate cholera and plague; many have learned to unite against slavery and intemperance. All these are but gropings and first steps in quest of a church of human brotherhood."[48]

---

[48] F. W. Newman. *Catholic Union: Essays towards a Church of the Future as the Organization of Philanthropy* (London, 1854), pp. 4–6.

Despite his eccentric views, Frank won praise from notable quarters. George Eliot was fond of referring to him as "our blessed St. Francis," whose "soul is a blessed *yea*."[49] The positivist Frederic Harrison was convinced that "In mental activity—undoubtedly in mental versatility and culture—Francis very much surpassed the Cardinal. There can be no question that, in learning and variety of gift, the two cannot be placed on the same level."[50] Mrs Gaskell "reverenced" his "holiness" and thought his non-dogmatic religion "the church of the future."[51] Thackeray regarded him as "a very pious loving humble soul . . . with . . . a beautiful love and reverence."[52] His friend Holyoake recalled a conversation he had at one of Gladstone's famous breakfasts in Harley Street, in which the Grand Old Man, inquiring after Newman's brothers, singled Frank out for lavish praise. "'When you write again to . . . Francis,'" Holyoake recalled Gladstone telling him, "'convey to him for me the assurance of my esteem. I am glad you believe that the cessation in his correspondence was not occasioned by anything on my part or any change of feeling on his. I must have been mistaken if I ever described Mr Francis Newman as 'a man of considerable talent.' He was much more than that. His powers of mind may be said to amount to genius.'"[53] One of his later admirers, Basil Willey, the historian of ideas, writing from Cambridge in 1956, agreed, hailing Frank as a pioneer:

> His difficulties may have ceased to terrify, and his conclusions—many of them— are now the unquestioned data of every beginner. Yet it remains an interesting and touching spectacle to watch a pioneer winning, inch by inch, the vantage- ground we now occupy. Moreover, in enjoying our present immunities, we may easily forget how they were gained, and how recently; and it is salutary to look back with gratitude on the costly struggles which purchased for us what now we take for granted. Newman's struggle commands our respect and sympathy all the more because it was, on the whole, worked out in solitude and estrangement. He lacked the intellectual supports enjoyed by later liberals.[54]

Newman also regarded Frank as a pioneer. In choosing to champion the fallacies of private judgement, Frank became a harbinger of "the plague of unbelief" that would afflict all of England's Christian communities in the nineteenth century and beyond.[55] Yet, on a more personal level, in letter after letter, throughout his long life, Newman grieved for his brother and for the loss of his faith. To his sister Jemima, he wrote: "Of course I was sadly and painfully interested in your account of Frank Newman. His joining the Unitarians is now in the Papers. The Unitarians are pious Deists now – believing in our Lord as an eminent teacher, greater, but not in a higher sense, than

---

[49] Cross's *Life* (London, 1885), 1, pp. 193–4.
[50] Frederic Harrison. *Realities and Ideals: Social, Political, Literary and Artistic* (New York, 1908), p. 374.
[51] ODNB.
[52] Thackeray to Mrs Brookfield (2–3 September 1849) in *The Letters and Private Papers of William Makepeace Thackeray*. ed. Gordon Ray (Harvard, 1946), I, p. 581.
[53] *Bygones*, 2, p. 14.
[54] Basil Willey. *More Nineteenth-Century Studies: A Group of Honest Doubters* (London, 1956), p. 18.
[55] LD, 27:102 JHN to Mrs Wilson (3 August 1874).

Socrates. Humanly speaking, there he will remain, unless, when death comes, God has mercy upon him, and the Saviour whom he has disowned. For that great Mercy one must pray."[56]

Stella Matutina

In 1824, two years before Frank graduated from Oxford, the brothers came to a crossroads that would divide them for life. "While I was arranging furniture in my rooms," Frank recalled, "I suddenly found a beautiful engraving of the 'Blessed Virgin' fixed up. I went to the print shop and begged its immediate removal, and then learned that my brother had ordered it. I am sure he thought me an ungrateful brother. My own act made me unhappy, yet the more I ruminated, the more I judged that to resist from the beginning was my wisest way. Before he was ordained, our intercourse was comparatively easy, and . . . on equal terms; so that if he quoted Scripture unconvincingly, I said my say naturally. Since his maiden sermon, I had felt less free. But after my repulse of his engraved Virgin, he came out with an attack on Protestants collectively, saying that they forgot that sacred utterance, 'Blessed art thou among women,' and I answered, 'Dear John, I do not forget it, but I remember also, that to like words from another woman, Christ replied, "Yea rather, blessed are they who hear the Word of God, and keep it."' Our Lord did not approve of honouring his mother."[57] In 1883, Newman disputed his brother's version of events, explaining that he purchased the picture without "any religious intention in doing so." When he went down to Smith and Parker's, the print sellers, at the corner of High Street and Long Wall, and asked to look at some engravings, he was shown several full portfolios, from which he chose David Wilkie's "Rent Day" (an apt choice considering his straitened finances) and Correggio's "La Madonna col Divoto." The latter, as Newman recalled, was "in no sense a devotional picture, such as is used by Catholics at prayer. It took my fancy as an artistic work; and I recollect feeling some scruples on the score of its subject . . ."[58]

When Frank refused to accept the print, Newman took it back and hung it up in his rooms in Oriel before taking it with him to the Oratory in Edgbaston where it hangs still. Despite its factual inaccuracy, Frank's version vividly reiterates the anti-Marian prejudices of most English Protestants. Charles Kingsley gave memorable expression to such prejudices when he took issue with a Catholic priest advising one of his female correspondents to pray to the Virgin. A muscular Christian, Kinglsey equated devotion to Mary with weakness and counselled the woman, "If your head had once rested on a lover's bosom, and your heart known the mighty stay of a *man's* affection, you would have learnt to go now in your sore need, not to the mother, but to the Son—not to the indulgent virgin, but to the strong man, Jesus Christ."[59] Apropos Kinglsey's impatience with the mother of God, his biographer Susan Chitty rightly

---

[56] LD, 28:112 JHN to Mrs John Mozley (10 September 1876).
[57] *Contr*, pp. 18–19.
[58] LD, 30:232 JHN to The Editor of the Fortnightly Review (14 June 1883).
[59] Susan Chitty. *The Beast and the Monk: A Life of Charles Kingsley* (New York, 1974), p. 237.

observes that "In his muddled way Kinglsey connected the honouring of the Virgin with. . . effeminacy"—precisely because he feared what he considered effeminate tendencies in himself. Despite the fact that Kingsley never met Newman, before or after impugning his veracity in *Macmillan's Magazine* in 1864, he was convinced that Newman epitomized everything he abominated. "In him and all that school," Kingsley wrote in 1852, "there is an element of foppery—even in dress and manner; a fastidious, maundering die-away effeminacy, which is mistaken for purity and refinement; and I confess myself unable to cope with it."[60] Anyone who has seen photographs of Newman must wonder where Kingsley got the notion that he paid undue attention to his dress.

One could see the fear Marianism inspired in those intent on maintaining Great Britain's Protestant order in a letter William Gladstone wrote to James Hope commenting on John Dalgairns' life of St Stephen Harding. "I am repelled by the introduction with apparent approval of particular points and phrases of Roman doctrine more or less opposed by the Church of England," Gladstone wrote, "such as the devotion to St. Mary, as interwoven parts of the narrative. . . . I dread most painfully the establishment in the popular mind of the conclusion, that we can have no reintroduction of holy personal discipline, no communion with the saints of the middle ages, except under such a condition."[61] When Newman was made privy to this letter—Hope shared it with him— he must have seen it as proof that Dalgairns' work had hit its mark; he also told Hope, accurately enough, that "G's remarks have shown me the *hopelessness*, by delay or any other means, of escaping the disapprobation of a number of persons whom I very much respect."[62] Newman, for his part, had always had a devotion to Our Lady, even as an Anglican, noting in the *Apologia*, as he said, how, "In spite of my ingrained fears of Rome, and the decision of my reason and conscience against her usages, in spite of my affection for Oxford and Oriel, yet I had a secret longing love of Rome, the Mother of English Christianity, and I had a true devotion to the Blessed Virgin, in whose College I lived, whose Altar I served, and whose Immaculate Purity I had in one of my earliest printed Sermons made much of."[63]

Frank's decision to resist his brother's influence was driven by more than the usual Protestant hostility to the woman whom Wordsworth nicely called "our tainted nature's solitary boast."[64] For Frank, resisting Newman's influence was always bound up with sibling rivalry, though for Newman, the issue at stake was infinitely greater than a younger brother's *amour propre*. In his subsequent meditations on the Blessed Virgin, Newman can be seen appealing not only to his brother but to all the Protestant English "to estimate the holiness and perfection of her, who was chosen to be the Mother of Christ . . ." He also put a very pointed question: "What must have been her gifts, who was chosen to be the only near earthly relative of the Son of God, the only one whom He was bound by nature to revere and look up to; the one appointed to train and educate Him, to instruct Him day by day, as He grew in wisdom and in stature? This

---

[60] Ibid., p. 236.
[61] LD, 10:43 William Ewart Gladstone to James Robert Hope (3 December 1843).
[62] LD, 10:45 JHN to James Robert Hope (5 December 1843).
[63] *Apo.*, p. 53.
[64] See Wordsworth's lovely poem, "The Virgin."

contemplation runs to a higher subject, did we dare follow it; for what, think you, was the sanctified state of that human nature, of which God formed His sinless Son . . ."[65] Here, Newman was clearly appealing to Frank to mind what he was doing when he denigrated the Virgin. In "The Theory of Developments in Religious Doctrine" (1843), the 15th of his *University Sermons*, Newman might have been speaking directly to his brother:

> Mary is our pattern of Faith, both in the reception and in the study of Divine Truth. She does not think it enough to accept, she dwells upon it; not enough to possess, she uses it; not enough to assent, she develops it; not enough to submit the Reason, she reasons upon it; not indeed reasoning first, and believing afterwards, with Zacharias, yet first believing without reasoning, next from love and reverence, reasoning after believing. And thus she symbolizes to us, not only the faith of the unlearned, but of the doctors of the Church also, who have to investigate, and weigh, and define, as well as to profess the Gospel; to draw the line between truth and heresy; to anticipate or remedy the various aberrations of wrong reason; to combat pride and recklessness with their own arms; and thus to triumph over the sophist and the innovator.[66]

Over 20 years later, in his *Letter to Dr. Pusey* (1866), Newman responded to the charge of his old Anglo-Catholic friend Edward Pusey that unity between the Anglican and the Roman Catholic Church was impossible so long as the latter connived in exorbitant devotion to the Blessed Virgin by reminding his friend that these devotions, however extravagant, were the effusions of love. "Religion acts on the affections; who is to hinder these, when once roused, from gathering in their strength and running wild? They are not gifted with any connatural principle within them, which renders them self-governing, and self-adjusting. They hurry right on to their object . . . Their object engrosses them, and they see nothing else. And of all passions love is the most unmanageable; nay more, I would not give much for that love which is never extravagant, which always observes the proprieties, and can move about in perfect good taste, under all emergencies. What mother, what husband or wife, what youth or maiden in love, but says a thousand foolish things, in the way of endearment, which the speaker would be sorry for strangers to hear; yet they are not on that account unwelcome to the parties to whom they are addressed . . . Burning thoughts and words are as open to criticism as they are beyond it. What is abstractedly extravagant, may in particular persons be becoming and beautiful, and only fall under blame when it is found in others who imitate them. When it is formalized into meditations or exercises, it is as repulsive as love-letters in a police report."[67] In his *Summa Theologica*, St Thomas said much the same thing about whether we should seek to temper our love of the Virgin's Son: "God himself is the rule and mode of virtue," St Thomas wrote; "our faith is measured by divine truth, our hope by the greatness of his power and faithful affection, our charity by His goodness. His truth, power, and goodness outstretch any

---

[65] "The Reverence Due to the Virgin Mary," (1832) *PS*, 2, p. 311.
[66] "The Theory of Developments in Religious Doctrine" (1843), in *US*, pp. 211–12.
[67] *VM*, ii, p. 81.

measure of reason. We certainly never believe, trust, or love God more than, or even as much as, we should. Extravagance is impossible. Here is no virtuous moderation, no reasonable mean; the more extreme our activity, the better we are."[68]

The upshot of Newman's response to Pusey was to argue that no unity would be possible between Anglicans and Catholics *without* devotion to the Blessed Virgin. That Newman had his brother in mind when he was writing the *Letter to Pusey* is also clear from his other remarks about the significance of Mary for his anti-Marian contemporaries: "Here our Lady is represented as rescuing a holy soul from intellectual error," he wrote his old Tractarian friend. "This leads me to a further reflection. You seem, in one place of your Volume, to object to the Antiphon, in which it is said of her, 'All heresies thou hast destroyed alone.' Surely the truth of it is verified in this age, as in former times, and especially by the doctrine concerning her, on which I have been dwelling. She is the great exemplar of prayer in a generation, which emphatically denies the power of prayer *in toto*, which determines that fatal laws govern the universe, that there cannot be any direct communication between earth and heaven, that God cannot visit His own earth, and that man cannot influence His providence."[69]

While showing how much the Fathers honoured Mary, whom they regarded "as the Church's deepest origin and unbroken kernel,"[70] Newman stressed how Mary renews the living tradition of the Faith. This was an important point because one of the most persistent criticisms lodged against Newman, whether as an Anglican or Roman Catholic, was that his faith was superannuated, not a living faith but quixotic medievalism. In his history of Victorian England, A. N. Wilson reiterates this charge, claiming that Newman and his Tractarian friends were engaged in "a form of mental Eglinton Tournament in which young men of the railway age tried to adopt the mentality of medieval monks or the Fathers of the Church in Late Antiquity . . . While the Irish starved, [Newman] worried his mind about Augustine's controversy in the fourth century with the Donatists . . ."[71] Newman, in other words, betrayed the real needs of his liberal age by immersing himself in what Wilson dubs "esoteric ecclesiastical controversies."[72] Presumably, he would have been more profitably employed in some form of famine relief. But whether he was remiss in choosing to read the Fathers instead of agricultural manuals, it is clear that there was nothing medievalist in his recognition of the role the Blessed Virgin plays in renewing the Faith.

And now, when I could wish to proceed, she seems to stop all controversy, for the Feast of her Immaculate Conception is upon us; and close upon its Octave, which is kept with special solemnities in the Churches of this town, come the great Antiphons, the heralds of Christmas. That joyful season, joyful for all of us, while it centres in Him who then came on earth, also brings before us in peculiar prominence that Virgin Mother, who bore and nursed Him. Here she is not in the background, as at Easter-tide, but she brings Him to us in her arms. Two great

---

[68] *St. Thomas Aquinas: Theological Texts.* ed. Thomas Gilby (Oxford, 1955), p. 182.
[69] *VM*, ii, p. 76.
[70] Nicolas L. Gregoris. *"The Daughter of Eve Unfallen:" Mary in the Theology and Spirituality of John Henry Newman* (Pennsylvania, 2003), p. 497.
[71] A. N. Wilson. *The Victorians* (Folio Society, 2008), p. 90.
[72] Ibid., p. 89.

Festivals, dedicated to her honour, tomorrow's and the Purification, mark out and keep the ground, and, like the towers of David, open the way to and fro, for the high holiday season of the Prince of Peace. And all along it her image is upon it, such as we see it in the typical representation of the Catacombs. May the sacred influences of this tide bring us all together in unity! May it destroy all bitterness on your side and ours! May it quench all jealous, sour, proud, fierce antagonism on our side; and dissipate all captious, carping, fastidious refinements of reasoning on yours! May that bright and gentle Lady, the Blessed Virgin Mary, overcome you with her sweetness, and revenge herself on her foes by interceding effectually for their conversion![73]

What alarmed and indeed angered Newman's contemporaries about his Catholic faith was not that it was antiquarian but that it was so insistently 'here and now.' In this, it resembled the *Hail Mary*. If the first part of the prayer is about the Incarnation, the second, as A. N. Gilbey reminded his readers, is about "this very present moment of time, over which alone we have control, and the hour of death, that moment of time when we pass into eternity, a moment which will seal our fate forever."[74] Unlike so many figures of the Gothic revival, Newman was not interested in returning to any imaginary past, even an imaginary Catholic past. He is quite clear about this in a fascinating letter that he wrote to the Catholic convert, T. W. Allies. In response to a book that Allies had sent him praising what he regarded as the exemplary Catholic civilization of the Middle Ages, *The Formation of Christendom* (1865) Newman wrote back "I do not see my way to hold that 'Catholic civilization,' as you describe it, is *in fact* (I do not say in the abstract), but in fact, has been, or shall be . . . desirable." And to argue his case, Newman wrote his friend: "You say 'Catholic civilisation . . . was the ideal which the Church aimed at in the Middle Ages, and which she worked into the laws, manners, institutions, public policy, or public opinions of Europe.' Now that it is the tendency of Christianity to impress itself on the face of society, I grant: but so, in like manner, it is the tendency of devotion to increase Church lands and property, and to multiply religious houses; but as the state of the recipient (i.e. a given population *hic et nunc*) may hinder the latter tendency from working well (*e.g.* may lead to secularity and corruption in the clergy), so may certain peculiarities in this or that age or place interfere with the beneficial effect of the former, that is, it is not necessarily a good." One will look in vain among the writings of Pugin or any of the other devotees of the Neo-Gothic for a critique of the impact of the faith on the Middle Ages that is as incisive as this. Moreover, Newman wrote, while "Christianity in the middle ages impressed its image on society, it did not succeed equally with literature and science. Society at the time bore witness to this serious incompleteness in the regeneration of human nature . . . And no one will deny that, as in primitive and in these times, the intellect of the world in the medieval period was untamed. If then Christianity has not compelled the intellect of the world, viewed in the cultivated classes, to confess Christ and follow His teaching, why insist, as some triumphant success that it has influenced the soldier and the magistrate? If there was to be a grand progress according to which

[73]   *VM*, ii, p. 118.
[74]   A. N. Gilbey. *We Believe* (London, 1983), p. 144.

first the individual, the family, then civil polity, was to be converted, why was the conquest of literature and science to have no place in the series of triumphs?" For Newman, "since the object of Christianity is to save souls, and St. Paul says that he endures all things for the sake of the elect, I ask what reason have we to suppose that more souls were saved, relative to the number of Christians, under the Catholic theocracy, than under the Roman Emperors or under the English Georges. There are no means of course of proving the point, but we ought to have some good reason for answering in the affirmative, before we lay any stress upon the glories of the medieval system."[75]

In "The Second Spring" (1852), his great sermon hailing the English hierarchy's reconstitution, in which he directly appealed to the Mother of God, Newman looked beyond the ruins of the medieval to something much more timeless.

Arise, Mary, and go forth in thy strength into that north country, which once was thine own, and take possession of a land which knows thee not. Arise, Mother of God, and with thy thrilling voice, speak to those who labour with child, and are in pain, till the babe of grace leaps within them! Shine on us, dear Lady, with thy bright countenance, like the sun in his strength, *O stella matutina*, O harbinger of peace, till our year is one perpetual May. From thy sweet eyes, from thy pure smile, from thy majestic brow, let ten thousand influences rain down, not to confound or overwhelm, but to persuade, to win over thine enemies. O Mary, my hope, O Mother undefiled, fulfil to us the promise of this Spring. A second temple rises on the ruins of the old. Canterbury has gone its way, and York is gone, and Durham is gone, and Winchester is gone. It was sore to part with them. We clung to the vision of past greatness, and would not believe it could come to nought; but the Church in England has died, and the Church lives again. Westminster and Nottingham, Beverley and Hexham, Northampton and Shrewsbury, if the world lasts, shall be names as musical to the ear, as stirring to the heart, as the glories we have lost; and Saints shall rise out of them, if God so will, and Doctors once again shall give the law to Israel, and Preachers call to penance and to justice, as at the beginning.[76]

Four years earlier, Newman wrote Henry Wilberforce from Maryvale, describing how Ambrose St John and he had gone to Bologna to visit Loreto "to get the Blessed Virgin's blessing on us. I have ever been under her shadow . . . My College was St. Mary's, and my Church, and when I went to Littlemore, there, by my own previous disposition, our Blessed Lady was waiting for me . . ."[77] Mary was central to Newman's understanding of himself and of his faithful progress through life—not a summons to try to recreate an ideal medieval Catholicism.

In his memoir of his brother, Frank recalled, "The more my brother argued about Invocation (not that I dare to say he ever urged me to practice it: I think he stopped short in refuting my objections) the more uneasy he made me, till one day,

75 LD, 19:420–3 JHN to T. W. Allies (22 November 1860).
76 *OS*, pp. 177–8.
77 LD, 12:153 JHN to Henry Wilberforce (12 January 1848).

wearied with the topic, I broke out in clearer opposition than usual, saying 'But, my dear John, what can be the use of invoking a Being who cannot hear you? The Virgin is not omnipresent.'[78] Here was the skepticism—the "captious, carping, fastidious refinements of reasoning"—that prevented Frank and so many of his contemporaries from heeding the "sacred influences" of "that bright and gentle Lady." Later, Frank was convinced that he had uncovered the source of Newman's otherwise unaccountable devotion to Mary when he went to Ireland "and saw popular Catholic manuals. From them I concluded he had pilfered his arguments."[79]

The Twisted Thread

Newman had additional personal reasons for wishing that Frank had not turned his back on the Mother of God. In a poem that he wrote to Frank on his 21st birthday in 1826, he spoke of another maternal love:

> My brother, 'tis no recent tie
>   Which binds our fates in one,
> E'en from our tender infancy
>   The twisted thread was spun;–
> Her deed, who stored in fond mind
> Our forms, by sacred love enshrined.
>
> In her affection all had share,
>   All six, she loved them all;
> Yet on her early-chosen Pair
>   Did her full favor fall;
> And we became her dearest theme,
> Her waking thought, her nightly dream.
>
> Ah! Brother, shall we e'er forget
>   Her love, her care, her zeal?
> We cannot pay the countless debt,
>   But we must ever feel;
> For through her earnestness were shed
> Prayer-purchased blessings on our head. . .
>
> So it is left for us to prove
>   Her prayers were not in vain;
> And that God's grace-according love
>   Has come as gentle rain,
> Which, falling in the vernal hour,
> Tints the young leaf, perfumes the flower . . .[80]

---

[78] *Contr*, p. 21.
[79] F. W. Newman quoted in Brian Martin. *John Henry Newman: His Life and Work* (London, 1990), p. 33.
[80] *VV*, pp. 12–15.

In April 1840, when Frank wrote of how haunted he was by his mother's death, Newman must have felt particularly aggrieved. "How have I mourned," Frank wrote, "that our most beloved mother, (whose value every day I seem more to know,) was snatched away not only from her children's love, but from being a promoter of their love! Bitterly, dear John, have I grieved, and perhaps shall never cease to grieve, that an erring judgment, and a conscience thereby misled, made me a less dutiful son to her, and at the same time, as I fully acknowledge, a more willful brother towards you."[81] Here was moving proof that, for all his contrarieties, there was great good-heartedness in Frank Newman, which could only have made his estrangement from his brother doubly painful.

First Principles

Once it became clear that Frank had repudiated Christianity, Newman came to realize that the religious differences between them were the result of different first principles— or what he defined as "opinions . . . held without proof as if self-evident," which could be true or false.[82] As an example, he cited Dr Johnson's holding that "the devil was the first whig"—a proposition which no one could prove or disprove but which still, for many, had the axiomatic force of truth. Newman gave another even more vivid example from the field of battle.

> The celebrated Roman patriot Cato stabbed himself when besieged at Utica, rather than fall into the hands of Cæsar. He thought this a very great action, and so have many others besides. In like manner Saul, in Scripture, fell on his sword when defeated in battle; and there have been those who have reproached Napoleon for not having blown out his brains on the field of Waterloo. Now, if these advocates of suicide had been asked why they thought such conduct, under such circumstances, noble, perhaps they would have returned the querist no answer, as if it were too plain to talk about, or from contempt of him, as if he were a person without any sense of honour, any feeling of what becomes a gentleman, of what a soldier, a hero, owes to himself. That is, they would not bring out their First Principle from the very circumstance that they felt its power so intensely; that First Principle being, that there is no evil so great in the whole universe, visible and invisible, in time and eternity, as humiliation.[83]

Frank recognized that first principles did stand in the way of his brother and him coming to any understanding on matters of faith. Once, he told Newman that he had explained their differences to an acquaintance thus: "I said I thought my differences from you almost turned on matters of fact, when in appearance we agreed as to sentiment and principle. We seem to look out on different worlds. Of course we fall in with totally different circles."[84] Frank found what he understood to be Newman's

---

[81] LD, 7:307 FWN to JHN (15 April 1840).
[82] *Prepos.*, p. 279.
[83] Ibid., p. 281.
[84] *Family*, p. 207.

first principles unpersuasive. "Ever since his first sermon, he never could get any starting point from me. His weakness and credulity as to First Principles were to me lamentable." And as an example, Frank cited Newman's willingness as a boy to credit the existence of ghosts. "I remember at Brighton one year he kept us all agog by a tale of ghosts which seemed inexplicable except by believing in the spirits; then, after two or three weeks, he suddenly told us he found it all to be false. I suppose he was ashamed; for he would not tell us either how he had been deluded or how undeceived. But that an educated man, not reared in Egypt or Abyssinia, should believe that an outward touch, whether by consecrated oil or a holy thumb, could affect the state of the soul and its acceptance with its Supreme Lord, seemed to me as base a folly as any magic. He did not see, that to deny such occult power is now a reasonable First Principle."[85]

But, of course, Newman did see this. Among his contemporaries, rejection of the miraculous was widespread. He also saw that, to many of the approved thinkers of his age, his own respect for the miraculous made him seem irrational. The agnostic philosopher and jurist, Frederic Harrison (1831–1923), for example, while conceding that Newman was "a brilliant controversialist, a subtle fencer, a splendid rhetorician, and a most enthralling preacher," nevertheless contended that "By these popular gifts he has blinded the opinion of his contemporaries to his extravagant hallucinations and passionate defiance of common sense and coherent thought."[86] About the irreconcilability of Harrison's first principles and his own, Newman would have agreed. Yet unlike Harrison he saw this divide in a far more critical, far-reaching light. Writing to Richard Simpson in 1859, when Simpson was reviewing for *The Rambler*, Newman put the absence of consensus regarding first principles in historical perspective. "I am glad you are going to grapple with [John Stuart] Mill – but he is not a common opponent, I am sure. In medieval times you might appeal to supernatural principles as axioms, and start from them. At a later date you might speak of the moral sense, and take truths for granted on the ground that every one held them. You might speak of the idea of a Supreme Being as common to the whole human family – but now nothing is received as true without and before proof, except what the senses or our consciousness conveys to us, for nothing else is universally held. I do not mean to say that Mill does not make assumptions as much as another – but it is easy, like Kilkenny cats, for two combatants to demolish each other – and one does not wish to propagate scepticism, which is the obvious result of such a process of mutual destruction."[87]

Newman also recognized that the nineteenth-century English, after the subsidence of the religious reawakening of the 1830s and 40s, were breaking with the Christian past by choosing to deny the reality of sin, and he had Frank in mind when he described how this first principle might affect relations between otherwise close individuals: "Sometimes two friends live together for years, and appear to entertain the same religious views; at the end of the time they take different courses; one becomes an unbeliever, the other a Catholic. How is this? Some latent and hitherto dormant First

[85] *Contr*, p. 46.
[86] Frederic Harrison. *Realities and Ideals: Social, Political, Literary and Artistic* (London, 1908), p. 374.
[87] LD, 19:169 JHN to Richard Simpson (6 July 1859).

Principle, different in each, comes into play, and carries off one to the East, the other to the West. For instance, suppose the one holds that there is such a thing as sin; the other denies it,—denies it, that is, really and in his heart, though at first he would shrink from saying so, even to himself, and is not aware he denies it. At a certain crisis, either from the pressure of controversy or other reason, each finds he must give up the form of religion in which he has been educated; and then this question, the nature of sin, what it is, whether it exists, comes forward as a turning-point between them; he who does not believe in it becomes an unbeliever; he who does, becomes a Catholic."[88] It is interesting that one of Newman's contemporaries who did not share her compatriots' indifference to iniquity was Lady Chatterton (1805–76), the popular travel writer and novelist whose portrait still adorns the walls of the recusant manor house, Baddesley Clinton in Warwickshire. In her lively memoirs, she opens by recalling how

> My first recollections are of the house in which I was born—24, Arlington Street. It looked into the Green Park, and had a little garden of its own, full of old-fashioned sweet smelling flowers. At least, it was always sweet whenever my father and mother used to stay in Arlington Street with my uncle and aunt Pitt. Every fine day, I used to be turned out into the sweet-scented garden to run wild and play with my doll, and look at the crowd of carriages that seemed to be always driving along Piccadilly—fine old carriages, and vis-a-vis, and state coaches, driven by powdered coachmen sitting on splendid hammercloths, and footmen with tall canes and cocked hats standing behind. Most of the carriages had coronets, or crests, at the four corners of the roof. No cabs, or omnibuses, or even hackney coaches can I remember. To my childish eyes all was glitter and show, and the crowd seemed composed of none but ladies and gentlemen bent on amusement. Yet there was a mysterious something beyond that often made me cry without any apparent reason. I learned afterwards what it was—it was the atmosphere of sin which hung about the great city, and which was as perceptible to my moral sense as its fogs of to-day are to my sight.[89]

Mary Gladstone (1847–1927), the Prime Minister's discerning third daughter, who would marry Harry Drew, the curate of Hawarden, recognized the much more widespread refusal to acknowledge sin in Ruskin, about whom she recalled, "He talked about sins and ugly things in the world all as mistakes or misprints, and utterly condemned the way in which they are dwelt upon and collected. 'You can see the beauty of a rose without a nasty dripping fungus near it,'" she remembered the sage declaring.[90] The denial of sin on the part of the Victorian English also caught the attention of Henry Mayhew, the author of *London Labour and the London Poor* (1851–62), who quoted a street entertainer on how the popular Pelagianism was vitiating the art of Punch and Judy.

> Punch, you know, sir, is a dramatic performance in two hacts. It's a play, you may say. I don't think it can be called a tragedy hexactly; a drama is what we names it.

---

[88] *Prepos.*, p. 286.
[89] *Memoirs of Georgiana, Lady Chatterton* (London, 1878), p. 7.
[90] *Mary Gladstone (Mrs. Drew): Her Diaries and Letters.* ed. L. Masterman (New York, 1930), p. 129.

There is tragic parts, and comic and sentimental parts, too. Some families where
I performs will have it most sentimental . . . . They won't have no ghost, no coffin,
and no devil; and that's what I call spiling the performance entirely. It's the march
of hintellect wot's doing all this—it is, sir.[91]

Having been a member of the Oriel Senior Common Room when it was dominated
by such Noetics as Richard Whately and Blanco White, Newman knew all about "the
march of intellect." In his attitude towards this triumphal march, he set himself apart
not only from Frank but from his entire age:

This is what we call an enlightened age: we are to have large views of things;
everything is to be put on a philosophical basis; reason is to rule: the world is
to begin again; a new and transporting set of views is about to be exhibited to
the great human family. Well and good; have them, preach them, enjoy them,
but deign to recollect the while, that there have been views in the world before
you: that the world has not been going on up to this day without any principles
whatever; that the Old Religion was based on principles, and that it is not enough
to flourish about your "new lamps," if you would make us give up our "old" ones.
Catholicism, I say, had its First Principles before you were born: you say they are
false; very well, prove them to be so: they are false, indeed, if yours are true; but
not false merely because yours are yours. While yours are yours it is self-evident,
indeed, to you, that ours are false; but it is not the common way of carrying on
business in the world, to value English goods by French measures, or to pay a
debt in paper which was contracted in gold. Catholicism has its First Principles,
overthrow them, if you can; endure them, if you cannot. It is not enough to call
them effete because they are old, or antiquated because they are ancient. It is not
enough to look into our churches, and cry, "It is all a form, *because* divine favour
cannot depend on external observances;" or, "It is all a bondage, *because* there
is no such thing as sin;" or, "a blasphemy, *because* the Supreme Being cannot
be present in ceremonies;" or, "a mummery, *because* prayer cannot move Him;"
or, "a tyranny, *because* vows are unnatural;" or, "hypocrisy, *because* no rational
man can credit it at all." I say here is endless assumption, unmitigated hypothesis,
reckless assertion; prove your "because," "because," "because;" prove your First
Principles, and if you cannot, learn philosophic moderation. Why may not my
First Principles contest the prize with yours? they have been longer in the world;
they have lasted longer, they have done harder work, they have seen rougher
service. You sit in your easy-chairs, you dogmatize in your lecture-rooms, you
wield your pens: it all looks well on paper: you write exceedingly well: there
never was an age in which there was better writing; logical, nervous, eloquent,
and pure,—go and carry it all out in the world. Take your First Principles, of
which you are so proud, into the crowded streets of our cities, into the formidable
classes which make up the bulk of our population; try to work society by them.
You think you can; I say you cannot—at least you have not as yet; it is yet to be
seen if you can. "Let not him that putteth on his armour boast as he who taketh

---

[91] *London Characters and Crooks by Henry Mayhew*. ed. C. Hibbert (Folio Society, 1996), p. 257.

it off." Do not take it for granted that that is certain which is waiting the test of reason and experiment. Be modest until you are victorious. My principles, which I believe to be eternal, have at least lasted eighteen hundred years; let yours live as many months. That man can sin, that he has duties, that the Divine Being hears prayer, that He gives His favours through visible ordinances, that He is really present in the midst of them, these principles have been the life of nations; they have shown they could be carried out; let any single nation carry out yours, and you will have better claim to speak contemptuously of Catholic rites, of Catholic devotions, of Catholic belief.[92]

Here is a fair sample of Newman's controversial skills: opponents with any ear for music must have listened to this and felt like Odysseus listening to what the Sirens sang.

It was characteristic of Newman's even-handedness to concede his brother's contention that the evidence for the truth of the Creed might be minimal; still, whatever the evidence, it was sufficient for those disposed to believe. Frank had asserted that "Reasons for our faith we must have; valid ones, which will bear keenest scrutiny." To which Newman replied: "Granted, but a faint reason may be a valid reason. I conceive that such reasons for believing are sufficient which make it more probable, ever so little, that the Catholic Creed is true than that it is false. I conceive that if a man rejects such a mere preponderance of probability, this is a proof that he has no great desire to attain the truth in the matter in hand; and his fault becomes a moral one. Moreover I conceive that God will always put 'the love of the truth' . . . into the hearts of a sufficient number while the world lasts, so that they will close with this mere probability, even supposing the evidence for the Creed be only this. Whether it be more or not, I am not sollicitous to establish, though I believe that in matter of fact it is much more."[93]

Richard Whately, the most formidable of the Noetics, and the man about whom Newman wrote in his *Apologia*, "He, emphatically, opened my mind, and taught me to think and to use my reason," was critical of what he considered both brothers' neglect of evidence.[94] "It is curious to observe how the brothers Newman, starting east and west, have gone so far that they have nearly met. Both have come to the conclusion that there is nothing of what is commonly called evidence for Christianity; the one resting his belief (if he has any) of that, and of the silliest monkish legends alike, on the Church; and the other on the infallible oracle within him. The disparagement of evidence among persons who are professed believers is characteristic of the present age . . . . And there are some very good people who, though they do not themselves feel all evidence for Christianity (as F. Newman says) 'crumble away under them,' yet regard it as a great triumph of their religion that it should so recommend itself to the inward feelings of those who hold that no reason can be given for their hope, and that yet do believe it. But if my tenants were to deny that I had any legal claim to my rents, and call my title-deeds mere waste paper, but to offer to hand me the money as a free gift, because they thought me a worthy man, I should decline the compliment; because next

[92] Ibid., pp. 293–5.
[93] LD, 7:414 JHN to FWN (22 October 1840).
[94] *Apo.*, p. 23.

year they might think I only deserved half the sum, and the year after, perhaps, none at all."[95] In Newman's analysis of the issue of evidence, we can see his response not only to Frank and Whately but to all the rationalists of his age and indeed ours. In Sermon 10 of the *University Sermons*, "Faith and Reason, Contrasted as Habits of Mind" (1839), he distinguished between two powers that are often confused by rationalists. Even Frank conceded that his brother would have made a splendid barrister. Here, he makes his case with masterly judiciousness.

> Now, in attempting to investigate what are the distinct offices of Faith and Reason in religious matters, and the relation of the one to the other, I observe, first, that undeniable though it be, that Reason has a power of analysis and criticism in all opinion and conduct, and that nothing is true or right but what may be justified, and, in a certain sense, proved by it, and undeniable, in consequence, that, unless the doctrines received by Faith are approvable by Reason, they have no claim to be regarded as true, it does not therefore follow that Faith is actually grounded on Reason in the believing mind itself; unless, indeed, to take a parallel case, a judge can be called the origin, as well as the justifier, of the innocence or truth of those who are brought before him. A judge does not make men honest, but acquits and vindicates them: in like manner, Reason need not be the origin of Faith, as Faith exists in the very persons believing, though it does test and verify it. This, then, is one confusion, which must be cleared up in the question,—the assumption that Reason must be the inward principle of action in religious inquiries or conduct in the case of this or that individual, because, like a spectator, it acknowledges and concurs in what goes on;—the mistake of a critical for a creative power.[96]

This is more persuasive than Whately's title-deed analogy, which, if pursued to its logical end, would make faith otiose. Newman never followed Whately in imagining that reason could somehow *prove* the objects of faith. Moreover, Whately was wrong to assert that Newman denied the evidence for Christianity. On the contrary, he accepted the evidence for what it was worth and argued that it tested as much as it confirmed faith.[97] The courses pursued by Charles and Frank sufficiently showed what unbridled scepticism could result if evidence was applied to for what only faith could supply. This was not to say that the extant evidence could not be compelling; only that it had to be seen in proper perspective. Here, he rehearsed arguments that he would marshal more fully in *A Grammar of Assent* (1870): "Nothing need be detracted from the use of the Evidences . . . much less can any sober mind run into the wild notion that actually no proof at all is implied in the maintenance, or may be exacted for the profession of Christianity. I would only maintain that that proof need not be the subject of analysis, or take a methodical form, or be complete and symmetrical, in the believing mind; and that probability is its life. I do but say that it is antecedent probability that gives meaning to those arguments from facts which are commonly called the Evidences of Revelation; that, whereas mere probability proves nothing, mere facts persuade no one;

[95] *Life and Correspondence of Richard Whately* (London, 1866), v. 2, pp. 154–5.
[96] *US*, p. 131.
[97] Cf. Richard Swinburne. *Was Jesus God?* (Oxford, 2008), an entertaining *tour de force*.

that probability is to fact, as the soul to the body; that mere presumptions may have no force, but that mere facts have no warmth. A mutilated and defective evidence suffices for persuasion where the heart is alive; but dead evidences, however perfect, can but create a dead faith."[98]

In Sermon 4 of the *University Sermons*, "The Usurpations of Reason" (1831), Newman put the rise of rationalist objections to faith in some historical context. "The usurpations of the Reason may be dated from the Reformation. Then, together with the tyranny, the legitimate authority of the ecclesiastical power was more or less overthrown; and in some places its ultimate basis also, the moral sense. One school of men resisted the Church; another went farther, and rejected the supreme authority of the law of Conscience. Accordingly, Revealed Religion was in a great measure stripped of its proof; for the existence of the Church had been its external evidence, and its internal had been supplied by the moral sense. Reason now undertook to repair the demolition it had made, and to render the proof of Christianity independent both of the Church and of the law of nature."[99] Yet Newman recognized that there were perils inherent in attempting to make the reason of men the measure of the claims of faith. "Our great danger is, lest we should not understand our own principles, and should weakly surrender customs and institutions, which go far to constitute the Church what she is, the pillar and ground of moral truth,—lest, from a wish to make religion acceptable to the world in general, more free from objections than any moral system can be made, more immediately and visibly beneficial to the temporal interests of the community than God's comprehensive appointments condescend to be, we betray it to its enemies; lest we rashly take the Scriptures from the Church's custody, and commit them to the world, that is, to what is called public opinion; which men boast, indeed, will ever be right on the whole, but which, in fact, being the opinion of men who, as a body, have not cultivated the internal moral sense, and have externally no immutable rules to bind them, is, in religious questions, only by accident right, or only on very broad questions, and tomorrow will betray interests which today it affects to uphold."[100] Here, again, was a fundamental difference between the brothers: Frank insisted that Christianity be recast to satisfy the dictates of public opinion; Newman insisted that those dictates could have no authority whatever on matters relating to Revealed Religion.

Citing what Christ says in the Gospel of St Matthew, "Wisdom is justified of her Children," Newman argued that: "There is no act on God's part, no truth of religion, to which a captious Reason may not find objections; and in truth the evidence and matter of Revelation are not addressed to the mere unstable Reason of man, nor can hope for any certain or adequate reception with it. Divine Wisdom speaks, not to the world, but to her own children, or those have been already under her teaching, and who, knowing her voice, understand her words, and are suitable judges of them. These justify her."[101] In Sermon 12 of the *University Sermons*, "Love the Safeguard of Faith against Superstition," (1839) Newman put the matter even more straightforwardly.

[98] *US*, pp. 141–2.
[99] Ibid., p. 57.
[100] Ibid., p. 60.
[101] Ibid., p. 54.

"It is new life, and not the natural reason, which leads the soul to Christ. Does a child trust his parents because he has proved to himself that they are such, and that they are able and desirous to do him good, or from the instinct of affection? We *believe,* because we *love.* How plain a truth! What gain is it to be wise above that which is written? Why, O men, deface with your minute and arbitrary philosophy, the simplicity, the reality, the glorious liberty of the inspired teaching?"[102]

Here, Newman might have been addressing not only Frank but all the rationalists of whom Frank was so fond, from James Martineau and G. J. Holyoake to Charles Kingsley and Frederic Harrison. Later, in the *Tamworth Reading Room* (1841), the series of letters he wrote *The Times* refuting Robert Peel's contention that science could somehow take the place of faith, he renewed his attack against the misguided trust that rationalists invested in reason as a principle of action. "Many a man will live and die upon a dogma; no man will be a martyr for a conclusion. A conclusion is but an opinion . . . This is why a literary religion is so little to be depended upon; it looks well in fair weather, but its doctrines are opinions, and, when called to suffer for them, it slips them between its folios, or burns them at the hearth . . . After all, man is *not* a reasoning animal; he is a seeing, feeling, contemplating, acting animal."[103] In this, Newman was at one with Queen Victoria who wrote her daughter Vicky in 1878 of how "Science is greatly to be admired and encouraged, but if it is to take the place of our Creator, and if philosophers and students try to explain everything and to disbelieve whatever they cannot prove, I call it a great evil instead of a great blessing."[104] Later still, in his *Apologia*, Newman even admitted that he might have relied too heavily on reason himself after he felt his growing sense confirmed that "my mind had not found its ultimate rest" in the Anglican Church. Still, the intimations he received as far back as 1829 that he was being "led on by God's hand blindly, not knowing whither he [was] taking me" forced on him a crisis and it was understandable that he should want to test his instincts: "The one question was, what was I to do? I had to make up my mind for myself, and others could not help me. I determined to be guided, not by my imagination, but by my reason. And this I said over and over again in the years which followed, both in conversation and in private letters. Had it not been for this severe resolve, I should have been a Catholic sooner . . ."[105]

Bishops

The disparate first principles of the brothers were aggravated by tensions that arose as a result of their rooming together at Searle's Coffee House at the Corner of Broad Street and Holywell. In letters home to his parents Newman always insisted that the cost of keeping Frank had been negligible. "He is no inconvenience to me. He is incurring no great expense. No bills are owing by him except the tailor's and one for

---

[102] Ibid., p. 163.
[103] *DA,* pp. 293–4.
[104] *Letters to Vicky: The Correspondence between Queen Victoria and her Daughter Victoria, Empress of Germany 1858–1901.* ed. Andrew Roberts (Folio Society, 2011), p. 497.
[105] *Apo.,* p. 112.

a hat.[106] He now owes nothing for board or lodging: and what is incurring this term, I expect to be able to pay before he goes down for Christmas. He has been now above a year at Oxford without any inconvenience or trouble to me . . . Looking at things merely in a human light, if we have got through the last year so well, much shall we the year to come. *Everything* then as far as relates to Francis and myself is to be cut off from your anxiety."[107] And yet writing his Aunt Elizabeth of this period, Newman revealed that "I had . . . no provision for the morrow. I was sensible that everything even I ate, I had no idea how it was to be paid for. I knew that every day was adding to what was owing, and I saw no quarter from which relief would come."[108] In the diary he kept in 1823, he wrote: "Praised be Thy name for the temporal blessings in which for the last year and a half, Thou has sustained Francis and myself. How wonderfully thou hast brought us through, beginning with nothing . . . By some mistake my pupil has not paid me yet—so that at present I have hardly more than a sovereign."[109] Clearly, Newman sacrificed a fair amount to keep his brother and, to his credit, Frank gratefully acknowledged as much, admitting even in his otherwise abusive memoir how, as he said, "In my rising manhood I received inestimable benefits from this (my eldest) brother. I was able to repay his money, but that could not cancel my debt, for he supported me not out of his abundance, but when he knew not whence weekly and daily funds were to come. I have felt grateful up to his last day, and have tried to cherish for him a sort of *filial* sentiment."[110]

There were a number of reasons why Frank could only feel "a sort of filial sentiment" for his brother. In *Phases of Faith*, he conceded that his brother "might have seemed my natural adviser . . . As a warm-hearted and generous brother, who exercised towards me paternal cares, I esteemed him and felt a deep gratitude; as a man of various culture and peculiar genius, I admired and was proud of him; but my doctrinal religion impeded my loving him as much as he deserved, and even justified my feeling some distrust of him."[111] In particular, he recalled that one difference that kept him from confiding in his brother was the respect Newman was prepared to show bishops—though Frank always misread the import of this respect. While still an Anglican, Newman put obedience to episcopal authority in some perspective.

> There is no room for eclecticism in any elementary matter. No member of the English Church allows himself to build on any doctrine different from that found in our book of Common Prayer. That formulary contains the elements of our

---

[106] Frank's fondness for hats never went unnoticed. Mrs Georgina Bainsmith, who did the bust of Frank Newman in University College, recalled: "Another day I came into the room and heard the Professor say to my mother quite seriously: 'I never can understand how it is that my hat always interests the idle little boys in the street. They say as I pass them, 'Where did you get that hat?' Everyone wears a hat of one shape or another, and I really fail to see why *mine* should be so very interesting.' He was wearing a soft felt hat with a very broad brim, set far back on his head; and with his peculiar American-looking beard and thick grey locks that came down over the high Gladstone collar which he always wore, and a black and white shepherd's plaid scarf round his neck and twisted over in front with its ends tucked into his waistcoat, he looked sufficiently odd." See Sieveking, pp. 125–6.

[107] LD,1:154–5 JHN to Mrs Jemima Newman (5 November 1822).

[108] LD, 1:138 JHN to Elizabeth Newman (28 April 1822).

[109] *AW*, p. 190.

[110] *Contr*, vi.

[111] Ibid., p. 7.

theology; and herein lies the practical exercise of our faith, which all true religion exacts. We surrender ourselves in obedience to it: we act upon it: we obey it even in points of detail where there is room for diversity of opinion. The Thirty-nine Articles furnish a second trial of our humility and self-restraint. Again, we never forget that, reserving our fidelity to the Creed, we are bound to defer to Episcopal authority. Here then are trials of principle on starting; so much is already settled, and demands our assent, not our criticism.[112]

In April 1844, when he was moving closer and closer to Rome, Newman reaffirmed his respect for bishops in a letter to Jemima, "No one can accuse me of not obeying St. Ignatius's rule—indeed the words constantly in my mind have been 'He who trifles with the Bishop, trifles with the Bishop invisible'. . . I wish to be subject and submissive to the one Bishop set over me—and for the same reason I should, if a Roman Catholic, be not a Gallican, but obey submissively and unreservedly the 'one Bishop' in the person of the Pope, as the representative of the Bishop unseen."[113] This was Newman's serious understanding of the role of the episcopate. But what Frank never appreciated—by all accounts, he was oddly bereft of any sense of humour—was the rather less serious view that Newman took of episcopacy. Describing a divine once to his sister Jemima, Newman observed that "he is a very episcopal looking man—(was he always so?) and might easily be made an Archdeacon or Dean. Some men have to grow into those things. I mean by the episcopal shape, height f. 5.11—slimness—firmness of step, uprightness, and length of legs—roundness or rather ovalness of head, or rather ovalness by roundness, height of forehead, and prominence of eyebrow.—and I mean by the episcopal air, gravity, decision, self possession, a certain dryness of manner, and a reserved courteousness. The episcopal dress completes the picture, consisting in long black gaiters . . ."[114] This was the episcopacy of old stagers, not the authoritarianism of which Frank so vehemently disapproved. To his mother in 1827, Newman wrote: "The new Bishop presented himself in his wig in Church last Sunday – he is much disfigured by it . . . Do you know that Bishop's wigs are made of cowhair? I have it from the best authority – nay from cow tail?"[115] Then there was Newman's description of the impetuous Richard Simpson, the wayward editor of the often provocative *Rambler*: "I DESPAIR of Simpson being other than he is – he will always be clever, amusing, brilliant, and suggestive. He will always be flicking his whip at Bishops, cutting them in tender places, throwing stones at sacred Congregations, and, as he rides along the high road, discharging pea shooters at Cardinals who happen by bad luck to look out of window."[116]

What is also missing from Frank's reading of his brother's attitude to episcopacy is any acknowledgement of the amount of distrust that Newman provoked in not only Anglican but Roman bishops. That this was provoked, on the whole, unintentionally does not diminish the independence with which Newman tempered

[112] *VM*, i, p. 24.
[113] LD, 10:213 JHN to Mrs John Mozley (19 April 1844).
[114] LD, 3:82 JHN to Jemima Newman (27 August 1832).
[115] LD, 2:10 JHN to Mrs Jemima Newman (30 March 1827).
[116] LD, 20:4 JHN to Sir John Acton (5 July 1861).

his submission to authority. Frank's object in charging that his brother was too submissive to episcopal authority was to question his brother's independence, yet the wholesale condemnation with which the Anglican bishops responded to Tract 90 and the continual opposition that Newman encountered from bishops when he was a Catholic clearly confute this charge. In both cases, Newman might have said, with Henry Adams, "It is devilish disagreeable to act the part of Sisyphus especially when it is our own friends who are trying to crush us under the rock."[117] As it was, in a journal entry for 29 January 1868, Newman made light of his abiding frustrations with his episcopal superiors: "I should be so out of my element if I were without that cold shade on the side of ecclesiastical authority, in which I have dwelt nearly all my life, my eyes would be so dazed, and my limbs so relaxed, were I brought out in the full sun of ecclesiastical favour, that I should not know how to act and should make a fool of myself."[118]

If Newman saw episcopal authority as at once profoundly necessary and incidentally comic, Frank saw it as intrinsically corrupt. After he was confirmed in the Anglican Church, he recalled how scandalized he was "by the lawn sleeves, wig, artificial voice and manner" of William Howley (1766–1848), the Bishop of London, whom he thought "a made-up man and a mere pageant."[119] This was hardly fair to Howley, who would later go on to become Archbishop of Canterbury. In fact, of all nineteenth-century archbishops, Howley was one of the most admirable. He stood by the doctrine of baptismal regeneration when it was neither popular nor profitable. He opposed Charles Grey and his whiggish friends for their usurpatory reforms of the Established Church. He staunchly opposed Catholic Emancipation and had nothing but contempt for the First Reform Bill. And he opposed Lord John Russell's recommendation that education be supplied along secular lines. As for Howley's scholarly attainments, Hugh James Rose considered him one of the best classical scholars that he had ever encountered.

In his contempt for bishops, Frank differed even with such a supple Anglican as F. D. Maurice, who reaffirmed the utility of episcopacy in his "Three Letters to the Rev. W. Palmer" (1842) at the height of the Jerusalem bishopric controversy.[120] "We

---

[117] Henry Adams to Charles Francis Adams, Jr. (20 November 1861) in *The Civil War: The First Year Told By Those Who Lived It* (New York, 2011), p. 651.

[118] *AW*, p. 264.

[119] *Phases,* p. 12.

[120] The Jerusalem Bishopric was a joint Prussian and Anglican bishopric installed in Jerusalem in 1842 to give Protestantism some representation in the Holy Land, which historically had been the preserve of the Eastern Orthodox and Roman Churches. Maurice's son attests how congenial the scheme was to his broad church father: "His contention was . . . that the nation is Protestant, the Church Catholic, and that the two are not contradictory, but complementary truths; the protest of the nation being that God, and not the Pope, is the King of its king; the catholicity of the Church consisting in a divine constitution under the head which the nation claims also as its head—its invisible King. To him, moreover, it was peculiarly satisfactory that in consequence, as he believed, of the catholicity of the order of bishops, it should be felt by the Prussian King to be inevitable that the union for which all Christians were seeking should be in that order." See Frederick Maurice. *The Life and Letters of F.D. Maurice* (London, 1884), v.1, p. 320. Newman's reading of the matter was starkly different. For him, the purpose of the scheme was "to collect a communion out of Protestants, Jews, Druses, and Monophysites, conforming under the influence of our war-steamers, to counterbalance the Russian influence under the Greeks, and the French through the Latins . . ." See LD, 8:292 JHN to S. F. Wood (10 October 1841).

cannot . . . recognize a Church without Bishops," he wrote "We cannot do it for our own sakes, because we believe that we have a solemn trust and responsibility to uphold this great institution of Episcopacy; because we believe that it has been preserved to us in a wonderful manner for the last three centuries, when there was scarcely anything in our minds to make its meaning intelligible; because we believe that all the circumstances of the age are declaring to us its purpose and its necessity."[121] Frank would only have considered this an unpersuasive appeal to tradition, against which he fulminated in his autobiography:

> For a century after the death of Edward VI the bishops were the tools of court-bigotry, and often owed their highest promotions to base subservience. After the Revolution, the Episcopal order . . . might be described as a body of supine persons, known to the public only as a dead weight against all change that was distasteful to the Government. In the last century and a half, the nation was often afflicted with sensual royalty, bloody wars, venal statesmen, corrupt constituencies, bribery and violence at elections, flagitious drunkenness pervading all ranks, and insinuating itself into Colleges and Rectories. The prisons of the country had been in a most disgraceful state; the fairs and waits were scenes of rude debauchery, and the theatres were—still, in the nineteenth century—whispered to be the haunts of the most debasing immorality. I could not learn that any bishop had ever taken the lead in denouncing these iniquities . . . Neither Howard, Wesley and Whitfield, nor yet Clarkson, Wilberforce, or Romilly, could boast of the Episcopal bench as an ally against inhuman or immoral practices . . .[122]

Frank's animus against episcopacy was at the heart of his inability to agree with his brother on religious matters. "In the World, I expected pomp and vain show and formality and counterfeits," he wrote, "but of the Church, as Christ's own kingdom, I demanded reality and could not digest legal fictions." How Frank "demanded reality" in this or in anything else is not clear. In his skeptical nominalism, he tended to treat reality as a fairly malleable property: this is one reason why he was always so intent on the search for truth, rather than on the thing itself.

When the brothers were at Oxford together, Frank recalled making some remark disparaging to bishops and Newman remonstrating with him, which led to a tell-tale passage in *Phases of Faith*:

> I was willing to honour a Lord Bishop as a peer of Parliament; but his office was to me no guarantee of spiritual eminence. To find my brother thus stop my mouth was a puzzle; and impeded all free speech towards him. In fact, I very soon left off the attempt at intimate religious intercourse with him, or asking counsel as of one who could sympathize. We talked, indeed, a great deal on the surface of religious matters; and on some questions I was overpowered and received a temporary bias from his superior knowledge; but as time went on, and my own intellect

---

[121] F. D. Maurice from *To Build Christ's Kingdom: F. D. Maurice and His Writings*. ed. Jeremy Morris (London, 2007), p. 11
[122] *Phases*, p. 12.

ripened, I distinctly felt that his arguments were too fine-drawn and subtle, often elaborately missing the moral points and the main points, to rest on some ecclesiastical fiction; and his conclusions were to me so marvelous and painful, that I constantly thought I had mistaken him. In short, he was my senior by a very few years: nor was there any elder resident at Oxford, accessible to me, who united all the qualities which I wanted in an adviser. Nothing was left for me but to cast myself on Him who is named the Father of Lights, and resolve to follow the light which He might give, however opposed to my own prejudices, and however I might be condemned by men. This solemn engagement I made in early youth, and neither the frowns nor the grief of my brethren can make me ashamed of it in my manhood.[123]

This gives a misleading impression of Frank's religious development. In fact, after failing to find any sustainable faith in Darbyism, Frank reverted to the bibliolatry of his adolescence and when that proved untenable, he consulted various Unitarians for religious guidance. Claiming, as he does here, that he resolved "to follow the light which He might give, however opposed to my own prejudices and however condemned I might be by men" was false: his highly subjective religion was never condemned by his colleagues. His good friend James Martineau might have found *Phases of Faith* "wholly destructive" but he also considered it a book which put one "in the presence of a mind wholly incapable of the least moral unfairness or ingenious self-deception, and devoted with absolute singleness to the quest of the true and the good." He even urged that the book be read twice.[124] Frank's friend Holyoake was similarly laudatory, treating his subjectivism in religion as though it were a badge of integrity. When Frank wrote him of how his rejection of the Christian belief in resurrection "cost me the regard of all who do not know me intimately," Holyoake insisted on seeing it as proof of "his lofty fidelity" to conscience. "Whatever might be his interest in a future life, if it were the will of God not to concede it, he held it be the duty of one who placed his trust in Him to acquiesce. The spirit of piety never seemed to me nobler, than in this unusual expression of unmurmuring, unpresuming resignation."[125] There was nothing condemnatory in that appraisal.

Frank's contention that his brother's view of episcopacy was founded on an "ecclesiastical fiction" was also false. In the *Apologia*, Newman freely conceded that "at first sight" many outside the Church might be inclined to imagine that inside the Church "the restless intellect of our common humanity is utterly weighed down, to the repression of all independent effort and action whatever, so that, if this is to be the mode of bringing it into order, it is brought into order only to be destroyed."

But this is far from the result, far from what I conceive to be the intention of that high Providence who has provided a great remedy for a great evil,—far from borne out by the history of the conflict between Infallibility and Reason in the past, and the prospect of it in the future. The energy of the human intellect "does from opposition grow;" it thrives and is joyous, with a tough elastic strength,

---

[123] Ibid., p. 8.
[124] James Martineau. *Miscellanies* (Boston, 1852), p. 218.
[125] *Bygones*, 1, p. 196.

under the terrible blows of the divinely-fashioned weapon, and is never so much itself as when it has lately been overthrown. It is the custom with Protestant writers to consider that, whereas there are two great principles in action in the history of religion, Authority and Private Judgment, they have all the Private Judgment to themselves, and we have the full inheritance and the superincumbent oppression of Authority. But this is not so; it is the vast Catholic body itself, and it only, which affords an arena for both combatants in that awful, never-dying duel. It is necessary for the very life of religion, viewed in its large operations and its history, that the warfare should be incessantly carried on. Every exercise of Infallibility is brought out into act by an intense and varied operation of the Reason, both as its ally and as its opponent, and provokes again, when it has done its work, a re-action of Reason against it; and, as in a civil polity the State exists and endures by means of the rivalry and collision, the encroachments and defeats of its constituent parts, so in like manner Catholic Christendom is no simple exhibition of religious absolutism, but presents a continuous picture of Authority and Private Judgment alternately advancing and retreating as the ebb and flow of the tide;—it is a vast assemblage of human beings with wilful intellects and wild passions, brought together into one by the beauty and the Majesty of a Superhuman Power,—into what may be called a large reformatory or training-school, not as if into a hospital or into a prison, not in order to be sent to bed, not to be buried alive, but (if I may change my metaphor) brought together as if into some moral factory, for the melting, refining, and moulding, by an incessant, noisy process, of the raw material of human nature, so excellent, so dangerous, so capable of divine purposes.[126]

Newman's view of episcopacy, as this demonstrates, was based, not on "ecclesiastical fiction" but on divine and indeed human truths. He may have had a respect for the authority of bishops but he did not regard bishops themselves with anything like the uncritical deference that Frank imagined. Once again, Frank was attempting to caricature his brother. To find a figure truer to his caricature, we must go to that memorable character in *The Pickwick Papers* (1836–7), Nathaniel Pipkin, whom Dickens describes as having seen "a bishop—a real bishop, with his arms in lawn sleeves, and his head in a wig. He had seen him walk, and heard him talk, at a confirmation, on which momentous occasion . . . [he] was so overcome with reverence and awe, when the aforesaid bishop laid his hand on his head, that he fainted right clean away, and was borne out of the church in the arms of the beadle."[127]

Frank and the Darbyites

Frank's dim view of bishops was all the more distressing to Newman in light of the high hopes that he had held out for his brother's future when they were at Oxford

---

126 *Apo.*, pp. 225–6.
127 Dickens. *The Pickwick Papers* (Penguin, 1972), pp. 309–10.

together. When Frank became a Fellow of Balliol in 1826, Newman fully expected him
to take orders. In his poem for his brother's 21st birthday, he wrote:

> Dear Frank, we both are summon'd now
>> As champions of the Lord;—
> Enroll'd am I, and shortly thou
>> Must buckle on thy sword;
> A high employ, nor lightly given,
> To serve as messengers of heaven.[128]

But Frank had other plans. "I longed to be a missionary for Christ among the heathen—a
notion I had often fostered while reading the lives of missionaries."[129] In 1827, while
tutoring Lord Congleton's sons in County Wicklow, Frank met precisely the sort of
missionary he had in mind in John Nelson Darby (1800–82), a young Anglo-Irishman
who spent his days in the Wicklow Mountains converting Irish peasants to the Church
of Ireland. It was only after William Magee, the Archbishop of Dublin insisted that all
legal converts first swear allegiance to George IV that the defections ceased. Darby
would be surprised to see the popularity the Church of Ireland has gained among
Ireland's new middle classes, though it is clear that this has been the result of clerical
scandal, not the old Bible-thumping that infused Darby's proselytism.

Frank describes young Darby in *Phases of Faith* as "a most remarkable man
who . . . gained immense sway over me . . ." Dressed in crumpled old tweeds and
invariably unshaven, Darby made his way through the drawing rooms of the
Ascendancy on crutches preaching an evangelical faith that could not have been more
different from the usual Church of Ireland latitudinarianism. Some of his appeal must
have come from his looks, especially his gaunt physiognomy. Looking at photographs
of Darby, one can understand what the poet Yeats was getting at when he described one
of his aging beauties as having

> Hollow of cheek as though it drank the wind
> And took a mess of shadows for its meat . . .

For Frank, Darby was missionary Christianity personified. "Every evening he sallied
forth to teach in the cabins, and roving far and wide over mountain and amid bogs,
was seldom home before midnight . . . his whole frame might have vied in emaciation
with a monk of La Trappe."[130] Educated at Trinity College, Dublin, he was nevertheless
dismissive of learning. "He had practically given up all reading except that of the Bible,"
Frank recalled, "and no small part of his movement towards me soon took the form of
dissuasion from all other voluntary study."[131] For Darby, "the highest Christian must
necessarily decline the pursuit of science, knowledge, art, history,—except so far as any
of these things might be made useful tools for immediate spiritual results."[132] Later,

---

[128] *VV*, p. 15.
[129] *Phases*, p. 17.
[130] Ibid., pp. 17–18.
[131] Ibid., p.18.
[132] Ibid., p. 23.

Darby would secede from the Church of Ireland altogether to form the Plymouth Brethren, a non-denominational sect convinced that priests were an affront to the Holy Ghost and that the faithful should organize around a simple sharing of the bread and wine and dedicate themselves to the letter of Scripture, unconstrained by dogma or ecclesiastical rites. He was also a fair poet, a quality which must have endeared him to the Irish. One of his poems, entitled "Devil's Shooting Excursion," has a memorable opening

> The month was November, the morning fine,
> The clock had just struck half-past nine,
> The devil had swallowed his coffee and toast,
> And sat by the fire perusing the Post.[133]
> "A rare morning", cries he, "ho! my dog and my gun,
> I vow I must forth for a taste of fun."

It is a shame that Darby did not devote himself more to mocking the Ascendancy at prayer: he had a talent for writing satirical *jeux d'esprit*. Instead, he gave all his energies to spreading his peculiarly gloomy *sola scriptura* religion. When Frank argued that riches could be justified on the grounds that they provided means for educating the young, Darby was scornful: "If I had children, I would as soon see them break stones on the road, as do any thing else, if only I could secure them the Gospel and the grace of God."[134] Asked whether every word in the Bible was true, Darby was categorical: "Every word, depend upon it, is from the Spirit, and . . . for eternal service."[135] Frank found the monomaniacal intensity of the man irresistible. "For the first time in my life I saw a man earnestly turning into reality the principles which others confessed only with their lips. . . . But for a few weaknesses . . . I could have accepted him as an apostle commissioned to reveal the mind of God."[136]

Darby would convince Frank that the Bible could serve as a proper basis for Christian faith, even though Newman warned his brother against what he called this "low arrogant cruel ultra-Protestant principle" as early as 1835.[137] On what ground of reason or Scripture, Newman asked his brother, "do you say that every one may gain the true doctrines of the gospel for himself from the Bible? where is illumination promised an individual for this purpose? where is it any where hinted that the aid of teachers is to be superseded? where that the universal testimony of the Church is not a principle of belief as sure and satisfactory as the word of Scripture?

> This is the πρωτον ψευδοσ [primary fallacy] of your notions. Till you give it up, till you see that the unanimous witness of the whole Church (as being a witness

---

[133] *The Post* was Dublin's popular Protestant paper.
[134] *Phases*, p. 18.
[135] Ibid., p. 19.
[136] Ibid, p. 21.
[137] Cf. W. R. W. Stephens. *Life and Letters of W. F. Hook* (London, 1879), p. 418. "Ultra-Protestantism demoralises the country. Its one doctrine is 'justification by the feelings'—'I feel happy, therefore I am saved, or I believe I am saved (which is only another mode of expressing the same thing), and therefore I am saved.' Here, in Leeds, this doctrine has blinded the moral perceptions of the Methodists and Evangelicals. They think themselves safe, when they have experienced certain feelings, whatever their conduct may be . . ." W. F. Hook to Wood (December 1844).

to an historical fact, viz that the Apostles so taught), where attainable, is as much the voice of God (I do not say as sacredly and immediately so, but as really) as Scripture itself, there is no hope for a clearheaded man like you. You will unravel the web of selfsufficient inquiry. You will tell me perhaps you must pursue the truth without looking to consequences – yet I cannot help begging you to contemplate whither you are going. Is it possible you are approaching Charles's notions? There will be this difference that you will admit the being of God – though this, I verily think, would be an inconsistency in you – but, admitting it, what else at least will you retain? Indeed my dear F., you are in a net which I do not like to think of. I do feel it to be a snare of the devil.[138]

This snare was not simply a figure of speech for Newman. Newman's conviction that religious error could be a trap laid by the devil gave his disagreements with his brother an urgency that is often overlooked. Too many have written of the brothers as though they were intellectual combatants engaged in some contest of wits.[139] From Newman's standpoint, nothing could have been further from the truth. He disputed various points of Christian doctrine with his brother not because he saw in him any redoubtable opponent—Frank was a poor disputant—but because he wished to salvage his deteriorating Christian faith, to rescue him from the devil's snares. And it is worth pointing out that Newman was not the only one who thought that his brother was flirting with the devil. In his later years, as I shall show, Frank would recommend practices that also put a staff writer at *Scribner's Monthly* in mind of the satanic.

Nevertheless, Frank chose to flout his brother's counsel and strode ever more recklessly into the labyrinth of private judgement, where he devised a subjective religion that even his Unitarian friends found *outré*. Frank, James Martineau complained, "exaggerates the resources of the purely subjective side of Religion, and undervalues its objective conditions. A spirit like his may doubtless draw, from the mere depth of its inner experience a faith and trust adequate to the noble governance of life. But just as the Intellect of mere metaphysicians, spinning assiduously from its own centre without fixed points of attachment for its threads, produces as many tissues of thought as there are original thinkers; so the Soul of spiritualists, in attempting to evolve every thing from within any datum of historical reverence, must create as many religions as there are worshippers."[140]

Richard Whately also recognized the thoroughly subjective cast of Frank's religious views. "F. Newman, we are told, is a very pious man. And so he is, in a certain way of his own. As far as I can judge from what I have read of him . . . his piety seems to consist mainly of a sort of self-adoration. His system seems to be that of 'every man his own apostle.'"[141] Nevertheless, it must be said that Frank was not unaware of the streak of egomania in his make-up. In 1871 when he was 66, he wrote Anna Swanswick, the proto-suffragette: "Every one of us who is to do anything worthy must forget self, and

---

[138] LD, 5:166–7 JHN to Francis William Newman (23 November 1835).
[139] See W. Robbins. *The Newman Brothers* (Cambridge, 1966) and F. Turner. *John Henry Newman: The Challenge to Evangelical Religion* (New Haven, 2002).
[140] James Martineau. Review of *Phases of Faith* from *The Perspective Review* for August, 1850 in *Miscellanies*. (Boston and New York, 1852), p. 279.
[141] *Life and Correspondence of Richard Whately* (London, 1866), II, p. 153.

above all, must not cast self-complacent glances on what he is, or does, or has done; and, in truth, I have so deep a dissatisfaction with what I am and have been, that my poor consolation is to think how much worse I might have been . . ."[142] This exhibits a side of Frank that was altogether winning; but whether this or the other less commendable aspects of the man were uppermost, Newman never abandoned his brother. Year after year, in both his Anglican and his Catholic writings, one can hear him calling out to Frank, warning him against "the all-corroding, all-dissolving scepticism of the intellect in religious enquiries."[143] Newman did not make such wholehearted appeals to win debating points. He made them out of fraternal love to help his brother, to respond to the "call of charity."

Frank saw matters differently. In his memoir, he recalled his brother's letter with a bitterness that proves that the offence it caused never went away. "I certainly do not wish to heap more odium on him than is inevitable," Frank wrote. "Grant that all was spontaneous: the sad fact remained that, whether he knew it or not, he was pushing on the Romish line in the garb of an Anglican." Then, again, Frank took issue with his brother for his "insidious invention of the term Ultra-Protestant to insult all that hold to the cardinal doctrine of Protestantism and common morality. Only when the *Apologia* came out in 1864, had I any idea that with him Protestant and Ultra-Protestant were identical. This invention of two names for the same thing, while the public use only one, could not advance Truth, but might cunningly aid error." This impatience with a perfectly reasonable distinction was typical of Frank, as was his conviction that "It was at last a relief to think him not actually fraudulent, but only fanatical . . . and the more acquaintance I made with his conveniently ambiguous words, the more this theory won on me: 'He is caught in his own net.'"[144]

Persian Adventure

The man who spoke of being caught in one's own net knew what he was talking about. What might be called his Persian adventure was a case in point. In 1829, Frank met Anthony Norris Groves, a Devonshire dentist who had written a tract called *Christian Devotedness*, urging readers to abandon their worldly goods and follow Christ. When Groves announced that he and fellow Darbyites—including Lord Congleton and Edward Cronin—were preparing to undertake a mission to Baghdad, Frank readily agreed to accompany them. He was at a turning point in his life. Eager to emulate Darby and convert souls to *sola scriptura* Christianity, he was also in the grip of an unrequited passion for Maria Giberne (1808–85), Newman's lifelong friend, who later converted to Catholicism. Thus, Frank's decision to pack up and commence missionary was driven as much by a broken heart as by zeal for converting Mohammedans.

In his reminiscences of the Oxford Movement, Tom Mozley vividly described the object of Frank's unrequited love: "In all this goodly array there was not a grander

[142] *Sieveking*, p. 156.
[143] *Apo.*, p. 218.
[144] *Contr*, pp. 22–3.

or more ornamental figure than Maria Rosina Giberne. She was, nay she is, the *prima donna* of the company. Tall, strong of build, majestic, with aquiline nose, well-formed mouth, dark penetrating eyes, and a luxuriance of glossy black hair, she would command attention anywhere."[145] Of Huguenot stock, like Newman's mother, Maria was one of Newman's earliest admirers and converted in December 1845, after meeting with the legendary Father Brownbill, S. J. of Farm Street. In 1846, she moved to Rome and lived with the Colonna family, supporting herself through painting. In 1851, she travelled to Italy to collect testimonies for Newman's Achilli trial. After spending 4 years in Rome, where she lived with the Borghese family, she decided to become a nun. Pius IX suggested the Visitation order and she was professed at Autun in 1863. Although she was one of Newman's most faithful correspondents, he was rather matter-of-fact about her sudden death. "We have this morning had a telegram from Autun with tidings of Maria Giberne's death," he wrote. "Miss Giberne died on 2 Dec. It was from an Apoplectic seizure. She had within the week written a clever critique on Emmeline Deane's portrait of me . . . I cannot be sorry at M. Gibernes death. She had had for near 30 years a life of penance, and her friends, who faithfully corresponded with her, were going or gone—her great friend, Lady Georgina Fullerton, lately."[146] That Newman said nothing more about the memory of a woman who had shown him so many kindnesses over the years does not do him much credit, though it has to be said that Maria could be tiresome. In one letter, in which he advised her to pay better attention to her health, the usually forbearing Cardinal lost his patience. "If you have not teeth, you cannot eat hard substances without danger. Unchewed meat is as dangerous to the stomach as brick or stone, or a bunch of keys. You are not an ostrich."[147]

Maria's strong attachment to Newman may very well have caused resentment in the jilted Frank. In any case, having decided against taking orders in the Church of England, he was ready to renounce his Oxford career. If he hated bishops, he was no fonder of the 39 Articles, which he regarded as a "trap for the conscience." Decrying the spectacle of educated Englishmen subscribing to tenets in which they did not believe, he deplored how the Articles "undermine truthfulness in the active thinker, and torture the sensitiveness of the tenderminded. As long as they are maintained, in Church or University, these institutions exert a positive influence to deprave or eject those who ought to be their most useful and honored members."[148] Frank was one of a number of Victorians who made their refusal to sign the Articles a badge of honour. James Martineau was particularly adamant against them, charging that they excluded those with "the very seal of God upon their foreheads . . . . It is precisely the men intellectually and spiritually incorruptible whom the ordeal of subscription and creeds pick out for rejection. A real *bona-fide* assent to all the doctrinal obligations is utterly impossible . . . it is fatal and blighting to embalm the obsolete."[149] F. D. Maurice, on the other hand, who held considerable sway over University College London, the godless

---

[145] Thomas Mozley, *Reminiscences of Oriel College and the Oxford Movement* (London, 1881), II, p. 42.
[146] LD, 30:98–9 JHN to Anne Mozley (3 December 1885).
[147] Joyce Sugg. *Ever Yours Affly: John Henry Newman and His Female Circle* (London, 1996), p. 287.
[148] *Phases*, p. 8.
[149] Vera Wheatley. *The Life and Work of Harriet Martineau* (London, 1957), pp. 306–7.

place in Gower Street, defended subscription to the Articles on the rather Newmanian grounds that they opposed "the glorification of private judgment."[150]

Before Frank left for Persia, Mrs Newman wrote a letter to her eldest son demonstrating that she had no illusions about how her younger sons regarded private judgement: "Charles is as earnest in Mr. Owen's plans, as Frank can be in his 'good cause,' yet it is very striking how similarly self-willed they each are. They each consider that they alone see things rightly."[151] Sensing that Newman might have misgivings about Frank's plans, she hoped that he would give the expedition his blessing. "His plans are ripening for his pursuing his wishes for devoting himself to a Missionary life," she wrote. "He is very anxious to tell you, but has always found you engaged . . . I write from my own feelings to apprize you that he must wish you to give him a little time, and I need not say how anxiously I hope you will hear and receive all he has to inform you with the cordiality of old and brotherly affection."[152] Newman was careful not to exacerbate his mother's anxieties. "Frank's departure has had its sufficient share in knocking me up, and much more will it, I fear, discompose you and my sisters," he wrote her in August 1830. "Still it is our great relief that God is not extreme to mark what is done amiss . . . He looks at the motive, and accepts and blesses in spite of incidental error. What indeed, else, would become of us!"[153] To Jemima, he was rather more candid: "My opinion on the subject, as far as I can make out under the scantiness of his intelligence is this – that, tho' the glory (so called) of the Missionary office is much exaggerated, yet that it is a necessary office, and supposes considerable self-denial – (in F's case I doubt not) – tho' from F's great dissatisfaction with every thing as it is, I doubt not it will be a relief to his mind to be free from the irritation which I believe the sight of every thing around him occasions . . ."[154] Privately, Newman doubtless agreed with his acerbic friend Hurrell Froude, who, in writing his father of Frank's proposed mission, confessed that he could not see "how this course can tend even to gratify aping vanity such as generally mixes with religious error."[155]

As it happened, Frank's mission was a fiasco. After barely surviving stoning by indignant Mohammedans, contemptuous of the well-meaning English travellers, the men of the party saw all three of their female companions die of exposure, overexertion and plague, including Congleton's fiancée, Nancy Cronin. To make matters worse, for over a year, the fallout from the Russo-Turkish war of 1828–9 delayed the missionaries in Aleppo, where most of their time was spent securing food and shelter. Frank left a memorable account of the one occasion on which he shared his missionary faith with one of the locals.

> While we were at Aleppo, I one day got into religious discourse with a Mohammedan carpenter, which left on me a lasting impression. Among other matters, I was

[150] *The Life of Frederick Denison Maurice*. ed. Frederick Maurice (London, 1884), 2, p. 214.
[151] LD, 2:263 Mrs Jemima Newman to JHN (9 August 1830).
[152] LD, 2:224 Mrs Jemima Newman to JHN (25 May 1830).
[153] LD, 2:284 JHN to Mrs Jemima Newman (27 August 1830).
[154] LD, 2:226 JHN to Jemima Newman (27 May 1830).
[155] Piers Brendon. *Hurrell Froude and the Oxford Movement* (London, 1974), p. 103.

peculiarly desirous of disabusing him of the current notion of his people, that our gospels are spurious narratives of late date. I found great difficulty of expression; but the man listened to me with much attention, and I was encouraged to exert myself. He waited patiently till I had done, and then spoke to the following effect: "I will tell you, sir, how the case stands. God has given to you English a great many good gifts. You make fine ships, and sharp penknives, and good cloth and cottons; and you have rich nobles and brave soldiers; and you write and print many learned books: dictionaries and grammars; all this is of God. But there is one thing that God has withheld from you, and has revealed to us; and that is the knowledge of the true religion, by which one may be saved."[156]

The moral Frank drew from this amusing exchange would inform a good deal of his subsequent thinking on religious matters. "His position towards me was exactly that of a humble Christian towards an unbelieving philosopher; nay, that of the early Apostles or Jewish prophets towards the proud, cultivated, worldly wise and powerful heathen. This not only showed the vanity of any argument to him, except one purely addressed to his moral and spiritual faculties; but it also indicated to me that Ignorance has its spiritual self-sufficiency as well as Erudition; and that if there is a Pride of Reason, so is there a Pride of Unreason. But though this rested in my memory, it was long before I worked out all the results."[157] After returning from the Middle East, Frank gradually gave up trying to reconcile himself to the Christian religion and chose instead to cobble together a highly idiosyncratic moralist religion of his own. When he told one correspondent, "Oh, I am anti-slavery, anti-alcohol, anti-tobacco, anti-everything!" he was accurately describing the viewiness that came to define this ethical pseudo-religion—what Newman himself in *The Idea of a University* (1852) defined as "spurious philosophism."[158] Women's rights, animal rights, the rights of Greece, the rights of Armenia, the cause of Mazzini, the cause of Kossuth—these would take the place of belief in dogmatic Christianity.

Frank's forays into comparative religion only hastened his abandonment of doctrinal religion. He might have found the different varieties of Christianity objectionable but he found Islam even worse. "I had resolved to read the Koran through—not in the original, but in translation—that I might get some insight into the Mussulman mind," he wrote. "But I confess to you I have broken sheer down in the attempt . . . the book makes no impression on my mind. I cannot find where I left off when I recur to it. That so tedious and shallow a work can meet such praises gives me a lower and lower idea of the power of mind in these nations. I now think the Arabs are captivated by the tinkle and epigrammatic point of an old and sacred dialect, while Turks and Persians take its literary beauty as a religious fact to be believed, not to be felt. How wonderful is the power of tradition!"[159] Indeed, as he wrote in his memoir of Newman, "To unlearn traditional folly may be the first necessary wisdom."[160]

---

[156] *Phases*, pp. 32–3.
[157] Ibid., p. 33.
[158] *Idea*, p. 12.
[159] *Sieveking*, p. 39.
[160] *Contr*, p. 49.

While in the Mediterranean, Newman entrusted St Mary's to the care of his curate, Isaac Williams, a fellow Tractarian and poet, who often joined Newman's mother and sisters at Rose Hill, their cottage in Littlemore to hear his letters read aloud when they arrived through the post. "At this time, while Newman was abroad," Williams wrote in his autobiography, "his brother Frank also was away in the East, having gone on a wild, enthusiastic expedition to Baghdad; and when his family were receiving letters from both brothers, I was struck with the contrast between the two. While our Newman, the eldest, had so much poetry, love of scenery, and associations of place and country, and domestic and filial affection, these qualities appeared to be wanting in his brother, who would have passed by Jerusalem and Nazareth without turning aside to look on them, or the most beautiful object in nature, or, at all events, would not deign to mention them, nor to cast any longing, lingering look to his home . . ."[161] The letters Newman wrote home abundantly bear this out. It is no wonder Williams recalled the letters so vividly nearly 20 years after he heard them read aloud: they are some of the most passionate Newman ever wrote. As he approached Syracuse, Newman wrote Harriett in April 1833, "the country got more and more striking . . . . The two last miles we

diverged from the road up a steep path and soon came to the ancient stone ascent leading to Taurominium. I never saw anything more enchanting than this spot – It realized all one had read of in books of the perfection of scenery – a deep valley – brawling streams – beautiful trees – but description is nothing – the sea was heard in the distance. But when after breakfast, with the advantage of a bright day we mounted to the theatre, and saw the view thence, what shall I say then? why that I never before knew that nature could be [so] beautiful, and that to have seen the view thence was a nearer approach to seeing Eden, than anything I had conceived possible. Oh happy I, it was worth coming all the way, to endure the loneliness and sadness of my progress and the weariness of the voyage to see it. I felt for the first time in my life with my eyes open that I must be better and more religious, if I lived there. Never before have I brought home to my mind the reality of foreign scenery. I mean that I have gazed on mountains and vegetation, and felt it was not English, yet could not believe it was not a dream – but now I see what real beautiful scenery is – long slopes which seem as if they never would end, cultivated to the top – or overhung there with jutting rocks – bold precipitous crags standing, because they choose to stand, independently – range after range of heights, so that you wonder the series does not proceed for ever.[162]

In contrast, Frank looked at Baghdad with the eyes of an exasperated city planner: "The political state of this city," he observed, "from within and without, is the very reverse of satisfactory."[163] Even when travelling from Tehran to Tabriz and being shown sculptures representing the conquest of Darius, he could not conceal his indifference.

---

[161] *Autobiography of Isaac Williams* (London, 1892), p. 60.
[162] LD, 3:303 JHN to Harriett Newman (25 April 1833).
[163] *Sieveking*, p. 49.

"Our caravan did not go close enough to see the sculptures; we were probably half a mile off, but the muleteers were careful to point to them and talk of them. So too in going from Babylonia into Media by the ancient pass of Zagros, they were eager to draw my attention to the sculptures in the lofty, apparently inaccessible rocks. 'Your uncle made those,' said a muleteer. At first I did not understand, but I found he meant by my uncle some infidel . . ."[164] These were dismal traveller's tales, though in one letter home he made the amusing observation of how, "A Turk was horrified at my tooth brush, which he instantly determined to be made of *pig's bristles*. All sorts of stiff brushes offend them on this ground. As they shave their heads, they can the better go without brushes."[165]

One hundred years later, another eccentric Englishman made another memorable sojourn to Persia, which he recounted in his classic travelogue, *Road to Oxiana* (1937). There, Robert Byron recalled how he and Christopher Sykes fell in with an Assyrian schoolmistress, who was returning from a missionary meeting in Teheran. They were in a lorry together when Byron and Sykes told her that they were chummy with the Patriarch of Assyria. She advised them not to speak of it, "since there was a persecution of Christians at the moment," a thought which caused both the lorry diver and the schoolmistress to begin singing *Lead, Kindly Light* in unison. When the schoolmistress informed her new companions that "she had taught the driver this to prevent his singing the usual drivers' songs," the response of the anti-Catholic Byron was characteristically caustic: "I said I should have preferred the drivers' songs."[166]

Frank returned home from Baghdad in June 1833 on the same day that John returned from Sicily. If the moral of Newman's Sicilian Expedition was that Rome was not the abominable imposture that Protestant bigotry had made it out to be, the moral of Frank's travels was that Protestantism was no more tenable than Catholicism—or 'Romanism', as he called it. And yet Frank also returned home convinced that both his family and his acquaintances had taken against him. In *Phases of Faith*, he describes feeling cut off from members of his family and being cross-examined by friends. "Not one who met me face to face had a word to reply to the plain Scriptures which I quoted. Yet when I was gone away, one after another was turned against me by somebody whom I had not yet met or did not know: for in every theological conclave which deliberates on joint action, the most bigoted seems always to prevail."[167] This sounds like garden variety persecution mania. Still, he was not easy company, as Jemima attested: "We get on as well with Frank, as the consciousness of having some forbidden subjects will allow. We keep from argument, which is a good thing. He knows we do not like it, and makes a point, I think, of avoiding bringing on a discussion. But today is the first day we have got him to talk easily on general subjects. Poor fellow, it is very difficult for him to know what to say to please us, when he thinks so differently."[168]

---

[164] Ibid., p. 52.
[165] F. W. Newman, *Personal Narrative, In Letters: Principally From Turkey, In The Years 1830–33* (London, 1856), p. 19.
[166] Robert Byron. *Road to Oxiana* (Oxford, 1982), p. 58.
[167] *Phases*, pp. 34–5.
[168] LD, 4:338 Jemima Newman to JHN (6 October 1834).

Marriage

In August 1833, after despairing of wooing Maria Giberne, Frank met and became engaged to Maria Kennaway, the daughter of Sir John Kennaway, an admirer of Darby's who had entered the East India service at the age of 14 and went on to have a distinguished diplomatic career, despite initially finding Indian life "extremely distasteful."[169] Frank and Maria married in December 1835. Before Sir John died in 1836, after going blind, he insisted that his son-in-law give up the missionary life that he had abjured himself. Then, again, the old diplomatist did not care for his son-in-law's outlandish views nor did his beautiful daughter, who was distressed by her husband's growing heterodoxy. Once, when James Martineau called on Frank at his home in Park Village, Regent's Park, his good friend Holyoake recalled, Maria "opened the window and stepped out on the lawn, rather than meet" the Unitarian sage.[170] Newman wished his brother's marriage well but continued to be concerned about where his scepticism was leading. "My brother Frank," he wrote his best friend, John Bowden, "was married three weeks since . . . I trust it may be of service in taking off his thoughts from the extravagances in which he has hitherto indulged. Whether he will ever approach nearer the Church, is another question. I am not sanguine."[171] Frank, for his part, was a happy husband: "For more than forty years I have been in possession of a heart that loved me ardently," he wrote in 1876 after Maria's death. On her tombstone, however, he inscribed the arresting words:

> With no superiority of intellect, yet by force of love, by sweet piety, by tender compassion, by coming down to the lowly, by unselfishness and simplicity of life, by a constant sense of God's Presence, by devout exercises, private and social, she achieved much of Christian saintliness and much of human happiness. She has left a void in her husband's heart.[172]

Only Frank would have commemorated a devoted wife by calling attention to her intellectual deficiencies.[173] No man had less *savoir vivre*. Yet the eccentricity of his religious views was not an anomaly. "I am ever in experiment on something," he once confessed. "At present it is on cacao butter and vegetable oils . . ."[174] Like Prince Charles, he had "a theory that plants feel pain, and that we should treat all vegetable life as if it were sentient."[175] He was also prone to sartorial theories. "I rather believe that man is a tropical animal, hairless, made for a climate warmer than ours, and needing much aid from clothing."[176] Accordingly, Frank never went out without a rug over his shoulders, with a hole in the middle for his head, underneath which he wore three overcoats. (Oddly enough, his brother Charles did the same; Gogol would have seen congenial spirits in both.) And yet when one considers the trappings of Frank's eccentricity—the

---

[169] DNB.
[170] *Bygones*, 1, p. 197.
[171] LD, 5:195 JHN to John William Bowden (10 January 1836).
[172] *Contr*, p. 59.
[173] *Sieveking*, p. 58.
[174] Ibid., p. 315.
[175] Ibid., p. 127.
[176] Ibid., p. 382.

silly theories, the rugs, the scrupulous diet, the commiserating with plants—it is hard not to see in them a kind of philosophical playacting: he had assumed the role of the contrarian sage that John Stuart Mill recommended in *On Liberty* (1859):

> Precisely because the tyranny of opinion is such as to make eccentricity a reproach, it is desirable in order to break through that tyranny, that people should be eccentric. Eccentricity has always abounded when and where strength of character has abounded; and the amount of eccentricity in a society has generally been proportional to the amount of genius, mental vigour, and moral courage it contained. That so few dare to be eccentric marks the chief danger of the time.[177]

Intellectual eccentricity always put Newman off. When he first broached the idea of publishing Hurrell Froude's papers to John Keble, for example, he observed: "They show how a person may indulge metaphysical speculations to the utmost extent and yet be practical. It might be a good lesson to various Cambridge men . . ."[178] Wordsworth was also unconvinced of the "genius, mental vigour, and moral courage" of eccentricity. In *The Prelude* (1805), he inveighed against its malign moral effects:

> I glance but at a few conspicuous marks,
> Leaving ten thousand others, that do each,
> In hall or court, conventicle, or shop,
> In public rooms or private, park or street,
> With fondness reared on his own pedestal,
> Look out for admiration. Folly, vice,
> Extravagance in gesture, mien, and dress,
> And all the strife of singularity,
> Lies to the ear, and lies to every sense—
> Of these, and of the living shapes they wear,
> There is no end. . .

On this score, both Wordsworth and Newman would have agreed with Richardson's Sir Charles Grandison, who observes how "Singularity is usually the indication of something wrong in judgment."[179]

Because Newman's own thinking "certainly did not run in tram-lines," as Owen Chadwick nicely put it, he would come in for a good deal of criticism himself for the sort of sophistry that he deplored in others.[180] In *Essays and Reviews* (1860), the Broad Church polemic published to contest the literal inspiration of the Bible and belief in Hell, Samuel Wilberforce, the flip-flopping Bishop of Oxford, nicknamed 'Soapy Sam' assured his readers: "Now we are not about to justify Number 90. So far from it, we consider it to be a singularly characteristic specimen of that unfortunate subtlety of mind which has since led its author into so many assertions and contradictions and

---

[177] John S. Mill. *On Liberty*. ed. David Bromwich and George Kateb (New Haven, 2003), p. 131.
[178] LD, 6:87 JHN to John Keble (30 June 1837).
[179] Samuel Richardson. *Sir Charles Grandison* (London, 1901), 6, p. 155.
[180] Owen Chadwick. *The Spirit of the Oxford Movement* (London, 1992), p. 30.

acts, which with the largest judgment of charity a plain man must find it hard to justify from the charge of moral dishonesty, except upon what we believe to be in this case the true plea – to use the ugliest word which we can employ – that of intellectual eccentricity."[181]

Writing in 1909, Frank's biographer, Sieveking observed how the English adopted more and more of Frank's eccentric views after his death. "It is strange to find, on looking through these letters," Sieveking wrote, "how advanced opinion is coming into line with his so-called outrageous ideas of a generation ago. It would have given him keen pleasure, if he could have lived till now, to see the strides that have been made of late years in the Women's Suffrage movement, and the admission of women to public bodies. In social and moral reform, and in the Temperance movement also, the progress has been very marked, and we may soon have an Act prohibiting the smoking of tobacco by young boys—a subject on which Professor Newman had very strong views. Last but not least, the Vegetarian movement, in which he took so keen an interest, has gained new vigour from the advocates of the simple life."[182]

On returning to England, Frank became tutor in Latin at Bristol College, a non-denominational school founded by Unitarians. Walter Bagehot was one of the star pupils. By the age of 15, he had read not only Homer, Demosthenes, Juvenal, and Cicero, but Newton's *Principia*.[183] Although no longer the bustling commercial city that Edmund Burke represented in the late eighteenth century, when it was full of rich merchants plying the West India trade, Bristol reinvented itself in the 1830s as a centre of scholarly Unitarianism.[184] It was in this congenial milieu that Frank fell out with Darby and his followers. Like many others familiar with Frank's heterodox views, the Darbyites could not help questioning the authenticity of his Christianity, convinced, as Frank himself admitted, that he "was endeavoring to sound the divine nature by the miserable plummet of human philosophy."[185] This was a fair paraphrase of Darby's essential criticism of *Phases of Faith*, about which he wrote, "The returning prodigal had his father on his neck while in his rags, and the best robe to enter into the house. It was his father's joy to have him back there. Such is the God revealed in Christ. Where is Mr. Newman's? It is a philosophical God, to be found by philosophers."[186] Later, perhaps still smarting from the sting of Darby's criticism, Frank complained of his "dwarfing men's understandings, contracting their hearts, crushing their moral sensibilities, and setting those at variance who ought to love . . ." Moreover, his disenchantment with the Darbyites was all the more galling when he recalled his initial fondness for the sect's leader: "How specious was it in the beginning! [Darby] only wanted men 'to submit their understandings to God,' that is to the Bible, that is, to his interpretation! From seeing his action and influence I have learnt that if it be dangerous to a young man . . . to have no superior mind to which he may look up with confiding reverence, it may be even more dangerous to think that he has

---

[181] LD, 20:29, Note 1.
[182] *Sieveking*, pp. 116–17.
[183] Alistair Buchan. *The Spare Chancellor: The Life of Walter Bagehot* (London, 1959), p. 28.
[184] Ibid., p. 27.
[185] *Phases*, p. 35.
[186] John Nelson Darby. *The Irrationalism of Infidelity: Being an Analysis of "Phases of Faith"* (London, 1853), p. 385.

found such a mind: for he who is most logically consistent, though to a one-sided theory, and most ready to sacrifice self to that theory, seems to ardent youth the most assuredly trustworthy guide . . ."[187] In trying to steer his brother clear of the shoals of Socinianism, Newman discovered the limits of influence. When Frank found that Darby was not, as he had hoped, "an apostle commissioned to reveal the mind of God," he discovered the limits of discipleship.[188]

Unreal Words

For Frank, if disengaging himself from Darby's *sola scriptura* bibliolatry proved difficult, resisting Newman's influence was relatively easy. From boyhood, he had caricatured his brother's thinking as authoritarian and reactionary and congratulated himself on taking what he considered a more independent, enlightened line. When Newman moved ineluctably towards Rome, Frank chose to regard him as a papist *malgré lui*. "Grant that all was spontaneous: the sad fact remained, that, whether he knew it or not, he was pushing on the Romish line while in the garb of an Anglican."[189] This was hardly an original slur: the charge that Newman had been a "crypto-papist," as Richard Whately put it, while still an Anglican, was a defamatory commonplace.[190] Despite his vaunted respect for the views of others, Frank never showed any serious interest in Newman's search for the truth. He showed no interest in his theory of development, which Newman first sketched out for him in a letter in 1840.[191] Nor did he ever show any interest in his Catholic faith, despite claiming to understand its main outlines. "I apprehend that I have read amply enough of your printed works to understand all your leading and fundamental principles as fully as I could by any conversation–If I fail, it is from the difficulty of putting our minds in juxtaposition, and not from want of information."[192] This is unconvincing: there is nothing in Frank's printed work or his correspondence to suggest that he read his brother's work with any fair attentiveness. Whenever Frank mentions Newman's Roman Catholic faith, it is to belittle it, referring to it as "fanatical," "sectarian," "puerile," or a form of "bondage."[193]

Newman's writings, on the other hand, abound in careful appraisals of Protestant objections to orthodox Christianity. Take, for example, the issue of private judgement, surely a pivotal point of disagreement between Newman and his brother, related as it was to the whole question of authority. Frank, like Gladstone, charged Newman with exercising the same private judgement that he proscribed in others. Newman's response could not have been less defensive. "Before I answer your question whether I do not go by private judgment though I proscribe it, I will put two . . . cases which though they do not immediately apply, yet are not quite off the point before us. Supposing I were in some inferior command in a battle, and from the smoke and noise could not make

---

[187] Darby, p. 21.
[188] Ibid.
[189] *Contr*, p. 22.
[190] See LD, 21:18 JHN to Edward Badeley (15 January 1864).
[191] See LD, 7:436–42 JHN to FWN (10 November 1840).
[192] LD, 7:319 FWN to JHN (29 April 1840).
[193] *Contr*, pp. 5, 9, 23.

out my commanding officer's signals, and could only act for the best, according to my best knowledge of what he was intending and what he was likely to intend, would this be to admit the principle that every one might fight, as he pleased, by himself?" Then, again, Newman posited another case, "supposing a pro-consul . . . in a falling empire, with usurpers rising around, and a weak government in the centre sending out contradictory orders, might he not be obliged to act, yet hardly know how, and be from time to time judging for himself, yet doing nothing to impair, nay doing all he could to honor and strengthen, the legitimate authorities and yet again be in a position, where, unless he were thoroughly honest, he might make his situation a pretence for following his own wishes?"

What Newman was at pains to argue was that submission to the authority of the Church did not always necessitate eschewing private judgement. "Again, there is nothing impossible in Almighty God having granted the Church a power of speaking truth within certain limits, viz on certain subjects or for a certain time, or under certain conditions; and that external to those limits private judgment should have its range. There may be moral uses in the freedom of judgment in some things as well as its restraint in others. As to the fact, whether Providence has thus appointed, and its antecedent probability, these are distinct and essential points of course; but I am describing a case in which a use of private judgment is not inconsistent with implicit submission to an external decision." These were the broad outlines of the issue, but Newman was not interested in codifying for the sake of codifying. In Newman's thinking, the personal always humanizes the philosophical. "I confess I wish to view the whole matter as a simple practical question coming home to every one according to his degree of information; what ought I to do under my circumstances?—I wish to set up no philosophy, or clearly arranged system—I am very ready to allow difficulties— but only ask myself in this mysterious world, what is most likely to be God's will, and how can I best please Him? Has He left me in utter ignorance about His will and my duty? or am I in a sort of twilight, in which I must do my best to move forward though at the risk of mistaking trees for giants, and in which I may expect His aid to enlighten my eyes if I am really in earnest at heart to do my best?"[194] This was not the language of polemical one-upmanship. Newman engaged his brother's objections forthrightly. There was no comparable show of generosity on Frank's part towards Newman and his faith.

Frank found it easy to resist Newman's influence, but he could not disengage so easily from Darby. Once the two separated, Frank claimed that he was "thus able again without disturbance to develop [his] own tendencies," but in reality what this meant was that he followed more desperately than ever the reliance on the Bible that Darby had instilled in him before he travelled to Baghdad.[195] Frank would spend eight long years wrestling with the contradictions of Darby's bibliolatry. "I reverenced the doctrine of the Trinity as something vital to the soul," he wrote in *Phases of Faith*, "but felt that to love the Fathers or the Athanasian Creed more than the Gospel of John would be a supremely miserable superstition. However, that Creed states that

---

[194] LD, 7:436–7 JHN to FWN (10 November 1840).
[195] *Phases*, pp. 28–9.

there is no inequality between the Three Persons; in John it became increasingly clear to me that the divine Son is unequal to the Father. To say that 'the Son of God' meant 'Jesus as man' was a preposterous evasion . . . ."[196] Having shared this with his readers, Frank observed how: "I afterwards remembered my old thought, that we must surely understand *our own words* when we venture to speak at all about divine mysteries."[197]

As it happened, these were not his own words but those that he had heard from his brother. In 1830, Newman had written Frank of the "multitudes in the so-called religious world . . . who think they know things because they can say them, and understand them because they have heard them—or account themselves Christians because they use Scripture phrases . . ."[198] When Newman turned his attention to the meaning of words, he wrote one of his most incisive sermons, "Unreal Words" (1839), in which he remarked:

> To make professions is to play with edged tools, unless we attend to what we are saying. Words have a meaning, whether we mean that meaning or not; and they are imputed to us in their real meaning, when our not meaning it is our own fault. He who takes God's Name in vain, is not counted guiltless because he means nothing by it,—he cannot frame a language for himself; and they who make professions, of whatever kind, are heard in the sense of those professions, and are not excused because they themselves attach no sense to them. "By thy words thou shalt be justified, and by thy words thou shalt be condemned." [Matt. xii. 37.]

The dangers against which Newman warns here are common. We are all prone to profess what we are not ready to practice, or to profess merely as a means of evading practice. Yet while Newman wrote his sermon to appeal to as wide an audience as possible—in 1868, he even included it with 12 other sermons in a collection of his favourite sermons—he also clearly had Frank in mind. In 1839, Frank was still Christian—tenuously perhaps but Christian nevertheless. Yet, even as a Christian, Frank's flippant professions—against the Athanasian Creed, against baptismal regeneration, against hell, against sin, against tradition—had already begun to jeopardize his faith. By 1840, when he became Professor of Latin at Manchester New College and began denying that Christ was the Son of God, he had decisively broken with any faith that could be identified as Christian. And yet he refused to admit as much, insisting that he abominated precisely the agnosticism to which he actually subscribed. In his memoir of his brother, he protested: "I have never ceased to regard Atheism as monstrous folly, and more than ever since in the last thirty years 'a self-acting Universe' is talked of. Concerning a Future Life, I hold the same conviction as I heard and approved of in Oxford sixty-five years ago, that without Supernatural Revelation it can only be a (pious) opinion, not a doctrine."[199] In June 1892, he wrote a correspondent, "Today I have received a letter and a book in Bengali from a

---

[196] Ibid., pp. 29–30.
[197] LD, 26:298–9 JHN to E. B. Pusey (27 April 1873).
[198] LD, 2:183 JHN to FWN (1830).
[199] *Contr*, p. 104.

believer in Theosophy, supposing me to be one of them! Hence, I was not too early in telling my friends that since the age of fourteen I became a Conscious Christian, no unbelief has made my hymns less precious . . . My change more than fifty years ago was on Historical arguments mainly."[200] So, while Newman may not have Frank in mind when he first addressed this issue of glib profession, he must have seen that his sermon prophetically anticipated the "unreal words" that actually came to define his brother's mature thinking. Addressing specifically the case of Christian profession, Newman wrote:

> This is especially a day of professions. You will answer in my own words, that all ages have been ages of profession. So they have been, in one way or other, but this day in its own especial sense;—because this is especially a day of individual profession. This is a day in which there is (rightly or wrongly) so much of private judgment, so much of separation and difference, so much of preaching and teaching, so much of authorship, that it involves individual profession, responsibility, and recompense in a way peculiarly its own. It will not then be out of place if, in connexion with the text, we consider some of the many ways in which persons, whether in this age or in another, make unreal professions, or seeing see not, and hearing hear not, and speak without mastering, or trying to master, their words . . . Of course it is very common in all matters, not only in religion, to speak in an unreal way; viz., when we speak on a subject with which our minds are not familiar. If you were to hear a person who knew nothing about military matters, giving directions how soldiers on service should conduct themselves, or how their food and lodging, or their marching, was to be duly arranged, you would be sure that his mistakes would be such as to excite the ridicule and contempt of men experienced in warfare. If a foreigner were to come to one of our cities, and without hesitation offer plans for the supply of our markets, or the management of our police, it is so certain that he would expose himself, that the very attempt would argue a great want of good sense and modesty. We should feel that he did not understand us, and that when he spoke about us, he would be using words without meaning. If a dim-sighted man were to attempt to decide questions of proportion and colour, or a man without ear to judge of musical compositions, we should feel that he spoke on and from general principles, on fancy, or by deduction and argument, not from a real apprehension of the matters which he discussed. His remarks would be theoretical and unreal.[201]

This is precisely the impression that one has when one reads Frank Newman essaying theological matters—the impression of someone taking up matters that he does not understand. Basil Willey referred to Frank as an "honest doubter," alluding to Tennyson's lines from *In Memoriam*, "There lives more faith in honest doubt/Believe me, than in half the creeds."[202] But professing to understand such mysteries as the Trinity or the Immaculate Conception sufficiently to account them irrational does not

---

[200] *Sieveking*, pp. 361–2.
[201] *PS*, 3, pp. 34–5.
[202] Alfred Lord Tennyson, *In Memoriam* (London, 1850), Section 96.

make for honesty. Newman was intent on warning his readers against the dangers of "unreal words" because he saw how flippancy could trivialize professions of doubt as easily as professions of faith.

> Let us avoid talking, of whatever kind; whether mere empty talking, or censorious talking, or idle profession, or descanting upon Gospel doctrines, or the affectation of philosophy, or the pretence of eloquence. Let us guard against frivolity, ve of display, love of being talked about, love of singularity, love of seeming original. Let us aim at meaning what we say, and saying what we mean; let us aim at knowing when we understand a truth, and when we do not. When we do not, let us take it on faith, and let us profess to do so. Let us receive the truth in reverence, and pray God to give us a good will, and divine light, and spiritual strength, that it may bear fruit within us.[203]

When Newman learnt that Frank was professing his own highly subjective form of Deism at Broadmead Chapel, he did not pull his punches. "I hope you understand that decidedly as I object to meet you in a familiar way or to sit at table with you, yet should you be coming here and wish to have any talk with me (not disputation) or in like manner of course to write to me, I shall be most happy. If I can be your servant in any way, so that I do not countenance your errors, you really may command me . . ." At the same time, it was a measure of the love that he felt for his brother that he should admit: "I write in great grief not knowing what best to say. . ."[204] In response, Frank was ambivalent. He pointed out in *Phases of Faith* that "The Tractarian movement was just commencing in 1833. My brother was taking a position, in which he was bound to show that he could sacrifice private love to ecclesiastical dogma; and upon learning that I had spoken to some small meetings of religious people . . . he separated himself entirely from my private friendship . . ." And, yet, Frank was honest enough to stress that "In my brother's conduct there was not a shade of unkindness . . ."[205] As his own doubts grew, he came to recognize that he might have been unfair in his criticisms of his brother. "I had a brother," he confessed in *Phases of Faith*, "with whose name all England was resounding for praise and blame: from his sympathies, through pure hatred of Popery, I had long since turned away. What was this but to judge him his creed? True, his whole theory was nothing but Romanism transferred to England: but what then? . . . the absolute excellences of her nuns and priests showed that Romanism as such was not fatal to spirituality. They were persecuted: this did them good perhaps or certainly exhibited their brightness. So too my brother surely was struggling after truth, fighting for freedom to his own heart and mind, against church articles and stagnancy of thought. For this he deserved both sympathy and love: but I, alas! had not known and seen his excellence. But now God had taught me more largeness by bitter sorrow working the peaceable fruit of righteousness; at last then I might admire my brother. I therefore wrote to him a letter of contrition. Some change, either in his mind or in his view of my position had taken place; and I was happy to find him once

---

[203] *PS*, 3, p. 45.
[204] LD, 5:167 JHN to FWN (23 November 1835).
[205] *Phases*, p. 34.

more able, not only to feel fraternally, as he had always done, but to act also fraternally. Nevertheless to this day it is to me a painfully unsolved mystery, how a mind can claim its freedom in order to establish bondage."[206]

A Fraternal Correspondence

In fact, it was Newman who sent the first conciliatory letter. On 11 April 1840, he wrote to tell his brother that since his Aunt had assured him that Frank was not preaching at the Broadmead chapel "all reason for my separating myself from your company is at an end . . ." Then, he continued: "let me express to you, my dear F. what is no great thing to say, my own consciousness of much infirmity in the details of my conduct towards you. In saying this, you must not suppose that I have changed my mind at all in regard to principles . . . But I am very sure that in my manner and my tone there was what there should not have been . . . Be sure that you are ever in my prayers . . ."[207] Frank responded with as much gratitude as misgiving. "Your letter this morning received excites at once joy and melancholy apprehension . . . Much as I desire to hold a brother's place with you, on the other hand I shrink with morbid fear from the attempt to claim it, lest bad be made worse. Men such as we are,—for this at least we have in common, the entering with great ardour into the highest interests of man, in this world and the next,—naturally find chief sympathy from agreement as to religious and political sentiments: and it is a hazardous experiment, to force those together as friends who clash too strongly on both points." Newman would hardly have agreed that Frank was as active as he imagined in "entering . . . the highest interests of man, in this world and the next," but he would have seen the point of steering clear of contentious ground. The problem was that this left the brothers with very little to talk about—though Frank was wrong when he suggested that Newman was somehow opposed to science; he was opposed to the misapplication of science but not to the thing itself. "Indeed I have much harmonious intercourse from time to time with some thus opposed to me," Frank wrote, "but then they have some literature or some science on which we meet. To science I have thought you were opposed, and your literature and history is all religious, and such as that on it we should probably differ. There remains no common topic, except such as are domestic and social. These I much value, and think it a duty diligently to cultivate, where no other link remains to fasten love, or say, to fasten down hatred . . ." Still, Frank was most perceptive about what antagonized him about his brother when he confessed that he bristled under what he considered his brother's imperious influence. "When once I was at Rosebank to hear you converse, I let you have all your own way, and therefore I believe you thought I agreed more than I did. I know it is harder for an elder brother to bear opposition, but it seemed to me as though you would not endure it; and while I feel this, I cannot be easy. It is not that I want to contradict you, when with you; but I want to feel that I am at liberty to do so, if I like; else it is slavery, not society on equal terms."[208]

---

[206] Ibid., p. 72.
[207] LD, 7:301–2 JHN to FWN (11 April 1840).
[208] LD, 7:308 FWN to JHN (15 April 1840).

Here, Frank clearly showed how much he resented his older brother, to whom he felt he was obliged to defer. Indeed, in the memoir Frank wrote of his brother in 1891, after Newman had been dead for a year, it still rankled: "If my brother had shown me as much courtesy as did my tutors at Worcester, or my senior Fellows at Balliol, instead of tormenting me by chidings as if I were a young child, he might have known me better." Frank was alluding to something Newman acknowledged in his letter of 11 April, in which he admitted: "I quite confess that especially in the years 1821–22 and later, I did not behave to you with that habitual meekness which was likely to inspire confidence in you towards me. I was very sorry for this at the time, but still that does not alter facts."[209] In his private journal, Newman continually remonstrated with himself over his unkindness to Frank. "I have gone on day after day so grievously sinning in ill temper that I have come to the resolution through God's grace to make an open confession to Francis, the first time I do so again."[210] When Mrs Newman informed him that Frank might not be returning to Oxford, Newman made no bones about his sense of guilt. "This is a severe stroke. Give me grace, Lord, to bear it. It is a just rebuke and punishment to me for the wicked ill nature and moroseness with which I treated him last term."[211] Of course, missing from the journal are any accounts of how provoking Frank could be. Peevishness, however, was absent from the letter that Frank wrote Newman in the spring of 1840, when some rapprochement between the brothers seemed possible. Certainly, Frank was comfortable enough with his brother to share with him the pain he suffered as the result of his break with the Darbyites. "Now, my dear John, I fear you may think that Aunt has misled you. I desire to avoid one of my great faults, of being blunt and harsh where I wish to be sincere: but the case is this. It is true that I see much sectarianism in dissenters, but I see a worse sectarianism in the Establishment. The former are narrow from want of information or misapplied principle; the latter, when they are so, are from false principle. My heart and understanding alike long for something larger far than either. I once thought I had found it in friends whom I loved more than brothers. Bitter experience showed me, that on the first trial, they threw up their own principles, or so explained them away so that they meant nothing at all . . . But you know not how I dread a renewed intimacy with you, lest a new rupture arise at any moment."[212]

What is striking about this letter is the degree of affection it demonstrates. Frank, in his torturous way, was fond of his eldest brother. "Now, my brother, I must once more say, I want to have you as a brother; if only I can keep you! I have always honored and defended you personally, while I could not defend your principles. I treasure the remembrance of all your affection to me, and cherish visions of the past, though generally sad, because they are often humbling and instructive, and bring before me your many noble qualities."[213] Some of the noble qualities that Frank praised in his brother were evident in Newman's response. "I agree with you that easy unrestrained intercourse between us is impossible and that to attempt it would be a

[209] LD, 7:302 JHN to FWN (11 April 1840).
[210] *AW*, p. 178.
[211] Ibid., p. 180.
[212] LD, 7:308 FWN to JHN (15 April 1840).
[213] LD, 7:309 FWN to JHN (15 April 1840).

great mistake. . . . I do not of course deny that restraint is painful, but is it not often salutary? It is painful to be with those to whom we fain would, to whom we cannot, dare not open our hearts, yet many good purposes are answered by it. Might it not in our case be a humiliation and so improve us? It might keep us too from thinking each other more estranged, whether in opinion or in affection, than we are. And it might keep up the wish to agree."[214]

Frank looked on the esteem and respect with which his contemporaries regarded his brother, especially after his deft response to Kinglsey's libels, with unbecoming resentment. The rivalrous attitude with which he regarded his brother only became more scabrous as he grew older. Confirmation of this can be found in a letter of February 1849 that the historian James Anthony Froude wrote to Charles Kingsley, in which he remarked, "My first book won me the regard of Frank Newman. My second has forfeited it, or nearly so. Strange he most resents my admiration of his brother."[215] This was especially noteworthy coming from Froude because, while he eventually chose a path quite different from the one Newman chose, he never lost his deep admiration for the former vicar of St.Mary's as a man and thinker. In 1882, he published his essay, "The Oxford Counter-Reformation," which brilliantly captured the power and appeal of Newman's genius.

> Newman's mind was world-wide. He was interested in everything which was going on in science, in politics, in literature. Nothing was too large for him, nothing too trivial, if it threw light upon the central question, what man really was, and what was his destiny. He was careless about his personal prospects. He had no ambition to make a career, or to rise to rank and power. Still less had pleasure any seductions for him. His natural temperament was bright and light; his senses, even the commonest, were exceptionally delicate. I was told that, though he rarely drank wine, he was trusted to choose the vintages for the college cellar. He could admire enthusiastically any greatness of action and character, however remote the sphere of it from his own. Gurwood's "Dispatches of the Duke of Wellington" came out just then. Newman had been reading the book, and a friend asked him what be thought of it. "Think?" he said, "it makes one burn to have been a soldier." But his own subject was the absorbing interest with him. Where Christianity is a real belief, where there are distinct convictions that a man's own self and the millions of human beings who are playing on the earth's surface are the objects of a supernatural dispensation, and are on the road to heaven or hell, the most powerful mind may well be startled at the aspect of things. If Christianity was true, since Christianity was true (for Newman at no time doubted the reality of the revelation), then modern England, modern Europe, with its march of intellect and its useful knowledge and its material progress, was advancing with a light heart into ominous conditions. Keble had looked into no lines of thought but his own. Newman had read omnivorously; he had studied modern thought and modern life in all its forms, and with all its

---

[214] LD, 7:309 JHN to FWN (16 April 1840).
[215] Froude to Charles Kingsley (27 February 1849) quoted in Waldo Hilary Dunn. *James Anthony Froude: A Biography* (Oxford, 1961), I, p. 134.

many-coloured passions. He knew, of course, that many men of learning and ability believed that Christianity was not a revelation at all, but had been thrown out, like other creeds, in the growth of the human mind. He knew that doubts of this kind were the inevitable results of free discussion and free toleration of differences of opinion; and he was too candid to attribute such doubts, as others did, to wickedness of heart. He could not, being what he was, acquiesce in the established religion as he would acquiesce in the law of the land, because it was there, and because the country had accepted it, and because good general reasons could be given for assuming it to be right. The soundest arguments, even the arguments of Bishop Butler himself, went no farther than to establish a probability. But religion with Newman was a personal thing between himself and his Maker, and it was not possible to feel love and devotion to a Being whose existence was merely probable.[216]

For Frank, the fact that such praise came from someone who shared his sceptical views must have been particularly galling. Indeed, he might even have been inspired to write his own denigratory reminiscences of his brother to try to discredit the favourable impression of Newman conveyed by Froude's sympathetic essay.

Notwithstanding Frank's tendency to berate his brother, the fragile reconciliation between the siblings produced revelatory exchanges. Frank was so convinced that the papacy was bogus that he could never understand how Newman accepted it. When Newman was offered the cardinalate in 1879, Frank advised his brother to refuse it on spiritual grounds. "You cannot help the Pope, nor (what is more important) do good to men's souls, by such an elevation; but you will lose a post of deep moral value, in which you are (I believe) a valuable counselor to numbers."[217] Newman was obliged to remind his brother: "You forget that I believe the Catholic Religion to be true . . . It is not that I am insensible to and ungrateful for the good opinion of Theists etc. but that Catholics are my brethren and I am bound to consult them first."[218]

Hobbies

Finding fault with a religion in which he had ceased to believe gave Frank grounds on which to justify his apostasy. It also prefigured his embrace of the many hobby-horses that exercised so much of his restless intellect. When it came to viewiness, Frank had no peer. Indeed, as the *Oxford English Dictionary* attests, Newman coined the word "viewiness" in his *Discourses on the Scope and Nature of University Education* (1852) to capture Frank's "spurious philosophism," which "shows itself in what, for want of a word, I may call 'viewiness.'" Frank's letters and books abound with views on everything from the evils of landlordism and the laws governing trollops, to women's rights and animal rights. In October 1866, Newman wrote Frank a playful letter gently mocking this viewiness—proof that he was prepared to practice what he preached

---

[216] J. A. Froude. *Short Studies on Great Subjects* (London, 1899) IV, pp. 279–81.
[217] LD, 29:44 FWN to JHN (27 February 1879).
[218] LD, 29:44 JHN to FWN (28 February 1879).

when it came to being "merciful towards the absurd."[219] "Your troubles in your new house are among the ordinary miseries of Human Life. Every one has to go through them, till his house, like a snail's shell, has become part of himself. I am surprised you say nothing about chimneys smoking. They are the opprobrium of this scientific age. They and sea-sickness are universal evils . . . Arabic in European type – it would be a great step in literary and social intercourse to have a common alphabet every where; but it seems at present impossible. Think of Greek – one should have to begin Greek again, if it were written in Roman type: even the Germans won't give up their exclusive alphabet, tho' they could do it so easily."[220]

As early as 1829, in a piece called "Signs of the Times," Thomas Carlyle rightly observed that "views" were exerting a new and potent force in modern life. "The true Church of England, at this moment," Carlyle observed, "lies in the Editors of its Newspapers. These preach to the people daily, weekly; admonishing kings themselves; advising peace or war, with an authority which only the first Reformers, and a long-past class of Popes, were possessed of; inflicting moral censure; imparting moral encouragement, consolation, edification; in all ways diligently 'administering the Discipline of the Church.'"[221] In 1852, Newman would memorably echo Carlyle in the preface to his *Discourses on the Scope and Nature of Univeristy Education*.

> An intellectual man, as the world now conceives of him, is one who is full of "views" on all subjects of philosophy, on all matters of the day. It is almost thought a disgrace not to have a view at a moment's notice on any question from the Personal Advent to the Cholera or Mesmerism. This is owing in great measure to the necessities of periodical literature, now so much in request. Every quarter of a year, every month, every day, there must be a supply, for the gratification of the public, of new and luminous theories on the subjects of religion, foreign politics, home politics, civil economy, finance, trade, agriculture, emigration, and the colonies. Slavery, the gold fields, German philosophy, the French Empire, Wellington, Peel, Ireland, must all be practised on, day after day, by what are called original thinkers. As the great man's guest must produce his good stories or songs at the evening banquet, as the platform orator exhibits his telling facts at mid-day, so the journalist lies under the stern obligation of extemporizing his lucid views, leading ideas, and nutshell truths for the breakfast table. The very nature of periodical literature, broken into small wholes, and demanded punctually to an hour, involves the habit of this extempore philosophy. "Almost all the Ramblers," says Boswell of Johnson, "were written just as they were wanted for the press; he sent a certain portion of the copy of an essay, and wrote the remainder while the former part of it was printing." Few men have the gifts of Johnson, who to great vigour and resource of intellect, when it was fairly roused, united a rare common-sense and a conscientious regard for veracity, which preserved him from flippancy or extravagance in writing. Few men are Johnsons; yet how many men at this day are assailed by incessant demands on their mental powers, which only

---

[219] *Idea*, p. 179.
[220] LD, 22:299 JHN to FWN (14 October 1866).
[221] Thomas Carlyle. *Selected Works, Reminiscences, and Letters* (Harvard, 1957), p. 39.

a productiveness like his could suitably supply! There is a demand for a reckless originality of thought, and a sparkling plausibility of argument, which he would have despised, even if he could have displayed; a demand for crude theory and unsound philosophy, rather than none at all. It is a sort of repetition of the "Quid novi?" of the Areopagus and it must have an answer.[222]

That Frank avidly patronized this pinchbeck wisdom surprised his brother. "I wonder you can for a moment lay stress on the dicta of reviewers," Newman wrote. "You must have had surely enough experience how utterly worthless, for the most part, the formal criticisms of the day are."[223] Yet Frank not only patronized such writing, he added to it, holding forth on everything from the American Civil War and the Government of India to contagious diseases and the Hebrew Monarchy. In one pamphlet, entitled "The Right and Duty of Every State to Enforce Sobriety on its Citizens," he enjoined his countrymen to put a legal stop to the "vice of drunkards," citing "the enormous extension" it gives to "Violent Crime, to Orphanhood, to Pauperism, to Prostitution, to disease in Children, and to Insanity," not to mention "an enormous expense for Police and Criminal Courts, for Jails and Jail-officers, for Magistrates and Judges, for Insane Asylums, and Poor Rates . . ."[224] Surely, Frank believed, this was a cause that should bring the Newman brothers together. Attending a temperance rally where Manning shared the platform with Protestants filled him with "enthusiasm and joy," though, as he recalled later, he "was merely a type of the thousands who listened in deep rapt silence to his magnificent speech."[225] Something had to be done to address "the sights that make the streets on Saturday evenings in England [such] a degrading scene."[226] Newman, however, would not join the crusade against dram drinkers and instead sent off one of his more memorable rebuffs: "As to what you tell me of Archbishop Manning, I have heard that some also of our Irish bishops think that too many drink-shops are licensed. As for me, I do not know whether we have too many or too few." For Frank, Newman's refusal to join forces with him over this issue was tantamount to his refusing to recognize the validity of his *Ersatzreligion*, which only aggravated the resentment he felt towards his brother.[227]

The Duty of Suicide

To grasp the nature of Frank's idiosyncratic faith, we need to keep in mind that he was a passionate advocate of euthanasia, a fact which throws a lurid light on his preoccupation with social justice. In 1873, he co-authored an article in the *Spectator* entitled "The Duty of Suicide," recommending that suicide and even murder be a legal

---

[222] *Idea*, pp. 13–14.
[223] LD, 19:343 JHN to FWN (22 May 1860). Cf. Wordsworth to Edward Quillinan (4 February 1830): "Who that ever felt a line of my poetry would trouble himself to crush a miserable maggot crawled out of the dead carcase of the Edinburgh Review . . ."
[224] *Sieveking*, p. 403.
[225] *Contr*, p. 110.
[226] *Sieveking*, p. 74.
[227] Frank's campaign to deny the bibulous drink was never as successful as he wished. In later life, he employed a secretary who claimed to be abstemious but whose rooms were found to be full of empty brandy bottles. See *Sieveking*, p. 362.

option for the old and infirm. The article set off a storm of indignation in the editorial pages of England and America. "Professor Francis Newman has lately startled the British public by an article in the *Spectator* in which he advocates suicide and murder under certain conditions," the *Newport Daily News* commented on 1 May 1873. "And this from a sense of duty. We remember a like case in the New York Tombs a few years ago when a culprit escaped 'the law's delay' by putting a end to his life and comforting his widow and children with a paper claiming that it was his duty to die." The editorialist then listed a number of comparably hard cases that might feel equally inclined "to get out of the world at their earliest opportunity"—including "sewing women who have a hard time of it in life . . . heart broken wives of drunken husbands . . . many husbands whose lives are well-nigh tormented out of them by fretting wives . . . many men embarrassed by pecuniary difficulties . . . [and] children whose homes are so dismal that the cemetery looks pleasant in comparison. . ."[228] The editorialist in *The Sun & Central Press* found Frank's article equally appalling. "Professor Newman deliberately declares that suicide is sometimes a duty. The sufferer from an incurable disease, the aged invalid who sees young health sacrificed in tending him, may justly consider it a duty to put themselves out of the world . . . A few old moral prejudices about the virtues of courage, honesty, generosity, fortitude and endurance must be cleared away, and then we shall dispose of 'that reluctance to shorten life' which Professor Newman thinks we overstrain, and which some mistaken mortals consider a part of civilization."[229] The satirical note here is tell-tale: for the moral imagination of the 1870s, the notion that there might be a legal right to suicide and murder was not only atrocious but fantastic. Then, again, the *Church Herald* saw the matter in amusingly blunt sectarian terms. Frank and his Euthanasian friends, the paper declared, "are only consistent Protestants, who claim the right to judge everything . . . The Reformation has made life such a dreary farce that they propose to put an end to it. From their point of view we think the Euthanasians are right. If, after abolishing everything else, they would be content to abolish themselves, the world could bear the loss. But before they begin to exterminate their fellow creatures, legally or otherwise, we hope they will give us timely notice."[230] Other editorialists were less jocose, choosing to excoriate the enormity of what Frank was advocating. The editorialist at *Scribner's Monthly* furnishes a good example.

A physician certifies that he is hopelessly diseased, his own consent is in some way obtained (and as he would be quite apt to be muddled by medicine it ought not to be a difficult thing to get that), the friends are all agreed, and an extra dose of chloroform closes the scene and relieves them, casting them at once into mourning, and into the sad and solemn duties of dividing such property as their much-lamented relative may have left behind him. In case the invalid were a mother-in-law, or an incompatible wife or husband, or an unwelcome baby, or a maiden aunt who had outlived her usefulness, or a family servant who lagged superfluous on the stage, and could not be sent to the poor-house without injuring the reputation

---

[228] "Killing the Useless," in the *Newport Daily News* (1 May 1873).
[229] "A New Duty," in *The Sun & Central Press*, London (24 February 1873), p. 9.
[230] "The Duty of Suicide," in *The Church Herald* (5 March 1873).

of those to whom he had given the services of a faithful life, the beauty of the arrangement would become still more obvious. There is not, of course, the smallest opportunity for abuse!

The editorialist at *Scribner's*, stressing that Frank's recommendation had come from a "learned man" who understandably regarded his view as "deserving dignified treatment," obliged by showing his euthanasia the respect it deserves. "Very well," he wrote, "let us try to formulate the principle involved in [these] doctrines and declarations."

> *When a life becomes exceedingly or hopelessly inconvenient to its owner or to society, it ought to be destroyed.* This seems to us a fair statement of the principle involved in Professor Newman's declarations concerning his supposed cases, and, if it be allowed to stand as such, we see at once to what awful absurdities it will lead us. It involves the destruction of millions of human beings in embryo, of a large class of children born into the world with diseased souls and bodies, of paupers by the hundred thousand, of all the idiots living, of half the insane, of all the bed-ridden and the helpless, and of all the beggars that swarm like vermin throughout the old world. On this principle, we could reduce the breadeaters of the world by many millions in a single day, and by recognizing the principle in law—as these philosophers suggest—we should so obliterate from the mind of the brutal masses the idea of the sacredness of human life, that it would be no longer safe anywhere. Recognize in law the principle that hopeless inconvenience in life justifies death, and the suicidal and murderous impulses hold the license of the widest havoc in their hands.[231]

When Frank died in 1897, the *Times* ran an obituary observing how "The lives of the two brothers are in a measure typical of the growth of the two great streams which English thought has tended to follow since they were up at Oxford together."[232] Those streams have since assumed a character that the *Times* obituarist could hardly imagine, though the Scribner editorialist saw them with an uncanny prescience: "If man is nothing but an animal, if this life is all there is of his existence, and the question simply concerns the amount of comfort to be got out of it in this transient world, why, let him do as he likes with himself and his friends; but he who regards the present scene as only the foreground of an infinite spiritual future . . . we say he will take life whether it be convenient or inconvenient, and hold it as the gift of God, inalienable by any reason of infirmity or suffering, or hopeless disease, or cost to other life through necessary ministry. The doctrines of Prof. Newman . . . are unchristian doctrines. They carry us back into barbarism—back into the darkness in which children killed parents that became a burden to them, and mothers strangled infants that could only inherit their own sufferings. It is an infamous criticism of the divine wisdom, an insult to Providence, an assault upon the safeguards of society, and a reflection upon human nature and human destiny from which all Christian manhood recoils as from the touch of a serpent."[233]

---

[231] "Thou Shalt Kill," in *Scribner's Monthly*, Volume 6 (May 1873), pp. 107–8.
[232] "The Death of Professor Francis Newman," in the *Times*, (6 October 1897).
[233] "Thou Shalt Kill," in *Scribner's Monthly*, Volume 6 (May 1873), pp. 107–8.

Heterodoxy and Doubt

Newman had seen his brother's heterodox faith developing for decades. As early as November 1840, he wrote his sister Jemima: "I wished before this to tell you about F. [Newman] It is most painful indeed. You cannot think how far he goes. Pray do not tell it, I have not told it except generally even to H. but I think you may perhaps see him as being nearer;—he doubts (if I understand him) whether the beginning of St John is written by the Apostle, whether it is inspired, and whether its doctrine is not taken from Philo. And he said in the course of his letter, God forbid he should ever doubt our Lord's resurrection. Indeed I do not see where he is to stop. It is like Bl. White. It is like the Genevese, the Germans, like Protestantism generally. Whether or not Anglicanism leads to Rome, so far is clear as day that Protestantism leads to Infidelity. With a clearheaded impartial man, or with a body of men on the long run, there is no resting place short of it."[234]

The American Episcopal Bishop Abram Newkirk Littlejohn (1824–1901), charged with overseeing the American Episcopal churches on the Continent, was similarly critical of Frank's resolutely undogmatical faith, regarding it as typical of what he described as a "tendency [that] is an old and frequent visitor in the Christian camp."

> It has done vast mischief, and threatens to do more. From age to age this undogmatic piety has left the same unvarying witness. Two, or at most three, generations are enough to include its start and its finish. Without exception its disciples have fallen away into unbelief . . . or have drifted into self-indulgent worldliness. Into one or the other the despisers of a positive faith have always declined by a law as irresistible as gravitation. The mystics of Port Royal, after a season of demonstrative fervour, fell off into coldness and indifference. Strauss, who could not endure the historic Christ, and would have Him a myth, was a grandson in the faith of Spener the pietist, who could find no room for dogma in his religion. Francis Newman, who ran through the various phases of unbelief, ending in naked Deism, began among those whose religion was so warm-hearted and elastic as to render them careless of the obligations of doctrinal standards.[235]

Yet, Newman recognized that the infidelity of so many freethinkers was curiously diffident. In 1860, Frank wrote Newman to give him what he thought some surprising news about Holyoake. "Now I will tell you an odd thing: take it as a compliment or the contrary. A man whose name is (unjustly) a horror to nearly all my friends, and to every class of religionists, Holyoake, the Atheist Lecturer, is a great admirer of you – and of me! . . . . He reads eagerly, not only your works on general subjects and your novels, but many of your sermons; has come far out of his way to hear you preach and me lecture; and he frankly told me, he found we had very much in common, as to method and style of mind, or, he did not know what; but so it was, he could always learn much from us, and feel quite sure, that what he did learn was substantial. Now who knows, how strangely, when your words fall flat on an audience of halfeducated

---

[234] LD, 7:454, JHN to Mrs John Mozley (30 November 1840).
[235] Bishop Littlejohn, *American Church Review* (January 1882).

selfsufficient gentry or tradesmen here or in Dublin, you may unawares be giving a secret but sound intellectual impulse to a body which at present has no religious beliefs whatever?"[236]

Ignoring Frank's slighting reference to the people who bought his books, Newman wrote back that the news was not as surprising as Frank might imagine. His response merits quoting at length because it shows not only Newman's recognition of the range of his influence but the quality of his correspondence. The nineteenth-century English produced first-rate letter writers, from Byron and Sydney Smith to Keats and Emily Eden.[237] But the richness and variety, the verve and incisiveness of Newman's letters put them in a class apart. Samuel Palmer, the English landscape painter and friend of Blake, who was a good letter writer himself, once said that "Letters should be artless . . . negligently elegant; they want a natty native-grace-Gainsborough-kind-of-touch . . ."[238] Well, Newman's letters exhibit this quality in abundance but they also have something else: a sustained brilliance that places them amidst his very best writing.

> I assure you I do not at all undervalue the interest which Mr Holyoake may take in my writings – More than most people have I had lessons through my life to "Cast my bread upon the waters", and "not to observe the winds." You may understand that my Creed leads me to feel less surprise at an Atheist than a Protestant feels. In truth, I think that logically there is no middle point between Catholicism and Atheism – At the same time, holding this, I hold of course also, that numbers of men are logically inconsistent; and, as I think many a Protestant has principles in him which ought to make him a Catholic, if he followed them out, so I think of an Atheist also – And, while you are wondering how I can be a Catholic, I on my own side may think that both you and (from what you say) Mr Holyoake may cherish that in your hearts, of which Catholicism alone is the full account. So far from thinking it little to advance him and his friends a step, I should think it a great favour shown me by Almighty God to be made the instrument of doing so – I should consider, that, as his disciples go further in the right direction than he, so their disciples again will go further than they, and so on; just as the lava of Vesuvius, after cooling is first covered with an almost invisible lichen, which becomes the mould of some higher vegetation, and that again of higher, till step by step we arrive at last to that rich fine soil which produces the lacryma.[239]

The doubts of freethinkers were always fascinating to Newman. Apropos the uncertainty of unbelief, he wrote Lady Herbert of Lea in August of 1879: "I think the

[236] LD, 19:286 FWN to JHN (17 January 1860).

[237] Readers who have not done so already must dip into the splendid letters of Emily Eden. Speaking of her time in India with her brother George, Lord Auckland, Governor-General of India from 1835 to 1841, Emily remarked how "George says he is sure that the staring, *round* look which everybody's eyes have here, is not, as is always supposed, occasioned by the heat or the shrinking of the eyelids, but the knack they have of wondering at everything. The least deviation from every day's routine puts them out." See entry for 16 August 1836.

[238] *The Oxford Book of Letters.* ed. Frank and Anita Kermode (Oxford, 1995), p. 296.

[239] LD, 19:286 JHN to FWN (18 January 1860) *Lacryma*, here, refers to *Lachryma Christi*, the strong sweet red wine of southern Italy.

great argument against this day's infidelity is that it does not, cannot believe in itself. I do not deny of course that there are certain minds who have as little concern about their religious ignorance and [are] as well satisfied with themselves, as are Unitarians, or Wesleyans etc etc in their own form of faith; but in the majority of unbelievers there is a deep misgiving that they are wrong or probably wrong."[240] This is evident even from the correspondence of Unitarians. In one letter, James Martineau wrote Frank: "Your remark as to the character of my Christian theology—that it is not a permanent structure, but a bridge to aid the timid—affects me with a certain sadness, which is perhaps an augury of its truth."[241] Newman would have seen his instincts richly confirmed if he had known of the number of fairly celebrated atheists who recanted. Joseph Barker, Thomas Cooper, J. B. Bebbington, Dr Sexton Townley, and J. H. Gordon all eventually grew unsure of their uncertainties and turned their energies to reaffirming Christian evidences for such Christian papers as the *British Banner* and the *Liberator*. Even Charles Southwell, the erstwhile champion of atheism, ended his days in New Zealand writing for a Wesleyan paper.[242]

Whether Holyoake had doubts about his doubts is arguable, though in his later years he did mitigate his attacks against Christianity. Frank, however, was a different case. Again and again, he tried to qualify his repudiation of Christian doctrine by asserting that he had never ceased being Christian. Sometimes, he sought to mask this inconsistency by explaining that he was in search of an ideal faith, "a religion which shall combine the tenderness, humility, and disinterestedness that are the glories of the purest Christianity with the activity of intellect and untiring pursuit of truth."[243] At other times, he went so far as to suggest that his eccentric Deism was the true Christianity and that orthodox Christians were the schismatics. In 1897, when Frank was 92, he wrote his friend Anna Swanwick a last letter insisting that he wished "once again definitely to take the name of Christian," which he defined as "'one who in heart and sympathy is a disciple of Jesus in upholding the prayer called the Lord's Prayer as the highest and purest in any known national religion.' I think J.M. [James Martineau] would approve this."[244] That Frank should cite the Unitarian Martineau as an authority on what defined a Christian speaks for itself. Nonetheless, such unreal words showed how uncomfortable Frank was with an apostasy that he could scarcely name, let alone acknowledge. In letter after letter throughout his life, he insisted that his free thinking had somehow left his Christian faith intact. Only once did he abandon this pretense and then he spoke with a pitiable remorse: "It is a sad thing to have printed erroneous fact. I have three or four times contradicted and renounced the passage . . . *but I cannot reach those whom I have misled*."[245] In light of this rueful admission, it is coincidental that George Eliot should have written a friend in 1874, "Poor Mr. Francis Newman must be aged now, and rather weary of the world and explanations of the world. He can hardly be expected to take in

---

[240] LD, 29:169 JHN to Lady Herbert of Lea (19 August 1879).
[241] *The Life and Work of Harriet Martineau* (London, 1957), p. 307.
[242] F. B. Smith, "The Atheist Mission 1840–1900," in *Victorian England: The Folio Society History of England* (London, 1999), p. 490.
[243] *Sieveking*, p. 341.
[244] Ibid., p. 215.
[245] Ibid., p. 342.

much novelty. I have a sort of affectionate sadness in thinking of the interest which, in far-off days, I felt in his 'Soul' and 'Phases of Faith,' and of the awe I had of him as a lecturer on mathematics at the Ladies' College. How much work he has done in the world which has left no deep conspicuous mark, but has probably entered beneficially into many lives!"[246]

The Search for Truth

In February 1848, Frank was appointed the first Principal of University Hall at University College, London, founded after the passing of the Dissenters' Chapels Act of 1844 to provide students with non-denominational theological instruction. The idea for the hall had first been broached at a meeting of the General Committee of the Presbyterian Union, where it was agreed "that, in viewing this measure [the Chapels Act] as the first legislative recognition of the great truth, that the sanctity of private judgement in matters of religion may be a principle in men's minds paramount to the holding of any peculiar dogmas, we would venture to suggest the formation of some permanent memorial, educational or otherwise, to perpetuate in the most useful form the great principle of unlimited religious liberty."[247] Subscribers to the Hall included James Martineau and Henry Crabb Robinson, the journalist and diarist. After hearing Frank's inaugural address, Robinson praised "the skill with which he asserted, without offence, the power of forming an institution open to all opinions whatever, even Jew and Mahometan."[248] Walter Bagehot, another subscriber, came away with a different impression, writing to a friend: "The only objection that any one could have to Newman as the head of a religious institution is that his own religion is such a thoroughly bad one. What he says about the magnanimity of founding an institution independent of opinion is marred for me by my being convinced that if the Council *had* known his creed they would never have appointed him."[249] As it happened, Frank resigned and the Hall appointed Arthur Hugh Clough in his place, largely because Clough was thought, as Crabb Robinson noted, "to have strong convictions of the truth of Christianity, but to be unfixed on points of doctrine."[250] The founders' commitment to "unlimited religious liberty" notwithstanding, they preferred Clough's private judgement to Frank's. The Unitarians of Gower Street were as baffled by Frank's Church of the Future as Darby and his friends had been. Sieveking, Frank's unflaggingly sympathetic biographer did not clarify matters when he noted how Frank "often described himself as holding Christianity without Christ."[251] Another friend recalled: "Not more than three or four years before his death I was sitting in an omnibus at Oxford Circus, when Dr. Martineau, accompanied by his daughter, got in and took seats by my side. After I had confessed my pleasure at seeing him, he said, 'I think you ought to know

---

[246] George Eliot to Sara Hennell (27 March 1874) in *The Writings of George Eliot As Related in Her Letters and Journals.* ed. J. W. Cross (New York, 1908), p. 161.
[247] Katherine Chorley. *Arthur Hugh Clough: The Uncommitted Mind* (Oxford, 1962), p. 170.
[248] *The Collected Works of Walter Bagehot* (London, 1986), XII, p. 279.
[249] Ibid., pp. 279–80.
[250] Chorley, p. 173.
[251] *Sieveking*, p. 361.

that the other day I had a letter from Frank Newman saying that, when he died, he wished it to be known that he died in the Christian faith.'"[252] The Rev J. Temperley Grey, who gave the eulogy at Newman's funeral at Weston-super-Mare in October 1897, admitted that:

> Theologically we were far apart, but we were entirely with him in his enthusiasm for righteousness, his sympathy with downtrodden and oppressed peoples ... We were with him also in his untiring efforts to secure for women their rightful place in the shaping of our national life, and in his splendid protests against the tortures inflicted in the name of science on the poor, helpless animals, our dumb bothers ... Those of us who were admitted into the inner circle of his friends were fondly impressed by his devoutness. He lived, as in the Presence of God, and his prayers in the home, were always a means of grace, a real refreshment ... He was a true philanthropist. He championed the cause of the oppressed everywhere .... A room in his house was set apart as a guest-chamber for persons needing a change to the seaside, but whose circumstances barred the way; and not a few were fresh equipped for the work and battle of life, as a result of his thoughtful hospitality ... Francis Newman stood by himself in his greatness, his simplicity, and we shall not find his like again ... Above all, our friend was a truth seeker. This was the ruling passion of his life.[253]

Frank would probably have approved of this summation of his faith, despite its studied vagueness. He was given to being vague himself. In 1847, he wrote Clough, "For myself, I look at it as a fixed certainty that all the idle janglings which ignorance now occasions will vanish with the progress of knowledge .... It will be in no small measure a work of destruction; but construction will go on pari passu: and perhaps the sons of our younger men will wonder at the blind bigotry of their grandshires."[254] Here was Lord Brougham's faith in the moral benefits of knowledge that Newman had skewered so splendidly in *The Tamworth Reading Room* (1841). As far back as 1828, the Tory *Morning Post* had anticipated Newman's satire, speaking of Brougham with mocking admiration. "He carries not in his satchel the tomes of antiquated philosophy, nor the venerable volumes of Revelation; they are to him as dust thrown into the eyes of reason, and as cobwebs that entangle the poor insect in its flight after truth ... The day is at hand when he shall stand forth the Great Captain of the Age, and at the head of his legions begin the march of intellect."[255] William Wordsworth also took issue with Brougham on this score, telling one correspondent that he was not convinced, as the reforming lord was, "that sharpening of intellect and attainment of knowledge are things good in themselves, without reference to the circumstances under which the intellect *is* sharpened, or to the quality of the knowledge acquired. 'Knowledge,' says Lord Bacon, 'is power,' but surely not less for evil than for good. Lord Bacon spoke like

---

[252] Ibid., p. 344.
[253] Ibid., pp. 345–6.
[254] *Correspondence of Arthur Hugh Clough* (Oxford, 1957), 1, p. 190.
[255] *The Morning Post* (28 February 1828) quoted in Rosemary Ashton. *Victorian Bloomsbury* (New Haven, 2012), p. 65.

a philosopher, but they who have that maxim in their mouths the oftenest have the least understanding of it."[256]

In *Phases of Faith*, Frank enunciated the propositions that would animate this new and improved faith: "Morality is the end, Spirituality is the means; Religion is the handmaiden to Morals: we must be spiritual, in order that we may be in the highest and truest sense moral."[257] In 1887, he wrote Mrs Charles Kingsley, ". . . the older I become (81 last June) the more painfully my creed outgrows the limits of that which the mass of my nation . . . account *sacred* . . . I uphold the *sacred moralities* of Jew and Christian, Hindoo and Moslem with all my heart. Two mottoes, or say three, suffice me:

> The Lord Reigneth.
> The righteous Lord loveth righteousness.
> The Lord requireth Justice, Mercy, Sobriety of thought, not ceremony or creed."[258]

Here, again, Frank was playing the contrarian sage, proud that he had not fallen prey to the outmoded creeds of his compatriots. Newman was never impressed by his brother's attitudinizing. In the autumn of 1840, when Frank first apprised him of the full extent of his Unitarianism, Newman wrote him back a letter full of prophetic foreboding. He did not subscribe to the notion that the search for truth was somehow an alternative to the truth itself. He did not believe that the Creator intended his creatures to spend their lives doubting the Revelation. He did not join the rationalists of the age in recommending doubt as a kind of surrogate religion. Nor did he believe that Christianity was a "handmaiden to morals." His rejection of these notions was at the heart of his understanding of his difference with his brother, and indeed with the age of profession of which Frank was so representative a figure. Of all Newman's various writings regarding his brother, this best captures how he saw his brother's rejection of Christianity and it merits quoting at length.

> Of course you can understand the pain your letter gave me, without my expressing it. Not that I am surprised at what you say of your present opinions; I was quite sure that you must arrive at them one day or other, if you continued in your adherence to those principles which for 14 years at least you have held. Nay unless withheld by divine grace you must go further still—your principles lead to scepticism on all points whatever, and this circumstance is to my mind a reductio ad absurdum of them. Whatever else is true, or false, man is made for religion; and your principles make religion impossible. I am not attempting to prove this; but I state my opinion for your information, as you have stated yours for mine. And this I wish you to understand of any thing else I shall say.
>
> I think your reasonings are irresistible, granting certain latent principles which you all along assume. And since I anticipate that these will be generally assumed by the coming age, as they are in great measure already, I am prepared for almost a downfall of Christianity for a time. Moreover do not let me hurt you if I say

---

[256] William Wordsworth to Hugh James Rose (11 December 1828) in *Letters of William Wordsworth.* ed. Philip Wayne (Oxford, 1954), p. 176.
[257] *Phases*, p. 44.
[258] *Sieveking*, p. 381.

that in the plain and undeniable irrationality of the religion of the Church, on the assumption of the principles alluded to, I see a vivid exemplification of what the Apostle meant when he said that the worldly wisdom knew not God, and spoke of the preaching of the Cross as foolishness.

And what I have said will serve to explain my own conduct towards what you justly call the English way of handling the Evidences, Canon, proof of doctrine etc. Considering that your conclusions are the legitimate issue of Protestant principles, when followed out, and that the English use and application of the latter is fallacious and ultimately untenable, I am not inclined to show mercy to what must one day be exposed and come to nought since it is better for men to be roused to a sense of their true state and to be shown whither they are drifting than to enjoy an hollow peace and dangerous rest some little time longer. Nor do I fear that such a course will eventually subserve your conclusions. Rather it will frighten men the other way. Latitudinarianism is an unnatural state; the mind cannot long rest in it; and especially if the fact of a revelation be granted, it is most extravagant and revolting to our reason to suppose that after all its message is not ascertainable and that the divine interposition reveals nothing. The more scepticism abounds, the more is a way made for the revival of a strong ecclesiastical authority; Christianity arose in the beginning, when the popular religions had lost their hold upon the mind. So strongly do I feel this, that, averse as the English people are to Romanism, I conceive that did their choice lie in the mere alternative they would embrace even Romanism rather than acquiesce in absolute uncertainty.

I have no fears then for the ultimate fortunes of Catholicism; I do but grieve and sigh over those who are destined to fall by the way in the wilderness.[259]

It is too soon to say whether Newman was being overly sanguine here: the Catholic Church might yet encourage the English people to rebel against their accustomed Latitudinarianism. Nevertheless, Frank's tolerance for "absolute uncertainty" was thoroughgoing, so much so that it blinded him to the true nature of his brother's conversion. One can see this in his letter of 6 August 1845, in which he actually tried to dissuade his brother from going over to Rome. If nothing else, it starkly demonstrates how entirely mistaken Frank was about the nature of his brother's search for truth. "I am about to address you on . . . your own position and your own future course," Frank wrote, with a sententiousness that must have amused his older brother. "You may be sure that I have no motive but a desire for your honour and usefulness—but I will add, that, unless I thought I could in some degree measure that usefulness by your own standard, I would refrain my pen. So also would I, if I thought that you had any real and decided necessity of conscience, determining you to join the Romanist body, other than the negative argument that nothing *better* is to be found . . ." It is clear from the recommendations that followed that Frank had only the foggiest notion of what Newman's "own standard" was in such matters. Certainly, to assume that his brother was converting, not because of dictates of conscience, but because "nothing better [was] to be found" said more about his own standards than those of his brother. But the whole letter is replete with unfounded assumptions. "If you chose

[259] LD, 7:412–13 JHN to FWN (22 October 1840).

the Romanish Communion as in *itself good*, you would be in it already, and would long and long since abandoned your ostensible position. It must needs have in it points which make you most reluctant to enter it. Assuming this, I say it would be far better for attaining what I believe to be your ends, not to join Rome, but to stay unconnected to any thing, until you can form and join some independent Episcopal system, similar to that of Scotland or New York." Here, Frank was addressing not his brother himself but the caricature he had formed of him. If it was episcopacy Newman wanted, Frank reasoned, he should pursue it in less disreputable places than in Rome. And if this argument did not persuade him, he should consider how Rome would discredit him in the eyes of his compatriots. "How vehement is the English repugnance to real and avowed Romanism, I need not tell you. I am but a sample of thousands, with whom it would be a clear reductio ad absurdum of Christianity, if Christianity logically led to Romanism—Hundreds of thousands, who have never presented the thought to themselves in this light, yet would feel certain there must be some most grave error in principles which terminated in such a practical conclusion. Hence by such a step you would *un*teach to multitudes those Church principles which they have learned from those who have hitherto in the main felt and acted with you. Your name would lose at once all influence with nine tenths of those who were used to respect you, and among Romanists you would be received with condescending pity as a novice who had yet much to learn and unlearn. In the cause of conscience, this and far more ought to be ventured and endured . . ."

As it happened, Newman was concerned that his conversion might unsettle the faith of Anglicans but he would not allow the preferences of others to sway his ultimate decision. And Frank's reference to the "cause of conscience" was adding insult to injury, especially after he had tried to suggest that his brother's allegiance to Rome was formed by neglecting that cause. "But I am presuming that it is with you in any case a choice of difficulties; a practical matter to be decided by a balance of arguments, and one in which expediency has a most legitimate place. 'Unity of the Church' (including a certain uniformity) I apprehend is your end—and the question is about means . . . You cannot really advance the end by joining Rome yourself; you may even throw it back." In reading this, Newman might have thought that his brother's impertinence had run its course but Frank was not finished. "Even . . . professing 'unity' as the end, I think you might boldly face the charge of 'Schism' (which no doubt would be thrown at you) if you took even a leading part in organizing the nucleus of an Anglo-Episcopal Free Church with succession of Bishops derived from New York or Scotland (and therefore, according to your views, from the Apostles)—provided that on the front of it no hostility to Rome were professed, but the whole question were kept carefully open . . . I have read enough of your writings to know what I suggest is *inconsistent* with what you have advanced publicly, but you have not scruples before you to avow changes of mind, and I do trust you will think SOLELY of what now recommends itself to you as wise and right, and not enslave yourself to your past words . . ."[260]

Towards the end of his life, in 1883, Newman would recall this letter and see it as emblematic of his brother's total failure to understand him: "As to [Frank's] insight

---

[260] LD, 10:744–5 FWN to JHN (6 August 1845).

into my habitual state of mind, nothing shows better his inability to enter it than that in 1845 he thought it worth while to advise me not to join the Catholic Church, but to set up a denomination of my own. I believe that in 1824 he knew just as much about my mind as in 1845."[261]

Taken as a whole, the letter is a kind of travesty of the letters that Newman wrote his brother Charles when Charles first broached leaving Christianity for Owenism. Now, Frank felt impelled to dissuade his older brother from taking what he considered an even more disastrous step. In response, Newman was characteristically forthright about what was truly guiding his conversion. "Thank you for your very kind letter, for which I am much obliged. I can assure you that the hypothesis which you have put aside as impossible, is literally true. It is from no idea of the Roman system being the most bearable of the existing forms of religion that I contemplate accepting it. I have always resisted, and do heartily resist, the notion of choosing a religion according to my fancy. I have no desire at all to leave the English Church. I feel the utmost disgust at the thought of forming a new sect. I have no temptation that way at all. My reason for going to Rome is this:—I think the English Church in schism. I think the faith of the Roman Church the only true religion. I do not think there is salvation out of the Church of Rome. This of course does not interfere with my thinking an exception is made for those who are in involuntary ignorance; but for myself, when I am once certainly convinced on the point [of the claims of the Roman Church], and I have given myself a long trail of my conviction, I am no longer in such ignorance."[262]

What is striking about Frank's response to Newman's imminent conversion was how typical it was of many in Protestant England. In his memoir about his brother, Frank recalled Oxford before his brother's conversion in a way that shows how conventional this otherwise wilfully eccentric man could be. Speaking of a time when Newman was undergoing the defining trial of his life, Frank could only recall, with malevolent relish, the popular contempt that greeted his brother as he prepared to secede from the Established Church.

> In my visit I found the atmosphere of Oxford most hostile to him. In the shops were caricatures and cartoons, with guideposts to show the way to Rome. The newspapers had bitter complaints from parents, who had believed that [Newman] had a special *via media* to save their sons from Rome, and, lo! It had led them thither. The general sentiment proclaimed him to be a wolf in sheep's clothing. The city seemed to cry to him, "Get out!" and his pupils from Rome to cry, "You are bound in honesty to come after us.". . . When I met him, his deportment to me was, greatly changed. He had come down from his high horse. I thought that first his humiliation about Tract XC might have done him good; but now far greater was the manifest contempt and aversion of the public. I frankly told him Rome was his only fit place: he did not resent it . . .[263]

[261] LD, 30:233 JHN to The Editor of the Fortnightly Review (14 June 1883).
[262] LD, 10:745 JHN to FWN (7 August 1845).
[263] *Contr*, p. 101.

John Newman Senior (Courtesy of Birmingham Oratory).

Family Residence, 17 Southampton Place (Courtesy of Birmingham Oratory).

Family Portrait by Maria Giberne (Courtesy of Birmingham Oratory).

Grey Court House, Ham (Courtesy of Birmingham Oratory).

Henry Brougham at the time of Queen
Caroline's trial.

Print of Holland House by Paul Fourdrinier of Charing Cross.

Oxford and Cambridge Coach.

Entrance to Oxford from London after
George Cooper (1817).

The Chapel, Trinity College (Courtesy of
British Museum).

View of the Chapel and Hall, Oriel College
(Courtesy of British Museum).

Charles Dickens by William Powell Frith.

Anthony Trollope by Samuel Laurence.

Edward Henry Manning by Richard Doyle
(Courtesy of British Museum).

James Joyce.

Fourdrinier Family Portrait by John Downman circa 1786. (Courtesy of National Portrait Gallery). Newman's mother, Jemima is third from the right.

Charles Newman (Courtesy of Birmingham Oratory).

Robert Owen (Courtesy of British Museum).

The Bank of England (Courtesy of British Museum).

Punch and Judy (Courtesy of British Museum).

Frank Newman as a Young Man Aged 46
(Courtesy of Birmingham Oratory).

John Nelson Darby.

Searle's Coffee House – Where Frank and
John roomed together at Oxford.

Maria Kennaway – Frank's First Wife.

Frank Newman as an Old Man (Courtesy of Birmingham Oratory).

La Madonna col Divoto after Correggio (Courtesy of Harvard University).

George Eliot – Thought Highly of "St Francis" (Courtesy of British Museum).

James Martineau – Frank's Unitarian Confidante (Courtesy of British Museum).

Tom, Harriett and Grace Mozley (Courtesy of British Museum).

Victorian Hats – Harriett was mad about bonnets (Courtesy of British Museum).

Thomas Mozley (Courtesy of Birmingham Oratory).

Henry Wilberforce at Oxford (Courtesy of Birmingham Oratory).

Mary Newman (Courtesy of Birmingham Oratory).

Minny Temple.

Hilaire Belloc.

Jemima (Newman) Mozley (Courtesy of
Birmingham Oratory).

Littlemore Village in 1840.

Image of Oratorian by Andrea Sacchi.

Alfred Tennyson by Richard Doyle (Courtesy
of British Museum).

The Martyrdom of Latimer and Ridley opposite Balliol (Courtesy of British Museum).

Lloyd's Caricaturist.)

(No. 1. Price 1d

POPERY OR NO POPERY? THAT IS THE QUESTION! OR JOHN BULL IN A FIX.

Popery or No Popery: That is the Question: John Bull in a Fix (Courtesy of British Museum).

John Rickards Mozley (Courtesy of Cambridge University Library).

King's College Chapel Cambridge (Courtesy of British Museum).

St Bartholomew Day's Massacre (Courtesy of British Museum).

Thomas Edward Brown.

Henry Sidgwick.

Montague Rhodes James.

Augustine Birrell by Spy (Vanity Fair).

Newman's Chapel at the Oratory with St Frances de Sales above the altar. (Courtesy of Birmingham Oratory).

St Philip Neri – (Courtesy of British Museum).

The Cardinal in his Study (Courtesy of
Birmingham Oratory).

Holy Family by Raphael 1518 (Courtesy of
Louvre Museum).

Despite the inaccuracy of that last line—Frank did not tell his brother to convert to Rome—this reveals a good deal. In the search for truth, to which Frank professed such passionate attachment, he was the brother who spoke of expediency. Newman, for his part, never allowed his choice of religion to be swayed by whether it would be popular with his compatriots. (Later, in *Loss and Gain*, he would have his hero Charles Redding observe how "what is very expedient, still may be very impossible."[264]) Nor did he consult his convenience. He "always resisted . . . the notion of choosing a religion according to . . . fancy." He chose to convert because he did "not think there is salvation outside the Church of Rome." There were exceptions, of course, but not for the voluntarily ignorant. That Frank could not grasp this was part and parcel of another difference between the brothers. Although grave in demeanour and never quick to see a joke, Frank was essentially frivolous. Newman recognized as much when he wrote atop Frank's letter of 6 August: "That I could be contemplating questions of Truth and Falsehood never entered into his imagination!"[265] For Newman, these questions were of the essence of any proper search for truth. Refuse to take them into consideration, refuse to answer them, refuse to act on them, and one might as well be playing a kind of hunt the slipper without the slipper. In rejecting the notion that the search for truth could have doubt as its object, Newman gave eloquent expression to his fundamental difference with Frank and with the principle of "philosophies and heresies" that so unsettled him.

That there is a truth then; that there is one truth; that religious error is in itself of an immoral nature; that its maintainers, unless involuntarily such, are guilty in maintaining it; that it is to be dreaded; that the search for truth is not the gratification of curiosity; that its attainment has nothing of the excitement of a discovery; that the mind is below truth, not above it, and is bound, not to descant upon it, but to venerate it; that truth and falsehood are set before us for the trial of our hearts; that our choice is an awful giving forth of lots on which salvation or rejection is inscribed; that "before all things it is necessary to hold the Catholic faith;" that "he that would be saved must thus think," and not otherwise; that, "if thou criest after knowledge, and liftest up thy voice for understanding, if thou seekest her as silver, and searchest for her as for hid treasure, then shalt thou understand the fear of the Lord, and find the knowledge of God,"—this is the dogmatical principle. . . . That truth and falsehood in religion are but matter of opinion; that one doctrine is as good as another; that the Governor of the world does not intend that we should gain the truth; that there is no truth; that we are not more acceptable to God by believing this than by believing that; that no one is answerable for his opinions; that they are a matter of necessity or accident; that it is enough if we sincerely hold what we profess; that our merit lies in seeking, not in possessing; that it is a duty to follow what seems to us true, without a fear lest it should not be true; that it may be a gain to succeed, and can be no harm to fail; that we may take up and lay down opinions at pleasure; that belief belongs

[264] *LG*, p. 221.
[265] LD, 10:745 Written atop Frank's Letter to Newman dated 6 August 1845.

to the mere intellect, not to the heart also; that we may safely trust to ourselves in matters of Faith, and need no other guide,—this is the principle of philosophies and heresies . . .[266]

In distorting these differences, Frank Newman would spend years distorting his brother and his brother's work. Yet, on 13 October 1845 in response to Newman's informing him of his conversion, Frank wrote a letter which, if it had been written at the end of his life, might have been a retraction of the many attacks he had made on his brother. As it was, it was followed by too many disavowals to constitute any repudiation of the antagonism that he had shown his brother throughout his long life. Still, it is worth quoting, if only because it shows that Frank was not entirely unsuccessful in his own search for truth.

> Your letter, though dated Octr 5 arrived only on the 11th. I have no doubt that you feel more happy for having made to me the confessions and apologies contained in it; and in so far, I cannot wish them unsaid. It is a healthy thing to have a far deeper sense of our own unworthiness than others have. I do not call it morbid in you, but on the contrary a condition without which we cannot struggle towards higher perfection.
>
> Yet I should not be happy to make any other reply than that I am utterly unaware of any such confessions or apologies being needed. I do not remember any "cruelties at school." It is credible that like other elder brothers you may have expected and enforced more obedience than the younger was always willing to yield; but I am certain that for one act of cruelty there were ten of protection, affection, and generosity. The collision between us when we were at College arose to the very full as much, as far more, from my harsh, blunt, inexperienced and heartless mode of following out dogmas which I received as axioms, than from any fault in you. You have ever had a far more refined and tender heart than I. . . . If in anything I have improved, it is by the grace of God acting by experience and by suffering. I must say I feel you were always a most affectionate and generous brother. I fully felt this, when I most rudely jarred against you; and, if I could think I had acted as well as . . . you to me, it would lessen many pangs of secret sorrow . . . .[267]

---

[266] *Dev.*, p. 357.
[267] LD, 11:309–10 Francis Newman to JHN (13 October 1845).

5

Mary Newman and the World to Come

Mary, the youngest of the sisters, was also the most beloved. Without Harriett's quick wit or Jemima's talent for music, Mary had nonetheless a sweetness and serenity that were remarked by all who knew her. Maria Giberne spoke for all of the Newman family when she wrote Newman in 1882: "Who could ever behold that dear sweet face for any length of time, and forget it again; and again who could ever have been acquainted with the soul and heart that lent their expression to that face and not love her."[1] Harriett may have been the sister with whom Newman was closest because of their proximity in age but it was Mary who was his favourite. For Newman, she was so "gifted with that singular sweetness and affectionateness of temper that she lived in an ideal world of happiness, the very sight of which made others happy."[2] In this chapter, I shall revisit Mary's life to show how she deepened Newman's understanding not only of life and death but of the life after death.

One of the reasons why Newman's contemporaries read him with such careful attention is that he addressed questions that they found addressed nowhere else with such compelling insight. The Unitarian Walter Bagehot could hardly be said to be favourably disposed to Roman Catholicism—or, for that matter, Anglicanism—but he read Newman avidly and closely precisely because he had questions of his own which the present world could scarcely answer. "Our senses teach us what the world is," Bagehot wrote in an essay on the French Romantic poet Béranger, "our intuitions where it is. We see the blue and gold of the world, its lively amusements, its gorgeous if superficial splendour, its currents of men; we feel its light spirits, we enjoy its happiness; we enjoy it; and we are puzzled. What is the object of all of this? Why do we do all this? What is the universe *for*?"[3] None of his siblings helped Newman to answer that importunate question more than Mary, and since hers was such a personal influence, Newman always spoke of the lessons of her loss with deep personal conviction.

Born on 9 November 1809, Mary left an indelible impression on Newman. After her death on 5 January 1828, when she was all of 19, Newman inscribed in his diary a laconic entry: "We lost my sister Mary suddenly." However, 50 years later, he would write how, as he said, "I have as vivid feelings of love, tenderness, and sorrow, when I think of dear Mary, as ever I had since her death."[4] Dorothea Mozley, the editor of

1 LD, 30:50 Maria Giberne to JHN (8 January 1882).
2 LD, 2:49 JHN to Robert Isaac Wilberforce (14 January 1828).
3 Augustine Birrell. "Walter Bagehot" (5 March 1901) in *Collected Works of Walter Bagehot* (London, 1986), XV, p. 201.
4 LD, 2:47 See Diary entry for 5 January 1828.

Newman Family Letters, recalls Mrs Newman's old teacher Mrs Magnoally gazing at Mary as a young girl and exclaiming, "Old Slyboots, who'd have thought of your growing so tall?" What seems to have made Mary especially charming was her gaiety. She liked to tell droll stories. Describing an Oxford rowing match, she wrote to Harriett of how the rowers were "so exhausted" at Vauxhall Bridge "that they thought they must give it up, but the cheers of the multitude, and a bumper of brandy each revived them," even though "when they arrived at the place they were obliged to be lifted out of the boat and immediately put to bed. How inglorious!"[5] She was also fond of nicknames, calling Harriett "Harry" and Jemima "Mum." As Mozley observes, "Not as clever as Harriett, less talented than Jemima," Mary nevertheless had "a simplicity, a directness, a sweetness and warmth of heart which endeared her to all whom she met. She was beloved by her family, and most of all by John."[6]

Something of Mary's charm is evident from her sense of fun, which had nothing of Harriett's tart derisiveness. In 1826, she wrote her eldest brother:

> Dear John how extremely kind you are – oh I wish I could write as fast as I think. I cannot tell why, but, whatever I write to you, I am always ashamed of. I think it must be vanity, and yet I do not feel so to most others. And now, all I have written, I should like to burn.
>
> Thank you for your long letter, which I do not deserve. I wish I could see your rooms. Are they called generally by the titles which you give them? I hope 'the brown room' is not quite so grave as its name would lead one to suppose. At least Harriett would not be in the number of its admirers. You know brown is not a great favorite of hers. I had no idea you lectured in your rooms . . .
>
> Oh how delightful if you can do as you say! it really will be quite astonishing to have you for so long – but poor Frank, I wish, oh that he might be with us too! . . .I did not imagine, John, that with all your tutoric gravity and your brown room you could be so absurd as your letter (I beg your pardon) seems to betray. . .
>
> . . .Well, I really think I have found out the secret of my difficulty in writing to you – it is because I never told that difficulty; at least I find I write much easier since my confession.[7]

There were times when Newman could be pompous. So Mary was within her rights gently to tease him about his "tutoric gravity." Harriett also poked fun at her brother for the same foible. "Dear John, take care of yourself and be sure you let me know from authority how you are."[8] Far from taking any umbrage at this, Newman enjoyed the opportunity his sisters gave him of putting aside his graver concerns. When he was 14, he wrote Mary from Ealing: "What had you on your birth-day? Let imagination answer. Perhaps you had apples, perhaps cakes, perhaps you had gingerbread, and perhaps you had – nothing at all. What had we? We had nothing. What shall we have? Difficult to answer. Perhaps we shall have a cake sent, and perhaps – nothing. Perhaps we may have our pay sent. Perhaps not. Perhaps we may have cake and pay, perhaps

---

5 *Family*, p. 5.
6 Ibid., p. xvii.
7 LD, 1:286 Mary Newman to JHN (5 May 1826).
8 LD, 1:300 Harriett Newman to JHN (25 September 1826).

so. I shall conclude and with the most profound respect am Your affectionate Brother John Newman."[9] In 1827, when he was an Oriel Fellow and surrounded by some of the finest minds in Oxford, he still enjoyed dashing off silly letters to his favourite sister. "I applaud your determination to pass an independent judgment on what you read," he wrote in one letter. "It is very necessary to keep in mind the necessity of making up one's mind for oneself; but I am rather stupid at this moment, or I would enter into a disquisition on the subject." However, that Newman and Mary saw eye to eye on a deeper level is evident from an extraordinary poem that Newman sent his sister in 1823 when she had just turned 20. (Mary was very keen on poetry.) In the light of future events, it was appallingly prophetic. Scarcely 5 years after he transcribed and sent the poem, Mary would be dead. Looking back at the poem, written by the Scottish poet and hymn-writer James Montgomery (1771–1856), Newman must have felt as though he had sent his young sister her own elegy. He had certainly sent her verses that would express much of his own heartbreak after she was gone.

> Night is the time for dreams –
> The gay romance of life,
> When truth that is and truth that seems
> Blend in fantastic strife –
> Ah! visions less beguiling far
> Than waking dreams by daylight are!
>
> Night is the time to weep –
> To wet with unseen tears
> Those graves of memory, where sleep
> The joys of other years –
> Hopes that were angels in their birth
> But finished young, like things of earth.
>
> Night is the time to watch –
> On ocean's dark expanse
> To hail the Pleiades or catch
> The full moon's earliest glance,
> That brings into the homesick mind
> All we have loved and left behind.
>
> Night is the time for care,
> Brooding on hours misspent –
> To see the spectre of despair
> Come to our lonely tent –
> Like Brutus, midst his slumbering host,
> Startled by Caesar's stalwart ghost.
>
> Night is the time to muse –
> When from the earth the soul

---

9   LD, 1:280 JHN to Mary Newman (14 November 1815).

Takes flight, and with expanding views
Beyond the starry pole,
Descries athwart the abyss of night
The dawn of uncreated light.

Night is the time to pray –
Our Saviour oft withdrew
To desert mountains far away –
So will his followers do –
Steal from the throng to haunts untrod
And hold communion there with God.

Night is the time for death –
When all around is peace,
Calmly to yield the weary breath,
From sin and suffering cease –
Think of Heaven's bliss, and give the sign
To parting friends . . . such death be mine![10]

Mary doubtless was appealing to the reader in her sister Harriett when she wrote to her in May 1824, "Perhaps you have not heard of Lord Byron's death. Papa told us of it late last night, a cold attended with inflammation carried him off in ten days; he was 37 years old." That she would be carried off herself in a mere night gave her own death a suddenness that her siblings could never forget. "I dare say strangers think us much at our ease and in good spirits," Jemima would say of the terrible aftermath, "but I always wish to say when I speak to any one who did not know her, 'Ah, you little think what she was to us all.'"[11]

Newman had always sensed that there was something special about Mary. After she had gone, he was convinced that what set her apart was her sanctity. "All that happened to her she could change into something bright and smiling like herself – all events, all persons (almost) she loved and delighted in – and thus, having lived in this world as if it were heaven, before she discovered (as she must in time) that it was not so, she has been translated into the real and substantial heaven of God. For myself indeed, I have for years been so affected with her unclouded cheerfulness and extreme guilelessness of heart that I have be[come] impressed with the conviction that she would not live long, and have almost anticipated her death."[12] An entry in his journal made after Mary's death corroborated this: "For some time I had a presentiment more or less strong that we should lose dear Mary. I was led to this by her extreme loveliness of character, and by the circumstance of my great affection for her. I thought I loved her too well, and hardly ever dared take full swing of enjoyment in her dear society. It must have been in October 1826 that, as I looked at her, beautiful as she was, I seemed to say to myself, not so much 'will you live?' as 'how strange that you are still alive!'"[13] As in

[10] LD, 1:168–9 JHN to Mary Newman (17 November 1823).
[11] *Family*, p. 24.
[12] LD, 2:50 JHN to Robert Isaac Wilberforce (14 November 1828).
[13] *AW*, p. 213.

the case of his mother's death, Newman's presentiments left him feeling at once guilty and admonished. He was always ready to read signs into the vicissitudes of those he loved and Mary's were of a radiant clarity. If the lesson of his father's life had been to renounce worldly success, the lesson of Mary's death was to see mortal attachments as intimations of immortal tidings to come. Despite the shock of her death, he still felt it was a shock for which he had been mercifully prepared. "Whether these anticipations ought to have been formed or not, certainly they have providentially prepared me for this most sudden event – which is thus rendered for me more tolerable, though still my sufferings. . . have been most acute."[14] The loss of Mary haunted Newman for the rest of his life. In 1882, when he was past 80, he confided in an old friend, "This is the anniversary of my dear Mary's death in 1828, an age ago, but she is as fresh in my memory and as dear to my heart as if it were yesterday, and often I cannot mention her name without tears coming into my eyes."[15] Yet in the poem that Newman wrote for his sister in April 1828—which is one of his best—there is not a touch of morbidity or mournfulness. For Newman, the "hurried road" on which Death took Mary to God's "eternal shore" is a bright road. In the very suddenness of her death, Newman saw at once cause for human consolation and an affirmation of divine approval, "Joy of sad hearts, and light of downcast eyes!"

> Death came and went:—that so thy image might
>   Our yearning hearts possess,
> Associate with all pleasant thoughts and bright,
>   With youth and loveliness;
>   Sorrow can claim,
> Mary, nor lot nor part in thy soft soothing name.
>
> Joy of sad hearts, and light of downcast eyes!
>   Dearest thou art enshrined
> In all thy fragrance in our memories;
>   For we must ever find
>   Bare thought of thee
> Freshen this weary life, while weary life shall be.[16]

The abiding depth of Newman's sense of loss recalls Henry James' response to the loss of Minny Temple, the young woman whom he told his mother was "the heroine of our common scene," who died of tuberculosis at 24 in 1870 when James was 26.[17] Minny would serve as the model for some of his greatest heroines, including Isabel Archer in *The Portrait of a Lady* (1882) and Milly Theale in *The Wings of the Dove* (1902). She "liked nothing in the world so much," James recalled in *Notes of a Son and Brother* (1914), "as to see others fairly exhibited; not as they might best please her . . . but as they might fully reveal themselves, their stuff and their truth . . ."[18] Indeed, he spoke of

[14] LD, 2:50 JHN to Robert Isaac Wilberforce (14 November 1828).
[15] LD, 30:48, JHN to M. R. Giberne (5 January 1882).
[16] VV, pp. 27–8.
[17] *Henry James: Letters* (Cambridge, 1974), I, p. 221.
[18] Henry James. *Notes of a Son and Brother* in Henry James. *Autobiography* (Princeton, 1983), p. 509.

her in terms that might almost have described Mary. In a letter to his mother, James recalled Minny as "a young and shining apparition," unaffected and unspoiled, "with a wonderful ethereal brightness of presence," whose zest for life endeared her to all who met her. "She certainly never seemed to have come into this world for her own happiness—as that of others—or as anything but as a sort of divine reminder and quickness—a transcendent protest against our acquiescence in its grossness."[19]

Yet, although they experienced loss with a similar intensity, Newman and James saw markedly different things in the death of youth. James would turn Minny into a gnawing might-have-been, which only confirmed his conviction that what mattered in life was not life itself—which could vanish in an instant—but what could be made of life. "I could shed tears of joy far more copious than any tears of sorrow," he boasted, "when I think of her feverish earthy lot exchanged for this serene promotion into pure fellowship with our memories, thoughts and fancies."[20] Living, James told his brother William, she was "the helpless victim and toy of her own intelligence."[21] Dead, she would be transformed into James's tragic muse. Yet the real tubercular woman went to her grave questioning nearly everything.

> Wasn't Christ the only man who ever lived and died entirely for his faith, without a shadow of selfishness? And isn't that reason enough why we should all turn to Him after having tried everything else and found it wanting? –turn to Him as the only pure and *unmixed* manifestation of God in humanity? And if I believe this, which I think I do, how utterly inconsistent and detestable is the life I lead, which, so far from being a loving and cheerful surrender of itself once for all to God's service, is at best a base compromise—a few moments or acts or thoughts consciously and with difficulty divested of actual selfishness. Must this always be so? Is it owing to the indissoluble mixture of the divine and the diabolical in us all, or is it because I am hopelessly frivolous and trifling? Or is it finally that I really *don't believe*, that I have still a doubt in my mind whether religion *is* the one exclusive thing to live for, as Christ taught us?[22]

As she lay dying a battle took place in the heart and mind of Minny Temple. In her last letters, regret for failing to enter into the reality of Christianity warred with a kind of Emersonian pantheism. "I am after all a good deal of a pagan," she wrote to William James, "certain noble acts of bygone stoics & philosophers call out a quick and sympathetic response in my heart. If I had lived before Christ, music would have come like a divine voice to tell me to be true to my whole nature—to stick by my keynote & have faith that my life would, in some way or other, if faithfully lived, swell the entire harmony. This is a greater music than the music of the spheres."[23] James found what he called Minny's "moral spontaneity" refreshing, though he never engaged her religious

[19] Ibid., p. 219.
[20] Lyndall Gordon. *A Private Life of Henry James* (New York, 1998), pp. 123–4.
[21] *Henry James: Letters* (Cambridge, 1974), I, p. 223.
[22] Henry James. *Notes of a Son and Brother*, in Henry James. *Autobiography* (Princeton, 1983), pp. 528–9.
[23] Gordon, p. 119.

doubts. Listening to his father natter on about Swendenborg when he was a boy had permanently put him off religion.[24] Nonetheless, he acknowledged that "Her life was a strenuous, almost passionate *question,* which *my* mind, at least, lacked the energy to offer the elements of an answer for."[25] The great thing for James was that Minny "did cling to consciousness; death, at the last, was dreadful to her; she would have given anything to live—and the image of this, which was to remain with me, appeared so of the essence of tragedy that I was in the far-off aftertime to seek to lay the ghost by wrapping it. . .in the beauty and dignity of art." For James, consciousness was a good in and of itself, perhaps the greatest good. "Art," he held, "*makes* life, makes interest, makes importance."[26] Indeed, he would proffer similar advice to Henry Adams, another friend who found himself down in the dumps. On the brink of the Great War, James wrote the disenchanted historian and friend of his youth, "*Of course* we are lone survivors, of course the past that was our lives is at the bottom of an abyss—if the abyss *has* any bottom; of course, too, there's no use talking unless one particularly *wants* to. But the purpose [of James' second volume of autobiography, *Notes of a Son and Brother*] was to show you that one can, strange to say, still want to—or at least can behave as if one did. Behold me therefore so behaving—and apparently capable of continuing to do so. I still find my consciousness interesting—under *cultivation* of the interest. Cultivate it *with* me, dear Henry. . ."[27]

Newman saw something altogether different in Mary's death. She would not become, as James resolved Minny Temple should become, "a steady unfaltering luminary in the mind. . . a sort of measure and standard of brightness and repose."[28] It might be true that Newman would think of his sister for the rest of his life. But he saw her as unveiling the world, not glorifying it.

> The country too is beautiful – the fresh leaves, the scents, the varied landscape. Yet I never felt so intensely the transitory nature of this world as when most delighted with these country scenes – and in riding out today I have been impressed, more powerfully than I had before an idea was possible, with the two lines – "Chanting with a solemn voice, mind us of our better choice." I could hardly believe the lines were not my own and Keble had not taken them from me. I wish it were possible for words to put down those indefinite vague and withal subtle feelings which quite pierce the soul and make it sick. Dear Mary seems embodied in every tree and hid behind every hill. What a veil and curtain this world of sense is! beautiful but still a veil. . .[29]

---

[24] Ironically enough, in her last illness, Minny came to see some merit in what she had heretofore found rambling in Henry James, Sr's views about Christianity. In one of her last letters, she wrote: "However it may turn out, whether it shall seem true or untrue to me finally, I am at least glad to be able to put myself intellectually into the place of the long line of Christians who have felt the need and the comfort of this belief. It throws a light on Uncle Henry's talk, which has seemed to me hitherto neither reasonable nor consoling . . . but ignoble and shirking . . . Now I say to myself: What if the good gentleman had all along really got hold of the higher truth, the purer spirituality?" See *Notes of a Son and Brother* in Henry James. *Autobiography* (Princeton, 1983), pp. 540–1.

[25] *Henry James: Letters* (Cambridge, 1974), I, p. 232.

[26] Leon Edel. *Henry James: The Master 1901–1916* (London, 1972), p. v.

[27] *Henry James: Letters* (Cambridge, 1974), V, pp. 705–6.

[28] Ibid., p. 227.

[29] LD, 2:69 JHN to Jemima Newman (10 May 1828).

In a letter to Edward Hawkins, whom he had helped elect Provost of Oriel, he was careful to remember the living woman. Hawkins had written to condole with Newman and Newman wrote back to thank him. "So sudden a loss of one so inexpressibly dear to us, is of course a bitter affliction – My sister had never known illness even of a day's duration – and she was carried off in 24 hours – we knew her extreme danger only four hours before she died: but of many troubles this is the most acute Providence has visited us with. Yet, thank God, from the very first we have one and all been enabled, not merely to acquiesce in His will, but even to thank Him for this His dispensation towards us." This may have been stretching the truth: it is unlikely that his atheist brother Charles saw Mary's death in these terms. Nevertheless, Charles certainly shared Newman's delight in their sister. Mary was a favourite of his, as he was of hers.[30] "All our recollections of my dear Sister are sweet and delightful," Newman told Hawkins. "After being our joy and delight in her lifetime, she consoled us by being able collectedly and calmly (on being told of her imminent danger) to review her life and faith, to confess the incompleteness and insufficiency of her obedience, and her full belief that in her Savior only could her sins be pardoned and her soul saved. – She said she could not help wishing to live, both to be with us, and in order that she might have time to grow more like her Savior and more meet for heaven – but that she felt that to depart and be with Him was far better. And she owned to us that she could not fully satisfy her mind as to the certainty of her salvation, and was in some fear – but her entire hope was in Christ. To understand fully the comfort all this gives us, a person must know (what few can know) the guilelessness and sweetness of her character, and the extreme conscientiousness which marked all she did. We do not grieve—as I write, I think we do not at all."[31] Once Hawkins became Provost, he objected to Newman exercising his tutorial duties along pastoral lines and later refused to send him students. Nevertheless, Newman's letter must have impressed on Hawkins more than his fraternal devotion: there was something steely about the faith of this otherwise shy young man.

To another correspondent, Newman spoke of Mary's death as a trial of divine love. "To us all her sudden death is of course a most bitter affliction – yet it is graciously softened by numberless merciful alleviations, and we one and all feel from our hearts. . . a strong conviction that it is most good and right and desirable – and we bless God for it – all our recollections connected with dear Mary are sweet – and our sorrow at her loss is borne down by the remembrance of what she was to us, our joy and delight, – and the hope of what she will be when we meet her before the throne of God. . ." Here, Newman, unlike James, was not promoting Mary to a place in his or any one else's thoughts: he was acknowledging that her being in heaven would encourage him and his family to reaffirm their faith. Of course, in the absence of their living sister their memories of Mary would be painful. "Yet I rejoice and will rejoice – . . . because whom God loveth He chastiseth, and because I feel I am especially honored by him and cared for, and that he is assuredly training me for usefulness here, and glory

---

[30] See Mary's letter to Jemima (24 May 1824) "The same day Charles took me into the long room at the Custom-House, thus showing me in the same day two objects I have so long wished to see." *Family,* p. 6.

[31] LD, 2:51 JHN to Edward Hawkins (18 January 1828).

hereafter. – More trials have I had and have, than most men and I can glory in them – nay almost boast of them as marks of the Lord Jesus. . . I see more trial in store, and the very death of this dear girl has accidentally disclosed to me (as I think) the elements of future tempests which may afflict me still more bitterly – God's will be done, only may *He give grace*."[32] The recipient of this heartfelt letter was Robert Isaac Wilberforce, the second son of William Wilberforce, who was also a fellow of Oriel with Newman and Hurrell Froude and a good friend of Henry Edward Manning. He eventually resigned his living as archdeacon of the East Riding and converted to Rome in 1854, though 3 years later he died suddenly of gastric fever weeks before being ordained a priest. After Wilberforce's death, Newman wrote how "The climate of Rome is very peculiar. It has been almost a medicine to Brownlow – to others it is in one way or another almost poison. I was never ill there – but I don't like the climate for all that. It would be a great thing for you to be near your friend. I doubt whether the living is cheap; and I know it is very bad. Robert Wilberforce was killed either by the climate or food, or both. A Milord Anglais will be served well – but seminarists, and persons who live quietly, are badly off."[33] The old *Dictionary of National Biography* gave Wilberforce a glowing send off, stressing how his "sudden death deprived the Roman church of a valuable recruit. He was utterly without ambition, but with a great power of identifying himself with any cause he took in hand. . . He was better trained in theological and other academic learning than either Newman or Manning; and. . . had he lived he would have become as prominent a figure in controversy. . . His own secession was a heavy blow to the church of England, and the attempt in his last book—on church authority—to destroy the position of those who uphold the royal supremacy on logical grounds remained for a long time unanswered." Throughout his long life, Newman was stalked by sudden death but the loss of Wilberforce was especially grievous.

Just over a month after Mary died, someone else close to him died suddenly: Walter Mayers, the Evangelical classical master at Ealing School who had been, as Newman said in his *Apologia*, "the human means of [the] beginning of divine faith in me. . ."[34] Mayers was only 38 when he handed in his dinner pail. Newman wrote his widow through the Vicar of Deddington, a man named Greaves.

> I am well aware, having but lately myself left the house of mourning, how vain all human consolation is at a season when dear friends are suddenly snatched from us – so that nothing I could suggest to Mrs Mayers or her sorrowing relations could in itself be of service to them. Still it will be relieving my own mind and indulging the grateful feelings with which I must ever think of one to whom I am so much indebted, if I am allowed to address this to Mrs Mayers through yourself. . .
>
> Assure Mrs Mayers that, though I have not been lately in the way of seeing her and my dear friend now taken from us, they have both been continually in my prayers. – Indeed to remember him affectionately before the throne of grace was but a poor return on my part for the great things which (under God's blessing) he had done for me. – Whatever religious feeling I have within me, to his kind

---

[32] LD, 2:50 JHN to Robert Isaac Wilberforce (14 January 1828).
[33] LD, 22:28 JHN to Henry Bedford (10 August 1865).
[34] *Apo*, p. 17.

instructions when I was at school I am especially indebted for it – and it may (I think) be safely said, that had it not been for my intimacy with him, I should not have possessed the comfort of that knowledge of God which (poor as it is) enabled me to go through the dangerous season of my Undergraduate residence here without wounding my conscience my any gross or scandalous sin – And when I think of the affection he always showed me, the anxious pains he took to be of service to me, the earnestness with which he seems to pray for me, and the readiness he ever manifested to assist me in any object I had in view, and again of his deep and spiritual views of religion, his great Christian love for all Christians, his humility, his singleness of mind and [purpose], and great generosity, I feel my heart quite [brea]k within me at the loss of him, and find words quite inadequate to express what I would say. But this is a gracious dispensation as concerns him, and his gain – and I will not be so selfish as to cherish grief; but will labour to look forward in hope, to meeting him again through grace in a happier state of being and before the visible presence of my God and Saviour; when we shall all meet others too from whom death, nay sudden death, has now separated us. For this world is but a shadow and a dream – we think we see things and we see them not – they do not exist, they die on all sides, things dearest and pleasantest and most beloved. But in heaven we shall all meet and it will be no dream.[35]

Eight years after the death of Mayers, Newman lost another formative influence on his religious life: Hurrell Froude, his best friend, "a high Tory of the Cavalier stamp," as Newman described him, who "delighted in the notion of an hierarchical system, of sacerdotal power, and of full ecclesiastical liberty" and scorned "the maxim 'the Bible and the Bible only as the religion of Protestants.'"[36] When it became clear that Hurrell had only days to live, Newman wrote his sister Jemima on his birthday, 21 February 1836: "Thanks too, and thank also my Mother and Harriet for their congratulations upon this day. They will be deserved, if God gives me the grace to fulfil the purposes for which He has led me on hitherto in a wonderful way. I think I am conscious to myself that, whatever are my faults, I wish to live and die to His glory – to surrender wholly to Him as His instrument to whatever work and at whatever personal sacrifice – though I cannot duly realize my own words when I say so. He is teaching me, it would seem, to depend on Him only – for, as perhaps Rogers told you, I am soon to lose dear Froude – which, looking forward to the next 25 years of my life, and its probable occupations, is the greatest loss I could have. I shall be truly widowed. . ."[37] When, on 17 May of the same year, his mother died, Newman wrote his sister Harriett: "Thank God, my spirits have not sunk, nor will they, I trust. I have been full of work, and that keeps me generally free from any dejection. If it ever comes, it is never of long continuance, and is even not unwelcome – I am speaking of dejection from solitude; I never feel so near heaven as then. Years ago, from 1822 to 1826, I used to be very much by myself; and in anxieties of various kinds, from money matters and other things, which were very harassing. I then on

[35] LD, 2:57–8 JHN to Richard Greaves (27 February 1828).
[36] *Apo.*, p. 34.
[37] LD, 5:240–1 JHN to Jemima Newman (21 February 1836).

the whole had no friend near me – no one to whom I opened my mind fully or who could sympathize with me. I am but returning at worst to that state. Indeed, ever since that time I have learned to throw myself on myself. Therefore, please God, I trust I shall get on very well, and after all this life is very short, and it is a better thing to be pursuing what seems God's call, than to be looking after one's own comfort. I am learning more than hitherto to live in the presence of the dead – this is a gain which strange faces cannot take away."[38]

Newman described what he had come to see as some of the lessons of bereavement in an extraordinary sermon entitled "Affliction, A School of Comfort" (1834), on which he would draw for the rest of his long life whenever he encountered others struggling with their own bereavement. He began with an eloquent commendation of the example of St Paul.

If there is one point of character more than another which belonged to St. Paul, and discovers itself in all he said and did, it was his power of sympathising with his brethren, nay, with all classes of men. He went through trials of every kind, and this was their issue, to let him into the feelings, and thereby to introduce him to the hearts, of high and low, Jew and Gentile. He knew how to persuade, for he knew where lay the perplexity; he knew how to console, for he knew the sorrow. . . "To the weak," he says, "became I as weak, that I might gain the weak. I am made all things to all men, that I might by all means save some." And so again, in another place, after having recounted his various trials by sea and land, in the bleak wilderness and the stifling prison, from friends and strangers, he adds, "Who is weak, and I am not weak? who is offended, and I burn not? If I must needs glory, I will glory of the things which concern mine infirmities." Hence, in the Acts of the Apostles, when he saw his brethren weeping, though they could not divert him from his purpose, which came from God, yet he could not keep from crying out, "What mean ye to weep, and to break my heart? for I am ready, not to be bound only, but also to die at Jerusalem, for the Name of the Lord Jesus." And even of his own countrymen who persecuted him, he speaks in the most tender and affectionate terms, as understanding well where they stood, and what their view of the Gospel was. "I have great heaviness and continual sorrow in my heart; for I could wish that myself were accursed from Christ for my brethren, my kinsmen according to the flesh." And again, "Brethren, my heart's desire and prayer to God for Israel is, that they might be saved. For I *bear them record* that they have a zeal of God, but not according to knowledge." And hence so powerful was he in speech with them, wherever they were not reprobate, that even King Agrippa, after hearing a few words of St. Paul's own history, exclaimed, "Almost thou persuadest me to be a Christian!" . . .And what he was in persuasion, such he was in consolation. He himself gives this reason for his trials. . ., speaking of Almighty God's comforting him in all his tribulation, in order that he might be able to comfort them which were in any trouble, by the comfort wherewith he himself was comforted of God.[39]

[38] LD, 5:312 JHN to Harriett Newman (21 June 1836).
[39] *PS*, v, pp. 300–2.

No one can read Newman's voluminous correspondence without seeing how much he emulated St Paul, especially in condoling with the sufferings of others, convinced as he was that "Man is born to trouble, 'as the sparks fly upward.' More or less, we all have our severe trials of pain and sorrow. If we go on for some years in the world's sunshine, it is only that troubles, when they come, should fall heavier. Such at least is the general rule. Sooner or later we fare as other men; happier than they only if we learn to bear our portion more religiously; and more favoured if we fall in with those who themselves have suffered, and can aid us with their sympathy and their experience. And then, while we profit from what they can give us, we may learn from them freely to give what we have freely received, comforting in turn others with the comfort which our brethren have given us from God." The many trials and tribulations that Newman would suffer bore this out, though he recognized that trials *per se* could not ensure sanctity, for "in speaking of the benefits of trial and suffering, we should of course never forget that these things by themselves have no power to make us holier or more heavenly. They make many men morose, selfish, and envious. The only sympathy they create in many minds, is the wish that others should suffer with them, not they with others." Indeed, Newman was tough-minded enough to recognize that "Affliction, when love is away, leads a man to wish others to be as he is; it leads to repining, malevolence, hatred, rejoicing in evil. . . .The devils are not incited by their own torments to any endeavour but that of making others devils also. Such is the effect of pain and sorrow, when unsanctified by God's saving grace."[40]

Then, again, Newman realized that even fasting and other mortifications did not necessarily conduce to holiness and genuine faith. After all, "A man may be most austere in his life, and, by that very austerity, learn to be cruel to others, not tender. And, on the other hand (what seems strange), he may be austere in his personal habits, and yet be a waverer and a coward in his conduct. Such things have been,—I do not say they are likely in this state of society,—but I mean, it should ever be borne in mind, that the severest and most mortified life is as little a passport to heaven, or a criterion of saintliness, as benevolence is, or usefulness, or amiableness. Self-discipline is a necessary condition, but not a sure sign of holiness. It may leave a man worldly, or it may make him a tyrant. It is only in the hands of God that it is God's instrument. It only ministers to God's purposes when God uses it. It is only when grace is in the heart, when power from above dwells in a man, that anything outward or inward turns to his salvation. . ."[41] Here, Newman exhibited something of the psychological insight that gives so many of his sermons their profound practical force.

Of course, Newman was ready to concede that "Sometimes we look with pleasure upon those who never have been afflicted. We look with a smile of interest upon the smooth brow and open countenance, and our hearts thrill within us at the ready laugh or the piercing glance. There is a buoyancy and freshness of mind in those who have never suffered. .." Still, Newman recognized that such innocence was "not the case of the many, whom earth soils, and who lose their right to be merry-hearted. In them lightness of spirits degenerates into rudeness, want of feeling, and wantonness. . . Pain and sorrow are the almost necessary medicines of the impetuosity of nature. Without

[40] Ibid., pp. 303–4.
[41] Ibid., pp. 304–5.

these, men, though men, are like spoilt children; they act as if they considered everything must give way to their own wishes and conveniences. . . . " Most of us can intimately verify the accuracy of these unsparing observations.

But then, Newman spoke of the mysterious uses of pain and trial in a way that describes how he himself acquired his own nearness to God.

> Such is worldly happiness and worldly trial; but Almighty God, while He chose the latter as the portion of His Saints, sanctified it by His heavenly grace, to be their great benefit. He rescues them from the selfishness of worldly comfort without surrendering them to the selfishness of worldly pain. He brings them into pain, that they may be like what Christ was, and may be led to think of Him, not of themselves. He brings them into trouble, that they may be near Him. When they mourn, they are more intimately in His presence than they are at any other time. Bodily pain, anxiety, bereavement, distress, are to them His forerunners. It is a solemn thing, while it is a privilege, to look upon those whom He thus visits. Why is it that men would look with fear and silence at the sight of the spirit of some friend departed, coming to them from the grave? Why would they abase themselves and listen awfully to any message he brought them? Because he would seem to come from the very presence of God. And in like manner, when a man, in whom dwells His grace, is lying on the bed of suffering, or when he has been stripped of his friends and is solitary, he has, in a peculiar way, tasted of the powers of the world to come. . . . He who has been long under the rod of God, becomes God's possession. He bears in his body marks, and is sprinkled with drops, which nature could not provide for him. . . . Surely this is a great blessing and cause of glorying, to be thus consecrated by affliction as a minister of God's mercies to the afflicted.[42]

Newman ends his sermon where he began by commending St Paul, who, as he says, "was consecrated by suffering to be an Apostle of Christ; by fastings, by chastisements, by self-denials for his brethren's sake, by his forlorn, solitary life. . ." Of course, he knew how repugnant such truths are to "men of the world, who are bent on gratifying themselves, and . . . think they have gained a point, and have just cause for congratulation, when they have found out a way of saving themselves trouble, and of adding to their luxuries and conveniences. But those who are set on their own ease, most certainly are bad comforters of others. . ." And for an example of this, Newman reminded his readers of how "the rich man, who fared sumptuously every day, let Lazarus lie at his gate, and left him to be 'comforted' after this life by Angels. As to comfort the poor and afflicted is the way to heaven, so to have affliction ourselves is the way to comfort them."[43]

At the same time, if Newman recognized that loss made us sympathetic to the loss of others, he also recognized that "affliction is sent for our own personal good also. Let us fear, lest, after we have ministered to others, we ourselves should be castaways; lest our gentleness, consideration, and patience, which are so soothing to them, yet

---

[42] Ibid., pp. 306–7.
[43] Ibid., pp. 310–11.

should be separated from that inward faith and strict conscientiousness which alone unites us to Christ;—lest, in spite of all the good we do to others, yet we should have some secret sin, some unresisted evil within us, which separates us from Him. Let us pray Him who sends us trial, to send us a pure heart and honesty of mind wherewith to bear it."[44]

Then, again, Newman's response to Mary's death can be contrasted with verses in Tennyson's great poem, *In Memoriam* (1850), where, he, too, after the death of his dear Cambridge friend Arthur Hallam, struggled to make sense not so much of the "presence of the dead," as their importunate absence, which, for the long-bereaving poet, was proof of their immortality.

> I cannot see the features right,
>   When on the gloom I strive to paint
>   The face I know; the hues are faint
> And mix with hollow masks of night;
>
> Cloud-towers by ghostly masons wrought,
>   A gulf that ever shuts and gapes,
>   A hand that points, and pallèd shapes
> In shadowy thoroughfares of thought;
>
> And crowds that stream from yawning doors,
>   And shoals of puckered faces drive;
>   Dark bulks that tumble half alive,
> And lazy lengths on boundless shores;
>
> Till all at once, beyond the will
>   I hear a wizard music roll,
>   And through a lattice in the soul
> Looks thy fair face and makes it still.[45]

When Tennyson himself was buried in Westminster Abbey beside the monument of Browning and Chaucer, his good friend Edward Burne-Jones was disappointed by the drab solemnity of the proceedings. For Burne-Jones, "there should have been street music, some soldiers and some trumpets, and bells muffled all over London, and rumbling drums. I did hate it so heartily, but as he sleeps by Chaucer I dare say they woke and had nice talks in the night."[46] Queen Victoria's response to Tennyson's meditation on death sheds a good deal of light on the age that she personified: "Next to the Bible, *In Memoriam* is my comfort," she wrote.[47] The Victorians may not have had much in the way of dogmatic faith but they followed their Queen in having an immense dedication to their dead. Carlyle exemplifies this, in his inimitable way, in

---

[44] Ibid., pp. 311–12.

[45] Alfred Lord Tennyson. "In Memoriam A.H.H." (London, 1850), p. LXX.

[46] Burne-Jones quoted in Fiona MacCarthy. *The Last Pre-Rapahaelite: Edward Burne Jones and the Victorian Imagination* (Harvard, 2012), p. 422.

[47] See Queen Victoria quoted in *Alfred Lord Tennyson: Selected Poems.* ed. Ruth Padel (Folio Society, 2006), p. xiv.

his *Reminiscences* (1881), which he wrote after the death of his acidulate wife Jane Welsh Carlyle (1801–66), who died after being knocked down by a horse-drawn London cab:

> Lonelier creature, there is not henceforth in this world; neither person, work or thing going on in it that is of any value, in comparison, or even at all. Death I feel almost daily in express fact, death is the one haven; and have occasionally a kind of kingship, sorrowful, but sublime, almost godlike, in the feeling that that is nigh. Sometimes the image of her, gone in her car of victory (in that beautiful death), and as if nodding to me with a smile, "I am gone, loved one; work a little longer, if thou still carest; if not, follow. There is no baseness, and no misery here. Courage, courage to the last!" that, sometimes, as in this moment is inexpressibly beautiful to me, and comes nearer to bringing me to tears than it once did.[48]

When Charles Dickens learned of Carlyle's loss, he wrote the heartbroken writer, "My dear friend my thoughts have been very much with you, for I truly love and honor you. To your great heart and mind, little can come out of mine but sympathy—That has been with you from the first, and ever will be while I live. Your truly affectionate friend. . ."[49]

That Newman and Tennyson (1809–92) never managed to meet is unfortunate because, for all of their differences, they had vital things in common. Besides being deeply affected by the loss of loved ones, they both had an extraordinary ear for the music of language, they lived outside the world, without ever turning their backs on its distress, and they abominated radicals. In 1888, the Earl of Carnarvon jotted down in his diary, apropos Tennyson: "He hates the modern Radicals, he has lost any admiration he may have had for Gladstone, and if he expresses an occasional belief in human or social progress, it's a very frigid and dubious profession. . ."[50] Newman similarly complained to their mutual friend Lady Simeon of how Gladstone had publicly vowed "to give the few remaining years of his life to preparing for eternity, but in no long time we find him setting out on his Scottish (Midlothian) expedition, and ever since he has been in the hands of the enemies of all religion. Alas, Alas . . ."[51] (Tennyson's son Hallam would leave behind an incomparable description of Gladstone, recalling how, "He has a face like a lion's; his head is small above it, though the forehead is broad and massive, something like Trajan's . . . Character, more than intellect strikes me in his physiognomy, and there is a remarkable duplicity of expression—iron, vice-like resolution combined with a subtle, mobile ingeniousness.")[52]

---

[48] From *Reminiscences* (1881) in *The Selected Writing s of Thomas Carlyle*. ed. Alan Shelston (Penguin, 1971), pp. 349–50.

[49] Dickens to Carlyle (30 May 1866) in *The Selected Letters of Charles Dickens*. ed. Jenny Hartley (Oxford, 2012), p. 403.

[50] See diary entry from Earl of Carnarvon (18 July 1888) in *Letters of Alfred Lord Tennyson*, III, p. 370 Carnarvon's son, the 5th Earl (1866–1923) sponsored the excavations of royal tombs at Thebes, which led to the discovery of Tut'ankhamun's tomb in the Valley of Kings in 1922.

[51] LD, 28:199 JHN to Lord Blachford (25 May 1877).

[52] See "Tennyson and Gladstone in Conversation, 8 December 1865," in *Alfred Tennyson: The Major Works* (Penguin, 2009), pp. 512–13.

Then, again, both Newman and Tennyson were deeply concerned about the rise of unbelief. Newman might be convinced that "utter unbelief has no root in the human heart," but he had to acknowledge that every year that passed saw a worsening of what he called the "epidemic" of unbelief. To his dear friend Emily Bowles, who left her comfortable London life to take up the unenviable position of Dame for his Oratory School, he confided, "We begin by asking 'How can we be sure that it is not so?' and this thought hides from the mind the real rational grounds, on which our faith is founded. Then our faith goes—and how in the world is it ever to be regained, except by a wonderful grant of God's grace. May God keep us all from this terrible deceit of the latter days. What is coming upon us! I look with keen compassion on the next generation and with, I may say, awe."[53] Tennyson, on the same subject, was a good deal blunter, telling Mary Gladstone when they were looking at old Chinese pictures together: "We shall all turn into pigs if we lose Christianity and God."[54] Indeed, whatever doubts the poet might have had with regard to the ancient faith, he knew that atheism was unacceptable. "I would rather know I was damned eternally," he avowed, "than not to know that I was to live eternally."[55] Then, too, Newman and Tennyson had beautiful voices. One auditor who was present when Newman delivered his sermon, "The Infidelity of the Future" (1873) left a vivid description of his delivery of it, recalling how Newman "had neither notes nor manuscript, but held a small Bible in his hand, where he sought out in a curiously eager fashion the texts which he was about to recite. His voice sounded low and clear, with exquisite modulations, as if he were thinking aloud."[56] Tennyson's voice also made a strong impression. Gladstone's daughter heard the great poet recite *Maud* one night in 1879, when he was 70, and confided to her diary afterwards how, "It was wondrous the fire and fervour and despair he put it into it. More like a passionate youth than a worn-out old man. We listened transfixed and I thought, apart from the strange, wild story, how astonishing the poetry was, even the 'Go not, happy day' seemed an inspired, rushing, ½ mad burst of exultation, and the lovely little tender similes and caressing words which he read in a sort of low, loving voice, gathered quite new meaning from his manner."[57] But what gave the two men their greatest common ground was their profound belief in the immortality of the soul, about which Newman wrote in one of his Anglican sermons, "Every one of us is able fluently to speak of this doctrine, and is aware that the knowledge of it forms the fundamental difference between our state and that of the heathen. And yet in spite of our being able to speak about it. . . there seems scarcely room to doubt that the greater number of Christians in no true sense realize it in their own minds at all. Indeed, it is a very difficult thing to bring home to us, and to feel, that we have souls; and there cannot be a more fatal mistake than to suppose we see what the doctrine means, as soon as we can use the words which

---

[53] LD, 29:169 JHN to Lady Herbert of Lea (19 August 1879) and LD, 30:102 JHN to Emily Bowles (5 June 1882).
[54] Diary entry of Mary Gladstone (4 June 1879) in *The Letters of Alfred Lord Tennyson*, III, p. 174.
[55] Tennyson quoted in Robert Bernard Martin. *Tennyson: The Unquiet Heart* (Oxford, 1980), p. 262.
[56] LD, 26:373, Note 1.
[57] See Mary Gladstone diary entry (22 March 1879) in *The Letters of Alfred Lord Tennyson*. ed. Lang and Shannon (Oxford, 1990), III, p. 170.

signify it."[58] Since a good deal of Tennyson's poetry is dedicated to arriving at a fuller understanding of this doctrine, it was only fitting that he should thank Newman for considering visiting him in a letter that speaks of the grave as though it were little more than a doorway.

> Aldworth, Haslemere, Surrey. Aug 20th 82
>
> My dear Cardinal Newman
>
> I and my wife and my son would have welcomed you to this house with more pleasure than I can well put into words. You and I are both of us old men, and I am the younger, and if you cannot come to me, I feel that some day or other I ought to go to you, for though, I dare say, there are a hundred things on which we might differ, there is no man on this side of the grave, more worthy of honour and affection than yourself; and therefore though I have never shaken you by the hand, let me subscribe myself
>
> Affectly Yours A Tennyson[59]

If Tennyson "heard, by secret transport led/Even in the charnels of the dead/The murmur of the fountain-head. . .," Newman recounted what the dead had taught him about love and faith in one of his best sermons, "The Invisible World," which he preached at St Mary's on 18 June 1837.[60] The sermon took as its text 2 Corinthians 4, in which St Paul encourages the faithful to take heart from the true import of their mortality. "We are afflicted in every way, but not constrained; perplexed, but not driven to despair;" St Paul wrote, "persecuted, but not abandoned; struck down, but not destroyed; always, carrying about

> in the body the dying of Jesus, so that the life of Jesus may also be manifested in our body. For we who live are constantly being given up to death for the sake of Jesus, so that the life of Jesus may be manifested in our mortal flesh. So death is at work in us, but life in you . . . Therefore, we are not discouraged; rather, although our outer self is wasting away, our inner self is being renewed day by day. For this momentary light affliction is producing for us an eternal weight of glory beyond all comparison, as we look not to what is seen but to what is unseen; for what is seen is transitory, but what is unseen is eternal.[61]

Newman opened his sermon by stressing the differences between the seen and the unseen. "There are two worlds," he told his listeners, "'the visible and the invisible,' as the Creed speaks, – the world we see, and the world we do not see; and the world which we do not see as really exists as the world we do see. . ." In making this distinction, Newman made no concessions to nominalism. The world we see, he insisted, is no illusion, no dream, no figment of our imagination. "We have but to lift up our eyes and look around, and we have proof of it: our eyes tell us. We see the sun, moon, stars, earth and sky, hills and valleys, woods and plains, seas and rivers. And again we see

---

[58] *PS*, I, 2. "The Immortality of the Soul," (1833).
[59] *The Letters of Alfred Lord Tennyson*, III. p. 225.
[60] See Tennyson's poem, "The Two Voices" and *PS*, iv, p. 13.
[61] 2 Corinthians 4: See *The Catholic Study Bible* ed. Senior and Collins (New York, 1990), pp. 1546–7.

men and the works of men." But if this world is real, there is another that is real as well, "quite as far-spreading, quite as close to us, and more wonderful than the world we see. . . All around us are numberless objects, coming and going, watching, working or waiting, which we see not: this is that other world, which the eyes reach not unto, but faith only."[62] When he spoke of these inhabitants of the immaterial world, he made oblique reference to all whom he had lost—his father, his mother, Mayers, Froude, and his beloved Mary.

> And in that other world are the souls also of the dead. They too, when they depart hence, do not cease to exist, but they retire from this visible scene of things; or, in other words, they cease to act towards us and before us *through our senses.* They live as they lived before; but that outward frame, through which they were able to hold communion with other men, is in some way, we know not how, separated from them, and dries away and shrivels up as leaves may drop off a tree. They remain, but without the usual means of approach towards us, and correspondence with us.[63]

And this brings with it the practical obligation to recognize the reality of the unseen, the eternal, the "heavenly places in Christ Jesus."

> The world of spirits, then, though unseen, is present; present, not future, not distant. It is not above the sky, it is not beyond the grave; it now and here; the kingdom of God is among us. "We look," says St. Paul, "not at the things which are seen, but the things which are not seen; for the things which are seen are temporal, but the things which are not seen are eternal." You see he regarded it as a practical truth, which was to influence our conduct. Not only does he speak of the world invisible, but of the duty of "looking at" it; not only does he contrast the things of time with it, but says that their belonging to time is a reason, not for looking at, but looking off them. . . In like manner, he says in another Epistle, "Our conversation is in heaven." And again, "God hath raised us up together, and made us sit together in heavenly places in Christ Jesus."[64]

For the English, poised to become Victorians, the very notion of heavenly places would become more and more disputed as the century progressed. In retrospect, there was something apt about Victoria inaugurating her long reign in 1837 with the administration of William Lamb, Lord Melbourne (1779–1848), an easy-going, jaded, irreverent Whig, who once famously complained that "Things have come to a pretty pass when religion is allowed to invade the sphere of private life."[65] Lytton Strachey painted a vivid picture of the old roué instructing the dutiful Victoria. "The man of the world who had been the friend of Byron and the Regent, the talker whose paradoxes had held Holland House enthralled, the cynic whose ribaldries had enlivened so many deep potations, the lover whose soft words had captivated such beauty and such passion

---

[62] *PS*, iv, pp. 200–1.
[63] Ibid., p. 203.
[64] Ibid., pp. 207–8.
[65] G. W. E. Russell. *Collections and Recollections* (London, 1898), p. 58

and such wit, might now be seen, evening after evening, talking with infinite politeness to a schoolgirl, bolt upright, amid the silence and the rigidity of Court etiquette."[66] When young and callow, Victoria hung on every word of her raffish Pygmalion but by the time Melbourne died in 1848, she saw him in more impartial terms. "Our poor old friend Melbourne died on the 24th," she wrote in her diary. "I sincerely regret him, for he was truly attached to me, and though not a firm Minister he was a noble, kind-hearted, generous being."[67] Melbourne was a throwback to the Regency and never comfortable with the middle-class proprieties that came to characterize Victoria's reign, but, after his death, his resolute indifference to religion became the norm. In this, he was less a remnant than a harbinger. Newman foresaw how his contemporaries would replace faith in God with faith in themselves, how they would make idols of themselves. "Men think this earth their property, and its movements in their power; whereas it has other lords besides them, and is the scene of a higher conflict than they are capable of conceiving. It contains Christ's little ones whom they despise, and his Angels whom they disbelieve; and these at length shall take possession of it and be manifested."[68]

Mortality and the pathetic pride of life put Newman in mind of change. He had a deep appreciation for change, especially the instructive part it plays in the working out of life, of history, of doctrine, of grace—an appreciation bred not only of his sense of loss and loneliness, but his trust in the transforming Providence of God's love.

> At present, "all things," to appearance, "continue as they were from the beginning of the creation;" and scoffers ask, "Where is the promise of his coming?" but at the appointed time there will be a "manifestation of the sons of God," and the hidden saints "shall shine out as the sun in the kingdom of their Father."[69]

With Mary's death in mind, Newman saw *suddenness* as the most characteristic emblem of change.

> When the Angels appeared to the shepherds it was a sudden appearance,— "*Suddenly* there was with the Angels a multitude of the heavenly host." How wonderful a sight! The night had before that seemed just like any other night; as the evening on which Jacob saw the vision seemed like any other evening. They were keeping watch over their sheep; they were watching the night as it passed. The stars moved on,—it was midnight. They had no idea of such a thing when the Angel appeared. Such are the power and virtue hidden in things which are seen, and at God's will they are manifested. They were manifested for a moment to Jacob, for a moment to Elisha's servant, for a moment to the shepherds. They will be manifested for ever when Christ comes at the Last Day "in the glory of His Father with the holy Angels." Then this world will fade away and the other world will shine forth.[70]

[66] Lytton Strachey. *Queen Victoria* (London, 1921), p. 90.
[67] Diary entry for 27 November 1848 from *Queen Victoria in Her Letters and Journals* (London, 1984), p. 79.
[68] *PS*, iv, p. 208.
[69] Ibid.
[70] Ibid., p. 209.

More than a sermon, "The Invisible World" was Newman's prayer for renewed faith, for renewed hope, for that "Eternal Spring," as he called it, "for which all Christians are waiting."

Once only in the year, yet once, does the world which we see show forth its hidden powers, and in a manner manifest itself. Then the leaves come out, and the blossoms on the fruit trees, and flowers; and the grass and corn spring up. There is a sudden rush and burst outwardly of that hidden life which God has lodged in the material world. Well, that shows you, as by a sample, what it can do at God's command, when He gives the word. This earth, which now buds forth in leaves and blossoms, will one day burst forth into a new world of light and glory, in which, we shall see Saints and Angels dwelling. Who would think, except from his experience of former springs all through his life, who could conceive two or three months before, that it was possible that the face of nature, which then seemed so lifeless, should become so splendid and varied? How different is a tree, how different is a prospect, when leaves are on it and off it! How unlikely it would seem, before the event, that the dry and naked branches should suddenly be clothed with what is so bright and so refreshing! Yet in God's good time leaves come on the trees. The season may delay, but come it will at last. So it is with the coming of that Eternal Spring, for which all Christians are waiting. Come it will, though it delay; yet though it tarry, let us wait for it, "because it will surely come, it will not tarry." Therefore we say day by day, "Thy kingdom come;" which means,—O Lord, show Thyself; manifest Thyself; Thou that sittest between the cherubim, show Thyself; stir up Thy strength and come and help us. The earth that we see does not satisfy us; it is but a beginning; it is but a promise of something beyond it; even when it is gayest, with all its blossoms on, and shows most touchingly what lies hid in it, yet it is not enough. We know much more lies hid in it than we see. A world of Saints and Angels, a glorious world, the palace of God, the mountain of the Lord of Hosts, the heavenly Jerusalem, the throne of God and Christ, all these wonders, everlasting, all-precious, mysterious, and incomprehensible, lie hid in what we see. What we see is the outward shell of an eternal kingdom; and on that kingdom we fix the eyes of our faith. Shine forth, O Lord, as when on Thy nativity Thine Angels visited the shepherds; let Thy glory blossom forth as bloom and foliage on the trees; change with Thy mighty power this visible world into that diviner world, which as yet we see not; destroy what we see, that it may pass and be transformed into what we believe. Bright as is the sun, and the sky, and the clouds; green as are the leaves and the fields; sweet as is the singing of the birds; we know that they are not all, and we will not take up with a part for the whole. They proceed from a centre of love and goodness, which is God Himself; but they are not His fulness; they speak of heaven, but they are not heaven; they are but as stray beams and dim reflections of His Image; they are but crumbs from the table. We are looking for the coming of the day of God, when all this outward world, fair though it be, shall perish; when the heavens shall be burnt, and the earth melt away. We can bear the loss, for we know it will be but the removing of a veil. We know that to remove the world which is seen, will be the manifestation of the world which is not seen. We know that what we see is as a screen hiding from us God and Christ, and His Saints and Angels. And we earnestly desire and pray for the dissolution of all that we see, from our longing after that which we do not see.[71]

Throughout his life, Newman was an inveterate keeper of anniversaries, commemorating not only the pivotal events in his own life but the birthdays and deaths of family, friends, and beloved saints. When Jemima's first child was born, Newman was asked to be the godfather and replied to John Mozley: "With the greatest pleasure will I stand sponsor – I wish I knew the day and hour. It is very pleasant to have Harriet and James as fellows. As to the name, since the remonstrance of Elizabeth's friends 'there is none of thy kindred that is called by that name,' I suppose all similar questions are silenced. As Jemima has a memory for days, let her know that the 2nd of May (which Arthur said was the day) is the feast of St Athanasius. I therefore propose he should be called Athanasius Mozley – Also tell her the 2nd of May was the day (I believe) I went to school – And the day on which I was knocked up 5 years ago at Leonforte in Sicily, where I remained three days helpless."[72] To Edward Pusey on 22 August 1867, he wrote: "My dear Pusey, I always remember your birthday, tho' I don't commonly write to you upon it; and this morning I have been saying Mass with the prayer that God will teach you and all yours His Blessed Will in all things. I think it is also Lockhart's birthday, and I fancy it is Sidney Herbert's death-day – and it was the day on which in 1845 I saw my way clear to put a miraculous medal round my neck."[73] Newman also made various interpolations into the copies of letters he kept of his vast correspondence, calling attention to the significance of dates. On 12 April 1836, his mother wrote him: "I dare say you remember that your dear Father used always to give this day the epithet of 'glorious.' I do not forget that it is the 14th Anniversary of a day and event that gave us great cause of gratitude. . ." This was the day in 1822 when Newman was nominated Fellow of Oriel; and beneath the letter, he wrote: "On the following April 28. 1836 my sister Jemima was married to John Mozley. On the following May 17, 1836 my Mother died."[74] As the years passed, his birthday, 21 February became an ever more insistent *memento mori*. "Birthdays as they come," he wrote to Maria Giberne in 1867, "are awful things now, as minute guns by night." But he also saw them as proof that time would be transcended. For myself, he wrote on the eve of his 60th birthday, "I remember my fourth birthday, my fifth, my sixth, my tenth, my eighteenth, as days shining out from the long lapse of time to which they belong – and, I suppose, it is some unconscious manifestation of the keen feeling which my birthday raises in me. . ."[75] For Newman, the evanescence of time was an intimation of timelessness; mortality of eternity. "What a wonderful thing time is," he wrote to Miss Giberne on 17 May 1867, "and life is every year more wonderful. The past is ever present—and life is at once nothing at all, and all in all."[76] In another letter, written in 1874, at the height of the controversy with Gladstone over the Vatican Decrees, Newman wrote: "What a long time is 29 years!

[71] Ibid., pp. 209–11.
[72] LD, 6:240 JHN to John Mozley (7 May 1838).
[73] LD, 23:318 JHN to E. B. Pusey (22 August 1867).
[74] LD, 5:276 Mrs Jemima Newman to JHN (12 April 1836).
[75] LD, 19:467 JHN to Isy Froude (20 February 1861).
[76] LD, 23:230 JHN to Maria Giberne (17 May 1867).

there is a new world since then, and this generation knows nothing of what happened in 1845 ... I see deaths in the newspapers almost weekly of members of that past age, my contemporaries—they are like minute bells tolling for the outgoing generation. A very few years, and the end must come."[77] To Henry Wilberforce, when he was 70, he wrote: "I wonder what day I shall die on – One passes year by year over one's death day, as one might pass over one's grave."[78] In his senescence, birthdays prefigured judgement. To Mary Holmes, he wrote: "A birthday is a very sad day at my age [he was 74] – or rather I should say a solemn day. When I call it sad, it is when it brings before me the number of friends who have gone before me – though this is a most ungrateful sadness, since I have so many affectionate and anxious friends left, who are so good to me. I think what makes me low, is the awful thought that where my departed friends are, there I must be – and that they can and do rejoice in their trial and their judgment being over, whereas I am still on trial and have judgment to come. The idea of a judgment is the first principle of religion, as being involved in the sentiment of conscience – and, as life goes on, it becomes very overpowering. Nor do the good tidings of Christianity reverse it, unless we go into the extreme of Calvinism or Methodism with the doctrine of personal assurance. Otherwise, the more one has received, the more one has to answer for. We can but throw ourselves on the mercy of God, of which one's whole life is a long experience."[79] Preoccupied as he was with time and memory, Newman saw an incomparable anniversary awaiting the faithful in heaven, and it was with a sense of festive expectancy that he ended his sermon.

> Who can imagine by a stretch of fancy the feelings of those who having died in faith, wake up to enjoyment! The life then begun, we know, will last for ever; yet surely if memory be to us then what it is now, that will be a day much to be observed unto the Lord through all the ages of eternity. We may increase indeed for ever in knowledge and in love, still that first waking from the dead, the day at once of our birth and our espousals, will ever be endeared and hallowed in our thoughts. When we find ourselves after long rest gifted with fresh powers, vigorous with the seed of eternal life within us, able to love God as we wish, conscious that all trouble, sorrow, pain, anxiety, bereavement, is over for ever, blessed in the full affection of those earthly friends whom we loved so poorly, and could protect so feebly, while they were with us in the flesh, and above all, visited by the immediate visible ineffable Presence of God Almighty, with His Only-begotten Son our Lord Jesus Christ, and his Co-equal Co-eternal Spirit, that great sight in which is the fullness of joy and pleasure for evermore,—what deep, incommunicable, unimaginable thoughts will be then upon us! what depths will be stirred up within us! what secret harmonies awakened, of which human nature seemed incapable! Earthly words are indeed all worthless to minister to such high anticipations.[80]

On 23 November 1828, ten months after the death of Mary, Newman wrote to his sister, Harriett: "My ride of a morning is generally solitary; but I almost prefer being alone.

---

[77] LD, 27:136 JHN to Maria Giberne (11 October 1874).
[78] LD, 25:294 JHN to Henry Wilberforce (26 February 1871).
[79] LD, 27:227 JHN to Mary Holmes (21 February 1875).
[80] PS, iv, pp. 212–13.

When the spirits are good, every thing is delightful in the view of still nature, which the country gives. I have learned to like dying trees and black meadows—swamps have their grace, and fogs their sweetness. A solemn voice seems to chant from every thing. I know whose voice it is—it is her dear voice. Her form is almost nightly before me, when I have put out the light and lain down. Is not this a blessing? All I lament is, that I do not think she ever knew how much I loved her."[81]

---

[81] LD, 2:108 JHN to Harriett Newman (23 November 1828).

6

Harriet Newman and English Anti-Romanism

In 1850, when Pope Pius IX reconstituted the Roman Catholic hierarchy in England and indignant Anglican churchmen responded with petitions decrying resurgent popery, Newman wrote the mother of a former student and dear friend: "I don't agree with you at being troubled at the present row. It is always well to know things as they are. The row has not unsettled a single Catholic or Catholicizing Anglican – rather it has converted and is converting many. It has but brought out what all sober people knew, though one is apt to forget it – that the English people is not Catholicly-minded. Many foreigners, many old Catholics, have thought they were – I dislike our smoothing over the nation's aversion to our doctrines, just as I dislike smoothing over those doctrines themselves. The real misery is the trouble it has introduced into families, the private persecutions, the alienation of friends, and the bitterness of feeling which the commotion has caused . . ."[1] No one drove home these truths more to Newman than his sister Harriett, whose anti-Romanism never allowed him to forget the force of what he called "that narrow, ungenerous spirit which energizes and operates so widely and so unweariedly in the Protestant community . . ."[2] Just as the reconstitution of the hierarchy impelled the English as a whole to revert to their customary anti-Catholicism, Newman's conversion caused his family to follow suit and recoil from a faith that they regarded as corrupt, irrational, blasphemous and un-English. To appreciate how Harriett's anti-Roman prejudices—even more than those of her siblings—helped Newman to appreciate the extent of his countrymen's prejudices, it is necessary to return to the family's history.

After his mother's death in May 1836, Newman wrote a characteristically candid letter to his sister Jemima reaffirming the deep love he felt for his mother. "I know in my own heart how much I ever loved her, and I know too how much she loved me—and often, when I had no means of showing it, I was quite overpowered from the feeling of her kindness. Mr. Wilberforce used to say that in heaven there will be no misunderstandings . . ."[3] Before misunderstandings set in, there was much amity within the Newman family. When he read over his correspondence during the writing of his *Apologia*, it is no wonder that Newman wept: it documented the life of a family that in its early days had been extraordinarily close-knit. And with no members of his

---

[1] LD, 14:161 JHN to Mrs Wood (7 December 1850).
[2] *Prespos.*, p. 236.
[3] LD, 5:313 JHN to Mrs John Mozley (26 June 1836).

family was he closer than with his mother and sisters. In a letter to his mother, written when he was 21, he gave heartfelt expression to this special bond.

> I am indeed encompassed with blessings for which I never can be properly thankful, but the greatest of them is so dear and united a home. If your fear is, lest my jesting letters to Harriett should unconsciously be written half in earnest, I can only protest, that however other places may agree with me, I am not in my own proper element when I am away from you and my sisters. Land animals may plunge into the water and swim about in it, but they cannot live in it; and, even for the short space they were in it, they must still drink in the air.[4]

It is a mark of the strength of the family that when troubles came, and came in force, the family's unity held. But what that unity could not survive were immitigable differences of faith, and when these emerged, the individual family members could only go their separate ways.

These differences hobbled Newman's relations with his brothers. So much of the fraternal correspondence was given over to unavailing debate. Newman admitted as much when he confessed to Charles, "I am indisposed again to expend time in stating to you arguments in behalf of religion, when I have already had experience of your being silenced without being satisfied . . ." To prove his point, he quoted from letters he wrote at the start of their epistolary debate and then 5 years afterwards. "In my letter of March 1825 on opening the controversy, I say, 'The most powerful arguments for Christianity do not convince only silence . . . . I do not expect so much to show Christianity true as to prove it rational.' I add, 'when I consider too the present flurried state of your mind to which I alluded in my last letter, I am still more bound to state these preliminary cautions.' In May 1830 I say, 'I have already had experience of your being silenced without being satisfied.' That is, I expected it, and I have experienced it. Whatever the cause of it be, the fact is a sufficient reason to myself for declining a renewal of the correspondence . . . However, in stating it to be such, I mean nothing contemptuous or offensive . . ." After all, he had been reluctant to enter into the debate in the first place. "I felt it would be a waste of time, health, and spirits. Never however did I show reluctance when it had once begun . . ."[5] Still, the upshot was always the same: Charles, like so many rationalists, refused to concede that faith could be rational. And he put his arguments, such as they were, with such stupefying prolixity. In 1829, Newman complained to Jemima: "Charles, poor fellow, has inflicted on me tractates and letters without end."[6] This sense of futility, which dogged Newman's correspondence with Charles, would also come to characterize his exchanges with Frank. Neither Charles nor Frank was prepared to reconsider his rejection of dogmatic Christianity; and since Newman could hardly enter into their peculiar enthusiasms— Owenism, vegetarianism, teetotalism, eugenics—their common ground was sparse. As a result, Newman was rarely entirely himself in his letters to his brothers, though it was a mark of his good faith that he did take the time to share with them fascinating

---

[4] LD, 1:151 JHN to Mrs Jemima Newman (5 November 1822).
[5] LD, 2:266–7 JHN to Charles Robert Newman (19 August 1830).
[6] LD, 2:142 JHN to Jemima Newman (7 May 1829).

dress rehearsals for such later finished productions as his *Essay on the Development of Doctrine* and his *Grammar of Assent*.

In his letters to Jemima and his other sisters—Harriett, the oldest, and Mary, the youngest—a different Newman emerges: exuberant, playful, chatty, charming, and brimming over with plans and projects. "I have brought home for my amusement the original Greek of Aeschylus," he tells Jemima in one letter, "and have begun learning his Choruses by heart; I have some thoughts of setting one or two of them to Music; then I have to compose a concerto; then to finish the treatise on Astronomy . . . then to peruse a treatise on Hydrostatics . . . then Optics; Euripides; Plato; Aristophanes; Hume; Cicero; Hebrew; Anatomy; Chemistry; Geology: Persian and Arabic; Law; I could mention many other things . . ."[7] And so that Jemima and his sisters should have no doubt as to where these labours of learning were to be undertaken, he describes his college rooms at Trinity with comic sumptuousness. "On reaching the outer door by the ascent of an elegant flight of stairs the stranger discovers an handsome mat to rub the shoes on, he knocks at the door which is opened by a gentleman of very prepossessing appearance immediately.—Who shall describe his amazement! – The room is lofty, and lighted by two windows, from which are seen the gardens of the college and the turrets of Wadham. Scarlet Morine curtains shed a rich glow over the apartment – Between the windows, half shadowed amid the rich red drapery hanging from the cornices, is seen the celebrated Venus of Canova, her hair tied and trussed in the Grecian fashion and her look averted from the entrance. – On turning to the right a massy chimney-piece of marble discovers itself surmounted by a handsome pair of bronze figures (holding nozzles brilliant with cut glass) and by the soft splendour of a vitreous reflection framed in bronze and gold. Above smiles forth the goddess of youth feeding the eagle of her father Jupiter with the viands of immortality . . ."[8]

After winning his Oriel fellowship, Newman wrote his brother Charles of his new colleagues, "I think myself honoured inexpressibly by being among such kind, liberal, candid, moderate, learned and pious men, as every act shows the fellows of Oriel as a body to be."[9] However, a few months later, Newman writes Harriett a letter after one of his pupils paid him £90 that shows that Oriel fellows could also be exultant: "Liber sum—my pupil having gone and I have been humming, whistling, and laughing out loud to myself all day. I can hardly keep from jumping about." And knowing that Harriett would share the letter with her middle sister, Newman was careful to add: "Jemima is an ingenious girl, and has invented a very correct illustration of every asymptotic curve."[10]

As this shows, with his sisters we see a more unbuttoned Newman. To neither of his brothers did Newman ever describe the authors he enjoyed with anything like this *brio*. "My attention is at present directed to Aeschylus, the great inventor of the Grecian drama," he writes to Jemima when he was nineteen. "Never have I read an author with whom I have been so much struck; I am lost in astonishment, I am stupefied, I am out

[7]   LD, 1:97 JHN to Jemima Newman (11 December 1820).
[8]   LD, 1:70 JHN to Jemima Newman (10 December 1819).
[9]   LD, 1:131 JHN to Charles Newman (13 April 1822).
[10] LD, 1:154 JHN to Harriett Newman (4 October 1822).

of breath . . . He is very fine, and in my judgement the dry, stiff, formal, affected, cold, prolix, dignified Sophocles must hide his diminished head . . ."[11] Later, when Newman became a fellow at Oriel College, he continued to share his literary discoveries with his sisters. "I commend to your notice," he tells Jemima, "if it comes in your way, Carlyle on the French Revolution—a queer, tiresome, obscure, profound, and original work. The writer has not very clear principles and views, I fear, but they are very deep."[12] Although not formally educated, Newman's sisters were well read. As Joyce Suggs points out, like Elizabeth Bennett and her sisters in *Pride and Prejudice*, "They read assiduously. All knew French. Harriett read Italian, working at Tasso and Manzoni's *I Promessi Sposi*, while Jemima knew some Latin and had a taste for mathematics."[13] One can also glean a good sense of the soundness of their early instruction from their mother from one of Harriett's tales, in which she observes of her heroine how "the steady uninterrupted routine of daily lessons, which her mamma pursued with her, had already accustomed her mind to do with ease, what many older cannot do with difficulty;—to concentrate her small powers upon the subject she had in hand, and not to be diverted from her task by outward objects. Mrs. Leslie had not studied the subject of education, like some mothers, and did not feel capable of forming any original plans. She only had a strong idea of the value of regular daily lessons; she had no plans about it; she did not talk about it; but she practised it. *Nothing*, we may say, interfered with the morning business. A mother differently circumstanced, could not herself have undertaken the office of instructress, with such unrelenting regularity."[14] It was similarly diligent instruction that enabled Newman's sisters to enter into his literary discoveries with such discerning zest.

Then, again, in a wonderful letter to his mother, describing his response to the Devonshire countryside where Hurrell Froude's father lived, Newman showed the extent to which his painter's eye was enchanted by the beauty of the natural world. Nowhere in his letters to his brothers do we encounter passages like this.

> What strikes me most is the strange richness of every thing. The rocks blush into every variety of colour—the trees and fields are emeralds, and the cottages are rubies. A beetle I picked up at Torquay was as green and gold as the stone it lay on, and a squirrel which ran up a tree here just now was not a pale reddish brown, to which I am accustomed, but a bright brown red. Nay, my very hands and fingers look rosy, like Homer's Aurora, and I have been gazing on them with astonishment. All this wonder I know is simple, and therefore of course do not you repeat it. The exuberance of the grass and the foliage is oppressive, as if one had not room to breathe, though this is a fancy—the depth of the valleys and the steepness of the slopes increase the illusion—and the Duke of Wellington would be in a fidget to get some commanding point to see the country from. The scents are extremely fine, so very delicate, yet so powerful, and the colours of the flowers as if they were all shot with white. The sweet peas especially have the complexion of a beautiful

[11] LD, 1:84–5 JHN to Jemima Newman (31 August 1820).
[12] LD, 7:66 JHN to Jemima Newman (23 April 1839).
[13] Joyce Sugg. *Ever Yours Affly: John Henry Newman and his Female Circle* (London, 1996), p. 11.
[14] *Fairy Bower*, p. 12.

face—they trail up the wall, mixed with myrtles, as creepers. As to the sunset, the Dartmoor heights look purple, and the sky close upon them a clear orange. When I turn back to think of Southampton water and the Isle of Wight, they seem by contrast to be drawn in india-ink or pencil.[15]

Such delight in the countryside was not universal. "The summer and the country . . . have no charms for me," Sidney Smith wrote in 1838. "I look forward anxiously to the return of bad weather, coal fires, and good society in a crowded city. I have no relish for the country: it is a kind of healthy grave. I am afraid you are not exempt from the delusions of flowers, green turf, and birds; they all afford slight gratifications, but not worth an hour of rational conversation; and rational conversation in sufficient quantities is only to be had from the congregation of a million of people in one spot. God bless you!"[16] Newman, with his love of Ham, would have agreed with Evelyn Waugh's mother, who, as her son wrote in his autobiography, always missed the natural beauty of the countryside, regarding towns as "places of exile where the unfortunate are driven to congregate in order to earn their livings in an unhealthy and unnatural way."[17] When Gladstone attempted to coax Newman to join him for one of his celebrity breakfasts (which often included Tennyson), Newman wrote back a letter revelatory of his view of London. "It pleases me much to know that you and Mrs Gladstone receive so kindly the gift I have ventured to make her," Newman wrote after he had sent a copy of his *Dream of Gerontius* (1864). "Certainly, I will avail myself of your permission to present myself at your breakfast table, should any thing call me in the season to London. What chance there is of that, I do not know—for my visit to London of last year was the first I had made, except for a few hours, for—what shall I say? twenty or thirty years."[18]

If Newman was not exactly keen on London, he was exceedingly fond of his mother and sisters. Eloquent proof of this can be found in a journal entry that he made in 1825, the year he took holy orders, when he wrote, "My Mother and Sisters came to Oxford the beginning of August, and stayed till the end of September. Jemima and Mary partook of the Sacrament for the first time . . . I administering it as a priest for the first time . . . O how I love them. So much I love them, that I cannot help thinking. Thou wilt either take them hence, or take me from them, because I am too set on them. It is a shocking thought."[19] His sisters fully returned their brother's love. "I wish I could say something to show you a little how I prize your affectionate kindness," Harriett wrote to John in 1829, "and how dear and happy to me is the thought of the love you bear me."[20] One of the reasons why Newman found his sisters so companionable is that they could enter into his ecclesiastical and literary interests. "The Miss Newmans are very learned persons, deeply read in ecclesiastical history, and in all the old divines, both High Church and Puritanical," Dr James Mozley wrote to his parents before Harriett

[15] LD, 2:343 JHN to Mrs Newman (7 July 1831).
[16] Sidney Smith to Miss G. Harcourt (July 1838) in *Selected Letters of Sydney Smith*. ed. Nowell C. Smith (Oxford, 1956), p. 254.
[17] See Evelyn Waugh. *A Little Learning* (London, 1964), p. 31.
[18] LD, 24:7 JHN to W. E. Gladstone (9 January 1868).
[19] *AW*, pp. 206–7.
[20] LD, 2:148 Harriett to JHN (13 June 1829).

and Jemima married his brothers Thomas and John; "Notwithstanding they are very agreeable and unaffected."[21]

Harriett, born in 1803, was generally considered not only the handsomest but the smartest of the sisters. Petite and delicate, she had bright blue eyes and fair lustrous hair. She wore her hair, as was the fashion then, in ringlets, and was mad about bonnets. "I hope you will like your Bonnets," she wrote Jemima. "Mamma and I think them very pretty and genteely fashionable. Miss A. calls them *cottage slouch* and says they are nearly the prettiest Bonnets she has made this season."[22] In another letter to Jemima, she dispensed strict sartorial advice: "You need not wear your gauze dress; only take great care of your gay one, and Mary also; as in case you have new Bonnets your dresses will look ashamed."[23] Prone to sleeplessness, Harriett suffered from prostrating headaches. Nonetheless, despite lingering ill health, including rheumatism and deafness, she was a gregarious woman, even if not all company suited her. Fond of London, she shuddered to think of what it would be like to live in the country "immured among boobies."[24] Yet after her marriage she grew so attached to the village of Cholderton in Wiltshire, where her husband, Tom Mozley was the parish priest, that when her family moved back to London in 1847, she was inconsolable, telling Jemima that it was the "bitterest moment of my life."[25]

Like Samuel Johnson, Harriett was enamoured of balloons.[26] "Mr. Graham ascended yesterday in his Balloon," she wrote Jemima; "we had a very good view of it; he alighted at Godstone, after having been an hour and a half surveying a splendid collection of clouds. I longed to be with him when I saw the Balloon ascending in such style . . ."[27] Early and late, she delighted in royalty, though never uncritically. In 1821, at the time of George IV's Coronation, she got up with the rest of the family at 3 o'clock in the morning to get a view of the royal procession. "When we had arrived very near our Places at 6 o'clock, we heard great applauses, and 'the Queen, the Queen,' resounded on all sides. She passed just before our Horses, so that we had a full view of her." Harriett did not describe this full view. Nor, a year earlier, did Charles Greville describe the view he had of the Queen, other than to say: "The Queen looked exactly as she did before she left England."[28] The innumerable caricatures of Gillray and Cruikshank doubtless made any description of her "sharp, sunken features and startlingly black eyebrows" superfluous.[29] Harriett did describe other members of the royal entourage, being "quite astounded to see how old, ill and *ugly* the King looks—indeed the whole Procession, [with the exception of] the Marquis of Londonderry, were the plainest set of Men I ever

[21] Wilfrid Meynell. *Cardinal Newman* (London, 1907), p. 93.

[22] *Family*, p. 7.

[23] Ibid., p. 6.

[24] Ibid., p. 9.

[25] Ibid., p. 178.

[26] "I have continued my connection with the world," Johnson told Hester Thrale's daughter, Queeney, in 1784, "so far as to subscribe to a new balloon . . . by which, I suppose, some Americo Vespucci, for a new Columbus he cannot now be, will bring us what intelligence he can gather in the clouds." See *Johnson and Queeney: Letters from Dr. Johnson to Queeney Thrale*. ed. Marquis of Landsdowne (London, 1932), p. 46.

[27] *Family*, pp. 6–7.

[28] *Greville's England: Selections from the Diaries of Charles Greville: 1818–1860* (Folio, 1981), p. 20.

[29] Flora Fraser. *The Unruly Queen: The Life of Queen Caroline* (London, 1996), p. 6.

beheld. . ."[30] Later, in 1843, when she was trying to cure herself of insomnia in France, she was fascinated by how Queen Victoria struck her Norman hosts. "I see all about the Queen in the French papers," she wrote back to Jemima, though she was indignant that there was no mention of her beauty. "What the French ladies were most struck with, and what was the greatest theme of admiration was her Majesty's teeth, which shone like pearls . . ."[31] On her return to England, she took her daughter Grace to see Victoria and Albert at Buckingham Palace. "The Queen and Prince came down half way on the Grand Staircase," she recalled. "Nobody before them, but two pages and four ladies following. The light was so bad that I could not catch a sight of her face—or in the least identify it with any portrait. The shape of her head seemed spoilt by a too large and round ugly coronet."[32] If the royal taste in dress exasperated Harriett—the lappets and feathers worn by the female royals particularly dismayed her—she was no more tolerant of other aesthetic lapses. Her letters attest how excruciating she found bad singing. "Oh the singing in church!" she lamented in one letter. "I was really quite mangled last Sunday. It was really like extemporaneous effusions, without tuning or concert . . ." In another, she complained of how "the Evening Hymn . . . was more disgraceful than I can describe. Master Abel screeched about 2 ½ notes above the pitch, sometimes attempting a counter tenor, sometimes treble, so that the whole gallery was in consternation, not knowing whether to try to reach him, or keep to us below . . ." Later, her delight in good singing would be richly gratified when she went to hear Jenny Lind in Essex Hall in London. "At last I have heard Jenny Lind," she wrote Jemima in 1849. "Altogether—from only this concert I should say her style is most glorious, the perfection of unadorned and unornamented singing."[33] Still, she never hesitated to find fault where she felt performers or composers fell short of her exacting standards. Since Lind was performing to set up a Mendelssohn scholarship (the first winner of which was young Arthur Sullivan), Harriett could not resist giving her opinion of the composer who had given Lind her start in Leipzig.[34] "I cannot admire Mendelssohn," she wrote to Jemima in 1849. "I may be astounded by his choruses and full pieces, but I cannot see genius or beauty in his music—it is *science* and *composition*, one never forgets the author. When Beethoven began one then felt what music was—nature opposed to skill and ease to effort. I never shall admire Mendelssohn . . ."[35] This echoed Wagner's criticism of Mendelssohn, whom he found a "musical landscape painter," lacking in profound feeling or depth.[36]

Headstrong and obdurate, Harriett was never averse to speaking her mind. Of all the sisters, she was the most acerbic. "We have been to the British Museum," she wrote Jemima in 1824. "There is no great alteration, except an addition of a polar Musk Ox and Bear, the former a fine animal and the latter a large one . . . as to the Elgin Marbles they do not improve by laying by . . . I will acknowledge that they have been admirable,

---

[30] *Family*, p. 4.
[31] *Family*, pp. 140–1. Newman also took a keen interest in Victoria, writing Maria Giberne in January 1854: "The report here is that the Queen is going mad, and that the people won't bear Prince Albert as Regent. Poor thing, a war will try her certainly, for she has had nothing but peace and plenty hitherto." See LD, 16:23 JHN to Maria Giberne (22 January 1854).
[32] *Family*, p. 161.
[33] Ibid., pp. 188–9.
[34] ODNB.
[35] *Family*, p. 185.
[36] See Wagner quoted in *Etude* (May 1922).

but to say that they *are*, demands too great a stretch of my charity—and I think it too bad that old wrinkled superannuated charmers should usurp the place of more youthful beauties . . .".[37] Yet she was no less critical of contemporary charmers. "Most of our Oxford friends are now gone," she wrote in one letter, "and now poor Oxford is quite desolate. It was a strange sight, so many ladies in the place. I wish they would not make themselves absurd or disagreeable. One would think they might behave like reasonable creatures in Oxford if nowhere else."[38] At a dinner party, she met someone called Mrs Pugh, whom she felt compelled to describe as "a very large, raw, handsome looking milkmaid. One could not but fancy they had just caught her, and clapt on a great velvet hat and white feather, and sent her in to graze—yet she looks so complete a raw girl that one cannot believe she has at home seven children."[39]

Harriett also had very decided literary views. In 1846, she wrote Jemima of the novelist with whom Newman would become very friendly in later life, "I quite expected Lady Georgiana to become a Romanist, after I heard she had written her Tale to enforce the desirableness of confession . . . It is just one of the fallacious and hollow arguments that would satisfy a Romanising mind."[40] In another letter to Jemima of 1849, she observed how "Miss Martineau has been writing a book on education from birth to manhood—a rather impertinent thing (as she has done it) for an unmarried person."[41] In still another of the same year, she informed Jemima how, as she said, "I am reading Macaulay's history and find it very odious . . . It is the fashion to call it interesting, but I feel pretty sure people skip the historical parts and read the scenes and the gossip, of which there is a sufficient sprinkling . . ."[42]

Clearly, Harriett had something of her eldest brother's talent for writing good colloquial mocking English. With this gift for pungent expression, it is not surprising that she turned her hand to fiction. Indeed, she wrote a number of novels, though she was always doubtful of their merit. Her stories, she feared, "were too deep for children, too shallow for grownups—just the unhappy medium."[43] Still, the great Dickens scholar Kathleen Tillotson considered Harriett's first novel, *The Fairy Bower, or the History of a Month* (1841), a "neglected minor masterpiece."[44] The book centres around Grace Leslie, who debates religious matters with her Evangelical cousins, Mary Anne and Constance while on holiday. "Introspectiveness in miniature is exquisitely traced in the moral dilemma of ten-year-old Grace," Tillotson wrote of the book in her survey of novels published in the 1840s, "and here, as not in many large-scale instances, the heroine's conflict of conscience is perfectly integrated with the narrative."[45] Harriett understood narrative in the same way as Ivy Compton-Burnett: "One difficulty I have

---

[37] *Family*, p. 7.
[38] Ibid., p. 39.
[39] *Family*, p. 80.
[40] *Family*, p. 170 Here, Harriett is referring to the English Catholic novelist Lady Georgiana Fullerton (1812–85) and her highly popular novel, *Ellen Middleton* (1844), which Gladstone and Lord Brougham could not resist praising for its handling of the auricular confession of which so many Victorians disapproved.
[41] *Family*, p. 182.
[42] Ibid., p. 188.
[43] Kathleen Tillotson, *Novels of the Eighteen Forties* (Oxford, 1954), p. 136.
[44] Ibid., p. 5.
[45] Ibid., p. 132.

is bringing out my story without implicating the actors in evil doings. You understand in order to do this all should be managed by *conversation*. Narrative almost inevitably betrays motive or gives a coloring."[46] In one conversation, Harriett nicely captured the exotic fascination with which Victorian England associated Catholic nuns.

"Do you mean to go on in this way, Constance?" said Emily; "*I* declare if you do, by the time you are grown up, you will be fit for nothing but a monastery, and you must leave the world, and shut yourself up in a convent."

"I hope I shall leave the world," returned her cousin, "but I hope I shall not shut myself up in a convent, and be any thing so shocking as a nun."

"Not be a nun!" cried Fanny, "not be a dear beautiful nun! oh, I had rather be a nun than any thing else in the whole world!"

"Really, Fanny, I am quite ashamed of you," said her sister. "Do you know what you are saying? Don't you know a nun is a Roman Catholic?"

"Oh, but a nun is the most unfortunate and interesting creature in the world!" cried Fanny, "and they all look so miserable, and wander about and sing all night, and they wear long black garments, with a streaming white veil, and an immense long string of beads, with a cross at the end of it; and they go about curing all sick people, and binding up their wounds."

"Fanny!" cried Emily, "what a medley you are making; I know what it is all from. *I* told you of a nun in one of Mrs. Ratcliffe's novels, and some one else has been talking to you of Madame de Genlis's 'Siege of Rochelle,' I am sure; but all that is not true of nuns!"

"No, to be sore not!" said Ellen, "first they would cut off all your hair, and then bury you, and shut you up in a convent, with bars, and you could never get out again."

"Yes," continued Grace, "and they would never let you see any of your friends, except before the abbess, and several others; they would not even let you speak alone to your papa or mamma, or brothers and sisters, and if you tried to do so, or to get out, they would clap you up in mortar, in a cellar, and leave you to starve. Oh! I would not be a nun for the whole world; how can you wish it, Fanny?"[47]

Newman, who was so friendly with so many Catholic nuns after he converted—bright, resourceful, faithful women—must have seen in this passage painful proof of the two very different worlds in which he and his sister moved.

In February 1841, Newman wrote from Oriel: "The Fairy Bower is making a sensation here—I have given away my editorial copy . . ."[48] In March, demand for the book had not abated: "Favorable opinions of that work flow in—the general opinion seems to be that it is of the school of Miss Austen—as occurred to you, and to me before you when I read it."[49] In November, he wrote Tom Mozley, "Our ultra friends here are enthusiastic in praise of the Fairy Bower. Ward of B. [Balliol] has but one draw back—Grace is his heroine—and someone suggested she was to marry—he has

---

[46] *Family*, p. 98.
[47] *Fairy Bower*, p. 293.
[48] LD, 8:34 JHN to Mrs John Mozley (12 February 1841).
[49] LD, 8:56 JHN to Henry Wilberforce (5 March 1841).

quite taken it to heart."[50] For Newman, Harriett had "brought out the *wooden* unelastic nature of both Mary Anne and Constance."[51] He tempered his praise, however, with a qualification, remaking that "H. understands girls well, but she does not understand boys. Hers are very unreal. She makes them talk, not like boys, but like Walter Scott's middle-age characters . . ."[52] This is reminiscent of Flannery O'Connor's objection to Henry James' *What Maisie Knew*, which anatomizes, through the eyes of a child, the baseness of divorcing adults: "You sometimes think the child must have a bald head and a swallow-tailed coat . . ."[53] Nevertheless, Newman thought *The Fairy Bower* "perfect" in its way.[54] Charlotte Yonge, the author of the Tractarian novel, *The Heir of Redclyffe* (1853), thought otherwise, finding *The Fairy Bower* a "curious study of antics and follies, enhanced by little domesticities . . . the ladies walk about in long ringlets and smoothed hair is the token of being religious."[55] This dismissive review appeared in 1890, long after Harriett's death, but it would probably not have surprised her, recognizing as she did that fiction demanded more concentration than she could muster. After the release of her last novel, *Louisa* (*1842*), which Newman thought "the best thing she has done,"[56] Harriett devoted herself to her own domesticities, looking after her daughter Grace, who would later move to Australia and become a concert pianist, and her husband, Tom Mozley, an Anglican divine, who was also editor of the Tractarian paper, *The British Critic*, before becoming a lead writer for *The Times*. Another, perhaps even more pressing reason why Harriett abandoned novel writing was that it aggravated her insomnia and gave her fierce headaches. "My mind is perfectly lacerated," she complained in the midst of finishing *The Lost Brooch*.[57]

However, in one posthumously published book of hers, *Family Adventures* (1852), she includes an amusing portrait of her eldest brother. As Wilfrid Ward noted in his biography, there Newman is described (at the age of 11) as "'a very philosophical young gentleman,' 'very observant and considerate.' He is fastidious and bored by general society. He is devoted to his mother, to whom he writes constantly when away from home and whom he delights in surprising with some gift which she will care for. He loves to read to the servants from serious books and to explain their meaning. He is tender and sympathetic to his sisters. 'You always understand about everything,' says one of them, 'and always make me happy when I am uncomfortable.'"[58] This was clearly the effect that Newman had on his many correspondents, if not always on his siblings, though the underlying contention of Harriett's book—that family can produce adventure just as much or more as romantic fiction—is one that her brother would have approved.

After Newman's beloved youngest sister Mary died suddenly in 1828 of appendicitis, Newman reaffirmed his special attachment to Harriett. "I cannot say how I love you. No

---

[50] LD, 8:356 JHN to Thomas Mozley (26 November 1841).
[51] LD, 8:422 JHN to Thomas Mozley (13 January 1842).
[52] LD, 10:75 JHN to Mrs John Mozley (31 December 1843).
[53] *Letters of Flannery O'Connor: The Habit of Being* (New York, 1979), pp. 332–3.
[54] LD, 10:75 JHN to Mrs John Mozley (31 December 1843).
[55] Charlotte Yong quoted in *Family*, p. 109.
[56] LD, 10:50 JHN to Mrs John Mozley (31 July 1842).
[57] *Family*, p. 108.
[58] Ward, I, pp. 27–8.

calamity, I think, could occur to me here so great, as to lose your love and confidence. For of all my brothers and sisters (from one cause or other,) you alone know my feelings and respond to them."[59] Harriett, who could be unsure of herself, despite her bold exterior, clung to her brother's good opinion. "I cannot tell you how dear to me is the assurance of your affection. I hoped you loved me, dear John, whenever I thought of it – but I could never persuade myself that there was any thing in me that could inspire the same feeling towards me that I feel for others, much more you. I cannot persuade myself so now."[60] Newman's own closeness to Harriett can be seen in his readiness to confide in her what was uppermost in his thoughts. Speaking of his painful experience of Mary's loss in relation to his faith, he wrote: "It is so difficult to realize what one believes, and to make these trials, as they are intended, real blessings."[61] Here was a confidence that summed up what animated a good deal of Newman's life as an Anglican. He also wrote Harriett brilliant letters while travelling abroad with the Froudes, like this one describing life aboard the 800-ton packet *Hermes*, on which he sailed from Falmouth to Italy in December 1832.

> I am but just now getting reconciled to my berth, which yet is very far superior to most if not all accommodations of the kind. I will not speak of its smallness, more like a coffin than a bed – nor its darkness; but first think of the roll of the vessel to and fro. The first night, my side was sore with the rub, rub of the motion. Then fancy the swinging, neverending swinging – the knocking your head, and bruising your arms, you all the while being shelfed in a cupboard six <five> feet from the floor. Then the creaking of the vessel. It is like half a hundred watchman's rattles, only far louder, mixed with the squeaking of several Brobdignag pigs, while the water dashes dash dash against the sides. Then overhead the loud foot of the watch, who goes tramping up and down the whole night more or less. Then (in the morning) the washing of the deck over your head. Rush comes an engine pipe on the floor above – ceases, is renewed, flourishes about, rushes again – then suddenly 1/2 a dozen brooms, wish, wash, wish wash, scrib, scrub, roaring and scratching alternately. Then the heavy flump, flump, of the huge dabbing cloth, which is meant to dry the deck in a measure instead of a towel or duster. Last and not least the smell. In spite of air, the berth will smell damp and musty – and at best close – there is no window in it – it opens into the cabin, which at night has been lighted with oil. Added to this the want of room for your baggage, and your higgledy piggledy state – and you will allow I have given you enough of discomforts – yet one day like yesterday outweighs them all, and in fact they are going fast. To be sure a valetudinarian could not possibly bear it. I think it would have quite knocked me up a year or two since – and as for those who in advanced stages of consumption are sent abroad, it must be a martyrdom – for I repeat our vessel is a peculiarly convenient one – but I am glad to say, I am getting over these things.[62]

[59] LD, 2:55 JHN to Harriett Newman (6 February 1828).
[60] LD, 2:55–6 Harriett Newman to JHN (14 February 1828).
[61] LD, 2:66 JHN to Harriett Newman (21 April 1828).
[62] LD, 3:134 JHN to Harriett Newman (12 December 1832).

However fond she might have been of her brilliant brother, Harriett looked askance at the Oxford Movement. As early as 1829, before the Movement got underway, she found Newman's sermons "very High Church. I do not think I am near so high, and do not quite understand them . . ."[63] In this, she might have agreed with that witty Anglican divine, Sydney Smith (1771–1845), the son of an equally witty Huguenot mother, who once preached against the Tractarians in St Paul's because, as he said, "they lessen the aversion to the Catholic faith . . . inculcate the preposterous surrender of the understanding to bishops . . . and make religion an affair of trifles, of postures and of garments."[64] Harriett also took a rather critical view of some of the Tractarians themselves, especially Hurrell Froude, whom she found arrogant. After besting him in some conversational exchange, she was exultant. "Off I stood master of the field," she wrote Jemima, "crowned with victory! I long to pique that proude froude and hope I shall have an opportunity . . ."[65] Harriett disliked in Froude what others disliked in her: flippancy. Still, when Newman brought out Froude's private journal, she regarded it as an indefensible violation of his privacy. "The only things I could never have guessed at and which I heartily grieve over (I mean their treacherous exposé) are painful littlenesses, which should never have been known. Only suppose handing about a private journal of daily faults, etc. etc. among friends, all of whose names are mentioned—could this be right?"[66] Doubtless, she would have felt the same about the publication of her own private correspondence, which, in its own way, exhibited even more "painful littlenesses."

Then, again, she was unimpressed with Edward Pusey, the patrician canon of Christ Church whom Newman dubbed "ὅ μέγας." In June of 1845, she wrote Jemima, "You heard of my meeting Dr. Pusey. He began to talk about J.H.N. but made a great mess of it, and if I had not known about things, and had not heard from other quarters of their having lately met and what passed, he might have made me very uneasy. A man of his station ought to have more sense and skill than to behave as he did. He went out of the room too, cutting all he called on but me, and squeezing my hand as if he loved me. Poor man he cannot please me you see."[67]

If Harriett disliked Froude and Pusey, she was altogether taken with Edward Caswall (1814–78), the Anglican vicar, Roman convert, Oratorian, humorist, and hymnologist, who gave such indispensable financial and administrative support to Newman and his Oratory, not to mention spiritual ballast. Harriett was at a decanal meeting at Netheravon with her husband in 1841, when Caswall first descended on her in all of his infectious bonhomie.

> I had not met him before. He lost no time in making up to me without any introduction and bounced at me into the thick of every thing, talking of his brother [Henry Caswall] and mine—and relating innumerable anecdotes, interspersed with reflections sentimental and moral, without end—he is a most entertaining and enthusiastic creature, at whom one can laugh, and with whom sympathise.

---

[63] *Family*, p. 33.
[64] *Selected Letters of Sydney Smith* (Oxford, 1956), p. 306.
[65] *Family*, p. 44.
[66] Ibid., pp. 73–4.
[67] Ibid., pp. 162–3.

He again got next to me at dinner, and hardly ate anything for talking—at least he dispatched each plate at the end while the things were clearing. He was resolved to get all he could out of me concerning J.H.N.—his birth, education and character and stuck at nothing so as he could get his curiosity appeased . . . He wanted to know if I knew what was *in* J.H.N. all his life, seeming to have a natural wonderment as to how he came to be what he is . . . You see I had an amusing companion.[68]

Something of Caswall's charm can be seen in his *Sketches of Young Ladies*, which Chapman & Hall commissioned him to write in 1837 under the pseudonym "Quiz" to piggyback on the success of Dickens' *Sketches of Boz* (1836). As it happened, the book was a tremendous success, going into eight editions in its first year alone. Harriett, who was never shy about calling attention to the follies of her sex, doubtless enjoyed Quiz's droll observations on this score, which, as Caswall admitted, were inspired by the classifications of zoologists and botanists.

We have often regretted that while so much genius has of late years been employed in classifications of the animal and vegetable kingdoms, the classification of young ladies has been totally and unaccountably neglected. And yet who can doubt but that this beautiful portion of the creation exhibits so many, if not more, varieties than any system of botany yet published? Nature, indeed, seems to have exhibited here, more than in any other part of her works, her uncontrollable propensity of ranging at freedom; and accordingly has beautifully diversified the female species, not only in respect to their minds and persons, but even n those more important points, their bonnets, gloves, shawls, and other equally interesting portions of dress.[69]

Thus, Caswall included sketches of "The Young Lady who Sings," "The Evangelical Lady," "The Literary Young Lady," "The Clever Young Lady," and "The Extremely Natural Young Lady." About this last creature, "Quiz" remarks how:

The extremely natural young lady is always doing some out-of-the-way thing, that she may appear simple and girlish. She is most particularly fond of romping; and, when you are out walking with her, is sure to run after a small donkey, or jump a ditch, or have her fortune told, or thrust herself bolt through a hedge; all which little exhibitions she esteems to be beautiful and touching pieces of rustic elegance. Then suppose she is able to sing, and comes to a green lane, forthwith she begins chirruping like a young sparrow; and if a cart pass by that particular time, ten to one she jumps and tells the boy to make the horses gallop. She enjoys nothing so much as getting her gown torn, and is particularly fond of arranging her hair out of doors. We have known her to stop on a common, give us her bonnet and cap to hold, and proceed to her toilet in the most simple, unaffected manner possible; all so delightfully natural; it was quite pleasant to see her setting her curls in their places, and wagging about her head right

---

[68] Ibid., pp. 103–4.
[69] Charles Dickens. *Sketches of Young Gentlemen and Young Couples with Sketches of Young Ladies by Edward Caswall* (Oxford, 2012), p. 5.

and left. When the natural young lady is in doors, she is always running out of doors, especially if it rains—that is perfection. She is delighted above all things with making snowballs. If there be a cow within a mile, she is sure to go some morning before breakfast and drink the warm milk, a feat of which she never ceases to talk for three months after. She will box a gentleman's ears and think nothing of it. She was never known to walk, but always hops and skips. Her utmost ambition is to be called a wild thing. . .[70]

Harriett was also very fond of Henry Wilberforce—perhaps because, unlike so many of Newman's Oxford friends, who could be intimidatingly bookish, he was easy to talk to. "Henry is my little friend," she wrote her Aunt Elizabeth in 1829, "who is no Don and never will be . . ."[71] Later, in 1836, when Mrs Newman died, Newman acknowledged the special friendship Harriett had with Henry by writing: "This is so bitter an affliction to both Harriett and me, that unless we knew Christ was coming, I do not know how we should bear it."[72] Nonetheless, that Harriett's judgement could be less than reliable is evident from her extravagant estimate of her husband, Tom, whose own judgement was notoriously erratic. In a letter to Jemima, Harriett praised her talkative husband. "Often I would never speak from the fear of stopping any thing so good or brilliant as his conversation. You have never heard him talk as he can, never heard the best of his moral maxims, and remarks on men and principles, endless and apt illustrations, and his extraordinary power of argument . . . I have lately been reading through two little volumes of Johnson from Boswell, and am greatly struck by his resemblance to my funny husband."[73] Doting wives often have exalted views of their husbands but they do not put them on a par with Samuel Johnson. Nevertheless, Johnson might very well have found the comparison flattering. Tom was a handsome, popular, clubbable man, who, to let off steam, often whipped his pretty young wife. "Tom has just been whipping Harriett round the garden with the new whip from the pony carriage," Aunt Charles Fourdrinier reported to Jemima. Harriett confirmed her husband's explosive impulses. "I could not tell you all I endure," she told her sister. "One day on the top of the plain, in full sight of the whole county, he lifted me over into a sheepfold, and would have left me among the animals only we expected someone to dinner and I should have been missed. Then he thinks nothing when in one of his passions, of throwing all the missiles within reach at me, one after another—they come like snow round me."[74]

These, however, were the complaints of a wife whose love for her husband was of an admirable loyalty. We can glean the depth of this love in the last letter she wrote Tom before they married, when there was some question as to whether they should go through with the marriage so soon after Mrs Newman's death. "You quite mistake me when you urge me to feel equal confidence with you," she wrote to her fiancé. "Surely I have shown enough—and I can only say what I feel, most truly, that

[70] Ibid., pp. 67–8.
[71] *Family*, p. 32.
[72] LD, 5:300 JHN to Henry Wilberforce (18 May 1836).
[73] *Family*, p. 63.
[74] Ibid., p. 62.

if you yourself, your family, and the whole world were to bear witness against you, I could not be persuaded that you are not what I believe you, or that you will ever be otherwise."[75]

Harriett was not the only one who thought highly of her husband: in a letter to Tom's father on the eve of his son's nuptials, Newman wrote:

> You indeed have known him some years longer than I have but I will not admit that any one can admire and honour him more than I do. I know no one of higher and more generous mind – and unless it were throwing words away in these common-place days to say so, of such heroic qualities – I mean I think him possessed of the most affectionate heart, and that he would do any thing, neglect himself, and go through all perils for those who are possessed of it. Every one who knows him at all must and does know this in a measure and though my words seem high flown, yet they are very true. With these convictions I am, as you may suppose, as much pleased for Harriett's sake at what is going to happen as for my own sake.[76]

Later, in 1882, after Mozley published his slapdash memoir of Tractarianism, which included erroneous references to Newman's father, Newman was understandably offended and his affection for Tom cooled, so much so that he stopped writing him, though Grace, his talented daughter, was the last person who would visit Newman at the Oratory before his death on 11 August 1890.

Frank Newman was also offended by Tom Mozley's unreliable reminiscences. "Now Mr Mozley is a very generous warm-hearted man;" Frank wrote to a correspondent, "and he is incapable of malice or any unkindness. I left Oxford myself in 1830, and ought to have been entirely left out of mention. We did know each other slightly when he was an undergraduate, but he does not refer to that. I am hardly a just critic of any thing to which he can claim memory. But I strongly repudiate his mention of things which he cannot pretend to remember, things of which he had no cognizance. My brother the Cardinal writes me words too strong to repeat, as to the impropriety of his lugging in my Father to his narrative; and says he has documents which prove him to be quite incorrect. For my part I strongly complain of his statement concerning my mother, and flatly deny it; both as untrue, and as a most gratuitous aspersion on her good sense. The religious training of us which he ascribes to her and the religious books to which he says she introduced us, – I entirely deny. I suppose he elaborated the fancy, out of the idea that sons who fall into Puritan reading must have got it from their mother, if one of her grandfathers fled from French persecution as a Protestant. Not one of the books he names was put into my hands by my mother, and if she ever read even one of them (which I doubt) it is likely to have been our introducing them to her. As to the Assembly's Catechism, I do not believe I ever set eyes on it, and am as ignorant of it as of the Westminster Confession." Frank also refuted Mozley's account of his relations with his eldest brother, pointing out "how much I owed at that time to his warm affection." Frank ended his letter with the corroboration of someone who had known both

---

[75] Ibid., pp. 59–60.
[76] LD, 5:323 JHN to Henry Mozley (13 July 1836).

Frank and Mozley at Oxford, "Mr [James Anthony] Froude tells me that whenever he has cognizance, he finds Mr M's memory to be at fault."[77]

What would gradually estrange Harriett from Newman was the development of his religious views. Newman sensed the break long before it came. "It is Sunday evening – the duties of the day are over," he wrote her as far back as November 1828, "and I am by myself. Can I raise my mind more entirely upwards than by writing to you? . . . Home has the memory of too many trying events to inspire a merely earthly pleasure. What confidence can I have, or you, or any of us, that we shall continue blest in each other's love, except as we are members of Him whose life and rule belong to another world?"[78] For Harriet, what made the break so bitter when it eventually came was the confidence she had that they were indeed "members of Him whose life and rule belong to another world;" though for her, as for so many English Protestants, this could never include Roman converts. Irony, consequently, suffuses their correspondence. In March 1829, after the storm over Catholic Emancipation erupted, Newman wrote Harriett: "I am clearly in principle an Anti-catholic; and, if I do not oppose the Emancipation, it is only because I do not think it expedient, perhaps possible, so to do. I do not look for the settlement of difficulties by the measure, they are rather begun by it, and will be settled with the downfall of the Established Church. If then I am for Emancipation, it is only that I may take my stand against the foes of the Church on better ground, instead of fighting at a disadvantage."[79] The idea that the writer of this bellicose admission would ever entertain joining the foes of the Established Church would certainly have struck Harriett and her sisters as incredible. Nor did his jolly letter of March 1833 sent from Rome to Jemima, which Harriett would naturally have seen, suggest that he was preparing to repudiate his Anglican allegiances.

> We are at present in good spirits about the prospect of the Church. We find Keble at length is roused, and (if once up) he will prove a second St Ambrose – others too are moving – so that wicked Spoliation Bill is already doing service, no thanks to it. We hear encouraging accounts about Prussia from M. Bunsen, who has received us very kindly. . . . there is every reason to expect the Prussian Communion will be applying to us for ordination in no long time. We hear much too about Germany . . . which leads us to hope that a high reverential spirit is stirring among them. And the W.W.s [Wilberforces] tell us that the recently ejected ministers of Geneva are applying to England for Episcopal ordination. Further our friend the Yankee (whom we again fell in with here) gave us so promising an account of the state of things in America, that we mean, when turned out of St Mary's, to go preaching thro' the Churches of the United States, "strengthening (if so be) the brethren." You can get over to New York for £10 about – and in such a work you would find board and lodging provided for you wherever you went. As to poor Italy, it is mournful to think about it. Doubtless there are the 5000 in Israel – and there are great appearances too of piety in the Churches – still as a system the corrupt religion (and it is very corrupt) must receive severe inflictions – and I fear

---

[77] LD, 30:99.
[78] LD, 2:108 JHN to Harriet Newman (23 November 1828).
[79] LD, 2:132 JHN to Harriett Newman (16 March 1829).

I must look on Rome, as a city, still under a curse, which will one day break out in more dreadful judgments than heretofore – yet doubtless the Church will thereby be let loose from the thraldom.[80]

Of course, this distrust of Romanism on Newman's part was of long-standing, as it was with most of his Protestant contemporaries. In the *Apologia*, he notes how his hostility to the Church of Rome stemmed, at first, from simple ignorance not only of what Catholics believed but of Catholics themselves, though, in his own case, he could see that even in childhood there were signs that he was not as opposed to the Church as he might have been. "I was very superstitious," he noted in a diary entry, "and for some time previous to my conversion [when he was fifteen] used constantly to cross myself on going into the dark." This would always leave him with a respect for superstition, which his contemporaries chose to see as simply deplorable. At the same time, he could never say from whom he had acquired this habit. "Of course I must have got this practice from some external source or other; but I can make no sort of conjecture whence; and certainly no one had ever spoken to me on the subject of the Catholic religion, which I only knew by name. The French master was an *émigré* Priest, but he was simply made a butt, as French masters too commonly were in that day, and spoke English very imperfectly. There was a Catholic family in the village, old maiden ladies we used to think; but I knew nothing but their name. I have of late years heard that there were one or two Catholic boys in the school; but either we were carefully kept from knowing this, or the knowledge of it made simply no impression on our minds. My brother will bear witness how free the school was from Catholic ideas."[81] At the same time, Newman appreciated that in fighting the forces of liberalism within the Anglican Church and Oxford, the "Anti-Catholic Party," as he called it, could learn from its Roman enemies. After admitting that he was resolved to "put down" the liberal Debating Society in Oxford, which he nicely refers to as "that spouting club," he confesses, "See what a bigot I am getting—I am more than ever imprest . . . with the importance of staying in Oxford many years . . . nay feel more strongly than ever the necessity of there being men in the Church, like the R. Catholic friars, free from all obstacles to their devoting themselves to its defence."[82]

But, then, beginning in the summer of 1839, the historian in Newman found himself fundamentally questioning the legitimacy of Anglicanism and he would spend the next 6 years fruitlessly trying to reconcile himself to an Anglicanism in which he no longer felt any confidence. Harriett, and many others, would look back on his Anglican career and see a pattern of dissimulation. Certainly, even when most critical of what he regarded as the flaws of the Roman Church, Newman was always moving towards Rome. That he was often unaware of this movement exculpates him from dissimulation. Nevertheless, Newman did recognize that Harriet and indeed his Mother and Jemima disapproved of the "catholic" aspects of the Tractarian movement almost from its inception. In 1873, in a memorandum entitled, "Apology for Myself," he looked back on this painful period and saw that "there was always the chance of

---

[80] LD, 3:264–5 JHN to Jemima Newman (20 March 1833).
[81] *Apo.*, p. 16.
[82] LD, 2:133 JHN to Jemima Newman (17 March 1829).

their not liking those whom I liked; and in matter of fact, they did not like some of my greatest friends. And again, from the first they did not like the distinctive principles of the Oxford Movement; and, the more it developed, the wider did their difference from me in respect to it grow."[83]

The first public turning point in the revolution of Newman's religious opinions occurred when he published Tract 90. In March, 1841, the indefatigable ecumenist Ambrose Lisle Phillipps published a letter in the *Tablet* recommending that the Anglican Church consider reuniting with the Roman Church, arguing in one passage, "Take the Church of England as her canons and her liturgy testify her to be, and I declare that the chasm which separates her from the Catholic Church is but small."[84] The letter put Anglican Oxford on tenterhooks. How would Newman respond? Newman responded with Tract 90 and the reaction could not have been more seismic. "I fear I am clean dished," Newman wrote Harriet. "The Heads of Houses are at this very moment concocting a manifesto against me."[85] Tract 90, the last of the *Tract of the Times*, which Newman and his fellow Tractarians wrote to renew the Church of England by returning it to its Catholic roots, argued that the 39 Articles of the Church of England "do not oppose catholic teaching: they but partially oppose Roman dogma: they for the most part, oppose the dominant errors of Rome." Newman wrote the Tract to dissuade some of his Rome-leaning friends from leaving the Church of England on the grounds that it was insufficiently apostolic; the Bishops read it as an attempt to undermine the Anglican Church by imposing a Catholic reading on Articles that they regarded as unambiguously Protestant. After the *Tract* was published, Newman was roundly condemned by both the bishops and the heads of the Oxford colleges. Three years earlier, the poet Coleridge had confided to his diary, "For a long time past the Church of England seems to me to have been blighted with prudence . . . I wish with all my heart we had a little . . . imprudence."[86] Had the poet lived to see Tract 90, he would have seen his wish come true.[87] Harriet, who had not yet read the Tract, wrote her brother on 14 March 1841: "We hear nothing but ill news, I think, on all sides of us just now. I am glad to hear you are not annoyed at your affairs, but it sounds formidable at a distance . . . The tug of war must come some day; let it be now, if you are prepared. And that I hope is the case. I trust to you, as a thousand others will, and you will have their good wishes and prayers, like mine, only better. I look to your late answer to the Roman Catholic's letters, as a pledge for your being carried through."[88] Days earlier, she had struck an even more optimistic note with Jemima. "J.H.N. has been writing privately a most triumphant and mastery answer to the Roman Catholic application, (I think you had better keep it as quite a secret, for I don't think he would like it to get

---

[83] LD, 5:314 "Apology for Myself" (June 1873).

[84] Rosemary Hill. *God's Architect: Pugin and the Building of Romantic Britain* (London, 2008), p. 249.

[85] LD, 8:67 JHN to Mrs Thomas Mozley (12 March 1841).

[86] *Samuel Taylor Coleridge. The Oxford Authors.* ed. H. J. Jackson (Oxford, 1985), p. 595.

[87] Coleridge died at the age of 62 on 25 July 1834. On 10 July, he wrote: "I am dying, but without expectation of a speedy release. Is it not strange that very recently bygone images, and scenes of early life, have blown from the spice-islands of Youth and Hope—those twin realities of this phantom world! . . . Hooker wished to live to finish his Ecclesiastical Polity: –so I own I wish life and strength had been spared to me to complete my Philosophy. For, as God hears me, the originating, and sustaining wish and design in my heart were to exalt the glory of his name . . ." See *Coleridge Select Poetry and Prose.* ed. Stephen Potter (London, 1933), pp. 520–1.

[88] LD, 8:67 Mrs Thomas Mozley to JHN (14 March 1841).

out by his means). My feeling of the matter is that a 'cardinal's hat' or rather more than that has been offered him direct from Rome, and I think he has looked upon it with an infinitely more single eye than did Laud. As simple as a child, and as bold as a lion, he has turned their inconsistency of principle on themselves; in such a way as, I think, must make all ashamed who have had a hand in the application . . . I should think they will see there is no hope for J.H.N. after all . . ."[89]

As it was, Tract 90 was nothing as anti-Roman as Harriett might have wished. Indeed, for her and for most other Anglicans, it seemed subversively papist. On 21 November 1841, Newman wrote a letter to Jemima gauging the probable backlash that would follow the publication of his Tract, which included the likely failure of Isaac Williams's bid to win the Poetry Professorship. Williams, Newman's curate at St Mary's and, later, Littlemore, was a learned, devout, unassuming poet, a Fellow at Trinity, and one of the writers of the "Tracts of the Times"; by rights he should have succeeded John Keble; but he was impelled to withdraw his name after it became clear that he would not win the requisite votes. The mere title of his Tract 80, "Reserve in communicating Religious Knowledge," which had actually been suggested by Newman, set off indignant protests throughout the country—to the English Protestant mind the word "reserve" connoted subterfuge. Williams was suspected of a duplicity of which he was entirely innocent. Later, he retired to Stinchcombe, near Durlsey, or "Stinkers," as Evelyn Waugh called it, where he devoted himself to writing sermons and poetry and educating his sons. Later, in 1865, Newman wrote Williams a year before he died to share with him the ordeal he was undergoing in writing the *Apologia*. "I hope you have guessed why I did not answer your very kind letter from Oxford. I never have had such a time. Under the lash of a printer, without any respite – and my matter growing under my hands, so that I thought it never would come to an end. And a dozen processes, efforts of memory, letter-hunting, planning, sketching, writing, correcting, transcribing, and correcting press, all going on at once. And then, it has affected and cut me up so cruelly, as no one can tell but those close about me."[90] Later, that same year, he wrote his old friend: "I don't forget, but remember with much gratitude, how for twenty years you are perhaps the only one of my old friends who has never lost sight of me – but by letters, or messages, or inquiries, have ever kept up the memory of past and happy days. How mysterious it is that the holiest ties are snapped and cast to the winds by the holiest promptings – and that they who would fain live together in a covenant of gospel peace, hear each of them a voice and a contrary voice, calling on them to break it!"[91] If this was true of his relationship with Williams, it was even truer of his relationship with his family.

Denying Williams the Poetry Professorship was Oxford's first salvo in its ultimately victorious counteroffensive against the Tractarians. Newman set out his sense of the imminent showdown in a letter to Jemima, which she shared with Harriett.

Our present great discomfort is the matter of Williams's election to the Poetry Professorship. I have been against his standing throughout, from a great dread of Convocation – but considering I am the cause of the opposition by Number 90, it

---

[89] *Family*, p. 101.
[90] LD, 21:119 JHN to Isaac Williams (17 June 1864).
[91] LD, 21: 442 JHN to Isaac Williams (31 March 1865).

would have been ungenerous to press my objection and I cannot complain of the difficulty though I foresaw it. I have a dread of Convocation exceedingly great – And now we hear that, if our opponents succeed in this contest, which I fear they will, there is already a plan to proceed to measures which are to have the effect of clean "driving us out of the University." . . . I fear some friends of mine, though they do not say so, would not be sorry for it. They feel the misery of the present state of the Church, with only half the robes of the Church Catholic upon her – they look out for signs of God's providence one way or the other – and, since they despair of the Church actually righting, they look with some sort of relief, as the second best event, for signs of her retrograding and withdrawing her notes. And though the mere defeat of a person in a University Election is a little thing enough, yet if there is a movement of the Church as a whole in all its ranks to disown Catholic truth, in its Bishops, Societies, popular organs and the like, the fact of a series of disavowals on the part of a University is an important fact as part of a series or collection. And it cannot be denied, I suppose, that a series of such facts might happen amounting to a moral evidence that our Church was quite severed and distinct from the Church of the first ages.[92]

After Harriett read the letter, she found her suspicions about her brother's evolving religious opinions confirmed. "I do not want to talk generally about my feelings on J.H.N.'s letter but only yourself and John if you please, consider them and compare them with your own, for I think I am more startled and frightened than you seem to be. It is true that he advances his arguments as from the part of the 'certain friends', but they are given too con amore for my taste. I hope it is all exaggerated, but I have always noticed things are thought one year, talked over the next and acted upon the third." Harriett accurately grasped the practical cast of her brother's thinking but she could not have disapproved more of what she suspected was its likely consequences. "The arguments throughout seem to me perfectly unsound, childish and pettish. Certainly such a step at such a time and under such circumstances must justly be considered to be taken in pique. These certain friends are impetuous undisciplined spirits, impatient and restless – and why is the whole thinking world to be sacrificed for a few such? All looks as near like expediency as any thing I can fancy. What is eight years? I heard in London in two quarters of these 'certain friends,' who are young undergraduates or nearly so – they laugh and talk and denounce F.R.[Rogers,] Mr Johnson, J.W.B.[Bowden] etc. etc. as slow and timid and halfhearted. I was told these young men go on at a wonderful rate. And there is a Cambridge set of the same, more ultra still. How can they talk in this way of the Church of Rome—as if, supposing they can fancy they find the other half of the apostolic robes there, they would not themselves be smothered with the extra garments with which they would, in her pale, find themselves daily encumbered."[93]

Tom shared Harriett's growing fears with Newman: "Harriett, I suppose, has disclosed to you all her anxieties about the ultras of our friends talking so seriously of going over to Rome. She heard a good deal in London about them . . . Your letter which

---

[92] LD, 8:339 JHN to Mrs John Mozley (21 November 1841).
[93] *Family*, pp. 113–14.

comes round through Jemima does not at all relieve her . . ."[94] Newman must have recognized that as he moved farther and farther away from the English Church there would be little he would be able to do to relieve Harriett's anxieties. Still, he did try to allay something of what he would later call her "mental fidget" by appealing to her sense of humour.[95] In July 1840, he described an extraordinary Sunday morning at the altar in Margaret Chapel. "While I was sitting in my surplice . . . during the first lesson a large cat fell from the ceiling, down close at my feet, narrowly missing my head. If I am not mistaken, it fell on its back. Where it came from, no one I have met can tell. It got [up] in no time, and was at the end of the Chapel and back again, before any one knew what the matter was. Then it lay down thoroughly frightened. I had heard a mewing since the beginning of the service. Mrs Bowden, who observed a large cat at S. Mary Maggiore at Rome, suggests that the Record may note it as an additional proof, that, in the Clerk's words, the Chapel in Margaret Street 'goes as near as ever it can to Roman Catholics.'"[96] In December 1841, Newman again sought to reassure Harriett that he would not act rashly, though he did not mince his words about what he saw as the clear threat posed by the Jerusalem Bishopric. "I have not yet had time to read carefully your letter, but lest you should think I am turning Roman outright, I send you last Sunday's Sermon—which let me have back (unread or read) at once—as people want it. I fully think that if this Jerusalem measure comes into full operation, it will all but unchurch us. I cannot help facts—it is not my doing, it is an external fact. And if it takes place, I think it clear that, though one might remain where one was, one-self – yet we should have no arguments to prevent others going to Rome. I am amused at your horror at our ultras—some of them are the very persons you would like, if you knew them."[97] On Christmas Eve, Newman shared with Tom his sense of the grave inadvisability of the Jerusalem Bishopric, at the same time that he counselled him to try to keep Harriett calm. "I assure you I think that Jerusalem question in its effects almost one of life and death—but I trust that it will be life—at all events the very way to die is to hush up the question and not dare to look the difficulty in the face. If the Church is to be saved, it is by saying that she is in danger. Shutting the eyes will not alter facts, but will hinder a remedy and kills hope. Tell H. [Harriett] this, if she is still anxious."[98]

The sermon that Newman sent Harriett was "The Invisible Presence of Christ," which he delivered at St Mary's on 28 November 1841.[99] Newman's object was to put aside the differences roiling the Church of England and look instead at religious division *per se*, though whether he succeeded is dubious. Partisans reading the sermon, whether of the Apostolical or the Protestant party, would not have come away without partisan reactions.

> . . . numbers among ourselves, though we profess the Gospel, are in that restless state, ever seeking, never finding! Look around you, my brethren, on every side: what, on the whole, is the religion of England? it is restlessness. Look round,

[94] LD, 8:361 Thomas Mozley to JHN (30 November 1841).
[95] LD, 15:127 JHN to Mrs J. W. Bowden (19 July 1852).
[96] LD, 7:353 JHN to Mrs Thomas Mozley (8 July 1840).
[97] LD, 8:361 JHN to Mrs Thomas Mozley (2 December 1841).
[98] LD, 8:385 JHN to Thomas Mozley (24 December 1841).
[99] *SD*, Sermon 21.

I say, and answer, why it is that there is so much change, so much strife, so many parties and sects, so many creeds? because men are unsatisfied and restless; and why restless, with every one his psalm, his doctrine, his tongue, his revelation, his interpretation? they are restless because they have not found. Alas! so it is, in this country called Christian, vast numbers have gained little from religion, beyond a thirst after what they have not, a thirst for their true peace, and the fever and restlessness of thirst. It has not yet brought them into the Presence of Christ, in which "is fulness of joy" and "pleasure for evermore." Had they been fed with the bread of life, and tasted of the honeycomb, their eyes, like Jonathan's, had been enlightened, to acknowledge the Saviour of men; but having no such real apprehension of things unseen, they have still to seek, and are at the mercy of every rumour from without, which purports to bring tidings of Him, and of the place of His abode. . . .

That Newman should have invoked Mary Magdalene in this description of his compatriot's religious muddle could not have pleased Harriett. "Mary wept because they had taken away her Lord, and she knew not where they had laid Him. She was in trouble because she sought Him, yet in vain. Poor wanderers, helpless and ill-fated generation, who understand that Christ is on earth, yet do but seek Him in the desert or in the secret chambers,—Lo here! and Lo there! O sad and pitiable spectacle, when the people of Christ wander on the hills as 'sheep which have no shepherd;' and instead of seeking Him in His ancient haunts and His appointed home, busy themselves in human schemes, follow strange guides, are taken captive by new opinions, become the sport of chance, or of the humour of the hour, or the victims of self-will, are full of anxiety, and perplexity, and jealousy, and alarm, 'tossed to and fro, and carried about by every wind of doctrine, by the sleight of men, and cunning craftiness whereby they lie in wait to deceive;'—and all because they do not seek the 'one body' and the 'one Spirit,' and the 'one hope of their calling,' the 'one Lord, one faith, one baptism, one God and Father of all,' and find rest for their souls!"[100]

This was an accurate description of the religious restlessness that did exercise the nineteenth-century English, though Harriett would not have found any consolation in it, nor in this, which would probably have confirmed her in her suspicion that her Rome-leaning brother was merely biding his time. "But you will, perhaps, ask, 'Is there no chance of Christ ever leaving a home where once He was? and if His Presence leaves it, must not we leave it also?' Yes, verily; did He leave His home, we must follow Him; who doubts it?" Another question posed in the sermon would also have fed, not alleviated Harriett's anxieties. "Let, then, the disorder in religious matters which now prevails among us, only lead each of us to ask himself this plain question, whether he may not have more tokens, real and intimate, that Christ is with himself and his brethren in our ordinances, than he has evidence in the present absence or mutilation of the truth, whatever it is, that Christ is not with him . . ."[101] This was hardly a plain question—and its clumsy, convoluted phrasing certainly did not make it any clearer; but its very knottiness would only have added to Harriett's unease.

---

[100] *SD*, p. 317.
[101] Ibid., p. 321.

Harriett's objection to considering Rome as a possible alternative to the Church of England was similar to the one Newman confessed he had had 2 years before, when he began to doubt the fundamental legitimacy of the Anglican Church. In some respects, Rome might supply what the English Church lacked, but it would come with other things as well, which, at least in 1839, Newman was not prepared to accept. In the *Apologia*, he wrote about this objection with perfect candour in a way that shows that he must have recognized many of his own earlier prejudices in those of Harriett and his other siblings.

Newman began to doubt the "tenableness of Anglicanism" in the summer vacation of 1839 after reading about the Monophysite heresy of the fifth century in his study of the Fathers. The Monophysites held that Christ had not two inseparable natures—one divine and one human—but only one divine nature.[102] At the Council of Chalcedon (451), the pope upheld Catholic orthodoxy by reaffirming Christ's human and divine natures and rejecting the Monophysite heresy; as a result, the Monophysites splintered into a radical and a moderate party. In this remote history, Newman saw a reflection of the divisions that were animating Christians in his own day: Protestants and Anglicans bore an uncanny resemblance to the radical and moderate camps of the Monophysite party, while Roman Catholics occupied the same Roman Church that they had occupied in the fifth century. The moral for Newman was inescapable: "I saw myself in the mirror and I was a Monophysite." This unsettling epiphany exploded the Anglo-Catholic *via media* that he had formed between Protestantism on the one hand and Roman Catholicism on the other. Yet if the untenability of his *via media* impelled Newman to consider whether "the other half of the apostolic robes" was in the Roman Church, he found himself confronted with a sizable hurdle: his long-standing anti-Romanism, which he shared not only with his brothers and sisters but with the majority of English Protestants. This put him in a quandary, which he described in his *Apologia*.

In revisiting his reasons for subscribing to Anglicanism, he identified "three original points of belief . . . the principle of dogma, the sacramental system, and anti-Romanism." Of these beliefs, he conceded that the first two were "better secured in Rome than in the Anglican Church." Newman felt that one might make a case for the Anglican Church comprising the "Apostolical Succession, the two prominent sacraments, and the primitive Creeds," but one could not deny that there was "far less strictness on matters of dogma and ritual in the Anglican system than in the Roman." Thus, Newman had to conclude that "my main argument for the Anglican claims lay in the positive and special charges, which I could bring against Rome. I had no positive Anglican theory. I was very nearly a pure Protestant. Lutherans had a sort of theology, so had Calvinists; I had none." Nevertheless, Newman was honest enough to admit that his "pure Protestantism" might have been "negative" but it was still "strong." He recalled that as a schoolboy, he "substituted epithets so vile" in some of his schoolbooks "that I cannot bring myself to write them down here." Despite publishing recantations of anti-Catholic statements he had made throughout his Anglican career, he regarded these youthful defacings as a "stain upon my imagination." To show how difficult it

---

[102] *Apo.*, p. 108.

was for him to root out his anti-Roman prejudices, Newman attested that as late as 1838 he was still convinced that "the spirit of the old pagan city, the fourth monster of Daniel . . . was still alive" in nineteenth-century Rome "and . . . had corrupted the Church which was planted there." It was only when he read of the Monophysite controversy and recognized the untenability of the *via media* that he "underwent a great change of opinion." But even after this revelation, he still could not shake his deep-seated conviction that Rome was the repository of corruption.

> I saw that, from the nature of the case, the Vicar of Christ must ever to the world seem like Antichrist, and be stigmatized as such, because a resemblance must ever exist between an original and a forgery; and thus the fact of such a calumny was almost one of the notes of the Church. But we cannot unmake ourselves or change our habits in a moment. Though my reason was convinced, I did not throw off, for some time after,—I could not have thrown off,—the unreasoning prejudice and suspicion, which I cherished about [the Roman Church] at least by fits and starts, in spite of this conviction of my reason. I cannot prove this, but I believe it to have been the case from what I recollect of myself. Nor was there any thing in the history of St. Leo and the Monophysites to undo the firm belief I had in the existence of what I called the practical abuses and excesses of Rome.[103]

Here, it is plain that, before Newman converted, he was exercised by many of the same prejudices that exercised Harriett. Even after the furore set off by Tract 90, both Newman and Harriett continued to share many of the same concerns. For example, for Harriett, flirting with Rome smacked of deluded impetuosity—something that Newman never entirely ruled out when he was deciding what he should do in that crucial period from 1839 to 1845. Newman also agreed with his sister that it was ill-advised to involve the Tractarian cause in a contest over the Poetry Professorship, which it was destined to lose. And Newman shared his sister's apprehensions about how the Roman leanings of the more advanced Tractarians might impact the faith of Anglicans generally. "To plan all as upon one throw—the election of the P[oetry]. P[rofessorhip]," Harriett wrote Jemima, "seems to me madness and those fierce spirits should be schooled and made to do penance. . . . The difficulties at present seem more fearful than ever – even driving the better part of the Church into the creed of ultra-protestantism, that of – no Church at all. Why is our Church with Episcopacy and the Apostolic succession to be treated as a pretender? and even at the worst that seems to be threatened, would she be, for one generation at least, worse than Rome at present? We can but act for our own generation and must leave the rest to Him who is the Ruler of all. I cannot say half I think on J.H.N.'s arguments. I would like to examine the letter more deeply. I have read it twice and that has been enough to keep me awake at night."[104]

Where Harriett and Newman disagreed was in their understanding of what 'Catholic' meant. What tended to be a term of clear approbation for Newman was always a red flag for Harriett. In March 1841, for example, Newman wrote Harriett expressing his gratitude to Walter Farquhar Hook, the Vicar of Leeds and James

---

[103] Ibid., pp. 113–15.
[104] *Family*, pp. 113–14.

Henthorn Todd, a Fellow at Trinity College for supporting him over Tract 90.[105]
Todd, in particular, Newman wrote, "has written me a warm letter, saying he fully
sympathized with me, and bore witness to the fact that Catholic feelings are springing
up every where quite mysteriously." Harriett would not have found this cause for
unalloyed rejoicing. Nor would she have altogether welcomed Todd's own reading
of the situation. "I cannot help writing to say how much I sympathize with you,"
Todd wrote Newman from Dublin, ". . . nothing can be more true than what you say,
that men's minds seem drawing towards a higher standard of Christian feeling, than
could satisfy the last generation . . . better views seem springing up in different places,
without any connection with others who held them before, as if the hearts of men were
stirred by some superior power, and a yearning created for Catholic truth, even before
it is known what Catholic truth or practice is . . ."[106] That last qualification would
have given Harriet pause. What indeed were Catholic truth and practice? If they were
nothing more than the same Roman abominations of approved Protestant prejudice,
she was not interested.

In May 1842, Harriett and her daughter Grace visited John at Littlemore, the quasi-
monastic retreat which he had set up outside Oxford. Although approving of the layout
of the place, she showed little interest in its purpose. The long, low former stables, she
told Jemima "looked like a wall" with "a dozen windows" and "one storey." "Inside it
is very pretty and neat—just my fancy. I do not wonder of John's present enthusiasm.
There are 4 or 5 sets of rooms—sitting and bedroom—all on the ground floor—the
door opening into a quadrangle into the verandah which runs all along, a length of
the diagonal of Oriel quad. The kitchen is in the middle—a pretty little garden before
the verandah. At right angles is he library, a large pretty room with a nice roof, the
sides covered with books."[107] Her husband, Tom, in his comments about the place,
went beyond interior decoration but not by much. Apropos the prurient gaping to
which Newman's monastic retreat gave rise, Tom was mordantly observant: "Newman
remarks upon the Oxford folks coming to Littlemore, peeping and prying about . . . and
even making their way into it, for mere curiosity. This however, is what English people
do with every convent they come across all over the world. It is a sort of unconscious
homage to the religious and catholic character of such institutions."[108]

In 1843, Harriet and Tom would pay some of that homage themselves when they
travelled to Normandy to try to find some respite for Harriett's worsening insomnia.
From the very moment that the two English Protestants disembarked at Havre, they
knew that they were in a country quite different from their own. "No words can express
the exhilaration I felt in the sights and sounds of a new world," Tom recalled in his
Reminiscences of Oriel College and the Oxford Movement (1882). "The air seemed

---

[105] Apropos Tract 90, Hook wrote Newman: "I write a line merely to express to you my most cordial
sympathy and my readiness to stand by my Friends at Oxford in any steps they may agree to take
at this painful Crisis. Our Enemies force us into the position of a Party and as a Party we must be
prepared to act: by which I mean, that in any ulterior proceedings little minor points of difference
must be forgotten and we must act as one man in asserting our general Principles." See LD, 8:98 W.F.
Hook to JHN (17 March 1841).

[106] LD, 8:105 J.H. Todd to JHN (18 March 1841).

[107] *Family*, pp. 121–2.

[108] *Rem*, ii, p. 215.

clearer, the sky brighter, the pace of life quicker, the voices sweeter, the manners and gestures those of ladies and gentlemen . . . The quay was lined with shops full of the things brought home by sailors; every variety of caged birds, monkeys, shells, corals, and the garments, ornaments, and weapons of natives. . . . Going up the harbour I came to a large dock crowded with ships, most of them with sacred names, one of them St. Augustine . . . The full figures of the saints, in many-coloured vestments, adorned the prows."[109] When he walked the streets beyond the docks, he saw abundant evidence of how the Catholic faith, even after the ravages of Jacobinism, continued to define the French. He noted the "colossal Crucifixes, painted to life, at the cross roads and other conspicuous points;" "representations of purgatory, in the rudest elemental form;" "little girls going about in their white Confirmation dresses."[110] Then he heard a bell and turning around saw "a little procession; a priest investments carrying something under a small canopy; an acolyte, a beadle or two, one of them perhaps carrying a tall staff surmounted by an ornamental lantern, such as one may see in the attics and lumber-rooms of our old country houses. As the procession passes the people stop a moment, take off their hats, and then walk on. This is the Host. It is the consecrated wafer, now become by Roman reckoning the very Body of our Lord. It is on its way to a sick or dying bed. The procession appeals alike to reverence, to the common sympathy with suffering, and to that sense of mortality which no profaneness can dispel or wholly deprive of its seriousness. Death is near, and the opportunity is taken to proclaim that here is Life."[111]

Harriet was similarly struck by the ubiquity of bells. "Certainly the Sunday bells are strange things to our notions," she wrote. Then she met her first French priest. "We dined at the Bowles and met M. le Cure of Notre Dame (Havre). One cannot but respect the French clergy—they work so hard, do such wonders in the way of teaching—and live on so little . . ." When the French priest learnt that Harriet was the sister of Newman, "he burst out into a strain I wish I could do justice to—'Quoi! M. New-man qui a . . . l'homme très célèbre . . .' ending with 'il est un de nos memes . . .'" However, the keenly sensitive Harriett sensed more than a hint of disapproval in her new French acquaintance: "I don't think the cure liked me as the wife of a priest."[112] After they visited a small cathedral at Ingouville, Harriett wrote a letter to Jemima that showed how French Catholic devotion rattled her otherwise complacent Protestantism. "We went into a large church . . . last evening in the dusk. No service was going on—no priests—but many in pews and side altars—in the last people seem most engrossed— almost always on their knees on the floor. A good deal of noise with people's creaking boots in walking, else it was a solemn scene and one to make one feel more and more

---

[109] Ibid., pp. 273–4.
[110] Ibid., pp. 321–6.
[111] Ibid., p. 327. By way of contrast, something of the English view of mortality can be seen in an entry that Duff Cooper made in his diary for 10 June 1919: "Another quiet and happy day. We did the Pitti gallery in the afternoon—we liked especially the Raphael picture of his mistress, and the Mantegna. We all went out after dinner and we had a happy evening together, except when talking about the dead as we often do. I suggested that we should imagine one or two of them sitting in the empty chairs around us. This was too much for Diana and made her cry. We were sitting on the terrace—it was a lovely night and after I had made this unhappy suggestion the unoccupied chairs looked terribly empty." See *The Duff Cooper Diaries* (London, 2005), p. 104.
[112] *Family*, p. 130.

the sinfulness which somehow or other brought on the present state of things as regards ourselves—for it seems to me no church man can doubt that here they have us at great advantage, and one must have a feeling of being in the *wrong* as it were—just as one feels in a quarrel, though ourselves may be ever so conscious of having the right on our side, and that on no account, under no temptation whatever, must one yield one's cause. There is nothing striking or exciting in the churches here to rouse any such extraordinary feelings—only the view of simple devotion in individuals as one *never* can see it exhibited at home . . . You must put my accounts and Tom's together. He sees more in every thing than I . . ."

Tom did indeed see a good deal. "Either on principle or for lack of opportunity, I had never before entered a Roman Catholic chapel . . . So what I now saw would come upon me with all the force of novelty, and it immediately had great fascination for me. This was truly worship! There was the sense of a Divine presence. All hearts were moved as one. . . . I had been prepared to be disappointed. I had repeatedly read and had partly believed that Roman Catholic worship was without reverence, unreal, and wholly beyond the understanding of all but a few scholars; that the clergy set the example of ill-behaviour, whether in church or out of it; that they talked, laughed, and took snuff at the most solemn parts of the service; that hardly ever was a man to be seen in church, certainly never a man of education; that the morals of Roman Catholic populations were flagitiously and shamefully bad."[113] This was an accurate catalogue of the prejudices shared by most English people about a faith which, since the Reformation, they had chosen to regard as synonymous with treachery and corruption. Yet Tom saw his own prejudices confounded. "I can only say that what I saw was the contrary of all this . . . The French appeared to me in the main a religious and orderly people, honest and polite . . . Their worship seemed to me hearty and intelligent . . ." This was precisely the impression that another Anglican had of French Catholicism. In June 1845, Thomas Allies visited France with Charles Marriott, where they spent a month "in searching out Catholic sights, and getting as far as we could at the interior life of the Catholic Church . . . . To the sight – nay, the hourly, daily, monthly feeling, and touch, and taste, and smell of Anglican penury, had succeeded a vision of Catholic wealth. And Marriott's kicks and struggles against the effect of what he saw with me, had their influence too. I used to put questions to him just as they occurred to me, and he would answer in a pet: 'I cannot reply to such questions as that while I am putting on my gloves.' Poor soul! It was his first principle, his αρχη of existence, that Pusey and Anglicanism must be right . . . Nevertheless, I believe that the dear and good Charles Marriott was the most conscientious of men. Perhaps such matters always made his head swim; he feared their physical effect upon him, and had reason for that fear."[114] Allies, who was nicknamed the 'Bantam Cock' because of his small stature and natty dress, converted to Rome in 1850 after the Gorham Trial, while Marriott worked closely with Pusey to keep Tractarianism alive in the wake of Newman's secession.

From the tenor of her correspondence it is clear that Harriett might have seen the allure of the French Catholicism that so beguiled Allies and Marriott but it was not an allure to which she would ever allow herself to succumb. In this respect, she was

[113] Ibid., pp. 319–24.
[114] LD, 29:232. T. W. Allies, *A Life's Decision*, pp. 73–4.

rather like Charlotte Brontë, who was amusingly categorical on how the English should regard the Roman faith of foreign lands. "People talk of the danger which protestants expose themselves to in going to reside in Catholic countries and thereby running the chance of changing their faith." she wrote her good friend Ellen Nussey from Brussels in 1842; "my advice to all protestants who are tempted to do anything so besotted as turn Catholic is to walk over the sea on to the continent—to attend mass sedulously for a time—to note well the mummeries thereof—also the idiotic, mercenary aspect of all the priests—& then if they are still disposed to consider Papistry in any other light than a most feeble childish piece of humbug let them turn papists at once . . . I consider Methodism, Quakerism, and the extremes of High and Low Churchism foolish, but Roman Catholicism beats them all."[115]

Pace Brontë, when Tom and Harriett visited Normandy, the self-sacrificing virtues of the French clergy that Hippolyte Taine described in his history of the French Revolution (1873) were still in evidence. "There was a *curé* or vicar in the smallest of the forty thousand villages," Taine wrote. "In thousands of small, poor, remote communes, he was the only man who could readily read and write; none other than he in many of the larger rural communes, except the resident seignior and some man of the law or half-way schoolmaster, was at all learned." For Taine, the very fact that a man was willing "to live isolated, and a celibate, almost in indigence, amongst rustics and the poor" proved the depth of his vocation. Thus, he was "a preacher of the Word, a professor of morality, a minister of Charity, a guide and dispenser of spiritual life." And Taine was convinced that history, "the supreme judge," as he called it, could show that "no heresy, no schism, not the Reformation nor Jansenism, had prevailed against the hereditary faith . . ." Indeed, "through infinitely multiplied and deeply penetrating roots," the Catholic faith in France had shown again and again that it "suited the national customs, temperament, and peculiar social imagination and sensibility. Possessing the heart, the intellect, and even the senses, through fixed, immemorial traditions . . . it had become an unconscious, almost corporeal necessity, and the Catholic orthodox *curé*, in communion with the Pope, was about as indispensable to the village as the public fountain . . ." Described thus, the contrast between France's priests and the easy-going Anglican parsons of England could not have been starker. Apropos this contrast, it is amusing that Leslie Stephen should have said of Charles Kingsley that "his ideal parson was to be no ascetic, but a married man with a taste for field sports. . ."[116] Taine's splendid conclusion was one with which Newman would have agreed.

> If we keep human weaknesses in mind, it may be said that nobleness of character in the clergy corresponded with nobleness of profession; in all points no one could dispute their capacity for self-sacrifice, for they willingly suffered for what they believed to be the truth. If, in 1790, a number of priests took the oath to the civil constitution of the clergy, it was with reservations, or because they deemed the oath licit; but, after the dismissal of the bishops and the Pope's disapprobation,

[115] *The Letters of Charlotte Brontë.* Volume One: 1829–47. ed. Margaret Smith (Oxford, 1995), pp. 289–90.
[116] Leslie Stephen. *Hours in a Library* (Folio Society, 1991), III, p. 45.

many of them withdrew it at the risk of their lives, so as not to fall into schism; they fell back into the ranks and gave themselves up voluntarily to the brutality of the crowd and the rigors of the law. Moreover, and from the start, notwithstanding threats and temptations, two-thirds of the clergy would not take the oath; in the highest ranks, among the mundane ecclesiastics whose scepticism and laxity were notorious, honor, in default of faith, maintained the same spirit; nearly the whole of them, great and small, had subordinated their interests, welfare and security to the maintenance of their dignity or to scruples of conscience. They had allowed themselves to be stripped of everything; they let themselves be exiled, imprisoned, tortured, and made martyrs of, like the Christians of the primitive church; through their invincible meekness, they were going, like the primitive Christians, to exhaust the rage of their executioners, wear out persecutions, transform opinion and compel the admission, even with those who survived in the eighteenth century, that they were true, deserving, and courageous men.[117]

The vitality of this French Catholic faith fairly made Tom's head swim. He described not only the Mass but what must have been peculiarly arresting for an English Protestant, "a large gaily-dressed doll, the very counterpart of which [could be seen] in many a London shop window, [before which] a crowd of women and children [were] on their knees, saying their prayers. It [was] the Virgin Mother . . ." Feeling an intruder in places of Catholic worship, Tom made a candid admission, which sheds light on the distance Newman travelled in overcoming his own prejudices against Rome. "The stranger may have heard of all this, and read of all this, and may have racked his brains about it to consider whether it comes within any reasonable comprehension. But there is a very old saying about the eyes doing their work quicker than the ears, and now you see it all. If the stranger has had to subscribe the Thirty-nine Articles, he has pronounced a very decided judgment on all this, and may justly have misgivings whether he has any right to be there, looking quietly upon what some of his neighbors at home call blasphemous mummery . . ."

This certainly was what Harriet considered the Roman Catholic faith to be. Dining with Charles X's former Prime Minister, Prince Jules de Polignac, who could not wait to see the back of Louis Philippe, Harriett conceded that both her French hosts and her husband and herself "felt equally and most sincerely the desire that the churches should be one . . ." But the grounds for any rapprochement struck Harriett as meagre. "I often try to think how far we might meet them in their doctrine and practices—but the more one thinks the more one's heart sinks within one." Harriett was particularly nettled when her French hosts suggested that the Puseyites would somehow lead the English into popery "unawares"—which she found "too absurd." "The infinity" of the French "ceremonies and forms" and "the complications" of their "traditional services" baffled her and "the notion of our doing anything of the kind in any of our churches" struck her as "too monstrous to dream of. There is nothing for those who would have such things but to go over at once to Rome."[118] In time, Newman and many others would agree.

---

[117] Hippolyte Taine, *The French Revolution* (Liberty Fund, 2002), III, pp. 1213–14.
[118] *Rem*, ii, pp. 134–5.

When Newman confided in his sisters that he would resign his St Mary's living in September 1843, Harriett was in Langrune and dismayed by how the news would be greeted by the French: "People here will be elated to the utmost."[119] Yet she claimed that she was reconciled to what she had seen coming: "I have long known it must be, and that now it was coming, and I feared it an experiment, but I trust it is not so." That Newman would have resigned his living as "an experiment" was a wild fear, which betrays how little Harriett appreciated her brother's thorough deliberations. Nonetheless, Harriett's letter confirms how closely Newman's career was followed in Europe. "M. Achille the other day showed me an Italian periodical with J.H.N.'s December letter translated with comments"—this was his "Retractation of Anti-Catholic Statements" which was published in the *Conservative Journal*. "It was very fairly written. They said that they were sure that such a learned and ingenious doctor would not stop there. He must go on and come over . . ."[120] Nearly 50 years later, in 1897, Oscar Wilde met a *curé* in Berneval-sur-Mer who was convinced not only that Edward Pusey was still alive but that God would convert the English "on account of England's kindness to the *prêtre exilés* at the time of the Revolution." It was to be "the reward of that sea-lashed land."[121]

Dispassionate though Harriett might have been about Newman's imminent resignation from St Mary's, she was incensed when Tom suddenly announced that he was contemplating converting to Rome himself. The devoutness of the French had made more of an impression on Tom than his wife dared to realize. "It all came upon me like a thunderclap on Tuesday," Harriett wrote Jemima. "He never gave me the slightest idea of what was passing in his mind—any more than always he is far more favorable and indulgent to the R.C.s than seems to me at all right. How he can possibly justify his step with regard to me I cannot imagine—lonely as I am in the midst of enemies. I only wish I were strong enough to put on paper what I see and hear every where of the workings of this wretched religion. Every hour is showing me what a showy, fallacious, false and hollow system it is."[122] Her husband's bombshell was all the more shocking because it was sent to her when she was alone in France—Tom had returned to England to attend to business relating to *The British Critic*. So she felt particularly betrayed, the victim of a plot that had been hatched in her absence.

Once Newman was apprised of what was happening, he counselled caution. "How unseemly to seem to be acting under excitement! If you ask me, I must plainly tell you that you *are* under excitement, and in no fit state to act for yourself."[123] Here, Newman was not giving any advice that he had not taken himself. "You cannot estimate, what so many (alas) feel at present," he told Jemima, "the strange effect produced on the mind, when the conviction flashes or rather pours upon it that Rome is the true Church. Of course, it is a most revolutionary, and therefore a most exciting tumultuous conviction. For this reason persons should not act under it. . ."[124] Tom must wait

[119] *Family*, p. 139.
[120] *Family*, pp. 139–40.
[121] *The Letters of Oscar Wilde* (London, 1962), p. 598.
[122] *Family*, p. 142.
[123] LD, 9:531 JHN to Thomas Mozley (21 September 1843).
[124] LD, 9:533 JHN to Mrs John Mozley (22 September 1843).

2 years and then decide. As it happened, Tom did wait and eventually decided to stay put in the Anglo-Catholic fold. Nevertheless, the episode rankled Harriett. Later, in Newman's resignation of his living at St Mary's, she saw papist betrayal, despite the clear honourable motives that prompted his decision. "I do so despair of the Church of England," Newman told her in a letter of 29 September 1843, "I am so evidently cast off by her, and on the other hand, I am so drawn to the Church of Rome, that I think it safer, as a matter of honesty, not to keep my living. This is a very different thing from any intention of joining the Church of Rome. However, to avow generally as much as I have now said would be wrong for ten thousand reasons . . . People cannot understand a state of doubt, of misgiving, of being unequal to responsibilities etc.—but they *will* conclude either that you have a clear view one way or the other. All I know is, that I could not without hypocrisy profess myself any longer a teacher in and a champion of our Church."[125] Harriett wrote Newman in late September asking him for some explanation as to what sparked his change of views, and Newman wrote back: "My present views were taken up in the summer of 1839 upon reading the Monophysite and Donatist controversies. I saw from them that Rome was the centre of unity and the judge of controversies. My views would not be influenced by the surface or the interior of the present French Church or of any other," an admission that seems to suggest that Harriett might have written to try to contest his views with some disparaging observations about the contemporary French Church, or at least the French Church she had recently witnessed. In all events, after Tom's sudden announcement, and Harriett's unfounded suspicion that Newman might somehow be partly responsible for her husband's abrupt change of allegiance, Harriett drew further and further away from her beloved brother. Of course, this was rash of Harriett, and unfair. As we have seen, Newman had nothing to do with Tom's decision and dissuaded him from doing anything in haste. Indeed, he had even offered to travel to France to speak with his distraught sister. But when it became clear that no mediatorial role from him would be welcome, Newman wrote Jemima on 29 September 1843: "Of course H's letter has *quite* made me give up any intention of going to her. Instead of being able to mediate, I find to my surprise that she considers me particeps criminis."[126] On 8 October 1843, Jemima responded apropos Tom: "If he will have patience, and wait the result of calm deliberation, he will do whatever he does in a better way, at any rate, not with unseemly speed, as if on the thought of the moment, the result of a childish admiration and novelty of foreign scenes . . ."[127]

Here, Jemima was too dismissive of how "foreign scenes" could affect a person's faith. After all, seeing Rome had been a milestone in the development of her brother's religious views. "What [can] I say of Rome," he had written Harriett in March 1833, when he finally reached the eternal city, "but that it is of all cities the first, and that all I ever saw are but as dust, even dear Oxford inclusive, compared with its majesty and glory. Is it possible that so serene and lofty a place is the cage of unclean creatures? I will not believe it."[128] Still, in warning Tom of what might be the likely consequence

---

[125] LD, 9: 537 JHN to Mrs Thomas Mozley (29 September 1843).
[126] LD, 9:536 JHN to Mrs John Mozley (29 September 1843).
[127] LD, 9:556 Mrs John Mozley to JHN (8 October 1843).
[128] LD, 3:230 JHN to Harriet Newman (4 March 1833).

of his converting, Newman described what would actually happen to him when he converted. "Now only think how any thing of this kind will prejudice those nearest and dearest to you against what you believe to be the truth . . . A deep, hopeless, bitter prejudice will sink into the minds of your whole family . . ."[129]

The references Harriett made to Newman in letters leading up to and following his conversion gave free vent to the bitterness she felt towards him and his new faith. Writing to Jemima in February 1845 of the encouragement John and Frank had given their brother Charles to try his hand at making a new career for himself in Germany, she could not resist getting in a dig at her eldest brother. "I think of late years Charles has struggled hard, and cannot now help what he is," she wrote of her inveterately hapless brother, but she thought "it a mistake to send him on his own resources to a strange country. It seemed to me a means of making the name notorious through Europe, as it has already through England . . ."[130] This showed not only her venom but her conventionality. The world mattered to Harriett, and it was perhaps inevitable that she should choose to regard Newman's conversion as a public embarrassment. "It is just like a disgraceful marriage," she told Jemima, "and he has been breaking it to his friends and to the world, just as a step of that kind is done." Preoccupation with the world and its good opinion also coloured Harriett's sense of humour. "I believe J.H.N. has been some time at Oscott," she wrote Jemima after Newman's conversion, "at least he was there a month or so ago. Do you know what they talk of doing? I believe it is the Pope's idea. Whosoever it is, it is a good one, and does credit to the wisdom of Rome, which I always respect. There is an old monastery at Oscott, which they think of repairing, and pitting therein all the new Anglican converts in a lump, with J.H.N. as Abbott. It is a most just, wise, and laughable scheme . . . One cannot think of it without amusement." Like Frank, Harriett was convinced that her brother's embrace of Roman Catholicism was something he would live to regret. . . "I do not understand," she wrote Jemima, "how it is you always say of J.H.N. 'I am afraid,' 'I fear he will be disappointed,' etc. etc. Surely you do not desire he should be satisfied? . . . He has chosen at a very mature age [Newman was 46]—he must abide by the consequences . . . We *know* he is wrong, and it seems unreal to say, 'I fear,' 'I'm afraid' . . ."[131]

Here, Harriett might have been speaking for many of her English contemporaries, who consoled themselves for the loss of Newman by predicting that the treacherous convert would come to a bad end in a church that could have no use for his compromised talents. The depth of Harriett's own prejudices against the Roman faith can be seen in her readiness to believe that her brother shared the same prejudices *after* he converted. To Jemima, she wrote: "I do not think you are right in talking about J.H.N.'s 'high theories of the Church of Rome.' I cannot tell what he may have said of late in letters to you. I cannot guess his tone—but in anything of his I have ever seen, he has a very low and degraded idea of the Church of Rome . . . The flagrant evil of his present step, as regards himself, is acting against his reason, and knowing it. If a man of reason (which

[129] LD, 9:531 JHN to Thomas Mozley (21 September 1843).
[130] *Family*, p. 155.
[131] *Family*, p. 165. Here, Harriet got her facts wrong: Oscott had never been a monastery: it was a school for the sons of Catholic nobility and gentry before Dr Wiseman offered it to Newman and other English converts as a place for study and meditation. Newman renamed the place Maryvale.

J.H.N. especially is) acts against his reason, suffer he must and ought. If he marries so, he does, and J.H.N. has a made a most disgraceful match—the consequences of which he must bear."[132] In this, she followed Frank, who could never convince himself that Newman really believed in what he regarded as the self-evident jiggery-pokery of papal Catholicism. This was a reaction to Newman's conversion shared by many of their English contemporaries. It is also why so many of these contemporaries were convinced that Newman, in his heart of hearts, was a sceptic. This was not simply a rhetorical slur, as some assume. Newman's contemporaries were convinced that he was one of them and in losing his faith in Anglicanism he had lost his faith altogether, and in this there was a kind of tribal pride: they refused to believe that one of their own, whatever his popish protestations, could truly believe in the Romanism that they themselves found so contemptibly unEnglish.

With views like these, it was perhaps understandable that Harriett should underestimate what would be the impact of her brother's conversion. "I feel sure that no step of J.H.N.'s . . . will effect people in general," she wrote Jemima. "A few partisans, who have been long hovering, like Oakeley, Dalgairns, St. John etc., most likely will accompany him. Private friends will more or less hold their tongues, but in general friend and foe will feel unmitigated displeasure, even disgust."[133] Later, in September 1846, she boldly predicted, "His influence will not be great any where . . . Most of the Anglicans who are inclined to use his name *have* taken their step, and the R.C.'s feel a just suspicion. . ."[134] By the same token, three years later, she was clearly disgusted by what she saw as the increasingly Romanizing character of the Tractarian party her brother had deserted. "I cannot help wondering what Dr. Pusey can say to it all," she writes to Jemima in March 1849. "He will *say* nothing, but somebody ought to make him. I cannot but think . . . that this public 'confession' of the Roman creed will have a good effect in making our foolish Crypto-Romanist party come to their senses and use of their own minds—those at least who are not like A. Froude, made unbelievers by the way."[135] When the hullabaloo surrounding the reconstitution of the English hierarchy was at its height, Harriett wrote Jemima in November of 1850 how, as she said, "I have had a great many calls lately and find every body up about the 'impudence' of the Pope and the Cardinal, 'St. Impudentia,' as he is called. The Pope has never made a false step, and that is saying a good deal." In her bitter aversion to this public demonstration of the revival of Romanism on English soil, Harriett was giving passionate voice to what her Huguenot mother would have felt if she had lived to see this revival. She also showed herself her mother's daughter when she wrote of how "After due defences of transubstantiation, purgatory, etc. etc. we shall have one on persecution. The Church of Rome has long wanted a Champion on all these points and for truth's sake she could never have so safe a one as J.H.N . . ."[136]

Harriett effectively broke off relations with her brother in 1843. Nine years later in July of 1852 she was dead of a heart attack. At the time, Newman was recovering from

---

[132] Ibid., pp. 165–6.
[133] Ibid., p. 163.
[134] Ibid., p. 175.
[135] Ibid., p. 186.
[136] Ibid.

the ordeal of the Achilli trial: during which he had been accused and convicted of libel by an apostate Italian priest, notorious for seducing women, in proceedings that remain some of the most egregious in English legal history. He was also completing his *Discourses on the Scope and Nature of University Education* (1852), which would later become the marrow of *The Idea of a University* (1873). Under normal circumstances, the sudden death of his sister would have been bad enough. But occurring, as it did, when so much else was happening in his life, Newman could scarcely take it in. "You may think how tried I am at this moment with my sister's death," he wrote Mrs.Bowden, after he received the devastating news. "I have not seen her for nine years. I have had a second letter this morning, but throwing no light upon it—I suppose she died worn out with years of mental fidget . . . All I know is . . . that her maid sat up with her, and at 5am finding her asleep, went to bed, too, and was found later in the morning by another servant asleep still, and Harriett by her dead."[137] It was fitting that he should have also shared the terrible news with Henry Wilberforce—one of Harriett's favourite people. "You will be greatly startled as I was to be told that my Sister Harriett died (I suppose) on Friday night in London . . . Poor Harriett, what a change from what it was, when first you knew us! What a world this is!"[138]

In a postscript, Newman added: "We ended the Synod yesterday in great triumph, joy, and charity." This was a reference to the first Provincial Synod of Westminster, held in July at Oscott. Earlier, in 1850, Nicholas Wiseman, the Vicar-Apostolic had been elevated to the cardinalate and instructed to reconstitute the territorial hierarchy in England. His pastoral letter announcing the reconstitution, "From out the Flaminian Gate," was met with raucous indignation throughout the country. Prime Minister Lord John Russell led the hue and cry by accusing Wiseman and his fellow Catholics of trying to subvert the country's Protestant order with what he called "papal aggression." *The Times* echoed Russell's indignation. "If this appointment be not intended as a clumsy joke, we confess that we can only regard it as one of the grossest acts of folly and impertinence which the court or Rome has ventured to commit since the Crown and the people of England threw off its yoke." Yet, at the same time, the *Times* was convinced that "The Pope and his advisers have mistaken our complete tolerance for indifference to their designs; they have mistaken the renovated zeal of the Church in this country for a return towards Romish bondage; but we are not sorry their indiscretion has led them to show the power which Rome would exercise if it could, by an act which the laws of this country will never recognize, and which the public opinion of this country will deride and disavow, whenever His Grace the titular Archbishop of Westminster thinks fit to enter his diocese." A few days later the paper returned to the subject by putting a very lively question, which must have caught Newman's eye: "Is it then here, in Westminster, among ourselves and by the English throne, that an Italian priest is to parcel out the spiritual dominion of this country—to employ the renegades of our national Church to restore a foreign usurpation over the consciences of men and to sow division in our political society?"[139]

[137] LD, 15:127 JHN to Mrs. Bowden (19 July 1852).
[138] LD, 15:126 JHN to Henry Wilberforce (18 July 1852).
[139] See *The Times*, 14 October 1850, quoted in Brian Fothergill. *Nicholas Wiseman* (London, 1963), p. 158 and *The Times*, 19 October 1850 quoted in Wilfrid P. Ward, *The Life and Times of Cardinal Wiseman* (London, 1912), 1, p. 540.

Newman responded to the furore the reconstitution set off with witty pugnacity. "As to the present row," he wrote one of his legal advisers, "I feel confident what our [Catholic] rulers have done is right . . . I have had nothing whatever to do with it . . . still I do believe that St Peter has come out of the Flaminian Gate, and not simply Nicholas Wiseman, and that he will be stopped by no 'Domine quo vadis?' outside the walls."

> And, to tell the truth, though I hate rows, I hate (I hope) humbug quite as much – and so much had got about lately at home and abroad to the effect that the British Lion had become a lamb, and that John Bull had become instinct with a diviner spirit, that liberals were Catholics, and the race of squires and parsons was extinct, that I do think it is a good thing to have matters put on their true basis. And then those wretched whigs, the μισητός στάσις of Hurrell Froude. I hope we are rid of them for ever. And then I suppose it will tend, especially if the row goes on, to bring together and consolidate the Catholic interest all over the Empire. The most serious thing is the collision with the radicals as far as there is one – but that must come – and there is not so much of it as I had expected. One thing the government may be quite sure of, that, though we shall try to escape breaking the law, if we can help, yet if they drive us to bay in a matter of principle, to a certainty we shall, whatever comes of it, though we are sent out after Smith O Brien.[140]

At the Synod, from Pugin's Chapel of St Mary's College, in one of his most powerful sermons, "The Second Spring," Newman hailed the phoenix-like recovery of the Church in England. Speaking of the Reformation, Newman reminded his listeners that "There was a struggle for a time" but the Church succumbed: "its priests were cast out or martyred."

> There were sacrileges innumerable. Its temples were profaned or destroyed; its revenues seized by covetous nobles, or squandered upon the ministers of a new faith. The presence of Catholicism was at length simply removed,—its grace disowned,— its power despised,—its name, except as a matter of history, at length almost unknown. It took a long time to do this thoroughly; much time, much thought, much labour, much expense; but at last it was done. Oh, that miserable day, centuries before we were born! What a martyrdom to live in it and see the fair form of Truth, moral and material, hacked piecemeal, and every limb and organ carried off, and burned in the fire, or cast into the deep! But at last the work was done. Truth was disposed of, and shoveled away, and there was a calm, a silence, a sort of peace;—and such was about the state of things when we were born into this weary world.[141]

The demise of the English Church was certainly unexpected, given its long history and its popularity with the people, but it was nothing as unexpected as its revival. "No one could have prophesied its fall, but still less would any one have ventured to prophesy

---

[140] LD, 14:154 JHN to Edward Badeley (3 December 1850). The Greek means "hateful faction." William Smith O'Brien (1803–64), an Irish nationalist, was convicted of high treason in 1848 and sentenced to be hanged, drawn and quartered until Queen Victoria commuted the sentence to transportation for life.

[141] *OS*, pp. 170–1.

its rise again. The fall was wonderful; still after all it was in the order of nature;—all things come to nought: its rise again would be a different sort of wonder, for it is in the order of grace,—and who can hope for miracles, and such a miracle as this? Has the whole course of history a like to show? I must speak cautiously and according to my knowledge, but I recollect no parallel to it."[142]

Yet, if this "Second Spring" was an answer to the prayer for renewal that Newman made in "The Invisible World," it was also an augury of sacrifices to come. The sacrifices that the English martyrs had made in the past could never be forgotten: "The long imprisonment, the fetid dungeon, the weary suspense, the tyrannous trial, the barbarous sentence, the savage execution, the rack, the gibbet, the knife, the cauldron, the numberless tortures of those holy victims . . ." At the same time, Newman hastened to make his listeners see that "Something . . . remains to be undergone, to complete the necessary sacrifice." He wished it were not so, "for this poor nation's sake.

> But still could we be surprised, my Fathers and my Brothers, if the winter even now should not yet be quite over? Have we any right to take it strange, if, in this English land, the spring-time of the Church should turn out to be an English spring, an uncertain, anxious time of hope and fear, of joy and suffering,—of bright promise and budding hopes, yet withal, of keen blasts, and cold showers, and sudden storms?
>
> One thing alone I know,—that according to our need, so will be our strength. One thing I am sure of, that the more the enemy rages against us, so much the more will the Saints in Heaven plead for us; the more fearful are our trials from the world, the more present to us will be our Mother Mary, and our good Patrons and Angel Guardians; the more malicious are the devices of men against us, the louder cry of supplication will ascend from the bosom of the whole Church to God for us. We shall not be left orphans; we shall have within us the strength of the Paraclete, promised to the Church and to every member of it.[143]

The sacrifices he himself had made had not been trifling. Scarcely 3 months after he converted, Maria Giberne had written to inform him that she had been left homeless as a result of her friend and roommate, Selina Bacchus marrying. Newman responded back that he and his fellow converts could entirely empathize with her. "Recollect that I, and all of us, have at this moment no home—or what is worse, are leaving what has been a pleasant home for some years. I felt nothing at leaving Oxford or St. Mary's— I feel a good deal leaving Littlemore." Although one can question whether he was being altogether truthful about Oxford and St Mary's, one cannot question the manifold bonds Newman had to see severed in order to enter the "One Fold of the Redeemer." It was in a spirit of hard-earned empathy, then, that he counselled his dear friend with words that he must often have applied to himself: "Take your present trial, as you do, as a gracious means of bringing you under the more intimate protection of your true friends, those Saints and Angels unseen, who can do so much more for you with God, and in the course of life, than any mere child of man, however dear and excellent."

[142] *OS*, p. 173.
[143] *SD*, p. 180.

In closing, Newman put his own sacrifices in perspective. "You speak as if I were not in your case, for, though I left Littlemore, I carried my friends with me, but alas! can you point to any one who has lost more in the way of friendship, whether by death or alienation, than I have? . . . So many dead, so many separated. My mother gone; my sisters nothing to me, or rather foreign to me; of my greatest friends Froude, Wood, Bowden taken away, all of whom would now be, or be coming, on my side. Other dear friends who are preserved in life not moving with me; Pusey strongly bent on an opposite course, Williams protesting against my conduct as rationalistic . . . Rogers and J. Mozley viewing it with utter repugnance. Of my friends of a dozen years ago whom have I now?" Still, Newman did not make this sad tally merely to grouse. The sacrifices had been bitter but the rewards were incomparably greater. "What did I know of my present friends a dozen years ago? why, they were at School, or they were freshmen looking up to me, if they knew my name, as some immense and unapproachable don; and now they know nothing, can know nothing of my earlier life; things which to me are as yesterday are to them as dreams of the past; they do not know the names, the state of things, the occurrences, they have not the associations, which are part of my own world, in which I live. And yet I am very happy with them, and can truly say with St Paul 'I have all and abound –' and moreover, I have with them, what I never can have had with others, Catholic hopes and beliefs – Catholic objects. And so in your own case, depend on it, God's Mercy will make up to you all you lose, and you will be blessed, not indeed in the same way, but in a higher."[144] However, if Newman was good at dispensing sound advice, he recognized that even sound advice was not always easily applied. When one of his younger friends, J. D. Dalgairns, who had been with him at Littlemore and joined him in the first English Oratory, lost his mother, Newman was front and center with heart-felt sympathy. "From what has befallen myself lately, I can do so better than any one else. After my sister's death, I lost an aunt [Elizabeth Good Newman died on August 1852], who had taught me to read and who lived with us till we grew up—my sister's death simply killed her."[145] Newman's troubles never came singly. In September 1852, he was looking at the very real prospect that he might be imprisoned as a result of the Achilli trial, and he was under attack by the unbalanced American convert Orestes Brownson for his theory of development. Moreover, knowing that he was being tried did not make the trial any less unbearable. Writing to Mother Margaret Mary Hallahan, he thanked her for her sympathy. "Indeed I need that sympathy, for things are getting worse daily . . ." Sometimes he even feared that he might not be up to the trial—a terrible thought for someone of Newman's fortitude. "I have felt from the first, I have for some time been braving the devil . . . There are times in one's life when, after the similitude of holy Job, one experiences a multitude of trials at once . . . And the worst of all is, I am not a bit the better for all this trouble—and seem to have no strength given me to bear it. So you see I really do need your prayers very much—and thank you for them."[146]

While adding to Newman's troubles at a time when they seemed scarcely endurable, Harriett exhibited something of the tenacity of English anti-Romanism. She also helped to acquaint her brother with reserves of strength that he may not have known

---

[144] LD, 11:102 JHN to Maria Giberne (28 January 1846).
[145] LD, 15:163 JHN to J. D. Dalgairns (12 September 1852).
[146] LD, 15:164 JHN to Mother Margaret Mary Hallahan (12 September 1852).

he possessed. But the greatest favour she paid him was helping him to see his own anti-Romanism, which would be the last obstacle he would scale before converting. Indeed, even as late as January 1840, he was "very rude to that zealous and most charitable man, Mr. Spencer, when he came to Oxford . . . to get Anglicans to set about praying for Unity." As Newman recalled in the *Apologia*, he might have been thrilled to see Spencer but he could not abide his conversion. "So glad in my heart was I to see him, when he came to my rooms with Mr. Palmer of Magdalen, that I could have laughed for joy; I think I did laugh; but I was very rude to him, I would not meet him at dinner, and that, (though I did not say so,) because I considered him 'in loco apostatæ' from the Anglican Church."[147]

The full extent of Newman's anti-Romanism has to be understood in order to understand how revolutionary his conversion was. Hilaire Belloc is useful in this regard. "You may potter about as much as you like with . . . half-truths and compromises," he wrote in an introduction to an American edition of the *Apologia* in 1928, "and all will be well; but make the great declaration of the Faith and you are in for martyrdom. Moreover, you strike a note quite different from anything the compromisers have ever heard before."[148] This was certainly Newman's case. When he finally repudiated the anti-Romanism at the heart of Oxford, he was met not only with fury but incomprehension. Again, Belloc was very clear-sighted on this crucial matter.

> If it be true that Anglicanism is the expression of English patriotism in religion, Oxford is, as I have called it, the very quintessence of Anglicanism: not of doctrines, for there are no doctrines, save repudiation of the Catholic Church. A man may deny the Resurrection, the Incarnation or what he will, so that he remain national and deny the Universal Church. Oxford means the very heart of this national thing, the Church of England.
>
> Now Newman was not only of Oxford, nor only in Oxford; he was, if one may use the metaphor, Oxford itself. He trembled with delight in his membership of this essentially anti-Catholic body; and when I say "essentially anti-Catholic" I mean the very word I use—"essentially." Not adventitiously, not as one out of many attributes, but as the very idea that makes Oxford what it is, you will there find opposition to the Catholic Church; to Ireland, to Poland, to Catholic culture as a whole, to Catholic history, to Catholic morals.
>
> Out of all that came Newman. To have been an undergraduate at an Oxford College was his happiest memory. To be elected a Fellow of an Oxford College his proudest moment. He lived within an extremely narrow Oxford circle, responding vividly to its every function. He was Oxford as Jane Austen was of the drawing room or Dickens of London. Even those parallels are not nearly strong enough. He

---

[147] *Apo.*, p. 117 George Spencer (1799–1864), younger son of Earl Spencer and brother of Lord Althorp, First Lord of the Admiralty, converted to Rome in 1829 and became a Passionist priest shortly thereafter. His descendants include not only Winston Churchill but Diana Spencer. Father Ignatius Spencer worked with Dominic Barberi, Ambrose Phillipps de Lisle and others to reconcile Anglicans to Rome in an effort to convert England. In 2007, his cause for canonization was submitted to Rome. See Margaret Pawley. *Faith and Family: The Life and Circle of Ambrose Phillipps de Lisle* (Norwich, 1993), pp. 48–98.

[148] Hilaire Belloc. Forward to *Apologia pro Vita Sua* (Chicago, 1930), p. ix.

was Oxford as Foch is of the French Army or as an intensely loving husband and father is of his own family . . . And out of that Newman came![149]

Again, one reason why Newman was accused so frequently of succumbing to scepticism was precisely because the Anglicans of his age could not imagine how anyone could repudiate the anti-Romanism at the core of Anglicanism and escape scepticism. Charles Kingsley expressed this view in a letter to Philip Gosse. "Many of your arguments," Kingsley wrote, referring to Gosse's book, *Omphalos* (1857), "are strangely like those of the old Jesuits, and those one used to hear from John Henry Newman fifteen years ago, when he, copying the Jesuits, was trying to undermine the grounds of all rational belief and human science, in order that, having made his victims (among whom were some of my dearest friends) believe nothing, he might get them by a 'Nemesis of faith' to believe anything, and rush blindfold into superstition. Poor wretch, he was caught in his own snare."[150] Harriett would not have disagreed.

Many things combined to show Newman the tragic enormity of English anti-Romanism, which, as one of Oxford's most loyal sons, he had made his own, but the cautionary example of Harriett's anti-Romanism might have been the most personally eye-opening. In all events, that he cared deeply for his sister and mourned her death cannot be doubted. Despite their estrangement, he thought of her continually.[151] If he made few references to her in his later correspondence, it was not for want of love but for the reticence of love. As was the case with all of his strongest feelings, he was silent about them out of respect for their preciousness.

·

[149] Ibid., pp. x–xi.
[150] Kingsley to Gosse (4 May 1858) in Edmund Gosse. *The Life of Philip Gosse* (London, 1890), pp. 281–2.
[151] LD, 11:112 JHN to Mr Thomas Mozley (13 February 1846). "Do not suppose I do not think of you and H. [Harriett] continually, because I do not write."

7

Jemima Newman and the Misery of Difference

In December 1852, Isaac Williams wrote Newman from Stinchcombe: "I can no longer forbear writing to you a few lines to express my deep sympathy and affection for you in your troubles—How can I forbear to do so when the mere thought of you fills my eyes as it has so often with tears? Of your trials I mean first and chiefly the loss of your sister Harriett, knowing what she once was to you and that you have so little remaining to fill up such a place in your mind . . ."[1]

However kindly meant, Williams' letter could only have brought back unhappy memories. Long before Harriett's death, Newman had seen their special bond disintegrate amidst bitter misunderstanding. To console himself, he turned to Jemima. Between 1839 and 1845, when he was deciding whether he could conscionably remain a teacher and minister within the Church of England, there was no correspondent with whom he wrote with greater candour than his dearly beloved middle sister. Between Newman and Jemima, there had always been a special affinity. Some could even detect physical similarities between the two.[2] Her future husband, John Mozley, the brother of Tom and James, wrote of her to his mother in 1835: "Miss Jemima is, as you have heard, not handsome, but is certainly a very pleasing person. She is more like Mr. Newman than her sister. At times there is both in expression and tone of voice a very strong resemblance."[3] Harriett referred to her as "quiet, sober, innocent Jemima."[4]

Like all of her brothers and sisters, Jemima was an avid reader, though she did not receive any formal education. Well-read in the English classics and familiar with Latin and French, she also had something of Newman's love of music (she played the piano) and was adept at mathematics. Far from stultifying the women of the early nineteenth century, such informal education often gave them a critical insight into the world around them that their more formally educated male counterparts lacked. This is one reason why so many were inspired to take up the literary profession: they needed a means to express this insight. Many exceptional female writers came into their own when the Newman sisters were growing up, including Jane Austen, Maria

---

[1] LD, 15:226–7 Isaac Williams to JHN (17 December 1852).
[2] Since James Anthony Froude thought Newman resembled Julius Caesar, this was hardly a resemblance that Jemima could find flattering.
[3] *Family*, p. 51.
[4] Ibid., p. xvii.

Edgeworth, Joanna Baillie, Elizabeth Gaskell, and Frances Trollope.[5] Harriett, as we have seen, attempted to join these writers when she turned to writing fiction of her own, though now her novels are all but forgotten. Nevertheless, we can see a good deal of the vivacious intelligence that animated the sisters from their correspondence. We can also see the great delight that their brother took in their discriminating society. When he was at Ealing School, he also appealed to their love of fun.

Ealing, April 12, 1815.

My dear Jemima,

It is always a great pleasure to me to write to you, for the following reason. If I write to Harriett she always requires a laughable letter, which is by no means suited to the dignity of my character, but you Jemima being conspicuously and wonderfully sedate yourself, always like a serious, sedate, sensible epistle. One thing in your letter disappointed me very much, and this it was. At the end you say, we all send our love with your affectionate sister, J. C. Newman. I consequently very naturally supposed that you were sent to me, as your letter seemed to imply it, and as there was a lumbering heavy lump of something or other at the bottom of the parcel, I concluded it must be you, and so I began to unpack this rapidly, to give you (as I thought) some fresh air, of which I did not doubt that you were in want. When to my surprise, having unpacked the said heavy lump, it proved to be a cake! And now I have touched upon the subject I will say two or three things about this said cake. I am very much obliged to Mama that she was so good as to be so punctual, then as to the cake itself I think it rather too much done, and that Mama must know if she has seen it. I liked Harriett's letter to Charles very much, excepting what related to Trusty, the trusty Trusty.[6]

Believe me ever, my dear Jemima, your affectionate Brother.[7]

The lively letters that went back and forth between Newman and Jemima in the pivotal years leading up to Newman's conversion and beyond are worth revisiting for a number of reasons. They show the special bond Newman and Jemima had. It was altogether characteristic of this bond, for example, that it should have been to Jemima that Newman wrote on 24 February 1841, his birthday: "I never had such dreary thoughts as on finding myself forty. Twenty-one was bad enough."[8] The letters show Newman's abiding need for sympathy at a time when he was contemplating a move that would separate him not only from St Mary's and his Oriel Fellowship but from friends and relatives of whom he was immensely fond, indeed an entire English way of life. They show Jemima's anguished inability to extend that sympathy to a brother whom she felt was leaving an imperfect for a false Church. They show how Jemima's refusal even to consider the claims of Rome informed Newman's later estimation of what the newly constituted English Catholic Church could expect from the English people as a whole. In a more general sense, they show what a vital constitutive role personal

---

5   For useful overviews of women in the early nineteenth century, see Joanne Shattock. *Women and Literature in Britain 1800–1900* (Cambridge, 2001) and "The Status of Women," in Boyd Hilton. *Mad, Bad and Dangerous People? England 1783–1846* (Oxford, 2006), pp. 371–53.
6   Trusty was the name of one of John Newman's horses.
7   LD, 1:16 JHN to Jemima Newman (12 April 1815).
8   LD, 8:44 JHN to Mrs John Mozley (24 February 1841).

experience played in the formation of Newman's thought. And, lastly, they corroborate and complement the account set out in his *Apologia Pro Vita Sua* of what Newman called "that great revolution of mind, which led me to leave my own home, to which I was bound by so many strong tender ties . . ."[9]

Welcoming the confidence her brother placed in her, Jemima was pleased to express her delight in the tremendous impact his work was having in what Newman would later refer to as the "Movement of 1833". "I am surprised yet pleased that you should think so much of what I say of your fifth volume of sermons," she wrote in January 1841, "because it shows how little you know of the estimation in which they are generally held. I think you will be glad to hear what I hear from all quarters, that they are more read than any of your writings; indeed it is a great comfort to me, for I cannot but think they are calculated to be of immense benefit . . . I am sure it is a great gift, that insight you show into human nature. When I think of people one calls decidedly 'clever men,' I see what I estimate in you is not their sort of talent; it is nothing intellectual; it is a sort of spiritual perception; and I wonder whether it is anything like the gifts in the Corinthian Church. Perhaps we might have the same gift in ours now if it was not so sadly neglected. Perhaps it may be met with in private clergymen, but I do not see it in any published sermons as strongly as in yours."[10]

This was accurately observed: Newman did manage to see more deeply into human nature by never overestimating the merely intellectual. Jemima's comments confirmed what Newman had argued in his fourth University Sermon, "The Usurpation of Reason" (1831), in which he wrote: "There is no necessary connexion between the intellectual and moral principles of our nature . . . on religious subjects we may prove any thing or overthrow any thing, and can arrive at truth but accidentally, if we merely investigate by what is commonly called Reason, which is in such matters but the instrument at best, in the hands of the legitimate judge, spiritual discernment."

When we consider how common it is in the world at large to consider the intellect as the characteristic part of our nature, the silence of Scripture in regard to it (not to mention its positive disparagement of it) is very striking. In the Old Testament scarcely any mention is made of the existence of the Reason as a distinct and chief attribute of mind; the sacred language affording no definite and proper terms expressive either of the general gift or of separate faculties in which it exhibits itself. And as to the New Testament, need we but betake ourselves to the description given us of Him who is the Only-begotten Son and Express Image of God, to learn how inferior a station in the idea of the perfection of man's nature is held by the mere Reason? While there is no profaneness in attaching to Christ those moral attributes of goodness, truth, and holiness, which we apply to man, there would be an obvious irreverence in measuring the powers of His mind by any standard of intellectual endowments, the very names of which sound mean and impertinent when ascribed to Him. St. Luke's declaration of His growth "in *wisdom* and stature," with no other specified advancement, is abundantly illustrated in St. John's Gospel, in which we find the Almighty Teacher rejecting with apparent disdain all intellectual display, and

---

[9] *Apo.*, p. 91.
[10] LD, 8:7 Mrs John Mozley to JHN (N.D.).

confining Himself to the enunciation of deep truths, intelligible to the children of wisdom, but conveyed in language altogether destitute both of argumentative skill, and what is commonly considered eloquence.[11]

J. C. Shairp, the Scottish literary critic and professor of poetry at Oxford, who wrote of "the beauty, the silver intonation of Mr. Newman's voice, as he read the lessons" at St Mary's, also saw the same insight into human nature that Jemima saw in her brother's sermons: "From his seclusion of study, and abstinence, and prayer, from habitual dwelling in the unseen, he seemed to come forth that one day of the week to speak to others of the things he had seen and known. Those who never heard him might fancy that his sermons would generally be about apostolical succession or rights of the Church, or against Dissenters. Nothing of the kind. You might hear him preach for weeks without an allusion to these things. What there was of High Church teaching was implied rather than enforced. The local, the temporary, and the modern were ennobled by the presence of the catholic truth belonging to all ages that pervaded the whole. His power showed itself chiefly in the new and unlooked for way in which he touched into life old truths, moral or spiritual, which all Christians acknowledge, but most have ceased to feel . . . Subtlest truths which it would have taken philosophers pages of circumlocution and big words to state, were dropt out by the way in a sentence or two of the most transparent Saxon."[12]

Newman and Jemima were also drawn together by memories of their beloved sister. In March 1828, 2 months after Mary's death, Jemima wrote her brother: "I cannot bear to think that I should ever cease to feel as much towards dear Mary, as I have all my life; but I think I am sure I shall not. I dare say strangers think us much at our ease, and in good spirits; but I always wish to say, when I speak to any one who did not know her, Ah you little think what she was to herself and to us all. Dear John, how you delighted me once, when you said 'she was so singularly good' . . ."[13] Nevertheless, despite their accord on this and so many other matters, their letters are full of the same portentous irony that informs the letters Newman and Harriett wrote one another. In 1826, Newman wrote Jemima about a project he was mulling over that he thought might take him 10 years to complete, which would "trace the sources from which the corruptions of the Church, principally the Romish, have been derived. The project would involve a reading of all the Fathers—200 volumes at least . . . all . . . the principle Platonists . . . an inquiry into Gnosticism . . . Rabbinical literature—and I know not what else . . ."[14] As it happened, it was his reading of the Fathers that first made him doubt the legitimacy of the Church of England. After the publication of *Lectures on the Prophetical Office of the Church* (1837), he wrote Jemima: "What you say about my book is very gratifying . . . I hear the same in various other quarters – and it is selling very well. It only shows how deep the absurd notion was in men's minds that I was a Papist; and now they are agreeably surprised. Thus I gain, as commonly happens in the long run, by being misrepresented . . . I shall take it out in an attack on popular Protestantism. I call the

[11] *US*, pp. 48–9.
[12] J. C. Shairp. *John Keble* (Edinburgh, 1866), pp. 13 and 15–16.
[13] LD, 2:62 Jemima Newman to JHN (17 March 1828).
[14] LD, 1:285 JHN to Jemima Newman (1 May 1826).

notion of my being a Papist absurd, for it argues on utter ignorance of theology. We have all fallen back from the Reformation in a wonderful way."[15]

The Cranmer Memorial gave proof that not everyone had "fallen back from the Reformation." Designed by Pugin's protégé Gilbert Scott (1811–78) to commemorate the deaths of Latimer, Ridley, and Cranmer, the three bishops burned at the stake by Queen Mary in 1555, the Memorial reaffirmed the Reformation's Protestant triumph. Pugin himself refused to take part in the Memorial, referring to the reformers in a pamphlet as "vile, blasphemous impostors pretending inspiration while setting forth false doctrines" and denouncing those who subscribed to it as "tyrants, usurpers, extortioners and liars."[16] Every English schoolchild knew what Hugh Latimer had told Nicholas Ridley moments before the venomous flames began to shrivel sinew and char bone: "Be of good comfort, master Ridley, and play the man. We shall this day light such a candle, by God's grace, in England, as I trust shall never be put out." The Memorial was designed to make sure that that light did not go out in Oxford. A clergyman named Pope, who had successfully put the touch on Newman for repairs to his church, wrote afterwards with an additional request: "Shall you be surprised to hear me say that I should much enjoy seeing your name on the list, if only to defeat the slanderers of yourself and friends . . . Do you not think my dear Newman *now* that Popery is avowedly making such rapid advance that a more decided Testimony than ever should be afforded from *every one* . . ."[17] Newman's response to this wheedling divine was fairly indignant.

> As to the Cranmer Memorial, it is in this place confessedly quite a failure–and before you ask me to subscribe, get the Dean and Students of Christ Church–the Fellows of Exeter–the Fellows of Trinity (Short, I believe is the sole subscriber) the Fellows of Oriel–the Fellows of Balliol . . . the Principal of Alban Hall . . . or the Provost of Oriel. . . . It is most preposterous to be called on to join so ramshackle tumbledown a concern got up by one or two men, and begun in spite against myself and others. They have only raised £5000, they want from £20,000 to £25,000. It would make me quite a laughing stock were I to join it . . . I care not if all the world, whom I know not, think me Papist–what is it to me? [No one] need commit himself to me or be implicated in my character. . . . To subscribe to this trumpery concern would be clean against my conscience, were it to save me from being proclaimed as a Papist at Paul's Cross. Never (as I think) will I do aught to imply any sort of liking for Cranmer.[18]

Even before the outcry over Tract 90 in 1841, Newman recognized that it was only a question of time before the Protestant party within the Anglican Church collided

---

[15] LD, 6:61 JHN to Mrs John Mozley (25 April 1837).
[16] Kenneth Clark. *The Gothic Revival: An Essay in the History of Taste* (London, 1962), p. 127.
[17] LD, 7:64 S. L. Pope to JHN (18 April 1839).
[18] LD, 7:64 JHN to S. L. Pope (21 April 1839) Apropos the subscription to the Memorial, a friend wrote Newman a letter that must have made him smile: "I say, old gentleman, I don't see your name among the subscribers to the Ridley and Latimer memorial (I can't afford it) –You must be a bit of a papist–Pray is Laud to be included among the list of Martyrs? What would I not give to have seen the effect produced by an amendment to that effect at the public meeting–" LD, 7:45 H. A. Woodgate to JHN (2 March 1839).

with what he followed his friend Richard Hurrell Froude in calling the "Apostolical party." In a letter to Jemima dated 17 November 1839, Newman gave an overview of the unhappy scene prior to Tract 90.

> The Heads of Houses are getting more and more uneasy. I should not wonder if the Bishop got uneasy (in which case, I suppose, I should resign the Living) and, I expect, the country clergy will be getting uneasy. I am quite in the dark what the effect of the new volumes of the Remains will be. They are much graver, but contain very strong opinions. I cannot guess where it will put us—I mean whether it will seriously displease influential people.—Then the question of the Fathers is getting more and more anxious. They are being published—and, for certain, persons will not find in them just what they expected. People seem to have thought that they contained nothing but the doctrines of Baptismal Regeneration—Apostolical Succession—Canonicity of Scripture and the like ... I cannot deny that from the first the Fathers do teach doctrines and a temper of mind which we commonly identify with Romanism. I never can be surprised, of course, at individuals going off to Romanism, but that is not my chief fear, but a schism in the Church i.e. those two parties, which have hitherto got on together as they could in the Church from the times of Puritanism downwards, gathering up into clear, distinct, tangible, forms—and colliding. Our Church is not at one with itself—there is no denying it. We have an heretical spirit in us. Whether it can be cast out, without "tearing" and destroying the Church itself, is quite beyond me. And then supposing on the other hand the Apostolical party be cast out, and without Bishops, what will they do?[19]

Newman's reference to the possible resignation of his living would certainly have alarmed Jemima, as would the prospect of an Anglican Church so divided that the Apostolical party would be "cast out . . . without Bishops." However, one assessed the situation, a set-to was imminent. Still, not all of Newman's letters to Jemima were taken up with the gathering conflict. He was always ready to share with her news of his parishioners. "Poor Mrs Quarterman is dead," he reported in one letter. "She went on month after month in the sad, uncomfortable, distressed way you recollect, always behind hand in her rent etc. At length I spoke to Pusey and he without my meaning it put her on his list of regular almswomen. This was a most exceeding great relief to her, and she was full of happiness and thanks; this was about a month since. Shortly after a place in the St Clement's Almshouses fell vacant, and the Master of University put her in. They say good fortune never comes single, but it was too much for her – she seems to have died of joy."[20] In March 1840, he decided to spend Lent at Littlemore, the chapel outside Oxford that was attached to St Mary's. In April 1835, the fellows of Oriel had provided land and partial support for the building of a new church in the village and in July of that year Mrs Newman laid the first stone after a grant from the Church Building Society contributed the necessary

---

[19] LD, 7:183 JHN to Mrs John Mozley (17 November 1839).
[20] LD, 6:225 JHN to Mrs John Mozley (6 April 1838). Newman's journal records the numerous occasions on which he visited Mrs Quarterman and left food packages for her.

balance. Newman's mother and sisters took a leading role in helping the poor of the neighbourhood, with funds generously donated by Newman. "The new Poor Law had not brought contentment to the countryside," Dorothea Mozley observed in her edition of the Newman family letters, "for even now labourers were only paid 1s. a day and pauperism was still encouraged."[21]

Harriett described the children of the neighbourhood as "red, dirty-cheeked, like bears."[22] In the letters that Newman wrote Jemima about the Littlemore schoolhouse he had set up he identified good grooming as his first priority. "My school perplexes me, at least the girl-school, for Mrs Whitman is perfectly incapable," he wrote. "I have been reforming, or at least lecturing against, uncombed hair and dirty faces and hands; but I feel I am not deep in the philosophy of school-girl tidiness, and do not expect the present air which the whole affair displays, will be much improved by my exertions. If I am obliged to take vigorous measures, which I cannot doubt I shall, I have this to back me, that the new Diocesan School Institution is about to send inspectors here, and that therefore all things must be put in the best possible trim." The man who would later write the greatest book on education in the language and found a university in Dublin dedicated to the teaching of universal knowledge was never above seeing to it that school children—whether at Littlemore or later at his Oratory School in Birmingham—were properly looked after. "The children are improving in their singing. I have had the audacity to lead them and teach them some new tunes. Also I have rummaged out a violin and strung it, and on Mondays and Thursdays have begun to lead with it a party of between 20 and 30, great and little, in the schoolroom. Moreover, I have just begun chanting and by way of experiment, a Gregorian Chant, which the children seem to take to, though they have not learned it yet—for, I see, it makes them smile—though that may be at me. I am catechizing them in Church too, and have got them on so far, that they take interest in it." Proof that he was making measurable progress inspired him to introduce other initiatives. "I have effected a great reform (for the time) in the girls' hands and faces – lectured with unblushing effrontery on the necessity of their keeping their work clean, and set them to knit stockings with all their might. Also, I am going to give them some neat white pinafores for Church use, and am going to contrive to make them make them. I saw some thing of the kind I liked at Bransgore in the Autumn, and have got [Mrs. Henry Wilberforce] . . . to send me a pattern with directions, which it would do your heart good to see . . . Also I have drawn up a sort of liturgy of School prayers varying with the seasons, on a hint I gained from some printed prayers etc. on pasteboard, done by some ladies in Sussex—and mean to have them hung up in the school room and used according to the day. I think I shall be a good deal here in future, for it does not do to begin and not go on. If I could get ground, I think I should build on it."[23] To his Aunt Betsey he admitted to feeling compunctious about how he was spending his Lent: "I have inflicted on Jemima a great deal of nonsense about my doings here. I am passing a most happy time. I came up here as a sort of penance during Lent; but though without friends or books, I have as yet had nothing but pleasure. So that it

---

[21] *Family*, p. 52.
[22] Ibid.
[23] LD, 7:285 JHN to Mrs John Mozley (1 April 1840).

seems a shame to spend Lent so happily."[24] Later, after he converted, he wrote from Edgbaston to his good friend Charles Marriott: "It is just possible one or two boys (G. Ryder's two sons . . .) may go from this place to Oxford tomorrow. Could you give them bread and cheese in the Porter's Lodge or elsewhere at 2 o'clock or 3 o'clock, if they make their appearance."[25] Little kindnesses of this sort for the children who passed through his life fill his letters. For Newman, the "simplicity of a child's ways and notions, his ready belief of everything he is told, his artless love, his frank confidence, his confession of helplessness, his ignorance of evil, his inability to conceal his thoughts, his contentment, his prompt forgetfulness of trouble, his admiring without coveting; and, above all, his reverential spirit, looking at all things about him as wonderful, as tokens and types of the One Invisible, are all evidence of his being lately (as it were) a visitant in a higher state of things."[26] In this delight in the wonder of children, Newman resembled G. K. Chesterton, who once spoke of how "The fascination of children lies in this: that with each of them all things are remade, and the universe is put again upon its trial. As we walk the streets and see below us those delightful bulbous heads, three times too big for the body, which mark these human mushrooms, we ought always primarily to remember that within every one of these heads there is a new universe, as new as it was on the seventh day of creation. In each of those orbs there is a new system of stars, new grass, new cities, a new sea."[27]

On 27 February 1841, Newman noted in his diary, "*this was the first day of the Number 90 row.*"[28] James Mozley, Newman's curate at St Mary's at the time and the younger brother of Tom and John Mozley, wrote his sister Anne the next day: "A new Tract has come out this last week, which is beginning to make a sensation. It is on the Articles, and shows that they bear a highly Catholic meaning; and that many doctrines, of which the Romanist are corruptions, may be held consistently with them. This is no more than what we know as a matter of history, for the Articles were expressly worded with a view to bring in R. Catholics. But people are astonished and confused at the idea now, as if it was quite new . . . Whether anything will really come of the matter I don't know. A hundred of the Tract sold in Oxford on Saturday. The Warden of Wadham is alarmed . . . ."[29] A few weeks later, alarm had turned to horror. "Those who have always thought the Articles ultra Protestant," Mozley wrote, "and have been accustomed to think so ever since they were born, are naturally horrified at the idea that even their stronghold does not protect them, and that the wolf may come in and devour them any day. The Heads have accordingly met, and very furious they were. The first day, I hear on good authority, some of them could not condescend even to a regular discussion of the question, so entirely had their vague apprehensions overpowered their faculties."[30] On 8 March, four college heads led by A. C. Tait of Balliol sent Newman a letter addressed "To the Editor of the Tracts of the Times," in which they charged that the Tract would "mitigate, beyond what charity requires, and to the prejudice of the pure truth of the

[24] LD, 7:286 JHN to Elizabeth Newman (1 April 1840).
[25] LD, 23:72 JHN to Charles Marriott (6 June 1853).
[26] "The Mind of Little Children" (1833) in *PS*, ii, p. 6, 65.
[27] G. K. Chesterton. "A Defense of Baby Worship," in *The Defendant* (London, 1903), pp. 112–17.
[28] LD, 8:45 Diary entry for Saturday, 27 February 1841.
[29] LD, 8:58 See *The Letters of the Rev. J.B. Mozley* (London, 1882), pp. 111–12.
[30] LD, 8:63 Ibid., pp. 112–13.

Gospel, the very serious differences which separate the Church of Rome from our own, and to shake the confidence of the less learned members of the Church of England in the Scriptural character of her formularies and teaching . . . In conclusion, we venture to call your attention to the impropriety of such questions being treated in an anonymous publication, and to express an earnest hope that you may be authorized to make known the writer's name. Considering how very grave and solemn the whole subject is, we cannot help thinking that both the Church and the University are entitled to ask that some person, besides the printer and publisher of the tract, should acknowledge himself responsible for its contents."[31] On 15 March, Frederick Temple (1821–1902), the fellow of Balliol and future Archbishop of Canterbury, who would later become a force among Liberal Anglicans, wrote to his mother, confirming Newman's prediction that renewed schism threatened to estrange those who did not share the Protestant view of the National Church:

> The disturbance about the Tract still continues, and I confess makes me feel very anxious . . . The Heads of Houses met the other day, and finding no one of their body knew anything of the Tract, separated to read it; but first voted a censure on Mr. Tait and the other three who had signed the Protest for not bringing it before them in the first instance, instead of referring in this way to public opinion . . . Newman will submit, I have no doubt, and withdraw the Tract, but the business will be very serious indeed if the matter is brought before University Convocation or before the Bishops; in the first case a schism in the Church would be almost inevitable, as there would be numbers coming up from the country to vote, who either believed Newman held correspondence with the Pope or else worshipped him. If it came before the Bishops I fear the result would be that Newman and his friends would leave the Church, and the reaction would be tremendous. I would not even express an opinion on the merits of the case; if you trust one party the Tract is a piece of the most complete Jesuitical juggling, if the other nothing can be more fair.[32]

Newman's own bishop, Richard Bagot was one of the latter, tacitly conceding that the reaction of the heads had been misguided, if understandable. "That the *object* of the Tract is to make our Church more Catholic (in its true sense) and more united," he wrote Newman, "I am satisfied,—and, as I have already said, I will not dispute upon what interpretations may or may not be put upon various articles,—but I cannot think it free from dangers, and I feel that it would tend to encreased disunion at this time. Under these convictions I cannot refrain from expressing my anxious wish that,—for the peace of the Church:—discussions upon the Articles should not be continued in the publications of the 'Tracts for the Times.'"[33] Newman agreed and thanked the Bishop for the "kind tone" of his letter. Jemima wrote Newman on 9 April commending him for his letter to the Bishop, which he had shared with her. "I really cannot but look upon that as a happy combination of circumstances which has extracted it from you,"

---

[31] LD, 8:59–60.
[32] LD, 8:78 and E. G. Sandford, *Frederick Temple: An Appreciation* (London 1907), pp. 58–9.
[33] LD, 8:94–5 Richard Bagot, Bishop of Oxford to JHN (17 March 1841).

she wrote, "for I think it tends more to set your *character* in a true point of view to well disposed persons than anything you have hitherto written."[34] Jemima might have particularly approved of the passage in which Newman wrote: "till we try to love each other, and what is holy in each other, and wish to be all one, and mourn that we are not so, and pray that we may be so, I do not see what good can come of argument."[35] "I knew all of this was in you," Jemima assured her brother, "but you must be aware that to persons who have not been brought up with you, or long accustomed to your manner of thought, yours is a difficult character. There is something which seems almost paradoxical which they cannot understand . . ."[36]

Bagot wrote Newman back a welcome letter. "Believe me that in anything I have said, or in anything I may hereafter suggest in a friendly manner, I am guided by a consideration for yourselves and the great good which it is in your power to effect, and which in many respects you have already done, as well as for the peace of the Church." Newman was grateful for this show of sympathy: "The kindness of your Lordship's letter of this morning brought tears into my eyes. My single wish . . . is to benefit the Church and to approve myself to your Lordship; and if I am not deceiving myself in so thinking, surely I shall in the end be blessed and prospered, however at times I may meet with reverses. I think of the text, 'Keep innocency, and take heed of the thing that is right, for that shall bring a man peace at the last.'"[37]

Whether Newman was aware of what the likely reaction to Tract 90 would be has always given rise to speculation. Isaac Williams, who was much in Newman's company at the time, cited the example of the private pamphlet Newman wrote on the Church Missionary Society in 1829, "recommending the clergy to join it, in order that, by their numbers, they might correct that Calvinistic leaven, on account of which they were opposed to it" to suggest that Newman could be very unaware indeed of how his writing might strike others. "This pamphlet (written in apparent simplicity as to its effect, like No. 90 afterwards) . . . would have entirely overturned that society . . ." Yet Williams doubted whether Newman was unaware of what the probable reaction to Tract 90 would be. Indeed, Williams claimed that before Newman wrote the Tract he had already resolved on converting to Rome. "He talked to me of writing a tract on the Thirty-Nine Articles, and at the same time said things in favour of the Church of Rome, which quite startled and alarmed me, and I was afraid he would express the same in this tract, with no idea (as his manner was) of the sensation it would occasion . . . On returning after the vacation, he said, 'I have written that tract after all, but you have no need to be alarmed, for I have got John Keble to look it over, and he says nothing against it.' . . . Yet, still, the sensation and the strong and bitter opposition it excited seemed to take Newman quite by surprise. . . . But his decided leaning to Rome came out to me in private, before that tract was written. . . . Nothing had as yet impaired our intimacy and friendship, until one evening, when we were alone in his rooms, he told me he thought the Church of Rome was right, and we were wrong,

[34] Mrs John Mozley to JHN (9 April 1841) in *Correspondence of John Henry Newman with John Keble and Others* 1839–1845 (London, 1917), p. 108.
[35] LD, 8:143 JHN to Richard Bagot (29 March 1841).
[36] Mrs John Mozley to JHN (9 April 1841) in *Correspondence of John Henry Newman with John Keble and Others* 1839–1845 (London, 1917), p. 108.
[37] LD, 8:101 JHN to Richard Bagot (20 March 1841).

so much so, that we ought to join it. To this I said that if our Church improved, as we hoped, and the Church of Rome also would reform itself, it seemed to hold out the prospect of reunion. And then everything seemed favorably progressing among ourselves. That mutual repentance must, by God's blessing, tend to mutual restoration and union. 'No,' he said, 'St. Augustine would not allow of this argument, as regarded the Donatists. You must come out and be separate.' This conversation grieved and amazed me . . ."[38]

Whether this is reliable is dubious. Williams wrote this account 10 years after Newman published Tract 90. Moreover, in his autobiography, written privately for the edification of his sons in 1851 but not published until 1892, Williams made no bones about how bitterly opposed he was to Newman's eventual secession. Even in the letter of condolence that he sent Newman after Harriett's death in December 1852, he could not resist adverting to their fallout: "My dear Newman, I do earnestly hope that we have a place in each others prayers—other offices of friendship have long ceased between us . . . of course there are many things which you think and do with which I cannot agree . . ."[39] Since one year prior to this, Williams was casting serious aspersions against Newman in his autobiography, it is difficult to resist the conclusion that Williams' anger at Newman for abandoning the Anglican Church coloured his recollection of events. For example, in the autobiography, he writes of Newman's intellectual development:

> The intellectual Oriel School, which had come through Whately, and in some degree infected Newman, was in the strongest contrast to that by which I had of late been trained. If my moral sense had been improved, not so the intellectual. And I find my Oxford sermons, for some time, were . . . directed against the pride of intellect and the dangers of theory and mere knowledge in religion, which is altogether a matter of practice. Yet this change that had been going on . . . in no way lessened by friendship and intimacy with Froude, but rather increased it; for, though naturally inclined to speculation, he was himself entirely of the Keble school, which in opposition to the Oriel or Whatelian, set ηθός above intellect; for I always looked upon the combination of these two schools in Newman, who was first a disciple of Whately's and then of Keble's, as the cause of such disastrous effects, which have now, in him, united German rationalism with the Church of Rome, in their full development.[40]

Many have put forward wild theses about Newman's thinking but Williams is the only commentator to claim that it resembles German rationalism.[41]

After publishing Tract 90, Newman found himself in an impossible position. Although increasingly convinced that the Church of Rome was the true Church, he

[38] *Autobiography of Isaac Williams* (London, 1892), p. 108.
[39] LD, 15:226 Isaac Williams to JHN (17 December 1852).
[40] *Autobiography of Isaac Williams* (London, 1893), p. 46.
[41] Cf. LD, 24:274 JHN to Louisa Simpson (25 June 1869) "I can never prophesy what will be useful to a given individual and what not. As to my Sermons, I was astonished and (as you may suppose) deeply gratified by a stranger, an Anglican Clergyman, writing to me a year or two ago to say that reading them had converted him from free thinking opinions, which he had taken up from German authors, or from living in Germany."

was still Vicar of St Mary's and sworn to uphold the Thirty Nine Articles. As he wrote to his fellow Tractarian Henry Wilberforce in 1843, "I am much out of heart . . . because I wish to be out of hot water and something or other is always sousing me again in it. It is so very difficult to steer between being hypocritical and revolutionary." Most fair-minded readers will see a kind of embattled integrity in Newman's handling of his predicament, though this did not stop M. G. Brock, editor of the nineteenth-century volumes of *The History of the University of Oxford* from claiming that "He stands in the Oxford tradition of Wycliffe and Wesley—inspired, disruptive and a stranger to moderation."[42] This is typical of the denigratory assessment of Newman and his conversion that still obtains in many quarters in his old university. A more balanced view of the matter can be found in the memoir of the Oxford Movement left behind by the fair-minded J. C. Shairp. Speaking of the years leading up to Newman's conversion, Shairp wrote: "Then followed the resignation of his fellowship, the retirement to Littlemore, the withdrawal even from the intercourse of his friends, the unloosing of all the ties that bound him to Oxford, the two years' pondering of that step he was about to take, – so that when in 1845 he entered the Church of Rome, he did it by himself, making himself as much as possible responsible only for his own act, and followed by but one or two young friends who would not be kept back. Those who witnessed these things, and knew that, if a large following had been his object, he might, by leaving the Church of England three years earlier, in the plenitude of his power, have taken almost all the flower of young Oxford with him, needed no *Apologia* to convince them of his honesty of purpose."[43]

If Tract 90 made Newman's position with regard to the Anglican faithful difficult, the Jerusalem Bishopric made it worse. Once the Prussian ambassador to Rome, Baron Bunsen broached the idea of a Jerusalem Bishopric, which would establish a joint Lutheran and Anglican Bishopric in the Holy Land, Newman wrote his good friend John Bowden: "It is quite plain that our Rulers can unchurch us, and I have no assurance that there is not a great scheme afloat to unite us in a Protestant League, the limits of which no one can see."[44] In November 1841, Newman wrote Jemima: "This Jerusalem matter is miserable . . . I have delivered in a formal protest to my bishop—which when it comes to be known will make a stir. It is to the effect that I consider the measure (if carried out) as 'removing the Church of her present position and tending to her disorganization.'"[45] Still, Newman counselled Jemima against making any rash inferences from this protest: "Do not believe any absurd reports. They talk in the papers of secession from among us to Rome. Do not believe it. Not one will go."[46] Jemima wrote back thanking her brother "for your interesting and important letter. It is the darkest view I have seen of things for a long time—that does not show it is not a true one . . . At any rate, John, I do not see how any decision of the University can affect you . . . while you are protected by your Bishop. Certainly, this Jerusalem Bishoprick seems a very superfluous wound to the Church . . ."[47] Here, Jemima misjudged.

[42] *The History of the University of Oxford.* Vol. 6: *Nineteenth-Century Oxford. Pt. 1.* ed Brock and Curthoys (Oxford, 1997), p. 69.
[43] J. C. Shairp. *John Keble* (Edinburgh, 1866), pp. 25–6.
[44] LD, 8:329 JHN to J. W. Bowden (13 November 1841).
[45] LD, 8:334–5 JHN to Mrs John Mozley (16 November 1841).
[46] LD, 8:334 JHN to Mrs. John Mozley (16 November 1841).
[47] LD, 8:341 Mrs. J. Mozley to JHN (23 November 1841).

The Jerusalem Bishopric ultimately contributed not only to Newman's decision to leave the Anglican Church but to Henry Edward Manning's and James Hope-Scott's. Jemima was on firmer ground when she spoke of matters closer the heart. "My great trust is that you will be supported through this trial, that you may act as firmly as you have hitherto done. You must not think that I am at all afraid of you, or doubtful of you. I only feel more and more thankful that you have more judgment and clearsightedness than the rest of the world, so as to steer through a most difficult course . . . . I often think what a wonderful creature you are, and what a singular history yours is–and then, I wish we were not so far apart."[48]

Why Newman continued to pledge allegiance to the Anglican Church when he disapproved so of its rejection of 'catholic' truth, of which the furore over Tract 90 and the Jerusalem Bishopric were only two examples, is a question which has prompted much conjecture. Many of his contemporaries, including some of his siblings, looked back on his Anglican career after he had converted and wondered if he had not been a papist all along only masquerading as an Anglican. On this matter, there is an interesting exchange between Newman and William Dodsworth, Pusey's curate at Christ Church, which suggests one reason why Newman remained loyal to the Anglican Church for as long as he did. "The Jerusalem matter . . . is what quite unnerves me," Newman told Dodsworth in December 1841. "It is so wanton an innovation. But I trust that Hope's pamphlet shows that we may weather the danger." James Hope [later, James Hope-Scott], a Tractarian and good friend of Newman, who later converted to Rome and donated the lion share of his considerable fortune to various Catholic charities, wrote a pamphlet questioning the legality of the Bishopric.[49] That Newman welcomed Hope's pamphlet showed how loyal he was to his "catholic" conception of the Anglican Church and how ready he was to see it rescued from its protestant foes. "I am sure that they are the worst friends of the Church who refuse to look dangers in the face," he wrote. "Her best friends are those who, instead of shutting their eyes, tell us when she is in danger. For centuries she has been wasting away, because persons have made the best of things and palliated serious faults. Of course directly one speaks out, one is accused of intending to Romanise—but I would speak out to prevent what silence would not tend a whit to prevent, but to excuse." For Newman, these contests between "catholicity" and Protestantism within the Anglican Church would only prove Romanizing if they were shirked. "Confidence is shaken," he conceded, "and when once a doubt of our Catholicity gets into the mind, it is like a seed—it lies for years to appearance dead—but, alas, it has its hour of germinating or is ever threatening. It should ever be borne in mind that no serious movement towards Rome took place, in fact, till the year 1841, when the authorities of the Church had more or less declared themselves against Catholic truth."[50]

William Dodsworth could not have agreed with Newman more. In a footnote to his sermon, "Allegiance to the Church," published in 1841, he confirmed "that no instance can be adduced of a well-instructed member of the Church of England, trained in Catholic principles, and of competent knowledge of Catholic antiquity, having ever

---

[48] LD, 8:363 Mrs John Mozley to JHN (3 December 1841).
[49] Hope's pamphlet was *The Bishopric of the United Church of England and Ireland at Jerusalem, Considered in a Letter to a Friend* (London 1841).
[50] LD, 8:392 JHN to William Dodsworth (27 December 1841).

joined the Church of Rome."[51] Indeed, Dodsworth was so intent on preserving "the good cause of Catholicism" within the Anglican Church that in November 1839 he shared with Newman the news that J. R. Bloxam, Newman's curate at Littlemore, had allegedly been seen bowing down at the elevation of the host at a mass at Alton Towers.[52] Bloxam's biographer, R. D. Middleton called Dodsworth a "heresy hunter," but the interesting thing about his report was not that it was the tattling of a busybody but that it showed that Dodsworth's High Church principles were not entirely dissimilar to Newman's Tractarian principles when it came to keeping the Anglican Church properly "catholic," an object, which, of course, the Jerusalem Bishopric threatened.[53] That Dodsworth ultimately followed Newman into the Catholic Church in 1851 after the Gorham Case confirms that there was no inconsistency between one's being loyal to the Anglican Church when it could still be considered recognizably "catholic" and switching one's allegiance to Rome after the Anglican Church clearly repudiated what Newman called "Catholic truth." In this regard, all of the conversions after the Gorham Trial, including Dodsworth's own, proved Newman's point that "we have raised desires, of which our Church does not supply the objects," and there would be some who would not be able "to keep from seeking those objects where they are supplied."[54]

A fairly succinct account as to why Newman took six years to convert can be found in the *Apologia*, where he addressed quite openly the related charge that he was slow to convert because he was somehow "shuffling" and "underhand." After observing that "I never had any suspicion of my own honesty . . ."[55] Newman accounted for his protracted deliberations thus: "I felt altogether the force of the maxim of St. Ambrose, 'Non in dialectica complacuit Deo salvum facere populum sum'—I had a great dislike of paper logic. For myself, it was not logic that carried me on; as well might one say that the quicksilver in the barometer changes the weather. It is the concrete being that reasons; pass a number of years, and I find my mind in a new place; how? the whole man moves; paper logic is but the record of it. All the logic in the world would not have made me move faster towards Rome than I did; as well might you say that I have arrived at the end of my journey, because I see the village church before me, as venture to assert that the miles, over which my soul had to pass before it got to Rome, could be annihilated, even though I had been in possession of some far clearer view than I then had, that Rome was my ultimate destination. Great acts take time."[56]

Apropos the charge that he delayed his conversion in order to bring as many converts with him as he could when he did convert, he was amusingly categorical: "if a man said to me, 'You tried to gain me over to your party, intending to take me with you to Rome, but you did not succeed,' I can give him the lie, and lay down an assertion of my own as firm and as exact as his, that not from the time that I was first unsettled, did I ever attempt to gain any one over to myself or to my Romanizing opinions, and

51 LD, 8:392, See Note 1.
52 LD, 7:xix and LD, 7:184 William Dodsworth to JHN (18 November 1839).
53 R. D. Middleton. *Magdalen Studies* (London, 1936), pp. 40–1.
54 LD, 7:186 JHN to William Dodsworth (19 November 1839).
55 *Apo.*, p. 153.
56 Ibid., pp. 155–6.

that it is only his own coxcombical fancy which has bred such a thought in him . . ."[57] The record corroborates Newman on this. If anything, while still an Anglican, he was careful to dissuade would-be Catholics from converting, though John Keble was a notable exception.[58]

By February 1842, Newman had decided to move to Littlemore. "'I am going up to Littlemore', he wrote Jemima, and my books are all in motion . . . It makes me very downcast—it is such a nuisance taking steps . . ."[59] Newman's stock taking could only have exacerbated Jemima's apprehensions. "For some years," he wrote, "I have felt that I am out of place at Oxford . . . Every one almost is my junior. And then added to this is the hostility of the Heads, who are now . . . taking measures to get the men from St. Mary's. But I think I have made up my mind . . . to anticipate them by leaving off preaching at St. Mary's. I shall tell no one—being here is an excuse—and I can at any time begin again. But I think my preaching is cause for *irritation*."[60] Jemima assured him that his preaching had a profound impression on her, especially his *Oxford University Sermons*, in a letter which demonstrates that she understood her brother's thinking very much better than Isaac Williams did. "I am sufficiently advanced in your University Sermons," she wrote, "to say how very much pleased I am with them . . . I do not know any volume I have ever read that was so attractive and satisfying to my mind except Butler's Analogy. It makes deep things so very simple. I was particular pleased with your second sermon ["The Influence of Natural and Revealed Religion Respectively"], as laying down principles so clearly. It seems to account for things one has wondered at all one's life . . . I tell you this because I think you sometimes like to know the impression your works make on readers . . . I have mentioned one sermon only, though there is a good deal to remark on in each. Each seems to have a little world of its own . . ."[61]

Proof that Jemima was not the only one deeply affected by his sermons came two months later in May 1843, when John Joseph Gordon, William Dodsworth's curate at Christ Church, St Pancras, wrote Newman. "Few things would have given me so much pleasure, as to have had the opportunity of expressing in person the debt of gratitude I . . . owe to you for the blessing of your books, especially your sermons . . . Being in Oxford I cannot bring myself to leave it, without . . . conveying my most sincere thanks . . ."[62] Four years later, Gordon would convert to Rome and, a year after that, he joined the Birmingham Oratory. After joining the Oratory, he was dispatched to Italy to collect evidence for Newman's defence in the Achilli trial. In his diary, he recorded the impression Newman's sermons left on him before he converted: "I was not in the least disappointed by my anticipations, which is saying a great deal. I thought I should have wept at times from mere fullness of heart . . ."[63] In 1847, Gordon was instrumental in converting George Tylee, whom he had known at Cambridge. Tylee, who retired

---

[57] Ibid., p. 153.
[58] See Edward Short. *Newman and his Contemporaries* (London, 2011), pp. 22–83.
[59] LD, 8:456 JHN to Mrs John Mozley (6 February 1842).
[60] LD, 8:463 JHN to Mrs John Mozley (15 February 1842).
[61] LD, 9:294 Mrs John Mozley to JHN (25 March 1843) Jemima was referring to Joseph Butler's *The Analogy of Religion Natural and Revealed to the Constitution and Course of Nature* (1736).
[62] LD, 9:360 John Joseph Gordon to JHN (28 May 1843).
[63] LD, 12:431.

from the Army with the rank of Major-General, married Catherine Ward in 1857. Ward converted in July 1849, after being influenced herself by Newman's sermons and by his wonderfully catechetical letters. Here were only three people whose lives were permanently changed by reading Newman; the total number, even during his own lifetime, would be impossible to tally.

As 1843 progressed, Newman began to reconsider the object he had set himself of rescuing the Anglican Church from its Protestant proclivities. On 28 August, he wrote Jemima: "There are reasons enough to make me give up St. Mary's, but, were there no other, this feeling would be sufficient, that I am not so zealous a defender of the established and existing system of religion as I ought to be for such a post."[64] In expressing her confidence that Newman's Anglican allegiance would somehow survive this insuperable objection, Jemima clearly showed that she did not grasp what her brother was trying to tell her. "I am very anxious, dear John, but not anxious" she blithely wrote. "It seems odd, but I cannot have that sort of feeling about you. You have been brought through so many strange situations, that I trust you will be preserved in what is to come. I shall be sorry if you give up St. Mary's in compliment to clamor."[65] Later, she was more hopeful still. "You are indeed in a wonderful position—may you be enabled to bear up in the same, as one of the true champions of our Church, not tired by all the opposition and calumny which have assailed you on all sides."[66] When it became clear that her optimism was not well-founded, Jemima took another tack. "Your letter has, as you may imagine, concerned me greatly. I do hope you may not have quite settled on the step of giving up St. Mary's just at this critical time. I know you have long had thoughts turned to this point, and I have by degrees learned to reconcile myself to the prospect; but I cannot think you are aware of the effect of every thing you do upon people in general . . ."[67] This must have struck Newman as cruelly wide of the mark: of course, he was aware of how his actions affected others; but that did not make his decision any easier.

> "My dearest Jemima, my circumstances are not my making. One's duty is to act *under* circumstances."
>
> Is it a light thing to give up Littlemore? am I not providing dreariness for myself? If others, whom I am pierced to think about, because I cannot help them, suffer, shall I not suffer in my own way?
>
> Everything that one does honestly, sincerely, with prayer, with advice, must turn to good. In what am I not likely to be as good a judge as another? In the consequences? True—but is not this what I have been ever protesting against, going by expedience, not by principle? . . . if this be a case of duty, and if I be able to judge whether or no it is, I must leave the consequences to Him who makes it a duty.[68]

That what Newman seemed set to do was already affecting others was clear from a letter that Jemima received from an aggrieved Tractarian lady. "There is something

[64] LD, 9:479 JHN to Mrs John Mozley (28 August 1843).
[65] LD, 9:361 Mrs John Mozley to JHN (28 May 1843).
[66] LD, 9:441 Mrs John Mozley to JHN (27 July 1843).
[67] LD, 9:489 Mrs John Mozley to JHN (30 August 1843).
[68] LD, 9:490–1 JHN to Mrs John Mozley (31 August 1843).

sad enough and discouraging enough in being shunned and eyed with distrust by neighbors, friends, and clergy—but, while we have had some one to confide in, to receive instruction from, this has been borne easily. A sound from Littlemore and St. Mary's seems to reach us even here, and has given comfort on many a dreary day—but, when the voice ceases, [some] of the words it has already spoken will lose some of their power—we shall have sad thoughts when we read them. Such was our guide, but he has left us to seek our own path—our champion has deserted us—our watchman whose cry used to cheer us is heard no more."[69] Then, Jemima's brother-in-law James Mozley wrote, making sure that Newman had no doubt as to the sense of betrayal which his own doubts were causing the Tractarian remnant. For Newman to give up Littlemore and St Mary's "does seem to me a heavy blow and grievous loss," wrote James, "not to yourself—for I can easily understand that [you] will be glad to get rid of the responsibilities in the present state of things—but to us and the cause of Oxford."[70] By the late summer and early autumn of 1843, Newman had reconciled himself to abandoning the cause of Oxford. On 7 September, he wrote his bishop, Richard Bagot, "I shall give your Lordship much pain, by the request which it is necessary for me to make of your Lordship, before I proceed to act upon a resolution on which I have made my mind up for a considerable time. It is to ask your Lordship's permission to resign the living of St. Mary's." A week later, Newman put this momentous decision into some perspective in a letter to his sister. "If there were no other reason in the world, why I should not undertake a parochial cure in our Church, this alone would suffice for the future that there is no confession. I cannot understand how a clergyman can be answerable for souls, if souls are not submitted to him. There is no real cure of souls in our Church."[71] Although St. Augustine, the great proponent of auricular confession, would have approved, Pusey braced himself for the worst. "It seems as if heavy times were coming," he wrote John Keble, "and that we were but at 'the beginning of sorrows.'"[72]

To give Pusey his due, although he mischievously charged that undue sensitivity swayed Newman's decision, he also acknowledged the part that conviction played. In the *English Churchman*, he wrote to his fellow Anglo-Catholics of how, as he said, "We ought not indeed to disguise the greatness of [our loss]. It is the intensest loss we could have had. Those who have won him knew his value. It may be a comfort to us that they do . . . Our Church has not known how to employ him . . . He is gone unconscious (as all great instruments of God are) of what he himself is. He has gone as a simple act of duty, with no views for himself, placing himself entirely in God's hands. And such are they whom God employs."[73]

Later, on his first anniversary as a Catholic, Newman looked back on his days as an Anglican with astonished recoil: "In my dealings with my people [that is to say, with his erstwhile Anglican brethren] I so keenly felt the want of ecclesiastical authority over them, the need of obligatory confession to know their state, that the cure of souls

---

[69] LD, 9:491 See "From a Lady to Mrs. John Mozley" (30 August 1843).
[70] LD, 9:491 James B. Mozley to JHN (31 August 1843).
[71] LD, 9:523 JHN to Mrs John Mozley (15 September 1843).
[72] LD, 9:534 E. B. Pusey to J. Keble (23 September 1843).
[73] Henry Tristram. *Newman and his Friends* (London, 1933), p. 53.

was always a dreadful burden. I had the responsibility without the means to fulfill it."[74] The antipathy of the English to the Roman confessional was nicely articulated by the Third Marquess of Salisbury in the House of Lords in 1877 when the great conservative Prime Minister spoke of how, "It so happens that this practice is deeply opposed to the peculiarities and idiosyncrasies which have developed among the English people ever since they became a free people. The English people are specially jealous of putting power unrestricted into the hands of a single man. More than any other system the practice of habitual confession does put unrestricted and irresponsible power in the hands of a single man. An Englishman values and cherishes the private independence of his family life; he looks with abhorrence upon any system that introduces another power into that family life, that introduces a third person between father and daughter, between husband and wife."[75] That Lord Salisbury should have cited the interests of the family as grounds for rejecting auricular confession would not have surprised Newman: it was commonplace among English prejudices. In his own catalogue of Protestant misconceptions of the Catholic faith, *Present Position of Catholics in England* (1851), Newman took up the issue of confession to put the Protestant revulsion from it in some perspective.

> How many are the souls, in distress, anxiety or loneliness, whose one need is to find a being to whom they can pour out their feelings unheard by the world? Tell them out they must; they cannot tell them out to those whom they see every hour. They want to tell them and not to tell them; and they want to tell them out, yet be as if they be not told; they wish to tell them to one who is strong enough to bear them, yet not too strong to despise them; they wish to tell them to one who can at once advise and can sympathize with them; they wish to relieve themselves of a load, to gain a solace, to receive the assurance that there is one who thinks of them, and one to whom in thought they can recur, to whom they can betake themselves, if necessary, from time to time, while they are in the world. How many a Protestant's heart would leap at the news of such a benefit, putting aside all distinct ideas of a sacramental ordinance, or of a grant of pardon and the conveyance of grace! If there is a heavenly idea in the Catholic Church, looking at it simply as an idea, surely, next after the Blessed Sacrament, Confession is such. And such is it ever found in fact,—the very act of kneeling, the low and contrite voice, the sign of the cross hanging, so to say, over the head bowed low, and the words of peace and blessing. Oh what a soothing charm is there, which the world can neither give nor take away! Oh what piercing, heart-subduing tranquillity, provoking tears of joy, is poured, almost substantially and physically upon the soul, the oil of gladness, as Scripture calls it, when the penitent at length rises, his God reconciled to him, his sins rolled away for ever! This is confession as it is in fact; as those bear witness to it who know it by experience; what is it in the language of the Protestant? His language is, I may say, maniacal; listen to his ravings, as far as I dare quote them, about what he knows just as much of as the blind know of colours: "If I could

[74] LD, 11:258 JHN to Miss Parker (9 October 1845).
[75] Salisbury quoted in Geoffrey Best. "Popular Protestantism," in *Ideas and Institutions of Victorian Britain: Essays in Honour of George Kitson Clark* (London, 1967), p. 137.

follow my heart wherever it would go," he cries about the priest, "I would go into his dark and damnable confessional, where my poor Roman Catholic countrymen intrust their wives and daughters to him, under the awful delusion of false religion; and, while the tyrant is pressing his . . . infernal investigation, putting the heart and feeling of the helpless creature on the moral rack, till she sink enslaved and powerless at his feet, I would drag the victim forth in triumph from his grasp, and ring in the monster's ear, No Popery!"[76]

Nearly 3 years after his conversion, Newman wrote Henry Bourne, a convert, who had heard rumours that Newman regretted his conversion: "I have not had any feeling whatever but one of joy and gratitude that God called me out of an insecure state into one which is sure and safe, out of the war of tongues into a realm of peace and assurance." Nevertheless, Newman did regret having to leave so many good people behind: "it pierces me to the heart to think that so many excellent persons should still be kept in bondage in the Church of England, or should, among the many good points they have, want the great grace of *faith*, to trust God and follow His leadings. This is the state of my mind, and I would it could be brought home to all and every one, who, in default of real arguments for remaining Anglicans, amuse themselves with dreams and fancies."[77]

On 25 September 1843, at Littlemore, Newman preached his last Anglican sermon, "The Parting of Friends," in the peroration of which he implored his hearers to pray for him.

And, O my brethren, O kind and affectionate hearts, O loving friends, should you know any one whose lot it has been, by writing or by word of mouth, in some degree to help you thus to act; if he has ever told you what you knew about yourselves, or what you did not know; has read to you your wants or feelings, and comforted you by the very reading; has made you feel that there was a higher life than this daily one, and a brighter world than that you see; or encouraged you, or sobered you, or opened a way to the inquiring, or soothed the perplexed; if what he has said or done has ever made you take interest in him, and feel well inclined towards him; remember such a one in time to come, though you hear him not, and pray for him, that in all things he may know God's will, and at all times he may be ready to fulfil it.[78]

This was a genial conclusion. In an earlier section, however, to remind his auditors that there had been bitter aspects about his Anglican tenure, he cited barbed references to St Luke: "O Jerusalem, Jerusalem, which killest the prophets, and stonest them that are sent unto thee, how often would I have gathered thy children together, as a hen doth gather her brood under her wings, and ye would not! Behold, your house is left unto you desolate." Describing this vehement leaves-taking, Pusey wrote his brother William: "The sermon was like one of Newman's" in the sense that "self was altogether repressed," though "it showed all the more how deeply he felt all the misconceptions

---

[76] *Prepos.*, pp. 351–2.
[77] LD, 12:218–19 JHN to Henry Bourne (13 June 1848).
[78] *SD*, p. 409.

of himself. It implied, rather than said, Farewell. People sobbed audibly, and I who officiated at the altar, could hardly help mingling sorrow with even that Feast."[79] If there was sobbing, there was also smarting. Newman's valedictory was not without undertones of recrimination.

Two days before resigning his living, Newman had written James Hope: "I ought to write . . . to say that the movement is going so fast, that some of the wheels are catching fire . . ."[80] When William Lockhart, who had joined the Littlemore community in July of 1842, suddenly converted, despite promising that he would make no move for 3 years, Newman was put into what he recognized was an untenable position: "It is a very great scandal under the circumstances," he wrote Jemima, "and I could not hold up my head again as Vicar of St. Mary's."[81] It was also at this time that his brother-in-law, Thomas Mozley announced that he was considering converting, which put Newman in a false position with his sister Harriett, who wrongfully assumed that Newman had had something to do with her husband's precipitate decision. "Your letters are indeed sad to for me to read," Jemima wrote Newman on 30 September 1843. "I feel I am very unfit to judge of what you say. As Harriett requests you to be candid, you cannot say less than you have."[82] Newman's candour, however, did not get him very far with Harriett. "My present views were taken up in the summer of 1839 upon reading the Monophysite and Donatist controversies," he explained to her in October, "I saw from them that Rome was the centre of unity and the judge of controversies. My views could not be influenced by the surface or the interior of the present French Church or of any other."[83] But apparently no explanations would satisfy her. Three months later, Newman was constrained to write: ". . . My dear H. do not think me unkind, but kind, in saying I have no wish to continue the subject, which forms the chief portion of your notes. It is an interchange of words in which nothing is gained and something may be lost."[84]

That Newman's resignation was also opening a rift between him and Jemima can be seen in her response to his offer to come and explain to her in person why he had resigned the living. This rift would never be as irreparable as the one that opened between Harriett and Newman, but it would be a rift nonetheless. "As to your coming here," Jemima wrote, "you tempt me strongly to accept . . . but I have some scruples— It is taking advantage of your kindness when I know you would not have come but for these late events . . . I had thought this many times, till today's letter, and now I seem bewildered—I fear you may only be called upon in a way painful to yourself to anticipate events and disclosures . . . I have not concealed anything from John [her husband] . . ."[85] Newman offered to write her "the history and state of my thoughts," with, however, the honest proviso that "I doubt whether it will be wise in you to ask what it will be painful for you to read."[86] Jemima, in turn, was equally honest in her

---

[79] R. D. Middleton. *Newman at Oxford: His Religious Development* (Oxford, 1950), p. 217.
[80] LD, 9:503 JHN to James Robert Hope (5 September 1843).
[81] LD, 9:504 JHN to Mrs John Mozley (5 September 1843).
[82] LD, 9:542 Mrs John Mozley to JHN (30 September 1843).
[83] LD, 9:546 JHN to Mrs Thomas Mozley (2 October 1843).
[84] LD, 10: 97 JHN to Mrs Thomas Mozley (22 January 1844).
[85] LD, 9:543 Mrs John Mozley to JHN (30 September 1843).
[86] LD, 9:551 JHN to Mrs John Mozley (5 October 1843).

response. If she was prepared to respect his decision, she still found it bewildering. "Knowing all I do of you and your present opinions, I do not call in question any thing you have done, or your manner of doing it. I may deeply lament, but I cannot find fault. I cannot accuse you of being impatient, precipitate, or insincere . . . I cannot say you have not acted wisely under the circumstances . . . But . . . for many years I have anxiously watched the course, and endeavoured to ascertain particulars concerning converts to Romanism, and I must say, I have never heard of any one like yourself. . ." She granted that the conversion of George Spencer in 1830 had been "respectable."[87] Yet "All other conversions I have known . . . seem more the fruit of excitement and restlessness than of straightforward, honest conviction. Their character seems to degenerate after their change, and, if they do not behave as disgracefully as Mr. Sibthorp, who is no credit to any communion, one has reason to fear it may not be from the best motives."[88]

For Anglicans leaning to Rome, the career of Richard Waldo Sibthorp became the great cautionary tale. A Fellow of Magdalen College, Sibthorp was received into the Roman Church by then Bishop Nicholas Wiseman on 27 October 1841 and ordained a priest in 1842. After breaking the news to his friends and associates, Sibthorp sought to soften the blow by vowing ever afterwards to pray for his college, "Floreat Magdalena." Once installed in St Chad's in Birmingham, however, he found himself in an uncongenial milieu. As Christopher Sykes, Evelyn Waugh's friend noted, "Throughout his career he had been used . . . to clerical companions drawn from county families and from the upper middle class, gentlefolk whose behaviour was informed by the graceful reserve peculiar to the Church of England. Here in the Birmingham clergy house he was thrown amid coarse people. His companions were Irishmen from rough humble homes. There was no friend for Dr. Routh's lost sheep. There was none who knew or cared about the Universities, none sharing any of his other secular interests. He had known few Catholics before conversion. He was not prepared for the fact, which met him forcibly among these priests, that as a result of many years of penal legislation most Catholics in England were grossly uneducated. They were ignorant and common, and he minded it."[89] Shortly thereafter, while holidaying on the Isle of Wight, Sibthorp had another revelation. In 1843, he converted back to Anglicanism, and later read out a public letter at a Church Missionary meeting in Bath, confessing how, as he said, "The conviction I am come to after most painful deliberation is that the Church of Rome is the Harlot and Babylon of the Apocalypse. I believe her to be an adulterous and idolatrous Church, especially as it respects Mariolatry."[90] When Wiseman learned of the embarrassing *volte-face*, he took to his bed. For Newman, "poor Sibthorp should be taken as a warning to all of us against sudden moves." And yet he also put Newman in mind of another lesson. "Our Lord tells us to count the cost. How can you tell whether it is His voice or that of a deceiving spirit? It is a rule in spiritual matters to reject a suggestion at first to any thing extraordinary from the certainty that if it is from

---

[87] George Spencer (1799–1864), the youngest son of the second Earl Spencer, was educated at Eton and Cambridge and after converting in 1830 became a professor at Oscott.

[88] LD, 9:556 Mrs John Mozley to JHN (8 October 1843).

[89] Christopher Sykes. *Two Studies in Virtue* (London, 1953), pp. 50–1.

[90] Sykes, p. 58.

heaven, it will return."[91] A few days after Sibthorp's farcical reversion, the *Tablet* noted how "Those who know their man and see us snap up a Sibthorp, laugh at us and say: 'How dreadfully these poor Papists must be off for decently educated priests, when they make such a pother about a Sibthorp.'"[92]

Such a ludicrously abortive conversion could only have made Newman warier still of his own leanings towards Rome. In May 1844, he tried to explain his dilemma to Jemima: "I am very sorry to make you anxious, but do not know what to do. I don't like you to be ignorant of my state of mind, yet don't like to tease you with any rigmarole statements." Since 1839, he had sought to be at once candid and reassuring about his developing religious opinions; now, he was not so ready with reassurance. "If I judge of the future by the past, and when I recollect the long time, now nearly 5 years, that certain views and feelings have been more or less familiar to me and sometimes pressing on me, it would seem as if any thing might happen. And I must confess that they are very much clearer and stronger than they were even a year ago."[93] In June 1844, he all but admitted that reassurances might be a thing of the past: "You must not be surprised, if I should determine on giving up my Fellowship"—an admission that could not have allayed Jemima's anxieties. In July 1844, Newman wrote his Aunt Elizabeth: "May we all meet again in peace, when this troublesome world and its many contentions are over. I really do think I am destined to be a 'man of strife.'"[94]

If Newman caused others anxiety, he remained equable himself. "The truth is (thank God) I *am* cheerful," he told Jemima, "and though it so entirely depends on Him that I might be cast down for good and all any day, and know not of course what is before me, yet having sound sleep at night and quiet days and trying to serve Him without aims of this world, however imperfectly, how can I be but cheerful . . ."[95] This is revealing because it shows how trial brought out not only his native buoyancy but his humility, his trust in God's will. The architect John Hungerford Pollen, who was privy to the many frustrations Newman experienced while Rector of the Catholic University in Dublin, where he served as Professor of Fine Arts and helped design the University Church, recalled: "He shed cheerfulness as a sunbeam sheds light, even while many difficulties were passing."[96] In this, Newman emulated his patron saint, Philip Neri, whose cheerfulness was legendary.[97] One proof of Newman's cheerfulness can be found in his writing, which throughout this punishing period retained a marked rhetorical ebullience—always a sign of conviction in Newman. For example, in July 1844 Newman drew up a memorandum that was very similar to the "history and state

[91] LD, 9:555 JHN to Thomas Mozley (7 October 1843).
[92] Sykes, p. 58.
[93] LD, 10:247 JHN to Mrs John Mozley (21 May 1844).
[94] LD, 10:304 JHN to Aunt Elizabeth Newman (25 July 1844).
[95] LD, 10:255–6 JHN to Mrs John Mozley (3 June 1844).
[96] Meriol Trevor. *Newman: Light in Winter* (London, 1962), p. 61.
[97] See *MD*, p. 106. "Sometimes [St. Philip] left his prayers and went down to sport and banter with young men, and by this sweetness and condescension and playful conversation gained their souls. He could not bear anyone to be downcast or pensive, because spirituality is always injured by it; but when he saw anyone grave and gloomy, he used to say, 'Be merry.' He had a particular and marked leaning to cheerful persons. At the same time he was a great enemy to anything like rudeness or foolery; for a buffooning spirit not only does not advance in religion, but roots out even what is already there."

of my thoughts" that he had promised Jemima, and it is full of a sprightly candour, which entirely refutes the charge that in converting Newman was guilty of duplicity. Speaking of his long period of deliberation, starting with the day in 1839 when he had had his Monophysite epiphany, he wrote:

> I have waited till I could act without doubt or hesitation, I have waited with much dreariness though not in sadness for–years, I have not waited in order at the end of that time to get into controversy about myself. Still, those who think well of me and wish me well have a claim on me to say how it is I have come to hold what once I disowned . . .
>
> I cannot be ashamed that my first efforts were to support that Church within which I was born or that I came to her system with a confidence it was true, and studied it with prepossessions in its favor, and accepted it with my heart as well as with my intellect. I was zealous for her, I reverenced her divines, I entered into their ecclesiastical and theological theory—I admired its internal consistency and beauty, I read the Fathers through them; I read the history of the first centuries with their eyes. My object was in what I wrote to serve them, and their and my Church; to develop their views and to supply and harmonize what was wanting or what was faulty in them . . .
>
> But so it was in June or July 1839 reading the Monophysite controversy, I found my eyes opened to a state of things very different from what I had learned from my natural guides. The prejudice . . . which had been too great for conviction from the striking facts of Arian history, could not withstand the history of St. Leo and the Council of Chalcedon. I saw that if the early times were to be my guides, the Pope had a very different place in the Church from what I had supposed . . . When this suspicion had once fair possession of my mind . . . the whole English system fell about me on all sides, the ground crumbled under my feet, and in a little time I found myself in a very different scene of things. What had passed could not be recalled.[98]

This is entirely consistent with the account Newman gave of what he called his Anglican "death-bed" in his *Apologia Pro Vita Sua*, where he wrote: "A death-bed has scarcely a history; it is a tedious decline, with seasons of rallying and seasons of falling back; and since the end is foreseen, or what is called a matter of time, it has little interest for the reader, especially if he has a kind heart. Moreover, it is a season when doors are closed and curtains drawn, and when the sick man neither cares nor is able to record the stages of his malady. I was in these circumstances, except so far as I was not allowed to die in peace . . ."[99] What Newman omitted to point out in the *Apologia* but which is abundantly clear from his correspondence is that his Anglican death-bed was also a Catholic cradle where his new faith was gradually taking shape with the help of the *Spiritual Exercises* of St Ignatius Loyola. As he told Miss Holmes, the governess with whom he corresponded throughout his life, "Religious truth is reached, not by reasoning, but by an inward perception. Any one can reason; only

---

[98] LD, 10:305 Memorandum (28 July 1844).
[99] *Apo.*, p. 137.

disciplined, educated, formed minds can perceive."[100] He elaborated on what he meant to John Keble: "I have for some time past been studying Loyola's Exercises and I may say in a certain sense making use of the hints they contain—and I must own my great admiration of them, or rather my sense of their extreme utility. He, and his followers after him, seem to have reduced the business of self-discipline to a science—and since our Enemy's warfare upon us proceeds doubtless on system, every one, I suppose, must make a counter system for himself, or take one which experience has warranted."[101]

Two months after drawing up his memorandum, in September 1844, Newman wrote Jemima of the growing sense of estrangement he felt from the scenes of so many of his earlier Tractarian battles. "I do fancy I am getting changed," he wrote. "I go into Oxford, and find myself out of place. Every thing seems to say to me, this is not your home. The College seems strange to me, and even the College servants seem to look as if I were getting strange to them. I cannot tell whether it is a fancy or not, but to myself I seem changing."[102] Two years earlier, in September 1842, he had made a complaint that he would repeat often throughout his vigorous prime: "If I come to you, I think you will think me vastly aged in this last year and a half. I begin to think of myself as an old man."[103] But in 1844 he made an arresting observation. "I am so much more easily touched than I used to be. Reading St. Wulstan's Life just now almost brought tears into my eyes. What a very mysterious thing the mind is! Yet nothing that my feelings suggest to me is different from what has been engraved more or less strongly on my reason long ago."[104] For all the sense of change he felt, he was also aware of mysterious continuity. This has always made dating his conversion with any precision difficult. When did it truly begin? And when it finally impelled him to embrace Rome, was he embracing something new or something "engraved more or less strongly on [his] reason long ago"?

Still, Newman was not quite ready to take the final step. In August 1844, his friend and confidant, Edward Badeley, a member of the Inner Temple, who would counsel him throughout the Achilli trial, put the case for remaining within the Anglican fold in terms that Newman must have found tempting, especially considering his aversion to what he called the "nuisance" of "taking steps."[105] First, Badeley argued, "The Jerusalem Bishopric . . . the most detestable of all the late innovations, seems already to have well nigh come to nought—it is likely to *die of inanition*—and I very much doubt whether the experiment in any shape will ever be repeated." On this score, Badeley was proved right. Then, he argued that fancying Rome preferable to England might be delusive. "Perplexed indeed should I be, if I came to such a conclusion," Badeley wrote, "for according to my present notions, I should find at Rome, if I sought refuge there, as many difficulties as I should have in England—Doubtless we are bad enough, but I trust not past recovery—and when I look at the immense change for the better which has been effected within a few years, I am inclined to take courage." To drive home his point, he

[100] LD, 9:274 JHN to Miss Holmes (8 March 1843).
[101] LD, 9:307–8 JHN to John Keble (15 April 1843).
[102] LD, 10:312 JHN to Mrs John Mozley (13 August 1844).
[103] LD, 10:97 JHN to Mrs John Mozley (17 September 1842).
[104] LD, 10:312 JHN to Mrs John Mozley (13 August 1844).
[105] LD, 8:456 JHN to Mrs John Mozley (6 February 1842).

added: "Those who leave us, retard our recovery . . . they withdraw that vital energy which is so much needed, and which might impel us to work out our restoration . . ."[106] This encapsulated the view that most Tractarians and indeed High Churchmen had of Newman's dilemma. Whatever his reservations might be with regard to Anglicanism, he should be mindful that Catholicism bristled with even more difficulties; therefore, he should stay put. Ironically, after representing Henry Phillpotts, the Bishop of Exeter in the Gorham Case, and failing to get the Court to overturn the Privy Council's ruling on baptism, Badeley would find his rationale for staying put confounded, and in 1852 he converted himself. After the death of Badeley, Bellasis and Hope-Scott, the three convert lawyers who meant so much to him, Newman, wrote: "To inspire love was their special characteristic; they were so honest and so true."[107]

While still an Anglican, Newman could always point to reasons of his own for staying put. "I believe all my feelings and wishes are against change," he wrote Jemima in November 1844. "I have nothing to draw me elsewhere. I hardly ever was at a Roman service, even abroad—I know no Roman Catholics. I have no sympathy with them as a party."[108] Then again, Newman was appalled by the turmoil the mere prospect of his moving was causing others. "Besides the pain of unsettling people, of course, I feel the loss I am undergoing in the good opinion of friends and well wishers—though I can't tell how much I feel this. It is the shock, surprise, terror, forlornness, disgust, scepticism, to which I am giving rise—the difference of opinion—division of families—all this makes my heart ache."[109] Why, then, did he not make a decision: either to remain in the Anglican fold or to go over to Rome? "I cannot make out that I have any motive but a sense of indefinite risk to my own soul in remaining where I am," Newman confided to Jemima. "As far as I can make out, I am in the state of mind which divines call 'indifferentia;' inculcating it as a duty, to set upon nothing, but to be willing to take any step whatever Providence wills." Yet no sooner did Newman formulate this reasoned explanation than he questioned the very notion that he should even entertain moving. "How *can* I, at my age, and with my past trials, be set upon any thing? I really don't think I am." So, rather than make any move he might regret, he waited. "What keeps me here, is the desire of giving every chance for finding out, if I am under the power of a delusion."[110]

Jemima tried to respond to her brother's candour with candour of her own, though the ground on which Newman's deepening doubts about Anglicanism placed her made this increasingly difficult. "This is my especial trouble, that I cannot defend you as I would desire through everything, and I have to throw a damp of reserve and

---

[106] LD, 10:327 Edward Badeley to JHN (28 August 1844) After he converted, Newman addressed this objection in *Difficulties of Anglicans* "It is a very common difficulty which troubles men, when they contemplate submission to the Catholic Church, that perhaps they shall thus be weakening the communion they leave, which, with whatever defects, they see in matter of fact to be a defence of Christianity against its enemies. No, my brethren, you will not be harming it; if the National Church falls, it falls because it is national; because it left the centre of unity in the sixteenth century, not because you leave it in the nineteenth. Cranmer, Parker, Jewell, will complete their own work; they who made it, will be its destruction." Lecture 1, p. 32.

[107] JHN quoted by Henry Tristram. *Newman and His Friends* (London, 1933), p. 175.

[108] LD, 10:435 JHN to Mrs John Mozley (24 November 1844).

[109] LD, 10:334–5 JHN to Mrs John Mozley (24 November 1844).

[110] LD, 10:435 JHN to Mrs John Mozley (24 November 1844).

discouragement on unsuspicious and generous spirits who are ready to answer for your steadfastness. I am afraid of adding to your trouble, but I really do wish you would take the whole matter into account, and consider it, not merely as counting the cost, but,,, whether such impediments as the troubling the minds of the better sort of people and long chosen friends etc., may not be providential warnings of the course in which we should walk." Here, for all her solicitude for her brother, Jemima was making an unpersuasive appeal. Newman might wish to avoid unsettling the faith of Anglicans but he would not let "the minds of the better sort" or even "long chosen friends" dissuade him from the admonitions of conscience. Jemima must have known as much, because at this point she left off trying to persuade her brother and spoke frankly of her own settled opposition to the course he seemed prepared to take.

> For myself I cannot help going a little further, hoping, dear John, I shall not shock you by this confession. I cannot help feeling a repulsion from that Church which has so many stains upon her. I do not, of course, believe all the vulgar charges which prejudice and bad feeling have brought against her during the last three centuries; but things which Roman Catholic themselves admit, and which seem to me as contrary to the spirit Christians should cultivate as the practices of ultra Protestants . . . But you must also believe that I can, in spite of all this, appreciate the pain and struggle which causes your suffering, and indeed sympathize entirely with it, looking upon it, in your case, as truly a matter of conscience.[111]

However admirably said, this was not the whole truth, as Jemima admitted. Pausing in her letter and thinking over what she had written, she resumed with an exclamation that must have cut Newman to the quick. "Would it were not so, and that you were more like other men!" Here was the cry of love that made their irreconcilable paths so harrowing. Of course, no one knew better than Jemima how *unlike* other men her brother was—this "wonderful creature," as she described him. "Your way of going on," she wrote, "ought in justice to do credit to a cause." The problem was that the cause he was preparing himself to champion was one that she was resolved to oppose, however much she appreciated his gallant defence of it. This was why, for Jemima, "We do really seem in a desperate state of things, when even Christ's little flock must bite and devour one another. How difficult it is to believe that our times are not indeed worse than those that have gone before." Whether the Anglican Church was less or more unified before the Tractarians came along is a nice question.[112] Still, Jemima, unlike Frank, did recognize that her differences with her brother began and ended with truth—not the search for truth, or the tenability of doubt as an alternative to truth, or even the idea of truth but the real, uncompromising, divisive thing itself. "I hope you will forgive anything wrong I have said in this letter," Jemima told her brother, "and believe that my first wish is that you should see the truth, whatever it is. I hope and trust that I desire this for you above all things."[113]

---

[111] LD, 10:439 Mrs John Mozley to JHN (29 November 1844).
[112] LD, 10:439–40 Mrs John Mozley to JHN (29 November 1844).
[113] LD, 10:440 Mrs John Mozley to JHN (29 November 1844).

This sympathy was vital to Newman. The deep chord it struck within him can be seen in a letter he wrote to Jemima on 22 December 1844. Well aware of the rumours circulating about him—what he once called "the tin-kettle accounts of me which rattle to and fro in the world"—he was eager to share with Jemima what he truly thought and felt.[114] Acknowledging that "the *onus probandi*" was on him to explain why he was contemplating leaving the Anglican Church, Newman assured his sister that it was not because he was "disappointed, or restless, or set on a theory, or carried on by a party, or coaxed . . . by admirers, or influenced by any number of the ten thousand persuasives, which are as foreign from my mind as from my heart, but which it is easy for others to assign as an hypothesis."[115] Walter Bagehot's Aunt Reynolds was one of many Anglicans who thought that Newman's change of allegiance was not entirely conscientious. "She believes that Newman is most likely bribed to become a Roman Catholic," Bagehot told his mother, "that he will be no loser in money matters by the change." At the same time, the economist in Bagehot knew the Vatican finances well enough to know that the "Pope is bankrupt" and that "it seems unlikely he should have much spare cash to send over to bribe English heretics . . ."[116]

However nettled by the misconceptions that always seemed to dog him, Newman was nonetheless confident that when people came to know him, personally or through his writings, they would see that "these suppositions do not hold . . . they will be led to see that my motive simply is that I believe the Roman Church to be true—and that I have come to this belief without any assignable fault on my part. Far indeed am I from saying 'without fault' absolutely—but I say without fault that can be detected and assigned. Were I sure that it was without fault absolutely, I should not hesitate to move tomorrow . . ."[117]

This was where Newman stood: waiting. But where did he stand in relation to others? "If God gives me certain light, supposing it to be such, this is a reason for *me* to act—yet in so doing I am not condemning those who do not so act." Frank and others in the rationalist camp liked to accuse Newman of bigotry and fanaticism because he affirmed the oneness of truth; well, here was proof that there was no bigotry or fanaticism in his apprehension of that oneness. At the same time, he would never subscribe to the rationalist view that truth could somehow be unobtainable or merely subjective or, worse, relative. "There *is* one truth," he told Jemima, "yet it may not please Almighty God, to show every one in the same degree or way what and where it is. I believe our Church to be separated from Catholic communion; but still I know very well that all divines, ancient and modern, Roman as well as our own, grant even to a Church in schism, which has the Apostolical Succession and the right form of consecrating the sacraments, very large privileges. They allow that Baptism has the gift of the Holy Spirit, and the Eucharist the Real Presence—What they deny to such a Church is the power of *imparting* these gifts . . . Our Church may be a place of grace and security to another, yet not to me."[118] Newman could not have set out the lines of difference between Jemima and himself, between Anglicans and himself, with more

---

[114] LD, 7:183 JHN to Mrs John Mozley (17 November 1839).
[115] LD, 10:467 JHN to Mrs John Mozley (22 December 1844).
[116] Mrs Russell Barrington. *Life of Walter Bagehot* (London, 1914), p. 147.
[117] LD: 10:467 JHN to Mrs John Mozley (22 December 1844).
[118] LD, 10:468 JHN to Mrs John Mozley (22 December 1844).

tactful clarity. But he did so not to justify himself but to reach beyond himself: he had been engaged for so long in so solitary an ordeal. "Now, my dear J, I am sure you feel that I am not arguing, but I wish you to understand where I stand, and what I feel—for my own comfort. I have never wished there should be any reserve between us—it is most repugnant to my nature to conceal things. Long indeed I had this sad secret, when I thought it would be wrong to mention it. By degrees, often without my intention, it has come out—and growing conviction has justified me in mentioning it. And since now it is out, it is a great comfort if you let me be open with you and to tell you what the state of my mind is. Indeed, there can be no exercise of love between persons without this openness."[119]

Newman was prepared to be equally open with close friends. To John Keble, to whom he confided most in this period of careful deliberation, he confessed: "No one can have a more unfavourable view than I of the present state of the Roman Catholics— so much so, that any who joined them would be like the Cistercians at Fountains, living under trees till their house was built."[120] If this was his view of the Roman Church, why should he contemplate joining it? In a letter to Maria Giberne, written a few weeks later, Newman explained that what was swaying him was not preference for the Catholic Church. "This I am quite sure of . . . nothing but a simple, direct call of duty is a warrant for any one leaving our Church—no preference for another Church, no delight in its services, no hope of greater religious advancement in it, no indignation, no disgust at the persons and things among which we find ourselves in the Church of England. The simple question is, can *I* (it is personal, not whether another, but, can *I*) be saved in the English Church? am I in safety, were I to die tonight? is it a mortal sin in me, not joining another Communion?"[121]

However bewildering Jemima found her brother's openness, she still felt the pull of his influence, so much so that she deliberately set about resisting it. As she explained in a letter of 8 January, 1845: "If I seem hard or wanting in sympathy, I do believe it is that fear I have lest I should be tempted to allow your influence to have more weight with me than it ought. I feel this has led me to speak more decidedly than I otherwise should do."[122] This must have come as a surprise to Newman because there is nothing in his letters to suggest that he was trying to influence his sister at this point, though he would have seen the accuracy, indeed the heartbreak, in this observation of Jemima's: "All I know, dear John, is that it is a great grief to me to feel as if we had two paths and two objects instead of one in common; I try to think of it as *really* one, though unfortunately we appear asunder—"[123] Soon these appearances would become realities. In response, Newman wrote: "Far indeed am I from being unwilling that you should fear my influence. I have quite enough responsibility about myself without being in a measure to answer for others. It is my principal trouble, as you know, what effect I may have on others. And I have looked forward to it as one especial test of the strength of my convictions, whether I could *bear* that others should be influenced by me."[124]

[119] Ibid.
[120] LD, 10:476 JHN to John Keble (29 December 1844).
[121] LD, 10:485 JHN to Maria Rosina Giberne (8 January 1845).
[122] LD, 10:485 Mrs John Mozley to JHN (8 January 1845).
[123] Ibid.
[124] LD, 10:509 JHN to Mrs John Mozley (23 January 1845).

Jemima could not entirely put his mind at rest on that score: "I must say my worst fears did not warn me of . . . the bad feelings of some few, and the infatuation of many more. I hardly know what terms to apply to the agitators of the movement, and indeed do not like to characterize them at all—but I really could not have believed that such cowardly persecution [could be set on foot] . . . I am pained to think of your being exposed to such vicious clamour, though I dare say you think less about it almost than any one else in the Kingdom."[125] As it happened, Newman was unconcerned about the dramatic events taking place in Oxford. In February 1845, Convocation condemned W. G. Ward's book, *Ideal of a Christian Church, considered in Comparison with Existing Practice* (1844), which argued that the Church of Rome was the ideal Church, and stripped him of his Balliol degree and fellowship. When the vote to censure Tract 90 came up, it was vetoed, as Newman expected. "I suppose that the Proctors will veto— and a large number of persons . . . will come forward to support them. If I wished people to be unsettled and inclined towards Rome, I could not have better fortune than a condemnation of Number 90."[126] Newman's heart and mind were elsewhere. Days before Convocation met, Newman wrote Jemima: "The Heads of Houses can do me neither good nor harm—I have distresses which they cannot increase or cure."[127] To Manning, he confessed the same indifference: "Real inward pain makes one insensible to such shadows."[128] Nonetheless, Newman was very much concerned about the "jealous controversy" that he thought would follow "about my conduct since Number 90 . . ."[129] To John Keble, he had written in November 1844: ". . . the only thing I *feel*, is the charge of dishonesty. Really no one but O'Connell is called so distinctly and so ordinarily a liar, as I am. I think nothing tends to hurt my spirits but this, I am not treated merely as a gentleman . . ."[130] To Jemima, he expressed the same unavailing indignation: "Now I really am conscious of nothing which I am ashamed of, and trust I should come out of the closest scrutiny undamaged—but yet one cannot help disliking such enquiries . . . I am not bound to come forward to play the scaramouch for the amusement of the Standard and Record papers . . ."[131]

Jemima, for her part, could not think that far ahead: she was too appalled by his imminent conversion. Writing Newman in March 1845, she told him that he was right to expect that this bitter news "would give me a great deal of pain." She could "think of nothing else."

> Yet I can hardly say why it is so, for I am far from taken by surprise; indeed, I have been dreading to hear something of this sort for some time past. You have sufficiently warned me of it. Yet I have so much sanguineness in my composition that I always hope the worst misfortunes may be averted till they are irremediable. And what can be worse than this? It is like hearing some dear friend must die. I cannot shut my eyes to this overpowering event that threatens any longer . . .

---

[125] LD, 10:533 Mrs John Mozley to JHN (7 February 1845).
[126] LD, 10:546 JHN to Mrs John Mozley (11 February 1845).
[127] LD, 10:542 JHN to Mrs John Mozley (10 February 1845).
[128] LD, 10:541 JHN to Henry Edward Manning (9 February 1845).
[129] LD, 10:547 JHN to Mrs John Mozley (11 February 1845).
[130] LD, 10:425 JHN to John Keble (21 November 1844).
[131] LD, 10:547 JHN to Mrs John Mozley (11 February 1845).

O, dear John, can you have thought long enough before deciding on such a step which, with its probable effects, must plunge so many into confusion and dismay?

I know what you will answer—that nothing but the risk of personal salvation would lead you to it; and I quite believe it. I know you have all along had the greatest regard for others, and acted upon it for some time past. But think what must be our feelings who cannot entertain your view, but can only deplore it as a grievous mistake! And I feel bitterly how many good sort of people would not do you justice, but judge you very hardly indeed. It is a real pain and grief to think of you as severed from us, as it were, by your own sentence. I am much afraid, dear John, you may be taken by surprise by what I say, and expect I shall receive this event more easily. Indeed I cannot; it is to me the great proof of the world and the unfortunate times that we live in, that such a one as you should take the line you have taken.[132]

This was powerful proof that when Newman said he dreaded how his secession would divide families he was not speaking lightly. What made matters worse for Jemima, rightly or wrongly, was that she doubted she could even get a proper hearing from her brother. "How sad it is to me that I cannot say these things to you without your thinking me in error and in the wrong way . . . Is there not enough in the world to make one weary of it, to all who try to see things as they really are?"[133] Jemima's wail of frustration measured the chasm that now separated them.

Newman wished he "saw any way of making things easier . . ." but in trying to explain himself he gave way to an exasperation of his own. "As to my convictions, I can but say what I have told you already, that I cannot at all make out *why* I should determine on moving except as thinking I should offend God by not doing so. I cannot make out what I am *at*, except on this supposition. At my time of life, men love ease—I love ease myself. I am giving up a maintenance, involving no duties, and adequate to all my wants; what in the world am I doing this for, (I ask *myself* this) except that I think I am called to do so? I am making a large income by my Sermons, I am, *to say the very least*, risking this—the chance is that my Sermons will have no further sale at all. I have a good name with many—I am deliberately sacrificing it. I have a bad name with more—I am fulfilling their worst wishes, and giving them their most coveted triumph—I am distressing all I love, unsettling all I have instructed or aided—I am going to those whom I do not know and of whom I expect very little—I am making myself an outcast, and that at my age . . ."[134] Here, the controversialist in Newman could not help putting Jemima's objections to his move better than Jemima herself. None of these objections, however, could still the insistent promptings of his unbiddable conscience.

If Jemima pleaded with her brother to understand her predicament, Newman made an even more desperate plea of his own. "Pity me, my dear Jemima—what have I done thus to be deserted, thus to be left to take a wrong course, if it be wrong. I began by

132 LD, 10:594–5 JHN to Mrs John Mozley (13 March 1845).
133 LD, 10:594–5 Mrs John Mozley to JHN (13 March 1845).
134 LD, 10:595 JHN to Mrs John Mozley (15 March 1845).

defending my own Church with all my might when others would not defend her. I went through obloquy in defending her. I in a fair measure succeed—at the very time of this success, before any reverse, in the course of my reading, it breaks upon me that I am in a schismatical Church. I oppose myself to that notion—I write against it—Year after year I write against it—and I do my utmost to keep others in the Church—From the time my doubts come upon me, I begin to live more strictly—and really from that time to this, I have done more towards my inward improvement, as far as I can judge, than in any time in my life." And yet still he is fearful that some unsuspected fault is deluding him. "The human heart is most mysterious. I may have some deep evil in me which I cannot fathom—I may have done some irreparable thing which demands punishment." This was one of the supreme trials of Newman's life and he met it with impassioned prayer.

> Continually do I pray that He would discover me, if I am under a delusion—what can I do more? What hope have I but in Him? to whom should I go? who can do me any good? who can speak a word of comfort but He? Who is there but looks on me with sorrowful face? but he can lift up the light of His countenance upon me. All is against me—may He not add Himself as an adversary!—may He tell me, may I listen to Him, if His will is other than I think it to be.[135]

The following day, 16 March, Palm Sunday, a day of "wind and January snow," as Newman recorded in his diary, he began to see his trial in some perspective. "Have not there after all been persons in my case before now, and were they not right? Were persons never in a schismatical or heretical Church, and would not their trial, when they came to their state, be exactly like mine? Have Jew never had to turn Christian, and been cursed by their friends for doing so? Can I shock people so much as they did? Is the Church of Rome, can it be, regarded more fearful than Jews regarded Christianity, than Jews regarded St. Paul?—was he not the prince of apostates? . . . Nay is not this the peculiar trial which happens in Scripture to be set upon a Christian . . . the quitting of friends and relations and houses and goods for Christ's sake? Surely all the distress and unsettlement I shall give, however great a warning to me not to act hastily, cannot be a *real reason* against moving, for it is . . . the very conditions under which a follower of Christ is drawn in Scripture . . ." This new perspective also caused him to see Jemima's veiled censures in a different light. "So, my dear Jemima, if you can suggest any warning to me which I am not considering, well, and thank you—else do take comfort, and think that perhaps you have a right to have faith in me—perhaps you have a right to believe that He who has led me hitherto, will not suffer me to go wrong. I am some how in better spirits this morning, and I say what it occurs to me to say at the time." Indeed, he did not mince his words. "Have I not a right to ask you not to say, as you have said in your letter, that I shall do *wrong*? What right have you to judge me? . . . I may be wrong, but He that judgeth me is the Lord, and judge nothing before the time."[136]

This elicited a letter from Jemima of heartfelt humility, which nevertheless only accentuated the revulsion with which she regarded her brother's contemplated move.

---

[135] LD, 10:595–7 JHN to Mrs John Mozley (15 March 1845).
[136] LD, 10:597 JHN to Mrs John Mozley (15 November 1845).

Brother and sister began here a dance of elaborate, cordial disagreement that would characterize most of their letters until Newman converted, after which they tended to avoid the topic of religion altogether. "Many thanks for your kindness in writing to me so promptly and at such length," Jemima began. "I feel most vexed with myself for having said anything that should have, as it were, compelled you to write so much, and I fear I cannot altogether receive all you say as you would wish." This was putting it mildly. Still, she did wish to clarify a few matters about which he seemed unclear. "I must say, thinking as you do, with such a strong view of what is right, I cannot ask or wish you to act otherwise than you contemplate. If my former letter seemed urgent it was because I hoped to draw from you something different from what I have drawn. I know on a point of conscience we must not be drawn aside by persuasions or arguments, which tell with others, but which are only mere excuses if we act by them when they do not touch ourselves." There was a certain impertinence in that last observation, however unintended. Indeed, even when taking the long view, Jemima could not avoid contentious ground. "I do take comfort in feeling how short-sighted we are in judging only of a few passing years. What signify the pains and trials of the next four or five years for those who live to see them, if it pleases God to bring good to His Church out of them?" Certainly, what Jemima understood to be "His Church" did not comprise Rome. And then she followed this up with an aside that seemed to suggest that if she had been on some more equal footing with her brother, she would be in a better position to make her opposition to his views tell. "All this strikes me as a bystander; of course if I were a man or a clergyman, or if events arose to compel me to be an actor, I [should] have a weight of responsibility which would make me feel differently." But this was secondary to her primary complaint. "Then, dear John, you attack *me* and wish me to ask myself whether after all you may not be right—and indeed I do often put it to myself in that light. I know how ignorant I am, and worse than ignorant, how little I ought to assume I am right in any one thing. Yet there are some things one dare not doubt, and some things it is one's highest happiness to believe and try to realize. So, however unworthy I am, I feel we must in some measure go by our own faith and our own light, though that light be little better than darkness . . ." Newman would certainly have rejected that assertion. If we were destined to be guided by light "little better than darkness," what was the purpose of Revelation? Newman would later skewer this muddled reasoning in lectures he gave to the London Oratory 5 years after he converted. Then, Jemima spoke directly of the point in contention: Rome. "I dare say . . . I may be prejudiced, it is most likely—we have one-sided views from birth and education; but I really do not think I am aware of any strong or hostile feelings against Rome, which some would not scruple to entertain." Here, she could not help but acknowledge her brother's influence. "I have been unlearning such [prejudices] the last dozen years and have thought them criminal since I ceased to believe Rome to be Antichrist—that is, since I read your sermons." Still, she had to admit, "I have no bias towards Rome, nor see any compensation in Rome to make up for the defects of our Church. I am afraid of paining you by saying she does not approve herself to me as at all fulfilling what she pretends to—far from it—She seems to me to contain Anti-Christian elements, which, as long as she cherishes them, seem an absolute barrier to her converting the world. I know I am talking in ignorance . . . Yet I feel a strong and what seems an insurmountable disapprobation of her, as of a guide with whom one dare not trust oneself."[137]

Newman's response was at once conciliatory and brisk. First, he wished to clarify something he had said. "I am sorry to see I have not guarded against your mistaking me in one point. When I said 'fancy the perplexity of my being right,' I did not mean 'fancy your being wrong.' Surely I have enough to do just now to look to myself—and it was in answer to your saying I was mistaken that I wrote, not dreaming of others. You do agree with me in feeling that this is a case where every one must stand by himself—As you are obliged to form your own judgement, so you must let me form mine, and that is all I meant to say; and as it does not come into my mind to take the responsibility of judging you, so you must not . . . judge me." This was a preventive truce: Newman was recommending that they agree to disagree, before their disagreements escalated—though, of course, this resolved nothing, as he conceded. "It is indeed a great perplexity, how what is a rule for me is not a rule for another—as if there were two truths—but, alas, any how we are in a state of perplexity—and we must submit to what is at present a sort of mystery." About Jemima's other points, Newman was perhaps understandably dismissive. "I could not get myself to read that portion of your letter which was a defense of yourself, for, believe me, I had no intention whatever of attacking you." So, there would be no debate on her "insurmountable disapprobation" of Rome—now or indeed ever. Newman closed the letter by suggesting that she might be good enough to break the news of his moving to their Aunt, only adding that it might be "best to say the plain reason"—that is to say, "I find it necessary for my salvation."[138]

The perplexity Newman articulated here would cast a pall over nearly all of Newman's old Tractarian associates. Jemima's brother-in-law, James Bowling Mozley would vividly attest to the sense of disaster that Newman's imminent conversion caused. Writing to William Scott, the editor of the Tractarian paper, *The Christian Remembrancer* on 14 May 1845, he confirmed that the rumours of Newman's moving were "too true." Now it was only a question of time before it took place. "I ought to have written and talked about the subject with you before now," he wrote, "but it has been such a painful one to me, that I have never been able to do it, and even now it is a great effort to me to write about it. I have known of the tendency so long myself, indeed, that I hardly feel more acutely about it now than I did a year ago. I have got used to it in a way. But it is something like getting used to being hanged." This was how Jemima and her other siblings experienced the impending conversion as well. After Jemima broke the news to Elizabeth Newman that her nephew had resigned his Oriel Fellowship and that his conversion would follow any day, she wrote her brother: "I wish I could give you a comfortable account of her—it grieves me to pain you, but it would not be right to conceal from you that she is greatly overcome by the news . . . She says it is the greatest grief that has ever befallen her . . ." Newman forthwith sent his aunt a note, "written with a trembling hand and great intensity of feeling," assuring her that it was only by converting to Rome that he could prepare himself to stand before God's judgement seat. "He alone knows how much you are in

---

[137] LD, 10:605–6 Mrs John Mozley (21 March 1845).
[138] LD, 10:606–7 JHN To Mrs. John Mozley (22 March 1845).

my heart, or how it pierces my heart so to distress you."[139] Elizabeth Good Newman
(1765–1852), his father's sister, to whom Newman was devoted—she gave him his
love of the Bible and first religious instruction—was synonymous for him with the
"strong tender ties" of home, which, of course, he was compelled to sever when he
converted. In 1811, when he was 10, he wrote her from Ealing School: "The joyful
21 again approaches when our books are closed according to delightful custom, and
when I hope for the additional pleasure of seeing you all well and happy at home.
Already in imagination I pay my respects to the mince Pies, Turkies, and the other
good things of Christmas. In the mean time the Notches on my wooden Calendar
diminish apace, but not so the duty and affection with which I am, Dear Aunt, Your's
ever John H. Newman."[140] Memories of those happy days must surely have been in
Newman's thoughts when he wrote his aunt news of his imminent conversion. James
Mozley spoke for the bereft Tractarian faithful when he wrote Scott: "So now he has
come to a point where I cannot follow him. It is a pain, indeed, to be in a church
without him. But I cannot help that. No one, of course, can prophesy the course of his
own mind; but I feel at present that I could no more leave the English Church than
fly. What the upshot of this is we have yet to see. We are in a struggle. One's spiritual
home is a stormy and unsettled one; but still it is one's home. At least it is mine."[141]
Scott responded with even more anguished disbelief. "Of course . . . one had for some
time attempted to realise what must be, but it is just the same as attempting to realise
losing wife or child. I for one have always, in my measure, leant upon Newman—
though I am scarcely acquainted with him—lived upon him, made him my other, and
better nature; so the crash is to me most overpowering. I dare not criticise any action
of his; he is in gifts and acquirements and in all ways so infinitely above me that I
cannot argue about the matter, only feel, and this of course selfishly, I cannot follow
him. I have no calls that way . . ."[142] Here, Scott spoke for the thousands who had come
to know and revere and love Newman through his sermons, which, throughout his
Anglican years and beyond, sold like hot cakes.

One of these was Charles Crawley, who had made some modest fortune as a
merchant in Spain before setting himself up as a squire in Littlemore. Newman had
written to his Aunt Elizabeth about Crawley back in 1843 apropos Littlemore, which
even ascetic Italian visitors found scarcely habitable: "Our garden improves—we have
no snowdrops but crocuses in plenty. We have gained a squire lately, of the name of
Crawley, a very excellent man and his wife too. They are friends of Copeland's and
will be a great 'acquisition', as it is called, to the place . . . So we are progressing, and
in a few years, when we have found a spa, we shall be a fashionable watering place."[143]
In June 1845, Newman confirmed a meeting with Jemima in Oxford and then added,
"I am very seldom indeed in Oxford—but shall not be sorry of the excuse of your
being there, to take a last look at the Common Room . . . I hope the Crawleys will
be there . . . they are such nice people." When Crawley first learned that Newman

---

[139] LD, 11:14, See Note 4.
[140] LD, 1:9–10 JHN to Elizabeth Newman (6 December 1811).
[141] LD, 10:660 James Bowling Mozley to William Scott (14 May 1845).
[142] LD, 10:660 William Scott to James Bowling Mozley (17 May 1845).
[143] LD, 10:251 JHN to Elizabeth Newman (22 February 1843).

was contemplating leaving the Anglican Church—from Newman himself, on one of their walks together—he wrote his neighbour an impassioned letter warning him of the consequences of so imprudent a course.

> Here at home in our own Communion, what confusion to our Friends—What triumph to our Enemies! and to Rome what an argument to confirm her in her errors and abuses!
>
> What hope, humanly speaking, can remain to our poor humbled Church after such a blow! And now that She is beginning to shew signs of life and raise her drooping head, to find herself all at once despaired of and deserted by her best champion; one who, under Providence, has been the chief instrument in raising her from her degraded state, and, as it were, breathing into her afresh the breath of life! Surely the bare thought of this is enough to make the whole head sick, the whole heart faint.—But I cannot I will not yet believe that such a fearful calamity is in store for us—. I take heart from your own words—from expressions in your own writings which absolutely forbid it.[144]

When Newman converted and moved to Birmingham, Crawley bought his land at Littlemore. Then, in 1861, after an interval of nearly 20 years, he contacted Newman at the Oratory to wish him well and Newman wrote him back: "Thank you for your expressions of friendship and good will. Alas – what a history has past [sic] before us, and is over, since I saw you! As to Oxford, I feel bitterly its present state. But it must be so in the nature of things – Those infidel principles have an enormous force, and a dreadful battle is coming. If I had thought that the weapons which Anglicanism gave me were equal to meeting it, I never should have left persons and scenes so dear to me."[145]

After Newman resigned his Oriel Fellowship on 3 October 1845, he received a letter from the Provost, Edward Hawkins, which was a fair specimen of the reaction he could expect from many Oxford quarters.

> You say nothing of your present position or intentions. Possibly you are thinking of retiring into Lay Community; and against this, if you hold the opinions which I suppose, I could say nothing. But your letter is so strong a confirmation of the rumours I have heard of your intention to join the Roman Church, that I venture to write to you as if it were so. And indeed, in any other case, where I could speak officially or as a friend, I should do what I could to dissuade any member, much more any minister, of the Church of England, from what you know I cannot but regard as very grievous error. It is not from want of regard for you, if I forebear to say anything in your case, but only because I despair of doing any good, when you have been so long studying all questions of this kind; and indeed much more, and more anxiously, no doubt, than I have myself. And yet I cannot forbear expressing the most earnest hope (in all sincerity and feelings of real kindness) that, whatever course you have resolved upon, you may still at

---

[144] LD, 10:428–9 Charles Crawley to JHN (21 November 1844).
[145] LD, 19:453 JHN to Charles Crawley (15 January 1861).

least be saved from the worst errors of the Church of Rome, such as praying to human Mediators or falling down before images—because in you, with all the great advantages with which God has blessed and tried you, I must believe such errors to be most deeply sinful.[146]

For his part, Newman bore no grudges. As he told Pusey in 1882: "I have never ceased to love Hawkins to this day." Nor did he regret helping get Hawkins elected Provost, a position he held for life: "I can't say I ever wished the election undone. Without it there would have been no Movement, no Tracts, no Library of the Fathers." As this shows, Hawkins proved a useful fulcrum. Then, again, it was profoundly characteristic of Newman to send off a heartfelt letter of condolence to Hawkins' wife after the former provost died on 18 November 1882. "What wonderful kindness it is in you to write to me in your present deep distress," Newman wrote, "it has touched me greatly. I thought of writing to *you*, when I heard yesterday of your loss, but on second thoughts I did not dare. Now by your own letter you give me leave, or rather invite me. Your dear husband has never been out my mind of late years. When the first snow came down some weeks back, I thought what the effect of it might be upon him, and only last week, I quoted to a friend with reference to him (thinking at the same time of my own case) a Greek poet's words, 'A light stroke puts to sleep aged men.'"[147] Newman's reminiscences of his former colleague were wonderfully generous, considering Hawkins' thoroughgoing opposition not only to Newman's conversion but to his pastoral understanding of the tutorial charge.

> I have followed his life year after year as I have not been able to follow that of others, because I knew just how many years he was older than I am, and how many days his birthday was from mine.[148] These standing reminders of him personally sprang out of the kindness and benefits done to me by him close upon sixty years ago, when he was Vicar of St Mary's and I held my first curacy at St Clement's. Then, during two Long Vacations, we were day after day in the Common Room all by ourselves, and in Ch Ch [Christ Church] meadow. He used then to say that he should not live past forty; and he has reached, in the event, his great age. I never shall forget to pray for him, till I too go, and have mentioned his name in my Obituary book, which dear Mrs Pusey made for me in her last illness.
>
> May God be with you, and make up to you by His grace this supreme desolation
>
> Most truly Yours John H Card. Newman

If Hawkins could never reciprocate Newman's sympathy, there were other Oxford friends who did, even if they could not support Roman Catholicism. Charles Marriott (1811–58) was perhaps the most notable. Privately educated at Rugby by two aunts

---

[146] LD, 10:782 Edward Hawkins to JHN (6 October 1845).

[147] LD, 30:152–3 JHN to Mrs Edward Hawkins (21 November 1882) Newman was alluding to 'σμικρὰ παλαιὰ σώματ' εὐνάζει ροπή' from Sophocles, *Oedipus Tyrannus*, p. 961.

[148] Hawkins was born on 27 February 1789.

after the death of both his parents, Marriott entered Exeter College in 1829 before winning an open scholarship at Balliol. George Moberly, Keble's good friend, was one of his tutors. Marriott had a brilliant academic career, though he fell short of the double first that most expected of him. At Easter 1833, he was elected fellow of Oriel and appointed mathematical lecturer before taking holy orders. At Oriel, he became a close ally of Newman and the Tractarians, writing Newman in December 1833, "I am sorry to interfere with the quiet enjoyment of freedom from Undergraduates and crackers; but perhaps you will be so good as to leave me the means of getting a stock of Tracts for Warwickshire and Shropshire, and advice as to saying any thing about them to booksellers."[149] From 1839 to 1841, he was Principal of the recently founded Chichester Diocesan College, the planning for which had been drawn up by Henry Edward Manning. Marriott was also an avid patristic scholar and one of the principal editors of the Library of the Fathers. Richard Church, who devoted an entire chapter to Marriott in his classic history, *The Oxford Movement: Twelve Years 1833–1845* (1891), described him as "a man who was drawn into the movement almost in spite of himself, by the attraction of the character of the leaders, the greatness of its object, and the purity and nobleness of the motives which prompted it . . . a man of metaphysical mind, given almost from a child to abstract and indeed abstruse thought." One of Mariott's relatives told Church that "questions about trade used to occupy him very early in life. He used to ponder how it could be right to sell things for more than they cost you." Later, this dubious view of trade would hamper the Anglican printing press that he established at Littlemore after Newman's departure and involve him in one of Oxford's first cooperatives, which had a marvellous name, "The Universal Purveyor." George Jacob Holyoake, the confessed atheist, who was a good friend of Frank Newman, praised Marriott for lending his support to the scheme, which showed, he thought, "great disinterestedness."[150] Later, Marriott would try to set up a hall in Oxford for poor students.

In thus uniting great learning and great charity in his undertakings, Marriott embodied one of the best traditions of Tractarianism. Newman thought well enough of his friend to recommend him to the legendary Dr Routh of Magdalen, to whom he described him as "a grave, sober and deeply religious person; a great reader of ecclesiastical antiquity," with "more influence with younger men than any one perhaps of his standing."[151] (Newman was attempting, unavailingly, to help his Oriel colleague obtain the vacant chair of Moral Philosophy.) Even after the forces of liberalism there had shown Tractarianism the door, Marriott remained devoted to Oxford. "For my own part," he confessed in 1845, "though I may be suspected, hampered, worried, and perhaps actually persecuted, I will fight every inch of ground before I will be compelled to forsake the service of that mother to whom I owe my new birth in Christ . . . I will not forsake her at any man's bidding till she herself rejects me."[152] Mark Pattison

[149] LD, 4:145 Charles Marriott to JHN (17 December 1833).
[150] George Jacob Holyoake. *The History of Co-operation in England: Its Literature and Its Advocates* (London, 1879), p. 203.
[151] LD, 8:334 JHN to M. J. Routh (15 November 1841).
[152] DNB.

recalled the aftermath of Newman's epochal defection with donnish mordancy. "The neophytes," he wrote, "were . . . scattered like chaff.

> Ward and Oakeley had gone before, but there still remained a small band of us more stable, to keep each other in countenance and meet at Manuel Johnson's for our Sunday dinner—Church, Marriott, Copeland, myself, and others. M. Johnson jocularly proposed to write the history of Absquatulation. He called upon Marriott to provide a theory to cover us. Marriott, who could not see a joke, answered seriously, "We are in a state of appeal—appeal to a general council." When this was repeated to Lewis, who was strong in canon law, he said, "Didn't Marriott know that an appeal must be lodged within thirty days?"[153]

If this was the sort of persecution Marriott suffered, he got off lightly. In all events, after Newman's absquatulation, Marriott became vicar of St Mary's and was instrumental, together with James Mozley, John Keble and Edward Pusey, in keeping the Tractarian faith alive. On 15 January 1845, Marriot wrote Newman a moving letter, which he included in his *Apologia*.

> You know me well enough to be aware, that I never see through any thing at first. Your letter to [Edward Badeley, a good friend of Newman's who gave him good legal advice during the Achilli trial] casts a gloom over the future, which you can understand, if you have understood me, as I believe you have. But I may speak out at once, of what I see and feel at once, and doubt not that I shall ever feel: that your whole conduct towards the Church of England and towards us, who have striven and are still striving to seek after God for ourselves, and to revive true religion among others, under her authority and guidance, has been generous and considerate, and, were that word appropriate, dutiful, to a degree that I could scarcely have conceived possible, more unsparing of self than I should have thought nature could sustain. I have felt with pain every link that you have severed, and I have asked no questions, because I felt that you ought to measure the disclosure of your thoughts according to the occasion, and the capacity of those to whom you spoke. I write in haste, in the midst of engagements engrossing in themselves, but partly made tasteless, partly embittered by what I have heard; but I am willing to trust even you, whom I love best on earth, in God's Hand, in the earnest prayer that you may be so employed as is best for the Holy Catholic Church.[154]

Apropos the unavoidably discordant issue of his conversion, it was one of the undoubted disappointments of Newman's long life that he never received a letter of any comparable fair-mindedness from any of his siblings.

On 8 October 1945, Newman wrote from Littlemore: "My dearest Jemima, I must tell you what will pain you greatly, but I will make it as short as you wish me to do. This night Father Dominic the Passionist, sleeps here He does not know of my intention, but I shall ask him to receive me into what I believe to be the One Fold of the Redeemer." Jemima's response showed that none of her bracing for the dreaded day mitigated its

---

[153] Mark Pattison. *Memoirs of an Oxford Don* (London, 1988), p. 113.
[154] *Apo.*, p. 210.

anguish when it finally came. "Dear John," she wrote her brother, "when you spoke in the name of our Church your exhortations were all powerful, your voice seemed the voice of an angel, you touched a chord in all our hearts—you seemed to know our very hearts. Since your new views gained the ascendancy how great the change! . . . Now I do not mean to say your influence will not be very great. Your talents, experience, and depth of mind must make your words powerful; but you will not influence the same class of minds that you have in times past. Believe me, it is very painful to me to contemplate all this, much more write it down. But I love my Church dearly, and place confidence in her as a chosen vessel, whom the Lord will not forsake though He bring her to an extremity . . . I am afraid my letter must give you pain; how can it be otherwise? This is the misery of difference in the most important of all subjects, the one thing needful for us all."[155]

In this otherwise moving letter, Jemima revealed an aspect of herself that can be seen in other letters as well: she was something of a snob. When she said that by going over to Rome her brother's influence would dwindle, what she meant was that he would not influence "the same *class* of minds." Earlier, in 1841, when she praised Newman for his sermons, she wrote: "I think you will be glad to hear what I hear from all quarters, that they are more read than any of your writings; indeed it is a great comfort to me, for I cannot but think they are calculated to be of immense benefit *to the most important class*." When she tried to impress upon her brother the damage he was doing to the Anglican Church by even considering defecting to Rome, she wrote: "I am afraid of adding to your trouble, but I really do wish you would take the whole matter into account, and consider it, not merely as counting the cost, but,,, whether such impediments as *the troubling the minds of the better sort of people* and long chosen friends etc., may not be providential warnings of the course in which we should walk." Of course, it is speculative to say but the memory of these invidious distinctions might very well have been in Newman's mind when he wrote his splendid rejoinder to George Talbot:

> July 25, 1864
>
> Dear Monsignor Talbot,
> I have received your letter, inviting me to preach next Lent in your Church of Rome, to 'an audience of Protestants more educated than could ever be the case in England.'
> However, Birmingham people have souls; and I have neither taste nor talent for the sort of work, which you cut out for me; and I beg to decline your offer.
> I am &c. JHN[156]

On the combustible issue of class, Newman might have been inclined to agree with Queen Victoria, who wrote to her daughter Vicky on 18 December 1867 of how "The higher classes—especially the aristocracy (with of course exceptions and honourable ones)—are so frivolous, pleasure-seeking, heartless, selfish, immoral and gambling that it makes one think (just as the Dean of Windsor said to me the other evening) of

---

[155] LD, 10:783 Mrs John Mozley to JHN (11 October 1845).
[156] LD, 21:167 JHN to George Talbot (25 July 1864).

the days before the French Revolution." Whether Newman would have entirely agreed with her on another aspect of class is rather less clear. "The lower classes," she was convinced, "are becoming so well-informed, are so intelligent and earn their bread and riches so deservedly—that they cannot and ought not to be held back—to be abused by the wretched, ignorant, high-born beings who live only to kill time."[157] Harriett's observation about Victoria would have struck Newman as much more to the point: "The height of praise for her mind and principles is her liberality in religion," Harriett wrote Jemima in 1843. "They say she has effected a reformation in the morals of the great! It makes one savage . . ."[158]

When Newman received Jemima's letter predicting that his conversion would diminish his influence—a prediction made as well by Harriett and Frank and many others—Newman wrote back: "Nothing you can say about my loss of influence has any tendency to hurt me, as you kindly fear it should. I never have thought about any influence I had had—I never have mastered what it was—it is simply no effort whatever to give it up. The pain indeed, which I knew I was giving individuals, has affected me much—but as to influence, the whole world is one great vanity, and I trust I am not set on any thing in it . . ."[159] This was not false modesty on Newman's part. However aware he was of how profound his influence was, it made him uneasy. "I have never wished to make myself of authority or the head of a party," he confided, though he became a very redoubtable leader indeed. Nevertheless, Newman recognized how influence can miscarry. Many Anglicans, for example, who swore by his sermons and held him in the highest regard imaginable, could not fathom why he should even consider converting. One correspondent, in a long, rambling, minatory letter, wrote Newman to urge him against making his final step to Rome, "You cut yourself off and you carry your writings with you—and your example—and your holy life. It will all be called unholy: it will be called wrong because it led you to Rome." In the letter's margin, Newman provided future scholars with a helpful gloss to this epistolary impertinence: "Well-intentioned fellow, came up to Littlemore and preached to me."[160]

Still, Newman recognized that he had an obligation to exert the legitimate influence he had responsibly, and to do that without converting would have been inconceivable. "Nor have I thrown influence away, if I have acted at the call of duty. This I have done. With what conscience could I have remained? how could I have answered it at the last day, if, having opportunities of knowing the Truth which others have not, I had not availed myself of them? What a doom would have been mine, if I had kept the Truth a secret in my own bosom, and when I knew which the One Church was, and which was not part of the One Church, I had suffered friends and strangers to die in an ignorance from which I might have relieved them! impossible. One may not act hastily and unsettle others when one has not a clear view – but when one has, it is impossible not to act upon it."[161] Again, what was at issue was truth: one could not compromise with error.

[157] *Letters to Vicky: The Correspondence between Queen Victoria and Her Daughter Victoria, Empress of Germany, 1858–1900.* ed. Andrew Roberts (Folio Society, 2011), p. 261.
[158] *Family*, p. 141.
[159] LD, 11:16 JHN to Mrs John Mozley (14 October 1845).
[160] LD, 10:717–20 John William Burgon to JHN (27 June 1845).
[161] LD, 11:16 JHN to Mrs John Mozley (14 October 1845).

That this and other letters bearing on faith had not met with any favourable response from his intransigent sister is evident from a letter that Newman sent on 16 August 1846, in which he complained:

I have ever been very ready to give you a full account of myself and my doings, but you have behaved towards me in a way which has been a virtual rejection of my offers.

It is now going on for three years since you knew of my extreme want of confidence in the English Church; and nearly from that time, or soon after, I said to you something like this: "I do not want to discuss religious points with you – I wish simply, letting you have your opinion and keeping my own, to put you in possession of what I feel, and what I am doing, and to write easily to you, as if (as far as might be) there were no differences between us." One time I recollect, in 1844, thinking you cold, I remonstrated about it to John, saying I really could not tell you more about myself, if you responded so little. You replied by saying it was a mere accident. This I refer to as showing the footing on which I all along wished to stand towards you . . .

Then, when my great trial came, my own relations, and they only, were those who could find the heart . . . to write censoriously to me. Others, agreeing with me or not, thought that something was due to my long suffering; it was otherwise with those on whom I had nearer claims. You were their organ; for I will not believe of so gentle and kind a heart that all you said was your own. I will not believe that it was you, though it was your hand, in answer to my own affectionate and confidential letters of many months, that wrote to me in so cruel a way – that wrote, for instance, so prematurely about my remaining at Littlemore, as if it were modest or seemly in you to advise in a matter of detail one from whom you differed so widely in the greatest matters, or as if the World, which had parted company with me, had any claim to know my mind at once on a point of expedience.[162]

What Newman was referring to here was Jemima's asking him whether he did not agree that staying at Littlemore, after he converted, would be ill-advised, which, under the circumstances, was rather tactless. In any case, after Newman left the Tractarian camp, it is clear that Jemima became the mouthpiece of her husband and brother-in-law James Mozley, neither of whom could be sympathetic to Newman's abandonment of the Tractarian colours to which they remained so loyal.

With these sad matters harrying his thoughts, Newman departed England in the autumn of 1846 with a certain relief. Together with his good friend and fellow convert, Ambrose St John, he sailed for Rome in September. Cardinal Wiseman was keen that he report to the College of the Sacred Congregation of the Propaganda to prepare for ordination as a Roman Catholic priest. The two converts made their leisurely way in stages, first by diligence to Rouen, then by rail to Paris, then to Besançon, then Jura, then Lausanne. From the Simplon Pass they walked to Milan, where Newman wrote Jemima a letter which must have reminded her of earlier letters he had sent describing his experiences at Oxford, though the new Catholic world he was now describing could

---

[162] LD, 22:87 JHN to Mrs John Mozley (16 August 1846).

only have sharpened her sense of what an utterly different civilization his brother had now embraced.

> It is so great a thing to be in the city of St Ambrose. I never was in a city which has so enchanted me. To stand before the tombs of such great saints as St Ambrose and St Carlo – and to see the places where St Ambrose repelled the Arians, where St Monica kept watch through the night with the "pia plebs" as St Augustine calls them, and where St Augustine himself was baptized. Our oldest Churches in England are nothing in antiquity to those here, and then the ashes of the Saints have been scattered to the four winds. It is so great a thing to be where the "primordia," the cradle, as it were, of Christianity is still existing. There is a Church here founded only eight years after the date when Constantine from this very place published the Edict of Toleration in favor of Christianity. At Monza, 12 miles off, there is the iron crown composed of one of the nails which Constantine placed in his diadem as one of the nails of the True Cross, and there are some gifts which Pope Gregory the Great sent to the Lombard Queen Theodelinda. – And at Pavia, where we were on Friday, lie the relics of St Augustine, 20 miles from the place of his conversion, having stopped on the way for some centuries on Sardinia. And the old Ambrosian Liturgy, or Mass, still goes on, carrying one back to the very date of that great Saint. In some respects I like it better than the Roman. I mean, there are one or two peculiarities which are more striking. The washing of the hands takes place just before the consecration, and immediately after it the priest stretches out his arms in the form of a cross – thus indicating, the whole length of the Duomo, what is taking, or has taken, place. This supersedes, partly, the use of bells. I have been very much surprised at the number of communions – they are not only daily, but the rail is filled many times in the course of an hour.[163]

Now that so many of Newman's dearest friends and relatives were either dead or estranged from him, he reached out to the saints, who befriended him in ways that the living could not. Charles Borromeo (1538–84) was a case in point. Related on his mother's side to the Medicis, St Carlo was born into the aristocracy in the castle of Arona on Lake Maggiore, and, after becoming Archbishop of Milan, proved one of the most effective reformers of the Counter-Reformation, as influential, in his way, as St Ignatius Loyola or St Philip Neri. His brief, assiduous life was devoted to clerical education and catechizing. At his death, in his Milan diocese alone, 40,000 students were studying under 3,000 teachers at 740 schools. He also had English connections: In 1580, he was sought out by a company of English recusants, including Ralph Sherwin and Edmund Campion, both of whom would later go on to die for the Faith during the Elizabethan terror. St Carlo also had a special devotion to another English martyr, St John Fisher. So, it is not surprising that this extraordinary administrator and educator, reformer and saint, so much of whose influence was trained on the practical care of souls, should have held a special place in Newman's heart.

> Milan is a most favored place, as having been blessed with that wonder Saint St Charles. I have been reading a good deal of a very accurate life of him. A great

---

[163] LD, 11:264 JHN to Mrs John Mozley (22 October 1846).

Saint indeed. For 80 years before his time there was no Bishop at all here – and the city was in a state of the most frightful disorder. In the course of twenty years he had stamped his character on every thing – and it remains. He died in the midst of a great career of reform at the early age of 46 – but he lives still. The actual memorials of him, his sacred vestments, or shoes with which he passed the Alps, or his mitre, or the Cross with which he stayed the plague, and again the buildings he raised, the institutions he formed, are on all sides of one. When he was taken ill, it was near his native place, Arona – he was scarcely brought to Milan. His people would not believe the news of his danger. When it broke upon them, the utmost distress prevailed – the Churches were crowded all night; at length in the midst of their suspense and anguish, the great bell of the Duomo told them their prayers had not been answered. There he lies; you see him, if you apply for it; any how you see his Coffin; there he lies in his silent shrine, under the pavement of the Cathedral. You see it from above – you can descend down to it, into a still chapel, he is just beyond the altar of the Chapel – and the chapel lies just in the centre of the Duomo, where Lord Nelson lies in St Paul's.[164]

In sharing his fondness for St Carlo with Jemima, Newman was sharing with her the life of a man whose example he had been unwittingly emulating for years. "There was a connexion between him and us," Newman wrote another correspondent, ". . . he was raised up to resist that dreadful storm under which poor England fell—and as he in his day saved his country from Protestantism and its collateral evils, so are we now attempting to do something to resist the same foes of the Church in England—and therefore I cannot but trust he will do something for us above . . ."[165] That Newman noted this connection with another correspondent and not Jemima shows how careful he was to avoid broaching issues with her that might exacerbate old differences.

Then, again, Newman shared with Jemima how St Philip reminded him of someone whom the Tractarians would always revere. "This great Saint," he wrote her in 1847, "reminds me in so many ways of Keble, that I can fancy what Keble would have been, if God's will had been he should have been born in another place and age; he was formed on the same type of extreme hatred of humbug, playfulness, nay oddity, tender love for others, and severity, which are the lineaments of Keble."[166]

Indeed, in the years after his conversion, Newman wrote Jemima of his new Catholic world with the same detail and zest that he had written to her of Oxford when he was an undergraduate. Then he had spoken of Aeschylus, "the great inventor of the Grecian drama; he is the hardest Greek author in the opinion of many, but his obscurity arises from his sublimity; he is a dark gloomy thunder-cloud through [which] the sheet and forked lightnings glare and dart at intervals, awfully magnificent, sternly beautiful, terribly pathetic. Never, I think, have I read an author with whom I have been so much struck; I am lost in astonishment, I am stupefied, I am out of breath; with much of the style and the genius of Shakespeare he has the advantage over him in coming to

---

[164] LD, 11:265 JHN to Mrs John Mozley (22 October 1846).
[165] LD, 11:250–1 JHN to W. G. Penny (24 October 1846).
[166] LD, 12:25 JHN to Mrs John Mozley (26 January 1847).

us in the garb of a foreign language, for every thing is novel and strange."[167] Yet, for Jemima, the Roman Catholicism to which her brother was trying to introduce her was infinitely newer and stranger, especially when Newman dilated on the different orders of Catholic priests, orders which, for centuries, the English had been encouraged to regard as agents of corruption. Newman conceded that some of these caricatures were not entirely groundless. "As far as I can make out the Roman Parochial clergy here are very exemplary, but Rome is a centre to which all persons come, and the foreign clergy are no ornament to the place. They have left their own neighbourhoods perhaps for no pleasant reason, and live here without public opinion upon them . . . But the worst set of all I suppose, (I speak of them as a body) are a number of fellows, part clergymen part laymen . . . called Monsignors – They are often regularly bad fellows – and these are the persons whom the English generally come across, and from whom they take their ideas of a Roman priest." But there were other more admirable orders. "The Capuchins are the order to which Fra Christoforo belongs in the Promessi Sposi. They keep up the reputation which they had in that 16th century; they have indeed the greatest reputation in Rome. Men of noble birth and wealth give up every thing and join them, and they do a great deal of good among the poor – Their dress is very ugly – it is well represented in the pictures attached to the Promessi Sposi – I don't like the Jesuit dress either – but the Dominican is very handsome, being the greater part white. Before I came to Italy, I had a great wish to like the Dominicans, for the sake of St Dominic and St Thomas, but I don't. They are a rising body through Italy, and have a good name – but they seem at present a dry technical school, rigorists in doctrine, and so fierce on their own points, as even (before now) to have plucked a person in examination, because he would not take up a Dominican opinion. It is plain I am only speaking of them as a body – for individuals of course in it are very different. Don't suppose I am set on writing a panegyric upon the various orders – but I have been exceedingly pleased to find that with but few exceptions they are so correct in their life . . . The Jesuits of course are the most wonderful and powerful body among the regulars. It seems pretty clear I shall never be a Jesuit, but I never can cease to admire them. They are a real working body, and mixing devotion with work. In their noviciate they are given up to meditation and prayer – then for seven years (I think) they go to the Roman College, where they go through their philosophical and theological schools, and then, lest their devotional character should have worn off, they go up to St Eusebio for retreats, to live awhile in the unseen world again."[168]

Then, in September 1850, two years after he had founded the Birmingham Oratory, "when," as he said, "I cannot shut my eyes to the possibility of my being put into situations, in which I should have no leisure whatever for ever again recurring to matters of a private or personal nature, and from which I should only be released by death," he decided to speak candidly to Jemima in one of the most powerful letters he ever wrote to her.

> You are quite right in saying that I do not and cannot forget those, who by death have been taken from me. You might have said more; – I think of them with far greater

---

[167] LD, 1:84 JHN to Jemima Newman (31 August 1820).
[168] LD, 12:26 JHN to Mrs John Mozley (26 January 1847).

comfort than of the living. Of them I can think without pain. They were taken away before the truth was offered to them; they were taken away in their ignorance. They had no warnings to look out elsewhere, for the True church of God. They died in good faith. They had not the call, year after year, month after month, sounded in their ears, by means of the successive conversion of their teachers and friends, to put their souls, their faith, their prospects, into God's hands, to do with them what He would. They had not that experience of the heterodoxy and the impotence of their own communion and its authorities, which now grows broader and clearer daily. Of them, alas, it must be said, "Blessed are your eyes, for they did not see, and your ears, for they did not hear." They never came to the determination that they would not let the idea of Catholicism being true ever enter into their mind, and turned away from it, (lest they should "see with their eyes and hear with their ears, and understand with their heart, and be converted,") and that, from an intimate sense of the misery of that inward unsettlement, and confusion on all sides of them and in all their relations, which would be the first immediate consequence of their admitting the thought. They never cherished their dislike of those doctrines and usages of the Catholic Church, which are difficult to Protestants, instead of making an effort to see if they were not really pious and true, in order that they might have thereby an excuse for remaining where they were. And so, [[as to them, (in the words of Scripture)]] "Weep not for the dead, neither bemoan him; but weep sore for him who goeth away," who turns his back on his true home, and refuses to give ear to the voice which calls him thither.[169]

In quoting Jeremiah, Newman, as he said, "was thinking especially of T. Mozley,"— Thomas Mozley, Harriett's husband, who nearly converted to the Church of Rome after visiting Normandy with his wife in September 1843. Newman, as we have seen, counselled him against any impetuous going over and told him to wait. As it happened, Mozley waited and did not convert. This was a source of distress to Newman, but the fact that Jemima would not so much as consider Rome caused him even greater distress.

You say, you are "only half resigned to an ever new misfortune." And do you think that I have not a portion of the Apostle's "great heaviness and continual sorrow, for his brethren, his kinsmen according to the flesh," who are losing what they might claim, and, instead of being first, are making themselves less than the last. O my dear Jemima, bear with me in thus writing to you; you have led me to do so. I have few opportunities of doing so; you will not be troubled with such words often, but I should have to answer for it, if I did not avail myself of an opening such as you have given, to set you right in a most serious matter, and to remind you how I view matters, which, surrounded by influences so fatal to you, you seem to forget can be viewed in any other way than your own.

That God may touch your heart is the constant prayer of Yours ever affectly John H Newman[170]

---

[169] LD, 14:78: JHN to Mrs John Mozley (28 September 1850).
[170] LD, 14:79 JHN to Mrs John Mozley (28 September 1850).

That this appeal fell on deaf ears was evident from a letter that Newman sent Maria Giberne three years later. "Jemima passed through Birmingham the other day in her way to Mr Johnson's at Oxford to stand for his child. He married one of the Miss Ogle's. Dr Ogle has just had a slight paralytic attack. She came up here, and sat with me for some hours – She inquired much after you and took down your direction. She would ask not a single question about my friends here whom she had known. She would not return a civil answer to a proposal I made about Mrs Wootten – she would not ask a word about Ireland – she would not notice even the house, except to ask how high the room was. We had the greatest difficulty to find talk; for all subjects were forbidden of any interest."[171] The wall between them was up to stay and there was nothing Newman could do to tear it down.

"When two Englishmen meet," Samuel Johnson once observed, "their first talk is of the weather." When irreconcilable siblings correspond, they also tend to talk of the weather, though Newman did so with characteristic panache. "Birmingham weather is generally very dull and harsh," he wrote Jemima in the winter of 1863; "but we have had a splendid fortnight. My room is now as bright as a Chinese lantern." In another letter, he mused: "An honest frost I can enjoy—a soft rain I can bear; but a harsh raw thaw, damp cold, is intolerable—worse than the East wind—unpleasant as very dry cold is. And we have a great deal of this weather here; there is no climate like the southern counties; when I have got through the Reigate Tunnel, I always seem to myself in another part of the world, and am tempted to regret the accident which placed me here."[172] Jemima, for her part, sought to beguile the awkwardness she felt regarding her brother by sending him marmalade. In letter after letter, year after year, Newman duly thanked her for these gifts of marmalade, until, finally, in 1867, he put his foot down: "You must not send me any more marmalade. My doctor won't let me eat it. The sugar is bad for me."[173]

Still, despite all of their differences Newman fared better with Jemima than Gladstone fared with his sister Helen, who not only renounced his beloved National Church but also converted to Catholicism, which enraged her brother. Indeed, to provoke him further, Helen tore pages out of the books of Anglican divines and used them as bum fodder. And when she received her portion of her father's estate, she made over £2,000 to Father Manning and bequeathed her Monkland Railways shares to Cardinal Wiseman.[174] Although subject to bouts of insanity—most spectacularly in Royal Leamington Spa, where she resided for a time in the 1840s—she regained command of herself in Scotland after the health of her domineering father collapsed. "The crumbling of the immense figure of John Gladstone gave her release," as S. G. Checkland wrote in his superb family biography of the Gladstones. "She now had a function at Fasque," the family seat.[175] Still, many Catholic Scots attributed her recovery not to her father's decline but to her regimen of fasting, prayer and visits to a nunnery in Edinburgh. In any event, nothing unnerved her brother like Helen's

[171] LD, 15:504 JHN to M. R. Giberne (14 December 1853).
[172] LD, 21:59 JHN to Mrs John Mozley (24 February 1864).
[173] LD, 23:53 JHN to Mrs John Mozley (5 February 1867).
[174] S. G. Checkland. *The Gladstones* (Cambridge, 1971), p. 375.
[175] Checkland, p. 363.

Roman piety. Jemima may have dismayed Newman but she did not taunt him the way Helen taunted William, especially when she added opium addiction to her delight in relics.[176]

In the various works that Newman addressed to Anglicans during his Catholic career, one can see him resuming debates that he had begun earlier with his siblings. Thus, in his *Letter to Pusey* (1866), he returned to the debate over the Blessed Virgin that he had begun with Frank when they roomed together at Oxford. In his *Lectures on Certain Difficulties felt by Anglicans in submitting to the Catholic Church* (1850), he returned to the debate as to whether Tractarians should remain within the Church of England, even after it became clear that the English Church had repudiated "Catholic truth," which he had begun with Jemima in their epistolary exchanges.[177] On what motivated Newman to write that pivotal book, Ian Ker is incisive:

> What makes him speak out "is my intimate sense that the Catholic Church is the one ark of salvation, and my love for your souls." And whose writings can he more fairly refute than his own, "without misrepresenting him or hurting his feelings"? As for his own conversion, he can state from experience that it was the Fathers, the very fount of Tractarian theology, who far from proving an obstacle had in fact been the ultimate cause of his submission to Rome. And so it is Newman's own eloquent testimony to the story of his conversion that forms the climax of the book. It is not an account of how he fell in love with the papacy or the medieval Church; it is rather the history of an Oxford patristic student whose first "vision of the Fathers" as a boy remained with him until the scales fell from his eyes and he realized that with all his ingenious and learned controversies on behalf of Anglicanism against the Roman Church he "was but forging arguments for Arius and Eutyches, and turning devil's advocate against the much-enduring Athanasius and the majestic Leo . . . whose image was continually before my eyes, and whose musical words were ever in my ears and on my tongue!"[178]

The vividness with which Newman depicts the false position of the Anglo-Catholics is masterly. Imagining what those who continued to cling to the "Movement of 1833" might have to say for themselves, especially in the wake of the Gorham Case, Newman replicates their accustomed reasoning with nice satirical mockery.

> Their opponents may triumph, if they will; but, after all, there certainly must be some satisfactory explanation of the difficulties of their own position, if they did but know what it was. The question is deeper than argument, while it is very easy to be captious and irreverent. It is not to be handled by intellect and talent, or decided by logic. They are undoubtedly in a very anomalous state of things, a state of transition; but they must submit for a time to be without a theory of the Church, without an intellectual basis on which to plant themselves. It would be an utter absurdity for them to leave the Establishment, merely because they do not at the moment see how to defend their staying in it. Such accidents will from time to time

[176] Ibid., pp. 326, 329, 377–8.
[177] For an incisive reading of Newman's lectures on the *Difficulties of Anglicans*, see Ian Ker. *John Henry Newman: A Biography* (Oxford, 2009), pp. 350–9.
[178] Ian Ker, *John Henry Newman*, p. 356.

happen in large and complicated questions; they have light enough to guide them practically,—first, because even though they wished to move ever so much, they see no place to move into; and next, because, however it comes to pass, however contrary it may seem to be to all the rules of theology and the maxims of polemics, to Apostles, Scripture, Fathers, Saints, common-sense, and the simplest principles of reason,—though it ought not to be so in the way of strict science,—still, so it is, they are, in matter of fact, abundantly blest where they are . . ."[179]

In this sardonic monologue, it might seem that Newman was having one-sided fun; but he hardly spares himself; he was, after all, the acknowledged leader of the Movement of 1833. Accordingly, he quotes passages from his own sermons to show that "one inward evidence at least Catholics have, which this writer had not, – certainty. I do not say, of course, that what seems like certainty is a sufficient evidence to an individual that he has found the truth, for he may mistake obstinacy or blindness for certainty; but, at any rate, the *absence* of certainty is a clear proof that a person has not yet found it, and at least a Catholic knows well, even if he cannot urge it in argument, that the Church is able to communicate to him that gift. No one can read the series of arguments from which I have quoted, without being struck by the author's clear avowal of *doubt*, in spite of his own reasonings, on the serious subject which is engaging his attention. 'What want we,' he exclaims, 'but faith in our Church? With faith we can do everything; without faith we can do nothing.' So all these inward notes which he enumerates, whatever their prima facie force, did not reach so far as to implant conviction even in his own breast; they did not, after all, prove to him that connection between the National Church and the spiritual gifts which he recognized in his own party, which he fain would have established, and which they would fain establish . . ."[180] By taking himself to task for his own role in the "Movement of 1833," Newman gives his elucidation of Anglican objections to Roman Catholicism an authenticity that is at once impartial and compelling.

Still, Jemima, together with many others, was indignant that Newman should seem to deprecate the good that Anglicans had accomplished in their attempts to revive the English Church. Newman did not deny the spiritual gifts gained by his former associates. He acknowledged the "clear evidences of the influences of grace" in their hearts; their conversion "from sin to holiness;" the "great support" they had received and "comfort under trial." Nevertheless, he had to admit that the Wesleyans and the Methodists and "even old Bunyan" could produce followers with as many or more gifts. So, his old friends and relatives should not put their faith in such dubious evidences. They should trust to their own well-founded misgivings about the Established Church. "If, my brethren, your reason, your faith, your affections, are indissolubly bound up with the holy principles which you have been taught, if you know they are true, if you know their life and their power, if you know that nothing else is true; surely you have no portion or sympathy with systems which reject them. Seek those principles in their true home. If your Church rejects your principles, it rejects you;—nor dream of indoctrinating it with them by remaining . . . You cannot change your Establishment into a Church without a miracle. It is what it is, and you have no means of acting upon it; you have not what Archimedes looked for, when he would move the world,—the

---

[179] *Diff.*, pp. 72–3.
[180] *Diff.*, pp. 79–80.

fulcrum of his lever,—while you are one with it. It acts on you, while you act on it; you cannot employ it against itself. If you would make England Catholic, you must go forth on your mission *from* the Catholic Church. You *have* duties towards the Establishment; it is the duty, not of owning its rule, but of converting its members. Oh, my brethren! life is short, waste it not in vanities; dream not; halt not between two opinions; wake from a dream, in which you are not profiting your neighbour, but imperilling your own souls."[181] Here, Newman's clear solicitude for his audience tempered his lectures, without taking away any of their hortatory edge.

Although many of Newman's letters to Jemima after his conversion were fairly trivial, there were exceptions. In 1870, he shared with his sister the fitful genesis of his *Essay in Aid of a Grammar of Assent* (1870): "I have been writing it ... this thirty or forty years," he wrote, "and never succeeded. I attempted it in my Oxford University Sermons – stopped after the first of these upon it in 1832, managed to get a little further in 1839 or thereabouts, and did no more. I have attempted it again more times than I can count, and have a pile of MS on the subject, in 1846, in 1850, in 1853, in 1859, in 1861, in 1865 – but I could not get on – it was like tunnelling through the Alps ...." He also shared with her his resolution to keep his book trained on his own findings. "It touches on a number of subjects, on which there has been much written in this day – but I have carefully kept myself from reading what any one else has published, because I wished to bring out my own view, and I was sure that, if once I began to read, I should so get confused in the terms and language of others, so mixed up in their controversies, and carried away with the views which they opened, that my own work would vanish. Of course I have the consequent inconvenience that I may be saying what others have said before me, and saying what others have disproved – but it was a choice of difficulties, and I think I have done what is best." Writing on his birthday, Newman could not help but remark the passage of time. "Our violin boys are vanishing, for time with boys is not stationary – as it is with old men." Typically, he ended with some practical advice. Jane Gertrude Mozley, Jemima's fourth child, was feeling poorly, and Newman recommended that Jemima "take her to the Alps, the Bel Alps or St Moritz for two or three months in the summer ... it would set her up."[182] All sickly children should have the benefit of such civilized good counsel.

Then, too, it is interesting that it should have been to Jemima that Newman articulated his view of biography. For Newman, a man's correspondence revealed the truth about him better than the narratives of biographers because "Biographers varnish; they assign motives; they conjecture feelings; they interpret Lord Burleigh's nods; they palliate or defend."[183] In one his own letters, he made the point that "letters always have the charm of reality. I have before now given this as the reason why I like the early Fathers more than the Medieval Saints viz: because we have the letters of the former. I seem to know St. Chrysostom or St. Jerome in a way in which I never can know St. Thomas Aquinas."[184] What Newman omitted to acknowledge is that letters can come with their own distortions. Samuel Johnson, for example, showed how Swift's correspondence misrepresented not only his own small circle but an entire

---

[181] *Diff.*, 1, p. 66.
[182] LD, 25:35–6 JHN to Mrs John Mozley (21 February 1870).
[183] LD, 20:443 JHN to Mrs John Mozley (18 May 1863).
[184] LD, 22:73 JHN to Mrs Sconce (15 October 1865).

age. "From the letters that pass between him and Pope," Johnson wrote, "it might be inferred that they, with Arbuthnot and Gay, had engrossed all the understanding and virtue of mankind, that their merits filled the world, or that there was no hope for more. They shew the age involved in darkness, and shade the picture with sullen emulation."[185] Still, Newman was not so much saying that letters are more objective than biographies as that they reveal their subjects more accurately, even when they misrepresent. This is why he was an advocate of letting the epistolary record speak for itself. "For myself, I sincerely wish to seem neither better nor worse than I am. I detest suppression . . ."[186] If a letter writer presents himself or others in a certain light, let him be seen doing so in his own words. He will reveal himself—as Swift revealed himself—better than any biographer. In this impromptu disquisition, Newman was also trying to forestall biographers from distorting his own life by stressing that all subjects have something about them that is inscrutable. J. C. Shairp, the Scotch outsider who recorded his impressions of the Oxford Movement with such shrewd detachment, recognized that a good deal of Newman's power derived precisely from his inscrutability. "It was this mysteriousness," he recalled, "which, beyond all his gifts of head and heart, so strangely fascinated and overawed,—that something about him which made it impossible to reckon his course and take his bearings, that soul-hunger and quenchless yearning which nothing short of the eternal could satisfy. This deep, resolute ardour of soul was no doubt an offence not to be forgiven by older men, especially by the wary and worldly-wise; but it was the very spell which drew to him the hearts of all the younger . . . ."[187] To make his point about the necessary mysteriousness of the biographical subject Newman used an old proverb: "It may be said that to ask a biographer to edit letters is like putting salt on the bird's tail." This accurately describes the many biographers who have tried and failed to get close enough to Newman to put salt on his tail. Here, again, Newman was arguing for an understanding of the genuine complexity of any biographical subject and the limitations of even the most even-handed biographer. "How can you secure his fidelity? He must take care not to hurt people, make mischief, or get into controversy. Hence men, like Talleyrand, have forbade the publication of their correspondence till a thirty years have passed since their death, that the existing generation may have fairly died out. But party interests and party feelings never die out; and how can one promise oneself that men thirty years hence, whom one has never seen, into whose hands one's MSS come, will be above the influence of party motives, at a time when personal delicacies and difficulties are in their graves?"[188] "Party interests and party feelings" have always been ready to distort Newman's legacy. If during his own lifetime, Protestants put it about that he was an unhappy papist and ready to return to the Church of England, since his death, liberal Catholics have continually sought to misrepresent his understanding of conscience and authority. Fortunately, Newman's vast epistolarium, splendidly edited in 33 volumes,

---

[185] Samuel Johnson. *The Lives of the Most Eminent English Poets; With Critical Observations on Their Works.* ed. Roger Lonsdale (Oxford, 2006), III, pp. 212–13.
[186] LD, 20:443 JHN to Mrs John Mozley (18 May 1863).
[187] J. C. Shairp. *John Keble* (Edinburgh, 1866), p. 11.
[188] LD, 10:443–4 JHN to Mrs John Mozley (18 May 1863).

preserves his own record of his life and work unvarnished. That Newman did indeed "detest suppression" is nowhere clearer than in the letters he wrote to Jemima, many of which were expressly written to establish a full and reliable record. In the case of the letter that he wrote to her in October of 1865, however, the record could not have been sadder. After the warm reception that greeted the *Apologia*, when Newman found himself suddenly welcome in quarters that had formerly spurned him, Jemima invited him to her home in Derby, where Frank was visiting, and his response was understandably aggrieved.

At the end of more years than I can count I have an invitation from you to Derby. About two years ago indeed, when you were so ill, you half suggested, if I went from home, my coming your way, and that was all. Never an invitation from your husband. You have let your children grow up, and I not know them. They have ever been in my prayers. When you came here in 1853, I asked you why you had not brought one of them with you, and you repelled or evaded the question. When you came on that occasion, you pointedly refused to see Mrs Wootten or Mr St John, both of whom you knew. You said as plainly as possible, "I come to see you, because you are my brother, but I will have none of your belongings." It was the same when John (your husband) came here – he seemed afraid every minute that I was going to commit him to some recognition of me, as what I am. I turned up last year a copy of a letter of mine to you written (I think) in 1846. There I say to this effect, "I have wished to write frankly, and tell you every thing about myself leaving the difference of religious sentiment on one side, but I can't, if you don't write naturally, and show interest yourself." I did not ignore the Church of England, but you persisted in ignoring my religion. Well, you wrote a sort of explanation – and I began to be full in my communications again. I wrote you detailed accounts of my goings on, when I was at Rome. On my return, you expressed interest in the descriptions in Loss and Gain. Accordingly I at once sent you the book. The way you thanked me was to write me word that "I must not think that it would have any effect on your religious convictions," as if I had said or thought any thing leading to such a remark. This sort of ignoring what I am, and antagonism to me, you continue down to this day. You never, down to the letter of this morning, direct to me as "Dr Newman", or as at "the Oratory."

This being so, since you have let me alone so many years, since you have let all your family grow up and I not know them, it is not wonderful that I should be surprised at your wishing me to come to you now – surprised in a double way, – because you do so much, and because you don't do more – for who ever heard of an invitation except from the master of the House?

I know how this letter will pain you, but it is impossible I can write any thing else. It would not be honest, if I wrote otherwise. None have so acted towards me as my near relations and connexions. Did I wish to revive the past I could say a great deal – and on some occasions, when I have appealed to you, and tried to get you to make matters better, you have declined to interfere.

Of course it much pleases me to have a change in you, however late – but you cannot bring back past years. I am old now . . .

As to the present moment, my duties keep me here – even were there no difficulties about my health. It is impossible I should come – but I am glad to have what I never have had for so long.[189]

This *cri de coeur* gave voice to decades of unvoiced hurt. Yet after sharing his wounded feelings so candidly, Newman characteristically reopened relations with Jemima on a more congenial footing, entertaining her and her only daughter Janie to lunch at the Plough and Harrow next to the Oratory and inviting them to Rednal, the Oratorians' retreat house.[190]

Nevertheless, the frustration that Newman had experienced in trying to share his Catholic faith with Jemima would inform his response to many in the Anglo-Catholic and convert camp who wrote him over the years suggesting either that Anglicanism and Catholicism might find some common ecumenical ground or that the English were somehow inclined to Rome. To the convert E. S. Ffoulkes, he wrote in December of 1861: "I understand you to conceive, that the English people had tendencies towards Catholicism, meaning by Catholicism either our communion or our faith. And next, that a co-operation with certain educated persons, say of the University of Oxford, would elicit and strengthen those tendencies. Now I do not see how you support these two positions . . .

I do not see how such facts as the observance of Sunday, family prayers etc in England, prove or tend to prove the former. Nor do I see that such facts as Bull's Treatises, Bingham's Antiquities etc and their history prove the latter.

On the other hand my own experience goes to show me, first, that the present tendencies of the English people are from, not towards Catholicism; and secondly, that the writings of learned and reflecting men have no influence upon the English people considered in its classes and professions.

And, since every one judges by his own experience, I cannot do more than state my judgment – and need not trouble you with more words in a matter on which you have a different judgment from my own.[191]

It was perhaps only fitting that Ffoulkes should eventually leave the Roman Church and return to the Anglican Communion, "a re-converted pervert," as Newman described him, who gave his confused allegiances a farcical end by becoming vicar of St Mary's. In these painful reminders of the "Movement of 1833," Newman could not have avoided recalling his unavailing attempts to rescue Jemima from what he regarded as the empty blandishments of the Established Church, with which, after all, he too had been beguiled before he joined what he called the "one true Fold of the Redeemer."[192] But he also recognized that the appeal of Anglicanism was bound up with love of home and that taking issue with that did not endear him to either his siblings or his

[189] LD, 22:86–8 JHN to Mrs John Mozley (31 October 1865).
[190] Meriol Trevor. *Newman: Light in Winter* (London, 1962), p. 506. Learning that Janie suffered from asthma, Newman wondered if her mother had considered sending her to the Alps, though he was not fond of them himself. "As to Switzerland, I should consider it a simple penance to be for six weeks in the monotonous grim glare of those awful white mountains, which are well enough as sights, not as companions — but I believe the air is a wonderful medicine." LD, 24:221 JHN to Mrs. John Mozley (21 February 1869).
[191] LD, 20:79–80 JHN to E. S. Ffoulkes (8 December 1861).
[192] LD, 11:9 JHN to Mrs John Mozley (8 October 1845).

contemporaries. One of Newman's ablest critics, the poet, historian and Broad Church Dean of St Paul's, Henry Hart Milman (1791–1868) took particular umbrage at this aspect of Newman. In the opening paragraph of his attack on Newman's theory of development, Milman gave it as his "solemn prayer and hope" that Newman might

> escape all the anguish of self-reproach and the reproach of others—self-reproach for having sown the bitter seeds of religious dissension in many families;—the reproach of others who, more or less blindly following his example, have snapt asunder the bonds of hereditary faith and domestic attachment, and have trodden under foot the holiest charities of our being; who have abandoned their prospects in life, many of them—from their talents and serious character—prospects of most extensive usefulness to mankind; and who *may* hereafter find, when the first burst of poetry and of religious passion has softened down, that the void was not in the religion of their fathers but in themselves; that they have sought to find *without,* what they should have sought *within;* and will have to strive for the rest of their lives with baffled hopes, with ill-suppressed regrets; with an uneasy consciousness of their unfitness for their present position, and want of power or courage to regain that which they have lost; with a hollow truce instead of a firm peace within their conscience; a weary longing for rest where rest alone can be found.[193]

However harsh, this description of the inherent divisiveness of the Catholic faith was not one with which Newman would have disagreed. After all, his own Catholic faith had been deeply divisive within his own family, though he would come to appreciate that his own part in that division did not warrant self-reproach. By the same token, he could understand why others thought differently. Writing to Lord Coleridge of an Anglican woman whom he had met once in 1839, Newman observed in November 1878, a year before Jemima died on Christmas day:[194] "I can quite understand such good people not becoming Catholics, from the *home* feeling which was so strong in Keble, and is so very sweet. Yet alas, alas! that we should be so divided, and that a long separation has created such a divergence between the religious ἦθος of English people, and that of foreign Catholicism."[195] For Newman, this was the misery of difference.

---

[193] Henry Hart Milman. "Newman on the Development of Christian Doctrine" (1846) in *Savonarola, Erasmus and Other Essays* (London, 1870), pp. 296–7.

[194] When Frank heard the news of Jemima's death, he wrote a friend, "This black edge is for my only surviving sister, whose death is just announced to me. She was my fondest object of boyish love, and it is impossible not to grieve . . . I believe she was loved, and respected by everyone who knew her, as she truly deserved to be." See *Family*, p. 208.

[195] LD, 28:418 JHN to Lord Coleridge (9 November 1878).

8

John Rickards Mozley and
Late Victorian Scepticism

When Newman complained that Jemima and her husband John had seen to it that their six children should have nothing to do with him when they were growing up, lest he pervert them, as they might have put it, he was only speaking the truth. "Englishmen," he observed in one letter, "allow children to be Anglicans, Baptists, Wesleyans, Presbyterians, Unitarians; not, if they can help it, Catholics."[1] However, in April 1874, Newman had occasion to enter into an extraordinary correspondence with Jemima's second son, John, which gave him an opportunity to share his views with a nephew that had been shaped by the scepticism of Victorian Cambridge. In this regard, Mozley is an important figure in the scheme of Newman's family because he would adopt many of the heterodox views that Newman first recognized in his brother Frank, particularly the notion that Christianity could only survive as a kind of Unitarian moralism. As one reviewer pointed out in summing up one of Mozley's later books, "He is sympathetic towards religious symbolism, but places the emphasis on moral rectitude as the one thing that finally determines the worth of a man's religion. The miraculous element, excepting wonderful acts of healing, is excluded from religion. The resurrection of Jesus is not excepted . . ."[2] Indeed, Mozley's Christianity had a lot in common with that of Charles Dickens, about whom Ruskin once remarked: "He knew nothing of the nobler power of superstition . . ." For the great art critic, the Christmas of the great novelist "meant mistletoe and pudding—neither resurrection from dead, nor rising of new stars, nor teaching of wise men, nor shepherds."[3] In one letter to a correspondent who had criticized him for failing to use his characters to recommend Christianity, Dickens confirmed Ruskin's point when he assured his epistolary critic that "With a deep sense of my great responsibility always upon me when I exercise my art, one of my most constant and most earnest endeavors has been to exhibit in all my good people some reflections of the teachings of our great Master, and unostentatiously to lead the reader up to those teachings as the great source of moral goodness. All my strongest illustrations are derived from the New Testament: all my social abusers are shown as departures from its spirit; all my good people are humble, charitable, faithful, and forgiving."[4] Mozley subscribed to a similarly moralistic pastiche of Christianity and

---

[1] LD, 30:18 JHN to John Rickards Mozley (3 November 1881).
[2] *Hibbert Journal*, Volume 15, (1916–17).
[3] *Letters of John Ruskin to Charles Eliot Norton* (London, 1905), p. 5.
[4] *Selected Letters of Charles Dickens.* ed. Jenny Hartley (Oxford, 2012), p. 364.

yet like the poet Arthur Hugh Clough, about whom he wrote with such sympathetic insight, he was never entirely comfortable with the scepticism that this moralism masked, which gives added interest to his epistolary exchange with his uncle. In this chapter, I shall revisit Mozley's life, as well as some of the men who influenced him, to show how in corresponding with him, Newman encountered precisely the scepticism that unsettled so many of his late Victorian contemporaries.

If much of Newman's work is prophetic, Mozley bore out a good deal of its graver prognostications with respect to the infidelity to which scepticism inclines. Born in 1840, Mozley was the son of John Mozley (1808–79), who took over the family printing business in Derby and whose daughter Ann would edit Newman's Anglican letters. Mozley's father had two well-known brothers, Thomas Mozley (1806–93), who married Newman's eldest sister, Harriett and became a leader writer for the *Times* and James Bowling Mozley (1813–78), the frequent contributor to the Tractarian paper, the *Christian Remembrancer* and the leading Tractarian theologian, who, in R. W. Church's estimation, was, after Newman, the "most forcible and impressive of the Oxford writers."[5] At Eton, Mozley studied under the legendary Edward Craven Hawtrey (1786–1862), who, though "singularly ugly," was "curiously dandified"; he also lisped.[6] Nevertheless, according to his biographer, he was "beyond his fellows candid, fearless and bountiful; passionate in his indignation against cruelty; ardent in admiring all virtue and all show of genius."[7] After Eton, Mozley went on to King's College, Cambridge, where in 1862 he was 12th Wrangler and 5th Classic. In addition to winning the Chancellor's medal, he won the Lebas Prize in 1863 for an essay entitled "The Study of Classics regarded as an instrument of Education," about which Newman wrote his mother, Jemima, "I was very glad to have John's Essay, and wrote to him to Cambridge to acknowledge it—it seems to have a good deal of thought in it."[8] A Fellow of King's from 1861 to 1869, Mozley went to Dresden in 1862 to improve his German. There, he encountered Oscar Browning (1837–1923), the fellow of King's College and, later, assistant master at Eton, whom Virginia Woolf took to task in *A Room of One's Own* (1929) for confessing that "the impression left on his mind, after looking over any set of examination papers, was that, irrespective of the marks he might give, the best woman was intellectually inferior to the worst man."[9] The editors of Tennyson's letters characterize Browning as "a gossip and a lion hunter" and quote a reviewer's quip that "OB had met more distinguished people *once* than any other living man," though, in their estimation, he was also "self-indulgent, and, finally, a bore and intellectual derelict."[10] From 1865 to 1885, Mozley was Professor of Pure Mathematics at Owen College, Manchester and in 1864 he was also Mathematics Master at Clifton School in Bristol, where he made long-lasting friends. Beginning in 1871, he was also Inspector of workhouse schools under the Local Government Board in Leeds. In 1868, he married Edith Merivale, daughter of Bonamy Price (1807–88), the quixotic economist, about

---

[5] R. W. Church. *The Oxford Movement* (London, 1891), p. 188.
[6] ODNB.
[7] Ibid.
[8] LD, 21:4 JHN to Mrs John Mozley (2 January 1864).
[9] Virginia Woolf. "A Room of One's Own," in *Three Guineas* (Penguin, 1998), p. 69.
[10] *The Letters of Alfred Lord Tennyson*. ed. Lang and Shannon (Oxford, 1990), I, pp. 1–2.

whom Gladstone observed in his speech on the Irish Land Law (7 April 1888), that he was "the only man—to his credit, let it be spoken—who has had the resolution to apply, in all their unmitigated authority, the principles of abstract political economy to the people and circumstances of Ireland, exactly as if he had been proposing to legislate for the inhabitants of Saturn or Jupiter."[11] That Mozley's wife did not share his heterodox religious views was a source of abiding tension between them. With Edith Mozley in mind, Newman wrote a charming letter in 1881 in which he captured something of the interconnectedness of family.

> It is odd that during the last fortnight I have been wondering in vain what was my Mother's Mother's maiden name. I lament the little curiosity I had to ask my Mother questions, which none but she could answer. She used to talk as if she knew Norwich well, and (I think) Ipswich—but it never occurred to me to pursue the subject. She once gave me a breast pin, which had belonged to her mother, with a small head in enamel of (as I understood) of her mother upon it. This too might have led me to inquire, but, strange to say, it did not. I gave this pin to Edith Mozley on her marriage with Jemima's John. It is odd too that in these later years, I have never thought of asking Jemima any question, since from her good memory, she would be sure to recollect every word my Mother let drop. But it was not my mother's way to talk of herself without pressing. She told me more about herself when I was a school boy than at any other time. I think the troubles of life had so oppressed, so crushed her, that she had no heart to look back at all at any thing.[12]

The "troubles of life" would escort Edith to her grave in 1911. Mozley died 20 years later at Headingley, Leeds at the age of 91.

In an autobiographical postscript to *The Divine Aspect of History*, Mozley left behind some interesting testimonials to the difficulties he had encountered in his religious life. "In the summer of 1866," he writes, "I spent a month at Bangor on the Menai Straits, trying to solve the mystery of the universe. I did not solve it. I have often thought of those lines of Heine, inimitable in their mixture of pathos and mockery, in which he describes a young man such as I was—"

> By the sea, by the wild sea, dark in the night,
> Stands a youth,
> His breast full of sadness, his head full of doubt,
> And with mournful lips he questions the waves;
> "O solve for me the riddle of life,
> The tormenting primaeval riddle,
> Over which so many heads have puzzled,
> Heads in hieroglyphic caps,
> Heads clad in turban and black biretta,

[11] DNB.
[12] LD, 29:364–5 JHN to Louisa Deane (16 April 1881).

> Bewigged heads,
> And a thousand other poor, perspiring human heads;
> Tell me, what is the meaning of Man?
> Whence has he come? whither does he go?
> Who lives there aloft on the golden stars?"
> The waves murmur their eternal murmuring,
> The wind blows, the clouds are borne along,
> The stars glitter, indifferent and cold,
> And a fool waits for the answer.

After reciting this wonderfully apt poem, Mozley made a very Newmanian observation. "I confess my method had been wrong; for action must be added to thought if the depths are to be fathomed."[13] This echoes something Newman wrote in *The Tamworth Reading Room* (1841). "Logic makes but a sorry rhetoric . . . first shoot round corners, and you may not despair of converting by a syllogism . . ."[14] In this, Newman was one with Pascal, who observed in his *Pensées* (1670) how "It was amusing to think that there are people in the world who have renounced all the laws of God and nature only to invent laws for themselves, which they scrupulously obey, as for example, Mahomet's soldiers, thieves and heretics, and likewise logicians."[15] Recalling perhaps Richard Whately and the Noetics with whom he shared Oriel's Senior Common Room and for whom logic meant so much, Newman wrote of how, "Logicians are more set upon concluding rightly, than on right conclusions. They cannot see the end for the process. Few men have that power of mind which may hold fast and firmly a variety of thoughts. We ridicule 'men of one idea;' but a great many of us are born to be such, and we should be happier if we knew it. To most men argument makes the point in hand only more doubtful, and considerably less impressive. After all, man is *not* a reasoning animal; he is a seeing, feeling, contemplating, acting animal."[16] Newman would make this point again and again in his letters and published works. Mozley exemplified it in his own way when he recalled what he called "the first religious act which I ever did in my life."

> After the acceptance by my future wife of my offer of marriage, I went to chapel at my college in Cambridge. I had done the same thing hundreds of times before, but now first I did it with a motive properly my own. For I felt, "I am a man full of infirmities. I have not been very successful in my practical life hitherto; I am entering on a life wholly unknown to me, and I know well that it is possible to make shipwreck of married life; surely I need protection." It was divine protection that I sought; I doubt if I expressed this in words; but I did seek it, and this was a true religious act.[17]

One of the primary strains in the marriage was caused by Edith's refusal to share his Unitarian views. "My wife had never been in the sceptical atmosphere at all; she had

13 J. R. Mozley. *The Divine Aspect of History* (Cambridge, 1916), II, p. 468.
14 *DA.*, p. 294.
15 Pascal. *Pensées* (Folio Society, 2011), p. 251.
16 *DA.*, p. 294.
17 J. R. Mozley. *The Divine Aspect of History* (Cambridge, 1916), II, p. 469.

embraced religion, as so many have done, and as I myself had done originally, in the High Church form; but the many years of thought and reading through which I had emerged out of those opinions had no parallel in her life. . . . Well do I remember my first experience of the strength which comes through prayer, when these difficulties first began to assume a dangerous form. I had all in my power; but had I remained quiescent, all manner of doubts and temptations were ready to assail me; it was only prayer that these were averted. . . . My wife, I know, prayed too, and there was hope in us both."[18] Tragedies, however, would follow. In 1879, his eldest son died; then in 1881, their eldest daughter fell ill and died 5 years later. Throughout these trials, Mozley could never move his wife "from that central belief which the Nicene creed expressed." In this, Edith resembled Frank Newman's first wife Maria Kennaway, who was equally loth to share her husband's heterodox views. Then, again, as Mozley confided, "Of all our points of difference there was nothing on which I was so anxious to attain agreement as in respect of something known to us both, but to one else, to which I attributed a vital significance and value, which she did not accord to it. It will be understood that this was not a matter relating to religion; and we did arrive at a perfect understanding of each other's position in respect of it, and an allowance of each other's position, though not to absolute agreement." What this could have been is anyone's guess: if it was something only he and his wife knew it would have to have been very secret indeed. Yet he ends his two-volume history with an admission that casts his affirmation of prayer in a strange light: "I am asking my reader to take something on trust, but is unavoidable. The proof of what I believe, that my wife is still present with me, can only be obtained by experience that real force lies in this belief in the way of organising the things known to me; and to win this experience is necessarily a matter of time."[19]

Here one can see that if Mozley had difficulty crediting "that central belief that the Nicene creed expressed," he had no hesitation in crediting what the Irish historian Roy Foster nicely refers to as "Protestant magic,"—the table tapping and grave-faced hocus-pocus that attracted so many sceptical Victorians from William Butler Yeats and Bram Stoker to Henry Sidgwick and Arthur Conan Doyle. Foster quotes a letter Yeats wrote to the Roman Catholic Lionel Johnson, in which the Anglo-Irishman explained how, "My position is that an idealism or spiritualism which denies magic . . . is an academical imposture. Your Church has in this matter been far more thorough than the Protestant. It has never denied *Ars Magica*, though it has denounced it."[20] Such kind words for the ancient faith must have pleased Johnson, who was fond of relating imaginary conversations he had had with Cardinal Newman to his fellow poets at the Cheshire Cheese. In one of these imaginary conversations, Johnson had Newman telling him how, "I have always considered the profession of a man of letters a third order of the priesthood," an absurdity which Newman would have found highly grotesque.[21] Mozley, in this regard, may not have been quite so generous to the Roman faith but he certainly shared Yeats' belief in mesmerism. In his later years, he would

---

[18] *Divine Aspect*, II, p. 469.
[19] Ibid., p. 472.
[20] R. F. Foster. *Paddy & Mr. Punch: Connections and Irish and English History* (London, 1993), p. 220.
[21] W. B. Yeats. *Autobiography* (London, 1965), p. 203.

write of his good friend Henry Sidgwick, the Cambridge don, "The days of one's youth cannot but recur to one; and though in one sense they never return, in another sense they are perpetually with one. I never think of Henry Sidgwick as dead, or otherwise than as living, though beyond our ordinary knowledge."[22]

One of Mozley's sons John Kenneth Mozley (1883–1946) also ended his days a widower, though it is not clear whether he also believed that his wife, Mary Geraldine, daughter of John William Nutt, sometime Fellow of All Souls College, remained somehow physically present after death. Educated at Malvern College, Leeds Grammar School, and Pembroke College, Cambridge, Kenneth went on to become a canon of St Paul's and the author of many works of Anglican theology, including a book about the Atonement. From 1905 to 1906, he was President of the Cambridge University Liberal Club. According to one contemporary, although Kenneth "was a scholarly theologian and churchman he had nothing of the 'highbrow' or ecclesiastic about him."[23] A devoté of the German theologian Albrecht Ritschl (1822–89), he followed his father and indeed his grandfather in laying great emphasis on ethics in religion, though his theological views were not quite as heterodox as theirs. He was in St Paul's during the night bombing raids of 1941, which led to his wife's sudden death and impelled him to resign his canonry. While hunkered down beneath that nightly barrage, Kenneth might have recalled a poem that his father had written in the prior century, entitled "In The Night," which captures the crisis of faith that perplexed so many of his contemporaries.

> Gone is the twilight glimmer, and no more
> Hangs the bright crescent with her glowing horns
> Above the western verge; the night is full,
> And all the mighty hills in darkness lie.
> Ye stars! the hour is yours. Immeasurable,
> In the interminable depths unseen,
> Recede your glories, myriad, myriad waves
> Flowing in one, the infinite revealed
> To mortal eyes. And has the Spirit eterne,
> Parent of life, our life, in whom we trust,
> Has he deserted your bright tabernacles,
> Left you as idle signs of barren being,
> Soulless and heartless? Or not rather, full
> Of living impulse and sweet harmony,
> Flash ye your messages athwart the night,
> Unknown, mysterious, undecipherable
> To us poor nurslings of earth's stony breast?[24]

From his many published writings, both poetry and prose, it is clear that Mozley had a passionate love of literature, as well as a fascination with the rise of scepticism, on which he was convinced that literature shed much misunderstood light. Speaking of Goethe's

[22] Mozley to Alfred Marshall (29 September 1916) in *The Correspondence of Alfred Marshall: Toward the Close 1903–1924* (Cambridge, 1996), p. 304.
[23] ODNB.
[24] J. R. Mozley. *A Vision of England and Other Poems* (London, 1898), p. 45.

Faust, for example, he wrote of how "he who wishes to understand the revolutionary epoch in which it was written (one of the most important in the world's history) will find the whole poem instructive in the very highest degree. The vehement resentment against the despotisms of the past, the personal passion, the fervid humanitarianism, of the revolution, are all represented in some part or other of Faust's career; complex characters such as Rousseau and Shelley have their counterpart in it. With all this, there is a steady determination on Goethe's part to show that the new principles are not really antagonistic to the old; that Christianity, from an inner sphere of light, radiates upon the most deeply agitating movements of modern society. Whatever confusion there may be in Goethe's method, whatever weaknesses in his character, he certainly lays a firm grasp on every kind of problem which the modern intellect has set before itself, and looks at the world with a clear and (whatever may have been said) by no means a hard or an unloving eye . . . A volume might be taken up with describing all its touching scenes, philosophic observations, lyrical outbursts! But, if what has here been written leads one person more to study the greatest work of one of the greatest writers of this or any century, it will not have been written in vain."[25]

In one of his last works, an immense two-volume disquisition on the history of religion, *The Divine Aspect of History* (1916), one can get a good sense of the convictions of the man. Speaking of the Great War, he was convinced that "Had that movement prospered, which grew up in the first half of the nineteenth century, to bring the religious spirit of Great Britain into fruitful contact with the religious spirit of Germany, the Reformed religion in both countries being recognized as inheriting the Christian promise, I can not but think that the Christian spirit would have replaced the military spirit in Germany, and our own country would have profited also." This gives a fair indication of how the old whiggish illusions survived even the shambles of the Somme.[26] In this same sprawling history, Mozley has some interesting things to say of Newman and his brother Frank. Speaking of the rise of scepticism in eighteenth and nineteenth-century Great Britain, he argues that it may have been slowed by Wesleyanism as well as the strong Christianity of influential individual Christians, including Samuel Johnson, William Cowper and those whom he refers to as "clerical supporters of the creeds," most notably members of the Oxford Movement, including Keble, Pusey and Newman, but it could not be entirely impeded. Then, he allowed himself a personal aside: "Of one of these John Henry Newman, known in his later years as a cardinal of the Roman church, I may say something more, mainly on account of his eminence; but partly also because he was my uncle, and I hold him in great esteem and affection.

> The criticism I make on him is (and this applies to the whole of his life) that while himself personally most humble and self-sacrificing, he yet expected and demanded of the Christian society an open and obvious imperial character, which it was not possible for that society to have. I do not think I need say more than this; but I should like to set by the side of his name that of his brother (also my uncle) Francis William Newman, a sceptic as to Christianity but deeply interested in it,

---

[25] *The Living Age*, Volume 194, 1890, p. 501.
[26] *Divine Aspect*, II, pp. 445–6.

valued by me not less than his brother, who however was more famous. Of Francis
William Newman I would say this, that while the style of his writing was sometimes
rash and to be regretted, his religious sentiment was sincere and his criticism often
perspicacious; nor did he ever forget that religion demands fearlessness and that
practical good must be our aim as well as theoretical truth. I have always lamented
that these two uncles of mine could not have interwoven, and by interweaving
have modified their respective first principles.[27]

The idea of Newman and his heterodox brother Frank "interweaving" is difficult to
conceive—they were so incompatibly different—but it does show the extent to which
Mozley had more in common with Frank than with his other more orthodox uncle.

Something of Mozley's conscientious character can be gleaned from the reports
he prepared for the Local Government Board in Leeds, when he was the Inspector
of Work House Schools. In one, he writes: "I have at the present time (January, 1903)
been an inspector of schools under your Board for upwards of thirty-one years;
and since my retirement from my present office cannot be very far distant, I should
like to make some general remarks (the result of an experience imperfect, indeed,
but still gathered according to my best ability) on a subject which comes under my
inspection, and on which I have to report to your Board, and which is the most
important, though also the most difficult, of all subjects taught in schools, namely,
the religious instruction.

Religious instruction, as everyone knows, is not one of the subjects which enter
into the code of the Board of Education; it lies outside the subjects which that
Board undertakes to inspect; so it has been ever since Mr. Forster's Education
Act of 1870 . . . As long as schools undertake to teach matters which pertain
to the affections and emotions (and history and poetry, which are recognised
subjects in schools, are barren if not interpenetrated with emotion), how is it
possible wholly to exclude from education the subject which deals with the point
in which all the emotions centre? To take English history and English authors
alone; according as men think differently about religion, so will they think
differently about such important characters as Henry II and Beckett, about Henry
VIII, Edward VI, Mary, Elizabeth, about Charles I, and Oliver Cromwell. To
attempt to eliminate religion from the controversies which these names indicate
is perfectly idle. Authors are implicated nearly as much, one way or another, in
religion; is it possible to read *Paradise Lost* and avoid all manner of questioning
on the religion which that great poem teaches? Thus the difficulty which exists
in the teaching of religion, and still more in the inspection of religious teaching,
overflows more or less into all subjects which have to do with the spiritual or
the emotional nature of man. Would it not be a one-sided view of education
which excluded all such subjects from its contents? I grant that children below
fifteen years of age (such as those who form the mass of those educated in our

---

[27] Ibid., pp. 446–7.

elementary schools) are generally better able, when they get beyond technical rules, to understand science than to feel the meaning of emotions; but children, even in tender years, have soul as well as mind, heart no less than intellect; and it is not right that the emotional side of man should be left uncultivated. Thus, with all the difficulties attending it, I think there is something to be said for the cognisance, on the part of the State, of that subject which lies at the root of man's emotional nature, namely, religion.[28]

This plea for the "emotional" value of religion shows the extent to which Mozley was influenced by Matthew Arnold, who was convinced that Christianity could only offer "spells for the heart and imagination."[29] Indeed, he once gave out that "the prevailing form for the Christianity of the future will be the form of Catholicism; but a Catholicism purged, opening itself to the light and air, having the consciousness of its own poetry, freed from its sacerdotal despotism, and freed from its pseudo-scientific apparatus of superannuated dogma."[30] Newman's understanding of the place of religion in education could not have been more different, though he would certainly have been struck by his nephew making a case for its inclusion, even on the wrong grounds, in an educational climate where the natural sciences had already begun to push religion out of the school curriculum altogether. Newman might also have appreciated Mozley's citing as "an example of voluntary help on a large scale," the "assiduous care which the Roman Catholic authorities take of the children in the certified schools, a care which I believe is extended into their after career."[31]

The photograph that Joseph Rosemont of Bond Street, Leeds took of Mozley when he was in his 60s shows him to have been a handsome, elegant, dapper man with piercing eyes and an air of assured intelligence. He is also bearded, which would have amused his uncle. "Every body is wearing moustache or beard now—all the snobs in Birmingham," Newman told his friend Maria Giberne in 1854. "Today I heard that my dear brother Frank wears a moustache!"[32] In another letter to the convert, T. W. Allies, Newman wrote, apropos his friend Edward Pusey, "it is harsh to call any mistakes of his, untruthfulness. I think they arise from the same slovenly habit which some people would recognise in his dress, his beard etc."[33] Certainly, many in Cambridge shared Newman's dim view of beards. As J. W. Clark pointed out in his lively history of nineteenth-century Cambridge, "Until the popularity of the Volunteer movement cast a military air over civilian manners, the cultivation of beards and moustaches was not allowed by the authorities. Dr. Whewall set his face steadily against the practice; and as late as 1857 a scholar of Trinity, who was afterwards elected to a fellowship,

---

[28] "Education Report for the year 1902, by Mr. J. R. Mozley, Inspector of Poor Law Schools for the Northern District, and Temporary Inspector for the Metropolitan District," in *Annual Report of the Local Government Board* (Leeds, 1903), pp. 158–9.
[29] Matthew Arnold. *Mixed Essays, Irish Essays and Others* (London, 1904), p. 87.
[30] Ibid., p. 90.
[31] "Education of Children under the Poor Law, No. 40, Report for the Year 1902, by Mr. J. R. Mozley, Inspector of Poor Law Schools of the Northern District and the Temporary Inspector for the Metropolitan District."
[32] LD, 16:23 JHN to Maria Giberne (22 January 1854).
[33] LD, 22:158 JHN to T. W. Allies (19 February 1866).

having returned at the beginning of the October term with these two ornaments on his countenance, was requested by the Dean to remove them. He was a good-looking fellow, and deeply deplored the loss of so important an addition to his personal attractions."[34] However, by the time Mozley became a don, the college's disapprobation of facial hair had clearly waned: Henry Sidgwick's beard was positively prophetical.

In its obituary of Mozley, the *Times* claimed that he "suffered from incurable shyness and consequently no one even of his Cambridge contemporaries became intimately acquainted with him. He would express his opinions directly and forcibly at College meetings, but was ill at ease in ordinary society. Undergraduates watched him with curiosity as he started on his solitary walks."[35] This may have been true of the Cambridge Fellow, but it was certainly not true of the man as a whole. On the contrary, like his uncle, Mozley was a gregarious man who saw his development in terms of the influence that others had had on him. Accordingly, it might be helpful, preliminary to looking at his correspondence with his uncle, to consider some of these friends and acquaintances, particularly Thomas Edward Brown, Henry Sidgwick, John Grote, and Montague Rhodes James. They shed interesting light on Mozley himself and provide invaluable context for the various influences that helped to shape him.

It was after he had married and moved to Clifton School that Mozley met the poet and history master Thomas Edward Brown (1830–97). Although Mozley left Clifton in 1865 to become Professor of Pure Mathematics at Manchester University, he often visited Brown in the Isle of Man. In a letter to their mutual friend, Henry Graham Dakyns (1838–1911), the classical master at Clifton, Mozley recalled the "series of walks in the Isle of Man which has left in my mind memories like a rhythm of music."[36] Brown is an interesting figure in his own right, especially with regard to Newman, because he was deeply influenced by the Oxford Movement. After taking a double first in classics and law and history at Christ Church in 1853, where he suffered a good deal of unforgettable ignominy as a servitor, Brown became a fellow at Oriel in 1854, when an Oriel fellowship still carried great prestige. Looking back on his Oxford career after the death of Benjamin Jowett (1817–93), the legendary master of Balliol, he wrote one correspondent, "I was sorry to see Jowett's death in the paper. Nothing that has yet appeared does justice to the subject . . . I always owe Jowett for his kindness when he withdrew me gently, but firmly, from the grim talons of Mark Pattison."[37] Brown also had occasion to look back fondly on what he regarded as the indispensable work of the stalwart Tractarian and Canon of Christ Church, Edward Pusey, which necessarily redefined Newman's early influence on him. "I send you a copy of . . . an article by me on Pusey's Life, which I hope and think you will like. Before writing it, I really read the book, and steeped my mind in all the tenderest and sweetest of my old Ch. Ch. and Oriel recollections. Liddon [Pusey's biographer] writes like a gentleman, and has affected me much by certain suppressions which are obvious enough to the initiated. As to Pusey, I stand amazed. Church (!) had left me unconvinced, Newman, Burgon,

---

[34] J. W. Clark. *Cambridge: Brief Historical and Descriptive Notes* (London, 1883), p. 78.
[35] *The Times* (27 November 1931), p. 14.
[36] *Newly Discovered Letters of T.E. Brown* (Isle of Man, 2004).
[37] *The Letters of T.E. Brown*. ed. S. T. Irwin. (London, 1900), I, p. 217.

the Mozleys had hardly shaken me; but now before the man himself thus revealed (and the revelation is unquestionably genuine), I throw up my hands, and fall upon my knees. Yes, here was a *good, good, real* man! And from a Patriotic point of view, what are we not to think of the patience, the firmness, the absolute confidence in his fellow-countrymen with which he waited, bestrode that fiery Pegasus, rode the great race, and won, while Newman lay sprawling on the Via Sacra? This is the unmistakable Englishman, this dogged Pusey; dogged, but did you see the tenderness! God forgive me! When I think of my blindness! Well, well, 'there's a dale that'll have to be forgiven at some of us—aye, a dale.' But, bedad, sor, I'm as thrue a Protestan' as the wan o' ye, for all that. I feel sure that no man did anything like as much as Pusey to stave off Popery in England. Don't you agree with me?"[38] Here was another expression of that tribal English Protestantism that Newman had encountered in his sisters Harriett and Jemima.

Even though he was ordained in England in 1855, Brown never became a priest in the Isle of Man; the Manx church refused him preferment, ironically enough, out of distrust of what they thought his unreliable Tractarianism. Instead, he devoted himself to school-mastering and poetry. In his collection of narrative poems, *Fo'c'sle Yarns* (1889), the occasional bawdiness of which was carefully bowdlerized by his publisher, Macmillan, he brilliantly preserved the vitality of the Manx dialect. Quiller-Couch was a great admirer of Brown, as were George Eliot and Tennyson's wife. In the *New Oxford Book of Victorian Verse*, Christopher Ricks includes a number of good poems by this unjustly neglected poet, especially some delightful stanzas from a piece called "Roman Women," the opening of which is splendid:

> O Englishwoman on the Pincian,
> I love you not, nor ever can–
> Astounding woman on the Pincian!
> I know your mechanism well-adjusted,
> I see your mind and body have been trusted
> To all the proper people:
> I see you straight as is a steeple;
> I see you are not old;
> I see you are a rich man's daughter;
> I see you know the use of gold,
> But also the use of soap-and-water;
> And yet I love you not, nor ever can—
> Distinguished woman on the Pincian!

Unlike the English in Rome that Arthur Hugh Clough described with such nice mockery in *Amour de Voyage* (1858), who, in their jaded ennui, consider that "Rome is better than London, because it is other than London," even if it is, as Claude says to his friend, Eustace, "Merely a marvelous mass of broken and castaway wine-pots," Brown's Englishwoman is far too insular even to allow for that exiguous concession. Still, if there is something wanting in these paragons of propriety—"how the progress of

[38] Ibid., I, pp. 216–7.

civilization/Has made you quite so terrible/It boots not ask"—there is also something admirable:

> ... for still
> You gave us stalwart scions,
> Suckled the young sea-lions,
> And smiled infrequent, glacial smiles
> Upon the sulky isles ...

In the *Oxford Book of English Verse* (1900), Quiller-Couch quoted another brief poem of Brown's, "My Garden," which can be read as proof that his scepticism was susceptible of distinct misgivings.

> A Garden is a lovesome thing, God wot!
>   Rose plot,
>   Fringed pool,
> Fern'd grot—
>   The veriest school
>   Of peace; and yet the fool
> Contends that God is not—
>   Not God! in gardens! when the eve is cool?
>   Nay but I have a sign;
> 'Tis very sure God walks in mine.

Brown came to such certainty late, even though his God was hardly the God of most Anglicans, even Broad Church Anglicans. Although he was curate of St Barnabas, Bristol from 1884 to 1893, he subscribed to a Christianity that was always highly idiosyncratic. In a memoir, Quiller-Couch wrote that Brown "belonged ... to what we may call the tradition of Clough (his predecessor of the Oriel time); and that period was preoccupied with intellectual doubt, religious questioning, a general malaise ..." Indeed, for Q, despite "filial ties" and "the pull of old remembrance" (Brown's father was vicar of Kirk Braddan in the Isle of Man, a well-regarded poet and preacher), the poet "never surrendered himself to the Church of his fathers. His hesitancy in proceeding to Priest Orders, his twice refusing to be made Archdeacon would indicate this, even did his poems not prove it. In short, he was born a Pantheist (with something of the Pagan, even the Faun, in him) and indulged throughout life his natural sense of God inhering in all things—in the sea, for example, in the poor folk plying their trades on it, in the very fish they took –'. . . from Ocean's gate/Keen for the foaming spate/ The true God rushes in the salmon.'"[39] An even better example of this can be found in a poem of his called "Clifton," where the natural world is invoked not so much as a substitute but a spur to faith.

> I'm here at Clifton, grinding at the mill
> My feet for thrice nine barren years have trod,

---

[39] See A. Quiller-Couch, "Memoir," in *Thomas Edward Brown: A Memorial Volume 1830–1930* (Cambridge, 1930), p. 70.

But there are rocks and waves at Scarlett still,
And gorse runs riot in Glen Chass—thank God!

Alert, I seek exactitude of rule,
I step, and square my shoulders with the squad,
But there are blaeberries on old Barrule,
And Langness has its heather still—thank God!

There is no silence here: the truculent quack
Insists with acrid shriek my ears to prod,
And, if I stop them, fumes; but there's no lack
Of silence still on Carraghyn—thank God!

Pragmatic fibs surround my soul, and bate it
With measured phrase that asks the assenting nod;
I rise, and say the bitter thing, and hate it,
But Wordsworth's castle's still at Peel—thank God!

Oh, broken life! oh wretched bits of being,
Unrhythmic patched, the even and the odd!
But Bradda still has lichens worth the seeing,
And thunder in her caves—thank God! thank God![40]

Mozley deeply sympathized with his friend's unconventional faith and its uneasy evolution. "When I first knew him, in the year 1864," Mozley recalls in *Clifton Memories*, his book of pen portraits of the men he had known at Clifton School in Bristol, "he was in deacon's orders, but the sceptical bias was strong in him, as in other clergymen of that time; and even as late as the year 1880 he had no belief in a future life . . . What was it that made Brown change his opinion? There may have been more than one reason for his doing so; but I find it impossible not to think that the death of his wife, which happened when he was fifty-eight years old (in the year 1888) had a great deal to do with so profound a change . . ."[41] After his wife's death, Brown wrote Mozley, "One thing emerges—my absolute belief in immortality. I am not naturally a materialist; that is a plant not native to my mind; but scales of materialism have sometimes grown upon my eyes. They now vanish utterly. . . . Death is the key to another room, and it is the very next room. I wish words could convey to you how intensely and profoundly I feel this."[42] The extent to which this echoes Tennyson is striking. Then, again, Newman, whose own understanding of immortality was so deepened by the loss of his sister, Mary, would doubtless have appreciated the force of this testimony. He would also have seen corroboration for his view of the impracticality of universal doubt in another of Brown's letters, which he wrote to a lady who had expressed doubts about the after life. "To those who have no aptness for metaphysical speculation," Brown wrote, "I would say, 'Stop where you are . . . The greatest thinkers of all ages have believed in the future

---

[40] "Clifton," in T. E. Brown. *Old John and Other Poems* (London, 1893), p. 140.
[41] J. R. Mozley. *Clifton Memories* (London, 1924), pp. 38–9.
[42] *Letters of T.E. Brown*, II, p. 129.

state. They have thought it out for you, be content. In a hundred difficult matters you act upon similar testimony.'"[43] Of course, this may not have been the sort of assent that Newman had in mind when he wrote the *Grammar of Assent* (1870) but it was proof of the untenability of unbelief, even if Brown was convinced that "it is not parsons and such folk that have passed through the region of shadows into the light of the eternal day; no, but the great fixed stars of the human race, pondering, reflecting, judicious." In any event, for Brown, "If, at the end of their great communings, somewhat of a rapture of intoxication has seized them, what wonder? They have seen the king in His beauty... With tottering steps I have accompanied them. But that was years ago. Now I don't want to totter, but to walk steadily. Therefore I say unhesitatingly, 'I believe.' I have encouraged the glimpses; stored them up for the periods of depression which will inevitably break in upon me. Must I always be breaking stones upon the road to heaven? examining and re-examining every inch of the way? proving every rung of the Jacob's ladder? Well, no, I have other things to do."[44]

One can see in this why Quiller-Couch likened Brown to Clough, who spent a good deal of his short life "breaking stones upon the road to heaven." Many passages could be cited to illustrate this aspect of Clough's work. In *Amours de Voyage*, there is one in which the speaker asks if Rome holds out some path to what Brown called "the light of the eternal day":

> Is it illusion? or does there a spirit from perfecter ages,
>   Here, even yet, amid loss, change, and corruption abide?
> Does there a spirit we know not, though seek, though we find, comprehend not,
>   Here to entice and confuse, tempt and evade us, abide?

In light of Brown's affinity for Clough, it is worth noting that Mozley was one of the first people to write about Clough's poetry. In an unsigned essay written for the *Quarterly Review* in 1863 entitled "Modern English Poetry," Mozley focused on an aspect of Clough's talent that would have interested the author of the *Oxford University Sermons* (1843).

> Certainly he had in the strongest measure that bias of the intellect, from which all great discoveries have sprung, which in its results is so potent and so beneficial, but which, nevertheless, renders so many of those over whom it dominates restless and unhappy, and most especially those who, having it, are yet unrewarded by any signal success; that instinct of solitary thought, that desire to understand fully before proceeding to action, the possessors of which are unintelligible to the crowd, and not less unintelligible in themselves even should their achievements have gained them honour and fame. If we look at the portrait of such a man as Newton, we shall see on it, indeed, a noble repose—the consciousness of triumph after labour; but we shall see also on the face of this the most successful of the masters of intellect, the traces, visibly written, of much failure and defeat; as if for one hour of rewarded energy he had had ninety-nine of painful waste, the pain of which could not be annihilated and wiped away by the highest glory that a man

---

[43] Brown quoted in *Thomas Edward Brown: A Memorial Volume 1830–1930* (London, 1930), p. 55.
[44] *Letters of T.E. Brown.*, II, pp. 215–16.

could possibly win. And if the triumphant are so worn, what must those be who are defeated? Yet these also will win honour, not from the unintelligent, but from those who know and can understand their toil and endeavour.

For Mozley, "in Clough, as in Lucretius, the poetry and the philosophy are inextricably intertwined." And to explain what he meant he pointed out how, "These two men were philosophers, not from the desire of fame, not from the pleasure of intellectual discovery, not because they hoped philosophy would suggest thoughts that would soothe some private grief of their own, but because it was to them an overpowering interest to have some key to the universe, because all even of their desires were suspected by them until they could find some central desire to which to link on the rest; and love and beauty, and the animation of life, were no pleasure to them, except as testifying to that something beyond of which they were in search."[45] Of course, Newman found this all-revealing key in the Church of Rome but he recognized how, even in an age of scepticism, the hunger for some such key would persist. Scepticism might corrode faith in Christianity but it could not undermine the religious impulse itself. At the same time, he was acutely conscious of the difficulties that arose "where the exercise of Reason much outstrips our Knowledge; where Knowledge is limited, and Reason active; where ascertained truths are scanty, and courses of thought abound; there indulgence of system is unsafe, and may be dangerous. In such cases there is much need of wariness, jealousy of self, and habitual dread of presumption, paradox, and unreality, to preserve our deductions within the bounds of sobriety, and our guesses from assuming the character of discoveries. System, which is the very soul, or, to speak more precisely, the formal cause of Philosophy, when exercised upon adequate knowledge, does but make, or tend to make, theorists, dogmatists, philosophists, and sectarians, when or so far as Knowledge is limited or incomplete."[46] Mozley may have been one of the first of Clough's commentators to grasp the nature of his philosophical predicament, but Newman had diagnosed the predicament as early as the writing of his *Oxford Univeristy Sermons* in the 1830s. It took Graham Greene, a century later, to see how this quintessentially Victorian malady would persist into the twentieth century and beyond.

> While the Texan talked across the car, my neighbor stared out of the window. He had a sensitive sick face, an air of settled melancholy. He looked like a Victorian with religious doubts, somebody like Clough, but he had no side-whiskers and his hands were practical hands—not the pretty hands of a writer or a theologian. He said he had been traveling for eight thousand miles, all round the United States by train in a great loop. One more loop and he'd be home . . .[47]

It is interesting that Henry Sidgwick (1838–1900), the moral philosopher and fellow of Trinity, Cambridge who could never quite bring himself to believe in his own unbelief, singled out Mozley's article on Clough because he suffered from many of the same problems that Mozley identified in Clough, particularly muddle and indecisiveness,

---

[45] *Quarterly Review*, CXXVI (April 1869), p. 348.
[46] *US*, pp. 294–5.
[47] Graham Greene. *The Lawless Roads* (Penguin, 1982), p. 26.

though, at the same time, like Clough, he could exhibit surprising shrewdness. "The more he studied the brochures for utopia," Stefan Collini observes of the critic of enthusiasm in Sidgwick, "the more he warmed to the idea of staying at home."[48] Besides being one of the leading lights of late nineteenth-century Cambridge (and the brother-in-law of Arthur Balfour), Sidgwick was the person with whom Mozley chose to share his epistolary exchange with Newman before publishing it in the *Contemporary Review* (1899). Coincidentally enough, he was also in Dresden studying Arabic when Mozley was there studying German. Born in Skipton, Yorkshire on 31 May 1838, the third son of the Rev William Sidgwick, headmaster of the Skipton Grammar School and Mary (née Crofts), Sidgwick would lose his father when he was 3 years of age. Edward White Benson, a cousin of the Sidgwicks and later Archbishop of Canterbury would have an immense influence on him. Fond of books and indifferent to games, Sidgwick resolved to follow in his cousin's scholarly footsteps while still at Rugby. He went on to have a brilliant career at Cambridge and, after being elected fellow of Trinity, he was instrumental in establishing the school of Moral Sciences, which allowed undergraduates to focus on natural philosophy. Like many of his generation, he was profoundly influenced by the utilitarianism of John Stuart Mill (1806–73), which sought to explode the pretensions of liberal Protestantism with the same critical ruthlessness that one finds in Newman's criticism of those pretensions in his *Lectures on the Difficulties of Anglicans* (1850), the only difference being that Mill believed that the unsustainability of those pretensions justified the jettisoning of dogmatic religion altogether, while Newman believed that an illegitimate religion like Anglicanism necessarily abandoned men to false notions of reason. "The whole of the prevalent metaphysics of the present century," Mill argued in 1833, "is one tissue of suborned evidence in favour of religion; often of Deism only, but in any case involving a misapplication of noble impulses and speculative capacities, among the most deplorable of those wretched wastes of human faculties which make us wonder that enough is left to keep mankind progressive, at however slow a pace." He continued:

It is time to consider, more impartially and therefore more deliberately than is usually done, whether all this straining to prop up beliefs which require so great an expense of intellectual toil and ingenuity to keep them standing, yields any sufficient return in human well being; and whether that end would not be better served by a frank recognition that certain subjects are inaccessible to our faculties, and by the application of the same mental powers to the strengthening and enlargement of those other sources of virtue and happiness which stand in no need of the support or sanction of supernatural beliefs and inducements.[49]

At the same time, Mill was equally critical of the Tractarians, charging that they were attempting to found "a new Catholic school without the Pope," which, again, is not dissimilar from the criticism of Tractarianism that Newman mounted in his *Anglican Difficulties*. Both men were intent on exposing an imposture, though for different reasons.

---

[48] ODNB.
[49] J. S. Mill. *Three Essays on Religion* (London, 1885), p. 73.

However persuasive Sidgwick might have found Mill's critique of English Protestantism, he was never altogether comfortable with his agnosticism. Something of his critical view of the utilitarian philosopher can be seen from a letter in which he told his correspondent, "You may say, perhaps the question is not whether we should like or find it convenient to believe in God, but whether such a belief is true. To this I answer, What criterion have you of the truth of any of the fundamental beliefs of science, except that they are consistent, harmonious with other beliefs we find ourselves naturally compelled to hold."[50] Mill would have answered that this criterion was sufficient. Certainly, in mapping out his own surrogate ethical religion, he did not allow any other criteria of truth to get in the way of his boldly utilitarian cartography. The striking thing about Mill from a Newmanian standpoint is how he confirms Newman's warnings against the dangers of private judgment. As the historian Jose Harris observes, Mill's writings on ethics and religion "were to be a powerful force for translating religious belief into the purely private sphere and generating a pervasive culture of 'agnosticism.'"[51]

Sidgwick's doubts about the tenability of Mill's scepticism notwithstanding, it was a mark of his integrity that in 1869 he resigned his Trinity fellowship, convinced as he was that he could not in good conscience comply with the university's religious tests. Cambridge would drop the tests in 1871, though it was not until 1882 that clerical fellowships ceased to predominate.[52] (Winstanley, in his rather plodding history of Victorian Cambridge, thought it "impossible to exaggerate the moral splendor" of the resignation.)[53] Sidgwick, for his part, would continue to lecture at the university and exert considerable influence on undergraduates and colleagues alike, though he also worried about the future of learning there. "It seems that every show place gets every year more and more throned," Sidgwick observed of the Cambridge colleges in 1869; "and it seems our destiny to turn into a show place. Learning will go elsewhere and we shall subside into cicerones. The typical Cambridge man will be the antiquarian personage who knows about the history of colleges, and is devoted to '*culture des ruines*.'"[54] Despite such baleful predictions, Sidgwick was keen on having women educated at Cambridge, and in 1879, thanks largely to his own munificent support, Newnham College opened its doors. In the same year, he married A. J. Balfour's sister, Eleanor, who would edit his letters after his death.[55] Later, he sat on the councils of the women's college at Girton. He was also a founding member of the Apostles, the Synthetic Club, and the Metaphysical Society, all of which gratified his delight in gregarious inquiry.

[50] Sidgwick quoted in Max Egremont. *Balfour: A Life of Arthur James Balfour* (London, 1980), pp. 24–5.
[51] ODNB.
[52] V. H. H. Green. *Religion at Oxford and Cambridge* (London, 1964), p. 297.
[53] Denys Arthur Winstanley. *Later Victorian Cambridge* (Cambridge, 1947), p. 67.
[54] Christopher Brooke and Roger Highfield. *Oxford and Cambridge* (Cambridge, 1988), p. 320.
[55] Apropos Balfour, who shared many of Sidgwick's sceptical views, Henry James once observed in a letter of 1888, "I spent 2 days in the autumn at a country house with [Balfour] & Wilfrid Blunt . . . Blunt is a humorless madman & a very disagreeable person. Balfour I should think indeed a prodigy of amiable heartlessness. It all comes back to *race*—high Scotch Tory ancestry, lands & dominions. The lands, ancestry & Toryism give the insolence, & Scotland the *mind*. See *Henry James: A Life in Letters*. ed. Philip Horne (London, 1999), p. 199.

It is a pity that Newman never met this endlessly deliberative man because, for all of their differences, they had some notable things in common. Both were men of extraordinary charm. E. F. Benson recalled Sidgwick's "gentle voice, his wise and kindly air . . . his lazy and contented laugh, the backward poise of his head, his up-drawn eyebrows . . ." Leslie Stephen was another admirer, recalling how "Besides his dialectical ability, he was delightful . . . in social occasions." He was also "a first rate talker," with "a singular ingenuity and vivacity of thought and constant play of humour . . ."[56] Wilfrid Ward, one of the best of Newman's early biographers, corroborated this impression, recalling how "With Sidgwick conversation never ceased. His fertility was endless."[57] Then, again, as the great constitutional historian F. W. Maitland recognized, Sidgwick had Newman's keen interest in the views of others. His wonderfully incisive review of Matthew Arnold's *Culture and Anarchy* (1869) exemplifies this, especially where he remarks how "many who love culture much—and respect the enthusiasm of those who love it more—may be sorry when it is brought into antagonism with things that are more dear to them even than culture. I think Mr. Arnold wishes for the reconciliation of antagonisms: I think that in many respects, with his subtle eloquence, his breadth of view, and above all his admirable temper, he is excellently fitted to reconcile antagonisms; and therefore I am vexed when I find him, in an access of dilettante humour, doing not a little to exasperate and exacerbate them, and dropping from the prophet of an ideal culture into a more or less prejudiced advocate of the actual."[58]

Another good example of Sidgwick's respect for the views of others can be found in a letter he wrote to Ward congratulating him on the publication of *William George Ward and the Oxford Movement* (1889). "I think your book is one of a rare class—the class of biographies which are good in the sense in which good novels are good . . . which give the peculiar pleasure and instruction that can only be given by the full unfolding of the intellectual and moral quality of a rare mind . . ."[59] That the conscientious sceptic in Sidgwick had a soft spot for the ardent Catholic in Ward says something about the catholicity of his judgement. For Maitland, Sidgwick's "range of sympathy was astonishingly wide. He seemed to delight in divining what other people were thinking, or were about to think, in order that he might bring his mind near to theirs, learn from them what he could learn, and then, if argument was desirable, argue at close quarters."[60]

One can see this same readiness to enter into the views of others again and again in Newman's correspondence, and not least in the exchange of letters that he had with his nephew. Then, again, both men took a deep interest in the way men actually reason, as opposed to how they should like to reason. The third book of Sidgwick's *Methods of Ethics* (1874) examines how men arrive at moral decisions—often unconsciously—in a way that is not dissimilar to Newman's examination in the *Grammar of Assent* (1870) of the way that men arrive at religious certitude.[61] Moreover, Newman and Sidgwick

56 DNB.
57 Wilfrid Ward. *Last Lectures* (London, 1918), p. xiv.
58 "The Prophet of Culture," in Matthew Arnold. *Culture and Anarchy* (Penguin, 2006), pp. 157–72.
59 F. W. Maitland. "Henry Sidgwick," in *The Independent Review*, Vol. 9 (April-June 1906), p. 330.
60 Ibid., p. 326.
61 *The Cambridge History of English Literature* (Cambridge, 1907–21).

were keenly aware of the demands of good writing. If Newman famously likened literary composition to a kind of child-birth, Sidgwick once told Lady Welby, apropos his literary endeavours, "It is a difficult matter to persuade a plain man to go through the process necessary to attain precision of thought: it requires great literary skill in presenting the process. I tried to do something of this sort in my *Principles of Political Economy* but I fear I bored the reader horribly."[62] But there was another similarity still. Sidgwick agreed with Newman (and, for that matter, Huxley) that Protestantism was an untenable half-way house between rationalist atheism on the one hand and Roman theism on the other, understandable, perhaps, as a necessary compromise for Anglican sceptics like Benson, who could never entirely part company with some vestige of Christian faith, but inconceivable for rigorous positivists like Mill and Comte. After Mozley shared with Sidgwick his epistolary exchange with his uncle, the Cambridge philosopher must have startled his younger colleague when he confided how, if he could embrace theism, "I really think the haven of rest that I should seek would be the church of Rome, just because of the insistence on authority of which your uncle speaks. There seem to me only two alternatives: either my own reason or some external authority; and if the latter . . . I should not hesitate to choose the Roman Church on broad historic grounds."[63]

This highlights another attractive trait about Sidgwick: he was intellectually honest. Maitland quotes him confessing in another instance, "Well, I myself have taken service with Reason, and I have no intention of deserting. At the same time, I do not think that loyalty to my standard requires me to feign a satisfaction in the service which I do not really feel."[64] Such candour would doubtless have endeared Sidgwick to Newman.

Where Sidgwick differed with Newman was in failing to recognize that if Protestantism could offer no alternative to the stark choice between Catholicism on the one hand and atheism on the other neither could liberalism, which, as Newman recognized, was cobbled together out of the ruins of Protestantism. Newman is very insightful about this in the *Apologia*, in which he candidly shares with his readers how his conversion willy-nilly helped disillusioned Protestants by pointing them in the direction, not of Rome—which they refused to consider in any case—but liberalism, which after Newman's departure from Oxford went from strength to strength in both Oxford and Cambridge. "The most oppressive thought, in the whole process of my change of opinion," Newman wrote in his great intellectual autobiography, "was the clear anticipation, verified by the event, that it would issue in the triumph of Liberalism." In accounting for this unintended consequence, Newman showed his own intellectual honesty, which is one of the hallmarks of his autobiography and indeed his work as a whole. "Against the Anti-dogmatic principle I had thrown my whole mind," he recalled, "yet now I was doing more than any one else could do, to promote it. I was one of those who had kept it at bay in Oxford for so many years; and thus my very retirement was its triumph. The men who had driven me from Oxford were distinctly the Liberals; it was they who had opened the attack upon Tract 90, and it was they who would gain a

---

[62] Bart Schultz. *Henry Sidgwick: Eye of the Universe* (Cambridge, 2004), p. 790.
[63] D. G. James. *Henry Sidgwick: Science and Faith in Victorian England* (Oxford, 1970), p. 18.
[64] See F. W. Maitland. "Henry Sidgwick," in *The Independent Review*, Vol. 9 (April–June 1906), p. 330.

second benefit, if I went on to abandon the Anglican Church."[65] This is borne out by Dean Church's history of the Oxford Movement, where he speaks of how it was out of the "feuds and discords" that preceded and followed Newman's secession that "the Liberal party which was to be dominant in Oxford took its rise, soon to astonish old-fashioned Heads of Houses with new and deep forms of doubt more audacious than Tractarianism, and ultimately to overthrow not only the victorious authorities, but the ancient position of the Church, and to recast from top to bottom the institutions of the University."[66] But for Newman, "this was not all." The peculiar character of his responsibility for this new order bore out one of his core convictions, a conviction shared by Sidgwick and Huxley. "As I have already said, there are but two alternatives, the way to Rome, and the way to Atheism: Anglicanism is the halfway house on the one side, and Liberalism is the halfway house on the other. How many men were there, as I knew full well, who would not follow me now in my advance from Anglicanism to Rome, but would at once leave Anglicanism and me for the Liberal camp. It is not at all easy (humanly speaking) to wind up an Englishman to a dogmatic level. I had done so in good measure, in the case both of young men and of laymen, the Anglican *Via Media* being the representative of dogma. The dogmatic and the Anglican principle were one, as I had taught them; but I was breaking the *Via Media* to pieces, and would not dogmatic faith altogether be broken up, in the minds of a great number, by the demolition of the *Via Media*? Oh! how unhappy this made me!"[67] When Newman returned to Oxford for his honorary degree in 1877, the High Churchman Frederick Meyrick pointed out the irony of how

> At dinner his health was given by Professor Bryce, who congratulated him on having brought about a state of theological liberalism or indifferentism in Oxford, the one thing which from the beginning of his life to its end he abhorred. In the course of the day he paid a visit to his old and beloved friend, Dr. Pusey. 'Newman,' said Pusey, after the first greetings, 'the Oxford Liberals are playing you like a card against us who are trying to preserve the religious character of the University.' He was made much of during this visit. College Gardens were lighted in his honour, and he held receptions of admirers. But it was his old enemies, whom he had fought *a l'outrance*, and whose principles he hated now from the bottom of his heart, who flocked round him as their champion, and thanked him for what he had done in demolishing the power of the Church of England in Oxford.

For Meyrick, "It is an entire mistake to suppose that the religious movement in Oxford of the last century owes its origin to Newman, or required his help for its success. It would have taken place had Newman not existed, though the fire would not have blazed up so rapidly nor so fiercely if he had not been there to feed it."[68] Here, one can see plainly that it was from Meyrick that Peter Nockles took his thesis for *The Oxford*

---

[65] *Apo.*, p. 184.
[66] R. W. Church. *The Oxford Movement* (London, 1922), p. 393.
[67] *Apo.*, pp. 184–5.
[68] Frederick Meyrick. *Memories of Life at Oxford and Experiences in Italy, Greece, Turkey, Germany, Spain and Elsewhere* (London, 1905), p. 26.

Movement in Context (Cambridge, 1994), though he omits to acknowledge as much in that elaborately misleading study.

Frank Turner, the late Yale Professor of History, suggests that Newman's account of the Movement of 1833 in the *Apologia* is unreliable because it is self-serving. Citing Newman's admission to a correspondent that he did not have a "sufficiently vivid memory of the Tracts for the Times," tracts which were written by various hands at various times for various purposes, Turner proceeds to assert, in his own highly polemical edition of the *Apologia* that "There is no reason to doubt that similar failures of memory . . . shaped the contours of the *Apologia* in 1864 and 1865." But there is every reason to doubt this when one considers how Newman's account tallies not only with those of Dean Church and Frederick Oakeley but those of various Tractarians, Liberals, and High Churchmen as well.[69] For Turner to give out that the reader should assume that Newman was *a priori* guilty of "selective use of memory," "consciously chosen areas of silence," and "polemical intentions" is proof of his own flagrant bias.[70] Newman's account of the part he played in handing Oxford over to scepticism and infidelity is, after all, self-deprecatory. Speaking of the many people that had looked to him for guidance and support when he was still vicar of St Mary's, he put very pointed questions, none of which were flattering to himself: "How could I ever hope to make them believe in a second theology, when I had cheated them in the first? with what face could I publish a new edition of a dogmatic creed, and ask them to receive it as gospel? Would it not be plain to them that no certainty was to be found any where? Well, in my defence I could but make a lame apology; however, it was the true one, viz. that I had not read the Fathers cautiously enough; that in such nice points, as those which determine the angle of divergence between the two Churches, I had made considerable miscalculations."[71] This is admission of error, honestly avowed, and a demonstrably accurate account of the consequences that flowed from the error, not self-vindication. Here, Newman was only exemplifying La Rochefoucauld's *aperçu* that "Nothing ought to damp our self-conceit more effectually than to observe that we now condemn what we formerly approved."

Before Newman summoned the clarity of purpose necessary to convert, which he drew, in part, from that most unEnglish of books, the *Spiritual Exercises* of St Ignatius Loyola, Newman initially held back from taking the final step to Rome because he was worried about how such a step might affect the faith of his Anglican contemporaries, though he eventually concluded that unsettling their faith might actually be a good thing, considering its accustomed latitudinarianism. Sidgwick held back from embracing atheism for reasons that were not dissimilar. "The reason why I keep strict silence now for many years with regard to theology," he wrote Mozley in 1881, "is that while I cannot myself discover adequate rational basis for the Christian hope of happy immortality, it seems to me that the general loss of such a hope from the minds of average human beings as now constituted, would be an evil of which I cannot pretend to measure the

---

[69] Here I have in mind Edward Pusey, John Keble, J. B. Mozley, Lord Blachford, William Copeland, Mark Pattison, Anthony J. Froude, Frederick Meyrick, and Richard Holt Hutton, all of whose accounts of the movement generally corroborate that of Newman, with, of course, incidental differences.
[70] *Apologia Pro Vita Sua and Six Sermons*. ed. Frank Turner (New Haven, 2008), p. 5.
[71] *Apo.*, p. 185.

extent. I am not prepared to say that the dissolution of the existing social order would follow but I think the danger of such a dissolution would be seriously increased, and the evil would certainly be very great." Newman never thought in such condescending terms of "average human beings"; no one can read his vast correspondence without appreciating the respect he showed his highly diverse correspondents, whether dukes or dustmen; and he certainly never imagined that anyone should be prepared to accept that "the Christian hope of happy immortality" had somehow become untenable. Still, he agreed with Sidgwick that the evils that would accompany the abandonment of this hope would be incalculable. Indeed, he saw those evils with a prescience that was unusual for a man of his age. But then Sidgwick went on to write in the same letter that he was "not," as he said, "prepared to say that this will be equally true some centuries hence; in fact I see strong ground for believing that it will *not* be equally true." And his explanation for this extraordinary statement was wonderfully revealing. "The tendency of development," he wrote, "has been to make human beings more sympathetic; and the more sympathetic they become, the more likely it seems to be that the results of their actions on other human beings (including remote posterity) will supply adequate motives to goodness of conduct, and render the expectation of personal immortality, of God's moral order more realised, less important from this point of view. At the same time a considerable improvement in average human beings in this respect of sympathy is likely to increase the mundane happiness for men generally, and to render the hope of future happiness less needed to sustain them in the trials of life."[72] One of Sidgwick's more recent commentators offers an arrestingly fatuous gloss on these bold prognostications: "moral maturation will yield an increase in general and individual happiness," he states, "rendering the problem of self-sacrifice less compelling."[73]

It is not difficult to imagine what Newman would have made of such views, especially in light of his conviction that "utter unbelief has no root in the human heart."[74] Nevertheless, it is important to keep Sidgwick's sweeping, if uneasy scepticism in mind when we revisit Newman's letters to his nephew because Mozley would have been surrounded by the same scepticism not only at Cambridge but at Manchester where he taught subsequently.

It is also worth noting that, months after writing to Mozley, Sidgwick wrote another correspondent: "We are now alone again, and I am labouring slowly at my *Political Economy*. But the great event that has occurred to me is that my interest in Spiritualism has been revived!"[75] When editing her husband's letters, Sidgwick's wife Eleanor explained that "This renewed interest in 'Spiritualism' was mainly due to experiments by Professor W. F. Barrett of Dublin, which seemed to show that 'thought transference'—the influence of one mind upon another, apart from any recognised mode of perception—was a reality. The interest of Sidgwick and others in this was part of the impulse that, through the zeal and energy of Professor Barrett, led to the foundation of the Society for Psychical Research. At a conference convened by the latter, and held on January 6, 1882, the Society was planned, and it was definitely

[72]   Arthur and Eleanor Mildred Sidgwick. *Henry Sidgwick: A Memoir* (London, 1906), pp. 357–8.
[73]   Schultz, p. 269.
[74]   LD, 29:169 JHN to Lady Herbert of Lea (19 August 1879).
[75]   *Henry Sidgwick: A Memoir*, p. 358.

constituted in February of that year, with Sidgwick as its first President, and with the declared object of 'making an organised and systematic attempt to investigate that large group of debatable phenomena designated by such terms as mesmeric, psychical, and spiritualistic.'" That one of the most esteemed and beloved dons of late nineteenth-century Cambridge was seriously interested in such patent charlatanism says something about the rigour of the science with which the place was enamoured, though, as we have seen, it was something that Mozley credited as well. Apropos this, A. N. Wilson makes an amusing point when he calls attention to "What seems so characteristic of the age"—namely "the attempt to confirm one type of belief by means of an essentially alien mental process: enlisting science to verify the resurrection of the body and the life everlasting," an absurdity tantamount to "appointing mystics to a chair of Physics." And to put this in some historic perspective, Wilson reminds his readers how "the 1880s were an era of kaleidoscopic muddle when the future of Ireland or the Liberal Party was determined not by political discussion but by sex scandals. Aesthetics turned from wallpaper design to redesigning society. One of the most famous atheists of the age became a convert to Theosophy. And journalism, that ultimate fantasy magic lantern, laid its first serious claims to be not simply a purveyor of news, but a moral mirror to society as a whole."[76] Another explanation might simply be that Sidgwick, like so many Cambridge men of his generation, misunderstood the place of theology within the scheme of universal knowledge so fundamentally that he misconceived not only the reach but the very nature of science. As Newman pointed out as far back as 1851, "University Teaching without Theology is simply unphilosophical."[77] Sidgwick all but conceded this in a piece that he wrote for the *Mind* in 1876, when he quipped, "If any one fifty years ago had been called upon to write a paper on Philosophy at Cambridge, he might reasonably have felt that he had been set to the ancient tyrannical task of making bricks without straw."[78] Of course, the university had paid some attention to John Locke's *Essay on Human Understanding* (1690) and William Paley's *Evidences of Christianity* (1794), as well as William Whewell's *Elements of Morality* (1855), but, for Sidgwick, until he and John Grote set about reordering the place, a reordering which would open the door to the mandarin ethics of G. E. Moore, "the educational movement in Cambridge was entirely absorbed in developing and determining the mutual relations of Classics, Mathematics and Physics: and was content to leave Ethics and Metaphysics to the care of Scotland and Germany."[79] Nevertheless, it is worth pointing out that before he died in 1900— that legendary year, when, according to the poet Yeats, "everybody got down off his stilts," and "henceforth nobody drank absinthe with his black coffee; nobody went mad; nobody committed suicide; nobody joined the Catholic Church . . ."—Sidgwick directed that his burial be accompanied with words that put his alleged scepticism in a most ambiguous light.[80] "Let us commend to the love of God with silent prayer the soul of a sinful man who partly tried to do his duty. It is by his wish that I say over

---

[76] A. N. Wilson. *The Victorians* (Folio Society, 2008), pp. 413–4.
[77] *Idea*, p. 50.
[78] Sidgwick, "Philosophy at Cambridge," in *Mind* (London and Edinburgh, 1876), p. 235.
[79] Sidgwick in *Mind* (London and Edinburgh), p. 236.
[80] *The Oxford Book of Modern Verse*. ed. W. B. Yeats (Oxford, 1936), p. xi.

his grave these words and no more."[81] Here, one can see why Newman never entirely despaired of the English tiring of Latitudinarianism.

Lytton Strachey and his Bloomsbury friends would mock Sidgwick for personifying what they called the "Glass Case Age," for living out his days in speculative futility, for his "refusal to face any fundamental question fairly—either about people or God."[82] But this is hardly fair. Sidgwick did attempt to face a number of fundamental questions, however agonizingly and with whatever dubious success. Indeed, he once admitted, apropos the problem of immortality, that "It is extremely difficult to state what sort of *hope* I have and I can readily believe that my idiosyncratic indifference regarding immortality makes my attitude of faith unintelligible."[83] Unlike so many Victorian sceptics—Jowett and Huxley come to mind—Sidgwick had nothing of the doctrinaire about him and made no bones about his doubts about his doubts. For this very reason, of all of the rationalists in his midst, Newman might have found Sidgwick the least objectionable. After all, when it came to "reason as it acts in fact and concretely in fallen man," Newman was never surprised by the sort of frank scepticism in which Sidgwick engaged. While he was the first one to appreciate "that even the unaided reason, when correctly exercised, leads to a belief in God, in the immortality of the soul, and in a future retribution," he was also aware, as he said, that "actually and historically . . . I do not think I am wrong in saying that its tendency is towards a simple unbelief in matters of religion."[84] Moreover, so much of Sidgwick's career bears out Newman's contention that "unbelief is in some shape unavoidable in an age of intellect," especially since "faith requires an act of the will, and presupposes the due exercise of religious advantages."[85] Considering the fact that Sidgwick received his early education at Rugby under Edward Benson, who revered Dr Arnold, Newman would have appreciated the distinct disadvantages under which the Cambridge moralist laboured. Sidgwick's career also bore out Newman's recognition that "Latitudinarianism is an unnatural state; the mind cannot long rest in it; and especially if the fact of a revelation be granted, it is most extravagant and revolting to our reason to suppose that after all its message is not ascertainable and that the divine interposition reveals nothing."[86] At the same time, Newman might have given Sidgwick credit for never entirely turning his back on the Christianity that so much of his rationalism told him was untenable, a piece of obduracy which exasperates many of his more recent commentators. "I sometimes say to myself, I believe in God," the perplexed moralist once told a correspondent, "while sometimes again I can say no more than I hope this belief is true, and I must and will act as if it was."[87] Indeed, in a letter to Tennyson he went much further, writing how "I am haunted by a dread that it is only a wild dream, all this scientific study of human nature, a dream as vain and unsubstantial as alchemy. At such moments, if I had been

[81] ODNB.
[82] Strachey to Keynes in Michael Holroyd. *Lytton Strachey: A Critical Biography* (London, 1995), p. 140.
[83] Schultz, p. 463.
[84] *Idea*, p. 218.
[85] Ibid., p. 382.
[86] LD, 7:412 JHN to FWN (22 October 1844).
[87] Henry Sidgwick, "Thomas Henry Green," in *Mind*, Vol. 17 (London, 1908), p. 94.

brought up a Roman Catholic, I might have become a Jesuit in order to get a definite object in life."[88] The thought of what the Society of Jesus would have made of Henry Sidgwick joining their ranks is profoundly amusing.

Strictly on philosophical grounds, Newman might also have given Sidgwick some credit, for on those grounds he could show genuine intellectual probity. For the Scottish philosopher, Alasdair MacIntyre, the moral philosophy of Sidgwick was the culmination of the scrutiny and re-scrutiny of the great nineteenth-century utilitarians, even though "it is with Sidgwick that the failure to restore a teleological framework for ethics finally comes to be accepted." And MacIntyre locates the cause for this failure in something very much like Newman's recognition of the force of first principles in matters where reason cannot have the final say. For Sidgwick, according to MacIntyre, "At the foundation of moral thinking lie beliefs in statements for the truth of which no further reason can be given." Borrowing from Whewell, Sidgwick named these statements *intuitions*. At the same time, "Sidgwick's disappointment with the outcome of his own inquiries is evident in his announcement that where he had looked for Cosmos he found only Chaos." And MacIntyre also points out that it was from Sidgwick that G. E. Moore took his ethical arguments for his *Principia Ethica* (1903), the only difference being that "what Sidgwick portrays as failure Moore takes to be an enlightening and liberating discovery." However, the proponents of Moore's hedonism failed to appreciate that, if Moore's ideas liberated them from Christianity and utilitarianism, they also "deprived" them "of any grounds for claims to objectivity" and opened the door to "emotivism"—the calamitous fancy that ethical judgements are simply expressions of feeling.[89]

Nevertheless, although MacIntyre is helpful in showing how Sidgwick's failure became Moore's bright idea, he gives his readers a false impression when he says that Sidgwick was merely *disappointed* with the "outcome of his own inquiries." One can see from the ending of *The Methods of Ethics* that Sidgwick's plight was much more radical and far-reaching: it was a disillusionment with rationalist enquiry *per se*, which, again, redounds to his intellectual honesty. Here is not a paraphrase of the passage but the passage itself.

Hence, the whole system of our beliefs as to the intrinsic reasonableness of conduct must fall, without a hypothesis unverifiable by experience reconciling the Individual with the Universal Reason, without a belief, in some form or other, that the moral order which we see imperfectly realized in this actual world is yet actually perfect. If we reject this belief, we may perhaps still find in the non-moral universe an adequate object for the Speculative Reason, capable of being in some sense ultimately understood. But the Cosmos of Duty is thus really reduced to a Chaos: and the prolonged effort of the human intellect to frame a perfect ideal of rational conduct is seen to have been foredoomed to inevitable failure.[90]

---

[88] Wilfrid Ward. *Ten Personal Studies* (London, 1905), p. 87.
[89] Alasdair MacIntyre. *After Virtue* (South Bend, 2007), pp. 64–5.
[90] Henry Sidgwick, *The Methods of Ethics* (London, 1873), p. 473.

In being thus forced to admit the limitations of intellect, Sidgwick was striking a very Newmanian note. We can hear it in Newman's letters not only to his nephew but to his rationalist brothers Charles and Frank and to so many of his other contemporaries. G. M. Young was not invariably right about different aspects of Newman but he was brilliantly right when he wrote of how Newman in *The Idea of a University* "employs all his magic to enlarge and refine and exalt [his] conception of intellectual cultivation as a good in itself, worth while for itself, to be prized and esteemed for itself beyond all knowledge and all professional skill; while, all the time, so earnestly does he affirm its inadequacy, its shortcomings on the moral side; its need to be steadied and purified by religion, that at the end we feel that what we have heard is the final utterance, never to be repeated or needing to be supplemented, of Christian Humanism; as if the spirit evoked by Erasmus had found its voice at last."[91] And what makes Newman's critical reevaluation of the intellect all the more striking is that it should have been mounted in the wake of 1848, *la révolution des clercs*, with all its false trust in the intellect's ability to reorder society, to defy what Hardy called "the ancient pulse of germ and birth."[92] Newman's distrust of intellect stemmed, in part, from his insistence that the individual was something more than intellectuals were prepared to appreciate, and in this he agreed with Dryden, who was convinced that "Every man, even the dullest, is thinking more than the most eloquent can teach him how to utter."[93]

In summing up Sidgwick's work, the philosophical historian Frederick Copleston again puts one in mind of Newman. "If we look at Sidgwick's moral philosophy," Copleston observed, "in relation to what was to come later . . . we shall probably lay more stress on his method."

He laid emphasis on the need for examining what he called the morality of common sense; and he attempted to discover the principles which are implicit in the ordinary moral consciousness, to state them precisely and to determine their mutual relations. His method was analytic. He selected a problem, considered it from various angles, proposed a solution and raised objections and counter-objections. He may have tended to lose himself in details and to suspend final judgment because he was unable to see his way clearly through all difficulties. To say this, however, is in a sense to commend his thoroughness and careful honesty. And though his appeal to self-evident truths may not appear very convincing, his devotion to analysis and clarification of the ordinary moral consciousness puts one in mind of the later analytic movement in British philosophy.[94]

The "ordinary moral consciousness" is something to which Newman paid careful attention—he appealed to its actual operations, as opposed to theories of its operations, throughout that bravura epistemological essay, the *Grammar of Assent* (1870). But what differentiates Newman from so many of his rationalist neighbours was his deep

---

[91] G. M. Young, "Newman Again," in *Last Essays* (London, 1950), p. 100.
[92] See Lewis Namier. *1848: The Revolution of the Intellectuals* (Oxford, 1946).
[93] See the entry for *dull* in Johnson's Dictionary. See also A. D. Nuttall. *Shakespeare The Thinker* (New Haven, 2007), which brilliantly discusses Shakespeare's profound distrust of intellect.
[94] Frederick Copleston. *History of Philosophy* (London, 1967), pp. 100–1.

respect for the primacy of action. Indeed, he might have been addressing Sidgwick directly when he wrote in *The Tamworth Reading Room* (1841):

It surely cannot be meant that we should be undecided all our days. We were made for action, and for right action,—for thought, and for true thought. Let us live while we live; let us be alive and doing; let us act on what we have, since we have not what we wish. Let us believe what we do not see and know. Let us forestall knowledge by faith. Let us maintain before we have demonstrated. This seeming paradox is the secret of happiness. Why should we be unwilling to go by faith? We do all things in this world by faith in the word of others. By faith only we know our position in the world, our circumstances, our rights and privileges, our fortunes, our parents, our brothers and sisters, our age, our mortality. Why should Religion be an exception? Why should we be unwilling to use for heavenly objects what we daily use for earthly? Why will we not discern, what it is so much our interest to discern, that trust, in the first instance, in what Providence sets before us in religious matters, is His will and our duty; that thus it is He leads us into all truth, not by doubting, but by believing; that thus He speaks to us, by the instrumentality of what seems accidental; that He sanctifies what He sets before us, shallow or weak as it may be in itself, for His high purposes; that most systems have enough of truth in them, to make it better for us, when we have no choice besides, and cannot discriminate, to begin by taking all (that is not plainly immoral) than by rejecting all; that He will not deceive us if we thus trust in Him.[95]

That Sidgwick and so many of his Cambridge generation suffered from their neglect of these elemental truths is borne out by Sidgwick himself in something, which, although written when he was only 29, still captures a good deal of the dilemma that defined his life as a whole. "I have not progressed since I saw you except backwards," he wrote a friend. "At my age it is a great thing even to progress backwards; it shows that one is not stagnating. I mean, in respect of thought I feel more like a young man (in all the points in which youth is inferior to age) than I did in June. In the first place I have less of a creed, philosophically speaking. I think I have more knowledge of what the thoughts of men have been, and a less conscious faculty of choosing the true and refusing the false among them." The problem was that his inability to make up his mind on any of the questions he essayed became something of a besetting sin. "I wonder whether I shall remain a boy all my life in this respect," he writes in the same letter. "I do not say this paradoxically, but having John Grote in my mind, who certainly retained, with the freshness, the indecisiveness of youth till the day of his death. I wonder whether we are coming to an age of general indecisiveness; I do not mean the frivolous scepticism of modern Philistines (I almost prefer the frivolous dogmatism of ancient ditto), but the feeling of a man who will not make up his mind till mankind has. I feel that this standpoint is ultimately indefensible, because mankind have never made up their mind except in consequence of some individual having done so. Still there seems to me to be the dilemma. In the present age an educated man must either be prophet or persistent sceptic, there seems no *media via*. I have sold myself to

[95] *DA.*, pp. 214–15.

metaphysics . . . I do not yet regret the bargain. Take notice that I have finally parted from Mill and Comte . . ."[96]

Reading this marvellously revelatory passage, one begins to see why Sidgwick felt such a strong affinity with Clough. Indeed, Sidgwick might have stepped straight out of Clough's witty novel in verse, *Amours de Voyage* (1858), in which the morbidly analytical hero Claude spends most of his time trying (unsuccessfully) to respond to the amorous attentions of a fellow traveller named Georgina Trevelyan, while questioning the very possibility of action, faith and love. In this regard, Sidgwick and Clough put one in mind of something Gladstone once said to Tennyson, "I have . . . toiled in the circuitous method; but unfortunately with this issue, that, working round the labyrinth, I find myself at the end where I was at the beginning."[97] The novelist Julian Barnes, in an essay on Clough, whom he dubs "the 'unpoetical' poet," summarizes the long poem's theme in a way that drives home the striking resemblance between Claude and Sidgwick. "At the poem's centre is a debate about 'exact thinking', and how such thinking translates into action, and whether emotion as opposed to reason is ever justifiable ground for action and whether action is worth it in the first place—though of course if it were to be so, then it must first be based on absolutely exact thinking . . ."[98] Newman, too, came to see the futility of such overly intellectual *fiddle-faddling* (to use Clough's term) after he tried to establish his Anglo-Catholic *via media*, which he would later dismiss as an exercise in paper logic, the "paralogisms of our ecclesiastical and theological theory."[99]

It is coincidental that Sidgwick should have singled out Grote in his comment about the indecisiveness of his age because Grote had a tremendous impact on Mozley. In 1866, Mozley wrote to his Cambridge colleague Henry Bradshaw (1831–86), the librarian of the university and an expert on early printed books, Chaucer and liturgical history, "I was exceedingly sorry to see Grote's death in the paper; there are not many people at Cambridge from whom I have gained as much, directly or indirectly. It was premature too; just as he was in the middle of a philosophical work."[100]

John Grote (1813–66), the eldest brother of George Grote, the celebrated historian of Greece, was a philosopher and fellow of Trinity College, Cambridge. After being appointed to the perpetual curacy of Wareside, near Ware, he succeeded to the college living of Trumpington, near Cambridge. At Trumpington, Grote and fellow dons, including Mozley, formed a reading club, at which they read philosophical papers. His sudden death in 1866, while engaged in writing the first part of *Exploratio Philosophica: Rough Notes on Modern Intellectual Science* (1865), devastated Mozley. The ODNB is right to say that Grote's death "robbed philosophy of a unique and fertile mind which new scholarship and close study of the modern Cambridge tradition could and should revive."[101] He was a deft critic of Mill and his Utilitarianism. The old DNB remarked how "In private his moral sensitiveness and fervour, joined with dialectical subtlety, gave

---

[96] Schultz, p. 98.
[97] Gladstone to Tennyson (15 November 1884), in *Collected Letters of Alfred Lord Tennyson*. ed. Lang and Shannon (Oxford, 1990), III, p. 304.
[98] Julian Barnes. *Through the Window: Seventeen Essays and a Short Story* (New York, 2012), p. 24.
[99] LD, 10:426 JHN to John Keble (21 November 1844).
[100] See unpublished letter from Mozley to Bradshaw (27 August 1866) in Cambridge University Library, 89161/C33.
[101] ODNB.

him great influence over the minds of others; he was especially consulted by friends in cases of conscience."[102] One of his philosophical contentions was that "as words mean what they are used to mean in ordinary conversation, we should study divergent and changing usage and the ever changing play of the sound word (phonem) and the thought word (noem or meaning)."[103] This is an intriguing theory, especially when one recalls the stammering that has always been typical of Oxbridge dons.[104] Sidgwick had a rather flamboyant stammer, as his good friend Wilfrid Ward vividly recalled. One night in 1893 they were at dinner at the Cambridge home of Baron Anatole von Hügel, Isy Froude's husband when, as Ward relates, Sidgwick's stammer was "perhaps more marked than usual . . . Towards the end of dinner Tennyson's poetry was discussed, and something led us to the *In Memoriam*. There was then a remarkable change in his manner. Something of inspiration came into his face . . . and the discussion passed to a higher plane. It soon gave place by general consent to almost a monologue, and Sidgwick's stammer entirely ceased as he recited in illustration of his remarks stanza after stanza of that great poem."[105] From listening to Sidgwick's inspired conversation, Grote may very well have derived his theory regarding the relationship between the sound and import of spoken words. In any case, Grote remains an unjustly neglected figure. According to the Australian empiricist John Passmore (1914–2004), "For his methods and style of patient clarification of issues and language . . . for his common-sense approach and avoidance of philosophic allegiances, doctrines, and sectarianism, and for his rebuttal of positivism, phenomenalism, and utilitarianism, we can concur with the claim that Grote's philosophy is in manner an early, perhaps the first, example of that Cambridge spirit . . . which was to reach its culmination in the work of G.E. Moore."[106]

Whether Grote would have found this altogether complimentary is doubtful. He may have rebutted the fallacies of others, but it is unlikely that this broad churchman would have credited Moore's evasive ethics, which amounts to a kind of morality without morality. In any case, it is amusing that Newman should have anticipated the Pelagian fallacy of Moore's "science of ethics" in his *Oxford University Sermons*, where he freely concedes that "Morals may be cultivated as a science; it furnishes a subject-matter on which reason may exercise itself to any extent whatever, with little more than the mere external assistance of conscience and Scripture. And, when drawn out into system, such a moral teaching will attract general admiration from its beauty and refinement; and from its evident expediency will be adopted as a directory (so to say) of conduct, whenever it does not occasion any great inconvenience, or interfere with any strong passion or urgent interest." By the same token, Newman recognized that "love

---

[102] DNB.
[103] ODNB.
[104] See the last stanza of "Victorian and Edwardian Oxford" (1971) by John Betjeman:

> 'Is it from here the people come,
> Who talk so loud, and roll their eyes,
> And stammer? How extremely rum!
> How curious! What a great surprise!'

[105] *The Dublin Review*, Vol. 139, p. 28.
[106] J. Passmore. *A Hundred Years of Philosophy* (London, 1966), p. 54.

of virtue is no test of a sensitive and well-instructed conscience,—of nothing beyond intellectual culture. History establishes this: the Roman moralists write as admirably, as if they were moral men."[107] The same, of course, can be said for the Bloomsbury set, for whom Moore was a kind of ethical god.

In light of these distinctions, it is worth noting that Mozley wrote to Dr Neville Keynes in 1905 about his eldest son John Maynard, the future economist, who spent most of his time at Cambridge with fellow Apostles Lytton Strachey and Leonard Woolf reading and rereading Moore's *Principia Ethica*, which appeared in 1903, Keynes' second year. "Though your son has (I feel) not got quite so high a place in the mathematical tripos as you hoped, it is a place which I ought to be the last person to disparage, for it is the exact place [twelfth] which I had in the mathematical tripos forty three years ago," Mozley wrote. "Please give your son my best regards and say that I hope he will have a brilliant career in the future."[108] Later, after that brilliant career was in full swing, Keynes had occasion to recall the Cambridge dons who had taught him in his youth; and about Sidgwick, in particular, he observed: "He never did anything but wonder whether Christianity was true and prove that it wasn't and hope that it was."[109] If they had read rather than sneered at Sidgwick, Keynes and his Bloomsbury friends might have seen their own moral and intellectual muddles with a good deal more clarity.

Then, again, Mozley also corresponded with Montague Rhodes James (1862–1936), the erstwhile Cambridge don who became at once Provost of Eton and a famous writer of ghost stories. "I have delayed long in writing to you my congratulations; but in truth I was for a long time ignorant at what date you ceased to be Provost of Kings, and became Provost of Eton. But an old colleger and Kingsman . . . was calling on me a few days ago, and certified to me that you were now actually Provost of an institution more famous perhaps than Kings but not dearer to my heart. He told me that, among other things, you hoped to have more time for literary work there than you had had at Cambridge . . . No doubt Eton is a more beautiful place than Cambridge, taken together . . . and though Cambridge is not to be despised . . . you cannot . . . wander into the wilds which you can in Windsor Forest." Mozley's uncle would have been struck by the letter's next passage. "Of all the subjects in which you are proficient, the Gnostics and Aramaic papyri are those in which I am most interested."[110] In his novel, *Callista* (1856), which he set in third-century Africa during the persecutions of Christians under Decius, Newman describes the Gnostics as making off with "the clever youths and restless speculators" of the place, which could fairly describe his view of nineteenth-century Cambridge as well.[111] Mozley then went on to tell James what fans his daughter and two sons were of his ghost stories before signing off.

That Mozley was friendly with James is interesting vis-à-vis Newman because in his antiquarian travelogue *Suffolk and Norfolk* (1930), he took great pains to recapture the

---

[107] "Evangelical Sanctity" (1831) in *US*, pp. 40–1.
[108] See unpublished letter from Mozley to John Neville Keynes (14 June 1905) in Cambridge University Library, Add 7562 184.
[109] R. F. Harrod. *The Life of John Maynard Keynes* (London, 1951), p. 135.
[110] See unpublished letter from Mozley to M. R. James (7 October 1918) in Cambridge University Library, Add 7481.
[111] *Call*, p. 20.

Catholic legacy of East Anglia, from which Newman's ancestors hailed, though, as a broad church Anglican, he had little time for the theological claims of Rome. In 1909, when he was Provost of King's, he refused to allow Elgar's *The Dream of Gerontius* to be performed in Chapel because, as he said, it was "too papistical." Nevertheless, he retained a lifelong fascination with the pagan superstitions that never entirely left Livermere, the Suffolk village in which he spent his childhood and which inspired so many of his ghost stories.[112] Indeed, in his treatment of ghosts in his stories, he expressed over and over again his impatience with the late nineteenth-century materialism that sought to reduce everything to a level with mathematics and science. As Penelope Fitzgerald once observed, "From his schooldays onward he not only disliked but detested maths and science."

In *Eton and King's* [his autobiography] he reduces both these subjects and their teachers to a stream of mildly satirical stories . . . T. H. Huxley he referred to as a "coarse nineteenth century stinks man." Mathematics he equated with suffering. He extended his disapproval, which was more like an intense physical reaction, to philosophy. When he was Dean of King's he overheard two undergraduates disputing a problematic point, and, according to his colleague Nathaniel Weld, he rapped on the table sharply with his pipe and called out, "No thinking, gentlemen, please!"[113]

In one of his ghost stories, "The Vignette" (1935), after passing a gate and seeing a face, "not monstrous, not pale" but "fleshless, spectral," and with eyes that "were large and open and fixed," the narrator asks himself a question that goes to the very heart of James' peculiar interest in the supernatural.

That I was upset by something I had seen must have been pretty clear, but I am very sure that I fought off all attempts to describe it. Why I make a lame effort to do it now I cannot very well explain: it undoubtedly has had some formidable power of clinging through many year to my imagination. I feel that even now I should be circumspect in passing that Plantation gate; and every now and again the query haunts me: Are there here and there sequestered places which some curious creatures still frequent, whom once on a time anybody could see and speak to as they went about on their daily occasions, whereas now only at rare intervals in a series of years does one cross their paths and become aware of them; and perhaps that is just as well for the peace of mind of simple people.[114]

To contrast this with Newman's interest in the world "behind the veil," which Mary's death first awakened in him, is to see how different his own view of the supernatural was, though, at the same time, James in his writing of ghost stories, like Sidgwick in his table tapping, was always at pains to acknowledge that the world beyond the grave did actually exist, which was not inveterately conceded in a Cambridge milieu that was becoming increasingly agnostic.

---

[112] Michael Cox. *M.R. James: An Informal Portrait* (Oxford, 1983), p. 72.
[113] See Penelope Fitzgerald. *The Afterlife: Essays and Criticism* (London, 2003), p. 139.
[114] "The Vignette," in M. R. James. *Casting the Runes and Other Ghost Stories*. ed. Michael Cox (London, 1987), pp. 297–8.

Newman, with his wonderful sense of humour, would have deeply appreciated another of James' stories, "Oh, Whistle and I'll Come to You My Lad" (1904), the ending of which leaves a so-called Professor of Ontology at St. James' College badly shaken, even though a Colonel staying at the hotel intervenes and saves him from an even worse fate. As the narrator relates it, "Exactly what explanation was patched up for the staff and visitors at the hotel I must confess I do not recollect. The Professor was somehow cleared of the ready suspicion of delirium tremens, and the hotel of the reputation of a troubled house." Then, the narrator, musing on the spectral creature that had so terrified the professor, observes how "There seemed to be absolutely nothing material about it, save the bed clothes of which it had made itself a body," before adding, "The Colonel, who remembered a very dissimilar occurrence in India, was of opinion that if [the Professor] had closed with it it could really have done very little, and that its one power was that of frightening. The whole thing, he said, served to confirm his opinion of the Church of Rome." In all events, the narrator concludes, ". . . the Professor's views on certain points are less clear cut than they used to be. His nerves, too, have suffered . . ."[115] If the episode marked a defeat for the materialist prejudices embraced by Mill and his followers, it was a triumph for another, older prejudice. In its anti-Romanism, expressed so confidently by the Colonel, we can see an amusing confirmation of Newman's own understanding of that inexpellable force in English life.

When Newman first laid eyes on Cambridge, he must have felt as though he were rubbing shoulders with the ghosts of St John Fisher (1469–1535) and Lady Margaret Beaufort (1443–1509), who not only founded Christ's College and St John's College but renewed the pastoral life of the university as a whole.[116] To his mother, Newman wrote in 1832:

> Having come to this place with no anticipations, I am quite taken by surprise, and overcome with delight. This doubtless you will think premature in me, inasmuch as I have seen as yet scarcely any thing . . . But, really, when I saw at the distance of four miles, on an extended plain, wider than the Oxford, amid thicker and greener groves, the Alma Mater Cantabrigiensis lying before me, I thought I should not be able to contain myself, and, in spite of my regret at her present defects and past history, and all that is wrong about her, I seemed about to cry out, "Floreat æternum!" Surely there is a genius loci here, as in my own dear home—and the nearer I came to it, the more I felt its power. I do really think the place finer than Oxford, though I suppose it isn't, for every one says so. I like the narrow streets— they have a character—and they make the University buildings look larger by the contrast. I cannot believe that King's College is not far grander than any thing with us—the stone too is richer, and the foliage more thick and encompassing. I found my way from the inn to Trinity College, like old Œdipus, without guide, by instinct; how I know not. I never studied the plan of Cambridge.[117]

[115] "Oh Whistle, and I'll Come to You, My Lad" (1904) in M. R. James. *Casting the Runes and Other Ghost Stories* (Oxford, 1987), pp. 57–77.
[116] Newman's friend, the convert T. W. Allies was instrumental in promoting the beatification of St John Fisher and the English martyrs, which finally took place in 1888. See LD, 29:181.
[117] LD, 3:66–7 JHN to Mrs Jemima Newman (16 July 1832).

Later, in 1861, when so much of his Catholic life seemed to have culminated in failure, Newman revisited the place for only the second time in his life, and recollected his first visit in 1832, when, as he said, "my allegiance to Oxford was shaken by the extreme beauty of the place. I had forgotten this—but a second sight has revived the impression. Certainly, it is exquisitely beautiful."[118]

When it came to the thinking of Cambridge, however, Newman had distinct qualms. Early on, he recognized the allure that fashion had for many of its fellows and undergraduates. Writing to his sister Harriett in 1839, he described how "Some junior Cambridge men are taking up Church principles, and, as they do every thing, too much in the way of a fashion, as a theory or literature. If so, it will run its course and come to an end. These Cambridge men have such a want of seriousness. They are Utilitarians, Shelleyans, Coleridgians, Mauricians by turns—and may be any thing else."[119] That one of his most reckless critics, Charles Kingsley, took a classical first at Magdalene College, Cambridge, may not have surprised Newman, though he might have been amused by the fact that Kinglsey's mathematics tutor, Samuel Waud would customarily greet his earnest young charges by crying out, "Come to my rooms, and we will have a problem or two and an oyster and cigar."[120]

Then, again, Newman could not have been unaware of the part that Cambridge played in the celebrated Gorham Case, which revealed anew the Erastian character of the National Church. In 1847 when Henry Phillpotts (1830–69), Bishop of Exeter, a former Fellow of Magdalen, refused to install the antiquary and divine George Gorham to the living of Exeter because of his Calvinist views on baptismal regeneration, he was rejecting a graduate of Queen's, Cambridge, who was reaffirming what he had learnt from the Evangelical president, Isaac Milner. Moreover, when Gorham appealed the ruling, and the Judicial Committee of the Privy Council overruled the bishop, the man who wrote the judgement was a fellow of Gonville and Caius, Lord Langdale, who exploded the queer Tractarian notion that the English Church should somehow enjoy autonomy from the English State. Of course, Newman had already converted by the time the Gorham Case occurred, but it must nevertheless have amused him to see what an unwitting ally Cambridge had been in his own demolition of the theological pretensions of the Anglo-Catholic party. By the same token, Newman never despaired of Cambridge coming round to a more lively apprehension of the claims of faith. When he was still an Anglican, he wrote to one correspondent in 1835:

High and true principle there is all through the Church, I fully believe, and this supported and consecrated by our great writers of the seventeenth century . . . Not a month passes without our hearing of something gratifying in one part of the kingdom or another. I am quite surprised when I think how things have worked together, and this in minute ways . . . . If it be not presumptuous, I should say the hand of God was in it. I suppose Knox is tempted to say what he says about schism from a wish *to see* what is good in everything . . . He is a remarkable

---

[118] LD, 15:17.
[119] LD, 7:19 JHN to Mrs Thomas Mozley (27 January 1839).
[120] Susan Chitty. *The Beast and the Monk: A Life of Charles Kingsley* (London, 1974), p. 51.

instance of a man searching for and striking out the truth by himself. Could we see the scheme of things as angels see it, I fancy we should find he has his place in the growth and restoration (so be it) of Church principles. Coleridge seems to me another of the same class. With all his defects of doctrine, which are not unlike Knox's, he seems capable of rendering us important service. At present he is the oracle of young Cambridge men, and will prepare them (please God) for something higher. Both these men are laymen, and that is remarkable. The very stones cry out.[121]

Newman showed his unshakable faith in Cambridge when he wrote Christopher Scott, a native of Cambridge who had been converted to Catholicism after reading Newman's confutation of the branch theory in his *Lectures on Certain Difficulties felt by Anglicans in submitting to the Catholic Church* (1850) and taken orders shortly thereafter:

Rednall Aug 29. 1884

Dear Dr Scott

I rejoice to hear from you that the work which your Bishop has committed to you, of providing for Cambridge a larger Church than the present has had so favorable and promising a commencement.

In an evil day, such as this, when a new and plausible form of infidelity is in our midst, the Catholic faith and worship is the only availing refuge of religion, and our Universities are the natural seat of that conflict, which now, as at other times, is the condition of victory.

The Cambridge Catholics have a great mission before them, and I pray with all my heart that the fulness of the Divine Blessing may be with them for the fulfilment of it

I am, dear Dr Scott

Your faithful Servant John H. Card. Newman[122]

Later, when he heard that a subscription was being proposed to support the building of the church, Newman wrote Scott again of how "Cambridge, as being the seat of a great University, has a hold on the hearts and minds of Catholics in all parts of England. This is why I feel a special satisfaction in learning from you that with your Bishop's sanction you are receiving subscriptions with a view to building there a new Church on a new site, an undertaking, which, though local in its purpose, is not local in the interest which attaches to it, nor in the call which it makes on our co-operation. I pray God to bless so important a work, and I beg of you to accept from me in aid of it the inclosed offering".[123] Newman subscribed £20, which in today's money would be about £380. Built to the designs of Dunn & Hansom of Newcastle between 1885 and 1890, Our Lady and the English Martyrs was founded by Mrs Yolande Marie Louise Lyne-Stephens, a former ballet dancer at the Paris Opera and Drury Lane, and widow

[121] LD, 5:26–7 JHN to Samuel Rickards (9 February 1835).
[122] LD, 8:394 JHN to Christopher Scott (29 August 1884).
[123] LD 30:398 JHN to Christopher Scott (12 February 1884).

of a wealthy banker. She promised to begin building the church on the feast of Our Lady of the Assumption, while Scott, who was rector from 1883 to 1922, chose to have the church commemorate the Catholic Martyrs, many of whom had been in residence at the university at the time of their murders during the Tudor Terror between 1535 and 1603.

When Mozley wrote his uncle, in 1875, he had left Cambridge and was Professor of Pure Mathematics at Owens College, Manchester, but one can see from the tenor of his correspondence that Cambridge had made an indelible imprint on his thinking. It is true that he did not accept all of the scepticism that was gaining ground there, but he was still deeply influenced by its moral objections to the Church of Rome, as well as its conviction that Christianity must somehow be reconciled to rationalism. Newman, for his part, was always at pains to differentiate rationalism from reason.

> As regards Revealed Truth, it is not Rationalism to set about to ascertain, by the exercise of reason, what things are attainable by reason, and what are not; nor, in the absence of an express Revelation, to inquire into the truths of Religion, as they come to us by nature; nor to determine what proofs are necessary for the acceptance of a Revelation, if it be given; nor to reject a Revelation on the plea of insufficient proof; nor, after recognizing it as divine, to investigate the meaning of its declarations, and to interpret its language; nor to use its doctrines, as far as they can be fairly used, in inquiring into its divinity; nor to compare and connect them with our previous knowledge, with a view of making them parts of a whole; nor to bring them into dependence on each other, to trace their mutual relations, and to pursue them to their legitimate issues. This is not Rationalism; but it is Rationalism to accept the Revelation, and then to explain it away; to speak of it as the Word of God, and to treat it as the word of man; to refuse to let it speak for itself; to claim to be told the *why* and the *how* of God's dealings with us, as therein described, and to assign to Him a motive and a scope of our own; to stumble at the partial knowledge which He may give us of them; to put aside what is obscure, as if it had not been said at all; to accept one half of what has been told us, and not the other half; to assume that the contents of Revelation are also its proof; to frame some gratuitous hypothesis about them, and then to garble, gloss, and colour them, to trim, clip, pare away, and twist them, in order to bring them into conformity with the idea to which we have subjected them.[124]

If Newman's interactions with his contemporaries show his interest in the experience of true faith, it also shows his interest in the many ways in which the would-be faithful could be seduced into settling for counterfeit faiths. And here his own experience with the *via media*, that mediatorial half-way house between Rome and Augsburg, which he would later abandon as an untenable theory, helped him to see how susceptible we all are to succumbing to false gods. Throughout my previous book, *Newman and his Contemporaries*, I show how various figures in the nineteenth century—from Thomas Huxley to Matthew Arnold to A. M. Fairbairn—took it into

---

[124] *Ess.*, i, p. 32.

their heads to make a religion of knowledge. Newman is one of the most discerning of all English authors precisely because, like Shakespeare, he never overestimated the claims of reason, though, of course, in giving reason its proper due, he never lost sight of how it cooperates with and indeed nourishes faith.[125] In Sermon 10 of the *University Sermons*, "Faith and Reason, Contrasted as Habits of Mind" (1839), he distinguished between two powers that are often confused by rationalists. Many were convinced that Newman would have made a splendid barrister. Here he makes his case with masterly judiciousness.

> Now, in attempting to investigate what are the distinct offices of Faith and Reason in religious matters, and the relation of the one to the other, I observe, first, that undeniable though it be, that Reason has a power of analysis and criticism in all opinion and conduct, and that nothing is true or right but what may be justified, and, in a certain sense, proved by it, and, undeniable, in consequence, that, unless the doctrines received by Faith are approvable by Reason, they have no claim to be regarded as true, it does not therefore follow that Faith is actually grounded on Reason in the believing mind itself; unless, indeed, to take a parallel case, a judge can be called the origin, as well as the justifier, of the innocence or truth of those who are brought before him. A judge does not make men honest, but acquits and vindicates them: in like manner, Reason need not be the origin of Faith, as Faith exists in the very persons believing, though it does test and verify it. This, then, is one confusion, which must be cleared up in the question,—the assumption that Reason must be the inward principle of action in religious inquiries or conduct in the case of this or that individual, because, like a spectator, it acknowledges and concurs in what goes on;—the mistake of a critical for a creative power.[126]

This clear-sighted appreciation of the limits of reason informed Newman's break not only with the liberal Noetics that he had encountered in the Senior Common Room of Oriel in the 1820s and 1830s—men like Richard Whately and Edward Hawkins—but with the rationalists and agnostics who would succeed them as the nineteenth century progressed.

No one saw the battle lines forming between Catholicism and its liberal enemies as clearly as Newman, battle lines which his correspondence with his nephew also adumbrated. Towards the end of his life, he took up this theme with great rhetorical brio. "I look out, then, into the enemy's camp, and I try to trace the outlines of the hostile movements and the preparations for assault which are there in agitation against us. The arming and the manœuvring, the earth-works and the mines, go on incessantly; and one cannot of course tell, without the gift of prophecy, which of his projects will be carried into effect and attain its purpose, and which will eventually fail or be abandoned."[127] Nevertheless, Newman could delineate the main lines of the liberal philosophy that would seek to discredit and dislodge the one holy catholic and apostolic faith.

[125] Cf. A.D. Nuttall. *Shakespeare the Thinker* (New Haven, 2007).
[126] *US*, p. 131.
[127] *Idea*, p. 313.

"You may have opinions in religion, you may have theories, you may have arguments, you may have probabilities;" Newman portrayed his suppositious rationalist arguing, "you may have anything but demonstration, and therefore you cannot have science. In mechanics you advance from sure premises to sure conclusions; in optics you form your undeniable facts into system, arrive at general principles, and then again infallibly apply them: here you have Science . . ." But for the rationalist, "it is absurd for men in our present state to teach anything positively about the next world, that there is a heaven, or a hell, or a last judgment, or that the soul is immortal, or that there is a God."[128] And in capturing the ethos of this anti-Christian rationalism, Newman captured the skepticism not only of his own age but ours as well.

Well, then, if Religion is just one of those subjects about which we can know nothing, what can be so absurd as to spend time upon it? what so absurd as to quarrel with others about it? Let us all keep to our own religious opinions respectively, and be content . . . upon no subject whatever has the intellect of man been fastened so intensely as upon Religion. And the misery is, that, if once we allow it to engage our attention, we are in a circle from which we never shall be able to extricate ourselves. Our mistake reproduces and corroborates itself. A small insect, a wasp or a fly, is unable to make his way through the pane of glass; and his very failure is the occasion of greater violence in his struggle than before. He is as heroically obstinate in his resolution to succeed as the assailant or defender of some critical battlefield; he is unflagging and fierce in an effort which cannot lead to anything beyond itself. When, then, in like manner, you have once resolved that certain religious doctrines shall be indisputably true, and that all men ought to perceive their truth, you have engaged in an undertaking which, though continued on to eternity, will never reach its aim; and, since you are convinced it ought to do so, the more you have failed hitherto, the more violent and pertinacious will be your attempt in time to come. And further still, since you are not the only man in the world who is in this error, but one of ten thousand, all holding the general principle that Religion is scientific, and yet all differing as to the truths and facts and conclusions of this science, it follows that the misery of social disputation and disunion is added to the misery of a hopeless investigation, and life is not only wasted in fruitless speculation, but embittered by bigotted sectarianism.[129]

Here, one can see not only the satirical reader of Hume but something of the genius with which Newman entered into the rationale of his opponents, and it is this critical clairvoyance that makes him such an incomparable guide to the pretensions of the rationalism of his age. Indeed, in the *Grammar of Assent*, he speaks of the allure of scepticism with a psychological sympathy that one will search for in vain in the attacks on faith mounted by his critics. "Are there pleasures of Doubt?" he asks. "In one sense, there are. Not indeed, if doubt simply means ignorance, uncertainty, or hopeless suspense; but there is a certain grave acquiescence in ignorance, a recognition of our

---

[128] Ibid., pp. 314–15.
[129] Ibid., pp. 315–16.

impotence to solve momentous and urgent questions, which has a satisfaction of its own. After high aspirations, after renewed endeavours, after bootless toil, after long wanderings, after hope, effort, weariness, failure, painfully alternating and recurring, it is an immense relief to the exhausted mind to be able to say, 'At length I know that I can know nothing about any thing'—that is, while it can maintain itself in a posture of thought which has no promise of permanence, because it is unnatural. But here the satisfaction does not lie in not knowing, but in knowing there is nothing to know. It is a positive act of assent or conviction, given to what in the particular case is an untruth. It is the assent and the false certitude which are the cause of the tranquility of mind. Ignorance remains the evil which it ever was, but something of the peace of Certitude is gained in knowing the worst, and in having reconciled the mind to the endurance of it."[130]

This sympathy with the scepticism of his opponents did more than give his prose its rhetorical equipoise: it led him to question what the practical issue of such doctrinaire anti-Catholicism would be. "Where men really are persuaded of all this, however unreasonable, what will follow?" For Newman, liberal relativism would not be inconsequential and the accuracy of his predictions can be verified by our own increasingly tragic experience. "A feeling, not merely of contempt, but of absolute hatred, towards the Catholic theologian and the dogmatic teacher," he foresaw, would come to characterize the new sceptical consensus. "The patriot abhors and loathes the partizans who have degraded and injured his country; and the citizen of the world, the advocate of the human race, feels bitter indignation at those whom he holds to have been its misleaders and tyrants for two thousand years."[131] Here, Newman clearly had not only Hume but all of his rationalist progeny in mind. For the rationalist, the "new teacher," as Newman called him, those who upheld Catholic doctrine were nothing short of "enemies of the human race," and here his ability to express the objections of his opponents better than the opponents themselves is given free ironical rein. "'But for Athanasius, but for Augustine, but for Aquinas,'" he has his new teacher contend, "'the world would have had its Bacons and its Newtons, its Lavoisiers, its Cuviers, its Watts, and its Adam Smiths, centuries upon centuries ago. And now, when at length the true philosophy has struggled into existence, and is making its way, what is left for its champion but to make an eager desperate attack upon Christian theology, the scabbard flung away, and no quarter given? and what will be the issue but the triumph of the stronger,—the overthrow of an old error and an odious tyranny, and a reign of the beautiful Truth?' Thus he thinks, and he sits dreaming over the inspiring thought, and longs for that approaching, that inevitable day"—a scene which Newman must have seen played out many times in his encounters with his radical brothers, who shared this new teacher's contempt for "a Power which Julian and Frederic, Shaftesbury and Voltaire, and a thousand other great sovereigns and subtle thinkers, have assailed in vain."[132]

In publishing the epistolary exchange in the *Contemporary Review*, Mozley gave centre stage to his own ethical objections to Roman Catholicism, explaining how,

---

[130] *GA*, p. 137.
[131] *Idea*, p. 317.
[132] Ibid., pp. 317–18.

as he said, "I had asked whether the real conduct of the visible Church – i.e., in his view, of the Church of Rome – had been in accordance with that spirit of morality and goodness which should mark a divine example and a divine teacher. I pointed to facts in the history of the Church which appeared to me to be symptoms of a faulty nature. I referred to the condition of the countries most obedient to Rome – Spain under Philip II, France up to the first Revolution, Italy up to the middle of the nineteenth century – as exhibiting a tremendous total of misdoing, partly traceable directly to the influence of the highest authorities of Rome, partly permitted by them without protest or repudiation . . . . How came it that the members of an organisation, to which the divine promises were believed to have been entrusted, should not only have committed such grave offences in the past, but should be so unwilling to confess them in the present, except as bare facts, and without any sense of the disrepute thereby attaching to themselves, and to the society they looked upon as divine?"[133]

Newman answered his nephew in a series of marvellously far-ranging letters. In the first, written on 19 April 1874, he observed how "Our Lord Himself foretold that His net would contain fish of every kind – He speaks of rulers who would be tyrannical and gluttonous – and it was one of the first great controversies of the Christian Church, issuing in the Novatian schism, whether extraordinary means should or should not be taken to keep the Church pure – and it was decided in the negative, as (in fact) a thing impossible. Now when this is once allowed, considering how evil in its own nature flaunts itself and is loud, and how true virtue is both in itself a matter of the heart and in its nature retiring and unostentatious, it is very difficult to manage to make a 'Note of the Church' out of the conduct of Catholics viewed as a visible body. Besides it must be recollected that the Church is a militant body, and its work lies quite as much in rescuing souls from the dominion of sin as in leading them on to any height of moral excellence."[134]

Here, Newman might also have responded by calling his nephew's attention to a sermon of his entitled "Men, Not Angels, the Priests of the Gospel," which he had preached at the Church of the Birmingham Oratory in 1849. Nowhere else does Newman more brilliantly disabuse his Protestant contemporaries of their moralist misconceptions of the Church, a Church about which St Paul told the Corinthians: "We preach not ourselves, but Jesus Christ our Lord; and ourselves your servants through Jesus. God, who commanded the light to shine out of darkness, He hath shined in our hearts, to give the light of the knowledge of the glory of God in the face of Christ Jesus: *but* we hold this treasure *in earthen vessels*." Mozley wished to imagine that these vessels somehow discredited the Roman Church: Newman recognized that they confirmed the Love on which the Church was founded.

> Had Angels been your Priests, my brethren, they could not have condoled with you, sympathised with you, have had compassion on you, felt tenderly for you, and made allowances for you, as we can; they could not have been your patterns and guides, and have led you on from your old selves into a new life, as they can who come from the midst of you, who have been led on themselves as you are to

---

[133] LD, 27:259, See Note 1.
[134] LD, 27:56 JHN to John Rickards Mozley (19 April 1874).

be led, who know well your difficulties, who have had experience, at least of your temptations, who know the strength of the flesh and the wiles of the devil, even though they have baffled them, who are already disposed to take your part, and be indulgent towards you, and can advise you most practically, and warn you most seasonably and prudently. Therefore did He send you men to be the ministers of reconciliation and intercession; as He Himself, though He could not sin, yet even He, by becoming man, took on Him, as far as was possible to God, man's burden of infirmity and trial in His own person. He could not be a sinner, but He could be a man, and He took to Himself a man's heart that we might entrust our hearts to Him, and "was tempted in all things, like as we are, yet without sin."[135]

This was the elemental reality of the Incarnation that Edward Hawtrey and Eton's other masters had somehow never shared with Mozley. As a result, he could only regard the Church and its human pockmarks, like so many of his contemporaries, with pharisaical disapproval. Newman, for his part, was never unprepared to admit the Church's human flaws. As he conceded in the *Letter to the Duke of Norfolk* (1875), "the Rock of St. Peter on its summit enjoys a pure and serene atmosphere, but there is a great deal of Roman malaria at the foot of it."[136] Indeed, far from trying to palliate the Church's sins, he held them up as proof of Christ's love.

Ponder this truth well, my brethren, and let it be your comfort. Among the Preachers, among the Priests of the Gospel, there have been Apostles, there have been Martyrs, there have been Doctors;—Saints in plenty among them; yet out of them all, high as has been their sanctity, varied their graces, awful their gifts, there has not been one who did not begin with the old Adam; not one of them who was not hewn out of the same rock as the most obdurate of reprobates; not one of them who was not fashioned unto honour out of the same clay which has been the material of the most polluted and vile of sinners; not one who was not by nature brother of those poor souls who have now commenced an eternal fellowship with the devil, and are lost in hell. Grace has vanquished nature; that is the whole history of the Saints. Salutary thought for those who are tempted to pride themselves in what they do, and what they are; wonderful news for those who sorrowfully recognise in their hearts the vast difference that exists between them and the Saints; and joyful news, when men hate sin, and wish to escape from its miserable yoke, yet are tempted to think it impossible![137]

If Newman did not cite this sermon, he did argue that the good effects of the Roman Church on Western Civilization as a whole spoke for themselves. After all, as he said, "in the course of 1800 years it has managed to impress its character on society, so that when countries fall away from its communion, the virtues, which it has created in their various people and civil polities, continue on by a kind of inheritance . . ."[138] Here, by the way, it is interesting to note that John Grote agreed,

---

[135] *Mix.*, p. 48.
[136] *Diff.*, ii, p. 297.
[137] "Men, Not Angels, the Priests of the Gospel" (1849) in *Mix.*, pp. 47–9.
[138] LD, 27:56 JHN to J. R. Mozley (19 April 1874).

arguing that "Christianity has been the nurse not only of benevolence, of meekness, and peaceableness, but of every variety of elevated character and generous action: it has strung up the fibres of man's moral being to every form of virtue, as well as guided him in each point of justice. 'Render to all their dues' is as cardinal a principle of it as 'Love your neighbor.'"[139] What would have shocked Mozley is that this was an estimate with which even his uncle Frank Newman agreed. "That Catholicism was not only *an* influence, but the chief influence of good to Medieval Europe," Frank wrote Newman in 1858, "I have always held, and hold as strongly as you, though with infinitely less knowledge."[140]

Then, again, for Newman, "civilisation itself, that is, the cultivation of the intellect, has a tendency to raise the standard of morals, at least in some departments, as we see in the history of philosophy, e.g. in the Stoics, in Juvenal, Persius, Epictetus &c. and as regards the minor virtues of gentlemanlikeness &c. &c., and this again tends to blur the contrast, which really exists between nature and grace, the special characteristic of the latter lying in the motive on which actions are done." Then, before signing off, he specified where he thought his co-religionists distinguished themselves: "Lastly, if, after these remarks, I am asked in what I conceive in matter of fact consists the superiority of well-conducted Catholics over Protestants, I should answer, in purity of intention, in faith, in humility, in contrition, in chastity, in honesty, in command of the tongue."[141]

At the same time, Newman shared with his young nephew the same "first principles" that he had shared 30 years before with his brother Frank, though now those principles elicited from him an even deeper humility. "First then I grant that I do assume certain first principles as the starting points from which my convictions proceed, and I don't see who can arrive at any conviction without making assumptions. I assume that there is a truth in religion, and that it is attainable by us: that there is a God, to whom we can approve ourselves and to whom we are responsible. On the other hand I find, in matter of fact and by experience, that there are great difficulties in admitting this first principle; but still they are not such as to succeed in thrusting it out from its supremacy in my mind. The most prominent difficulty in Theism is the existence of evil: I can't overcome it; I am obliged to leave it alone, with the confession that it is too much for me, and with an appeal to the argumentum ab ignorantiâ, or in other words, with the evasion or excuse, not very satisfactory, that we have not the means here of answering an objection, which nevertheless, if we knew more, we should doubtless have the means of answering . . ."[142] Acknowledging evil, without presuming to know why evil should exist, Newman proceeded to answer his nephew's question. "I allow, then (and for argument's sake I allow more than facts warrant) the existence of that flood of evil which shocks you in the visible Church; but for me, if it touched my faith mortally in the divinity of Catholicism, it would, by parity of reason, touch my faith in the Being of a Personal God and Moral Governor. The great question to me is, not what evil is left in the Church, but what good has energized in it and been practically

---

[139] John Grote. *An Examination of the Utilitarian Philosophy* (Cambridge, 1870), pp. 240–1.
[140] *Family*, p. 207.
[141] LD, 27:56 JHN to J. R. Mozley (19 April 1874).
[142] LD, 27:259–60 JHN to John Rickards Mozley (11 April 1875).

exercised in it, and has left its mark there for all posterity. The Church has its sufficient work, if it effects positive good, even though it does not destroy evil except so far forth as it supplants it by good."[143]

By the same token, Newman cited an essay by none other than Lord John Russell to argue that ordinary Catholics could show extraordinary sanctity. "As to the virtues of Catholics, I have lately been reading the following words of Lord Russell, an impartial witness, from his 'Essay on the Christian Religion,'" and there Russell had described how: "There is among Roman Catholics, in their relations to each other, a pure essence of affection which does not appear in the moral writings of Greece and Rome. The Roman Catholics, who have never practised or have relinquished the vices of erring youth, are humble, loving, compassionate, abounding in good works, kind to all classes of their fellow creatures, ever ready to say, 'God be merciful to me a sinner,' ready to give of their substance to the needy, ready to forgive others their trespasses, and kneel in humble devotion to their Maker." Newman's response to this surprising praise from an altogether surprising quarter is charmingly grateful. "He speaks as if there were no middle class among us; but, if we were not living in sin, we were almost saints."[144]

Then, Newman invoked the testimony of history. Thus, "leaving the highest and truest outcome of the Catholic Church and descending to history," he maintained "with most writers on the Evidences, that, as the Church has a dark side, so (as you do not seem to admit) it has a light side also, and that its good has been more potent and permanent and evidently intrinsic to it than its evil. Here, of course, we have to rely on the narrative of historians, if we have not made a study of original documents ourselves. It would be a long business (assuming their correctness), but an easy business too, to show how Christianity has raised the moral standard, tone, and customs of human society; and it must be recollected that for 1500 years Christianity and the Catholic Church are in history identical. The care and elevation of the lower classes, the championship of the weak against the powerful, the abolition of slavery, hospitals, the redemption of captives, education of children, agriculture, literature, the cultivation of the virtues of piety, devotion, justice, charity, chastity, family affection, are all historical monuments of the influence and teaching of the Church." And the individual historians he cited reflected his own deep reading in an historical record that was hardly uncritical of the Church of Rome. "Turn to the non-Catholic historians, to Gibbon, Voigt, Hurter, Guizot, Ranke, Waddington, Bowden, Milman, and you will find that they agree in their praises, as well as in their accusations, of the Catholic Church. Guizot says that Christianity would not have weathered the barbarism of the Middle Age but for the Church. Milman says almost or altogether the same. Neander sings the praises of the monks. Hurter was converted by his historical researches. Ranke shows how the Popes fought against the savageness of the Spanish Inquisition. Bowden brings out visibly how the cause of Hildebrand was the cause of religion and morals. If in the long line there be bad as well as good Popes, do not forget that long succession, continuous and thick, of holy and heroic men, all subjects of the Popes, and most of them his

---

[143] LD, 27:261 JHN to J. R. Mozley (1 April 1875).
[144] LD, 27: 261–2 JHN to J. R. Mozley (1 April 1875).

direct instruments in the most noble and serviceable and most various works, and some of them Popes themselves, such as Patrick, Leo, Gregory, Augustine, Boniface, Columban, Alfred, Wulstan, Queen Margaret of Scotland, Louis IX., Vincent Ferrer, Las Casas, Turibius, Xavier, Vincent of Paul—all of whom, as multitudes besides, in their day were the life of religion."[145]

In his letter of 4 April 1875, Newman responded further to his nephew's ethical objections to Rome. "In what I wrote to you the other day I said that both good and bad were to be expected in the Catholic Church, if it came from our Lord and His Apostles, whereas you had ignored the good altogether, and had insisted there was in it an actual tradition or abiding system of bad, forming a whole and giving the Church a character; and worse, that, though it was so, Catholics would not confess it and renounce it. Now I do confess that bad is in the Church, but not that it springs from the Church's teaching or system, but, as our Lord and His Apostles predicted it would be, in the Church, but not of it. He says, 'It must *needs be* that scandals come;' 'many are called, few are chosen;' 'the kingdom of heaven is like a net which gathereth of every kind.' Good men and good works, such as we find them in Church history, seem to me the legitimate birth of Church teaching, whereas the deeds of the Spanish Inquisition, if they are such as they are said to be, came from a teaching altogether different from that which the Church professes."[146]

Newman similarly argued that the Massacre of St. Bartholomew's Day could hardly be cited as representative of Church teaching, even though many in Protestant England might wish to contend otherwise. At the same time, the psychological historian in Newman could appreciate how the upheavals of the Reformation betrayed the papacy into approving the indefensible. "I think such insane acts as St. Bartholomew's Massacre were prompted by mortal fear. The French Court considered (rightly or wrongly) that if they did not murder the Huguenots, the Huguenots would murder them. Thus I explain Pope Gregory's hasty approbation of so great a crime, without waiting to hear both sides. After a period of luxury and sloth, the sudden outburst of the Reformation frightened the Court of Rome out of its wits, and there were those who thought the one thing needful was to put it down anyhow, as the destruction, at least eventually, of all religion, morality, and society."[147] Having thus rejected any justification for the massacre, Newman insisted that Catholics remained more critical of other Catholics than was usually appreciated. For Newman, "among controversialists, there is no want of candour and frankness among us; witness the fact that Protestant attacks on us generally are drawn from the admissions of Catholics. Baronius, writing under the Pope's eye, speaks in the strongest terms of the evil state of the Popedom in the dark age; Rinaldus, his continuator, speaks against Alexander VI.; St. Bernard, St. Thomas, and many others speak against the conduct of the Roman See in their own times. So do Pope Adrian VI., Paul IV, &c. So do holy women in their writings, such as St. Bridget." Newman himself would continue this tradition by conceding the human weaknesses of the Church where he felt concessions warrantable, though he saw a good deal of

---

[145] LD, 27:262–3 JHN to J. R. Mozley (1 April 1875).
[146] LD, 27:264 JHN to J. R. Mozley (4 April 1875).
[147] LD, 27:265 JHN to J. R. Mozley (4 April 1875).

disingenuous, indeed hypocritical criticism of the Church, especially from English and German quarters.

As to the state of Catholic Europe during these last three centuries, I begin by allowing or urging that the Church has sustained a severe loss, as well as the English and German nationalities themselves, by their elimination from it; not the least of the evil being that in consequence the Latin element, which is in the ascendant, does not, cannot know, how great the loss is. This is an evil which the present disestablishment everywhere going on may at length correct. Influential portions of the Latin races may fall off; and if Popes are chosen from other nationalities, other ideas will circulate among us and gradually gain influence.

As to the unbelief of France, Italy, and Spain, allowing it to the extent facts warrant, still I had fancied that *England*, the most fiercely Protestant country of Europe, had begun the tradition of infidelity in Europe in its school of Deists in the seventeenth and eighteenth centuries; and that *Germany*, the native soil of the Reformation, was now the normal seat of intellectual irreligion. Is it not something the case of the pot and the kettle?[148]

Nevertheless, Newman did not wish to give his nephew the impression that the vitality or, as the case may be, debility, of the pope's temporal power decided his own faith. "The temporal prosperity, success, talent, renown of the Papacy did not make me a Catholic, and its errors and misfortunes have no power to unsettle me. Its utter disestablishment may only make it stronger and purer, removing the very evils which are the cause of its being disestablished."[149]

In his next letter, dated 21 April 1875, Newman returned to the ethical objection to Roman Catholicism. "You now ask me whether I agree or disagree with your judgment 'that the Church of Rome, as a society, has sometimes done, more often sanctioned, actions, which were wrong and injurious to mankind.' I find no difficulty in answering you. I should say that the Church has two sides, a human and a divine, and that every thing that is human is liable to error . . ."

I grant that the Church's teaching, which in its formal exhibitions is divine, has been at times perverted by its officials, representatives, subjects, who are human. I grant that it has not done so much good as it might have done. I grant that in its action, which is human, it is a fair mark for criticism or blame. But what I maintain is, that it has done an incalculable amount of good, that it has done good of a special kind, such as no other historical polity or teaching or worship has done, and that that good has come from its professed principles, and that its shortcomings and omissions have come from a neglect or an interruption of its principles.[150]

The question, however, that Mozley wished to put to his Catholic uncle was whether it is "really necessary for Roman Catholics both to be and to proclaim themselves to be

[148] LD, 27:266 JHN to John Rickards Mozley.
[149] LD, 27:267 JHN to J. R. Mozley (4 April 1875).
[150] LD, 27:282–3 JHN to John Rickards Mozley (21 April 1875).

at war with the new methods and organisations of society, with the spirit of material science in its speculations and hopes of future discoveries?"[151] Newman's response was of a disarming candour: "Your letter puts me into a great difficulty. It is my heart's desire to bring you nearer to me in opinion, and so to explain my own religious views as to excite in you interest and sympathy for us; to reduce difficulties, and to inspire hope that Catholics and Protestants are not so far apart from each other as is commonly said; in a word to throw myself into the sentiment which has led you to write, and to cooperate with it. But I cannot feel you have gone to the bottom of the matter, and it would not consist with that truth and frankness due to all men, and especially to one with whom I am so united in affection as yourself, not to say so."[152] At the same time, in response to the deference Mozley was prepared to show what he called "the new methods and organisations of society" and "the spirit of material science," Newman might very well have referred his nephew to words that he had written 34 years before in *The Tamworth Reading Room* (1841), the collected letters he had written to Sir Robert Peel and Lord Brougham in the *Times* attacking their scheme for a non-denominational library from which all books of theology would be barred, which did indeed go to the "bottom of the matter." In that satirical *tour de force*, Newman had called into question the claims of secular advancement held out by the natural sciences.

Now, independent of all other considerations, the great difference, in a practical light, between the object of Christianity and of heathen belief, is this—that glory, science, knowledge, and whatever other fine names we use, never healed a wounded heart, nor changed a sinful one; but the Divine Word is with power. The ideas which Christianity brings before us are in themselves full of influence, and they are attended with a supernatural gift over and above themselves, in order to meet the special exigencies of our nature. Knowledge is not "power," nor is glory "the first and only fair"; but "Grace," or the "Word," by whichever name we call it, has been from the first a quickening, renovating, organizing principle. It has new created the individual, and transferred and knit him into a social body, composed of members each similarly created. It has cleansed man of his moral diseases, raised him to hope and energy, given him to propagate a brotherhood among his fellows, and to found a family or rather a kingdom of saints all over the earth;—it introduced a new force into the world, and the impulse which it gave continues in its original vigour down to this day. Each one of us has lit his lamp from his neighbour, or received it from his fathers, and the lights thus transmitted are at this time as strong and as clear as if 1800 years had not passed since the kindling of the sacred flame. What has glory or knowledge been able to do like this? Can it raise the dead? can it create a polity? can it do more than testify man's need and typify God's remedy?[153]

Instead, Newman chose to tell his nephew that in this matter Catholics were starkly different from Protestants, though not for the reasons usually adduced. "I go far beyond

---

[151] LD, 27:385–6.
[152] LD, 27:386.
[153] *DA.*, pp. 270–1.

you in holding, that the difference between Catholics and Protestants is an ethical one: for I think that in pure Catholics and pure Protestants, (I mean, by so speaking, that most Protestants are tinged with Catholicity, and most Catholics with Protestantism) this difference is radical and immutable, as the natures of an eagle and a horse are, except logically, two things, not one. Opposition to physical science or to social and political progress, on the part of Catholics, is only an accidental and clumsy form in which this vital antagonism energizes—a form, to which in its popular dress and shape, my own reason does not respond. I mean, I as little accept the associations and inferences, in which modern science and politics present themselves to the mass of Catholics, as I do those contrary ones, with which the new philosophy is coloured . . ."[154]

Then, again, Newman was careful to disabuse his nephew of the notion, to which both his brothers subscribed, that Christianity, if no longer theologically tenable, could be kept alive as a kind of philanthropic concern, a summons to what social reformers, then, as now, call 'social justice,' as though Jesus Christ were little more than a Victorian reformer before his time, a sort of first-century Lord Shaftesbury. "When we go on to inquire what is the ethical character, whether in Catholicity now or in Christianity in its first age, the first point to observe is that it is . . . in utter variance with the ethical character of human society at large as we find it at all times. This fact is recognized, I say, by both sides, by the world and by the Church. As to the former of the two, its recognition of this antagonism is distinct and universal. As regards Catholicism, it is the great fact of this very day, as seen in England, France, Germany, Italy, and Spain. On the other hand, we know that in the Apostolic age Christians were called the 'hostes humani generis' (as the Quarterly called Catholics within this two years), and warred against them accordingly."[155] Doubtless, Mozley had never seen these distinctions drawn quite so sharply. Nevertheless, here Newman denounced the ethical religion espoused by Mill and so many of his acolytes, the primary object of which was to serve the putative well-being of men in the world.

> This antagonism is quite as decidedly acknowledged on the side of the Church, which calls society in reprobation "the world", and places "the world" in the number of its three enemies, with the flesh and the devil, and this in her elementary catechisms. In the first centuries her badge and boast was martyrdom; in the fourth, as soon as she was established, her war-cry was, "Athanasius contra mundum": at a later time her protests took the shape of the Papal theocracy . . . In the recent centuries her opposition to the world is symbolized in the history of the Jesuits. Speaking then according to that aspect of history which is presented to the eyes of Europeans, I say the Catholic Church is emphatically and singularly, in her relation to human philosophy and statesmanship, as was the Apostolic Church, "the Church militant here on earth."

This recalls Newman's great regard for what he took to be the two most powerful maxims of Thomas Scott, "Holiness rather than peace" and "Growth the only evidence of life," both of which animate Newman's understanding of the character and mission

---

[154] LD, 27:386 JHN to J. R. Mozley (3 December 1875).
[155] LD, 27:387 JHN to J. R. Mozley (3 December 1875).

of the Church militant, which he proceeded to define in greater detail by telling his nephew that "what is a remarkable feature in her ethos now and at all times" is that "she wars against the world from love to it. What indeed is more characteristic of what is called Romanism now than its combined purpose of opposing yet of proselytizing the world? –a combination expressed in our liturgical books by the two senses of the word 'conterere,' that of grinding down and of bringing to contrition." Then, again, Newman was careful to differentiate the purposes of the Church Militant from those of the world. "This will be still clearer as we examine the details of our ethics," Newman pointed out, "as developed from our fundamental principles. The direct and prime aim of the Church is the worship of the Unseen God; the sole object, as I may say, of the social and political world everywhere, is to make the most of this life. I do not think this antithesis an exaggeration when we look at the action of both on a large scale and in their grand outlines. In this age especially, not only are Catholics confessedly behindhand in political, social, physical, and economical science (more than they need be), but it is the great reproach urged against them by men of the world that so it is. And such a state of things is but the outcome of apostolic teaching. It was said in the beginning, 'Take no thought for the morrow. Woe unto those that are rich. Blessed be the poor; to the poor the gospel is preached. Thou hast hid these things from the wise and prudent. Not many wise men, not many mighty, not many noble are called. Many are called, few are chosen. Take up your cross and follow Me. No man can have two masters – he who loveth father or mother more than me is not worthy of me. We walk by faith, not by sight; by faith ye are saved. This is the victory that overcometh the world, our faith. Without holiness no man can see the Lord. Our God is a consuming fire.'"[156] Needless to say, this is not an ethical system of which Mill would have approved, or Paley or Bentham.

At the same time, Newman was intent on stressing that he did not imagine that the Church rejected the secular simply because it was secular. "I am far from saying that it was not from the first intended that the strict and stern ethos of Christianity should be, as it was in fact, elastic enough to receive into itself secular objects and thereby secular men, and secular works and institutions, as secondary and subordinate to the magisterium of religion – and I am far indeed from thinking that the teaching and action of the world are unmixed evil in their first elements (society, government, law, and intellectual truth being all from God) and far from ignoring the actual goodness and excellence of individual Protestants, which comes from the same God as the Church's holiness; but I mean, that, as you might contemplate the long history of England or France, and recognize a vast difference between the two peoples in ethical character and national life and consequent fortunes, so, and much more, you can no more make the Catholic and Protestant ethos one, than you can mix oil and vinegar. Catholics have a moral life of their own, as the early Christians had, and the same life as they – our doctrines and practices come of it; we are and always shall be militant against the world and its spirit, whether the world be considered within the Church's pale or external to it."[157] And from this it followed, as Newman pointed out, "that,

---

[156] LD, 27:389 JHN to J. R. Mozley (3 December 1875).
[157] Ibid.

though our opposition to science etc. ceased ever so much, we should not thereby be more acceptable in our teaching to the public opinion of the day."[158]

In October 1877, in an article in the *Quarterly Review* entitled "The Three Extreme Ideals," Mozley returned to his charge by claiming that while "in past times the Church of Rome . . . has taken no small part in the formation of our modern order, when the standard of justice among men and nations was lower than it is now," in more recent times, the Church had turned its back on this order.[159] In his rejection of this assertion Newman could not have been more categorical: "I do not at all allow that now, any more than in the middle age the Church makes light of secular progress," he wrote. Then and now, "its supreme end has been to inculcate the maxim, 'Seek ye first the Kingdom of God and His righteousness.' What Catholics see in this age is a generation fascinated, intoxicated, carried away by its own great achievements in secular knowledge, and in the means of material happiness. If there is any point on which Scripture is strong, it is on the real danger of wealth and of the desire of wealth, using the word 'wealth' in a large sense, and who can deny that the pursuit, the acquisition, the engagement, the pride of wealth is the characteristic feature of this age. Of course we regard it with distress, with great jealousy, with fear. But there is nothing to show that we are opposed to secular advancement, as such, and in subordination to what is higher than it."[160]

In defending his own promotion of certain secular studies within the scheme of universal knowledge, Newman called into sharp contrast the record of Cambridge with regard to the same scheme. "You say you thought of me as you wrote. Well, I wrote 20 years ago a book on Universities, to which I refer you, its object being to show that intellectual truth is the one business of University education. Of course I there say that there is something better than those branches of knowledge which are secular, in the spirit of the lines occurring in one of Handel's Oratorios 'What tho' I knew each leaf and flower, That drinks the morning dew, Did I not own Jehovah's power How vain were all I knew!' But still it is a phenomenon running counter to your view of me, that I should leave my own home and go to Ireland and incur great trouble and vexation, in order to advocate, as I did especially in a Catholic institution the direct and earnest cultivation of the physical sciences and the useful arts. It is also true of course that I was strong also in demanding that, among the branches of intellectual knowledge, theology should have a place, but the ground on which I rested this demand was that a University was a place for all knowledge and therefore for theological inclusive. And I strenuously resisted the notion that physical science or other department of knowledge was to be sacrificed to theology. I said that theology must not encroach upon their provinces any more than they upon its."[161]

Mozley had complained that the Church of Rome "uses all the material appliances and mental gains of civilization but gives no word of gratitude to those who have laboriously discovered them."[162] To which, Newman replied: "You say that such men as I are not grateful for the secular benefit which we have gained from the researches

---

[158] Ibid.
[159] LD, 28:265, Note 2.
[160] LD, 28:266 JHN to John Rickards Mozley (10 November 1877).
[161] Ibid.
[162] LD, 28:266, Note 3.

and genius of men of science. I do not allow this. What I say of Bacon in my volume shows both my gratitude to them and my jealousy of their excesses. . . . You speak as if you had never seen this book. I will ask your acceptance of it." Here, Newman was alluding to a passage in the *Idea of a University* in which he commended the "mission" of Francis Bacon, referring to it as "the increase of physical enjoyment and social comfort." Indeed, looking back from the vantage point of the nineteenth century on the contributions that this seventeenth-century savant had made to science, Newman freely conceded that Bacon had "fulfilled his conception and his design," as he said, "most wonderfully" and "most awfully." The proof for this was ubiquitous. "Almost day by day have we fresh and fresh shoots, and buds, and blossoms, which are to ripen into fruit, on that magical tree of Knowledge, which he planted, and to which none of us perhaps, except the very poor, but owes, if not his present life, at least his daily bread, his health, and general well-being. He was the divinely provided minister of temporal benefits to all of us so great, that, whatever I am forced to think of him as a man, I have not the heart, from mere gratitude to speak of him severely."[163]

Here, the differences between uncle and nephew could not have been starker. And yet Mozley treated the differences without rancour. It is "a real question," he wrote in his article, "for those who hold with us that the Papacy is a human accident and not a divine institution, what they are to think of Roman Catholics? whether there is any possible appeal to them that we can make, independently of a demand that they shall abandon their characteristic doctrine? There is, it is plain, a division between us and them, which extends beyond the bounds of theology, which deeply affects social and political life, and the individual temper of men. Can we narrow this breach? In our opinion—and in this perhaps they will agree with us—it is not to be narrowed, in the first instance, by theological argument."[164] Here, Mozley was attempting to bridge a divide that his mother Jemima and Uncle Frank had despaired of bridging and in a way that was suffused with the painful feelings of an entire extended family. Speaking of those who had converted to Roman Catholicism in general, and of his uncle in particular, Mozley wrote, "Let us be permitted to leave general propositions."

We see before us men gentle, benign, affectionate. We hear their voices, sounding with longing towards the past; and can we indeed repudiate the past? Can the age that now is say to the age that begot it and reared it, "Away! I am a new thing; I have no need of thee"? No; we, as they, have our thoughts continually upon the past; upon the past, but none the less upon the future also, whither our desires tend. But again, these men, so gentle and so kindly, are also loyal with the extreme of devotion to that which they once have taken for their ideal; to their Church they

---

[163] *Idea*, p. 118. Francis Bacon (1561–1626), English philosopher and statesman, was educated at Trinity College, Cambridge and Gray's Inn. "His greatness," according to Magnus Magnusson, "consists in his insistence on the facts, that man is the servant and interpreter of Nature, that truth is not derived from authority, and that knowledge is the fruit of experience; and in spite of the defects of his method, the impetus he gave to future scientific investigation is indisputable. He was the practical creator of scientific induction. An unparalleled belief in himself, which justified to himself all ignoring of all ordinary laws of morality, is the leading feature in the character of this 'wisest, brightest, meanest of mankind.'" See *Chambers Biographical Dictionary*. ed. Magnusson (London, 1990), p. 88.

[164] *Quarterly Review* (October 1877), p. 390

give up everything that they can honestly give. Nor, let us at once admit it, does this loyalty to their Church imply disloyalty to the truth, as it comes before their eyes; they will allow, if challenged, the faults of their Church, as they allow their own faults; they are no defenders of persecution and falsehood. The divine element, they say, exists in the Church, in spite of these faults; the Spirit promised by the Master cannot fail; how shall we desert it? And indeed it is to be perceived that these men do not spare themselves; and if labour and self-devotion and mutual affection are signs of the true spirit, are not these men in possession of it?

One can see here the fruits of Mozley's epistolary exchange with his uncle, and the deeper insight it gave him into his uncle's crisis of faith. And it was this insight that enabled Mozley to see that, for Newman and the other converts from the Anglo-Catholic party, "in presence of an ideal that they deemed loftier, the tenderest ties could not avail to bind and retain where they stood. Let others speak as they will, we at least cannot help honouring these men, knowing that they acted thus with sincerity and in deep pain . . . ." Nevertheless, this passage, for all its conciliatory generosity, only accentuated the differences between the two men, especially when Mozley spoke of "the fatal seed of division between us and sincere and honest Roman Catholics," and concluded that it was a difference of worldview. "We look on the world with hope and delight, they look on it with mourning and apprehension. To us, the earth is in its green youth, expecting, it is true, the still better and worthier future, but expecting it with that reasonable confidence which is present happiness; to them the earth is in mourning for its sins, and the joy of it is hollow and vain." Mozley was willing enough to concede that "There are indeed griefs and miseries, villanies and rascalities, weaknesses and follies in abundance in the world." Still, he was adamant that "as we understand the matter, the primary position of a man, as respects hopefulness or the contrary, depends on something in himself, and not in what he sees around him. There is a glow of faith and of inward strength in the hearts of some, by which, as a thing that cannot die, they feel assured that the flame of happiness ever increasing, of energy ever victorious, shall spread over the world."[165] Here was the belief in private judgement and in progress that animated so many in the nineteenth century. That such convictions should have come to smash in the trenches of Flanders was a tragic irony that would not have been lost on Newman, who never ceased to marvel at the way his contemporaries idolized not only their rationalism but the glorious moral benefits that were expected to issue from it.

Apropos his nephew's claim that his uncle took an unduly negative view of the world, Newman remarked, "Your analysis of my mental position in your last letter made me smile, but how in the world did it become our subject? I thought you were advancing and I answering a definite allegation against the Catholic Church and Catholics. Is it not well in controversy to keep to the point?"[166] Mozley conceded that he had wandered from the point, but nonetheless he was convinced that his uncle had before his "eyes the image of an exalted self-denial" and did not sufficiently "admire conduct which is not animated by a conscious recognition of God." And then he added: "Now I am

---

[165] Ibid., pp. 390–1.
[166] LD, 28:328 JHN to J. R. Mozley (10 March 1878).

going to what appears to me the bottom of the matter, when I say that you do not take as much pleasure in pleasurable things as you naturally would, and as God desires us all to take (and indeed takes himself, if I may venture to say so, as I most firmly believe) because you have the will of God before your eyes out of season and in season."[167] Newman's *Letters and Diaries* include no response to this but in one of his very first sermons about the trials of the pastoral office Newman related how priests "have to convert and admonish those, who (without God's grace) oppose the very efforts that are made for their good. Thus in one sense they are at war with the very individuals they love. They have to wrestle with the pride and selfishness of the heart. They have to probe before they can cure. They are seemingly unkind. Thus they must be content with the affection of some, and meekly bear the opposition of many. They must not wonder if they are misunderstood and misrepresented."[168] Nevertheless, in March of 1884, the priest in Newman was clearly very pleased indeed when he received a letter from his nephew saying "The following letter was in answer to one in which I had expressed my belief in that doctrine which, as I suppose, is the primary addition which Christianity makes to simple Theism; the indispensability, namely, of the personal help of Jesus Christ for our permanent welfare; and I had said that I judged so by my own experience." To which Newman warmly replied:

March 14, 1884

My dear John,

You are quite right in thinking I should be deeply interested in your letter, and grateful to you for writing it. It is that which all these scientific men need, and which is hid from them, the experience of the religious soul. . . . Of course what are called "experiences" involve often much that is enthusiastic and wild, but *usum non tollit abusus.*

For myself, now at the end of a long life I say from a full heart that God has never failed me – never disappointed me – has ever turned evil into good for me. When I was young, I used to say (and I trust it was not presumptuous to say it) that our Lord ever answered my prayers. And what He has been to me, who have deserved His love so little, such He will be, I believe and know, He will be to every one who does not repel Him and turn from His pleading.

And now I believe He is visiting you, and it rejoices me to think He will gain you.

Yours very affectionately John H. Card. Newman[169]

Penelope Fitzgerald, in her delightful portrait of her extraordinary uncles, *The Knox Brothers* had occasion to comment on the ethos of Cambridge, which had such a tremendous impact on Mozley. Fitzgerald's novels concern themselves more with questions than answers. "If a story begins with finding," the narrator of *The Blue Flower* (1995) observes, "it must end with searching." Yet the answers against which her novels warn are not the answers of belief but those of disbelief, the axiomatic

---

[167] LD, 28:328 J. R. Mozley to JHN (10 February 1877).
[168] See Sermon 1, No. 42, "On Attending the Ordinances of Grace," preached 12 December 1824 *in John Henry Newman: Sermons 1824–1843* (Oxford, 2011), IV, p. 9.
[169] LD, 30:324 JHN to J. R. Mozley (14 March 1884).

answers of a modern age that prides itself on its spirit of inquiry yet rejects out of hand the claims of faith. In her portrait of her uncle Dilly, she recalls his undergraduate years at King's College, Cambridge. "The college finances were depressed, the food uneatable, and Hall so crowded that waiters and diners were in constant collision, but the prevailing air was one of humanism and free intellect, and many felt, as Lowes Dickinson had described it, that 'the realization of a vast world extending outside Christianity was like a door that had once or twice swung ajar, and now opened and let me out.'" To which Fitzgerald adds the one withering sentence: "But across the way their magnificent chapel stood in all its beauty, a perpetual reproach to them."[170]

In the course of his correspondence with John Rickards Mozley, Newman made a comment that nicely sums up not only his avuncular but his pastoral care for a young man whom he scarcely knew but cared for deeply. It also suggests that there might have been distinct limits to the influence that Cambridge had on the nephew of Blessed John Henry Cardinal Newman, limits of which even he himself might not have been aware. "I was rejoiced to be told by you that you recognised the truth of the power of prayer," Newman wrote. "Nothing else will clear our religious difficulties."[171]

After Mozley's mother Jemima died on Christmas Day, 1879, Newman sent a letter to the family telling them that he would say Mass for his sister, which somehow the family construed as unfeeling. "This simply puzzled him," as Meriol Trevor wrote in her biography of Newman; "he never could realise that people do not believe in the feelings of others unless they are expressed in recognized phrases of exaggerated sentiment and mourning—just what always seemed to him 'unreal words.' And the older he grew, the less Newman attempted to put feelings into words. To say Mass for his sister meant everything to him; he did not realize to his Protestant nephews it seemed a mere formality."[172] For Newman, as for Willis in *Loss and Gain*, nothing was "so consoling, so piercing, so thrilling, so overcoming, as the Mass . . ." It was "not a mere form of words" but "a great action, the greatest action that can be on earth . . . the evocation of the Eternal." God Himself was "present on the altar in flesh and blood, before whom angels bow and devils tremble."[173] The Mozley family, like most of Newman's Protestant contemporaries, could scarcely enter into these realities. For them, the Mass might be an impressive spectacle but its very grandeur was inseparable from the corruption of the Roman Church, a corruption that reinforced the indifference to the sacrifice of the Mass that Fanny Kemble noticed among her compatriots at St Peter's in Rome during Holy Week of 1846. What particularly struck the actress was "their total apparent forgetfulness of the sacred purposes to which the place . . . was dedicated, the coarse levity of their observations and comments upon what was going on; their determined perseverance in their own flirtations and absurd conversation in the midst of the devotions of the people whose church they were invading . . ."[174] Something of this same tragic illiteracy characterized the

---

[170] Penelope Fitzgerald. *The Knox Brothers* (London, 1977), p. 68.
[171] LD, 27:267 JHN to J. R. Mozley (4 April 1875).
[172] Meriol Trevor. *Newman: Light in Winter* (London, 1962), p. 580.
[173] LG, pp. 327–8.
[174] Fanny Kemble quoted in John Pemble. *The Mediterranean Passion: Victorians and Edwardians in the South* (Oxford, 1987), p. 212.

Mozleys' view of the Mass, and in a subsequent letter to his indignant nephew, one of the most moving he ever wrote, Newman summed up his feelings not only towards Mozley but towards his family as a whole.

The Oratory, Febr 26. 1880.

My very dear John,

Thank you for your affectionate letter, which I am glad to have, tho' how to answer it I scarcely know, more than if it were written in a language which I could not read. From so different a standpoint do we view things.

Looking beyond this life, my first prayer, aim, and hope is that I may see God. The thought of being blest with the sight of earthly friends pales before that thought. I believe that I shall never die; this awful prospect would crush me, were it not that I trusted and prayed that it would be an eternity in God's Presence. How is eternity a boon, unless He goes with it?

And for others dear to me, my one prayer is that they may see God.

It is the thought of God, His Presence, His strength which makes up, which repairs all bereavements.

"Give what Thou wilt, without Thee we are poor,
And with thee rich, take what Thou wilt away."[175]

I prayed that it might be so when I lost so many friends 35 years ago; what else could I look to?

If then, as you rightly remind me, I said Mass for your dear Mother, it was to entreat the Lover of souls that, in His own way and in His own time, He would remove all distance which lay between the Sovereign Good and her, His creature. That is the first prayer, sine quâ non, introductory to all prayers, and the most absorbing. What can I say more to you?

Yours affectly John H. Card. Newman

P. S. Cardinals don't wear mourning.[176]

Here is an epitome not only of the differences that Newman encountered in his family but the readiness with which he responded to them as to the "call of charity." If one is looking for an understanding of what motivated the *caritas* that animates his work, one will not find a better example than this: "Looking beyond this life, my first prayer, aim, and hope is that I may see God. . . . And for others dear to me, my one prayer is that they may see God." That is the essence of Newman's vocation *cor ad cor* and nowhere did he practice it more lovingly than within his own fractious family.

---

[175] These lines are from "The Winter Morning Walk," in *The Task* (1785) by William Cowper, a poet of whose work Mozley was also fond.

[176] LD, 29:241 JHN to J. R. Mozley (26 February 1880). This was a nice riposte to Mozley's earlier claim that Catholics were somehow mournful.

Epilogue: Family, Faith, and Love

After Newman died on the evening of Monday, 11 August 1891, the newspapers and periodicals of Great Britain recalled the life of a man who had had an enormous influence on his contemporaries. "Throughout his long and useful career," the *Edinburgh Evening Dispatch* noted in a typical obituary, "even when his polemical contentions were at their fiercest, Cardinal Newman enjoyed the privilege of winning to himself the respect and affections of others besides his co-religionists. Beloved and revered by all who were ever brought into intimate association with him, he all along secured to himself by his writings the personal sympathy—in many instances it might even be said the tender veneration—of multitudes who never once came face to face with him, who never felt the pressure of his cordial hand, or listened to the vibration of his earnest voice."[1] Whoever reads Newman's massive correspondence can attest to the accuracy of this claim. Thousands of Protestants were devoted to him and his work, and indeed even those of no faith at all. As William Lockhart, the first of the Tractarians to abandon the *via media* for Rome, noted, "No one who knew him could doubt that he was one in whom 'wisdom had built herself a house'; as the Incarnate Wisdom says of the man who loves God: 'My Father will love him, and we will come to him, and make our abode with him.'" After his death, the *Belfast News* recalled a reception that the Duke of Norfolk gave Newman on his return from receiving his red hat at which Matthew Arnold and Lord Ripon were present and at which his admirers from Australia presented him with a testimonial in silver and gold. "The gentle voice and the sad smile that played upon his face had great effect upon all present," the paper recalled. "It was a wonderful face, with its asceticism toned down by an every-day manner. The eye was large and steady, of bluish tint, and full of depth. He read his little speech of thanks to the deputation in a clear, nervous voice, and when all was over he bowed everybody gracefully out of the apartment. It was easy to perceive the great influence that such a man could exercise over his fellow-creatures."[2] And yet there was one group over whom this "great influence" failed, and that was his family, who bore out the great truth that "A prophet is not without honour, save in his own country, and in his own house."[3]

For Newman, this was a heartbreaking irony, but it was tempered by the fact that it was his family that had helped to make him a prophet in the first place by acquainting him with the real condition of an English people that had, for the most part, known

---

[1] See LD, 32:595.
[2] LD, 32:580.
[3] St Matthew, Ch. 13, v. 57.

little of their traditional faith for over 300 years. Lockhart is good on the lengths to which Newman had to go to overcome this condition himself.

> For aboriginal Catholics, it is not easy to understand many of the characteristics of the life and influence of John Henry Newman; especially the long course of years it took him, and many others who are now Catholics, to find their way through the tangled mazes of religious error in which they had been brought up, and reach, at last, the City of God, which to Catholics seems so manifestly "the City set upon a hill which cannot be hid." The Catholic who has received the Faith in his baptism, and has adhered from the earliest opening of his reason to the *motivum credendi*, *i.e.*, God speaking to him by the Light of Faith within his soul, and by His infallible Church, cannot easily place himself in the position of a convert, who has climbed up to the high mountain, whence by the intuition of faith he sees God and the things of God, and holds them no longer as *opinions*, but as *verities*.[4]

For Lockhart, "Newman was leader of a band of pioneers who cut their way, with great expenditure of time and labour, through the tangled forest that had grown up during three hundred years, between the insular Christianity of England and Catholic Christendom." Then, again, "it must be remembered that men in Newman's position, who come into the Catholic Church chiefly through the elaborate study of the Fathers and of ecclesiastical history, find many difficulties that have to be reconciled, knotty points of history that have to be disentangled; especially, since many of the most telling arguments of Protestants against the Church are drawn from an elaborate, if onesided, study of Ecclesiastical History, of documents of Fathers and of Popes . . ." One reason why Newman had taken six deliberative years to make the final step to Catholicism was to verify the theological grounds on which he would break not only with the National Church but with an entire way of living. Lockhart took this into consideration when he observed how: "A real survey of the almost boundless field of history is a gigantic work; and it is this which detained Newman so long upon the road. But it is not the road for ordinary wayfarers. It had to be done once for all, and John Henry Newman has done it, and has made a high-road for all time, by which men of good-will can easily find their way, even through the mazes of history, from the City of Confusion to the City of Truth . . . ."[5]

Newman might have been amused to hear his old acolyte sum up his work in such sanguine terms, but it is doubtful whether he would have credited them. After all, his brothers and sisters were "ordinary wayfarers" and, despite his best efforts, none of them found any "high-road" to what Newman called the "one true Fold of the Redeemer."[6] One fundamental conclusion that emerges from my study is that if Newman's life and work helped many to persevere in the trials of conversion, his own family proved that the road from "the City of Confusion to the City of Truth" could be strewn with insuperable obstacles. For Newman, conversion required a genuine change of heart and his family showed him again and again how extraordinarily difficult that could

---

4   William Lockhart. *Cardinal Newman: Reminiscences of Fifty Years Since* (London, 1891), pp. 19–20.
5   Ibid., pp. 21–3.
6   LD, 11:3 JHN to Henry Wilberforce (7 October 1845).

be. Towards the end of his life, Newman described the scarcely discernible birthpangs of conversion when he spoke of how "the faint initial stirrings of religion in the heart, the darkness, the sense of sin, the fear of God's judgment, the contrition, the faith, hope and love, need not be a conscious, clearly defined, experience, but may be, and commonly is, a slow and silent growth, not broken into separate and successive stages, but as regards these spiritual acts composite, and almost simultaneous, strengthening with the soul's strength, advancing with advancing years, till (after whatever relapses and returns, or whatever unswerving fidelity) death comes at length, and seals and crowns with perseverance and salvation what from first to last is a work of grace. Grace is the beginning and the end of it."[7] For Newman, as for St Augustine, conversion was an arduous, lifelong process.

No one brought home the necessity for assiduity on this score better than Frank Newman, whose abandonment of orthodox Christianity for the surrogate religion of social reform ended at last, as we have seen, in his support for euthanasia, the apotheosis of precisely the sort of factitious pity that fuels our own culture of death. Frank's biographer endeavoured to put Frank's unorthodox religion in some respectable light by arguing that "The real valour of his life was shown in the splendid aspects of Social Reform which he . . . was ever preaching and writing about." Yet if Frank "was the Perseus of To-Day whose wholehearted efforts were spent in freeing Andromedas from their antiquated bonds and fetters; whose good sword was ever pointed at the throats of the dragons which lift their ugly heads against freedom— against reforms of all sorts; the dragons who take so long in dying," his brother spent his days working to achieve a simpler and yet infinitely more difficult object: reform of the heart, without which conversion is impossible.[8] In a letter to William Froude's daughter Elizabeth, who experienced some of the same difficulties with respect to conversion that so many of her Anglican contemporaries experienced, Newman wrote: "If you go on to ask *why* we are commanded to believe on authority, instead of holding on proof, it is enough to answer that such a duty is a trial of our trust and obedience to Him, who has a right to demand our trust and obedience. But I add, ex abundanti, that such a belief, bringing in a new set of motives, has an important effect upon our moral state, or tends, to use the common phrase, to change the heart etc etc." This was precisely the argument that Newman had used with Frank and Charles, when they found orthodox Christianity objectionable. But it was only after he encountered his brothers' scepticism first-hand that he could counsel Isy on the pressing appeal of conversion.

> Our Lord asked the faith of those whom he healed, first . . . as an act of submission and devotion to Himself, and secondly because we may suppose that in some cases that faith may have been the medium of the cure.
>
> This applies to the Athanasian Creed, "Whosoever wishes to be saved, before all things etc."; that is Almighty God *wills* to exact this act of supreme devotion to Him of every one whom He admits to the privileges of the Gospel. He has a right to do so—and, moreover, He has in part allowed us to see *why* He exercises here

[7] LD, 30:225 JHN to George T. Edward (2 June 1885).
[8] *Sieveking*, p. 340.

His right. Amid the multitude of errors in to which the mind falls on the subject of religion, who is likely to go right, if left to himself?

This is the very meaning of Revelation. It is made to *teach* us something, which otherwise we should not know,—for our soul's good, for the education of our soul—for our preparation for heaven . . .[9]

The way in which Newman's family deepened his understanding of conversion is one example of how they influenced my subject; there are others. His parents imbued him with his deep distrust of the world without ever diminishing his abiding conviction that the world could not be evaded or ignored. If there is one characteristic about Newman that is most compelling to believers and non-believers alike it is his respect for the way that men and women actually believe or do not believe. In entering into the various religious difficulties of his siblings, Newman prepared himself for many of the religious difficulties that he would later address in the world beyond the family, of which his family became a microcosm. His brothers acquainted him with aspects of that "all-corroding, all-dissolving scepticism of the intellect," a scepticism that lay waste so much orthodox Christianity among the nineteenth-century English and gave rise to the surrogate faith that still fascinates our own contemporaries, which Newman defined as "liberalism"—the "doctrine that there is no positive truth in religion, but that one creed is as good as another."[10] Another Froude, Anthony, one of Newman's liveliest critics, recognized how much this fundamental scepticism put Newman on his mettle.

What a sight must this age of ours have been to an earnest believing man like Newman, who had an eye to see it, and an ear to hear its voices? A foolish Church, chattering, parrot-like, old notes, of which it had forgot the meaning; a clergy who not only thought not at all, but whose heavy ignorance, from long unreality, clung about them like a garment, and who mistook their fool's cap and bells for a crown of wisdom, and the music of the spheres; selfishness alike recognized practically as the rule of conduct, and faith in God, in man, in virtue, exchanged for faith in the belly, in fortunes, carriages, lazy sofas, and cushioned pews; Bentham politics, and Paley religion; all the thought deserving to be called thought, the flowing tide of Germany, and the philosophy of Hume and Gibbon; all the spiritual feeling, the light froth of the Wesleyans and Evangelicals; and the only real stern life to be found anywhere, in a strong resolved and haughty democratic independence, heaving and rolling underneath the chaff-spread surface. How was it like to fare with the clergy gentlemen, and the Church turned respectable, in the struggle with enemies like these? Erastianism, pluralities, prebendal stalls, and pony-gigging parsons,—what work were they like to make against the proud, rugged, intellectual republicanism, with a fire sword between its lips, bidding cant and lies be still; and philosophy, with Niebuhr criticism for a reaping sickle, mowing down their darling story-books? High time it was to move indeed. High time for the church warriors to look about them, to burnish up their armour, to seize what ground was yet remaining. . . .[11]

[9] LD, 26:287 JHN to Isy Froude (9 April 1873).
[10] *Apo.*, p. 218.
[11] James Anthony Froude. *The Nemesis of Faith* (London, 1849), pp. 152–3.

If none in Newman's experience confirmed the contagion of this "proud, rugged, intellectual republicanism" more than Charles and Frank, none proved more how necessary it was to repudiate a communion that "mistook their fool's cap and bells for a crown of wisdom." To this extent, Charles and Frank paved the way for Newman's conversion by showing him how the unbelief of scepticism could only be answered by the faith of the one true Church. And in the last chapter of the *Apologia*, he could not have been more candid about how this skepticism had led him to recognize the salutary force of infallibility.

> Supposing then it to be the Will of the Creator to interfere in human affairs, and to make provisions for retaining in the world a knowledge of Himself, so definite and distinct as to be proof against the energy of human skepticism, in such a case, –I am far from saying that there was no other way, –but there is nothing to surprise the mind, if He should think fit to introduce a power into the world, invested with the prerogative of infallibility in religious matters. Such a provision would be a direct, immediate, active, and prompt means of withstanding the difficulty; it would be an instrument suited to the need; and, when I find that this is the very claim of the Catholic Church, not only do I feel no difficulty in admitting the idea, but there is a fitness in it, which recommends it to my mind. And thus I am brought to speak of the Church's infallibility, as a provison adapted by the mercy of the Creator, to preserve religion in the world, and to rescue it from its own suicidal excesses. . . I say, that a power, possessed of infallibility in religious teaching, is happily adapted to be a working instrument, in the course of human affairs, for smiting hard and throwing back the immense energy of the aggressive, capricious, untrustworthy intellect. . .[12]

The influence that his sisters had on him was equally pronounced. Harriett mirrored his own sworn anti-Romanism, at a time when he needed to be able to assess his thinking with some reliable detachment, while Mary personified the sanctity with which he sought to overcome that stultifying prejudice. In Jemima, on the other hand, he saw what a tragic snare the bonds of family and country could become, if their inordinate affiliations were not resisted. Newman was always careful to denounce the pride inherent in inflated national identity. Historians like to rap the knuckles of jingoists, as though they had some monopoly in this line, but false nationalism came in many subtle varieties and one of the subtlest was Anglicanism. Apropos what he called the "odious self-conceit," the "low vainglory . . . of those who have not raised and purified their minds by the contemplation of that real spiritual perfection which Scripture sets before us," Newman could be withering. More than most of his contemporaries, he saw the terrible complacency that sustained so much nineteenth-century national belief or, perhaps one should say, nationalism as belief.

> Do not we constantly hear mention made of our glorious farspreading empire on which the sun never sets—of its inexhaustible resources, and its gigantic power!— Is there not unceasing clamorous exultation in our political privileges, our liberty

[12] *Apo.*, pp. 219–20.

of person and security of property, our right of interfering in matters of civil
government? Do we not pride ourselves in the energy, enterprise, perseverance,
and productiveness of our people . . .? are we not, as a nation, well satisfied with our
own mental powers and acquirements?—do we not think ourselves wise, sagacious,
enlightened, dexterous, beyond all former ages . . .?[13]

Nevertheless, although Newman himself, as Dean Church remarked, was always
ready "to detect and denounce what was selfish and poor in English ideas and action,"
he never left off taking a deep interest in "English literature, English social life,
English politics, English religion."[14] In his first letter to the Corinthians, St Clement
recounted how "Abraham . . . was found to be faithful when he became obedient
to God's words. In obedience, he left his land, his family, and his father's house,
so that by abandoning a paltry land, an insignificant family, and a small house he
might inherit the promise of God."[15] One of the paradoxes of Newman's life is that it
was only by renouncing many of the false allegiances of his own "paltry land" that
he could serve not only his English family but his English compatriots by sharing
with them the "promise of God." And in this duty, which he discharged in so many
brilliant sermons and other writings, he would often have to distinguish between the
religion of the State and the religion of God, as here in "Saintliness the Standard of
Christian Principle" (1848):

The national religion has many attractions; it leads to decency and order,
propriety of conduct, justness of thought, beautiful domestic tastes; but it has
not power to lead the multitude upward, or to delineate for them the Heavenly
City. It comes of mere nature, and its teaching is of nature. It uses religious
words, of course, else it could not be called a religion; but it does not impress on
the imagination, it does not engrave upon the heart, it does not inflict upon the
conscience, the supernatural; it does not introduce into the popular mind any
great ideas, such as are to be recognised by one and all, as common property,
and first principles or dogmas from which to start, to be taken for granted on all
hands, and handed down as forms and specimens of eternal truth from age to
age. It in no true sense inculcates the Unseen; and by consequence, sights of this
world, material tangible objects, become the idols and the ruin of its children, of
souls which were made for God and Heaven. It is powerless to resist the world
and the world's teaching: it cannot supplant error by truth; it follows when it
should lead. There is but one real Antagonist of the world, and that is the faith
of Catholics;—Christ set that faith up, and it will do its work on earth, as it ever
has done, till He comes again.[16]

Another striking paradox is that the force of Newman's distinctions should have
been grasped by Augustine Birrell, a liberal politician who had grown up in the

13 See Sermon 26, No. 273 in *John Henry Newman: Sermons 1824–1843*. ed. Francis J. McGrath, FMS
    (Oxford, 2010), III, pp. 172–3.
14 C. S. Dessain. *John Henry Newman* (London, 1966), p. 167.
15 See "First Letter of Clement," in *The Apostolic Fathers*. ed. Bart D. Ehrman (Loeb, 2010), I, p. 51.
16 *Mix.*, pp. 102–3.

Nonconformist tradition and never had the least intention of following the great convert into the Roman fold.

What Disraeli meant when he said that Newman's secession had dealt the Church of England a blow under which it still reeled, was that by this act Newman expressed before the whole world his profound conviction that our so-called National Church was not a branch of the Church Catholic. And this really is the point of weakness upon which Newman hurled himself. This is the damage he did to the Church of this island. Throughout all his writings, in a hundred places, in jests and sarcasms as well as in papers and arguments, there crops up this settled conviction that England is not a Catholic country, and that John Bull is not a member of the Catholic Church.

Birrell also understood that however indifferent many of the British people might be to the challenge Newman posed to his Anglican contemporaries—a challenge that he had first made to his brothers and sisters—there were others who would respond differently. Indeed, for Birrell, "to those who care about such things, who rely upon the validity of orders and the efficacy of sacraments, who need a pedigree for their faith, who do not agree with Emerson that if a man would be great he must be a Nonconformist—over these people it would be rash to assume that Newman's influence is spent. The general effect of his writings, the demands they awaken, the spirit they breathe, are all hostile to Anglicanism. They create a profound dissatisfaction with, a distaste for, the Church of England as by law established. Those who are affected by this spirit will no longer be able comfortably to enjoy the maimed rites and practices of their Church. They will feel their place is elsewhere, and sooner or later they will pack up and go. It is far too early in the day to leave Newman out of sight."[17] Birrell published that in 1902 but he could have written it yesterday.[18]

Of all the questions that grew out of my researches the one I asked myself most was what effect Newman's family *not* converting had on him. And several answers have occurred to me. Certainly, it broke his heart; it exasperated him; it intensified the loneliness that this most gregarious of men was prone to suffer; but, above all, it impressed upon him the power of the Cross. "Let me bear pain, reproach, disappointment, slander, anxiety, suspense, as Thou wouldst have me, O my Jesu," he writes in his *Meditations and Devotions.* "And I promise too, with Thy grace, that I will never set myself up, never seek preeminence, never court any great thing of the world, never prefer myself to others. I wish to bear insult meekly; and to return good for evil. I wish to humble myself in all things, and to be silent when I am ill-used, and to be patient when sorrow or pain is prolonged, and all for the love of Thee, and Thy Cross, knowing that in this way I shall gain the promise of this life and of the next."[19] Thus, the sorrows of the divisions of family deepened his humility.

---

[17] See Augustine Birrell, *Collected Essays* (London, 1902), p. 123.
[18] G. K. Chesterton credited Birrell with making him a Liberal, or, as he put it, someone who was "really full of something that was not liberalism but liberality." The shrewd critic in Chesterton also recognized that "Birrell was a Nonconformist with a very rich comprehension of Newman." See *Autobiography* (London, 1936), p. 280.
[19] *MD*, pp. 348–9.

Commentators often speak of Newman possessing a genius for religion. This is true but he also possessed a hard-won sense of the gift of religion. Consequently, the fact that this was not a gift that had been given in any comparable measure to his other family members could not but mortify him. This, I suppose, is something of what Frances Palgrave saw when he visited Newman at the Oratory in November 1887. "I was allowed an interview with Cardinal Newman at the Oratory," Palgrave noted in his diary.

There sat that aged man with his snow-white hair; he rose and thanked me for coming and for caring for him with a sort of young child's gracious simplicity. He was much changed, of course, since I had last seen him many years ago: the look of almost anxious searching had passed into the look of perfect peace. His mind was not only bright as ever, but with the cheerfulness and humour of youth. He talked of his old Oxford days . . . Then of [Dean] Church, "whom no one could know without loving". He spoke of his voyage long ago in the Mediterranean; how little he had, however, seen of Italy. We talked of Rome, of Varallo, when he at once recalled the Gaudenzio "Nativity" which I sent him last Christmas. He went on to speak of Creighton's "Papacy", and the Renaissance and its evils in high places; and he broke out, with a bright smile of tenderness: "How wonderful was the revival of the Church soon after under Loyola, St Philip Neri, San Carlo Borromeo!" Then he spoke of Tennyson, and said that in poetry one went back to what one knew in youth. I said Wordsworth perhaps—at which he smiled . . . He went on to say that Scott had been his favourite, and alluded playfully to his age (eighty-seven in January next) as a reason why he read less than he would have liked. He thanked me again for what he called my kindness in caring to see him. This great and perfect humility was almost overwhelming in its strikingness. No wonder he looked up with reverence to the two Borromei, whom he mentioned with special admiration. What a strange and beautiful union of the saint and the poet! His voice has much of its old strange sweetness, such as I heard it at Littlemore in my Oxford days—how far off for both of us!'[20]

Now that I am at the end of my study, I am more appreciative than ever of the whole families on whom Newman's influence did not fail. Many of my readers will know how beloved Newman was by members of the Froude, Pusey, Bellasis, Coleridge, Wilberforce, Bowden, Ryder, Hope-Scott, and Pollen families, to name only a few; but there were many more. On 6 January 1870, James Stewart, Professor of Greek and Latin at the Catholic University of Ireland, wrote to Newman a letter whose gratitude summed up that of many fathers of families in Newman's extensive circle of friends. "I cannot help thinking of you always on the Epiphany," Stewart wrote from Dublin, "for it was on that day I and my family were received into the Church, 20 years ago,

---

[20] Gwenllian F. Palgrave, _Francis Turner Palgrave_ (London 1899), p. 202. A good friend of Tennyson, Palgrave was a critic, poet and editor of the _Golden Treasury of English Songs and Lyrics_ (1861).

and we never can forget how entirely it was owing to you that humanly speaking we ever became Catholics.

Your sermons as a Protestant broke up the hardened protestant soil of my heart, and your sermons to mixed congregations was the last book I read before I became a Catholic; and my doubts and difficulties about the Blessed Virgin were dispelled by your two sermons in that volume, especially the one on "The Glories of Mary for the sake of her Son." You will never know how many people owe their conversion to you, mediately or immediately, till the day when all hearts are open. I fear you will think me almost impertinent, if I tell you with what veneration every Irish priest whether in Dublin or in the North, South or West speaks of you and I know as much as most people for I go to all quarters on behalf of the University every year. I won't say any more, but I could say much of the same kind, if I would.[21]

Newman responded with a letter full of solicitous affection. If his relations with his own family tended to be painfully vexed, especially after his conversion, his relations with those whom he had brought into the one true fold were of a compensatory joy.

The Oratory Jany 9. 1870

My dear Stewart

A happy new year to you and all yours. Thank you for your affectionate letter, and all you say of me. It is a great encouragement to believe I have the prayers of good people, especially now that I am so old. Just now give me some prayers for prospering in a work I am finishing. It is not much of a work in size, but I can't get to the end. I am a few yards from the shore, and the waves beat me back. [Here, Newman was referring to the finishing of his *Essay on the Grammar of Assent*, which he would publish on March, 15, 1870.] I rejoice you have got over your uneasiness about Mrs Stewart. Tell her, that, please God, I will say Mass for her on an early day. Thank you for telling me of your children. I, or rather we, shall rejoice to see you as you propose—though the time is so long off that one does not like to promise anything about oneself.

Best wishes to all friends Ever Yours affly
John H Newman[22]

Newman must have been particularly pleased when Stewart came to visit him at the Oratory on 28 September 1871 with his daughters in tow, one of whom, Isabella (1851–1932), was about to become a Benedictine at Princethorpe Priory, Warwickshire.[23] In 1871, Isabella became a Postulant there, and on 30 April 1872, she received the habit as Sister Mary John. She remained at Princethorpe for the rest of her days.[24] When she

---

[21] LD, 25:7 James Stewart to JHN (6 January 1870).
[22] LD, 25:7–8 JHN to James Stewart (9 January 1870).
[23] LD, 25:47, Note 1.
[24] LD, 26: 435.

received the habit, Newman wrote the Prioress of Pincethorpe to tell her how, as he said, "I rejoice to hear that Miss Stewart has attained so great a grace as to be admitted into the family of your glorious St. Benedict. Praise be to God—pray convey to her my kindest congratulations. I propose to say Mass for her on the 30th."[25] In this way, family by family, Newman put his own incomparable stamp on the Communion of Saints.

Then, again, the delight Newman took in families can be seen best in the love he showed their children. A charming example of this can be seen in a letter he wrote to Charlotte or "Chattie" Bowden (1848–1933), aged 15, who had made him a present of cakes:

Who is it that moulds and makes
Round, and crisp, and fragrant cakes?
One it is, for whom I pray,
On St. Philip's festal day,
With a loving heart that she
Perfect as her cakes may be,
Full and faithful in the round
Of her duties ever found
Where a trial comes, between
Truth and falsehood cutting keen;
Yet that keenness and completeness
Tempering with a winning sweetness.
Here's a rhyming letter Chat,
Gift for gift, and tit for tat.[26]

To Helen Church, the daughter of Dean Church, who had sent Newman a copy of Lewis Carroll's *The Hunting of the Snark* (1865), he responded with an equally charming letter, telling her how the Easter Greeting in the book "is likely to touch the hearts of old men more than of those for whom it is intended."

The second paragraph of this letter began "Do you know that delicious dreamy feeling when one wakes on a summer morning, with the twitter of birds in the air, and the fresh breeze coming in at the open window—when, lying lazily with eyes half shut, one sees as in a dream green boughs waving, or water rippling in a golden light? . . . ." I recollect well my own thoughts and feelings, such as the author describes, as I lay in my crib in the early spring, with outdoor scents, sounds and sights wakening me up, and especially the cheerful ring of the mower's scythe on the lawn, which Milton long before me had noted;—and how in coming down stairs slowly, for I brought down both feet on each step, I said to myself "This is June!" though what my particular experience of June was, and how it was broad enough to be a matter of reflection, I really cannot tell.

---

[25] LD, 26:57 JHN to the Prioress of Princethorpe (6 April 1872).
[26] JHN to Charlotte Bowden (26 May 1863) in *A Packet of Letters*. ed. Joyce Sugg (Oxford, 1983), p. 141.

Can't you, Mary, and Edith recollect something of the same kind? though you may not think so much of it as I do now? May the day come for all of us, of which Easter is the promise, when that first spring, may return to us, and a sweetness which cannot die may gladden our garden.[27]

Another conclusion occurs to me and that is how the pain Newman suffered with regard to his own family made him sympathetic to the pain that others suffered in theirs. A year before his death, he wrote Lord Blachford a letter that epitomizes this fellow feeling. Frederic Rogers (1811–90), I should remind my readers, was one of Newman's oldest and dearest friends, despite the fact that after Newman's conversion he refused to speak to him for 20 years. Nevertheless, when they finally reconciled in 1863, Newman was overjoyed, especially when then Lord Blachford, together with Dean Church, made him a present of a new violin. Something of the great love that Blachford bore Newman, for all his prejudice against the convert's Catholicism, is evident in a tribute he paid to him in one of his letters.

Newman seemed to have an intuitive perception of all that you thought and felt, so that he caught at once all that you meant or were driving at in a sentiment, a philosophical reflection or a joke . . . And so there was in talking with him that combination of liveliness and repose which constitutes ease; you seemed to be speaking with a better kind of self, which was drawing you upwards. Newman's general characteristics—his genius, depth of purpose; his hatred of pomp and affectation; his piercing insight into the workings of the human mind . . . his strong and tenacious . . . affection . . . are all matters of history.[28]

Hearing of the death of Blachford's youngest sister Sophie, Newman wrote to commiserate with his old friend, a year before his own death, assuring him, as he said, of how "I ever loved and felt attached to your home and family and I can understand your and their sorrow." Then, on learning that Blachford himself was declining in health, Newman responded, with wry wit: "My dear Blachford, I tried to write you a line, but the failure is no great loss. Tell me how you are." When Blachford wrote back, informing his old friend that "I ought to tell you that within the last two days, my doctors have told me plainly that I am not to recover," Newman thanked him for the precision of his report, a precision not lost on someone who had come to find letter writing so extremely difficult: "Your letter of this morning added of course to the griefs which for a long course of years have gathered heavily upon my mind. And though I knew all along what must take place any how some day or other to the destruction of my tenderest memories, yet, I was not the more prepared for your very kind and distinct announcement when it came to me." After which, he wrote to Lady Blachford, "Thank you for having me in memory amid your sorrow for one who is still dearer to

---

[27] LD, 28:52–3 JHN to Helen Church (19 April 1876) Newman alludes to Milton's *L'Allegro* (1645), line 66 "And the Mower whets his sithe . . ." Shane Leslie argued that in the trial of the Knave of Hearts, Lewis Carroll was satirizing Newman and the Tractarians' attacks on the 39 Articles. In this reading, the Articles are the tarts, against which a "knavish Ritualist" is accused of "having removed their natural sense." See Shane Leslie, "Lewis Carroll and the Oxford Movement," in *Aspects of Alice*. ed. Robert S. Phillips (New York, 1971), p. 216.

[28] *Letters of Lord Blachford* (London, 1896), p. 14.

you than a life long friend. I am always thinking of him, and together with him of those who are so dear to him." When Lady Blachford gave him the news that her husband was dead, Newman wrote her back: "I pray the blessing of God may come upon you and him and all dear to him. He is nearly the dearest as well as the oldest of my early friends." Blachford was also one who was very close to Newman's family—he delighted in his mother and sisters—so his death doubtless reminded him of their death as well, now that only he and his brother Frank survived.

Without his parents, without his brothers, without his sisters, Newman would have been a very different person, for it was each of them, in their different ways, who first helped him to see what would become his life's mission. In 1879, when he gratefully received his red hat from Pope Leo XIII, Newman told his Roman audience, "I have made many mistakes. I have nothing of that high perfection, which belongs to the writings of the Saints . . . but what I trust I can claim all through what I have written is this, -an honest intention, an absence of private ends, a temper of obedience, a willingness to be corrected, a dread of error, a desire to serve Holy Church . . . And I rejoice to say, to one great mischief I have from the first opposed myself. For 30, 40, 50 years I have resisted to the best of my powers the spirit of liberalism in religion." Critics of Newman have tried to cast doubt on the consistency and indeed the coherence of this claim. But his explanation of what he meant in what has come to be known as his Biglietto Speech is neither inconsistent nor incoherent. On the contrary, it gives to his work its unifying simplicity. Although he conceded that there are ideas attached to "the liberalistic theory" that are "good and true"—he cited "the precepts of justice, truthfulness, sobriety, self-command, benevolence," which he reminds his readers issue from "the natural laws of society" – he recognized in "liberalism in religion" a number of propositions, which, as he was loth to admit, were gaining increased acceptance, even by the "able," "earnest," and "virtuous," and he identified them thus:

> Revealed religion is not a truth, but a sentiment and a taste; not an objective fact, not miraculous; and it is the right of each individual to make it say just what strikes his fancy. Devotion is not necessarily founded on faith. Men may go to Protestant Churches and to Catholic, may get good from both and belong to neither. They may fraternise together in spiritual thoughts and feelings, without having any views at all of doctrine in common, or seeing the need of them. Since, then, religion is so personal a peculiarity and so private a possession, we must of necessity ignore it in the intercourse of man with man. If a man puts on a new religion every morning, what is that to you? It is as impertinent to think about a man's religion as about his sources of income or his management of his family. Religion is in no sense the bond of society.[29]

These were the captivating sophistries of "liberalism in religion," and in his published writings and in his letters, Newman shows how they deny objective truth, undermine the fellowship of truth, and confound religious certainty. He also shows how they can

---

[29] *Addresses to Cardinal Newman*, II, pp. 64–5.

deceive even those most avid for the truth. He had the example of his brothers to convince him of that. Only by studying Newman and his family can we appreciate why he entered the battle to defeat such sophistries with such wholehearted *caritas*. This is why my final chapter on Newman's correspondence with his nephew John Rickards Mozley was so necessary to my design. At Cambridge, Mozley imbibed a scepticism that left him unable to accept or reject Christianity, for which so much of his restless mind and heart yearned. One of my purposes in that chapter was to show that in his sceptical approach to scepticism he was more representative of his milieu than is generally appreciated. What is loosely termed Cambridge philosophy, at least in the late nineteenth century, was never entirely comfortable with thoroughgoing scepticism. The work of Henry Sidgwick and John Grote confirms Newman's great conviction that "unbelief has no root in the human heart" by corroborating G. E. Moore's and Wittgenstein's insights into the untenability of universal doubt.[30] "I can prove now, for instance, that two human hands exist," Moore famously claimed in "A Defense of Common Sense" (1925), "How? By holding up my two hands, and saying, as I make a certain gesture with the right hand, 'Here is one hand,' and adding, as I make a gesture with the left, 'and here is another.'" Wittgenstein would not entirely accept this common-sense claim in the terms in which Moore framed it but he did, in his own way, concede its point. "Scepticism," he declared in the *Tractatus*, "is *not* irrefutable"—a fact of which Newman was never unaware—"but obviously nonsensical, when it tries to raise doubts where no questions can be asked."[31] It meant a good deal to Newman that he should be able to share with his nephew, coming as he did from Cambridge's highly agnostic ethos, the promises of dogmatic Christianity, which Mozley was right to see encapsulated in one splendid sentence from his uncle's letters: "The *ethos* of the Catholic Church is what it was of old time, and whatever or whoever quarrels with Catholicism now, quarrels virtually and would have quarreled if alive 1800 years ago, with the Christianity of the Apostles and Evangelists."[32]

In this regard, Newman was carrying on something of a family tradition with his nephew, which he had inaugurated with his brother Charles in the 1820s and continued with Frank, Harriett and Jemima in the years leading up to and beyond his conversion: and that was sharing the gift of faith, the "pearl of great price," even when that gift was sorely misunderstood, or, perhaps one should say, *especially* when it was misunderstood, for this was not a tradition that met with much success. On the contrary, like so much else in Newman's life, it was riddled with failure. What is that wonderful quote from Chesterton? "The saint is a medicine because he is an antidote. Indeed, that is why the saint is often a martyr: he is mistaken for a poison because he is an antidote."[33]

And here I encounter another conclusion, but one which is more elusive than the others, calling to mind as it does something Newman told an old friend who was alone in the world, Miss Holmes, the governess, who, after sharing with her friend some

---

[30] LD, 29:169 JHN to Lady Herbert of Lea (19 August 1879).
[31] See how ably Ray Monk discusses these abstruse matters in *Ludwig Wittgenstein: The Duty of Genius* (London, 1990), pp. 556–7.
[32] LD, 27:387 JHN to J. R. Mozley (3 December 1875).
[33] *The Everyman Chesterton.* ed. Ian Ker (New York, 2011), p. 503.

scraps of family history, received a letter back in which he assured her how, "You were right in thinking that your family reminiscences would interest me. I think nothing more interesting, and it is strange to think how evanescent, how apparently barren and result-less, are the ten thousand little details and complications of daily life and family history. Is there any record of them preserved any where, any more than of the fall of the leaves in Autumn? or are they themselves some reflexion, as in an earthly mirror, of some greater truths above?"[34]

This was written in 1860, when the life of Newman's own family might have seemed very "result-less" indeed. His parents had died long ago, his father bankrupt and his mother estranged from the son whom once she had considered the "*silent* pride of my early life" and "the comfort and guide of my age."[35] His sister Mary had predeceased her parents, when she was all of 19. His sister Harriett died with a like suddenness but with complete contempt for the brother whom once she had been so fond. His feckless brother Charles had thrown his lot in with the Owenite socialists and made a spectacular mess of his life. His brother Frank had fared no better, ending his days a ruthless eugenicist. His sister Jemima, it is true, kept in contact with her brother, but she saw to it that her children had nothing to do with him. When her second son, John Rickards Mozley finally got around to corresponding with his uncle, he was 35 and frankly baffled by how anyone, even a Roman convert, could defend an institution as self-evidently vicious as the papacy.

Here is one version of the Newman family history, which can hardly be said to abound in happy issue. Yet there is another, more balanced version, and it can be seen in something Newman wrote in October 1836, six months after the death of his mother. In one of his own favourite sermons, "The Greatness and the Littleness of Human Life," based on the Scripture text, '*The days of the years of my pilgrimmage are an hundred and thirty years; few and evil have the days of the years of my life been*,' Newman observed how "the longest duration of this external world is as dust and weighs nothing, against one moment's life of the world within. Thus we are ever expecting great things from life, from our internal consciousness every moment of our having souls; and we are ever being disappointed, on considering what we have gained from time past, and can hope from time to come. And life is ever promising and never fulfilling; and hence, however long it be, our days are few and evil . . ." This might have been Newman's variation on Johnson's great adaptation of Juvenal, but instead of the vanity of human wishes, Newman shows us their promise, when conformed to the will of God.

Our earthly life then gives promise of what it does not accomplish. It promises immortality, yet it is mortal; it contains life in death and eternity in time; and it attracts us by beginnings which faith alone brings to an end. I mean, when we take into account the powers with which our souls are gifted as Christians, the very consciousness of these fills us with a certainty that they must last beyond this life; that is in the case of good and holy men, whose present state I say, is to them who know them well, an earnest of immortality. The greatness of their gifts, contrasted with their scanty time for exercising them, forces the mind forward to the thought

[34] LD, 19:415 JHN to Miss Holmes (4 November 1860).
[35] LD, 2:252 Mrs Newman to JHN (19 July 1830).

of another life, as almost the necessary counterpart and consequence of this life, and certainly implied in this life, provided there be a righteous Governor of the world, who does not make man for nought.[36]

And for an example, Newman pointed to the suppositious case of a man who might almost be the double of his father. "I mean," he explained, "when one sees some excellent person, whose graces we know, whose kindliness, affectionateness, tenderness, and generosity,—when we see him dying (let him have lived ever so long; I am not supposing a premature death; let him live out his days), the thought is forced upon us with a sort of surprise; 'Surely, he is not to die yet; he has not yet had any opportunity of exercising duly those excellent gifts with which God has endowed him.' Let him have lived seventy or eighty years, yet it seems as if he had done nothing at all, and his life were scarcely begun."[37] Of course, these are words that can apply to multitudes, but they especially evoke the talented, good-hearted, unfortunate man, whose enterprise and acuity were no match for the vagaries of the post-Napoleonic financial markets or the unpredictability of breweries.

He has lived all his days perhaps in a private sphere; he has been engaged on a number of petty matters which died with the day, and yielded no apparent fruit. He has had just enough of trial under various circumstances, to evidence, but not adequately to employ, what was in him. He has, we perhaps perceive, a noble benevolence of mind, a warmth of heart, and a beneficent temper, which, had it the means, would scatter blessings on every side; yet he has never been rich,—he dies poor. We have been accustomed to say to ourselves, "What would such a one be were he wealthy," not as fancying he ever *will* have riches, but from feeling how he would become them; yet, when he actually does die as he lived, without them, we feel somehow disappointed,—there has been a failure,—his mind, we think, has never reached its scope,—he has had a treasure within him which has never been used. His days have been but few and evil, and have become old unseasonably, compared with his capabilities; and we are driven by a sense of them, to look on to a future state as a time when they will be brought out and come into effect. I am not attempting by such reflections to prove that there is a future state; let us take that for granted. I mean, over and above our positive belief in this great truth, we are actually driven to a belief, we attain a sort of sensible conviction of that life to come, a certainty striking home to our hearts and piercing them, by this imperfection in what is present. The very greatness of our powers makes this life look pitiful; the very pitifulness of this life forces on our thoughts to another; and the prospect of another gives a dignity and value to this life which promises it; and thus this life is at once great and little, and we rightly contemn it while we exalt its importance.[38]

Moreover, for Newman, "There is something in moral truth and goodness, in faith, in firmness, in heavenly-mindedness, in meekness, in courage, in loving-kindness,

---

[36] *PS*, iv, pp. 214–16.
[37] Ibid., p. 217.
[38] Ibid., p. 218.

to which this world's circumstances are quite unequal, for which the longest life is insufficient, which makes the highest opportunities of this world disappointing, which must burst the prison of this world to have its appropriate range. So that when a good man dies, one is led to say, 'He has not half showed himself, he has had nothing to exercise him; his days are gone like a shadow, and he is withered like grass.'"[39] Learning these lessons required a fair amount of disillusionment and it was only by putting himself to the school of family, with all of its high hopes and bitter disappointments, that he made them his own. At the same time, the disappointments of family never prevented Newman from seeking to share with his own family the Faith he cherished so keenly. In 1870, when he republished his *Essay on the Development of Christian Doctrine*, which he had originally published in 1845, he could not have been unmindful that the appeal with which he ended his greatest work of theology was directed as much to his family as to readers as a whole, especially those Anglican readers with whom his sisters Jemima and Harriett had so much in common. Much is warrantably made of the personal character of Newman's work: not only the personal care that he invested in his work but the personal care with which he sought to address the practical needs of his readers.[40] Here, we can see how it was his deep love of his family that animated this care the most.

And now, dear Reader, time is short, eternity is long. Put not from you what you have here found; regard it not as mere matter of present controversy; set not out resolved to refute it, and looking about for the best way of doing so; seduce not yourself with the imagination that it comes of disappointment, or disgust, or restlessness, or wounded feeling, or undue sensibility, or other weakness. Wrap not yourself round in the associations of years past, nor determine that to be truth which you wish to be so, nor make an idol of cherished anticipations. Time is short, eternity is long.[41]

In another sermon, one of his most illuminating, "Faith and Love" (1838), a profound meditation on St Paul's text, "*Though I have all Faith, so that I could remove mountains, and have no Charity, I am nothing,*" he describes how faith without love is indeed insufficient; a truth on which a good deal of Newman's work meditates.[42] "Love is the true ruling principle of the regenerate soul, and faith ministers to it. Love is the end, faith the means; and if the means be difficult, much more is the end. St. Paul says that faith which could remove mountains will not avail without love; and in truth, faith is only half way (as it were) to heaven. By faith we give up this world, but by love we reach into the next world . . ."[43] This was the love that Newman brought to

---

[39] Ibid., p. 219.
[40] In this regard, Newman richly fulfills Aristotle's criteria for the good orator: "To carry conviction, a speaker needs three qualities—for there are three things that convince us, apart from actual proof— good sense, good character, and good will towards his hearers." See F. L. Lucas. *Style* (London, 1955), p. 50.
[41] *Dev.*, p. 445.
[42] One of the best of these is "Love: the One Thing Needful" (1839).
[43] *PS*, iv, p. 315.

all of his work throughout his long life, whether in Oxford or Littlemore, London or Edgbaston, Dublin or what he called that "virtual university" created beyond the university, and it was his family that first gave him the means to put it into practice.[44] In his sermon, "Love, the One Thing Needful" (1839), he shows how in this he was imitating Christ, for "Christ showed His love in deed, not in word, and you will be touched by the thought of His cross far more by bearing it after Him, than by glowing accounts of it."[45] By showing his father such loving empathy throughout his reversals; by bearing his mother's misunderstanding of his faith with patience and forbearance; by emulating the sanctity of his sister Mary; by bearing the slights of his sister Harriett without recrimination; by supporting his brother Charles despite his many self-inflicted misfortunes; by never turning his back on his brother Frank, who repaid his loyalty with contempt and contumely; by keeping close to Jemima, even though she contrived to keep him at a distance, Newman imitated Christ, knowing, as he wrote in his wonderful sermon, that "It is by such deeds and such thoughts that our services, our repentings, our prayers, our intercourse with men, will become instinct with the spirit of love. Then we do everything thankfully and joyfully, when we are temples of Christ, with His Image set up in us." And there was another good grace that followed from this love of family: "We are patient in bereavement, adversity, or pain, for they are Christ's tokens."[46]

No attribute of Newman's was more characteristic of the imaginative fellow-feeling of the man than the empathy he brought to the bereaving. As we have seen over and over again, his letters abound with examples of how he exercised this crucial virtue, but here is one of the most moving, which he wrote to a parishioner after Father Ambrose, his "dearest friend" died on 24 May 1875.

The Oratory June 19. 1875

My dear Miss Geoghagan

I am sure you will excuse my silence, when you know the cause of it. I have been afflicted suddenly by a great bereavement, as your sister has—the illness which has carried off my dearest friend is the same as that which has taken away her little child, and the suddenness of the blow has made me so confused in mind and unwell, and has involved so much work, that I could not till now write to you. Say every thing kind from me to your Sister, and tell her that, please God, I will say Mass for her and her intention tomorrow. I can quite understand how a little child twines round the hearts of parents from its innocent sweetness and helplessness—and that the more, because, in the account I gave some friends of the illness of the friend I have lost, I recognized in him just those same looks which made me say to them that his face had on it a child's expression, so tender,

[44] "We cannot then be without virtual Universities . . . the simple question is, whether the education sought and given should be based on principle, formed upon rule, directed to the highest ends, or left to the random succession of masters and schools, one after another, with a melancholy waste of thought and an extreme hazard of truth." See Newman quoted in Edward Short. *Newman and his Contemporaries* (London, 2011), p. 308.
[45] *PS*, v, p. 338.
[46] Ibid., p. 340.

gentle, and imploring. Thus both young and old, go "as little children" into the
presence of their God

> Ask her to pray for me in the greatest affliction I ever had, and believe me to be
> Most truly Yours in Xt John H Newman[47]

In entering into the sufferings of others, Newman showed himself a worthy successor
of St Paul, whom he resembled in so many vital ways. Indeed, one of the reasons why
it is untenable to claim that Newman's Anglican sermons are better than his Catholic
sermons is that it is only in the latter that he shares with his readers his deep insights into
the legacy of the great convert, a legacy that he could only entirely absorb after he had
converted himself. Then, the similarities between the two men became unmistakable.
Like St Paul, Newman began by extolling the faith of his fathers only to find that he
could not embrace that faith fully without entering into the very communion that his
own people reviled; he devoted his life after his conversion to trying to help those
whom his conversion had obliged him to leave; he delighted in his people's traditions,
but understood them in ways that his own people regarded as treacherous; he was
a great preacher; he was an inspired poet; he understood that without love men are
hollow and that the source of all love is Jesus Christ; he knew this because he had a
deep personal relationship with Christ; and he made it his special apostolate to share
this love of Christ not only with the faithful but with his unconverted brethren as well.
When St Paul uttered that most moving of laments, "I could wish that I myself were
accursed and separated from Christ for the sake of my brothers, my kin according
to the flesh," we can hear something of Newman's own lament for the unbelief of his
people but especially his family, who, in their way, had also been on the receiving end
of "the worship and the promises."[48]

Then, again, Newman's deep sense of the spiritual uses of failure also bound him
to St Paul, as he related to one of his most capable Oratorians, John Stanislas Flanagan
(1821–1905), who abandoned the hunting fields of Ireland to become a priest—first
with the Oratory and then with Lord Dunraven's parish, Adare in Country Limerick.
"Don't be cast down," Newman told Flanagan, "all will turn out well.

> Recollect, and let me myself recollect, that from the first it has been my fortune
> to be ever failing, yet after all not to fail. From the first I have had bad strokes
> of fortune—yet on the whole I have made way. Hardly had I begun life, when
> misfortunes happened to my family—then I failed in the Schools; then I was put
> out of office at College; then came Number 90—and later the Achilli matter. You
> talk of "brilliant success" as not our portion—it is not, because you are all joined
> to me. When I was a boy, I was taken beyond any thing in Homer, with Ulysses
> seeming "like a fool or an idiot," when he began to speak—and yet somehow doing
> more than others, as St Paul with his weakness and foolishness. I think this was
> from some presentiment of what was to happen to me. Depend upon it, we shall
> be happier and more blessed and more successful in my way then in any other.[49]

[47] LD, 27:323 JHN to Mrs Geoghagan (19 June 1875).
[48] Romans, 9:3–4.
[49] LD, 18:271 JHN to J. S. Flanagan (24 February 1858).

With all of these similarities to St Paul, it is not surprising that in another sermon, "St. Paul's Gift of Sympathy" (1857), preached before the Catholic University of Ireland in Dublin in the University Church, Newman should describe an aspect of the great saint that captures his own profound solicitude for the well-being of both his immediate and his pastoral family.

There are Saints in whom grace supersedes nature; so was it not with this great Apostle; in him grace did but sanctify and elevate nature. It left him in the full possession, in the full exercise, of all that was human, which was not sinful. He who had the constant contemplation of his Lord and Saviour, and if he saw Him with his bodily eyes, was nevertheless as susceptible of the affections of human nature and the influences of the external world, as if he were a stranger to that contemplation. Wonderful to say, he who had rest and peace in the love of Christ, was not satisfied without the love of man; he whose supreme reward was the approbation of God, looked out for the approval of his brethren. He who depended solely on the Creator, yet made himself dependent on the creature. Though he had That which was Infinite, he would not dispense with the finite. He loved his brethren, not only "for Jesus' sake," to use his own expression, but for their own sake also. He lived in them; he felt with them and for them; he was anxious about them; he gave them help, and in turn he looked for comfort from them. His mind was like some instrument of music, harp or viol, the strings of which vibrate, though untouched, by the notes which other instruments give forth, and he was ever, according to his own precept, "rejoicing with them that rejoice, and weeping with them that wept"; and thus he was the least magisterial of all teachers, and the gentlest and most amiable of all rulers. "Who is weak," he asks, "and I am not weak? who is scandalized, and I am not on fire?" And, after saying this, he characteristically adds, "If I must needs glory, I will glory of the things that concern my infirmity."[50]

When Newman wrote these deeply characteristic words, although he might have been thinking of his family, he was of course living at the Birmingham Oratory with the Fathers of the Oratory, in what he often referred to as *Santa Communità*, and in that life he had formed a new family. In 1879, he returned home to this family after receiving the red hat from Leo XIII and celebrated his homecoming in words that show that the home that he had shared with his mother and his father, his brothers and his sisters had prepared him for another more precious home:

MY DEAR CHILDREN,
I am desirous of thanking you for the great sympathy you have shown towards me, for your congratulations, for your welcome, and for your good prayers; but I feel so very weak—for I have not recovered yet from a long illness—that I hardly know how I can be able to say ever so few words, or to express in any degree the great pleasure and gratitude to you which I feel. To come home again! In that word "home" how much is included. I know well that there is a more heroic life than a

[50] *OS*, pp. 114–15.

home life. We know the blessed Apostles—how they went about, and we listen to St. Paul's words—those touching words—in which he speaks of himself and says he was an outcast. Then we know, too, our Blessed Lord—that he "had not where to lay his head." Therefore, of course, there is a higher life, a more heroic life, than that of home. But still, that is given to few. The home life—the idea of home—is consecrated to us by our patron and founder, St. Philip, for he made the idea of home the very essence of his religion and institute. We have even a great example in our Lord Himself; for though in His public ministry He had not where to lay His head, yet we know that for the first thirty years of His life He had a home, and He therefore consecrated, in a special way, the life of home. And as, indeed, Almighty God has been pleased to continue the world, not, as angels, by a separate creation of each, but by means of the Family, so it was fitting that the Congregation of St. Philip should be the ideal, the realisation of the family in its perfection, and a pattern to every family in the parish, in the town, and throughout the whole of Christendom. Therefore, I do indeed feel pleasure to come home again . . . I feel I may rejoice in coming home again—as if it were to my long home—to that home which extends to heaven, "the home of our eternity."[51]

---

[51] *Addresses to Cardinal Newman*, pp. 103–5.

Select Bibliography

Correspondence

The Letters and Diaries of John Henry Newman. ed. Dessain, Gornall, Ker, Kelly, Tracey, McGrath, 32 vols. (London and Oxford, 1961–).

Letters and Correspondence of John Henry Newman During His Life in the English Church. ed. Anne Mozley, 2 vols. (London, 1890).

The Letters of Queen Victoria. ed. A. C. Benson, Lord Esher, and G. E. Buckle: 1st series 1837–61, 3 vols. (1907), 2nd series 1861–85, 3 vols. (1926–8), 3rd series 1886–1901, 3 vols. (1930–2).

Letters to Vicky: The Correspondence of Queen Victoria and her Daughter Victoria, Empress of Germany: 1858–1901. ed. Andrew Roberts (London: Folio Society, 2011).

Newman Family Letters. ed. Dorothea Mozley (London, 1962).

Letters of Frederic, Lord Blachford. ed. George Eden Marindin, 2 vols. (London, 1896).

Life and Letters of Dean Church. ed. M. C. Church. (London, 1894).

Selected Letters of Charles Dickens. ed. Jean Hartley (Oxford, 2012).

George Eliot's Life as Related in Her Letters and Journals. ed. J. W. Cross, 3 vols. (Cambridge, 2010).

Mary Gladstone: Her Diaries and Letters. ed. Lucy Masterman (New York, 1930).

Correspondence on Church and Religion of William Ewart Gladstone. ed. D. C. Lathbury, 2 vols. (London, 1910).

Henry James: A Life in Letters. ed. Philip Horne (London, 2001).

Letters of the Rev. J. B. Mozley. ed. Anne Mozley (London, 1895).

Sieveking, I. G. *Memoir and Letters of Francis W. Newman* (London, 1909).

The Collected Letters of Alfred Lord Tennyson. ed. Cecil Lang and Roger Shannon (Cambridge and Oxford, 1981–90).

Newman Biographies

Dessain, S. *John Henry Newman* (Oxford, 1966).

Hutton, R. H. *Cardinal Newman* (London, 1890).

Ker, I. *John Henry Newman*, rev. ed. (Oxford, 2009).

Martin, B. *John Henry Newman* (London, 1982).

Trevor, M. *The Pillar of the Cloud* and *The Light in Winter* (London, 1962).

Ward, M. *Young Mr. Newman* (New York, 1948).

Ward, W. *The Life of John Henry Cardinal Newman*, 2 vols. (London, 1912).

Newman Anthologies

A Newman Anthology. ed. William Samuel Lilly (London, 1949).
The Genius of John Henry Newman. ed. Ian Ker (Oxford, 1989).
The Living Thoughts of Cardinal Newman. ed. Henry Tristram (London, 1948).
Newman: Selected Prose and Poetry. ed. Geoffrey Tillotson (London, 1957).
Realizations: Newman's Own Selection of His Sermons. ed. Vincent Ferrer Blehl, S. J. Foreword by Muriel Spark (London, 1964).

Primary Sources

Church, R. W. *The Oxford Movement* (London, 1920).
Dickens, C. *The Uncommercial Traveller and Reprinted Pieces* (Oxford, 1958).
de Vere, A. *Recollections* (New York, 1987).
Froude, J. A. *Short Studies on Great Subjects* (1867–83).
The Greville Memoirs 1814–1860. ed. L. Strachey and R. Fulford, 8 vols. (1938).
Grote, J. *Exploratio Philosophica: Rough Notes on Modern Intellectual Science*, 2 vols. (London, 1865 and 1900).
—*An Examination of the Utilitarian Philosophy* (London, 1870).
—*Treatise on Moral Ideals.* ed. Joseph Bickersteth Mayor (London, 1876).
The New Oxford Book of Victorian Verse. ed. Christopher Ricks (Oxford, 1987).
The Oxford Book of Victorian Verse. ed. C. Quiller-Couch (Oxford, 1912).
Maurice, F. *The Life of Frederick Denison Maurice Chiefly Told in his Own Letters*, 2 vols. (London, 1889).
Mayhew, H. *London Labour and the London Poor* (Folio Society, 1986).
Mill, J. *Autobiography* (Oxford World Classics, 1963).
—*On Liberty*, (Oxford World Classics, 1948).
Mozley, H. *The Fairy Bower* (London, 1841).
—*Family Adventures* (London, 1852).
Mozley, T. *Reminiscences, Chiefly of Oriel College and the Oxford Movement* (London, 1882).
Mozley, J. R. *Clifton Memories* (London, 1923).
—*The Divine Aspect of History*, 2 vols. (Cambridge, 1916).
—*A Vision of England and Other Poems* (London, 1898).
Murray, P. (ed.), *Newman the Oratorian: His Unpublished Oratory Papers* (London, 1980).
Newman, F. W. *Contributions to the Early History of the Late Cardinal* (London, 1891).
Oakeley, F. *Historical Notes on the Tractarian Movement* (London, 1865).
Ornsby, R. *Memoirs of James Robert Hope-Scott*, 2 vols. (London, 1884).
Pattison, M. *Memoirs* (London, 1885).
Sidgwick, H. *The Methods of Ethics* (London, 1907).
Tristram, H. (ed.), *John Henry Newman: Autobiographical Writings* (New York, 1956).
Trollope, A. *An Autobiography* (Oxford, 1953).
Wiseman, N. Pastoral Letter: "From the Flaminian Letter" (London, 1850).
—*Essays on Various Subjects*, 2 vols. (London, 1853).

Secondary Sources

Ackroyd, P. *Dickens* (London, 1990).

Alexander, M. *Medievalism: The Middle Ages in Modern England* (New Haven, 2007).

Ashton, R. *Victorian Bloomsbury* (New Haven, 2012).

Barrington, Mrs. R. *Life of Walter Bagehot* (London, 1914).

Batchelor, J. *John Ruskin: No Wealth But Life* (London, 2000).

Battiscombe, G. *John Keble: A Study in Limitation* (London, 1963).

Beard, M. *Faith and Fortune* (London, 1997).

Benson, A. C. *As We Were: A Victorian Peepshow* (London, 1930).

Best, G. *Mid-Victorian Britain 1851–75* (London, 1971).

Birrell, A. *Obiter Dicta* (London, 1884 and 1887).

—*In the Name of the Bodleian* (London, 1905).

Boyce, P. (ed.), *Mary: the Virgin Mary in the Life and Writings of John Henry Newman* (London, 2001).

Brendon, P. *Hurrell Froude and the Oxford Movement* (London, 1974).

Brock, M. G. and Curthoys, M. C. *The History of the University of Oxford. Volumes VI and VII Nineteenth-Century Oxford, Parts 1 and 2* (Oxford, 1997 and 2000).

Brooke, C. *Oxford and Cambridge* (Cambridge, 1988).

Buchan, A. *The Spare Chancellor: The Life of Walter Bagehot* (London, 1959).

Burn, W. L. *The Age of Equipoise: A Study of the Mid-Victorian Generation* (London, 1964).

Champ, J. *The Life of William Ullathorne* (London, 2006).

Chesterton, G. K. *Autobiography* (London, 1936).

—*Charles Dickens* (1906).

Clark, G. K. *The Making of Victorian England* (London, 1962).

Clark, J. W. *Cambridge: Historical and Picturesque Notes* (London, 1902).

Clark, J. C. D. *English Society 1688–1832: Ideology, Social Structure and Political Practice during the Ancient Regime* (Cambridge, 1985).

Cohen, D. *Household Gods: The British and their Possessions* (New Haven, 2006).

Copleston, F. *A History of Philosophy,* 9 vols. (London, 1946–75).

Cox, M. *M. R. James: An Informal Portrait* (Oxford, 1983).

David, M. *Catholicism in England 1535–1935* (London, 1936).

Davis, H. Francis. Foreword to *Newman on Tradition* by Gunter Biemer (New York, 1967).

Davies, H. *The English Free Churches* (Oxford, 1963).

Dunn, H. D. *James Anthony Froude: A Biography 1857–1894,* 2 vols. (Oxford, 1963).

Eden, E. *Up the Country: Letters Written to her Sister from the Upper Provinces of India,* 2 vols. (Cambridge, 2010).

Egremont, M. *Balfour: A Life of Arthur James Balfour* (London, 1980).

Edel, L. *The Life of Henry James,* 5 vols. (New York, 1950–78).

Ellmann, R. *James Joyce,* rev. ed. (Oxford, 1982).

Ensor, R. *England: 1870–1914* (Oxford, 1936).

Fenlon, D. "The Aristocracy of Talent and the Mystery of Newman" in Terrence Merrigan (ed.), *Louvain Studies,* vol. 15 (Louvain, 1990).

—"From the White Star to the White Rose: Newman and the Conscience of the State" in *Newman Studien,* vol. 20 (Munich, 2010).

—"De-Christianising England: Newman, Mill and the Stationary State" in Luke Gormally (ed.), *Culture of Life, Culture of Death* (London, 2002).

Fitzgerald, P. *The Knox Brothers* (London, 1977).

Flanders, J. *The Victorian House* (London, 2003).

Foster, R. F. *Paddy & Mr. Punch: Connections in Irish and English History* (London, 1993).

Fothergill, B. *Nicholas Wiseman* (London, 1963).

Galloway, P. *A Passionate Humility: Frederick Oakeley and the Oxford Movement* (London, 1999).

Gilbey, A. N. *We Believe* (London, 1983).

—*The Commonplace Book of A.N. Gilbey* (London, 1993).

Girouard, M. *Life in the English Country House* (New Haven and London, 1978).

—*The Victorian Country House* (New Haven and London, 1985).

Glendinning, V. *Anthony Trollope* (New York, 1993).

Green, V. H. H. *Religion at Oxford and Cambridge* (Cambridge, 1964).

Grote, J. *Exploratio Philosophica: Rough Notes on Modern Intellectual Science*, 2 vols. (London, 1865 and 1900).

—*An Examination of the Utilitarian Philosophy* (London, 1870).

—*Treatise on Moral Ideals*, ed. Joseph Bickersteth Mayor (London, 1876).

Hanham, H. J. *The Nineteenth-Century Constitution* (Cambridge, 1969).

Hilton, B. *A Mad, Bad, and Dangerous People? England 1783–1846* (Oxford, 2006).

Hilton, T. *John Ruskin: The Early Years 1819–1859* (New Haven, 1985).

—*John Ruskin: The Later Years* (New Haven, 2000).

Hart-Davis, R. (ed.), *The Letters of Oscar Wilde* (London, 1962).

Heffer, S. *Moral Desperado: A Life of Thomas Carlyle* (London, 1995).

Holmes, J. D. *More Roman than Rome: English Catholicism in the Nineteenth Century* (Oxford, 1984).

Hoppen, K. T. *The Mid-Victorian Generation: England 1846–1886* (Oxford, 1998).

Houghton, W. E. *Victorian Frame of Mind 1830–70* (Yale, 1957).

James, M. R. *Casting the Runes and Other Ghost Stories*, ed. Michael Cox (Oxford, 1987).

Joyce, S. *My Brother's Keeper* (New York, 1958).

Kennedy, M. *Portrait of Elgar* (Oxford, 1993).

Ker, I. *Newman and the Fullness of Christianity* (London, 1993).

—*Newman on Being a Christian* (London, 1990).

—*Newman and Conversion* (London, 1997).

Kingsley, M. *Travels in West Africa* (Folio Society, 2007).

Kynaston, D. *The City of London. Volume I: A World of its Own 1815–1890* (London, 1994).

Leslie, S. *Henry Edward Manning: His Life and Labours* (London, 1921).

Longford, E. *Victoria, R.I.* (London, 1964).

MacCarthy, F. *The Last Pre-Raphaelite: Edward Burne-Jones and the Victorian Imagination* (Harvard, 2012).

Maritain, J. *On the Use of Philosophy* (Princeton, 1961).

Matthew, H. C. G. *Gladstone 1804–1879* (Oxford, 1988).

—*Gladstone 1875–1898* (Oxford, 1995).

Middleton, R. D. *Magdalen Studies* (Oxford, 1936).

—*Newman and Bloxam: An Oxford Friendship* (Oxford, 1947).

—*Newman and Oxford: His ReligiousDevelopment* (London, 1950).

Muhlstein, A. *Balzac's Omelette* (New York, 2011).

Newsome, D. *The Parting of Friends: The Wilberforces and the Mannings* (London, 1966).

Norman, E. *The English Catholic Church in the Nineteenth Century* (Oxford, 1985).

—*Church of England and Society in England 1770–1970* (Oxford, 1976).

Norris, T. *Newman for Today* (New York, 2010).

O'Faolain, S. *Newman's Way: The Odyssey of John Henry Newman* (London, 1952).

Pawley, M. *Faith and Family: The Life and Circle of Ambrose Phillipps de Lisle* (Norwich, 1993).

Pemble, J. *The Mediterranean Passion: Victorians and Edwardians in the South* (Oxford, 1987).

Ponsonby, F. *Recollections of Three Reigns* (London, 1951).

Roberts, A. *Victorian Titan: Life of Lord Salisbury* (London, 1999).

Schlicke, P. *The Oxford Companion to Charles Dickens* (Oxford, 2011).

Schultz, B. *Henry Sidgwick: Eye of the Universe: An Intellectual Biography* (Cambridge, 2004).

Searby, P. *A History of the University of Cambridge* (Cambridge, 1997).

Searle, G. R. *A New England? Peace and War 1886-1918* (Oxford, 2004).

Short, E. *Newman and his Contemporaries* (London, 2011).

Slater, M. *Charles Dickens* (New Haven, 2009).

Smith, B. A. *Dean Church: The Anglican Response to Newman* (Oxford, 1958).

Strachey, L. *Eminent Victorians* (London, 1918).

—*Queen Victoria* (London, 1921).

Sugg, J. *Affly Yours; Newman and his Female Circle* (London, 1997).

Svaglic, M. J. "Charles Newman and his Brothers," MLA 71(3): (June 1956).

Sylva, J. A. C. *How Italy and her People Shaped Cardinal Newman: Italian Influences on an English Mind* (New Jersey, 2010).

Tillotson, K. *Novels of the Eighteen-Forties* (Oxford, 1954).

Thomas, Keith. *The Ends of Life: Roads to Fulfillment in Early Modern England* (Oxford, 2009).

Trevelyan, G. M. *English Social History* (London, 1942).

Tristram, H. *Newman and his Friends* (London, 1933).

—(ed.), *John Henry Newman: Centenary Essays* (London, 1945).

Waller, P. *Writers,Readers, & Reputations: Literary Life in Britain 1870-1918* (Oxford, 2006).

Ward, W. *Life and Times of Cardinal Wiseman* (London, 1897).

—*William George Ward and the Oxford Movement.* (London, 1890).

—*William George Ward and the Catholic Revival* (London, 1893).

—*Ten Personal Studies* (London, 1905).

—*Last Lectures* (London, 1918).

Watkin, E. I. *Roman Catholicism in England from the Reformation to 1950* (Oxford, 1957).

Willey, B. *Nineteenth-Century Studies: Coleridge to Matthew Arnold* (Cambridge, 1949).

—*More Nineteenth-Century Studies: A Group of Honest Doubters* (Cambridge, 1956).

Wilson, A. N. *The Victorians* (Folio Society, 2008).

Winstanley, D. A. *Later Victorian Cambridge* (Cambridge, 1947).

Woodward, L. *The Age of Reform*, second edition (Oxford, 1962).

Young, G. M. *Portrait of an Age* (Oxford, 1936).

—*Daylight and Champlain* (London, 1937).

—*Today and Yesterday* (London, 1948).

—*Last Essays* (London, 1950).

Index